Chronology of African History

Chronology
of African History

G.S.P. FREEMAN-GRENVILLE

OXFORD UNIVERSITY PRESS

1973

Oxford University Press, Ely House, London, W.1

GLASGOW   NEW YORK   TORONTO   MELBOURNE   WELLINGTON
CAPE TOWN   IBADAN   NAIROBI   DAR ES SALAAM   LUSAKA   ADDIS ABABA
DELHI   BOMBAY   CALCUTTA   MADRAS   KARACHI   LAHORE   DACCA
KUALA LUMPUR   SINGAPORE   HONG KONG   TOKYO

ISBN 0 19 913174 0

© *Oxford University Press* 1973

**Set by Gavin Martin Ltd. and printed and bound in Great
Britain by Pitman Press Ltd.**

To My Wife

Contents

Introduction

European and Islamic historians have at their disposal a substantial number of printed aids to study: historical tables, chronologies, genealogies, dictionaries and handbooks. One needs only to recollect such names as Capelli, Delorme, Lane-Poole, Philips, Powicke, Spuler, Steinberg, Stockvis, and Zambaur.[1] Although some of these mention some parts of the African continent, they provide no picture of its history as a whole. For myself, when I first begun to study African history twenty years ago, I found myself helplessly confused by the welter of events and nations in different parts of a continent which is far larger than Europe. These twenty years have seen the volume of both primary and secondary material grow greatly. Twenty years ago, indeed, African history was, to say the least, a novel and perhaps an eccentric subject. If this is no longer so, it must be recognized that our knowledge still suffers from many large gaps. These can be filled only by more extensive archival research, by more exacting examination of literary sources, by the collection or photography of the numerous documents known to exist in private hands in both eastern and western Africa, and equally by field work in the collection of oral traditions. Moreover, if a substantial number of ancient sites in Africa have now been surveyed, and some of them excavated, the archaeology of Africa as a whole, whether as prehistoric or historical archaeology, is still in its infancy. There is still much speculation which stands in need of verification.

Nevertheless, for very much of the continent sufficient research has been carried out for the broad outlines of the past three thousand years to be reasonably apparent, and some parts of these in considerable detail: the student or teacher of today is faced by a corpus far more complex than twenty years ago. It has become more difficult, not less, to view this corpus in proper perspective and to perceive the sequence of events in both their temporal and spatial aspects. Many of the difficulties arise because in earlier times we are dependent upon the interpretation of but a slender number of documents and other evidences: it is because of this that so much more has been written about the period after 1800. After this date evidences, especially in official archives, become far more numerous than before, but not to include the earlier period would be rather as if the play of *Hamlet* were given without reference to the murder of Hamlet's father.

1. A. Capelli, *Cronologia, Cronografia e Calendario Perpetuo,* 2nd edn., Milan, 1930; J. Delorme, *Chronologie des Civilisations,* Paris, 1949; S. Lane-Poole, *The Mohammedan Dynasties,* 1893; C.H. Philips, *Handbook of Oriental History,* 1951; F.M. Powicke, *Handbook of British Chronology,* 1961; B. Spuler, *Regenten und Regierungen der Welt,* 2 vols., Wurzburg, 1962; J.H. Steinberg, *Historical Tables,* 6th edn., 1961; A.M.H.J. Stockvis, *Manuel d'histoire, de généalogie et chronologie de tous les états du globe,* 3 vols., Leiden, 1888-91; E. de Zambaur, *Manuel de généalogie et de chronologie pour l'histoire de l'Islam,* 2 vols., 2nd edn., Bad Pyrmont, 1955.

The primary object of this work, then, is to supply the kind of aid to perspective that European and Islamic historians enjoy in their respective spheres. These historical tables display, in a calendrical fashion, the whole course, so far as it is known, of the principal events and dates in the whole continent of Africa from *c.* 1000 BC until the end of 1971. In this way it is hoped to provide an instrument that will be of use not only to students and teachers of African history, but also to all those who in different ways find an interest in the African continent and perceive the need to see it whole.

It was said, perhaps not unmaliciously, of a former Fellow of Worcester College, Oxford, that as a young don he sat down to write a work of which the only possible title could be *De omnibus rebus et quibusdam aliis*[2] : his objectives were so ambitious that it is hardly surprising that when he reached retirement he had not completed his first volume. In order to compile the present work in manageable form it has been necessary to impose rigid limitations upon it. No work could include every known event or every single ruler. Somewhere Professor Kenneth Ingham has remarked that African history 'began with Herodotus'. So be it. Here 1000 BC has been taken as a convenient and wholly arbitrary beginning. The year itself has no intrinsic significance. An earlier start would simply have been a chronology of dynastic Egypt and of near-by Asiatic peoples, and this is already available in Sir Alan Gardiner's *The Egypt of the Pharoahs,* 1961, and in many other works. The date arbitrarily selected is roughly when Egypt is known to have entered into and been affected by other regions of Africa, although she had connections with the south on a number of recorded occasions earlier. It enables one to account for the last millenium of the Pharaonic dynasties, for the long-lived Kingdom of Meroe and for the beginnings and course of the Carthaginian maritime empire, and its supercession by Rome. A later start would have excluded Carthage in its formative period; and would thus have left unexplained the commercial competition which not only made Rome the first imperial power in Africa, but which had consequences which are still apparent in the Empire of Ethiopia. An earlier start, too, would chiefly have involved that part of African prehistory which is strictly the province of prehistoric archaeologists. While it is impossible to draw any precise line, least of all in Africa, as to where prehistory ceases and history begins, some wholly arbitrary judgement was necessary: the point of departure is thus roughly where our earliest historical records begin.

One may sift from many sources a skeletal outline of datable events. Very many of these dates are speculative and must be treated with caution. The most numerous sources for African history, so far as chronology is concerned, derive from dynastic records. These, whether preserved in writing or as oral traditions — and, generally speaking, the greater number eventually can be found to depend upon the oral tradition of one time or another — have as their primary purpose the proof of the legitimacy of the claim of a particular line, or of a particular person, to power. Oral

2. 'Concerning all things and certain other matters.'

traditions are seldom, if ever, history or genealogy for its own sake. For our purpose, which is not of a political but of a historical nature, such records are very frequently defective in that the majority of the rulers are named without dates, or even without regnal years. J. S. Kirkman has written of the Swahili chroniclers that they wrote of the Swahili states as if each one had existed in 'planetary isolation' from all the rest. Throughout the continent indeed the majority of chroniclers and traditionalists have handed down their knowledge with a truly planetary disdain for the passage of time. Thus, the attempt to marry what we may ascertain with a fair certainty from chronologically reliable sources with material which by its very nature is a-chronological can often be misleading.

In the absence of known dates some scholars have believed that a reasonably accurate calculation might be made in terms of average generations or of average lengths of reign such as might be derived from genealogies or dynastic lists. [3] This sort of calculation can give rise to confusion of a serious kind, and, so far as the present writer is concerned, seems to be an instrument of very slight reliability. Except where there has been Islamic or early Christian influence, or, in more recent times, European influence, African genealogies are non-calendrical, and indications of the precise descent of rulers and their mutual relationships within a dynasty are only sporadically given. Many dynastic lists and genealogies are, in fact, compilations and recensions of different periods, so that legal and political points, now long forgotten, are being made which were relevant only at the different times of the different recensions. It is only when we possess a sufficient abundance of external sources from which checks can be made that we can feel any absolute conviction.

It is a matter of some notoriety that in times past in Europe the heralds would obligingly stretch a point or two so as to provide what amount to fictitious descents.[4]

3. C.F. I. Wilks, 'The growth of the Akwapim state: a study in the control of evidence', in J. Vansina, R. Mauny and L.V. Thomas, *The Historian in Tropical Africa*, 1964, pp.390-408, esp. p.408; Myron J. Echenburg. 'The application of normal probability theory to the problem of Wagadugu Mossi State origins', a paper contributed to the Conference on African Chronology arranged by Professor R.A. Oliver in 1966.

4. Humbert Wolfe embodies his conclusions in a parody:

The House of Lords
are waiting for
the newspaper
proprietor.

Soap! Attention!
Listen! Beer!
"Glory to the
new-made peer."

Hark! the Heralds'
College sings,
as they fake his
quarterings.

Humbert Wolfe, *The Uncelestial City*, 1930.

Inquiry by the writer of an official of the Irish Bloodstock Association elicited that racehorse owners not infrequently propose fictions in the pedigrees of bloodstock horses similar to those of certain European pedigrees. It is of particular interest that in them a process which may be described as telescopy is common: owners are careful to record the names of ancestors who have been winners whilst less successful animals tend to be omitted. It is in this way that individual names and even whole generations disappear, and this in a quite random fashion. This is not to say that the owners of Irish bloodstock are generally liars, or that African or European genealogists or chroniclers are or were purveyors of premeditated falsehoods: it is simply that the primary concern of the parties has been to make some particular point or sequence of points, and not merely to set out their material in terms of an objective world chronological sequence. To cite only three out of very many other possible examples, Sir E.E.Evans-Pritchard, P.Bohannan, and I.M.Lewis[5] have demonstrated in different ways a number of reasons for regarding traditional pedigrees amongst the Nuer, the Tiv, and the Somali respectively as unreliable. They have shown how what here we have called telescopy takes place: the founding fathers and their immediate descendants in the line are the best remembered, and then the generations nearest in time to the compiler of the pedigree: between these two areas names and generations become lost, and not in a regular or predictable manner, but in a random fashion just like the random closing of the sections of a portable telescope.

For any valid mathematical test the material must be known to be complete in all particulars: each stage in a pedigree therefore demands external verification. Even when this can be done, an average discovered from one dynasty could never be validly applied to another unless it could be shown, which is impossible, that all the circumstances of each succession were identical. There are in fact too many *imponderabilia* for any system of averaging to be effective. One line may produce men or women of great longevity: in another line generation succeeds generation with great rapidity: in another the fortunes of war or of duelling or of hunting will procure a rapid succession: marriage, whether monogamous, albeit sometimes frequently repeated, or polygamous, may take place late or early in life: war, plague, and famine can wipe out the greater part of a family: a young child and sometimes a posthumous child, may succeed and yet be of the same age as his own great-nephews. These chances, nor indeed any combination of these chances, do not exhaust all the possibilities. There is a contemporary case in Tanzania of an especially fertile father who, as quite a young man, was installed as a chief in 1917:

5. E.E. Evans-Pritchard, *The Nuer,* 1940, pp.195 ff., esp. pp.199-200; L. Bohannan, 'A Genealogical Charter', *Africa,* xxii, pp.301-15, esp. p.313; I.M. Lewis, 'Historical Aspects of Genealogies in the Northern Somali Social Structure', *Journal of African History,* III, 1, pp.35-48, esp. p. 43; and see the special number, Problems of African Chronology, *Journal of African History,* XI, 2, 1970, together with a number of yet unpublished papers contributed to the Conference on African Chronology, 1966; and, for further discussion, G. S. P. Freeman-Grenville, 'Coin Finds and Their Significance for Eastern African Chronology', *Numismatic Chronicle,* 1971, pp.283-301.

his youngest children attend school with his great-great grandchildren. There are many equally curious cases and much material for comparison in Burke's *Peerage* and *Landed Gentry* in more than two thousand pedigrees. Like African pedigrees, the original importance of them all lay in proving succession either to office or to the ownership of land. For the historian the value of these British pedigrees resides in that they have been carefully established by documentary means: where reliable documents are absent, this is clearly indicated. It is not infrequent that in earlier times the dates of birth or of marriage remain unknown. From them it is impossible in many cases to work out average lengths of tenure both of life and of office in different families. The length of tenure of peerages varies widely in a sample taken from a number of families which can be traced over the past three or four hundred years: the lowest average is eight years and the highest forty-four. It follows that any attempt to work out a general average would result in absurdity, and that its application would only serve to make works which are of the highest reliability wholly unreliable. As D.H. Jones has remarked:

> Given the small numerical scale of the calculations involved and the number of unknown variables, fancy mathematics can bring us no nearer to certainty than the commonsense of the experienced historian.[6]

To apply averages to African pedigrees or dynastic lists is simply to pursue a chimera.

It is not simply within the field of genealogy and of oral tradition that difficulties arise. Once one reaches the fifteenth century one is able to exploit the Portuguese archives, followed soon after by the archives of other European nations with interests in Africa. There are nevertheless many conflicts of date between what appear to be primary authorities. Before the fifteenth century many historians have perforce had to arrange their material in sequence and then assign what examination shows to be wholly arbitrary datings: an original statement, made with great caution, later tends to become canonized as a definitely known absolute date. Chronology has always been a matter for controversy, and it is safe to predict that it will continue to be. It is thus extremely difficult to be wholly precise, and indeed precision becomes more difficult as any study of chronology progresses. If the formality is observed, wars can be dated from the moment of declaration: yet sometimes the true date would seem to be the first minor clash of hostilities. Generally, laws are dated by their enactment; yet it is on their vesting date that they come into effect. The signing of treaties and their dates of ratification present similar difficulties. The dates in any given tract of history depend upon documents, whether historical or archaeological: even the dates of inscriptions are not invariably reliable: many can only eventually be traced to the opinion of an individual historian or archaeologist.

These historical tables contain over 12,000 entries, and consequently it has not been possible for the compiler to check each one of them at its ultimate and authoritative source. To a great extent he has been obliged to rely upon the best secondary authorities available. In some cases these authorities are themselves in conflict, or in fact can only give a date *à peu près*: in other cases the compiler

6. D.H. Jones, 'Problems of African Chronology', *Journal of African History*, XI, 2, 1970, p.168.

himself has felt misgivings about dates given quite confidently by both primary and secondary authorities. Such occasions of difficulty, which are numerous, have been indicated by the frequent use of *c. (circa),* together with, on occasions of extreme doubt, a mark of interrogation. In African history some dates have been inferred directly from oral traditions, or from oral traditions subsequently committed to writing, and these have invariably been marked *c.* There is no space here to enter into controversy about the merits or demerits of establishing dates by radio-carbon analysis. For the layman an admirable account of this method has been given by Roger Summers.[7] Since the method itself includes a mathematically calculated amount of error, all dates so established have been shown with the conventional sign ±, followed by the calculated amount of error.

My friend Robert Cornevin, who has been so courageous as to write a detailed and consecutive history of Africa single-handed, divides the continent into seven geographically distinct regions.[8] The divisions adopted in these historical tables are largely those of convenience. For optical reasons information conveyed on a single page or upon two pages facing one another becomes confusing to the eye if the number of columns exceeds six. This is not to dispute Cornevin's system: it is simply that one must choose, in attempting to display the history of Africa in tabular chronological form, that system which is most likely to produce clarity and ease of reference to the eye of the reader. From *c.* 1000 BC to AD 599 four columns only have been used: the first is employed for Egypt with the Sudan and the eastern side of Africa, the second for northern Africa and the western side. The third column is a selection of the more prominent items in the history of western Asia, without which the history of Egypt and the eastern side of Africa is not intelligible: the fourth column is used for items from the history of Europe, without which neither the history of Carthage and northern Africa, nor the history of Egypt, can properly be understood. In these two latter columns it is the purpose to give no more than the barest outline of events in western Asia or in Europe, and only in so far as they are relevant to Africa.

From AD 600 we become progressively more informed about Africa south of the Sahara, and this renders new divisions necessary. Until 1399 four columns are retained: Egypt and Sudan continue to occupy the first column and northern Africa the second: the third column is devoted to Africa south of the Sahara and now includes Ethiopia. The fourth column is entitled Other Countries. It is not intended to give an outline of the whole history of the rest of the world in this column. Rather, priority has been given to Egyptian and northern African activities in Europe and in the Near East, together with a selection of the main events and dates in European history in order to provide a background to the whole picture.

From 1400 new divisions again become necessary because of our increasingly

7. Roger Summers, *Zimbabwe: A Rhodesian Mystery,* Cape Town, 1963.
8. R. Cornevin, *Histoire de l'Afrique,* 4 vols., Paris, 1962 ff. (Vol. III forthcoming 1973), II, pp.23-7.

greater knowledge of events south of the Sahara. Of the six columns printed on opposite pages, three columns on each, Egypt and the Sudan retain the first column and Northern Africa the second. There are three separate columns for Eastern Africa, including Ethiopia, for Western Africa, and for Central and Southern Africa. The sixth column, entitled Other Countries, has as its priority events in Europe which have had a direct or an indirect effect upon Africa, and only thereafter such principal events in Europe which provide as it were a backcloth.

Finally, after 1800 our knowledge of datable events is greatly expanded in the area south of the Sahara, whilst their pace diminishes in the northern area. Therefore six new divisions have been adopted. Egypt and the Sudan have been included in a single column with Northern Africa, whilst Western Africa, Central Africa, Eastern Africa (Ethiopia included), and Southern Africa have one column each. Like its predecessors, the sixth column is entitled Other Countries. It is primarily devoted to events outside the continent which directly or indirectly have affected Africa. In addition there are also included other events, some of world importance, some of more local significance, so as to enable a coherent picture of Africa to emerge in a world context. This column could, of course, become so greatly expanded as to provide a chronology of the whole world, and it has been necessary to curtail and trim it greatly, often in a wholly arbitrary fashion, in order to preserve the balance of the work.

We are greatly indebted to J.D. Pearson for his *Index Islamicus* and for his *Guide to Manuscripts and Documents in the British Isles relating to Africa:* but we are equally in great need of a systematic bibliography of printed books concerning Africa, and of the contents of archives, in Africa as well as outside. It is to be hoped that the challenge will be taken up. If a complete bibliography of all the works, monographs and articles, consulted in preparing this volume were printed, it would occupy some three to four hundred pages. A bibliography of this size printed together with the tables would make the work unduly burdensome.

It is for the same reason that justificatory footnotes have not been given. There are, indeed, a number of useful select bibliographies already available in R. Cornevin, *Histoire de l'Afrique,* 4 vols, Paris, 1962 ff., (Vol.III forthcoming 1973); R.I. Rotberg, *A Political History of Tropical Africa,* New York, 1965; R.A. Oliver and J.D. Fage, *A Short History of Africa,* 1966 edn.; R.A. Oliver and A. Atmore, *Africa since 1800,* 1967. The most comprehensive bibliography available in handy form is in Robin Hallett, *Africa to 1875: A Modern History,* University of Michigan Press, 1970, and much of this refers also to the more recent period. It is a matter for regret that Hallett's second volume, announced as *Africa since 1875: A Modern History,* was not available at the time of going to press. If a select bibliography were to be drawn up for the present work, it would not mention any work of serious significance which is not already listed either in one or other of the foregoing, or in the *Journal of African History.*

The large number of abbreviations employed has been listed following this introduction. The index does not refer to page numbers because this would give the reader the unnecessary trouble of scanning an entire page for the reference sought. Instead, the index gives the briefest possible reference to personal or place names, followed by an entry showing the year in which that reference has been made. Where such mentions are very frequent, the terminal years between which the entries occur alone are shown. In this way the reader is guided instantly to the date which it is his object to verify, each year being printed in bold type so that it stands out on the page.

In a work of this kind the spelling of names presents much difficulty. There is great difference of convention between authors, and especially between English and French. For the sake of consistency it has been necessary from time to time to make arbitrary decisions, but generally the usage of the English authors referred to above has been followed. In the spelling of Arabic names and words the 'ain, hamza, diacritical marks, and indications of vowel length have been discarded. There are generally unintelligible to the non-Arabist. Generally the spelling of the *Encyclopaedia of Islam* has been followed, with the exceptions conventional amongst British Arabists, that *q* replaces *k*, and *j* replaces *dj*. But, especially in western Africa, there are many names of Arabic derivation which have been borrowed and adapted by the sound usages of local languages: in these the usage of the most reputable primary or secondary authority has been followed. In all deviations from the rule familiar conventions have been preferred to the unfamiliar. It would merely be affected, moreover, to write 'Adan for Aden, al-Makkah for Mecca (often pronounced in East Africa as Mekke), al-Madinah for Medina, and a score of other instances. It is to be noted that the conventional rulers for the orthography of African languages give for the most part, although not in all cases, a phonetic value for the vowels broadly similar to Italian. It is not possible here to provide rules for the pronunciation of all the foreign names recorded because at least 700 languages are involved.

There are many to whom I owe a debt of gratitude for having permitted me to consult them on different points, so many indeed that if here I have made some accidental omission I trust I may be forgiven. Some have allowed me to pick their brains in conversation, others have put themselves to the trouble of correspondence. I recollect with especial gratitude Archbishop David Matthew, whose *Ethiopia: The Study of the Polity,* 1947, first stimulated my interest in Africa, and his brother Gervase Matthew; Sir Mortimer Wheeler and the late Sir John Gray; Professors Eric Axelson, Douglas Dunlop, Sir Edward Evans-Pritchard, P.C. Garlick, Richard Gray, Ivan Hrbek, Dan McCall, Bradford G. Martin, Roland Oliver, the late Joseph Schacht, P.L. Shinnie, Jan Vansina, the late W.H. Whiteley, and Ivor Wilks; Drs G.A. Akinola, Barbara Dubins, J.R. Goody, D.H. Jones, J.S. Kirkman, Jan Knappert and D.C.H.O. McQueen; the late George Bennett, Mrs David Brown (formerly Miss Helen Mitchell), E. Cerulli, H.N. Chittick, R.Cornevin, the late Mrs R.L. Devonshire, G.O. Ekemode, T.R. Hodgkin, J.O. Hunwick, Paul Ozanne and Hamo Sassoon. I need hardly say that the opinions set down are wholly my own. I have received endless kindnesses from members of the staff of a number of libraries and archives, but as individuals their names have not always been known to me. I trust therefore they will recognize my gratitude if I mention their institutions: Ampleforth College; the *Archives de France*; the Archives of the Augustinian Generalate, Rome; the *Archivio Nacional da Tôrre do Tombo,* Lisbon; the Balme Library, University of Ghana; the *Bibliothèque Nationale,* Paris; the British Museum; the Butler Library, Columbia University, New York; Heythrop College; the J.B. Morrell Library, University of York; New York Public Library; Rhodes House Library, Oxford; the Sacred Congregation for the Evangelization of Peoples, Rome; the School of Oriental and African Studies, London; the Sojourner Truth Library, State University College, State University of New York, New Paltz; and the University of California, Los Angeles. By custom members of the staff of the Oxford University Press are not named by their authors, but I must acknowledge my special debt to the patience and kindness I have received at their hands and for many useful suggestions in the complex production of this work. I also thank my sister-in-law, Anne Deen, for having lent us her villa at Villefranche-sur-mer, thus enabling us to have delightful holidays and for myself a peaceful opportunity to bring this work to completion. I am grateful too to my old friend and colleague Charles Inge, who has made the index, and to my neighbour 'Elephant Bill' Lancaster, who kindly undertook the tedious task of reducing over 12,000 filing cards into a manageable typescript. I am likewise grateful to my son for help with proof-reading. This book is dedicated to my wife, not simply for checking the proofs, and the appalling task of checking the index, but as some small return for twenty-two years of happy married life in over thirty different houses, mostly in Africa.

Sheriff Hutton, York
8 September 1972   G.S.P.F.-G.

Abbreviations

±   a radio-carbon dating

ABAKO   *Association des Bakongo* (Congo, L)

Abp   Archbishop

AD   after the birth of Christ

ad int.   *ad interim*

AEF   *Afrique Equatoriale Française*

ALN   *Armée de Libération Nationale* (Algeria)

AML   *Amis du Manifeste et de la Liberté* (Algeria)

ANC   African National Congress (SA)

AOF   *Afrique Occidentale Française*

ante   before

b.   born

b.   bin (Arabic, son of)

BBC   British Broadcasting Corporation

BC   before the birth of Christ

BDC   *Bloc Démocratique Camerounais*

BDS   *Bloc Démocratique Sénégalais*

BMS   Baptist Missionary Society

Bp   Bishop

BSA Co.   British South Africa Co. Ltd

C   Central

C.   Cape

c.(cc.)   century, centuries

c.   *circa*

Capt.   Captain

CAR   Central African Republic

CATC   *Confédération Africaine des Travailleurs Croyants*

CDWA   Colonial Development and Welfare Act(s)

C.E.   Church of England

CEM   Congo Evangelistic Mission

CEMN   *Comite d'Entente des Mouvements Nationaux*

CFA   *Côte Française d'Afrique*

CFTC   *Confédération Française de Travail Catholique*

CGT   *Confédération Générale de Travail*

CGTA   *Confédération Générale des Travailleurs Africains*

CMS   Church Missionary Society

CNO   *Comité nationale d'organisation* (Cameroun)

CNRA   *Conseil National de la Révolution Algérienne*

Co.   Company

Congo (B)	Congo (Brazzaville)
Congo (K)	Congo (Kinshasa), later Zaïre
Congo (L)	Congo (Léopoldville), later Congo (K)
CPP	Convention People's Party (Ghana)
CRF	*Comité pour le Renaissance de France* (Algeria)
CRUA	*Comité Révolutionnaire pour l'Unité et l'Action* (Algeria)
CSSp	Congregation of the Holy Ghost, or Holy Ghost Fathers
d.	died
Dept	Department
DP	Destour Party (Tunisia)
Dr.	Doctor
DRC	Dutch Reformed Church
E	East
EA	East Africa
EEC	European Economic Community
EIC	East India Co.
ENA	*Etoile Nord Africaine* (Algeria)
ESAM	Evangelization South Africa Mission
ESOCAM	*Evolution Sociale Camerounaise*
FAK	*Federasie van Afrikaanse Kultur Verenigings*
FAO	Food and Agriculture Organization (UN)
FCA	Federation of Central Africa
FCS	Free Church of Scotland
FERDES	*Fonds d'équipement et de développement économique et sociale*
FIDES	*Fonds d'investissement et de développement économique et sociale*
FLN	*Front de Libération Nationale* (Algeria)
fl.	*floruit*, period during which an individual is known to have been living
Fr	Father
FRELIMO	Liberation Front of Mozambique
HAM	Heart of Africa Mission
HMS	Her (His) Majesty's Ship
IBEA	Imperial British East Africa Co.
IFAN	*Institut Français* (later *Fondamental*) *de l'Afrique Noir*
IOM	*Groupe Parlementaire Indépendent Outre-Mer*
Is.	Island, Islands
IWA	International Workers of Africa (SA)
KADU	Kenya African Democratic Union
KANU	Kenya African National Union
KAR	King's African Rifles
KAU	Kenya African Union
L.	Lake
LCATC	Livingstonia Central African Trading Co. Ltd.
Leg. Co.	Legislative Council

LIM	Livingstone Interior Mission
LMS	London Missionary Society
Ltd.	Limited
m.	million(s)
MANC	*Mouvement d'Action National Camerounaise*
MCP	Malawi Congress Party
Mgr	Monsignor
MMCC	Methodist Mission of Central Congo
MMSC	Methodist Mission of South Congo
MNA	*Mouvement National Algérien*
MPLA	Popular Movement for the Liberation of Angola
MSA	*Mouvement Socialiste Africain*
MTLD	*Mouvement pour le Triomphe des Libertés Démocratiques* (Algeria)
Mt(s)	Mount(ains)
N	North
NA	Native Authority
NAACP	National Association for the Advancement of Coloured Peoples
NAC	Nyasaland African Congress
NCSL	National Council of Sierra Leone
NDP	Neo-Destour Party (Tunisia)
NE	North-East
NFD	Northern Frontier Division (Kenya)
NLM	National Liberation Movement (Gold Coast)

NPP	Northern People's Party (Gold Coast)
NPPPP	Northern Province Progressive People's Party (Kenya)
OAS	*Organisation Armée Secrète* (Algeria)
OAU	Organization for African Unity
OCAM	*Organisation Commune Africaine et Malgache*
OFS	Orange Free State
OMI	Oblates of Mary Immaculate
OP	Order of Preachers (Dominicans)
ORAF	*Organisation de la Résistance de l'Algérie Française*
ORANA	*Organisation pour le recherche sur l'alimentation et la nutrition en Afrique*
ORS	Orange River Sovereignty
OS	*Organisation Spéciale* (Algeria)
OSB	Order of St Benedict
oz.	ounce
PCA	*Parti Communiste Algérien*
PPA	*Parti du Peuple Algérien*
PPAA	*Parti Populaire Algérien*
PAFMECA	Pan-African Freedom Movement for Eastern and Central Africa
PAFMECSA	Pan-African Freedom Movement for Eastern, Central, and Southern Africa
PFA	*Parti de la Fédération Africaine*

PPS	*Parti Populaire Sénégalais*	St	Saint
pop.	population	succ.	successor, succeeded
post	after	SYL	Somali Youth League
PPP	Progressive People's Party, Gambia	SVD	Divine Word Fathers
PRA	*Parti de Régroupement Africaine*	SWA	South-West Africa
R(s)	River(s)	TAA	Tanganyika African Association
RC	Roman Catholic	TANU	Tanganyika (later Tanzania) African National Union
RDA	*Rassemblement Démocratique Africaine*	UAC	United Africa Co.
Rev.	Reverend	UAP	Union of Angolan Peoples
RFMA	*Rassemblement Franco-Musulman Algérien*	UAR	United Arab Republic
Rt.	Right	*UGTA*	*Union Général des Travailleurs Algériens*
R.	Royal	*UDMA*	*Union Démocratique du Manifeste Algérien*
Sa.	*São, Santo or Santa*		
S	South	UK	United Kingdom of Great Britain and Northern Ireland
SA	South Africa		
SDA	Seventh Day Adventists	UMCA	Universities' Mission to Central Africa
SFIO	*Section Française de l'Internationale Ouvrière*	*UEAC*	*Union des Etats de l'Afrique Centrale*
SJ	Society of Jesus	*UNISCO*	*Union des interêts sociaux congolais* (Congo, L)
SLPP	Sierra Leone People's Party		
SMA	Lyons Missionary Society	UN	United Nations
SME	*Société des Missions Evangéliques de Paris* (Paris Missionary Society)	UNO	United Nations Organization
		UPA	*Union Populaire Algérienne*
		UPC	Uganda People's Congress
SNL	Somali National League	US	United States (of America)
SPG	Society for the Propagation of the Gospel	USA	United States of America

USC	*Union Sociale Camerounaise*
USSR	Union of Soviet Socialist Republics
USTA	*Union Syndicale des Travailleurs Algériens*
UTP	United Tanganyika Party
via	by way of
W	West
W.	Wadi
WAFF	West African Frontier Force
WF	White Fathers
WMS	Wesleyan Methodist Missionary Society
ZANU	Zimbabwe African National Union
ZAPU	Zimbabwe African People's Union

HISTORICAL TABLES

EGYPT, THE SUDAN & EASTERN AFRICA	NORTHERN AFRICA & WESTERN AFRICA	WESTERN ASIA	EUROPE
	*c.*1300—*c.*600 Saharan bronze age; mines in present Mauritania and Senegal probable source of copper. *c.*1100 Lixus and Utique (Utica) founded by Phoenicians.		
*c.*1087—*c.*954 Twenty-first dynasty in Egypt.			
		*c.*1010—*c.*970 Hebrew alphabet developed.	
*c.*1000 Stone Bowl culture in Kenya: cattle-owning agriculturalists.	*c.*1000 Gradual dessication of Sahara desert still progressing; drawings of horse-drawn carts show trade routes from Morocco to R Senegal and R Niger and from Tripoli through Ghadames to Gao on R Niger. Pre-Carthaginian settlement at Salammbo near Carthage.	*c.*1000 Jerusalem conquered by David. *c.*1000—800 R Ganges valley colonized by Aryans. *c.*1000—500 Apogee of Sidon as a trading state.	*c.*1000—800 Greeks adopt the Phoenician alphabet.
		*c.*970—*c.*930 Solomon, King of Israel: marries daughter of a Pharaoh. *c.*968—*c.*923 Hiram, King of Tyre, assists Solomon to build the Temple in Jerusalem. *c.*950 Queen of Sheba visits Solomon.	
*c.*945—*c.*730 Twenty-second dynasty in Egypt. *c.*945—*c.*924 Shoshenk I, Pharaoh; Upper and Lower Egypt unified. A section of the clergy of Amon takes refuge in Napata.			
		*c.*930 Death of Solomon. Palestine invaded by Shoshenk of Egypt; Jerusalem pillaged.	
*c.*924—*c.*888 Osorkon I, Pharaoh.			
		*c.*922 Kingdom of Israel separates from the Kingdom of Judah.	
*c.*920 Beginning of Kushite dynasty at Napata: tombs at El Kourrou.			
	c. 918±70 – 207± 50 Nok Figurine culture in present Nigeria; said to be the ancestors of the present Yoruba.		
		*c.*900 Beginning of Phoenician maritime expansion.	*c.*900 Celts arrive in Gaul. *c.*900—700 Ionian confederation formed.
*c.*888—*c.*881 Takelot I, Pharaoh. *c.*881—*c.*852 Osorkon II, Pharaoh. *c.*858 Takelot II, co-ruler with Osorkon II.		858—824 Shalmaneser III, King of Assyria. *c.*854 Samaria settled by Omri.	

EGYPT, THE SUDAN & EASTERN AFRICA	NORTHERN AFRICA & WESTERN AFRICA	WESTERN ASIA	EUROPE
		853 Battle of Karkar; Shalmaneser III beats coalition of Ahab, King of Israel, with Syrians and Egyptians.	
c.852—827 Takelot II, ineffective ruler: independent principalities in Egypt.			
			c.850 (or c.750—650) *Iliad* and *Odyssey* composed. c.850—800 Etruscans arrive in Italy.
c.827—788 Shoshenk III, Pharaoh. c.817—730 Twenty-third dynasty: period of anarchy.			
	814 Legendary date of the foundation of Carthage, seat of the Phoenician maritime trading empire.		
		805 Assyria invades Syria and Palestine.	
c. ante 800 Greek colony on Platea Is., Marmarica.			c.800 Foundation of Carthaginian trading colony at Nora, Sardinia. c.800 Etruscans settle between R Tiber and R Arno, and establish twelve cities.
c.788—782 Pemay, Pharaoh.			
		c.786 Growth of the Kingdom of Israel.	
c. 782—745 Shoshenk IV, Pharaoh. c.780 Sudanese Kashta intervenes in Theban politics.			
		c.776 Two-decked ship originated in Tyre.	c.776 First Olympic Games.
			c.753 Foundation of Rome.
ante c.751 Alara, chief of Kush; succ. by brother Kashta (—751); obtains control of Upper Egypt. c.751—730 Piankhy, King of Napata-Meroe.			
			c.750 Beginning of Greek colonization of the Mediterranean, with numerous settlements in southern Italy. Hesiod, poet.
		c.746—728 Tiglath Pilesar III, ruler of Assyria.	
			c.733 Foundation of Syracuse by Greeks.
		c.732 Damascus incorporated into the Assyrian Empire. c.731—722 Hoshea, King of Israel: alliance with Egypt.	
c.730 Piankhy invades Egypt: Delta and Middle Egypt, under several dynasties, do him homage. Piankhy reaches Memphis and Hermopolis; then returns to Napata. c.730—715 Twenty-fourth dynasty. Tefnakht submits to Piankhy as a vassal.			

EGYPT, THE SUDAN & EASTERN AFRICA	NORTHERN AFRICA & WESTERN AFRICA	WESTERN ASIA	EUROPE
		*c.*721–705 Sargon II of Assyria. 721 Israel taken into captivity by Sargon II of Assyria. 720 Battles of Karkar and Raphia: Egyptians and Jews beaten by Sargon.	
*c.*716–656 Twenty-fifth (Kushite)dynasty. *c.*716–695 Shabako (Sabacon) conquers the whole of Egypt: title, King of Kush and Misr.			
			*c.*708 Foundation of Tarentum by Greeks.
		*c.*704–686 Sennacherib, King of Assyria. 702 Fall of Tyre to Egypt. 701 Egyptians beaten by Sennacherib at Altakan; Kush receives assistance from Judah when Assyrians retreat as a result of plague.	
*c.*700 Shabako re-captures Bochchoris. 695–690 Shabataka (Shebitku) son of Piankhy. 689–664 Taharka, brother of Shabataka, associate ruler.			*c.*700 Arrival of the first Tyrians on Tuscan coast.
		689 Babylon destroyed by Sennacherib. *c.*686 Sennacherib d.: succ. by Esarhaddon (–668).	
*c.*685 Lowest level of temple at Kawa built; opened 679. 680–669 Esarhaddon of Assyria drives Taharka back to Egypt after his attack on Syria; Memphis destroyed; Egypt organized as an Assyrian colony. *c.*670 Possible beginning of iron-working at Meroe.			
		*c.*668–627 Ashurbanipal, King of Assyria. 667 Assyrians seize Tyre.	
*c.*667 Taharka regains Memphis; Ashurbanipal of Assyria retakes it, re-conquering most of Egypt; Tanuatamun (Urdamane), an Ethiopian, occupies Memphis (ruler, 664–656). *c.*664–525 Twenty-sixth dynasty. *c.*664–610 Psammetichus I, Pharaoh. *c.*663 Ashurbanipal drives Tanuatamun from Memphis and Thebes; immense booty carried off to Niniveh; Tanuatamun recovers, but retires to Napata; city of Miletus founds Greek colony at Naucratis.			
		*c.*660 Empire of the Medes emerges under Phraortes and Cyaxares.	*c.*660 Byzantium founded by Megarians.

GYPT, THE SUDAN & ASTERN AFRICA	NORTHERN AFRICA & WESTERN AFRICA	WESTERN ASIA	EUROPE
655 Psammetichus gains astery over other princes the Delta; treaty with yges, King of Lydia, for ercenaries.			
654 Tanwetamani, nephew f Taharka, hands over all aims to Egypt to sammetichus: retires to apata.			
		652—648 Babylon in revolt.	c. 650—560 Sappho, poetess.
650 Iron begins to be used Egypt. Tanwetamani d.; ynasty endures for another ,000 years at Napata and eroe.			
		648 Babylon recovered by Ashurbanipal.	
640 Syrian and Jewish olonists settle at Elephantine; ewish temple built; Greek ercenaries recruited; Ionian raders begin to settle.			
		631 Money invented by Lydians. Josiah, King of Judah, occupies former Kingdom of Israel.	
	630 Greeks found colony at Cyrene.		630 King of Tartessus visited by a Greek from Samos; obtains rich cargo of silver.
		627 Ashurbanipal d. 626 Chaldean dynasty founded by Nebuchadrezzar I (—605) at Babylon.	
			c. 621 Dracon, law-giver, at Athens. c. 616 Tarquin dynasty established at Rome. c. 612—599 Solon, law-giver.
10—595 Necho II, Pharaoh. .610 Necho II tries to link ile with Red Sea by a canal; hoenicians sent by him to ircumnavigate Africa; laimed to have done so in years.			
		c. 609—605 Egyptian campaigns against the Chaldeans. 605 Egyptians defeated at Carchemish. 605—602 Nebuchadrezzar II.	
01 Babylonians under ebuchadrezzar II attack gypt; driven off with eavy losses.			
			c.600 Marseilles founded by the Carthaginians.
597 Egyptian fleet onstructed by Necho II. 95—589 Psammetichus II, haroah; war with Napata- eroe.			

EGYPT, THE SUDAN & EASTERN AFRICA	NORTHERN AFRICA & WESTERN AFRICA	WESTERN ASIA	EUROPE
*c.*593—568 Aspelta, King of Napata-Meroe; temple of the Sun built at Meroe. 591 Psammetichus II sacks Napata; Meroe becomes the real capital. 589—568 Apries (Hophra); Egyptian expedition to Palestine to relieve Babylonian siege of Jerusalem; siege temporarily broken off.			
	*c.*588 Libyan alliance against Greeks of Cyrene ends in reconciliation.	*c.*588 Egyptian fleet supports Tyrians against Chaldeans. *c.*587 Jerusalem taken by Chaldeans; completely destroyed; Israel in captivity (to 539).	
*c.*587 Prophet Jeremiah and other Jews take refuge in Egypt.			
570—526 Amaris, Pharaoh; reaches throne by civil war; Apries put to death; treaty of alliance with Greeks of Cyrene; some towns in Cyprus conquered; Greek merchants confined to Naucratis.	*c.*570 Adicran, Libyan chief, applies to Apries for help against Greeks of Cyrene; Egyptian army over-whelmingly defeated.		
		561—542 Croesus, King of Lydia.	565 Cyprus captured by Egypt. 561—559 Pisistratus, tyrant of Athens. *c.*560 Carthaginians regain power in western Sicily.
		*c.*558-529 Cyrus II of Persia, the Great.	
*c.*550 Arabs from Yemen cross Red Sea and settle in Ethiopia; Habashat emerge as principal tribe; country called Habash (Abyssinia).	*c.*550 Euthymenes reaches Senegal; extension of Carthaginian dominions in Africa, Sicily, and Sardinia: Mogador, Tipasa, Hadrumetum, and Leptis founded; Carthaginian alliance with Persia; Malchus of Carthage's expeditions to set up bases in Sardinia and Sicily.	550 Cyrus II deposes King of Media.	*c.*556—552 Pisistratus again tyrant of Athens. *c.*550—500 Anacreon, poet.
		542 Cyrus seizes Lydia and deposes Croesus. 539 Babylon occupied by Cyrus II of Persia; Jewish captivity ended.	546 Sardis captured by Cyrus II of Persia. ?*c.* 542—528 Pisistratus again tyrant of Athens.
	*c.*539 Carthaginians defeated by Greeks.		
c. 538 Napata finally abandoned in favour of Meroe, already an important town.			
	*c.*533 Carthage enforces tribute from neighbouring tribes.		535 Carthaginians expel Phocaeans from Corsica. 533 War between Carthage and Syracuse for possession of Sicily.
		529 Cyrus II of Persia d.; succ. by Cambyses (529—522).	

EGYPT, THE SUDAN & EASTERN AFRICA	NORTHERN AFRICA & WESTERN AFRICA	WESTERN ASIA	EUROPE
526–525 Psammetichus III, Pharaoh.			
525 Battle of Pelusium; Cambyses conquers Egypt.	c. 525 Greeks in Libya declare themselves vassals of Persia.		c. 525 Aeschylus, dramatist, b.
525–404 Twenty-seventh (Persian) dynasty; Cambyses of Persia proclaimed Pharaoh; expedition sent to Siwa; commands expedition southward to Batn-al-Hagar.			
c.525 Camels introduced into Egypt from Persia.			
522 Persian satrap Aryandis put in charge of Egypt by Cambyses: declares himself independent: put down by Darius I.	522 Greeks in Libya revolt; Persians defeated.	522–486 Darius I of Persia.	
c.517 Darius I visits Egypt: laws of Egypt ordered to be put in writing; canal from Nile to Red Sea completed; a chief physician 'to relieve the sick' appointed; library rebuilt at Sais; many temples built.			
post c.510 Egyptian voyages to Punt (? Somalia or Hadhramaut).	c.510 Carthaginian alliance with Libyans against Greek principality near Leptis. c.510 Greek northern African colonies expanding trade.	c.510 Voyage of the Greek Scylax from R Indus to Suez; greatly increased trade between Egypt and the East: develops S Arabian Kingdoms.	c. 510 Carthaginians bar Greek access to Tartessus. 509 Foundation of the Roman Republic.
c.500 Aramaic used with Demotic for official documents in Egypt.	c.500 Barca founded; Carthaginians destroy attempted Spartan colony in Libya; tombs of Carthaginian settlers at Tipasa.	c.500 Palace of Persepolis built.	
? c. post 500 Proto-Karanga reaching Rhodesia and other Bantu-speaking groups beginning to spread in E Africa.			499–493 Ionian cities revolt against Persians: first Persian war, ending in defeat of Artaphernes. 490 Battle of Marathon.
486 Egypt revolts against Persians: time of confusion and trouble.		486–465 Xerxes I, King of Persia. 486 Babylon in revolt.	c.485 Syracuse the most prosperous trading city in the Mediterranean.
	c.484–483 Treaty between Carthage and Xerxes I of Persia. 480 29 Sept., Carthaginians defeated off Himera, Sicily.		480 Persian invasion of Greece; battle of Thermopylae; battle of Salamis (29 Sept.). 479 Battle of Plataea.
	c.479 New constitution in Carthage: Magonids replaced by 100 Judges (until c.279): forced to pay indemnity to Sicily: policy of retrenchment.		

EGYPT, THE SUDAN & EASTERN AFRICA	NORTHERN AFRICA & WESTERN AFRICA	WESTERN ASIA	EUROPE
	c. post **479** Expansion of agriculture by Carthaginians: conquest of area of present Tunisia and coastal Tripolitania; trading centres as far as Moroccan coast.		
			477 League of Delos founded. **471** Creation of Tribunes of the Plebs at Rome.
	*c.***470** Hanno the Carthaginian's voyage claimed to reach Mount Cameroun: extension of Carthaginian trade along western African coast.		
			*c.***468–399** Socrates, philosopher.
*c.***465–454** Inaros, a Libyan, sets up a fortress at Marea against Persians: takes possession of Delta: makes war on Persians in Cyprus: Athenian allies help Egyptians. **460** Egypt revolts against Persian satrap Achaemenes.		**465–424** Artaxerxes I, King of Persia.	
			459 Athenian expedition against Egypt. Greeks defeat Sicilian insurgents.
454 Persian general Megabyzus regains Egypt; Inaros crucified.			
			451–449 Decemvirs established at Rome.
*c.***450** Herodotus visits Egypt. Meroe trading with the Greek world.	*c.***450** Nasamones living in the Aujila oasis, as they still do; Garamantes making periodic wars in chariots on 'Ethiopians' from the Fezzan; customs post at Leptis taking one talent of gold (about £310) a day from trade between desert and Mediterranean. Claim by Herodotus that five Nasamones from Aujila had reached a land of pygmies with a river flowing westwards. Development of new Carthaginian trading centres: Sabratha, Tacapae, Thapsus, Leptis Minor, Hippo Diarrhytus, Hippo Regius, Rusicade, Saldae, Rusucurru, Rusguniae, Icosium, Iol, Cartennae, Tingi, Rusaddir, Sala, Ruzibis, as far as Tamusiga (Mogador). Carthaginians receiving tin from Brittany and Cornwall *via* Gades; Himilcon's expectation to Ireland.	*c.***450** Coinage begins to be minted by Phoenicians.	
		449–448 Peace between Persia and Athens.	**449** Greco-Persian treaty; Persians evacuate Europe. **447–438** The Parthenon built.

EGYPT, THE SUDAN & EASTERN AFRICA	NORTHERN AFRICA & WESTERN AFRICA	WESTERN ASIA	EUROPE
		c. post 445 Nehemiah, satrap of Jerusalem: the Temple rebuilt.	*c. post* 445 Herodotus, *The Histories* (various recensions) (—*c.*429). 443 Pericles (d.429), ruler of Athens. 441—439 The Samian war. 431 The Peloponnesian war. 428—347 Plato, philosopher. 427—424 Athenian expedition in Sicily.
		424 Xerxes II succ.; is assassinated: succ. Darius II (—404).	
			418—413 Athenian expedition in Sicily.
	*c.*415 Carthage builds new fleet and engages mercenaries for war on Sicily.		
410 Egyptian priests of Chnum at Elephantine bribe local commandant to destroy Jewish temple.			410 Democracy re-established in Greece.
	*c.*409 Carthaginian invasion of Sicily: war continues 100 years.		
		408 Cyrus the Younger, governor of Asia Minor.	408 Carthage takes Selinontum.
	405 Treaty between Carthage and Syracuse.		406 Carthage takes Acragas. 405—367 Dionysius of Syracuse. 405—404 Siege of Athens.
404—399 Twenty-eighth dynasty: Amyrtaeus of Sais, kinsman of Inaros, continues struggle against Persians. 404—369 Harsiyotef, King of Meroe: expeditions against Beja and Rehreh. 401 Battle of Cynaxa: insurgent Persian prince killed.		404—358 Artaxerxes II of Persia. 401 Revolt of Cyrus the Younger against Artaxerxes; retreat of the Ten Thousand.	
399—380 Twenty-ninth dynasty. 399 Nepherites I, prince of Mendes, expels Persians.			*c.*400 Agesilaus, King of Sparta. 400 Greeks of Sicily struggle against Carthage. *c.*399 Socrates condemned to death.
396—393 Egyptian treaty of alliance with Sparta.	396 Carthage makes peace with Syracuse. *c.*396 Tyrian cults being replaced by Greek cults at Carthage.	396 Persia and Sparta at war in Anatolia.	397 Thucydides, *Histories.* 396 First *Dialogues* of Plato.
393 Egyptian treaty with Salamis, Cyprus.			395 Beginning of the war with Corinth.
*c.*386—383 Egypt attacked by Persia; Egyptians carry war into Palestine.		386 Peace of Antalcidas between Persia and Sparta.	387 The Academy founded by Plato.
380 Peace with Persia.			384—322 Aristotle, philosopher. 381 Rome taken by Celts.

EGYPT, THE SUDAN & EASTERN AFRICA	NORTHERN AFRICA & WESTERN AFRICA	WESTERN ASIA	EUROPE
380—343 Thirtieth dynasty; oldest parts of temple at Philae built.			
	379 Revolt of Libyan mercenaries against Carthage; some small independent kingdoms in Morocco.		
378—360 Nectanebo I, Pharaoh. 378 Persian army defeated at Memphis. *post* 378 Many temples and buildings constructed. 373 Persians attack Pelusium and Memphis: forced to retreat by Nile floods.			
			369 Athens and Sparta ally against Thebes. *c.*367 Carthage begins to regain Sicilian possessions.
360 Agesilaus of Sparta arrives with 1,000 hoplites: joins in Egyptian attack on Phoenicia. 360—341 Nectanebo II: peace restored with aid of Greek troops. 360 First coinage struck in Egypt; taxes still raised in kind; wine, oil, pottery, and arms imported from Greece; cereals, papyrus, and ivory exported by Egypt.			
			359—336 Philip, King of Macedon.
		358—338 Artaxerxes III Ochus of Persia: Phoenicia and Palestine revolt.	
			356 Alexander the Great, b. 354 Demosthenes' first speech to the Assembly in Athens.
351 Persian invasion of Egypt prevented with aid of Spartan and Athenian mercenaries.			
	348 First trade treaty between Rome and Carthage.		
		345 Artaxerxes III occupies Phoenicia.	345—340 Carthage driven out of Sicily by Timoleon of Corinth. 343 Campania annexed by Rome. First Samnite war.
343 Persian campaign against Egypt; becomes a Persian province again. *c.*343—332 Thirty-first (Persian) dynasty.			
		338 Artaxerxes III murdered; succ. Arses (−336).	*c.*338 Beginning of rise of Macedon as a world power. 337 Philip of Macedon at war with Persia.
		335—332 Darius III Codomannus succ. Arses.	335 First coinage minted in Rome. Alexander the Great's campaign on the Danube.
		334 Alexander the Great begins to conquer Asia.	334 Philip of Macedon assassinated; succ. by Alexander the Great.

EGYPT, THE SUDAN & EASTERN AFRICA	NORTHERN AFRICA & WESTERN AFRICA	WESTERN ASIA	EUROPE
		333 Battle of Issus; Darius beaten by Alexander; Syria seized. 332 Tyre destroyed by Alexander.	
332 Alexander the Great reaches Egypt; accepted as Pharaoh; Cleomenes of Naucratis financial superintendent; Ptolemy in command of standing army.			
	331 Alexander visits Siwa; oracle confirms his divine origin.		
c.331 20 Jan., Alexandria founded; many Macedonians, Greeks, and Jews settle.			
			330 Democratic revolution in Syracuse.
328–308 Nastasen, last King to be buried at Napata.			
	327 Second trade treaty between Rome and Carthage.	327 Alexander the Great in India.	
		325 Nearchus's *Periplus*. Alexander the Great in Persia.	326 Second Samnite war.
323–285 Ptolemy I Soter of Egypt: Ptolemaic, or Lagid dynasty (to 30).	323 Carthage sends embassy to Alexander the Great.	323 Alexander the Great d. at Babylon; his empire divided among his generals.	
320 Ptolemy I Soter formally recognized ruler of Egypt; Libya included as a province. 320 Cleomenes put to death by Ptolemy.			321 The Caudine Forks. 320 Ptolemy I seizes Cyprus; aristocratic regime restored in Syracuse.
		319 Ptolemy I takes Syria.	
	314 Ptolemy loses control of Cyrene by a revolution: later regained.		317–289 Agathocles, tyrant of Syracuse. 314 Cyprus taken by Satrap Antigonus.
		312 Battle of Gaza: Syria lost by Egypt.	
	310–307 Agathocles, tyrant of Syracuse, attacks Carthaginians; takes Hadrumetum, Utica and Hippo Diarrhytus; then returns to Sicily; conquered territory sold to Carthage. c.308 Bomilcar's conspiracy in Carthage. c.307 Libyan war chariots replaced by cavalry. c.306 Trade treaty between Rome and Carthage defines spheres of commercial influence. 306 Peace between Carthage and Agathocles.		
305 Ptolemy proclaimed as Pharaoh. ante 300 Beja (Belhe or Medyat) raiding Kawa and other Nile settlements.	c.300 Carthaginian alliance with Egypt: great extension of commercial prosperity.	c.300 Great Wall of China built.	

EGYPT, THE SUDAN & EASTERN AFRICA	NORTHERN AFRICA & WESTERN AFRICA	WESTERN ASIA	EUROPE
c.300 Royal burials at Meroe begin. c.300 Mouseion library containing 500,000 mss founded at Alexandria; Zenodotus of Ephesus, Librarian, aided by poets Callimacus and Theocritus; Euclid, mathematician, teaching.	c.300 Rock paintings in central Sahara; elaborate cemetery with 45,000 graves of Garamantes at Garama.		
			295 Ptolemy recovers Cyprus. c.295 Rome leading power in all Italy. 294 Demetrius Poliorcetes, King of Macedon. 289 Agathocles plans attack on Carthage; dies before start; civil war and war with Carthage (−275).
287–212 Archimedes, mathematician. 285–247 Ptolemy II Philadelphus. 283 Ptolemy given a cult as Soter (Saviour). 280 Pharos (Lighthouse) built at Alexandria; Nile-Red Sea canal completed; great development of trade with India and Africa.	280 ± 120 Nok culture site at Tarunga, with abundant evidence of iron-working.		280 Celtic invasions.
		278 Galatians invade Asia Minor. 276–272 First Syrian war.	
c. 275 Manetho, *History of Egypt*. c.275–200 Eratosthenes of Cyrene, mathematician and philosopher.			c.275 Carthaginians fully re-established in Sicily with some gains.
		274–236 Reign of Asoka, conqueror of India: Buddhism spreads widely.	
			272 Rome captures Tarentum. c.270 Hieron, despot of Syracuse. 269–268 Carthaginian naval garrison at Messina.
c.269–264 Port of Ptolemais Epitheras (Ptolemais of the Hunts) founded on Eritrean coast.			
	264–241 First Punic war: Romans take many Carthaginian towns in Sicily.		265 Carthage reoccupies Messina. 264 Rome garrisons Messina: war with Carthage inevitable. 262–258 Roman naval actions against Carthage in the Mediterranean.
	260 Carthaginian fleet defeated by Romans at Myles, near Messina. 256 Roman army under Regulus disembarks at Clipea (Kelibia); pillages villas of Carthaginian nobility; 20,000 slaves taken; Xanthippus, a Spartan, beats Regulus in open country.	260–255 Second Syrian war. c.260 Asoka becomes a Buddhist.	

EGYPT, THE SUDAN & EASTERN AFRICA	NORTHERN AFRICA & WESTERN AFRICA	WESTERN ASIA	EUROPE
c.250 Hebrew scriptures translated by seventy scholars into Greek (Septuagint). 247—221 Ptolemy III Euergetes I: expedition to Red Sea to trade with Ethiopia; Roman port created at Adulis. c. 243 Leap year introduced in the Egyptian calendar.	post 255 Carthaginians make war on Sicily and into Calabria. c.250 Inscriptions in ancient Libyan in Fezzan and central Sahara related to present Tuareg script. 247—183 Hannibal.		
		246—241 Third Syrian war.	
	241 Carthaginian fleet beaten by Romans off Aegates Is.; Carthage made to abandon Sicily and pay 3,200 gold talents. 241—219 Peace between Carthage and Rome. 240—238 Revolt of Carthaginian mercenaries; Carthage and Tunis occupied: Utica and Bizerta besieged: Hamilcar Barca obtains support of Numidian cavalry: mercenaries destroyed at Scie.	c.240 Ceylon becomes Buddhist.	
			239 Rome takes Corsica and Sardinia from Carthage.
	238 Tunis recovered. 237 Victory of Hamilcar Barca over Libyan and other mercenaries.		237 Carthaginians conquer Spain.
		230—228 Attalus I conquers Asia Minor.	c.230 Hamilcar develops ports, mines and trade in Spain. c.226 Hasdrubal assassinated in Spain; Hannibal becomes general of the Carthaginian army. Carthage and Rome define their areas in Spain.
225—200 Arkamani (Ergamanes), King of Meroe; friendly relations with Alexandria. 221—200 Ptolemy IV Philopator; further expedition in Red Sea: Berenice (Adulis) and other trading stations set up. 217 Risings in Egypt.	218—201 Second Punic war. 215 Treaty between Carthage and Philip V.	223—187 Antiochus III. 221—217 Fourth Syrian war.	219 Hannibal takes Saguntum. 218 Hannibal marches on Italy: takes elephants across the Alps; battle of Trebia. 216 Battle of Cannae. 212 Archimedes d. at siege of Syracuse.

EGYPT, THE SUDAN & EASTERN AFRICA	NORTHERN AFRICA & WESTERN AFRICA	WESTERN ASIA	EUROPE
		210–205 Antiochus III's expedition to India.	209–206 Cornelius Scipio conquers Spain from Carthaginians.
	204–201 Scipio makes alliances for Rome against Carthage with Numidian chiefs: Syphax and Masinissa side with Carthage. 204 Scipio disembarks with two legions near Utica; Masinissa joins Romans. 203 (March) Scipio beats army under Hannibal and Syphax: conquers most of Carthaginian territory: Masinissa seizes Syphax: Carthage isolated.	203 Fifth Syrian war.	
	202 13 Oct., Battle of Zama: Hannibal defeated by Scipio; Carthage made to pay 20,000 gold talents and give up fleet; Masinissa, King of Numidia (201–148), ruling from Libya to Morocco, conquers Masaesyles; peace between Rome and Carthage.	202 Han dynasty founded in China.	202 Treaty between Philip V and Antiochus III against Egypt.
c.200 Nubai living in Dongola region. 200–181 Ptolemy V Epiphanes: commemorated on Rosetta Stone in hieroglyphic, demotic, and Greek.	c.200 Nok culture in Nigeria reaches fullest development.		c.200 Germans invade Bohemia. 200 Rome annexes Spain.
		c.198 Antiochus III seizes Phoenicia and Palestine.	
		196 Hannibal at the court of Antiochus III.	197 Andalusia in revolt. 196 Andalusian revolt put down by Cato.
195 Treaty between Egypt and Antiochus III.	195–184 Hannibal, suffete of Carthage. 191–148 Gradual encroachment of Masinissa on Carthaginian territory.		
			184 Cato censor: demands that Carthage be destroyed.
		183 Hannibal d. in Bithynia.	
181–145 Ptolemy VI Philometor: Jewish temple erected at Leontopolis. c.180 Cursive script replaces Egyptian hieroglyphic at Meroe.			
		175–164 Antiochus IV. 170–136 Mithradates I, King of Parthia. 169 Sixth Syrian war.	
169 Antiochus IV attacks Egypt. 168 Antiochus IV compelled by Rome to withdraw from Egypt.		168 Violent persecution of the Jews by Antiochus IV.	
		167 Beginning of the Maccabean revolt. 164 Freedom of worship restored to the Jews.	

EGYPT, THE SUDAN & EASTERN AFRICA	NORTHERN AFRICA & WESTERN AFRICA	WESTERN ASIA	EUROPE
	162 Masinissa seizes Syrta region.	162 Fresh revolt of the Jews. 161 Treaty between Rome and the Jews. 160 Judas Maccabeus defeated.	
	154 Carthage arms against Masinissa. 153 Masinissa takes region of Campi Magni (Dakhla). c. 153 Cato in Africa. 150 Carthaginians raise army against Masinissa: defeated: new Roman indemnity of 5,000 gold talents: Carthage ordered to be destroyed. 150–146 Siege of Carthage. 146 Carthage taken by Romans. 149–146 Polybius's voyage along western Africa as far as Argüin. 148 Masinissa d., leaving kingdom stretching from Morocco to Tripolitania. 148–118 Micipsa succ. Masinissa.		149 Death of Cato.
	146 North-western Tunisia constituted the Roman Province of Africa.		147 First consulate of Scipio.
145–116 Ptolemy VII Euergetes II. Jewish scholars invited to settle in Alexandria.		145 Revolt of Diodotus Tryphon in Syria. 143 Jonathan Maccabeus murdered. c. 143–142 Independence of Judaea recognized. 141 Hasmonean dynasty founded. c.134 Attalus III seizes Judaea. 133 Attalus III bequeaths Syria to Rome. 129 Judaea regains independence. 123–86 Mithridates II the Great, King of Parthia.	
			120 Rome annexes Transalpine Gaul.
119 Voyage of Eudoxus of Cyzicus from the Red Sea to India.			
	118–104 Jugurtha succeeds Micipsa: Jugurthine war. 118 Cirta revolts against Jugurtha.		
c. 117 Agatharcides, geographer. 116–108/7 Ptolemy VIII Soter II (first reign).			
	113–112 Siege of Cirta by Jugurtha. 111 Roman army in Numidia: Jugurtha visits Rome. 110–107 Roman army under Metellus in Numidia: no decisive action.	c. 111 Eudoxus of Cyzicus fails to reach India via the Cape.	113 Invasion of Cimbrians and Teutons.

EGYPT, THE SUDAN & EASTERN AFRICA	NORTHERN AFRICA & WESTERN AFRICA	WESTERN ASIA	EUROPE
108/7—88 Ptolemy IX Alexander I.	107 C. Marius in command in Africa. 106—80 Bocchus I, King of Mauritania. 105 Jugurtha captured: taken to Rome and strangled. 105—c. 88 Gauda, King of Numidia.	103 Alexander Jannaeus, King of Judaea.	107 First consulate of C. Marius. 106 Cicero b. 102 Marius beats the Teutons at Aix. 101 Cimbrians beaten at Verceil.
88—80 Ptolemy VIII restored.	97 Cyrenaica independent of Egypt. 96 Ptolemy Apion, King of Cyrene, makes Rome heir to his country in his will. *ante* c.88—c.68 Hiemsal, King of Numidia. c.86 Julius Maternus makes an alliance between the Romans and Garamantes against the 'Ethiopians' and reaches Agisymba (? Aïr). 82 Tingis (Tangier) occupied by Sertorius.	90 Pharisees revolt against Alexander Jannaeus.	
80 Ptolemy X Alexander II names Rome as heir in his will. Succ. Ptolemy XI Auletes, 80—51.	74 Rome annexes Cyrene.		80—72 Sertorius's revolt in Spain. 73 Servile war in Italy.
	c. 68 Juba I, King of Numidia: capital Zama.	67 Civil war in Judaea. 65 Pompey in the Caucasus. 64 Pompey seizes Syria. 63 Jerusalem taken by Pompey.	63 Cicero, Consul. 60 Cyprus taken by Rome from Egypt. 59 Julius Caesar, Consul.
59 Caesar compels the recognition of Ptolemy Auletes as ruler of Egypt.			58—51 Caesar's campaigns in Gaul: *de bello Gallico*.
56 Gabinius, Roman Proconsul of Syria, intervenes in Egypt.		57—55 Judaea revolts against Rome. 56—37 Orodes I of Parthia.	55—54 Caesar twice invades Britain.
		54 Crassus succeeds Gabinius as proconsul of Syria: campaign in Mesopotamia. 53 Orodes I defeats Romans at Carrhae; Crassus killed.	53 Quarrel between Caesar and Pompey.

EGYPT, THE SUDAN & EASTERN AFRICA	NORTHERN AFRICA & WESTERN AFRICA	WESTERN ASIA	EUROPE
51—30 Cleopatra last independent ruler of Egypt.			
	49 Juba I supports Pompey against Caesar: defeats Caesarion Curion.		**49** Caesar in Spain.
48 Pompey flees to Egypt and d. Alexandria revolts against Caesar. **48—47** Caesar in Egypt: rebellion quashed; library burnt at Alexandria.			**48** Caesar victorious over Pompey at Pharsalus.
	47 Sallust (86—35), historian, Governor of Africa. **46** 1 Jan., Caesar disembarks at Hadrumetum. **46** 4 Apr., Caesar defeats Pompeian army and allies at Thapsus: Juba commits suicide; twenty-two camels captured. **46** Caesar annexes region of Thabraca and Ampsage estuary; Cirta left to the bandit Sittius; Roman Africa reorganized to cover all of present Tunisia.		**46** Caesar made dictator for 10 years.
		44 Brutus and Cassius in the East. **42** Parthians occupy Syria and Judaea.	**44** Caesar murdered.
	42 and **38** Bogud, King of western Mauritania, takes part in expeditions in Spain.		
41 Marcus Anthony in Egypt.	**38** Bogud's kingdom seized by Bocchus II; Tingis (Tangier) given rights of a Roman city.		
37 Marcus Anthony marries Cleopatra.		**37** Herod, King of Judaea, under Roman protectorate. **36** Marcus Anthony's expedition against the Parthians. **35—33** Marcus Anthony's campaign in Armenia.	
			35 Quarrel between Marcus Anthony and Octavian, adopted nephew of Caesar. **35—33** Octavian's campaigns in Illyria.
34 Marcus Anthony divides the east between Cleopatra and her children.			
	33 Numidia annexed by Rome: Bocchus II dies; **33—25** Mauritania governed by two Roman prefects.		
32 Octavian declares war on Cleopatra.			**32** Marcus Anthony makes final breach with Octavian. **31** 2 Sept., Battle of Actium.
30 Egypt annexed to Rome by Octavian. **29** Aug., Cleopatra commits suicide; Marcus Anthony d.			**30—AD 14** Octavian ruler of Rome: Augustan Age: Livy, historian; Strabo, geographer; Ovid, Vergil, poets. **29** Vergil, *Aeneid*.

EGYPT, THE SUDAN & EASTERN AFRICA	NORTHERN AFRICA WESTERN AFRICA	WESTERN ASIA	EUROPE
	27 Roman African reorganized by Augustus.		27—AD 14 Roman Empire reorganized by Octavian; receives the name of Augustus. 27—25 Augustus's campaigns in Spain.
	c.25—AD 23 Juba II, King of Mauritania: placed on throne by Augustus; capital at Caesarea (Cherchel); a fleet sent to the Canary Is. post 25 Juba II explores Atlas Mts with his physician Euphorbius, author of numerous works now lost; coast of Morocco explored to Mogador.	25 Aelius Gallus's expedition to South Arabia. Indian embassy to Rome.	
			24—19 Spain in revolt.
23 Petronius defeats Candace, Queen of Meroe, and sacks Napata. c. 20—AD 15 Natakamani, King of Meroe: restores Lion Temple at Naga: Queen Amanitere, co-ruler: trade relations with India via Axum.		c.20 Temple at Jerusalem rebuilt by Herod. 20 R Euphrates established as eastern boundary of the Roman Empire.	
	c.19 Cornelius Balbus's expedition to the Fezzan: claimed to have reached R.Niger.		
			12—AD 6 Drusus and Tiberius subdue Germany.
		4 Herod the Great d.	
	1st c. AD The camel introduced into the Sahara. c.1 Raids by the Gaetuli on Numidia; Roman legions called on to suppress them.		c. AD 1 Ovid, Ars Amatoria. 1AD Beginning of the Christian Era according to the monk Dionysius the Little (5th c. AD).
		c.4 AD Birth of Jesus Christ.	4—6 Tiberius conquers Germany as far as the Elbe.
c. AD6 Hippalus discovers periodicity of the monsoons; increase of trade of Alexandria and the Roman world with the east.		6—9 Varus's expectation against Parthia. 6 Judaea annexed by Rome and made a province. 9 Varus taken prisoner.	
			14—37 Tiberius, Roman Emperor. 14—16 Germanicus's campaigns in Germany.
	17—24 Tacfarinas, leader of Musulames, revolts.		19 Strabo, Geography; Vergil d.
c.20—96 First datable iron-working in Zambia.			
	c.24 Tacfarinas killed in battle: revolt dissolves: Roman troops withdrawn.		
c.25 Greek, with Latin, official languages in Egypt.		c.25—30 or 33 Pontius Pilate, Procurator of Judaea.	

EGYPT, THE SUDAN & EASTERN AFRICA	NORTHERN AFRICA & WESTERN AFRICA	WESTERN ASIA	EUROPE
		*c.*27 John the Baptist beheaded. *c.*30 or 33 Crucifixion and resurrection of Jesus Christ.	
			36 Peace between Rome and Parthia. 37–41 Caligula, Roman Emperor.
40 Philo of Alexandria, Jewish Hellenistic philosopher, d. *c.*40 See of Alexandria claimed to be founded by St Mark. 41–54 Revolt of Jews in Alexandria. Porphyry quarries on Red Sea exploited and stone exported to Rome. *c.*41–54 Diogenes voyages from the Red Sea along the coast of eastern Africa as far as Rhapta (?R Rufiji).	40 Ptolemy, King of Mauritania, murdered on instigation of Caligula. 40–1 Aedemon's rebellion in Mauritania and Numidia. 41 Marcus Licinius Crassus beats Aedemon: conquers Mauritania: rebellion increases in Numidia: put down by Suetonius Paulinus.		41–54 Claudius, Roman Emperor.
	42 Mauritania (Morocco) annexed to the Roman Empire: capital Tingis (Tangier).		
			43 Romans begin conquest of Britain.
		*c.*45–57 Missionary travels of St Paul.	
	46 Mauritania divided into two provinces, Mauritania Caesariensis and Mauritania Tingitana.		
		*c.*47 Council of Jerusalem.	*c.*47 Pomponius Mela, geographer, *de Situ Orbis.*
*c.*50 Active trade between Alexandria and India.			
			54–68 Nero, Roman Emperor.
		57–63 Roman campaigns in Armenia and Parthia.	
60 Two Roman centurions sent by Nero to explore the Nile with object of reaching Ethiopia: unable to pass the Sudd.			60–1 Queen Boudicca (Boadicea) revolts against the Romans in Britain. 64 Rome burnt; Christians believed responsible and persecuted.
66 Rebellion of the Jews in Alexandria: 50,000 massacred.		*c.*65 St Mark's *Gospel.* 66–8 Judaea revolts against Rome.	
			67 Martyrdom of St Peter the Apostle, first Pope (*c.*42–67), and of St Paul.
	68 Revolt of Romans in N Africa. 69 War between Oea and Leptis. 70 Garamantes pillage Tripolitania: expedition under Septimus Flaccus pursues them to the Fezzan and perhaps Bilma.	70 Jerusalem destroyed by Titus.	69–79 Vespasian, Roman Emperor.

EGYPT, THE SUDAN & EASTERN AFRICA	NORTHERN AFRICA & WESTERN AFRICA	WESTERN ASIA	EUROPE
		c.75 Flavius Josephus, *The Jewish Wars*.	77 Pliny the Elder, *Natural History*.
79 Emperor Titus visits Egypt.			79—81 Titus, Roman Emperor. 79—85 Agricola, Governor of Britain, completes conquest of Britain as far as R Clyde and Firth of Forth.
		c.80 St Luke's *Gospel*.	
c.81—96 Temples erected by Domitian to Isis and Serapis.	c. 81—96 Wheat, olive-growing, and viticulture increased in Roman Africa to make it the granary of Rome.		81—96 Domitian, Roman Emperor.
		c.85 St Matthew's *Gospel*.	
90 ± 220 Zambezi Channelled Ware in the Machili Forest, Zambia. c.90—168 Claudius Ptolemy, geographer.		c.95 St John's *Gospel*.	
			96—8 Nerva, Roman Emperor. 98—117 Trajan, Roman Emperor; Roman Empire at its greatest extent. 98 Tacitus, *Histories*.
	98—117 Trajan alienates best lands in Africa to Romans and Berber allies of Rome: impoverishment of former landowners. 2nd century Magharibah Berbers and Mandingos begin to form population of (ancient) Ghana.	105 Rome annexes Nabataean Arabia.	
c. 1st to 6th centuries Stamped Ware Stone Age communities penetrate south of R Zambezi, and begin to mine gold, copper, and tin. c.106 *The Periplus of the Erythraean Sea* written by an anonymous official in Alexandria: describes the trade of the Red Sea, eastern Africa, and South Arabia with India and China. 115 General revolt of Jews in Egypt, N Africa, Palestine, and Cyprus. c.115 Trajan restores canal from Nile to Red Sea.	115 Jews revolt in Leptis Magna and Cyrene; some flee to Fezzan and Hoggar.	111—13 Persecution of Christians in Bithynia. 114—16 War between Rome and Parthia.	107 Martyrdom of St Ignatius of Antioch at Rome.
	118 Emperor Hadrian leads expedition against rebels in Mauritania: makes new road from Carthage to Tebessa.		117—38 Hadrian, Roman Emperor.
			122—6 Hadrian's wall built in Britain.

EGYPT, THE SUDAN & EASTERN AFRICA	NORTHERN AFRICA & WESTERN AFRICA	WESTERN ASIA	EUROPE
130 Hadrian visits Egypt: orders building of new capital for Upper Egypt at Antinopolis. *c.*130 Basilides, gnostic, d., after teaching at Alexandria.			
		132—5 Final diaspora of Jews from Palestine after Bar-Cochba's rising.	
			136 Valentinus, gnostic, teaching in Rome. **138—61** Antoninus Pius, Roman Emperor.
140—61 Valentinus, gnostic, teaching in Alexandria.			
	144—52 General revolt of Berbers in the Aurès Mountains.		
*c.*150 Original version of Claudius Ptolemy's *Geography* written in Alexandria. *c.*150—350 General economic decline in Egypt as a result of Roman corn tax: reflected in the decline in the Sudan. **150** St Clement of Alexandria b.			
			153 Justin, *Apology*.
		156 Martyrdom of St Polycarp in Smyrna.	
	*c.*160—230 Tertullian, theologian and writer, at Carthage.		
*c.*161 Revolt of peasants near Alexandria. **161** Valentinus d.			**161—80** Marcus Aurelius, Roman Emperor. **161** Gaius, *Institutiones*. **165** Persecution of Christians in Rome. **169** Invasion of Quadi and Marcomanni; Verus, co-emperor.
		*c.*172 Beginnings of Montanism in Phrygia: spreads later to Africa and (?) Gaul.	**172** Moors (Mauri) overrun much of Spain: Emperor Marcus Aurelius sends general Septimius Severus to restore order.
180±100 Iron working at Mabveni, Rhodesia. *c.*180 *Didaskaleion* or Catechetical School started at Alexandria under Pantaenus. *c.*185—251 Origen, theologian and biblical scholar. **186**±150 Channelled Ware at Lusu, near Sesheke (present Rhodesia) dates the end of the Wilton period: possible arrival of Bantu speakers.	**180** First African Christians martyred at Scilli.		*c.*180 Irenaeus, *Adversus Omnes Haereses*. **180—92** Commodus, Roman Emperor.

EGYPT, THE SUDAN & EASTERN AFRICA	NORTHERN AFRICA & WESTERN AFRICA	WESTERN ASIA	EUROPE
189 Demetrius, Bp of Alexandria.			
		195 Roman campaign against Arabs and Parthians.	
	c.196 Tertullian converted to Christianity: preaches Montanist doctrines in Carthage. c.197 Tertullian, *Apology.* c.197 Leptis Magna given *ius italica* in honour of being Septimius Severus's birthplace.		197–212 Septimius Severus, a Berber from Leptis Magna, Roman Emperor.
		c.198–200 Roman Empire reaches Nineveh. 198 Seleucia and Ctesiphon captured.	
?c. 3rd-4th c. Steles, throne and palace at Axum. c.200–15 St Clement, Bp of Alexandria. 202 Capitals of *nomes* made Roman municipalities. c.203 Fort erected at Premis, Nubia: furthest Roman penetration. Origen head of the Catechetical School of Alexandria. 205–70 Plotinus, philosopher.	203 Sts Perpetua and Felicity martyred at Carthage.		
			208–11 Roman campaigns in Britain. 212–17 Caracalla, Roman Emperor. 212–13 Caracalla's campaigns on R Danube. 212 Caracalla gives Roman citizenship to every free-born subject of the Empire.
c.212 Revolt in Alexandria: many massacred.		212–41 Ardashir I of Persia: coin found in Zanzibar.	
		c. 216–76 Mani, founder of the Manichee Gnostic sect.	
			217 Macrinus, Roman Emperor. 218–22 Elagabalus, Roman Emperor. 222–35 Alexander Severus, Roman Emperor.
c.222 Hoard of gold coins at Debra Damo imported from India. c.225 Origen, *Hexapla.*	225 or 230 Agrippinus, Bp of Carthage, holds a council.		
		227 Sassanid dynasty established at Ctesiphon, ruling Persian Empire until the Arab conquest. 228 Mani's first revelation.	
230 Origen exiled from Alexandria for heresy.	c. 230 Tertullian d. 231–2 War between Rome and Persia.	230 Origen teaching in Palestine (−251).	
c.232–304 Porphyry, philosopher, at Alexandria.			
	235 Revolt of imperial colonists at El Djem; Gordian, Governor of Africa, declared Emperor; defeated by Carpillinus.		235–8 Maximinus, Roman Emperor.

EGYPT, THE SUDAN & EASTERN AFRICA	NORTHERN AFRICA & WESTERN AFRICA	WESTERN ASIA	EUROPE
		238 Goths begin to invade Eastern Empire. 241—4 Second war between Rome and Persia. 242—73 Sapor I of Persia.	238—44 Gordian III, Roman Emperor. 244—70 Plotinus, philosopher, in Rome. 244—8 Philip, Roman Emperor.
247—65 Dionysius, Bp of Alexandria.	246 Cyprian becomes a Christian.		
		248 Origen, *Contra Celsum.*	248—51 Decius, Roman Emperor.
c.250 St Paul of Thebes (—c.299) becomes first hermit during Decian persecution. c.250 Aphilas, King of Axum; first Axumite ruler to issue coinage. c.250 (—356) St Anthony the Hermit, father of monasticism, b. in the Fayoum. c.250—350 Blemmyes (Beja) raiding Upper Egypt. c.250 First work on algebra by Diophantus of Alexandria. c.251 Latest known inscription in Nubia: subsequent relapse into illiteracy inferred. c.251—3 Embassy from Meroe to Rome.	250 Dionysius of Alexandria flees to Libya as a result of Decius's persecution. Persecution of Decius raises question of lapsed. c.250—325 Lactantius, writer.		c.250 Christianity spreading in Gaul. 250 Persecution of Christians by Emperor Decius; Pope Fabian martyred.
	251—8 St Cyprian, Bp of Carthage. 251 St Cyprian, treatises *On the Unity of the Catholic Church* and *On the Lapsed.* 253 Revolt in Numidia and Mauritania by Berbers: Aurès virtually independent to 262.	251 Origen d. in Palestine.	251 Emperor Decius defeated by Goths. 251—3 Trebonianus Gallus, Roman Emperor. 253—60 Valerian, Roman Emperor.
c.255 Plotinus, *Enneads.* c.256 Arius, originator of the Arian heresy, b. in Libya.	256 Controversy between St Cyprian and eighty-eight African bishops with Pope Stephen on the baptism of heretics. 258 14 Sept., St Cyprian martyred in Carthage.	254 Sapor takes Nisibis. 256 Sapor takes Antioch.	254 Assassination of the Moorish general Aemilianus who had proclaimed himself Emperor. 258 Persecution of Christians by Valerian: Pope Sixtus II martyred. 258—68 Roman Empire invaded by Franks.
		260 Emperor Valerian taken prisoner by Sapor.	260—8 Gallienus, Roman Emperor. 260 Gallienus issues edict tolerating Christians.
	262 Revolt near Sétif.	265—340 Eusebius of Caesarea, first ecclesiastical historian. c. 267 Zenobia, Queen of Palmyra: conquers Mesopotamia, Syria, and Egypt.	267 Goths invade Greece and reach Athens.

EGYPT, THE SUDAN & EASTERN AFRICA	NORTHERN AFRICA & WESTERN AFRICA	WESTERN ASIA	EUROPE
			268—71 Claudius II, Roman Emperor. 268 Claudius II defeats the Alemanni. 269 Goths defeated at Nish.
269—72 Time of troubles and weakness in Roman Empire. 270 St Anthony becomes a hermit. c.270—80 Porphyry, *Contra Christianos*.			
		273 Aurelian overthrows Palmyra.	271—5 Aurelian, Emperor.
274 Uprising in Alexandria led by Firmus; put down by Probus; Probus leads expedition against the Blemmyes. The Bible translated into Coptic.			274 Ethiopian captives from Palmyra brought to Rome.
			275—6 Tacitus, Roman Emperor. 276—82 Probus, Roman Emperor.
		281 Carus's campaign in Persia.	
		283 Carus recovers Seleucia and Ctesiphon.	282—3 Carus, Roman Emperor. 283—4 Numerian, Roman Emperor.
284 Beginning of the Coptic Era of the Martyrs (Coptic Calendar). Nobatae introduced into Lower Nubia to counteract raiding Blemmyes. c.285 First description of the cogwheel, lever, pulley, screw, and wedge, and theorems on areas and volumes by Pappus of Alexandria. Monasticism spreading rapidly in Egypt.	284 Roman provinces in N Africa reorganized by Diocletian: Mauritania Tingitana joined to Spanish province of Baetica.		284—305 Diocletian, Roman Emperor. Cult of the Roman Emperor as a god made compulsory throughout Roman Empire: persecution of Christians follows.
	289—95 Revolt of Berbers in region of Kabylia and Hodna.	c.290 Gupta Kingdom established in Bengal.	
292—346 St Pachomius, organizer of cenobitic monasticism. 292—3 Roman general Achilles proclaims himself Emperor; put down by Diocletian after 20 months siege of Alexandria: frontier withdrawn to Aswan: administration and currency reformed.			
			293 Roman Empire organized as a tetrarchy. 293—306 Constantius I Chlorus, Emperor.
296 Frontiers of Egypt contracted to fortress on Elephantine Is.: Kharqa oasis fortified and garrisoned with first camel corps: territory south ceded to Nobatae, who keep off Blemmyes.			

EGYPT, THE SUDAN & EASTERN AFRICA	NORTHERN AFRICA & WESTERN AFRICA	WESTERN ASIA	EUROPE
			297 Diocletian reforms the administration of the Roman Empire.
600±100—900±100 Ziwa culture at Inyanga. c.300 Kalomo, Zambia, first inhabited by mound-dwellers. c.300 King of Axum suzerain of Himyar, Saba, Raydan, and Salhen. c.300—11 Peter, Bp of Alexandria.	4thc.—c.750 Berber Maga dynasty ruling Mandingos as Kings of Ghana. c.300 Iron objects appear at Saharan sites. ?c.300—400 Beginnings of trans-Saharan camel-borne traffic in gold and salt.		
			303—11 Edict of Diocletian against Christians starts persecution throughout the Roman Empire: the 'Great Persecution'.
305 Domitius Alexander, general commanding Egypt, proclaimed Emperor: long struggle by Maxentius to recover all northern Africa. 306 Peter of Alexandria, Letter on Penitence.	305 Beginning of Donatist heresy: Donatus, Bp of Casa Negra, leads seventy-six Numidian bishops in movement of extreme moral rigidity.		306—37 Constantine the Great, Emperor. 306 Constantine's campaigns against the Franks and the Alemanni.
		309 Sapor II of Persia blocks an invasion of the Huns.	
311 Persecution of Christians by Maximinus Daia: St Anthony visits Alexandria to comfort Christians.	311 Caecilian, Bp of Carthage.		311 Emperor Galerius issues edict tolerating Christianity.
			312 Emperor Constantine sees a vision of the Cross before the battle of the Milvian Bridge. 313 Emperor Constantine publishes Edict of Milan recognizing Christianity as a lawful religion.
		314—?393 Libanius, philosopher, tutor of the Emperor Julian.	314 Council of Arles: Donatism condemned. 314 Partition of the Roman Empire.
c.318 St Pachomius organizes the first monastery at Tabennisi, near Thebes. 318 First discussion in Alexandria of doctrines of Arius. 319 Persecution of Christians in Egypt. 320 Synod of Alexandria condemns Arianism: Arius, two bishops and five priests expelled from Egypt. c.320—55 Aezanas, son of Ella Amida, King of Axum; kingdom includes Saba and Himyar as well as Beja. Many Syrian Christian merchants in Axum.	321 Edict of tolerance for Donatists.		320 Courts first forbidden to sit on Sundays. 321 Constantine attempts to heal Donatist schism.

EGYPT, THE SUDAN & EASTERN AFRICA	NORTHERN AFRICA & WESTERN AFRICA	WESTERN ASIA	EUROPE
			323 Constantine overthrows Licinius, becomes sole Emperor.
		325 First General Council of the Church at Nicaea. 327 Church of the Holy Sepulchre begun.	
328–73 St Athanasius, Bp of Alexandria.			328 Constantine pardons Arius.
		329–90 St Gregory of Nazianzen. *post* 329–*post* 394 St Gregory of Nyssa.	
330±90 Earliest traces of occupation at Engaruka. 330 ± 150 Gokomere ware found at Zimbabwe Acropolis, earliest known traces of its occupation.	330 Donatist Council at Carthage attended by 270 African bishops.	330–79 St Basil of Caesarea. *c.*330–400 Ammianus Marcellinus, soldier and historian.	330 11 May, Constantinople (Byzantium) founded as capital of the Roman Empire.
			331 Meetings of heretics forbidden by Constantine. First law against divorce. 332 Constantine victorious over Goths.
333–451 Schnoudi of Atripe, Abbot of the White Monastery, Sohag, and founder of numerous monasteries. 333 Frumentius converts King of Axum; conversion of Ethiopia slowly follows. 335 St Athanasius exiled to Trèves. 336 Arius d. Kingdom of Axum in correspondence with Constantinople.		335 Council of Tyre condemns St Athanasius.	336 Constantine declares that subjects of the King of Axum are to be treated as equals of Romans. 337 Death of Constantine the Great. 337–61 Constantius II, an Arian, and Constans (−350) Roman Emperors.
338 St Athanasius returns from exile: visited in Alexandria by St Anthony. 340 First monastery for women founded. c. 341–6 Frumentius, first Abuna of Ethiopia *(Abuna Salama)*, consecrated by St Athanasius.		338–50 War between Rome and Persia.	
		342 or 343 Council of Sardica.	*c.*344–407 St John Chrysostom.
	345 Donatist circumcellions begin pillaging the country-side near Carthage; confiscation of Donatist churches ordered by Emperor Constans. 347 Troops sent against Donatists.		
350 Meroe destroyed by Aezanas of Axum: campaign against *Noba*.			*c.*350 Huns invade Europe. 350 Constantius sole emperor: persecutes non-Arians.
	354–430 St Augustine, theologian, monk.		

EGYPT, THE SUDAN & EASTERN AFRICA	NORTHERN AFRICA & WESTERN AFRICA	WESTERN ASIA	EUROPE
	355 Death of Donatus.		
356 St Athanasius flees to the desert; George of Alexandria usurper bishop (to 361). 357 St Athanasius, *Life of St Anthony*.			
		359 Sapor II invades Mesopotamia.	359 Council of Rimini. *c.*360 Books begin to replace scrolls. 361–3 Julian the Apostate, Roman Emperor: temples reopened and paganism encouraged: Christians persecuted.
361 St Athanasius returns to Alexandria.			
	363 Leptis appeals for Roman help against the Austuriani raiding their territory. 364–75 Desert nomads invade the ports of Tripolitania; revolt in Kabylia led by Firmus; Caesarea and Icosium taken.	363 Julian attacks Persia; is killed in battle; peace made by Emperor Jovian (363–4).	364–75 Valentinian and Valens (−378), Roman Emperors.
373 St Athanasius d.	373–5 Two-year campaign of Theodosius to recover N Africa.		*c.*370 Beginnings of monastic life in the west. 373–97 St Ambrose, Bp of Milan.
		379 Sapor II of Persia d.; Persia the dominant power in the Indian Ocean.	378 Valens defeated and killed by Goths. 379–95 Theodosius, Roman Emperor.
			380 Theodosius makes Christianity the state religion. 381 Second General Council of the Church at Constantinople: condemns Macedonian and Apollinarian heresies. 388–407 Roman legions evacuate Britain. 383–7 Maximus, co-Emperor.
385 Theophilus, Patriarch of Alexandria.	386–7 St Augustine, *Philosophical Dialogues.* *c.*386 Gildon nominated Count of Africa.		386 Council of Trèves.
		387 Armenia partitioned between Rome and Persia.	387 Valentinian II, Western Roman Emperor.
389 Daughter Library destroyed at Alexandria. 391 Christianity proclaimed the official religion in Egypt: more than 40,000 statues and numerous temples destroyed.			391 Theodosius orders all pagan temples to be closed throughout the Roman Empire.
	393 Gildon refuses aid to Theodosius.		

EGYPT, THE SUDAN & EASTERN AFRICA	NORTHERN AFRICA & WESTERN AFRICA	WESTERN ASIA	EUROPE
395 Egypt and Cyrenaica in Eastern Roman Empire.	395 Africa in Western Roman Empire.	395 Huns invade the Eastern Empire and reach Antioch.	395—408 Arcadius, Eastern Roman Emperor; Honorius, Western Roman Emperor (—423); Stilicho *de facto* ruler of the west.
	396 St Augustine elected Bp of Hippo: first cathedral monastery founded. 396 Gildon revolts: grain convoys to Rome stopped: declared a public enemy by Rome. 397—8 St Augustine, *The Confessions.* 398 Gildon defeated by his brother Mascezel, ally of the Romans.		398—407 St John Chrysostom, Patriarch of Constantinople.
c. ante 400 Beginning of Iron Age A2 in Rhodesia. *c.*400 Kalambo Falls, Zambia, first settled. *c.*400 Claudius Ptolemy's *Geography* edited at Alexandria in its present form, describing Byzantine knowledge of Africa at that period. *c.*400 Estimated 5,000 monks and 500 nuns in Pachomian monasteries.		*c.*400—650 Ajanta paintings in India. *c.*400 St Jerome's (d.420) Latin translation of Bible *(Vulgate)*made at Bethlehem.	
	405 Donatists outlawed.		405 Ostrogoths defeated by Stilicho. 407 Vandals and Suevi invade Gaul. 408 Saxons invade Britain. Stilicho murdered. 408—50 Theodosius II. Eastern Roman Emperor.
		410 Council of Seleucia.	410 Rome captured by Alaric the Hun.
	411 Donatist schism healed by Council of Carthage.		
412—44 St Cyril, Patriarch of Alexandria.			412 Visigoths in Gaul.
	413—26 St Augustine, *The City of God.*		
415 Murder of Hypatia in Alexandria.			
			418—519 First schism between Rome and Byzantium.
*c.*420 Axum trading with Ceylon and India.			
		421—2 War between Rome and Persia. 422 100 years peace between Rome and Persia.	421 Constantius III, Western Roman Emperor.
			425—55 Valentinian III, Western Roman Emperor. Vandals take Seville and Cartagena.
	426—7 St Augustine, *Retractationes.* 427 Boniface, Count of Africa, recalled: refuses to leave: declared a public enemy.		

EGYPT, THE SUDAN & EASTERN AFRICA	NORTHERN AFRICA & WESTERN AFRICA	WESTERN ASIA	EUROPE
428 St Cyril of Alexandria disputes doctrines preached by Nestorius of Constantinople.	428 Sigisvult, Count of Africa, takes Hippo and Carthage.		428 Nestorius elected Patriarch of Constantinople. Genseric becomes King of the Vandals in Spain. *c.*429–38 Theodosian Code composed.
	429 Vandals disembark in N Africa under Genseric with 80,000 persons including 20,000 soldiers; Boniface restored as Count of Africa; besieged in Hippo; Genseric occupies whole country except Cirta and Carthage; ruler until 477.		
	430 28 Aug., St Augustine d.		
	430–1 Siege of Hippo by Vandals.		
	431 Relieving army under Aspar fails to help Boniface and is defeated; Boniface d.	431 General Council of the Church at Ephesus; Nestorius deposed and exiled.	
			432 Conversion of Ireland begun by St Patrick.
	435 11 Feb., Convention of Hippo: Vandals accorded rights as *federales*; occupy Mauritania and Numidia.		
436 Kharqa raided by Mazices (?Tuaregs).			
			438 Theodosian code published.
	439 19 Oct., Genseric seizes Carthage; builds fleet.		439 Genseric attacks Sicily and takes Lilybaeum.
			440–61 St Leo the Great, Pope.
			441 War between Attila and Theodosius II.
			*c.*441–2 Anglo-Saxons conquer southern and eastern Britain.
	442–55 Good relations between Romans and Vandals.		442 New treaty between Rome and Vandals signed in Ravenna; Vandals granted the most prosperous parts of N Africa.
444–51 Dioscorus, Patriarch of Alexandria.			
		448 Eutyches condemned for heresy.	
		449 'Robber' Council of Ephesus: Flavian of Constantinople deposed for Eutychianism.	449 The *Tome* of St Leo.
c. 450 Nobates and Blemmyes attacking Philae.			450–7 Marcion, Roman Emperor.
451 Coptic Church of Egypt separates as a result of Council of Chalcedon: Greek Christians known in Egypt henceforward as Melkites: Greeks only follow new Bp imposed by government, Proterios; Ethiopian Christians follow Copts.		451 Council of Chalcedon: Dioscorus of Alexandria deposed: Monophysitism condemned.	
		452 Death of Attila the Hun.	452 Attila the Hun in Italy: Rome occupied.

EGYPT, THE SUDAN & EASTERN AFRICA	NORTHERN AFRICA & WESTERN AFRICA	WESTERN ASIA	EUROPE
453 Roman expedition against Nobatae and Blemmyes (Beja): peace treaty for 30 years; rebellion in Alexandria. 454 Proterios assassinated. Uprising in Alexandria: henceforward two Patriarchs, Coptic and Melkite.			
	455 Genseric seizes Zingitana, expelling landowners, giving land to his soldiers. 455 Genseric mounts expedition against Rome.		455 2 June, Rome taken by Genseric.
457–60 Timothy, Monophysite Patriarch of Alexandria (–477). 460 Timothy exiled.	460 Majorian's expedition to Africa fails.		457–74 Leo I, Emperor.
		466 Byzantine army and fleet raised to recover Africa from Vandals.	
	468 Treaty between Genseric and Euric, King of the Visigoths. 468 Byzantine fleet under Basiliscus burnt by Genseric off Cape Bon.		
			474 Genseric raids Greek coast. 474 Leo II, Emperor; 474–91 Zeno, Emperor. 474 Zeno at war with the Goths. 476 Zeno makes peace with Genseric; Rome taken by Heruli.
	476 Genseric obtains from Emperor Zeno recognition of his rights over Africa, Corsica, Sardinia, Sicily, Balearic Is., and Ischia. 476 Masties, a Berber chief, proclaims himself Roman Emperor. 477 24 Jan., Genseric d. 477–84 Huneric, Vandal King: persecution of Catholics and Manicheans.		
477 Peter, Monophysite Patriarch of Alexandria.			
			c.480–577 St Benedict, father of western monasticism. 482 Emperor Zeno issues Henotikon, or Edict of Union.
	484–96 Gunthamund, Vandal king.		
			489 Invasion of Italy by Theodoric.
	496–523 Thrasamund, Vandal king; Berbers independent in many towns; Cabaon, with camel cavalry from Tripolitania, defeats Thrasamund.		
post 500 The Nine Saints translate the Scriptures and other religious works into Geez; 'silent trade' between Red Sea coast and inhabitants of interior.			post 500–post 562 Procopius, historian: De Aedificiis describes buildings in N Africa and elsewhere.

EGYPT, THE SUDAN & EASTERN AFRICA	NORTHERN AFRICA & WESTERN AFRICA	WESTERN ASIA	EUROPE
		502—6 War between Rome and Persia.	
c.514—43 Caleb, (Ela Atsbeha), King of Axum. 517 Caleb of Axum sends fleet against Yemen and defeats Dhu Nuwas: Yemen taken by Ethiopia (−c.570).		517 Dhu Nuwas, King of Yemen, persecutes Christians.	517 Justinian, nephew of Justin I, encourages Ethiopian expedition against Yemen. 518—27 Justin I, Emperor. c.post 523 Marriage of Justinian and Theodora.
	523—30 Hilderic, Vandal King; Berbers in control of all but the coastline.		
c.524 Cosmas Indicopleustes travels from north of Red Sea to Adulis and Axum, and thence to Ceylon: trade route Adulis—Colloe—Axum extends to interior.			
		c. 525 Caleb mounts successful expedition to restore Ethiopian suzerainty over Himyar.	
			527—65 Justinian I, Eastern Roman Emperor. 529 Abbey of Monte Cassino founded by St Benedict. 529—34 Justinian issues Institutes, Digests and Code.
530 ± 120 −840 ± 100 Gokomere culture in Mashonaland. 530 Expedition from Adulis to Ceylon organized by Emperor Justinian. 531 Justinian sends embassy to Axum asking an alliance against Persia.	530 Hilderic deposed; succ. Gelimer, 530—4.	531—79 Chosroes I of Persia. 532 Peace between Byzantium and Persia.	
	533 13 Sept., Gelimer defeated by Belisarius with Byzantine army of 16,000 men. Carthage taken by Belisarius: other Vandal possessions recovered for Byzantium. 534 April, Justinian reorganizes Africa under a prefect with seven provinces: Berber chiefs confirmed as vassals: Solomon prefect: general revolt in Numidia and Mauritania.		c.534 St Benedict, The Rule.
535 Empress Theodora nominates Timothy, a Monophysite, as Patriarch of Alexandria: uprising, with many thousands killed. 536 Persecution of Coptic Monophysites by Justinian.	536 Military revolt led by Stotzas put down by Belisarius.		536 Rome and Naples taken by Belisarius. 537 Italy conquered by Belisarius for Justinian.

EGYPT, THE SUDAN & EASTERN AFRICA	NORTHERN AFRICA & WESTERN AFRICA	WESTERN ASIA	EUROPE
	539 Solomon makes war on Iabdas in Aurès: complete victory; Solomon then killed at Tebessa.	539–62 Renewed war between Byzantium and Persia.	
c.540 Nubia divided between three Kingdoms: Nobatia, Alodia, and Mukurra (Dongola). Christian missions active (−580).			
c.540 Second embassy from Justinian to Axum.			
543 Conversion of Silko, King of the Nobatae, to Monophysite Christianity: capital shortly moved from Ballana to Bukharas (Faras).			543 Edict of *Three Chapters*.
545 Nobatae and Blemmyes stop receiving annual payments from Constantinople.			
	546–8 Campaigns of John Troglita against Berber insurgents.		546 Rome taken by Ostro-Goths. Peace between Byzantium and Persia.
c.547 Cosmas Indicopleustes' *Christian Topography* written in Alexandria.			547 Belisarius retakes Rome.
			548 Empress Theodora d.
c.550 Kingdom of Mukurra (Dongola) converted to Orthodox Christianity.		c.550 Turkish migrations from central Asia begin.	
			552 Defeat and death of Totilas; 552–5 Narses recovers Italy for Byzantium.
553–4 Justinian reforms administration of Egypt; temple of Isis at Philae destroyed.			
	565–78 Byzantine general Thomas prefect; Christianity reaches the Fezzan: Berber risings.		565–78 Justin II, Emperor.
		568 Turkish embassy to Justin II.	568–72 Italy invaded by Lombards.
c.569 Conversion of the Kingdom of Alodia to Christianity by the Monophysite Bishop Longinus; many temples made into churches.			
	c.570 Sef ibn Dhi Yazan, first reputed Mai of Maghumi (Sefawa) dynasty of Bornu.	c.570 Prophet Muhammad born at Mecca; Battle of the Elephant. Axumites defeated at Mecca: Yemen occupied by the Persians.	
		572 Persian fleet ends Axumite domination of Yemen; Persian domination of Arabia (−628).	
		572–91 War between Byzantium and Persia.	
578–604 Damian, Melkite Patriarch of Alexandria, a Monophysite.		578 Persians seize the Lakhmid Kingdom.	
			580 Council of Toledo.

EGYPT, THE SUDAN & EASTERN AFRICA	NORTHERN AFRICA & WESTERN AFRICA	WESTERN ASIA	EUROPE
	582–602 Africa reorganized in two provinces, less Tripolitania, transferred to Egypt.		
			584 Franks in Italy.
	587 Gennadius, Exarch of Carthage.		
		590–627 Chosroes II of Persia.	590–604 St Gregory the Great, Pope.
		590–627 Turks seize Bactria.	
		c.595 Amr b. al-As, conqueror of Egypt, b.	
		595 Muhammad marries Khadija.	
			596 St Gregory the Great sends St Augustine (of Canterbury) to evangelize Britain.
			597 Conversion of Ethelbert, King of Kent.

EGYPT & THE SUDAN	NORTHERN AFRICA	AFRICA SOUTH OF THE SAHARA	OTHER COUNTRIES
	c. 7th or 8th c. Zawila founded as a caravan post.	c. 7th c. Camels spread to Ghana and Sudan. Lemta and Howara Berbers said to have migrated from Tripolitania to Songhai; Dia Aliamen made ruler at Kukia. White nomads from Ethiopia and Tripolitania with some Umayyads arrive near L.Chad. So people living E of L.Chad. Berbers arrive near Gao.	
	c.600–1000 Tuareg men adopt the veil.	c.600–900 Oriental ancestors of the Yoruba believed to have left Near East.	
			602 See of Canterbury established by St Augustine.
			603 War between Persia and Byzantium.
			605–9 Persians occupy the eastern provinces of the Byzantine empire.
608 Alexandria taken by Berbers.	608–9 Aurelius, exarch of Africa, plots against Emperor Maurice; sends Berber troops into Egypt.		
			610–41 Heraclius, Roman Emperor.
			c.610 Muhammad starts preaching at Mecca.
			611–14 Persians again occupy the eastern Byzantine provinces.
			614 Two Seng-chi (Zanj) women brought to the court of China by Javanese envoys.
		615 Axum gives refuge to party of persecuted Muslims from Mecca.	

EGYPT & THE SUDAN	NORTHERN AFRICA	AFRICA SOUTH OF THE SAHARA	OTHER COUNTRIES
616–17 Persians under Chosroes II besiege Alexandria. 618 Alexandria taken. 619–29 Egypt occupied by the Persians.			618–900 Tang dynasty in China.
		c.620 Copper wire used at Dambwa, Zambia.	
			622 16 July, Muhammad leaves for Medina: official date for the beginnings of the Hijra, or Muslim era.
629 Egypt recovered by Emperor Heraclius. 630 Byzantine authority fully established in Egypt.		629 Muslim exiles return from **Axum** to Mecca. c.630 Kings of Gobir claim to have left Yemen for the Sudan. 630–40 Pirates active in Red Sea.	629 Chosroes II of Persia d.; Byzantines recover former territory. 630 Mecca occupied by Muslims. Battle of Muta: first clash between Byzantines and Muslims. c.630–1 The greater part of Arabia becomes Muslim.
			632 Muhammad d.; Abu Bakr, first Caliph, (632–4); attacks made on Persia and Palestine.
c.633 Monothelitism spreads in Egypt.		634 Massawa occupied by Arabs.	634–44 Umar, Caliph. 634 Basra and Kufa founded. Palestine taken by Arabs. 635 Sept., Damascus and Syria taken from Byzantines by Arabs. 636 20 Aug., Byzantines decisively beaten by Arabs at battle of Yarmuk and expelled from Syria. 638 Jerusalem captured: Caliph Umar respects Christian Holy Places.
638 Heraclius issues the *Ecthesis* in an attempt to conciliate Monophysites and Melkites. 639 12 Dec., Amr b. al-As enters Egypt at al-Arish. 640 Feb., al-Farama (Pelusium) and Belbeis taken by Amr b. al-As; Cyrus (al-Muqawqis) flees to fortress of Babylon, now Old Cairo; July, Amr takes Heliopolis: fortress of Babylon besieged. 641 6 Apr., Fortress of Babylon taken by Arabs. 8 Nov., Patriarch Cyrus surrenders Alexandria: Byzantine army allowed to embark: freedom of worship guaranteed. Abdullah b. Saad invades Nubia: tribute paid after initial resistance. 641–2 Mosque of Amr built in Old Cairo: canal from Nile to Red Sea cleared. 642 Amr takes Egyptian coastal towns; Sept., last Byzantines evacuate Alexandria; 29 Sept., Amr enters Alexandria in triumph; military base set up at Fustat, south of fortress of Babylon.	642 Barca and the Pentapolis conquered by Arabs: Berber tribes submit.	640 Arab fleet sent by Caliph Umar defeated by Ethiopians.	639 Muawiya made Governor of Syria. 641–43 Arabs conquer Persia.

EGYPT & THE SUDAN	NORTHERN AFRICA	AFRICA SOUTH OF THE SAHARA	OTHER COUNTRIES
643 All Egypt now under Arab control.	**643** Arabs raid the Fezzan from Egypt and take Tripoli by assault.		
			644–56 Uthman, Caliph.
645 Rising of Greeks in Alexandria; town retaken by Byzantine fleet; Byzantine army under Michael the Armenian recaptures Delta; defeated decisively by Amr at Nikiou. Arab expansion from Egypt westwards authorized. **645** Amr b. al-As relieved of command in Egypt. **645–55** Abdallah b. Saad, foster brother of Caliph Uthman, Governor of Egypt. **646** Alexandria retaken by Arabs under Amr, restored; again replaced by Abdallah b. Saad.	**646** Gregory, Governor of Africa, proclaims himself Emperor. **647** Abdallah b. Saad defeats Byzantines at Sbeitla; Gregory killed. **647–710** Long drawn-out Arab conquest of Berbers.		
			649 Cyprus taken by Arab fleet from Alexandria.
	*c.***650** Abdallah b. Saad subjugates part of Ifriqiya (Africa) and capital Qartajanna (Carthage).	*c.***650** Villages on Batoka plateau, Zambia, importing glass beads.	
651 Abdallah b. Saad leads expedition against Aloa and Nubia: King Kalidura of Nubia agrees to peace and an annual tribute of 400 slaves: tribute generally paid for the next 600 years. **652** Byzantine fleet repulsed in attack on Alexandria. **655** Byzantine fleet sent to recover Alexandria; 'Battle of the Masts': first Arab naval victory.			*c.***655** Final redaction of the Koran. **656–61** Ali, Caliph.
658 Muawiya, Governor of Syria, seizes Egypt from Caliph Ali. **658–64** Amr b. al-As, Governor of Egypt; moderate taxation; Trajan's canal re-opened; new capital built at Fustat; Copts conciliated.	**660–800** Governors of Ifriqiya appointed by Baghdad.		
			661–750 Umayyad Caliphate. **661–80** Muawiya usurps caliphate; capital Damascus. *c.***664–7** First Arab raids on India.

EGYPT & THE SUDAN	NORTHERN AFRICA	AFRICA SOUTH OF THE SAHARA	OTHER COUNTRIES
	665 Expedition of Muawiya b. Hodaij against the Berbers; Jaloula, near Hadrumetum, taken. 666 Uqba b. Nafi raids Fezzan as far as Kaouar; Djerma and Kaouar made to furnish 360 slaves.		
			668 or 669 Egyptian navy pillages Sicily. 669 Arabs attack Byzantium.
	670 al-Qayrawan founded by Uqba b. Nafi as military base for conquest of Ifriqiya; Uqba shortly replaced by Abu al-Muhajir as governor. 671 Kosaila, prince of the Aouraba, beaten and taken prisoner at Tlemcen by Abu al-Muhajir: converted to Islam.		
			672 Arabs capture Rhodes. 673 Arab fleet attacks Byzantium. 674—80 Arab 'Seven Years War' on Byzantium. 674 Arabs capture Crete.
		678 Translation of Bible into Geez completed with book of Ecclesiasticus.	
			680 Husain, grandson of the Prophet Muhammad, proclaims himself Caliph and is murdered at Medina: beginning of Shiism. 681 Council of Toledo: canons against the Jews.
	681 Uqba b. Nafi again Governor; campaign in Algeria; Kosaila becomes symbol of Berber resistance against Uqba. 683 Uqba b. Nafi d. in battle at Biskra against Kosaila. Ifriqiya in hands of Kosaila, with Qayrawan as capital.		
			685—705 Abd al-Malik b. Marwan, Caliph. c.685 Beginning of Kharijism. 687—91 Dome of the Rock (Haram al-Sharif) built in Jerusalem. 689 Oman conquered by al-Hajjaj b. Yusuf.
c.690 Zanafaj, a Beja tribe, penetrating Eritrea.		c.690 Gao said to be founded by Sorko under Faran Maka Bote and Bamba by Sorko Fono. c.691 Sulaiman and Said said to have left Oman for East Africa.	
	c.693—700 Hasan b. al-Numan al-Ghassani governor of Ifriqiya: reasserts Arab authority and puts down local resistance.		

EGYPT & THE SUDAN	NORTHERN AFRICA	AFRICA SOUTH OF THE SAHARA	OTHER COUNTRIES
	695 Hasan b. al-Numan takes Carthage; but is defeated by Kahina, woman Berber patriot leader.		695 First gold dinars and first silver dirhems struck at Damascus.
		c.696 Alleged settlement of Pate, Lamu, Kilwa, and thirty-two other towns by Syrians: possibly represents commercial relationship.	696–767 Abu Hanifa, jurist and theologian.
	702 Hasan b. al-Numan finally defeats Kahina; end of Berber resistance; Kahina d.	699 Jidda attacked by Ethiopian pirates. c.8th c. Sosso Kingdom of Kaniaga founded. ?c.700–1500 Madagascar populated from Indonesia. 702 Ethiopians sack Jidda and make pirate raids in Red Sea; Arabs occupy Ethiopian ports in revenge.	
	c.705 Musa b. Nusair, Governor of Ifriqiya: vigorous campaigns against Berbers; government extended to Atlantic and south to Sijilmasa; numerous conversions to Islam.		705–15 al-Walid, Caliph.
706 Arabic made the official language of Egypt.			
709 Last bilingual Greco-Arab papyrus.	707 Tangier taken by Musa b. Nusair: becomes base for Muslim assault on Spain. 709 Ceuta taken by the Arabs.		
			711 Tariq disembarks with largely Berber army at Gibraltar (Jabal al-Tariq): 19 July, Spanish army under King Roderick utterly routed. 712 June, Seville and Merida taken by Musa b. Nusair; autumn, Musa replaced as Governor of Ifriqiya and Spain by his son, Abd al-Aziz. c.712 or 719–91 al-Malik, theologian and jurist. c.714 North African Arabs in control of all of Spain.
715 Christian civil servants forcibly replaced by Muslims throughout Egypt.			715 Feb., Musa b. Nusair enters Damascus with 400 captive Visigoth princes and booty from Spain.
716 Nilometer built on al-Rawdah Is., Cairo.			716 Aug.–717 Sept., Syrian troops and an Egyptian fleet besiege Byzantium. 717 or 718 al-Hurr b. Abd al-Rahman al-Thaqafi crosses Pyrenees and raids France with Berber-Arab army. 717–41 Leo the Isaurian, Byzantine Emperor.

EGYPT & THE SUDAN	NORTHERN AFRICA	AFRICA SOUTH OF THE SAHARA	OTHER COUNTRIES
			717 Syro-Egyptian fleet loses 1,795 out of 1,800 vessels in storm off Syria; end of Arab sea power. 718 Battle of Covadonga: first Christian victory over Muslims in Spain. Leo the Isaurian defeats the Arabs outside Byzantium. 720—4 Yazid II, Caliph. 720 Berber-Arab raid from Spain captures Narbonne. *c.*721 Berber-Arabs besiege Toulouse.
722 Caliph Yazid orders destruction of Christian images and pagan statues. 725 Revolt of the Copts in Egypt.			724—43 al-Hisham, Caliph. 725 Berber-Arabs take Carcassonne and besiege Autun. 726 Arab offensive in Asia Minor. *post 727 Gesta Regum Francorum.*
		*c.*730 Alleged Arab settlement in Pemba.	731 Bede, *Ecclesiastical History.* 732 Bordeaux stormed by Abd al-Rahman; Tours taken; Oct., Berber-Arabs defeated at Poitiers by Charles Martel; end of impetus of Berber-Arab conquests. 732—55 Twenty-three Arab governors succeed one another in Spain, subject to Governor of Ifriqiya at Qayrawan.
	732—3 Muslim fleet reorganized at Tunis.		
	*c.*734—50 Habib b. Abi Ubaida's expedition to the Sudan; obtains considerable quantity of gold: fails to discover source of gold. 734—42 Berber insurrections against Arab rule, reaching also to Spain.	*c.*734—50 Some Arab soldiers settle at al-Honeihin.	
737 Crusade of Nubians and Ethiopians to free the Patriarch of Alexandria. 739 Further revolt of the Copts.	739—40 Maisara's insurrection against Arabs; Tangier taken; Maisara proclaimed Caliph; and then assassinated; beginning of Kharijite movement in N Africa. 740 Khalid b.Hamid succ. Maisara; Arabs defeated at Battle of the Nobles. 741 Caliph al-Hisham sends army of 27,000 Syrians to quell Ifriqiya: one-third cross to Spain.	*c.*740 Zaidites said to have settled on the East African coast.	737 Arabs defeated by Charles Martel near Narbonne.

EGYPT & THE SUDAN

745 Nubians invade Egypt: Cairo temporarily captured.

750 Jan., Caliph Marwan II takes refuge in Egypt after defeat by Abbasids; 1 Aug., killed; Abbasids take over Egypt.
c.754–75 Nile to Red Sea canal abandoned.

NORTHERN AFRICA

742 Khalid b.Hamid defeats Amir Kulthum at Baqdoura. Arabs defeat the Kharijites at El Qarn and El Asnam. Sijilmasa founded by the Midrarids of Tafilalet: centre for Tuareg trade in gold and salt.
744 Abd al-Rahman b.Habib, great-grandson of Uqba, proclaims himself independent at Tunis; stabbed to death by his brothers; Qayrawan seized by Kharijites. Kharijite Ibadites under Abu al-Khattab seize Tripoli; defeat two armies from Egypt.
c.744 Sahh, chief of the Berghwata tribe, translates Koran into Berber.

755 Abd al-Rahman, founder of the dynasty of Umayyad Caliphs of Cordova, arrives at Ceuta as a penniless refugee.

757 Tafilalet founded as a caravan 'port'.
757–923 Imams of Nefusa: founder Abu al-Khattab (757–61).
758 June, Abd al-Rahman b. Ibn Rustam, a Persian, named Governor of Qayrawan by Kharijites.

761 Ibn al-Ashatti, Governor of Egypt, leads army against the Kharijites; Aug., takes Qayrawan; Ibn Rustam escapes and founds kingdom at Tahert; Abu Qurra founds kingdom at Tlemcen.
761–908 Rustamid Imams of Tahart.

AFRICA SOUTH OF THE SAHARA

c.747–54 Qanbalu said to have been seized by Muslims, who enslaved the Zanj inhabitants.
?c.750 Earliest building at Zimbabwe.

OTHER COUNTRIES

744 Shiite rebellion in Persia.

746 Byzantine invasion of Syria.
747 Cyprus regained by Byzantium.

750 Abbasids replace Umayyads as Caliphs (−1258): Abu al-Abbas Abdallah al-Saffah, first Abbasid Caliph (−754).
754–75 al-Mansur, Caliph.

756–1031 Amirate of Cordova.
756–7 Abd al-Rahman conquers Spain; discards authority of Damascus and mention of Caliph in the khutbah: 14 May, Cordova taken.

759 Arabs expelled from Languedoc.

EGYPT & THE SUDAN	NORTHERN AFRICA	AFRICA SOUTH OF THE SAHARA	OTHER COUNTRIES
			762 Foundation of Baghdad as capital of the Abbasid caliphs.
		c.766 Alleged expedition by Caliph to secure loyalty of eastern African coastal towns.	
767 Cyrenaica annexed to Egypt. 767–72 Copts again in revolt.			
		c.770 Berber dynasty of Ghana driven out by Soninke of Wagudu: Soninke dynasty of Ghana. (–1240).	
	771 Kharijite-Berber alliance invests Qayrawan; Berbers again in control of Ifriqiya. Abbasid Caliph sends army under Yazid b.Hatim with 90,000 men; retakes Ifriqiya. 771–976 Midrarid rulers of Sijilmasa. 772–87 Yazid b.Hatim, Governor of Ifriqiya; central and western Morocco still independent. 772–4 Great Mosque of Qayrawan rebuilt except for the minaret and the mihrab.		
			c.773 First Abbasid contacts with India; Arabic numerals adopted in place of letters.
	776 Imams of Nefusa become subject to the Rustamids of Tahert.		
			778 Charlemagne campaigns as far as Saragossa: battle of Roncevaux. Byzantine invasion of Syria. c.780 Hindu learned writings translated into Arabic. 782 Short Arab campaign against Byzantium. 783 Charlemagne established at Aix-la-Chapelle.
		c.784–835 Dougou, first King of Saifawa dynasty of Kanem and later Bornu (–1846); capital, Njimi.	
785 Arab uprisings in Egypt in favour of an Umayyad pretender.	785 Idris b. Abdallah, a descendant of Ali, flees to Morocco after an insurrection in Medina. 786 Idris b. Abdallah settles at Oulili: becomes Imam of the Aouraba.	c.786–809 A number of eastern African coastal towns said to have been founded by Harun al-Rashid.	786–809 Harun al-Rashid, Abbasid Caliph. 786–803 Yahya, Barmecide vizier. 786 Byzantines renew war against the Arabs. 788 Great Mosque of Cordova begun. 788–96 al-Hisham I, Amir of Cordova.
	788–974 Idrisid dynasty founded by Idris b.Abdallah in Morocco: capital Fez; first Shiite dynasty.		

ЗYPT & THE SUDAN	NORTHERN AFRICA	AFRICA SOUTH OF THE SAHARA	OTHER COUNTRIES
			c.789 Monastic schools encouraged by Charlemagne.
	790–823 Abu Mansur al-Yasa, ruler of Sijilmasa.	c.790 Kaya Maghan Sisse, King of Ghana; extends boundaries in all directions.	
			791–795 War between Byzantium and Arabs.
	793–4 Idris b. Abdallah poisoned at instigation of Caliph Harun al-Rashid; succ. 2 days later by posthumous Idris II (–828).		
			796–822 al-Hakim I, Amir of Cordova. 798 Lisbon taken from Arabs by Christians. c. ante 800 Ptolemy's *Geography* translated into Arabic.
		ante 800 al-Fazari, astronomer, first mentions Ghana as the land of gold. c.9th c. Audaghost founded by Lemtuna Tuareg. 9th c. Copper mines in Katanga operating. 9th–11th c. Islamization of the Danakil and Somali.	
	c.800 Tiloutane creates a Berber empire in the western Sahara. 800–11 Ibrahim Ibn al-Aghlab, appointed Governor of Ifriqiya in 800, establishes Aghlabid dynasty (–909) in Tunisia; capital Qayrawan. 802 Rising of soldiers in Qayrawan.	c.800 Bornu invaded by Beri-Beri from Yemen: begin to expel So from north of L. Chad; Soninke move into Kaniaga. Agriculturalists inhabiting all of central Africa, contact with east coast evidenced by beads found at Kisale in rich burials.	800 25 Dec., Charlemagne crowned as Roman Emperor.
			803 Barmecide family massacred. Cyprus pillaged by Muslim fleet. 807 Muslim fleet pillages Rhodes.
	807 Ibrahim I, Aghlabid, builds al-Abbasia: entertains embassy from Charlemagne. 808 Idris II, Idrisite, has Abu Leila Ishaq, chief of the Aouraba, murdered. 809 Fez built by Idris II. 810 Rising of soldiers in Qayrawan; Ibrahim I, Aghlabid, flees, returning later.		810 Abu Nuwas, poet, d.
			813 Dar al-Hikma (House of Wisdom) established by Caliph Mamun at Baghdad. 814 (or 817-18) Revolt in Cordova led by a Berber *faqih*; 8,000 persons expelled to Morocco. Charlemagne d.
	814 (or 817–8) Refugees from Spain settle at Fez, and also at Alexandria and in Crete.		
815 Coptic weavers at Tanais complain to the Patriarch of being taxed five times the correct amount. 816–36 Nubia refuses tribute to Egypt.			

EGYPT & THE SUDAN	NORTHERN AFRICA	AFRICA SOUTH OF THE SAHARA	OTHER COUNTRIES
816 15,000 refugees from Umayyads in Cordova seize Alexandria; Abu Nasr b.Sari and Ali b.Abd al-Aziz, bandit leaders, seize Egypt; order restored by Abdallah b.Tahir.			
	817—38 Ziyadat-Allah I, Aghlabid. 817—9 Revolt of army against Ziyadat-Allah I. c. 817 Further building of the Great Mosque of Qayrawan begun. 818—25 Fez grows rapidly.		
			822—52 Abd al-Rahman II, Amir of Cordova.
		c. 825 ± 150 Dimple-based pottery used at Nsongezi, Uganda.	
827 Mosque of Amr at Fustat enlarged.			826 Arabs take Crete. 827 Sicily attacked by Ziyadat-Allah I, Aghlabid, and Sardinia seized; Sicily held until 909.
	828 Idris II d.; kingdom divided between his ten sons.		
829 Fresh revolts in Egypt; put down by Turkish troops. 831 Treaty between Beja chief Kanun Abd al-Aziz of Hajar and the Arab governor of Aswan: Beja to continue to pay tribute to Cairo and to stop raiding. 831—2 Revolt of Bachmouri between Rosetta and Damietta; last Coptic armed rising: rapid conversion of Egypt to Islam thereafter. 832—4 Kaider, first Turk to be governor of Egypt. 834 Beja raid Edfou and Esna and refuse tribute. 836 New treaty between Egypt and Nubia.	836 Great Mosque of Qayrawan greatly enlarged.		834 Jatt and Zott installed in the Shatt al-Arab. 836 Foundation of Samarra: Abbasid capital (—892). 838 Arabs take Ancyra and Amorium, Asia Minor. 840 Bari taken by Arabs.
		c. 840 Tiboutiane, chief of the Lemtuna branch of the Zenata, gathers large army; conquers western Sahara and twenty African chiefs.	
			842 Messina and Taranto taken by the Arabs. 845 Normans pillage Paris. 846 Arab raid on Rome.
		846 Ibn Khurdadhbih, director of posts in Baghdad, lists no towns to the south of Aden.	
			849—50 Arab raid on Provence.
c. 850 George son of Zakaria, King of Nubia, sends embassy to Baghdad to protest against stoppage of food supplies by Cairo.		c. 850 Saifawa supplant former dynasty of Bornu in Kawar. Zaghawa ruling Kanem.	

EGYPT & THE SUDAN	NORTHERN AFRICA	AFRICA SOUTH OF THE SAHARA	OTHER COUNTRIES
		c. 851–900 Betsine, son of Tiboutiane, Zenata ruler.	
853 Byzantine raid on Chata and Damietta. 854 Beja refuse tribute: Egyptian expedition enables opening of gold mines.		854 Ethiopia unable to obtain new Abuna because of conflict between Nubia and Egypt: Massawa and Adulis lost to Arabs.	
			855 Ibn Hanbal, jurist and theologian, d.
856–8 Alexandria and the Fayoum in revolt.			
			858 France invaded by Louis the German.
859 Byzantine raid on al-Farama (Pelusium).			
	862 Karaouine mosque built at Fez as a university with 514 rooms.		
			863 Tuan Cheng-Shih, *Yu-yang-tsu*, includes description of eastern Africa.
866 Apr. –868 June, revolts in Alexandria and the Fayoum. 868–905 Tulunid dynasty in Egypt. 868 Ahmad b.Tulun sent to Egypt as governor by Caliph al-Mutamid (–884).			868–92 Revolt of the Zanj slaves in lower Iraq.
	869 An Alid pretender raises a revolt at Barqa.		
c. 870 Ahmad b. Tulun refuses financial aid to the Caliph to put down Zanj rebellion: beginning of the emergence of Egypt as an independent state. Rebel Ibn al-Sufi beaten at Akhmim. c. 871 Ibn Abd al-Hakam, first historian of Arab conquest of Egypt. 872 Revolt of al-Umari. c. 872 al-Yaqubi describes the Kingdom of Axum.		872 al-Yaqubi's description of eastern Africa.	870–92 al-Mutamid, Abbasid Caliph. 870 al-Bukhari, theologian and traditionalist, d. 871–99 Alfred the Great, King of England.
	874–902 Ibrahim II, Aghlabid; Great Mosque of Qayrawan completed: capital at Raqqada.		
			875 Charles the Bald, Emperor.
876–9 Mosque of Ibn Tulun built, a palace, a hospital, and a race-course, with many other buildings in Katai quarter of Cairo.			
			877 Ahmad b.Tulun invades Palestine and Syria. Syria occupied by Egypt; Akka (Acre) becomes a naval base; Ibn Tulun's son Abbas revolts; seizes treasure and besieges Tripoli; brought back to Fustat (882).

AFRICA

EGYPT & THE SUDAN	NORTHERN AFRICA	SOUTH OF THE SAHARA	OTHER COUNTRIES
878 al-Umari, chief of an Arab band, pillages the gold mines in Nubia.			878 All Syria conquered by Ibn Tulun.
			880 Byzantines retake Taranto. Battle of the Lipari Is.
883 Egyptian expedition against Tarsus; Ibn Tulun taken sick; March 884 d. at Fustat. 884–95 Khumarawayh ruler of Egypt; reign marked by extravagance and luxury held impious by orthodox Muslims.		883 Eldad the Danite: first account of Ethiopian Jews.	
			885 Paris besieged by Normans. Syria conquered by Khumarawayh.
		c. 887 Foundation of Mogadishu; the Seven Brothers of al-Hasa said to have settled in eastern Africa. *c.* 890 Songhai Kings of Kukia extend dominions on right bank of R Niger to Gao.	*c.* 890 Abdallah al-Husain al-Shii, a Yemeni Ismaili, preaches sedition to Berbers on pilgrimage to Mecca.
	893 Dai Abu Abdallah preaching; campaign against the Kotama of Little Kabylia; beginning of Fatimid movement.		
		c. 898/7–1285 Makhzumi dynasty of eastern Shoa.	
897–961 al-Kindi, historian.			
			899 Qarmatian republic set up in al-Hasa: 30,000 Zanj slaves in state ownership.
	c. 900–3 Said b. al-Husain, a descendant of Fatima, daughter of Muhammad, disguised as merchant, travels in NW Africa; imprisoned at Sijilmasa. 900–19 Temem, son of Betsine, Zenata ruler.	*c.* 900–*c.* 1400 Kalomo culture in Zambia. ?*c.* 900 Foundation of Hausa Kingdom of Daura: Habe dynasty of seventeen queens and forty-seven kings to 1911. *c.* 900 Dimple-based ware in use in Congo, Kenya, Rwanda, Tanzania and Uganda. Iron industry on Bauchi plateau, Nigeria. Beginning of first Ogiso dynasty of Benin. *c. ante* 901–2 Trade treaty between Ethiopia and Yemen.	
	902 Mila taken by Dai Abu Abdallah. 903–9 Ziyadat-Allah III, Aghlabid. 904 Dai Abdallah takes Sétif.		902 Sicily conquered by Arabs.
904–5 Shaiban, ruler of Egypt: territory surrendered to Abbasid general Muhammad b.Sulaiman. 905–6 Precarious Abbasid rule in Egypt: former officers of Ibn Tulun attempt to gain control.	905 Dai Abu Abdallah takes Tobna and Belezina.		
	908 Tahert destroyed by Dai Abu Abdallah.		

EGYPT & THE SUDAN	NORTHERN AFRICA	AFRICA SOUTH OF THE SAHARA	OTHER COUNTRIES
	909 27 March, Raqqada captured by Dai Abu Abdallah. 26 Aug., Sijilmasa occupied by Fatimids; Iliasa II prisoner. Ziyadat-Allah III flees from advancing Fatimids without offering any resistance. Said b.Husain establishes himself in Tunisia as Fatimid Caliph; headquarters at Salamya: Ismaili propaganda organized by Abdullah al-Husain al-Shii. Said b. Husain rescued from prison by al-Shii; raises army and drives out Aghlabid dynasty; Said proclaimed as Imam Ubaidullah al-Mahdi (909–34). **910** Ubaidullah enters Raqqada. **911** Tahert destroyed; Kharijites continue to survive to the present in Jabal Nafusa, Jarba Is., Ouargla and Mzab; 31 Aug., Dai Abu Abdallah executed for treason; revolt of Kotama against Ubaidullah (to 912).		
912 Church at Tanais destroyed by the populace; rebuilt at the public expense.	**912** Tripoli declares against Kotama in favour of Ubaidullah. *c.* 912 or 915 Ubaidullah builds al-Mahdia as Fatimid capital. **913–14** Ubaidullah sends his son Abu al-Qasim against Egypt.		**912–61** Abd al-Rahman III, Amir of Cordova. **912–59** Constantine VII Porphyrogenitus, Byzantine Emperor.
913–4 Fatimid army under Abu al-Qasim occupies Alexandria and Fayoum, but driven back. **914** Ubaidullah takes Alexandria.			
		c. **915** Sofala already trading with S Arabia. al-Masudi visits E Africa as far as Qumr (? Madagascar or Comoro Is.) from Oman; area 'Zanj-speaking'.	**915–17** Abbey of Cluny built. **915** Arabs defeated by Byzantines at Garigliano.
916 Ubaidullah raids Delta, and also Malta, Sardinia, Corsica and Balearic Is. **919–20** Second Fatimid invasion repelled from Egypt; 11 May, Fatimid navy defeated at Rosetta.	**919** Temim massacred by Zenata chiefs.		
	c. **920–40 or 970** Tinyeroutane, King of Audaghost. **921** Ubaidullah instals himself at al-Mahdia; second Fatimid occupation of Sijilmasa; revolt of Abu Yazid.	**920–1050** Apogee of the Sarakole Empire of Ghana.	**920** Byzantium at war with the Caliphate.
922 al-Tabari, historian, d.	**922** Fatimids seize most of Morocco.		**922** Cordova independent of Baghdad.

AFRICA

EGYPT & THE SUDAN	NORTHERN AFRICA	SOUTH OF THE SAHARA	OTHER COUNTRIES
			929–91 Hamdanid dynasty in Mosul. 929 Abd al-Rahman III of Cordova proclaims himself Caliph. 930 Mecca taken by Abu Tahir.
	931 Ceuta annexed by Amirate of Cordova (–1031).		932 Abd al-Rahman III takes Toledo.
	933 Karaouine mosque at Fez rebuilt. Third Fatimid occupation of Sijilmasa. 934–46 Abd al-Qasim Muhammad al-Qaim, second Fatimid Imam; two unsuccessful campaigns against Egypt. 935 Indecisive Fatimid campaign against Sijilmasa.		934 or 935 Fatimid raids on French coast, Genoa and Calabria.
935–69 Ikhshidid dynasty in Egypt. 935–46 Muhammad b.Tughj, first Ikhshidid. 936 Alexandria taken by Berbers.			
			937 Navarre recognizes suzerainty of Abd al-Rahman III *post* 938 Constantine Porphyrogenitus, *The Book of the Ceremonies.* 939 Abd al-Rahman III defeated by Ramire II at Simancas.
c. 940 al-Masudi visits Egypt.			941 Egypt again seizes Syria. Byzantines retake Dara and Nisibis, and reach Aleppo. 942 Egypt seizes Mecca and Medina. 944–5 Byzantines defeated by Saif al-Dawla.
	944 Abu Yazid, the 'man on the donkey', besieges al-Mahdia with Berbers from Aurès; takes Tunis.	*c.* 945 Arabs trading in Madagascar. Indonesian raid against Waq-waq near Sofala.	945–1055 Buwayhids dominate Caliphate. 945–1267 Sung dynasty in China.
946–66 Real ruler of Egypt Abu al-Misk Kafur, Ethiopian eunuch. 946–60 Abu al-Qasim Unujur, nominal ruler.	946–52 Abu Abbas Ismail, Fatimid; title al-Mansur after defeat of Abu Yazid; Caliphate of Cordova in control of Moroccan coast. 946 Defeat of Abu Yazid at Qayrawan; returns to Hodna; Fatimid power now securely established. 947 Aug., Abu Yazid d.; al-Mansuria founded by Fatimid al-Mansur.		
c. 950 Egyptian tax revenue 45m. gold francs. 950 Nubian raid on Upper Egypt. *c.* 952 New ships built for Egyptian fleet at Maqs, predecessor of Bulaq naval arsenal.	*c.* 950 Algiers, Roman Icosium, refounded with name al-Jazair Bani Mazranna; whence corruption Aljazir (Algiers). 952–75 Abu Tamim Ma'add al-Muizz, Fatimid Imam; apogee of Fatimid power in N Africa.	*c.* 950 Federation of clans formed in Mogadishu against Somali pressure; Mogadishu trading with Sofala.	*ante* 950 First Persian version of the *Thousand and One Night.*

EGYPT & THE SUDAN	NORTHERN AFRICA	AFRICA SOUTH OF THE SAHARA	OTHER COUNTRIES
956 Aswan captured by the Nubians: punitive expedition from Egypt takes Qasr Ibrim.			955 Fatimid raids on Spain. 956 al-Masudi d.
	958 Morocco taken by Jafar for Fatimids; Fez, Tangier, and Ceuta taken.	c. 957 Kilwa founded by Ali b.al-Husain b.Ali.	
960–6 Ali b.Muhammad, nominal ruler of Egypt.			960 Crete recovered from Arabs by Byzantines. 961–76 al-Hakam II, Amir of Cordova. 962 Otho crowned emperor at Rome. 964 Nicephoras Phocas raids Syria and recovers Cyprus. 965 Nicephoras Phocas recovers parts of Asia Minor.
968–9 Ahmad, ruler of Egypt.			968 Nicephoras Phocas takes Laodicea, Hieropolis and Emesa.
969–1171 Fatimid dynasty Egypt. 969 Jawhar al-Siqilli (or Rumi), Fatimid general takes al-Fustat; building of al-Misr al-Qahira (Cairo) begun. 969–75 al-Muizz, Fatimid Caliph. 970 al-Azhar Mosque begun.			969 Fatimid raid into Syria; Damascus temporarily occupied. Byzantines take Antioch. 970 Fatimids take Damascus.
972 Caliph al-Muizz enters Cairo. 973 Cairo becomes Fatimid capital; bodies of earlier Fatimids moved to Cairo. 974–96 al-Aziz, Fatimid Caliph; public disputations between Christians and Muslims tolerated: library founded in Cairo containing 600,000 books. 975 al-Azhar mosque becomes a university. 976 al-Hakam d., leaving library catalogued in forty-four volumes.	972–1167 Zairite dynasty. Abu al-Futuh Yusuf Bulukin b.Zairi, Fatimid governor of Tripolitania. 973 Bulukin takes Fez and all Morocco. 976 Sijilmasa taken by Maghrawa under Khazrun b.Talful.		973–1048 al-Biruni, scholar. 976–1008 Hisham II, Amir of Cordova: al-Mansur, regent. 976 Fatimids take Palestine.
		c. 977–8 Zaila controlled by Ethiopians. 977 42,000 dinars of gold exported from Audaghost. 979 King of Ethiopia asks George, King of Nubia, to transmit letter to Coptic Patriarch to ask aid against Bani al-Hamuya raiders; Ethiopia devastated; new patriarch (Abuna) requested.	

EGYPT & THE SUDAN	NORTHERN AFRICA	AFRICA SOUTH OF THE SAHARA	OTHER COUNTRIES
			c. 980—1037 Ibn Sina (Avicenna), Persian philosopher 982 Bermuda II, Christian King of Spain.
c. 985 Ibn Salim, account of Nubia and other Sudanic Kingdoms. Simeon, King of Aloa; Muslim settlers from Egypt in northern Nubia; Nubians further south recently converted.	984—96 al-Mansur b.Bulukin succ. his father. 985 al-Mansur leads unsuccessful expedition against Fez and Sijilmasa.		
	986—8 al-Mansur fighting revolt of the Kotama.		
			987 Hugh Capet, founder of the French monarchy, crowned in Paris. 987—8 al-Mansur seizes the Christian Kingdom of Spain. 988 Fatimid conquest of Syria completed. c. 988 Ibn Hauqal, *Kitab Surat al-Ardh* (The Configuration of the World).
		c. 988 'Whites' alleged in Zanzibar by Ibn Hauqal. c. 990 Audaghost taken by the Emperor of Ghana; African governor installed.	
			991 Danish invasion of England.
996—1021 Abu Ali Mansur al-Hakim, Fatimid Caliph.	996—1016 Badis b.al-Mansur succ. al-Mansur.	c. 996—1021 Persecuted Copts settle in Ethiopia.	
			997 Shrine of St James of Compostela destroyed by al-Mansur. 997—1030 Mahmud of Ghazna.
11th c. Glass windows introduced in Cairo.		c. 11th c. Iron Age B folk, probably Shona speakers, arrive on Rhodesian plateau: theocratic state founded: trade in gold and ivory against imported cloth, beads and porcelain. c. 1000 Sanhaja Tuareg occupying Saharan caravan routes; Gao said to be capital of Songhai. Majority of Berbers in Audaghost region nominal Muslims.	
			1001 Treaty between Byzantines and Fatimids. 1003—14 Danish invasions of England.
1005 Dar al-Hikma or Dar al-Ilm (House of Wisdom or Science), centre at Cairo for teaching Shiite doctrine founded by al-Hakim: library contains 600,000 books. 1006 Abu Rukna's rebellion in Egypt; flees to Nubia; is imprisoned by King Raphael.			

EGYPT & THE SUDAN	NORTHERN AFRICA	AFRICA SOUTH OF THE SAHARA	OTHER COUNTRIES
	1007–9 Qala founded by Banu Hammad. 1007–1152 Hammadid dynasty.		
1008–14 Christians and Jews persecuted by al-Hakim.			
		c. 1009–10 Dia Kossoi of Kukia converted to Islam: capital transferred to Gao.	1009 Holy Sepulchre destroyed by Caliph al-Hakim.
	1011 Sidi Daudi, mystic, d. at Tlemcen.		1011 Controversy in Baghdad on genuineness of Fatimid descent: Caliph al-Qadir rules it spurious.
	1016–62 al-Muizz b.Badis, Zairite. 1017 Qala attacked unsuccessfully by Badis b. Bulukin.		
			1019 Canute unites England with Denmark.
		1020 Zenata chiefs elect Tarsina (or Tarshina) as ruler; becomes Muslim and makes pilgrimage to Mecca; killed in a raid, 1023.	
1021 al-Hakim, proclaims himself divine: organizes sect now known as Druse (al-Darazi): disappears mysteriously: body never found 1021–35 al-Zahir, Fatimid Caliph.			1021 In return for agreement to permit re-building of Holy Sepulchre, the Caliph's name mentioned in Friday prayers in mosques in Byzantine lands.
		1023 Yahya b.Ibrahim succ. Tarsina.	1025 Ferdausi, poet, d.
	1026 Zairite dynasty becomes independent from Fatimids under al-Muizz b.Badis.		
			1028–94 al-Bakri, geographer. 1031 End of the Umayyad dynasty of Cordova: Kingdoms of the Reyes de Taifas formed.
1035–94 al-Mustansir, Fatimid Caliph.		1034 Genoese and Pisan ships pillage Bône. c. 1035 Yahya b.Ibrahim brings Abdallah b.Yasin back from Mecca with him: beginning of Islamic military brotherhood al-Murabitun ('Almoravids'), established amongst Lemtuna in Lower Senegal. c. 1040 Mannu dynasty of Tekrur: War Djabi ally with the Almoravids; beginning of Islamization of Tekrur. 1042 Campaigns of Abdallah b.Yasin against pagan Zenata, Goddala and Lemtuna.	1035 Accession of William, VIIth Duke of Normandy.

EGYPT & THE SUDAN	NORTHERN AFRICA	AFRICA SOUTH OF THE SAHARA	OTHER COUNTRIES
		c. 1043 Mandingo empire of Jenne founded. c. 1045 Abdallah b. Yasin, expelled by Zenata, settles at Sijilmasa; Yahya b.Umar put in command of army; many local campaigns. c. 1047—8 Abdun, an adventurer, becomes Abuna of Ethiopia by means of forged documents.	post 1043 Fatimid power in Syria declines.
	1048 al-Muizz b.Badis forbids use of Fatimid currency. 1048 First campaign of the Almoravids.		
c. 1050 Egyptian tax revenue 56m. gold francs.			
	c. 1052 Banu Hilal and Banu Sulaim arrive in Ifriqiya from Egypt, sent by al-Mustansir. 1053 al-Muizz defeated by Banu Hilal near Gabès.		1052 Building of Westminster Abbey begun.
	1055 Sijilmasa taken by the Almoravids.	1055 ± 65 Population of Bambadyanalo on R Limpopo essentially Bush-Boskopoid. 1055 Audaghost seized by the Almoravids from the Soninke.	1054 Schism between Rome and Byzantium. 1055 Seljuqs effective masters of the Abbasid Caliphate: Baghdad seized.
	1056—1146 Almoravid dynasty. 1056—82 Invasion of Morocco and western Algeria by the Almoravids. 1057 Qayrawan taken by the Arabs. Zairites abandon Qayrawan to Banu Hilal: all N Africa in chaos; Zairites set up at al-Mahdia and take to piracy.		
		1058 ± 65 Earliest Mapungubwe culture, Rhodesia.	1058 Fatimids take Baghdad with Turkish mercenaries. 1058—1111 al-Ghazali, theologian and mystic. 1060—91 Norman conquest of Sicily. 1060 Baghdad retaken by the Seljuqs.
	1061—1106 Yusuf b. Tashfin. 1062 Yusuf b.Tashfin, having established Almoravid control throughout Senegal and western Sahara, builds Marrakesh as capital and re-founds Algiers. 1063 Fez taken.	1062 Tunka Menin succ. Tunka Bas, his uncle as King of Ghana. 1063 ± 65 Ngoro cave, Kenya: Ethiopian or Caucasoid burials: no negroid skulls in graves: Stone bowl culture.	
			1066 England conquered by the Normans; 25 Dec., William I, VIIth Duke of Normandy, crowned (1066—87).

GYPT & THE SUDAN	NORTHERN AFRICA	AFRICA SOUTH OF THE SAHARA	OTHER COUNTRIES
		c. 1067 empire of Kanem extends west to Niger, including most of Hausaland.	1067 Turks massacre their African mercenaries.
069–72 Famine in Egypt.			1071 Egypt loses Yemen and Syria to Abbasids. Battle of Manzikert. Sicily taken by Normans.
	1072 Bougie founded by al-Nasr.		
073–6 Badr al-Jamali, a Armenian officer, fective ruler of Egypt: stigated by al-Mustansir, assacres army officers, placing them with rmenians; Berbers, Turks ad negroes removed om the army; 50,000 ouble-makers sold as slaves.			1073–85 Pope Gregory VII (Hildebrand).
			1075 Seljuqs take Damascus. 1076 Seljuqs take Jerusalem.
077 Atziz invades Egypt: efeated by Badr al-Jamali.	1077 al-Bakri, geographer: description of northern Africa.	1077 Ghana seized by Almoravids after a long resistance; Berbers replace Soninke dynasty.	1077 Seljuq Sultanate of Iconium founded.
	c. 1078–c. 1130 Muhammad b.Tumert assumes title of Mahdi: and preaches return to Islamic orthodoxy: followers called Almohads (al-Muwahhidun).	c. 1078–80 Sosso Kingdom of Kaniaga founded by Kambine Diaresso.	
			1079–1142 Abélard, theologian and philosopher.
		1080 ± 180 Channelled ware found at Kalambo Falls.	
		c. 1080 Abba Sawiros, a Muslim imposter, Abuna of Ethiopia: constructs mosques; imprisoned by emperor.	
		c. 1085–97 Umme, 12th Mai of Bornu-Kanem; assumes title of sultan and is converted to Islam.	
		c. 1086 Attempt to enforce monogamy in Ethiopia.	1086 Ibn Tashfin defeats the Christian forces at Zallaca. *The Domesday Book.*
	1087 Fleet of 200 from Pisa and Genoa attack al-Mahdia to recover prisoners.	1087 Abu Bakr b.Umar d.; end of Almoravid dynasty in Ghana.	
	1090 Hammadid Amir al-Mansur moves capital to Bougie.		1090–1147 Almoravid dynasty in Spain; capital Seville. 1090 Beginning of Assassin (Hashshashin) movement. 1091 Norman conquest of Sicily completed.
		1093 Embassy from Egypt to Ethiopia, headed by Coptic Patriarch, begging king to let the Nile rise.	
094–1101 al-Mustali, atimid Caliph.			1094 al-Bakri, geographer, d. at Cordova.

EGYPT & THE SUDAN	NORTHERN AFRICA	AFRICA SOUTH OF THE SAHARA	OTHER COUNTRIES
1094–1121 Afdal b. al-Badr, effective ruler of Egypt.			
		1095–1134 Gojemasu, King of Kano; Kano city built.	1095 Emperor Alexius Comnenus appeals to Pope Urban II for aid against Seljuq Turks; 26 Nov., Urban calls for first crusade at Clermont. 1095–99 First Crusade. 1097–98 Byzantines recover Nicaea, Smyrna, Ephesus, and Sardis from Seljuqs. 1097 Conflict between Byzantine Emperor Alexis I and Crusaders in Asia Minor. 1098 Baldwin of Boulogne, Count of Edessa. Jerusalem taken by Fatimids. Antioch taken by Crusaders: Bohémond installed as Prince of Antioch. 1099 14 July, Jerusalem captured by Crusaders from Egyptian garrison of 1,000. Battle of Askelon.
12th c. Glass lamps introduced in Cairo.	12th c. Marabout cults begin to be popular in N Africa. 1100–66 al-Idrisi, geographer, born at Ceuta: passes life in Sicily at court of Roger II at Palermo.	c. ante 1100 Mapungubwe dominated by Shona peoples. 12th c. Timbuktu originated as a Tuareg watering-place. Mzizima, now Dar es Salaam, already occupied. Merca already occupied by Hawiye Somali. c. 1100 Antalaotes, mixture of Malagash, Arabs and Africans, develop in the Comoro Is. Earliest known Tonga settlement at Sebanzi Hill, Lochinvar, Zambia. Gedi, Kenya, inhabited. Dynasty of Habe Kings in Katsina (to present). Islam firmly established in all principal Sudanic states. post 1100 Antalaote trading-stations at Mahilaka and Nosy Manja (Lanjani) in Madagascar. 1100 Epitaph at Sane of Abu Abdallah Muhammad, King of Songhai.	1100–35 Henry I, King of England. 1100–18 Baldwin I, King of Jerusalem.
1101–30 al-Amir, Fatimid Caliph: aged five at accession.	1102 Hammadids take Tlemcen from Almoravids. 1104 Pisan and Genoese fleet leaves al-Mahdia.		1102 Almoravids take Valence. Fatimids defeated by Baldwin I at Ramleh: Caesarea taken. 1104–8 War between Byzantium and Bohémond, Prince of Antioc 1104 Crusaders take Acre and Byblos: defeated by Turks at Harran.
		1105 First dated Muslim epitaph at Barawa, Somalia.	

YPT & THE SUDAN	NORTHERN AFRICA	AFRICA SOUTH OF THE SAHARA	OTHER COUNTRIES
6 Ibn Tashfin d.			1106 Balaguer taken by French and Spanish. Almoravids take Seville. Apamaea taken by Tancred.
		1107 Original Friday Mosque at Kizimkazi, Zanzibar, completed, with dedicatory inscription in Persian style.	
		c. 1108 Jubbah (Argobbah) converted to Islam.	1108 Almoravids defeat Castilians at Ucles. Bohémond taken prisoner by Alexis I. Laodicea taken by Tancred. 1109–13 War between England and France. 1109 Crusaders take Tripoli and Beirut.
	c. 1110 Ibn Tumert, Berber religious reformer and originator of Almohad movement, goes to study in Damascus and Baghdad.	1110 ± 80 Iron in use at Talaky, Madagascar.	1110 Almoravids take Lisbon. Baldwin I takes Sidon.
			1111 Almoravids take Saragossa. 1113 Baldwin I defeated at Tiberias. 1114 Almoravids unsuccessfully besiege Barcelona. 1116–18 Baldwin I leads expedition against Egypt. 1117–18 Saragossa recovered by Christians. 1118–31 Baldwin II, King of Jerusalem. 1118–47 Christians steadily recover territory in Spain.
18 Baldwin I, King Jerusalem, leads edition against ypt; Pelusium burnt; of an accident.			c. 1119 Many wealthy persons in Canton possess E African slaves.
	c. 1120–1 Ibn Tumert preaching in Tlemcen, Oudja, Fez, and Marrakesh.	c. 1120 Kilwa ousts Mogadishu from the gold trade at Sofala and obtains a monopoly.	
21 Afdal b.Badr assinated.	1122 Zairites and Spanish Almoravids attack Sicily. 1123–68 Almohad dynasty.		1124 Tyre taken by the Crusaders.
	1125 Ibn Tumert preaching amongst Berbers of the Atlas Mts; claims to be the Mahdi.		c. 1126–98 Ibn Rushd (Averroes), philosopher: Commentary on Aristotle. 1126 Baldwin II besieges Damascus.

EGYPT & THE SUDAN	NORTHERN AFRICA	AFRICA SOUTH OF THE SAHARA	OTHER COUNTRIES
	1128–63 Muhammad b.Tumert d.; Abd al-Mumia b.Ali, of the Zenata tribe of Berbers, succeeds to religious leadership.		1128 Battle of São Mameda: Afonso Henriques of Portugal makes himself independent of Spain.
		c. 1129–31 Sulaiman, Sultan of Kilwa.	
1130 Caliph al-Amir murdered by the Assassins. 1130–49 al-Hafiz, Fatimid Caliph.	1130 Abd al-Mumin proclaims himself *Amir al-Muminin* in the Atlas Mts.		1130–65 Norman dynasty in Sicily. 1130–54 Roger II, King of Sicily. 1131–48 Fulk of Anjou, King of Jerusalem.
1134–92 Qadi al-Fadil, secretary to Saladin, owner of library containing 100,000 books.		c. 1131–70 Daud b. Sulaiman, former governor of Sofala, Sultan of Kilwa.	
	1135 Roger II of Sicily makes treaty with Zairite Hasan b.Ali. 1136 Great Mosque of Tlemcen built. Bougie attacked by Genoa. 1137 Attempted Norman invasion foiled at battle of Cape Dimas.	1137 Zagwa, of an Agao family of Lasta, founds 'Zagwe' dynasty of Ethiopia, with capital Roha.	
			1138 Saladin (al-Malik al-Nasir al-Sultan Salah al-Din Yusuf) b. on the Tigris.
		1140 Embassy from Ethiopia to Egypt asking the Coptic Patriarch for more bishops unsuccessful. c. 1140–1360 Archaic period of Benin art.	
	1141 Ahmad b.Arif, author of *Mahasin al-majalis* d.: introduces Sufi thought into N Africa. 1143 Coast of Tunisia ravaged by Roger II of Sicily.		1143 Dynasty of Aviz in Portugal: Afonso of Portugal recognized by Castile.
	1144–6 Abd-al-Mumin takes Tlemcen, Fez, Ceuta, Tangier, and Aghmat, defeating Almoravids. 1145–50 Abd al-Mumin sends army to Spain; acknowledged as overlord. 1146–58 Normans take Tripoli and Sfax (−1156). 1146–7 Eleven-month siege of Marrakesh: Abd al-Mumin defeats Almoravids and makes it his capital.		1146–8 Second Crusade.
			ante 1147 Portuguese from Lisbon trading with Madeira, Canary Is., and Morocco.

EGYPT & THE SUDAN	NORTHERN AFRICA	AFRICA SOUTH OF THE SAHARA	OTHER COUNTRIES
	1148 Roger II of Sicily takes al-Mahdia (–1160); all Tunisian coast except Tunis and Kelibia subject to him.		1148 Second Crusade checked at Damascus.
49–54 al-Zafir, Fatimid aliph.			1149 Lerida taken by Aragon.
	1150 Building of Rabat begun. c. 1150 Banu Marin (Marinids) wandering as nomads near Oran. 1151 Bougie taken by Almohads; end of the Hammadid Kingdom; al-Mahdia taken from Sicily. 1152 Abd al-Mumin defeats Banu Hilal at Sétif; conquers Algeria.	c. 1150 Yusa, King of Kano, completes town walls.	1150–1 Alphonso VII beaten by the Almohads.
		c. 1151 Dunama b. Umme, Mai of Bornu, drowned whilst on pilgrimage to Mecca.	
		1152 Sena (Siuna), Mozambique, already established as a trading centre with Africans, Arabs and Indians.	
154–60 al-Faiz, Fatimid aliph.	1153 Normans take Bône, Gabès and Jerba.		1153 Baldwin III takes Askelon. 1154–89 Henry II, King of England. 1154 al-Idrisi, *Kitab Rujar*. 1155–1227 Genghis Khan, ruler of the Mongols.
	1156 Normans lose Sfax. 1158 Abd al-Mumin conquers Tunisia.		1159 Siege of Antioch by Byzantines and Franks.
160–71 al-Adid, atimid Caliph. 161–69 Four attempts y the Crusaders to invade gypt.	1160 Abd al-Mumin conquers Tripoli and Libya: campaigns in Morocco. 1160–1212 Almohad dynasty.		1162 Abd al-Mumin takes Granada.
164 Saladin accompanies is uncle Ayyub on an xpedition to Egypt.	1163 Abd al-Mumin makes *Ribat-al-Fath* (Rabat) Almohad capital; then d. 1163–84 Abu Yaqub b.Abd al-Mumin, Almohad.		
167 Invasion of Egypt y Amalric, King of erusalem: Cairo taken. 168 Cairo lost by rusaders to Nur al-Din. 169 Revolt of African mercenaries in Egypt: put own by Turks under aladin.		1165 Alleged letter from 'Prester John' to Byzantium.	

EGYPT & THE SUDAN	NORTHERN AFRICA	AFRICA SOUTH OF THE SAHARA	OTHER COUNTRIES
1169–1252 Ayyubid dynasty in Egypt: Saladin, initially with title *Wazir*, first ruler (–1193).			
		c. **1170–88** Sulaiman Hasan b.Daud, Sultan of Kilwa; Kilwa fortified; many stone buildings erected.	**1170** Amalric beats Nur al-Din on the Dead Sea; and then Saladin at Gaza.
1171 10 Sept., by order of Saladin, the *Khutbah* pronounced in the name of the Abbasid Caliph; 13 Sept. last Fatimid d.; end of Shiism in Egypt. Turan Shah's campaign in Nubia; Red Sea and eastern Africa become a sphere of Egyptian trade influence. Benjamin of Tudela travels from Aidhab to Aswan.			**1171** Saladin dethrones Amalric, King of Jerusalem.
1172–3 Second expedition of Turan Shah against Nubia: Kasr Ibrim seized and pillaged.			**1172** All Spain subject to Almohads.
1174 Saladin declares Egypt independent of the Caliphate.			**1174** Saladin takes Syria, including Damascus.
1175 May, Saladin given control by Abbasid Caliph over Egypt, al-Maghrib, Nubia, western Arabia, Palestine and central Syria.			
1176 Building of the Citadel of Cairo begun.		*c.* **1176** Second dynasty of Benin founded by Oranmiyan.	
		1177 Letter of Pope Alexander III to Emperor of Ethiopia rebuking him for vain-glory and boasting.	**1177** Saladin beaten by Baldwin IV at Montgisard.
	1180 Portuguese attack Ceuta.		**1179** Saladin raids Tyre.
			1180 Truce between Saladin and Baldwin IV.
1181–1235 Ibn al-Farid, Egyptian mystical poet.			
1181 Latest dated Greek inscription in Nubia.			
1182 Crusaders raid Ailat and Aidhab.			**1182** Saladin raids Nazareth, Tiberias, and Beirut.
			1183 Saladin seizes Aleppo and ravages Samaria.
	1184 Abu Yusuf b.Abu Yaqub, Almohad, known as al-Mansur. Ali b.Ghaniya, Almoravid adventurer, seizes Bougie; allies with Banu Sulaim; all N Africa under control of nomads; revolt put down by Abu Yusuf.		**1184** Saladin ravages Galilee.
c. **1185** Jewish population of Egypt estimated to be 13,000; Copts estimated at 12m.			
			1186 Saladin's dominions reach Mosul.

;YPT & THE SUDAN	NORTHERN AFRICA	SOUTH OF THE SAHARA	OTHER COUNTRIES
			1187 3-4 July, Crusader army destroyed at the Horns of Hittin. Jerusalem captured by Saladin.
			1188 Saladin master of all former Crusader conquests except for Antioch, Tripoli, and Tyre.
			1189—93 Third Crusade.
			1189—99 Richard I, Coeur-de-Lion, King of England.
		1190—1225 Lalibela, Emperor of Ethiopia.	
		c. 1190 Kanem, helped by Tunis, subdues Saharan trade routes.	
		c. 1191—1215 al-Hasan b.Sulaiman II, Sultan of Kilwa.	1191 Philippe Augustus of France and Richard I retake Acre. Saladin beaten at Arsouf.
93 21 Feb., Saladin d.		1193—1210 Selma, Mai of Kanem, said to be the first black King of Kanem.	
93—8 al-Aziz Imad Din, Ayyubid ruler.			
	1196—1464 Marinid dynasty of Fez.		1196 Almohads under Abu Yusuf, assisted by Banu Marin, defeat Spanish at Alarcos.
	1196—1217 Abu Muhammad Abd al-Haqq b.Abi Khalid Mahin al-Marini.		
	c. 1197 Tlemcen becomes a centre of pilgrimage to the tomb of Sidi Bu Madian.		
98—9 al-Mansur hammad, Ayyubid er.	1198 Abu Midyan al-Ghawth, introducer of the Qadiriyyah Sufi order into Morocco, d.		1198 Trinitarian Order founded by St Jean de Matha for the redemption of Christian slaves.
99—1218 al-Adil I if al-Din, Ayyubid er.	1199—1222 Al-Nasir, Almohad; puts down revolt of Banu Ghaniya; retakes Tunis, Gafsa and al-Mahdia.		1199—1216 John, King of England.
		12th c. Ali b.al-Hasan, first Kilwa sultan to mint coins, otherwise unknown.	
		?late 12th c. Palace of Husuni built at Kilwa.	
		?13th c. Songye infiltrate Kalundwe and establish an empire.	
		early 13th c. Lalibela, King of Ethiopia, transfers capital from Axum to Lasta (Lalibela): great builder of churches; considerable literary activity.	
	c. 1200 Jews given special privileges in Morocco, which they have had ever since.	c. 1200 Churches at Lalibela of Abba Libanos, St George, the Virgin and the Cross. Nta or Ntafo, ancestors of the Akan, begin to disperse near Gonja. Eweka I, Oba of Benin: hereditary council to elect Obas instituted. Fulani begin to appear in Borgu and amongst Hausa.	

EGYPT & THE SUDAN	NORTHERN AFRICA	AFRICA SOUTH OF THE SAHARA	OTHER COUNTRIES
	post 1200 Morocco becomes Arabic speaking as a result of the invasion of the Maaqil Arabs.	*post* 1200 Sereres migrate and found kingdoms of Sine and Saloum. *c.* 1200–1300 Fulani entering Hausaland; a second group entering Senegambia. 1200–35 Soumangouroun; 1203, takes Ghana; Muslims migrate north.	1200 Yaqut, geographer, d.
1202–4 Famine in Egypt.			1202–4 Fourth Crusade: attacks Byzantium. 1203 Almohad conquest of the Balearic Is. 1204 Crusaders take Byzantium and establish Latin Empire (–1261). Sidon retaken. 1206 St Dominic preaching against the Albigenses. 1208 Order of Preachers founded by St Dominic. 1209 First Franciscan constitution drawn up. 1211 Crusade preached against the Almohads. 1212 Battle of Las Novas de Tolosa: Almohads expelled from Spain. 1215 King John of England signs *Magna Carta.*
	1204 Traditional date of foundation of Sultanates of Pate and Vumba, Kenya.		
	1209 Almohad victory over Banu Sulaim at Jebel Nefusa.		
1211 Ibn Surah, rare bookseller in Old Cairo, d.			
1215 Treaty of peace between al-Malik al-Adil and Frederick of Hohenstaufen.	*c.* 1215 or 1216 Banu Marin raid Almohad territory.		
	1217 26 Sept., Battle in Wadi Sebu between Almohads and Banu Marin: Banu Marin make local tribes vassals.		
1218–38 al-Kamil Muhammad, Ayyubid ruler. 1218 Fifth Crusade, led by Jean de Brienne; Damietta besieged. 1219 St Francis of Assisi visits Cairo and discusses religion with al-Kamil. 1219–21 5 Dec., Damietta occupied by the Crusaders.			1218 Order of *Nôtre Dame de la Merci* founded by St Peter Nolasco to redeem Christian captives in N Africa. 1219 Bokhara captured by Mongols. Franciscans spread into France and Spain.
		c. 1220 Ethiopia and Nubia invaded by Damdam. 1221–59 Dunama Dubalemi, seventeenth Mai of Kanem; empire of Kanem at its peak. *c.* 1224 Foundation of Walata.	
			1225–74 St Thomas Aquinas, theologian. 1226–70 St Louis IX, King of France. 1226 Chao Ju-Kua, *Chu-fan-chih,* includes description of Somalia and eastern Africa. 1227 Genghis Khan d.

YPT & THE SUDAN	NORTHERN AFRICA	AFRICA SOUTH OF THE SAHARA	OTHER COUNTRIES
28–9 Ambassadors from derick of Hohenstaufen eived in Cairo; Jerusalem ed secretly to him.	1228–1574 Hafsid dynasty of Tunis. 1228 Ifriqiya becomes independent under Abu Zakaria Yahya I, Hafsid, with capital at Tunis: commercial treaties made with Genoa, Pisa, Sicily, and Venice. 1229 Abu Zakaria takes Bougie and Algiers; Ghaniya destroyed. c. 1230 Ibn Ali al-Marrakushi, geographer.		1228–9 Sixth Crusade: led by Frederick of Hohenstaufen, King of Sicily, enters Jerusalem 17 March 1229.
		c. 1230 Sosso Kingdom includes Bagana, Diaga, Bakunu, and Gumbu: attack made on Nare Fa Maghan, King of the Mandingo.	
	1234 Commercial treaty between Abu Zakaria and Pisa. 1235 Abu Yahya Yaghmorasan, Amir of Tlemcen (1235–82), proclaims his independence of the Almohads: dynasty of Zenata of the Banu Abd al-Wad (Abdalwadids) (–1554). 1235–6 Genoese attack Ceuta. 1236–7 Abu Zakaria takes title of Amir (–1249): treaties of commerce with Genoa, Pisa, Sicily, and Venice.	c. 1235–55 Sundiata Keita, King of Mali. 1235 Sundiata Keita defeats Soumangouroun at Kirina near Kulikoro.	1235–9 Mongol conquest of Persia. 1236–46 Ferdinand III of Castile conquers Andalusia: Great Mosque of Cordova made a cathedral.
38–40 al-Adil I, yubid ruler.		1237 Embassy from Kanem to Tunis. 1238 Minaret of Friday Mosque at Mogadishu completed.	
40–9 al-Salih Najm Din, Ayyubid ruler; rried Shajar al-Durr.		1240 Ghana destroyed by Sundiata Keita, King of Mali, and incorporated in Mali: end of empire of Ghana.	1239 Pope Gregory IX preaches the Sixth Crusade: Crusaders halted at Gaza. c. 1240 Gunpowder introduced into Europe. 1240 Kiev taken by Tartars. Galilee ceded to Crusaders and Askelon to Egypt. 1244 Jerusalem captured by Turks.
	1244 Almohads attack and defeat Marinids near Fez. 1244–58 Abu Yahya Abu Bakr, chief of the Banu Marin: 1244 moves to near Meknès and seizes it. 1245 Abu Yahya Abu Bakr recognizes Hafsids as overlords. post 1248 Following capture of Seville, many Andalusian Muslims migrate to Tunis. 1248 20 Aug., Banu Marin take Fez; and then Taza, Rabat, and much of Morocco; Marinid dynasty (–1470).		1248 Seville taken by Ferdinand III. Louis IX in Cyprus.

EGYPT & THE SUDAN	NORTHERN AFRICA	AFRICA SOUTH OF THE SAHARA	OTHER COUNTRIES
1249 Sixth Crusade: 29 June, Damietta again occupied by Crusaders under Louis IX of France.	**1249–79** al-Mustansir, Hafsid.		
1249–50 Shajar al-Durr, widow of al-Salih, ruler: only woman to rule Egypt in Islamic times: 'Queen of the Muslims'. al-Muazzam Turan Shah, Ayyubid claimant murdered by his mother Shajar al-Durr,			
1250–2 al-Ashraf Musa; Ayyubid: nominal reign only, **1250–1390** Bahri Mamluk dynasty in Egypt. **1250** April, crusading army destroyed at al-Mansura, near Cairo; Louis IX of France prisoner with many others; released after one month for ransom and surrender of Damjetta. Shajar al-Durr, last effective, Ayyubid ruler, marries Izz al-Din Aybak, first Bahri Mamluk sultan.	**1250** Jan-Feb., Almohads temporarily reign Fez.	**1250–74** Ethiopia without an Abuna. *c.* **1250** Fakhr al-Din dynasty founded at Mogadishu by Abu Bakr b. Fakhr al-Din. Beginning of conversion to Islam and organization of constitutional government among the Hausa. *c.* **1250–1300** Mannu dynasty of Futa Toro. *c.* **1250–1468** Katsina subject to Bornu.	**1250** Mamluks seize Damascus. **1250–4** Louis IX of France in Syria.
	1253 al-Mustansir, Hafsid, takes title of Amir al-Muminin as Caliph; recognized by kingdoms of Tlemcen and Fez. Banu Marin defeat Almohads near Fez. **1254–5** Marinids take Sijilmasa and other towns.		**1253–8** Hulagu Khan seizes Persia and Mesopotamia.
			1254 Louis IX returns to France. **1254–1323** Marco Polo, traveller.
		c. **1255–70** Mansa Ule, King of Mali; Mansa becomes an official title; Timbuktu, Gao, Niani (or Mali), and Jenne flourishing.	
1257 Izz al-Din Aybak murdered in his bath because Shajar al-Durr hears he is taking a second wife; she herself is then battered to death.		**1257** Dunama Dubalemi, King of Kanem, sends a giraffe and other gifts to al-Mustansir, Hafsid, in Tunis.	
	1258–86 Abu Yusuf Yaqub, Marinid: controls all Marinid territory except Fez. **1258** Marinids control all Morocco: Tlemcen and Fez vassals of Hafsids.		**1258** Ali al-Shadhili, founder of the Sufi Shadhiliyyah order, d. 17 Jan., Baghdad sacked by Mongols.
1260 Mamluk Kutu recognizes al-Mustansir, Hafsid, as Caliph. **1260–77** Baybars (al-Malik al-Zahir Rukn al-Din Baybars al-Bunduqdari), Mamluk Sultan.	**1260** Marinid pretender at Salé; Sept., Salé temporarily occupied by Spaniards; retaken by Abu Yusuf Yaqub.	*c.* **1260** Korau, King of Katsina: war on the Kwararafa. Mansa Ule of Mali makes pilgrimage to Mecca. Kingdoms of Bambouk and Gangaram founded.	

EGYPT & THE SUDAN	NORTHERN AFRICA	AFRICA SOUTH OF THE SAHARA	OTHER COUNTRIES
1261 June, last Abbasid Caliph al-Mustansir moves from Damascus to Cairo: henceforward line of pseudo-caliphs in Cairo (–1517).			
	1262 Abortive Marinid attack on Marrakesh.		
			1263–71 Egyptian raids wear down Crusaders in Palestine.
	1264 Commercial treaty between Pisa and Hafsid al-Muntasir. 1265 Sijilmasa taken by Abdulwadids.	1265 Final date for a hoard of more than 250 Chinese coins found at Kajengwa, Zanzibar.	1265–6 First Parliament meets at Westminster. 1265–1321 Dante, poet. 1265 Baybars takes Caesarea and Arsouf.
	1266 Almohad Abu Dubbus takes Marrakesh.		
		1268 Mihrab of the Mosque of Arbaa Rukun completed at Mogadishu. 1269 Fakhr al-Din mosque completed at Mogadishu.	1268 Baybars takes Jaffa and Antioch.
1269 Mosque of Sultan Baybars, Cairo, built.	1269 8 Sept., Marrakesh taken by Abu Yusuf Yaqub, Marinid; takes title of Amir al-Muminin. 1270 Louis IX leads Eighth Crusade against Tunis; plague attacks invaders; 25 Aug., Louis IX d.; Hafsid army defeated by Charles of Anjou, followed by peace; Spanish occupy Larache.	c. 1270 Wati, then Khalifa, then Abu Bakr, Kings of Mali: expeditions against Gao and Tekrur. 1270–85 Yekuno Amlak, founder of the present Solomonic dynasty of Ethiopia; capital, Ankober.	1269 Hugh III of Cyprus, King of Jerusalem.
	1271 Hafsid trade with Aragon, Pisa and Venice restored. Abu Yusuf, Marinid, leads campaign in Wadi Dra. 1272 Hafsid trade with Genoa restored. 1273 Tangier and Ceuta taken by Marinids. 1274 Sijilmasa taken by Marinids.		1271–95 Marco Polo in China. 1273–1331 Abu al-Fida, geographer.
1275 David of Nubia refuses tribute to Egypt: Nubia invaded as far as Dongola.		1274–5 Yekuno Amlak corresponds with Mamluk Sultan Baybars requesting an Abuna; Ethiopian hostilities against Ifat; Baybars declines. c. 1275 Yoruba destroy Nupe Kingdom. 1275–6 Umar b.Dunya-huz, first of Walasma dynasty of Ifat, d.	1275 Marinid expedition to Spain.
1276 Further Egyptian campaign against Nubia: northern Nubia subjected to Egypt: Shemamun made puppet king. Ahmad al-Badawi, founder of the Ahmadiyyah Sufi order, d. at Tanta.	1276 New Fez (al-Fas al-Jadid) begun by Marinids; with kasba, castle and great mosque at Meknès; and a madrassah at Qayrawan.		1276 Hugh III abandons Syria.

EGYPT & THE SUDAN	NORTHERN AFRICA	AFRICA SOUTH OF THE SAHARA	OTHER COUNTRIES
		c. 1277–94 al-Hasan b. Talut, Sultan of Kilwa. 1277 Asma attacks Makhzumi sultanate of eastern Shoa.	1277–9 Second Marinid campaign in Spain. 1277 Pedro III of Aragon fights Moors in Andalusia. 1278–9 Abortive Spanish siege of Algeciras.
1279–90 Qalaun, Mamluk Sultan; trade with Genoa, Venice, and Barcelona greatly developed.	1279–1370 Anarchy in N Africa. 1279 Spanish occupy Ceuta.		
		c. 1280 Oguola, Oba of Benin: wars with the Ibo.	
	1281 Tlemcen besieged by Abdulwadids. 1282–1303 Abu Said Uthman, Abdulwadid: almost continuous war with Marinids.		1281 Egyptian army repulses Mongols at Homs. 1282–3 Third Marinid campaign in Spain. 1282 The 'Sicilian Vespers'. Ten-year truce between Egypt and the Crusaders.
		c. 1283 Kingdom of Zandoma founded by Rawa; walls of Benin built.	
1284 al-Maristan al-Mansuri, hospital with a school and mosque, built in Cairo by Qalaun.	1284 Abu Hafs grants land to Riya Arabs.		1284–95 Sancho IV, King of Castile: treaty with Aragon partitioning N Africa into spheres of influence. 1285–6 Fourth Marinid campaign in Spain.
		1285 Makhzumi sultanate of eastern Shoa destroyed by Asma. post 1295 Ifat sultanate conquers Adal, Mora, Hobat, and Jidaya. 1285–94 Yagbea Sion of Ethiopia: successful campaign against Zaila; truce made and an Abuna consecrated. c. 1285 –1300 Sakura, King of Mali.	
c. 1286 Egyptian embassies to Nubian princelets of Ador, Bara, Taka (?Kassala), Kaderu (?Kadaro), ?Uri, Anaj, and Keisa, and to Shemamun of N Nubia. c. 1287 Egyptian army sent against Dongola: Shemamun flees; replaced temporarily. by nephew. 1288–9 Abu al-Hasan Ali, dean of al-Maristan al-Mansuri, d.; his Sharh Tashrih al-Qanun describes the circulation of the blood. 1289 Further Egyptian expedition against Dongola: Shemamun flees but again re-established: tribute promised to Egypt. 1290–3 al-Malik al-Ashraf Khalil, Mamluk Sultan. c. 1291 Further Egyptian expedition against Shemamun and other Sudanese rulers.	1286–1307 Abu Yaqub Yusuf, Marinid.	c. 1286 Ibn Said records Indian settlers in eastern Africa.	c. 1286 Ibn Said, geographer, d.
			1287 Qalaun takes Laodicea.
		1289 Unknown travellers of Dombay mss. explore to south of Morocco.	1289 Qalaun takes Tripoli.
	1290 May-Oct., Marinids besiege Tlemcen.	1291 Vivaldi brothers reach Gozule and Cape Nun.	1290 University of Lisbon founded. 1291 Expedition of al-Malik al-Ashraf Khalil finally destroys Crusader principalities: Acre taken.

EGYPT & THE SUDAN	NORTHERN AFRICA	AFRICA SOUTH OF THE SAHARA	OTHER COUNTRIES
		c. 1291–1339 Fumomadi the Great, Sultan of Pate: coast controlled as far as Mogadishu. 1293–4 Sakura, King of Mali, makes pilgrimage to Mecca.	1291–3 Fifth Marinid campaign in Spain. 1293 Paper-making and printing factory established at Tabriz by Mongols: first banknotes made.
1295 Famine in Egypt. 1296 Famine again in Egypt: students sell books from Fadiliya library for food.			
		1298–9 Muhammad Abu Abdallah, a visionary, abortively collects an army to conquer Ethiopia.	1298 Marco Polo, *Travels,* written in Venice.
	1299–1306 Siege of Tlemcen by Marinids: rival capital al-Mahalla al-Mansura built.	*c.* 1299 Art of brass casting introduced into Benin from Ife. Empire of Kanem stretches from the Niger to the Nile, and from the Fezzan to Adamawa. 1299–1314 Wadem Arad of Ethiopia: makes treaty with Muslim Sultanate of Ifat.	1299 Damascus taken by Mongols.

EGYPT & THE SUDAN	NORTHERN AFRICA	WESTERN AFRICA
		14th to 15th c. Jenne develops as a market for the gold trade from the south. Maaqil Arabs move into Mauritania: Western Berbers Arabized.
c. **1300—1400** Guhayna and other Arabs migrating into Sudan to Darfur, Ethiopia and beyond.		*c.* **1300—1400** Ibo begin to move into present habitat.
		c. **1300** Ga migrate from Benin to Accra. Bedde, led by Ago, reach present habitat. Friday Mosque of Jenne built: Komboro Mana, chief of Jenne. Tondjoa arrive amongst Tekrur. Some Fulani migrate from Futa Toro to Bornu, entering Adamawa. Yoruba begin to infiltrate region of Benin.
1302 Treaty of commerce between Egypt and Venice.		
1303 Mosque of Qalaun built in Cairo. King Amai of Nubia sends embassy to Cairo with presents.	**1303—7** Abu Zayan, Abdulwadid.	
	1304—77 Ibn Battuta, greatest Arab traveller, b. at Tangier.	
	1306 Abu Yaqub, Marinid, assassinated before Tlemcen; end of siege; al-Mahalla al-Mansura demolished.	
	1307—8 Abu Thabit, Marinid.	**1307—32** Kankan Mansa Musa, ruler of Mali: seizes Songhai.
	1307—18 Abu Hammu Musa, Abdulwadid; Tlemcen strengthened in case of further siege; Constantine and Bougie attacked.	
	1308—10 Abu al-Rabi, Marinid.	
	1309 Marinids retake Ceuta.	
1310—41 Muhammad b.Qalaun, Mamluk Sultan; merchants from Barcelona, Marseilles, Pisa and Venice set up at Alexandria, Damietta and Rosetta. Copts persecuted.	**1310—31** Abu Said Uthman, Marinid.	
1311—12 Tribute sent to Cairo by Kerenbes, last Christian King of Dongola.		
		ante **1312** Maritime expedition from Mali to Morocco: all but one of 2,000 vessels lost.
		c. **1312** Ship from Cherbourg accidentally reaches Canary Is.
		c. **1313** Mossi Kingdom of Ourbri founded by Morho Naba.
	1314 Abortive Marinid attack on Tlemcen.	
1315 Kerenbes deported to Cairo: Abdallah b.Sanbu made King: Kanz al-Daula, chief of Kunuz, kills Abdallah; Abraam, brother of Kerenbes, regains throne briefly; Nubia usurped by Kanz al-Daula (—1323).	**1315** Abu Ali temporarily deposes Abu Said, Marinid: rebellion to 1322.	
	1316 Yahya b.Afzi declares Ceuta independent of Marinids (—1326).	
	1316—1401 Ibn Arafa, jurisconsult, at Qayrawan.	
	1318—36 Ibn Tashfin, Abdulwadid; Bougie and Constantine besieged; Tamzizdikt built.	

EASTERN AFRICA	CENTRAL & SOUTHERN AFRICA	OTHER COUNTRIES
14th c. *Kebra Negast* (Book of the Glory of the Kings of Ethiopia) compiled.	**14th c.** Kongo monarchy established by Ntinu (King) Wene, or Nimi a Lukeni: title Mani Kongo, or Ne Kongo; Kingdoms of Mpangu and Mbata incorporated.	
c. **1300** Beginning of dynasty of 'Shirazi' Diwans of Mkwaja by a settler from Baghdad.	*c.* **1300** Sena the residence of the King of Sofala.	*c.* **1300** Printing and banknote factory set up at Genoa. Cannon first used by Muslim armies. **1300** Ghazan takes Damascus.
		1301 al-Umari, geographer, b. Othman beats Byzantines at Nicomedia.
		1304—8 Duns Scotus teaching in Paris.
		1305 Clement V elected Pope. **1306** Mongol expedition checked in India. Jews expelled from France. Robert the Bruce crowned King of Scotland.
c. **1310—33** al-Hasan b. Sulaiman III, Sultan of Kilwa.		**1308** Coimbra University founded. **1309** Pope Clement V at Avignon. **1310** Knights Templar disbanded.
		1311 Barons revolt in England.
1312 Tekla Haimanot d.: greatest of Ethiopian saints: missionary amongst pagans of Shoa and Damot.		**1312** Order of Christ founded in Portugal to carry on work of Knights Templar.
1314—44 Amda Sion the Great of Ethiopia.		**1314** Battle of Bannockburn.
1316 Eight Dominicans set out for Nubia and Ethiopia.		
1321 Embassy from Ethiopia to protest against persecution of Copts.		

EGYPT & THE SUDAN	NORTHERN AFRICA	WESTERN AFRICA

1323 Kerenbes reinstated.

1324 Kankan Mansa Musa's pilgrimage to Mecca; mosque at Gao built by Ishaq al-Saheli.
1325 Gao captured by Ghana; Mali the effective centre of Saharan commerce.

c. 1327 Jingereber mosque built at Timbuktu.
1327—9 Muhammad, sultan of Kanem-Bornu: dynasty breaks into two opposing sections.

1330—50 Bartolomeo of Tivoli, Bishop of Dongola.

1331—48 Abu al-Hasan, Marinid: mother an Ethiopian.

c. 1331 Embassy from Mali to Fez.

1332—1406 Abd al-Rahman b. Khaldun of Tunis, historian: originates theory of historical development in *Muqaddamah.*

c. 1332—6 Magha, son of Mansa Musa, ruler of Mali; Timbuktu burnt by Mossi; Gao lost to Songhai.

c. 1335 Gao liberated by Ali Kolen, who takes the title of Sonni.

1336—7 Siege of Tlemcen by Marinids; Abu Tashfin and his three sons perish; Tlemcen annexed by Fez (until 1359); Great Mosque and Palace of Victory built.

1336—1433 Timbuktu under Mali.
ante 1336 Lanzarote Malocello settles in Canary Is. for twenty years.

1337 Voyage of Abu Abdallah Muhammad of Reggano, Vizier of Almeria, to region between Cape Timiris and Senegal.
1338 Timbuktu sacked by Mossi.

1340 5 April, Marinid and Hafsid fleet defeat Spanish off Gibraltar.

c. 1341 Voyage of Niccolosa di Recco and Angelino del Tegghra dei Corbizzi to Azores and Canary Is.
c. 1341—60 Sulaiman, King of Mali: domination of Mali re-established.
c. 1342 Majorcan voyages to the Canary Is.

EASTERN AFRICA   CENTRAL
     & SOUTHERN AFRICA   OTHER COUNTRIES

post 1321 Haqq al-Din, Sultan of Ifat,
invades Ethiopia and burns churches.
1322 Abu Bakr b.Muhammad, Sultan
of Mogadishu: first ruler known to
issue dated coins in east Africa.

1325 Amda Sion threatens to divert
the Nile if the persecution of
Christians in Egypt is not stopped.
c. 1325 Haqq al-Din, Sultan of Ifat,
again makes war on Ethiopia.

1326 Janissaries first recruited.
Ottoman Turks seize Brusa.

1327 Guillaume des Bons Mains
sent to Ethiopia by Charles V.

1328 Amda Sion takes Haqq al-Din of
Ifat prisoner and annexes Ifat and
Fatajar: Sabr al-Din Governor.
c. 1330 Sor Leone Vivaldi reaches
Mogadishu: refused passage to Ethiopia.
1331–2 Ibn Battuta visits Zaila,
Mogadishu, Mombasa and Kilwa from
Aden: sails direct from Kilwa to Dhufar.
c. 1332 St Ewostatewos, missionary
and founder of Ethiopian monasteries,
d. Collapse of Friday Mosque at Kilwa: no
facilities to restore it for 100 years.
c. 1332–8 Embassy from Ifat to Cairo
to ask aid against Ethiopia.
c. 1333–56 Daud b. al-Hasan, Sultan of
Kilwa: policy of economic retrenchment.

1330 Jordanus, a monk, describes
East Africa as 'India tertia'.

1333–7 Ottoman Turks take Mysia.
1333 Algeciras retaken by Fez.

1338 Ottomans reach the Bosphorus.

c. 1339–92 Omar b.Muhammad I, Sultan
of Pate: claims to control coast from
Mogadishu to Kerimba Is.

1340 Marinid campaign in Spain repulsed.

1344–72 Saifa Harud of Ethiopia.

1344 26 March, Spanish take Algeciras
after twenty month siege.

EGYPT & THE SUDAN	NORTHERN AFRICA	WESTERN AFRICA
		1346 Jac Ferrer, expedition to Rio d'Oro.
	1347 Abu al-Hasan, Marinid, takes Bougie, Constantine, and (18 Sept.) Tunis from Hafsids.	
1348–55 Black Death in Egypt. Some 900,000 die in Cairo.	1348 Marinids fail to take Qayrawan. 1348–57 Abu Ainan, Marinid. 1349 Ibn Battuta returns to Tangier from his eastern travels.	
		c. 1350 Guan established in their present habitat.
1352 Marcos, Coptic Patriarch, imprisoned.	1352 Abdulwadids retake Tlemcen but are expelled.	1352 Ibn Battuta visits western Africa.
	1353 Bougie revolts against Marinids.	1353–76 Idris, King of Kanem: visited by Ibn Battuta.
	1357 Campaign of Abu Inan against Constantine and Tunis. 1358–9 Muhammad, Marinid: aged 5 at accession: Marinid power begins to disintegrate through absence of leadership. 1358–89 Abu Hammu Musa II, Abdulwadid. 1359 Dawawida Arabs revolt against Marinids; Abdulwadids restored at Tlemcen.	
		1360–74 Mari Diata II, King of Mali. c. 1360–1500 'Precocious' period of Benin art. 1360 Embassy from Mali to Fez .
1362 Mosque of Sultan al-Hasan built in Cairo. 1364–5 Famine in Egypt. 1364–1442 al-Maqrizi (Taqir al-Din Ahmad al-Maqrizi), historian. 1365 Peter I of Cyprus pillages Alexandria. 1366 Southern Egypt ravaged by Kenuz and Ikrima Arabs; King of Nubia murdered: capital already moved from Dongola to Du.		1364–1413 Alleged trade between Dieppe and area between Cape Verde and the Gold Coast.
	1369–93 Abu al-Abbas Ahmad II, Hafsid: Bougie becomes the centre of organized piracy; Tunis and Bône regained. 1370–2 Marinids temporarily regain Tlemcen.	c. 1369–1437 Etsu Ede, King of Nupe.
1372 Bishop of Ibrim and Faras consecrated in Cairo.	1374–81 Musa II, King of Mali: Jata, Wazir. 1374 Jata's campaign against Bornu. 1377 Ibn Battuta d. at Marrakesh.	
		c. 1380 Forty Muslim missionaries working in Kano.
1382–99 Barquq, Mamluk Sultan. 1384 Mosque of Barquq built in Cairo.		

EASTERN AFRICA	CENTRAL & SOUTHERN AFRICA	OTHER COUNTRIES
		1346 Battle of Crécy. The Black Death. 1347–1490 Bahmanid sultanate of the Deccan.
		1348 Jews expelled from Italy. Black Death in England.
		1351 Laurentian portolan gives accurate outline of W Africa. Madeira and the Azores known to the Italians.
1352 Saifa Harud imprisons Egyptian merchants in Ethiopia as a reprisal for persecution of the Copts in Egypt, putting to death those who do not accept Christianity.		
		1353–6 Ottomans seize the Gallipoli peninsula. 1356 Battle of Poitiers.
		1360–61 Ottomans take Adrianople.
1364 First mention in literature of a pillar tomb in E Africa.		
		1366 Abortive crusade of Amadeus of Savoy against Ottomans in Gallipoli.
		1367–83 Ferdinand I, King of Portugal. 1368–1642 Ming dynasty in China.
1369 Monastery of St Tekla Haimanot built.		
1372–82 Neonya Mariam of Ethiopia: further troubles with Ifat.		1372 Anglo-Portuguese treaty of alliance.
		1380 Jews expelled from Holland.
1382–1411 David I of Ethiopia.		
		1383–1433 João I, King of Portugal; m. Philippa of Lancaster, daughter of John of Gaunt: third son, Henry the 'Navigator'.

EGYPT & THE SUDAN	NORTHERN AFRICA	WESTERN AFRICA
		c. 1386 Nomadic Arabs from Sudan help expel reigning family from Bornu, placing cadet branch on the throne.
1390—1517 Burji Mamluk dynasty.	1390 French and Genoese expedition against Bougie to put down piracy; repulsed by Abu Faris.	1390—1410 Kanajeji, King of Kano: first Hausa King to introduce quilted armour and iron helmets. 1391—2 King of Bornu complains to Cairo of Arab raiders from Egypt who sell his people as slaves.
	1393—1433 Abu Faris, Hafsid: Tripoli, Tozeur, Gafsa and Biskra retaken.	1394—8 Omar, King of Kanem: abandons Kanem and moves to Kagha. 1397 Kanem in revolt.
1397 Deposed King of Du flees to Cairo; Beni Kanz, Hawara and kindred tribes amalgamating with Nubians: Islam replacing Christianity.	1399 Tetuan taken by Henry III of Castile.	
		? early 15th c. Mande colonization of Begho. *c.* 15th c. Kingdom of Nikki established.
		c. 1400 Baga, Temne, Yalunka and Loko enter Sierra Leone region. Fante occupy Gold Coast. Sonni Ma Dogo of Gao raids Mali; Ijaw settle at Calabar. *c.* 1400—1500 Fula begin to accept Islam. *c.* 1400—50 Guan people of Ghana reach the sea.
1403 Famine in Egypt.	1402 Jean de Bethencourt's expedition to the Canary Is.; Château de Rubicon built on Lanzarote. 1404 Lanzarote taken by Jean de Bethencourt. 1405 Jean de Bethencourt raids interior from Cape Bogador. 1410 Algiers taken by Abu Faris, Hafsid.	

EASTERN AFRICA	CENTRAL & SOUTHERN AFRICA	OTHER COUNTRIES
		1385 Victory of Aljubarrota gives guarantee of Portuguese independence in the Iberian peninsula.
1386 Haqq al-Din of Ifat killed in battle with David I of Ethiopia.		**1386** Persia conquered by Tamberlaine (Timur-i-Leng).
1387 Embassy from Ethiopia to Egypt with twenty camel-loads of gifts.		**1387—1400** Geoffrey Chaucer, *The Canterbury Tales.*
	1388 ± 60 Second stage of Mapungubwe culture, Rhodesia.	
c. **1390** Nabhani mosque built on Songo Mnara Is.		
		1391 Jews expelled from Spain.
		1392 Zafar Khan founds dynasty in Gujerat, with trade links with East Africa.
c. **1394** Venice sends masons, painters and artisans to Ethiopia.		**1394** Prince Henry the 'Navigator', b.
	late 14th or early 15th c. Iron smelting introduced amongst the Bakongo. *c. ante* **1400** Tutsi arrive in Rwanda and Burundi. *c.* **early 15th c.** Ngoni settled in Natal. Iron Age B 2 beginning in Rhodesia. Sao living in the Logone valley: invaded by the Massa.	
c. **15th—18th c.** Movement of Lwoo-speaking Nilotic peoples from southern Sudan to present habitats in Uganda and Kenya. **15th c.** Controversy on the Three Births or Two Births of Christ divides Gojjam and Shoa from the rest of Christian Ethiopia.	*c.* **1400** Karanga occupy S and SW Rhodesia. Great enclosure built at Zimbabwe. Luba and Songye states near lakes in Katanga; Bolia in tropical forest; much of later Kongo, Loango, and Tyo (Teke) kingdoms on lower R Congo. *c.* **1400—***c.* **1600** Kangila people in Zambia.	
		1401 Statute *de heretico comburendo* in England.
1402 David I of Ethiopia sends four leopards and other gifts to Egypt.		
		1403 Jews expelled from France.
		1409 Council of Pisa. **1410** Battle of Tannenberg. **1411** John Huss excommunicated.

1415 Ceuta taken by the Portuguese.
Spanish take Tenerife.

1418 Canary Is. ceded to Castile.
1418–20 Tristão Vaz Teiveira and
Gonçalves Zarco rediscover and
colonize Madeira.

1422–37 Barsbay, Mamluk Sultan.

1427 –1550 Wattasid dynasty at Fez.
1427–49 Abu Zakaria b.Zayan
al-Wattasi: usurps last Marinid, an infant,
as mayor of the palace.

1431 Azores Is. discovered by Gonçalo
Velho.
1433–4 Gil Eanes reaches Cape Bogodor.

1433 Tuareg chief Akil takes Timbuktu;
Arawan, Walata and other areas also seized.
1433–68 Timbuktu under Maghcharen
Tuareg.
1434 Gil Eanes, first Portuguese to reach
Cameroun.

1435–87 Abu Umar Uthman, Hafsid;
Tunis, Bizerta and Bougie the principal
centres of piracy.
1436 Rio de Oro named by Afonso
Gonçalves Baldaya. Afonso Gonçalves
Baldaya reaches Angra dos Cavallos and
Pedra da Gale.

EASTERN AFRICA	CENTRAL & SOUTHERN AFRICA	OTHER COUNTRIES

c. 1412—21 al-Malik al-Adil Muhammad b.Sulaiman, Sultan of Kilwa; coins minted; first recorded appointments of wazirs and amirs, probably from Malindi immigrants.

1414—29 Yeshaq of Ethiopia; continues war with Zaila: arsenals established with Turkish Mamluk craftsmen; tax collection reorganized: Somali first mentioned in Ethiopic literature.

1414 Jews again expelled from Spain. Council of Constance.

1415 Yeshaq of Ethiopia besieges Saad al-Din II of Ifat in Zaila; Sultan killed; Zaila occupied.
c. 1415 Embassy from Malindi to China.
c. 1416 Walasma dynasty re-emerge as Sultans of Adal, with capital Dakar.
1417—19 Chinese fleet under Cheng Ho visits Mogadishu, Barawa and Malindi.

1415 An ambassador of Malindi at the Chinese court. Battle of Agincourt.

1416 Ottoman fleet destroyed by Venice off Gallipoli.

1419 Prince Henry the 'Navigator' sets up naval school and arsenal at Sagres.

c. 1421—42 Sulaiman b. Muhammad, Sultan of Kilwa; Friday mosque restored.
1421—2 Cheng Ho's fleet re-visits Mogadishu and Malindi.
1422 Ethiopia intensifies war against neighbouring Muslim sultanates.
1424 Ifat attacks Jedaya: brother of sultan taken prisoner: town sacked and inhabitants dispersed as slaves to Persia and India.
1427 Yeshaq of Ethiopia sends embassy to Alfonso V of Aragon and to the Duke of Berry to unite Christians against Islam.
ante 1428 Sidama Kingdom of Enarya conquered by Yeshaq.

1430 Shaikh Ibrahim Abu Zaharbui goes to Harar and converts many to Islam: buried later at Zaila.

1422 Jews expelled from England.

1424—6 Cyprus conquered by Barsbay of Egypt from house of Lusignan: king forced to pay ransom.

1428 ± 60 Third stage of Mapungubwe culture, Rhodesia.

1428 English besiege Orléans.

1429 Joan of Arc relieves Orléans.

1431 Colonization of the Azores begun by Goncalo Velho.
1433 Abortive Egyptian expedition against Syria. Council of Basle.
1433—8 Duarte I, King of Portugal.

1434—68 Zara Yaqub of Ethiopia: civil and religious reformer: war with Sultan of Adal: Sultan Badlai killed: end of Eustathian schism; Solomonic dynasty reaches peak: churches and monasteries built; literature and arts encouraged.

1435 Pope Eugenius IV orders the liberation of slaves in the Canary Is. Diocese.

EGYPT & THE SUDAN	NORTHERN AFRICA	WESTERN AFRICA

1437 16 Oct., Portuguese expedition against Tangier destroyed; Ceuta abandoned.

1439—41 Coptic representative sent to Council of Florence.

1439 Active colonization of the Azores by Portugal.

c. 1440 Ewuare the Great, Oba of Benin: traveller in Nigeria, Dahomey, Ghana, Guinea and Congo and warrior against surrounding peoples. Sidi Yahya mosque at Timbuktu built.

1441 António Goncalves and Nunes Tristão reach Porto de Cavaleiro.

1443 Nunes Tristão and Gil Eanes reach Arguin (Gete Is.).

c. 1443 Bolewa, claiming a Yemeni origin, move from Lariski or Wuyo to Daniski.

1445 Portuguese fort built at Arguin.

1445 João Fernandes, abandoned on the coast of the Gambia, penetrates to the Sahara and witnesses the salt trade of Teghazza and the gold trade of Bambouk. Mouth of R Senegal reached by Dinis Dias.

1446 Nunes Tristão and others killed, probably at mouth of R Gambia.

1447 Malfante, a Genoese, visits Touat.

1447 Fernando Alonzo makes contact with Sereres, vassals of Mali.

1448 Dinis Dias passes Cape Verde and reaches Sierra Leone.

c. 1450 Gold from Golam passes from Mali to Timbuktu, then to Mediterranean via Touat. Empire of Kanem reorganized. Ijebu conquered by Ozolua, Crown Prince of Benin.

1453 Cide de Souza's expedition to Guinea.

1455 March, Alvise de Cadamosto and Antoniotto Usi de Mare explore R Gambia.

1456 Further exploration of R Gambia by Cadamosto and Usi de Mare. Cadamosto in Cape Verde Is.

1458 Diego Gomez sails up R Gambia.

1460 Blessed Anthony Noyrot, OP, martyred at Tunis.

1460 Official discovery of Cape Verde Is. by António and Bartolemeo de Nola of Genoa. Voyage of Pedro de Cintra to Guinea.

1462—1517 Commercial correspondence between Pisa and Hafsids.

1462 Bissagos Is. discovered by Pedro de Cintra and Suero da Costa, probably reaching S Maria, Liberia.

1463—99 Mohamman Rumfa, King of Kano: patron of Shaikh Muhammad al-Maghili; indecisive eleven years war with Katsina, with intermittent hostilities to 1506: fortifies Kano and builds palace of Gidan Rumfa.

ASTERN AFRICA	CENTRAL & SOUTHERN AFRICA	OTHER COUNTRIES

OTHER COUNTRIES

1438 Council of Basle transferred to Florence.
1439 Abortive act of union between Rome and Constantinople.
1440 The caravel invented by Portuguese.

EASTERN AFRICA

439–41 Ethiopian representative ent to the Council of Florence.

CENTRAL & SOUTHERN AFRICA

c. 1440 Rozvi King Mutota of the Karanga established in Dande Region: takes title Mwene-Mutapa (Monomotapa): launches campaign to set up an empire.

1441 First negro slaves and gold dust arrive in Portugal. Ottoman siege of Constantinople.
1443 Bull *Rex regum* on Portuguese conquests in Africa. Council of Basle transferred from Florence to the Lateran.

445 Zara Yaqub of Ethiopia at var with Mogadishu and Adal.

1448 Battle of Kossovo.

?*c.* 1450 Metal used only for weapons in southern Africa.
c. 1450–80 Matope, second Monomotapa, establishes authority over Rhodesian plateau and S of R Zambezi: members of his family local governors.
1450 ± 150 Well-built daga huts and quantities of beads at Zimbabwe, Rhodesia.

452 Ethiopian embassies to Lisbon nd Aragon.
453 Zara Yaqub puts down Stephanist eretics who refuse devotion to the lessed Virgin.

1451–1506 Christopher Columbus.
1452 Rising in Constantinople against unity with Rome.
1453 29 May, Constantinople captured by Ottomans: end of Byzantine empire.

1454 Bull confirms Portuguese monopoly of trade with Indies.

1456 Further bull confirming Portuguese monopoly of trade with Indies.

1458 Ottomans occupy Athens.
1460 Prince Henry the 'Navigator' d.
1460–1524 Vasco de Gama.

460 ± 90 Earliest occupation of he circle at Engaruka.

1462 Slave trade in W Africa condemned by Pope Pius II.

EGYPT & THE SUDAN	NORTHERN AFRICA	WESTERN AFRICA
	1464 Nine chiefs of Canary Is. accept suzerainty of Spain.	**1464–92** Sonni Ali the Great (Ber), King of Songhai. **1465** Campaigns of Sonni Ali against Bandiagara, Hombori and Gourma. **1466** 12 June, Portuguese royal charter sets up administration in Cape Verde and Guinea.
1467–96 Qait Bey, Mamluk Sultan.		*c.* **1468** Sonni Ali drives Tuareg out of Timbuktu. Mahmud al-Kati, historian, b. **1468–93** Timbuktu under Songhai.
	1469 Portuguese take Anfa. **1470–1524** Muhammad al-Shaikh al-Bortugali, Wattasid: struggle to maintain power. **1471** Portuguese take Tangier, Arzila and Larache: Tangier held by Portuguese until cession to England in 1661.	**1469–70** Sonni Ali resists attacks of Mossi and Gourmantche. *c.* **1470** Ngazargarmu founded as new capital of Bornu: until *c.* 1810. **1470** Benedetto Dei, a Florentine, visits Timbuktu. Campaign of Sonni Ali against Gourma. **1471** João de Santarem and Pedro d'Escobar reach Elmina and mouth of R Niger. **1471–6** Seven-year siege of Jenne by Gao.
1472 Mosque of Qait Bay built.		**1472** Fernão da Po discovers the island now named after him. *c.* **1472** Ruy de Sequeira visits Benin. **1472–1504** Ali Ghadji (or Ghadjideni), King of Kanem: Nokena (council) reformed: residence at Ngazargarmu. **1473** Empire of Songhai free from Mali: boundaries extend from Bussa to Jenne. *c.* **1473** Jenne conquered by Sonni Ali. *c.* **1475** Warri founded by Ginuwa. son of an Oba of Benin. **1475** 25 Nov., Ruy de Sequeira reaches St Catherine; and, 21 Dec., São Tomé. **1476–1524** Spanish occupation of Canary Is. **1476** Campaign of Sonni Ali against Bandiagara and Hombori Ruy de Sequiera reaches São Antão Is., 17 Jan., later renamed Principe Is.
	1477 Revolt of Canary Is. put down.	**1477–83** Sonni Ali again resists Mossi and Gourmantche. **1479** July, Na'asira of Mossi takes Walata. *c.* **1480** Jekri (or Shekiri) kingdom founded by Oginuwa, son of Oluwa, Oba of Benin. Portuguese said to have made first visit to Kula.

EASTERN AFRICA	CENTRAL & SOUTHERN AFRICA	OTHER COUNTRIES

1468–78 Baeda Mariam of Ethiopia.
c. **1468** Sultan Muhammad b.
Badlai of Adal promises annual
tribute to Ethiopia.
post **1468** Baeda Mariam reorganizes
Shoa, Amhara, Damot, Tigre and
other provinces; capital peripatetic.

1473–4 Two Ethiopian armies
defeated in war with Adal.

c. **1475** Imports of Ming blue-and white
porcelain become common in E Africa.

1475 End of the 'Hundred Years War'.

1477 Charles the Bold d.

1478–94 Eskender, Emperor of
Ethiopia.

1479 Spain united by the marriage of
Ferdinand of Aragon and Isabella of
Castile.
1480 Portugal cedes Canary Is. to
Spain.

ante **1480** Changa, vassal ruler
of Guninswa, and Torwa (or Togwa)
of Mbire, begin to make themselves
independent of Monomotapa.
c. **1480** Monomotapa Matope d.; buried
in an *mhondoro* shrine attended by
professional mediums.

EGYPT & THE SUDAN	NORTHERN AFRICA	WESTERN AFRICA
1481 Qait Bay gives refuge to Ottoman pretender Jem, brother of Bayazid II.		**1481** John Tintam and William Fabian, first English interlopers on W African coast. *c.* **1481–4** Republican government in Benin.
		1482 Short-lived Portuguese fort on R Sierra Leone. Diogo de Azambuja builds fort at Elmina (Gold Coast); mouth of R. Zaïre (R. Congo) discovered 20 Jan.; first mass celebrated on the Gold Coast. **1483** Mossi raid as far as Walata; routed by Sonni Ali; battle of Kobi; Sonni Ali attacks Mossi town of Gourma.
		c. **1484–1504** Ozolua, Oba of Benin: civil wars. **1484** Campaign of Sonni Ali against Bandiagara and Hombori. *c.* **1485–6** João Afonso d'Aveiro said to have visited Benin and introduced guns and coconuts; Bini ambassador returns with him to Portugal. Trade in ivory and pepper; King of Benin corresponds with João II of Portugal; churches and monasteries established. **1485** São Tome colonized by João de Paiva and Mecia Paes. Diogo Cão reaches mouth of R Congo. Al-Hajj Ahmad, teacher at Sankore mosque, Timbuktu, visits Mecca; d. later, leaving 700 books. **1486** Wolof ruler of Bemoim visits Portugal and presents João II with 100 slaves. Elmina constituted a Portuguese city. **1487** Portuguese reach Wadan, near Abar: factory established.
	1488 João Bemoim, baptized Wolof prince, assisted by Pera Vaz da Cunha in trade between Senegal and Gambia.	**1488** Campaign of Sonni Ali against Gourma.
		1489–91 Kongo sends embassy to Portugal.
1490–91 Covilhão back in Cairo.	**1490** Palma, Canary Is., conquered by Spain.	
		1491 Portuguese expedition to Angola.

EASTERN AFRICA	CENTRAL & SOUTHERN AFRICA	OTHER COUNTRIES
	c. **1480—90** Monomotapa Nyuhama. *post* **1480** Changa takes the title Amir: Changamire dynasty founded.	
1481 Sumptuous Ethiopian embassy to Cairo to ask for a new Abuna.		**1481** 16 Nov., ambassador from Ethiopia received at Vatican. Embassy from Portugal to England, requesting England not to trade in the Gulf of Guinea. Inquisition established in Spain. Sale of arms in W Africa forbidden by Pope Sixtus IV.
	c. **1483** Diogo Cão erects padrão dated 1482 at Cape St Mary; sends delegation to Mani (King of) Kongo; hostages taken from Sonyo; continues voyage to Benguela.	**1483** Martin Luther b.
	1485 Diogo Cão brings four missionaries to Kongo, taking back four noblemen from Mpinda. *post* **1485** Portuguese criminals and Jews sent to colonize São Tomé; slave trade organized. Monarchy already established in Loango.	
	1487 8 Dec., Bartholemeu Dias reaches Walfish Bay; 21 Dec., Golfo de S. Tomé (Spencer Bay); 26 Dec., Elizabeth Bay; 31 Dec., Terra de Silvestre. Diogo Cão returns noblemen to Kongo and withdraws missionaries; ambassador sent from Kongo requesting missionaries and artisans.	**1487** Pedro da Covilhão and Afonso de Paiva dispatched from Lisbon to explore spice route and to search for Prester John.
1488—1518 Muhammad b.Azhar al-Din, Sultan of Adal: policy of neutrality towards Ethiopia. **1488—90 or 91** Pedro da Covilhão visits Zaila, Red Sea, and eastern Africa as far as Sofala, returning to Cairo.	**1488** Dias reaches: 6 Jan., Serra dos Reis; 3 Feb., Bay of São Bras (Mossel Bay); crew mutinies in Algoa Bay; March, homeward voyage begun; April, Cape of Good Hope first sighted.	**1488** Covilhão in Aden, Hormuz and Calicut.
	c. **1490** Changamire defeats Monomotapa Nyahuma: usurps empire for four years.	
	1491 Kongo embassy returns from Lisbon with missionaries and artisans; church built at Soyo; 3 May., Nzinga a Nkuwa, Mani Kongo, baptized as Afonso I; war against Tyo, now Stanley Pool; numerous conversions; first school built.	*c.* **1491** Ignatius Loyola b.

EGYPT & THE SUDAN	NORTHERN AFRICA	WESTERN AFRICA
	1492 Many Spanish Jews settle in N Africa.	**1492** Last campaign of Sonni Ali against Gourma: d. at R Koni.
		c. **1492–3 – 1541–2** Muhammadu Koran, first Muslim King of Katsina.
	1493 Tenerife taken by Spain.	*c.* **1493** Muhammad al-Maghili, *Obligations of Princes, Taj-al-Din.*
		1493 Sonni Baru succ. Sonni Ali Ber; refuses to become Muslim: 12 April, defeated at battle of Angoo; flees to Ayorou.
		1493–1535 Askia Muhammad of Songhai; first to adopt title Askia; Songhai empire reorganized: Sankore mosque developed as a centre of learning.
		1493–1591 Timbuktu under Songhai.
	1496 Spanish take Melilla.	
		1497 Askia Muhammad makes pilgrimage to Mecca.
		1499–1509 Abdullahi, King of Kano; war with Katsina.
c. **1500** Osman Kade, Bulala prince from Bornu-Kanem, makes himself ruler of Makada, probably Sennar.		**16th c.** Fulani (Fulbe) infiltrating between R Niger and R Bani.
		c. post **1500** Wolof kingdom between R Senegal and Cape Verde under Budumel dynasty; second Wolof kingdom between R Gambia and Cape Verde under another Budumel dynasty.
		early 16th c. Fulani begin to arrive on the Futa Jallon plateau.
		1500–31 French privateers raiding Portuguese Guinea fleets: 300 caravels taken.

EASTERN AFRICA	CENTRAL & SOUTHERN AFRICA	OTHER COUNTRIES
		1492 Christopher Columbus discovers America. End of the Nasrid Kingdom of Granada; Jews expelled from Aragon and Castile. 1493 Pope Alexander II divides discoveries between Portugal and Spain.
1494–8 Naod Emperor of Ethiopia. 1494 Covilhão reaches Ethiopia: kept at court by the Emperor (–1525).	1494–1506 Nzinga a Nkuwa reverts to paganism. c. 1494 Monomotapa Chikuyo kills Changamire: succ. Changamire II; war between them still continuing in 1502. 1494 Toroa of Butwa revolts against Monomotapa.	1494 7 June, Treaty of Tordesillas dividing discoveries between Spain and Portugal; Columbus in Jamaica.
1495–9 al-Fudail, Sultan of Kilwa.	1495 Correspondence between Kings of Kongo and Portugal.	1495–1521 Manuel, King of Portugal. 1495 West Africans ordained in Lisbon for mission work in Guinea. 1496 Jews expelled from Portugal. 1497 8 July, Vasco da Gama sails with a fleet of four vessels from Belem for India. John Cabot discovers Labrador.
	1497 22 Nov., Vasco da Gama reaches Cape of Good Hope; 25 Nov., Mossel Bay; 2 Dec., Great Fish River.	
1498 Vasco da Gama passes Kilwa, reaches Mombasa 7 Apr. and Malindi 14 Apr.	1498 25 Jan., Vasco da Gama reaches Quelimane; 2 March, Mozambique.	1498 Duarte Pacheco, *Esmeraldo de Situ Orbis*. 1498 22 May to 1498 29 Aug., Vasco da Gama at Calicut.
c. 1499–1506 Treasury at Kilwa controlled by Muhammad Rukn al-Din al-Dabuli and his brother. 1499 3 Jan., Vasco da Gama reaches Mogadishu on his return from India and bombards it. 1499 13 May, birth of the anonymous author of the *History of Kilwa*.		1499 9 Sept., Vasco da Gama returns to Lisbon.
	c. ante 1500 Dembo chiefdoms, Mutamba and Okango tributary to Kongo; Tyo (Teke), Loango, Ngoy, Kakongo and Bungu independent kingdoms. Revolt against Monomotapa. Bantu migration from R Lualaba region into NE Rhodesia; Luba empire founded by Kongolo: capital Mwibele. Ngola dynasty of Ndongo founded by Ngola Kiluanji.	
c. 1500 Dynasty of Shehe Mvita ruling in Mombasa. Bigo pottery widespread in W Uganda. Buganda a sub-kingdom of Bunyoro. First Bito dynasties in Uganda. Qadiriyyah order introduced amongst the Somali; Somali expanding and raiding Ethiopia; Galla pressed out of Ogaden and Banadir. *post* 1500 Muzaffarid dynasty replaces Fakhr al-Din dynasty at Mogadishu.	1500 or later. Mapungubwe abandoned: arrival of the Venda. c. 1500 Kakamas already in SW Africa. *post* 1500 Metal begins to be used for implements in S Africa. Maize introduced from Brazil. 1500 20-26 July, Cabral at Mozambique, then Sofala. Madagascar discovered by Diego Dias. 1500–1800 Peoples of Congolese origin move into Zambia.	1500 23 Apr., Pedro Alvarez Cabral takes possession of Brazil for Portugal. Charles V of Spain b.

EGYPT & THE SUDAN	NORTHERN AFRICA	WESTERN AFRICA
		c. 1500 Ayi Kushi, first chief of Accra: Ga begin to settle near Accra; Akwamu kingdom established. Portuguese fort built at Axim. Shaikh Mastarma b. Uthman, *History of Bornu.* Bini army penetrate Brass district and settle at Nembe. Bulwa expelled from Bornu.
		1503 Idris Katagarmabe, son of Mai Ali, succ.(—1526); regains Kanem for Bornu; Bulala installed as vassal Kings. Chief of Efutu baptized with 1,300 subjects.
1504 Alwa destroyed; Amara Dunkas, first Funj King of Sennar (—1534), replaces Christian Kings: possibly of Bornu origin.		*c.* 1504—50 Esigie, Oba of Benin: first Portuguese missionaries arrive at his request; Onitsha founded.
	1505 Banu Saad begin Holy War against Portuguese: origin of Sharifs of Morocco. 9 Sept. — 23 Oct., Mers el-Kebir taken by the Spaniards in revenge for a raid on Alicante. Portuguese take Agadir (S. Cruz de Aguer) and build fortress at Founti.	*c.* 1504 Benin at war with Udo. *c.* 1505—30 Muhamman Abu, King of Zaria; Zaria converted to Islam.
		1506 Tristão da Cunha discovers Tristão da Cunha Is.
	1508 Portuguese take Safi; Peñon de la Gomera temporarily occupied.	
	1509 Oran seized by army of Cardinal Ximénès under Pedro Navarro: under Spain until 1708. 1509—10 Algiers in Spanish hands under Pedro Navarro.	

EASTERN AFRICA	CENTRAL & SOUTHERN AFRICA	OTHER COUNTRIES
1500 Cabral visits Kilwa and Malindi *en route* for India.	**?c. 1500–1600** Chewa tribe reaches Zambia. **16th c.** Mpongwe already living near R. Ogooué.	
1502 King of Mombasa writes to King of Malindi urging unity against the Portuguese. Kilwa pays tribute of gold and jewels to Portugal: used to make Belem Monstrance. **1502–3** Ruy Lourenço Ravasco harries Zanzibar, which pays tribute to Portugal. **1503** Vicente de Sodre visits Socotra; Vasco da Gama passes within sight of Seychelles Is.	**1501** Ascension Is. discovered by João de Nova. **1502** St Helena discovered by João de Nova. 14 June-15 July, Vasco da Gama visits Sofala; and then Mozambique: factory established under Gonçalo Baixo.	**1501** First African slaves imported into Hispaniola. **1502** Vasco da Gama's second voyage to India; Columbus in Martinique. Muslims in Spain given choice between conversion to Christianity or exile. **1503–13** Pius III, Pope.
	1504 Portuguese forbid trade S of R Congo.	
1505 23 July, Francisco d'Almeida sacks Kilwa; 14 Aug., sacks Mombasa; Fort Santiago built at Kilwa: garrison installed (**to 1512**); ban on trade between Sofala and Swahili ports; two Franciscan friars, chaplains to fort, start missionary work.	**1505** St Helena occupied by the Portuguese. Sept., Pedro d'Anaia constructs fort at Sofala and instals factor and garrison; ?Dec., inhabitants attack fort, many killed; Shaikh of Sofala killed; Pedro d'Anaia d.; Manuel Fernandes, factor, temporary captain. Rui Dias Pereira in Madagascar with João Gomes d'Abreu; island explored on eastern side; d'Abreu d.; remainder make way to Angoche.	**1505** Francisco d'Almeida, first Viceroy of the Indies, builds forts at Angediva and Cananor; Lourenço d'Almeida reaches Ceylon: King of Kandi tributary to Portugal. Francisco d'Almeida sends his son to take the Maldives.
1506 Muhammad Rukn al-Din al-Dabuli, treasurer, made puppet Sultan of Kilwa by Portuguese; many inhabitants of Kilwa migrate to Malindi and Comoro Is.; Lamu and Pate capitulate to Portuguese; Oja and Barawa sacked; Nuno Vaz Pereira lifts trade ban with Sofala; forty persons converted to Christianity at Kilwa contrary to wish of sultan. **1506–8** Hinterland of Malindi in anarchy; João Gomes and João Sanchez unable to penetrate overland to Ethiopia. **1506–43** Imam Ahmad b.Ibrahim al-Ghazi nicknamed Gran (left-handed). **1507** Hajj Hasan b. Muhammad Rukn al-Din al-Dabuli made puppet Sultan of Kilwa after assassination of his father. Socotra occupied.	**1506** Fernão Soares explores east coast of Madagascar; Barawa taken. Diego d'Alcaçova reports to Portugal on the gold of Makalanga; 400 Arabs living at Sofala. **1506–43** Nzinga Mvemba Afonso I: requests priests, teachers, and artisans from Portugal; young Kongolese sent for education in Lisbon; payment made in slaves and copper *manillas.*	**1507** Lourenço d'Almeida killed and Portuguese defeated by Egyptian fleet off Chaul. Albuquerque takes Hormuz.
c. **1508** João Gomes and João Sanchez leave Malindi for Ethiopia. **1508–40** Lebna Dengel of Ethiopia.	**1507** Vasco Gomes d' Abreu, Captain of Sofala: fort completed; hospital, church, factory, warehouse and fort built at Mozambique. **1508** Annual expeditions from Lisbon to Kongo. Diogo Lopes de Sequeira in Madagascar. **1508–10** Friction between Kongo and Portugal begins.	**1508** Bull *Universali Ecclesiae.*
1509 Portuguese factory set up at Malindi. Matthew, an Armenian, sent to Lisbon as ambassador of Ethiopia.		**1509** Francisco d'Almeida defeats Egyptian fleet off Diu. Council of the Indies established in Spain. **1509–47** Henry VIII, King of England.

EGYPT & THE SUDAN	NORTHERN AFRICA	WESTERN AFRICA
	1510–1653 Sharifs of the Banu Saad, Hasani branch, Sharifs of Morocco. **1510–17** Abu Abdullah Muhammad, Saadi Sharif. **1510** Spaniards take Bougie and Tunis; Tripoli taken by assault. **1511** Spaniards checked at Jerba. Banu Saad take Sousse. Tenès, Delys, Cherchel, Mazagan and Algiers tributary to Spain; no further Spanish expansion.	
		1512 Askia Muhammad the Great, King of Songhai, conquers Hausa states of Katsina, Zaria and Kano, adding them to his empire but leaving local rulers in charge.
	1513 Portuguese take Azemmour.	**1513** 565 slaves dispatched from Guinea to Portugal.
	1514 Portuguese take Mazagan. Abu Yusuf Aruj b.Yaqub, known as Barbarossa, Turkish corsair, seizes Djidjelli.	**1514** 978 slaves dispatched from Guinea to Portugal.
	1515–1830 Turkish domination of Algeria and Tunisia. **1515–86** Algiers ruled by Turkish Beylerbeys and Pashas.	*c.* **1515–61** Muhammadu Kantu, first King of Kebbi: rebels against Songhai and takes Katsina, Kano, Gobir and Asben. **1515** 1,423 slaves dispatched from Guinea to Portugal. **1515–16** Benin at war with Idah.
1516–17 al-Ashraf Tuman-bay, last Mamluk Sultan of Egypt.	**1516** Aruj (Barbarossa) seizes Algiers: 30 Sept., Spanish relief expedition under Diego de Vera fails.	*c.* **1516** Surame, capital of Kebbi, built. **1516** 23 Dec., Annular eclipse of the sun recorded during the reign of Ali Kariagwa of Katsina.
1517 22 Jan., Tuman-bay defeated by Ottoman Selim I outside Cairo; 14 April, Tuman-bay hanged at Cairo. Cairo and Egypt seized and occupied by the Turks; Khair Bey appointed Viceroy; Egyptian administration little changed; first twenty-four beys created. **1517–1804** Turkish domination of Egypt. **1517–1773** Egypt under viceroys with title Pasha.	**1517** Tlemcen taken by the Spaniards.	**1517** 16 Dec., Portuguese merchants in Cape Verde forbidden to trade in Sierra Leone.
	1518 Aruj (Barbarossa) killed. Khair al-Din I Barbarossa captures Algiers, and offers it to the Turks; receives title Beylerbey (Bey of Beys) as confirmation, together with artillery. **1518 (or 1520)** 'Leo Africanus' captured and presented as a slave to Pope Leo X, who frees him.	

EASTERN AFRICA	CENTRAL & SOUTHERN AFRICA	OTHER COUNTRIES
	1510 Francisco d'Almeida killed in a fight at Table Bay. Mani Kongo requests Portuguese representative in Kongo to control Portuguese residents. **1510–30** Portuguese fail to put down smuggling from Angoche.	**1510** Afonso de Albuquerque takes Goa. First slaves from Guinea arrive in Haiti.
1511 Portuguese abandon Socotra.		**1511** Alburquerque takes Malacca. Cuba conquered. Cortes campaigns against the Aztecs.
1512 Portuguese fort at Kilwa dismantled; Franciscans leave Kilwa with garrison.	**1512–15** Soares, factor at Sofala. **1512** Dry stone building reported in the Monomotapa's territory. Simão de Silva sent as resident ambassador to Kongo.	**1512** Polyglot Bible published. **1512–17** Fifth Ecumenical Council at the Lateran. **1512–20** Selim I the Grim, Ottoman Sultan. *c.* **1512–15** Tomé Pirès gathering material from E Africa and the Indies for his *Suma Oriental* written at Malacca: mentions trade agents from Zaila, Malindi, Mombasa and Kilwa stationed there. **1513** The Psalms in Geez printed in Rome. Albuquerque's abortive expedition to Aden and the Red Sea. Balbõa reaches Pacific Ocean. **1514** Aug., Turks defeat Persians at Chaldiran.
	c. **1513** Bourbon (Réunion) and Cirne (Mauritius) discovered by Pero Mascarenhas: Is. named Mascarenhas (Mascarenes). Both uninhabited. **1514** António Fernandes explores Sofala hinterland and visits Mobara: sees copper trade; first contacts with Makalanga. Mani Kongo complains of extent of slave trade from Kongo to Portugal; Kongo at war with Ambundu.	
1516 Ethiopian embassy to Cairo: Adal prepares to attack Ethiopia, but defeated; Adal invaded; castle of Zankar destroyed.		**1515** Hormuz occupied by Portuguese; Albuquerque d. Ottoman fleet sent against Gujerat. Turks occupy Mesopotamia and parts of Persia. Uruguay discovered by Juan Dias de Solis. **1515–20** Tower of Belem built at Lisbon. **1516** Ottoman conquest of Syria. Mamluk Sultan Qansuh al-Ghauri leads Egyptian army to aid Persians at Aleppo; 24 Aug., battle of Marj Dabiq: Syro-Egyptian army defeated. 21 Dec., Egyptians defeated by Ottomans at Gaza.
1517 Zaila burnt by Portuguese under Lope Suarez.	**1517** Kongo again at war with Ambundu.	**1517** Portuguese expedition to China. al-Mutawakkil, last shadow caliph, taken from Cairo to Constantinople (d.1543). Martin Luther attacks indulgences. *c.* **1517–18** The *'Book'* of Duarte Barbosa: description of eastern Africa and India.
1518 Berbera burnt by Portuguese under Saldanha. Sultan of Adal murdered in a struggle for the throne. **1518–20** Five sultans of Adal.		

EGYPT & THE SUDAN	NORTHERN AFRICA	WESTERN AFRICA
	1519 Abortive Spanish attack on Algiers. Portuguese take Agouz.	1519 *Kitab al-Fattash* begun by Mahmud al-Kati.
1520 Funj defeated by Turks at battle of Hannak. *c.* 1520–7 Nubians appeal to Ethiopia for priests: last episode in the decay of Christianity in Nubia.	1520 Khair al-Din Barbarossa defeated by Hafsids; retires to Djidjelli.	*c.* 1520 Fula arrive in the present Portuguese Guinea.
	1521 Khair al-Din Barbarossa takes Collo, and, 1522, Bône.	
1522 Khair Bey d.; Mustafa Pasha, brother-in-law of Sultan Sulaiman, governor of Egypt: Mamluks revolt in Fayoum and western Delta.		1522–*fl.*1872 Sultanate of Baghirmi.
1524 Feb., Ahmad Pasha al-Khair claims sultanate of Egypt; captured and killed 6 March. 1525 Ibrahim Pasha, Vizier of Turkish Empire, inspects government of Egypt for three months: imperial firman establishes new organization as a *vilayet* (province): *Qanun-name* of Egypt codifies administrative practice. 1525–38 Seliman, Pasha of Egypt. *c.* 1525 Dongola said to possess 150 churches, but with vestigial Christianity only.	1525 Banu Saad take Marrakesh. Khair al-Din Barbarossa extends dominions. 1525–41 Abu Abdallah Muhammad al-Hasan, Hafsid.	
		1526–46 Muhammad Idris, Sultan of Bornu.
		1528 Musa b.Askia Muhammad rebels against his father; Askia Muhammad abdicates; Musa assassinated; Bankuri, usurper (–1536).
	1529 27 May, Khair al-Din Barbarossa takes Algiers; new port constructed; state organized, with little change until 1830; systematic piracy begun. Treaty between Antoine, King of Navarre, and Morocco. 1530–51 Knights of Malta occupy Tripoli.	1530 William Hawkins of Plymouth trading on Sestos river, Liberia. *c. post* 1530 First church built at Warri.
		c. 1531–91 Tsoede (Edegi), first Etsuzhi of Nupe: capital Nku.

EASTERN AFRICA	CENTRAL & SOUTHERN AFRICA	OTHER COUNTRIES
	1519 Export of goods from Kongo permitted only on royal Portuguese ships.	1519–56 Charles V, Holy Roman Emperor. 1519 Magellan's voyage round the world (–1522). Cortez conquers Mexico.
1520 Capital of Sultanate of Adal moved from Dakar to Harar by Abu Bakr b.Muhammad. 17 April, annular eclipse of the sun seen by Olimi I, fifth Bito Mukama of Bunyoro, in Ankole, and by Nyabugaro I of Ankole. *c.* 1520 al-Malik al-Adil Muhammad b. al-Husain Sultan of Kilwa. *c. post* 1520 *Kitab al-Sulwa fi Akhbar Kilwa* (History of Kilwa) written. 1520–7 Portuguese embassy under Rodrigo de Lima to Ethiopia; Francisco Alvares chaplain.	1520 Portuguese embassy to Ngola; Balthasar de Castro held captive (to *post* 1526).	1520 Luther excommunicated. 1520–66 Sulaiman I the Magnificent, Ottoman Sultan. 1520–1 Sequeira's expedition to the Red Sea.
1521 Tristao da Cunha forces Lamu to pay tribute to Portugal; paid in Venetian silver currency.	1521 Henrique, son of Afonso I of Kongo, returns from Lisbon as Bishop of Utica and Vicar Apostolic of Kongo (–*c.* 1526). 1522 Portuguese expedition under Pedro de Castro against Kerimba Is.	1521 Luther's translation of the Bible. First slaves from Guinea arrive in Cuba. 1521–57 Joao I, King of Portugal. 1522 Portuguese occupy Ternate, Molucca Is.
		1523–34 Clement VII, Pope. 1524 Vasco da Gama Viceroy of India; d. 25 Dec. Pizarro fighting Incas in Peru.
1525 Govenor of Zaila murdered: period of disorder follows; Ahmad Gran begins to make Hubat a centre of power.	1525 French ship lands at Mpinda and is seized by Portuguese.	
	c. 1526 Sofala blockaded by Inhamunda. 1526 Mani Kongo again complains of extent of Portuguese slave trade; attempt to expel Portuguese fails: slaving board set up; name *pombeiros* first given to slave traders; general unrest in Kongo.	1526 Leo Africanus, *Description of Africa*. Portuguese reach Canton.
1527 Army under Degalhan, Governor of Bali, invades Adal; decisively defeated by Ahmad Gran, who organizes Somali territory, raising larger army. 1528 Mombasa, Mtangata and Utondwe revolt against the Portuguese; second sack of Mombasa. First French vessel visits Kilwa. 1529–42 War between Ahmad Gran and Ethiopians. 1529 Ahmad Gran defeats Ethiopians at Shembura Kure.	1528 Shipwrecked Portuguese build fort at Fort Dauphin. 1529 Parmentier brothers set up at Maromoka, Madagascar.	1528 Order of Friars Minor Capuchin founded. 1529 Vienna besieged by Turks.
1531 Ahmad Gran occupies Dawaro and Shoa.	c. 1530 4,000 to 5,000 slaves shipped annually from Kongo, acquired from beyond boundaries by trade and raids; many local wars. 1531 Portuguese open market in Arab settlement of Sena.	1530 The Augsburg Confession. Portuguese begin to colonize Brazil. 1531 Henry VIII proclaimed Supreme Head of the Church of England.

EGYPT & THE SUDAN	NORTHERN AFRICA	WESTERN AFRICA
	1533–4 Abu Abdullah, last Nasrid ruler of Granada, d. at Fez. 1533 Embassy from Francis I of France to Morocco.	1533 Diocese of Cape Verde and Guinea established: Dom Braz Neto, first Bishop (–1540).
1534–51 Nail, King of the Funj.	1534 18 Aug., Tunis occupied by Khair al-Din Barbarossa; piracy organized. 1534–1705 Tunis ruled by Deys.	1534 Bishopric created at São Tomé.
c. 1535 End of Tungur Kingdom of Darfur; annexed to Empire of Bornu until 1603.	1535 Charles V of Spain's expedition to Tunis; many thousand Christian slaves liberated; Turkish garrison flees to Algiers; al-Hasan, Hafsid, a vassal of Spain. Treaty between Khair al-Din Barbarossa and France.	c. 1535–80 Yamta-ra-Wala the Great (Abdullahi) founds Amirate of Biu. 1535 Muhammad Idris of Bornu expands kingdom as far as Darfur.
	1536 Khair al-Din Barbarossa recalled to Constantinople to command Turkish fleet; succ. by Hasan Agha (–1541).	1536 Ismail b. Askia Muhammad, ruler of Songhai. c. 1536 Zaria town founded.
1538–49 David, Pasha of Egypt:		
	1540 Hafsid dominions disintegrating; Doria intervenes to recover Kelibia, Sousse, Sfax and Monastir for Tunis; Qayrawan independent with southern Tunisia. 1541 Charles V of Spain attacks Algiers; 3 Nov., decisively defeated. Fortifications of Algiers strengthened. Banu Saad take Agadir, Safi and Azemmour from the Portuguese. 1541–73 Ahmad b.Hasan, Hafsid.	post 1540 French privateers active on the Guinea coast.
		1542 French privateers attack Fogo Is., Guinea.
	1544–52 Hasan Pasha, son of Khair al-Din Barbarossa, Beylerbey of Algiers: first term.	

ASTERN AFRICA	CENTRAL & SOUTHERN AFRICA	OTHER COUNTRIES
	1532 Portugal forbids direct trade with Angola: all trade to be *via* Kongo.	
33 Ahmad Gran takes Amhara and sta, and Kingdoms of Bali, Hadya, lama and Gurage.		1533 Henry VIII of England excommunicated. Calvin declares himself Protestant. Bishopric of Goa created. 1534–49 Paul III, Pope. 1534 Ottomans take Baghdad. Khair al-Din Barbarossa attacks France. Luther's Bible completed.
35 Ahmad Gran seizes Tigrai; hiopia appeals to Portugal for help.	*c.* 1535 Portuguese begin to build at Tete.	1535 Anglican bishops renounce papal authority.
		1536 Inquisition established in Portugal. Calvin, *Institution Chrētienne*.
37 Galla said to have entered Bali.		1537 29 May, Pope Paul III excommunicates all Catholics engaged in the slave trade; 2 June, Paul III voids all contracts of Catholics who have deprived Africans of liberty or goods. Society of Jesus founded by St Ignatius Loyola. 1538 Egyptian expedition against Portuguese in Diu: Aden occupied for twenty days. Turks occupy Yemen. St Thomas More martyred.
40–59 Galawdewos (Claudius), son Lebna Dengel, Emperor of Ethiopia. 40 Turks raid eastern coast as far as lindi. 41–2 St Francis Xavier visits Malindi d Socotra. 41 Portuguese destroy shipping in gadishu: Barawa sacked. 400 Portuguese der Cristovão da Gama arrive at ssawa to help fight Ahmad Gran. 42 Occupied provinces of Ethiopia e against Ahmad Gran; indecisive battle th Portuguese at Anasa; Ahmad Gran tains Arab, Turkish and Albanian rcenaries; da Gama captured and rdered; Oct., Emperor Galawdewos and rtuguese take offensive.	1539 German reports Kongo wealth in copper, lead and silver exceeds Spain. 1540 Easter Sunday night, Portuguese attempt to murder Afonso I. *c.* 1540–75 Andriamanelo, first Merina ruler in Madagascar. *c.* 1540 New fortress begun in Mozambique. 1541–2 St Francis Xavier in Mozambique for 6 months.	1540 Society of Jesus established in Portugal. 1542–52 St Francis Xavier in India, Indonesia and the China Sea. 1542 Inquisition instituted in Rome.
43 21 Feb., Ahmad Gran killed in ttle by Pedro Léon; 100 Portuguese nilies settle at Frémonat; Wazir Abbas es to form Muslim state of Dawaro, tajar and Bali.	*c.* 1543–5 Pedro I, King of Kongo.	1543 Francis I of France hands Toulon over to Algerian fleet as winter quarters.
	1544 Portuguese factory established at Quelimane; Lourenço Marques travels coast from Sofala to Delagoa Bay, trading for ivory.	
45–7 Galla invade Dawaro, expanding rthwards. 45 Emperor Galawdewos defeats Wazir bas and recovers lost territory.	*c.* 1545–61 Diogo I, Mani Kongo.	1545–52 First session of the Council of Trent.

EGYPT & THE SUDAN	NORTHERN AFRICA	WESTERN AFRICA
		1546–63 Dunama, Mai of Bornu.
	1548–56 Abu Abdullah Muhammad I al-Mahdi, Sharif of Morocco. 1549–61 al-Fishtali, historian, poet and statesman.	
c. 1550 Ottomans take Ibrim and territory between Ist and 3rd cataracts: named Berberistan, with garrisons at Aswan, Ibrim and Say.	1550 Marseilles merchants set up agency at Algiers. Spanish take al-Mahdia from Dragut, pirate.	c. 1550 1,500 slaves sent annually from Guinea to Portugal. Manes invasion S of present Sierra Leone spreads northwards. Adansi Kingdom established. Some migrant Fulani reach Baghirmi; Yoruba defeated by Nupe and forced to leave Oyc Igboho (Bohoo) built. c. 1550–78 Orhogbua, Oba of Benin, educated by Portuguese, a Christian: visits Ijebu. 1550 Inspector sent from Portugal to examine finances in C. Verde.
	1551 First English merchants in Morocco. Sinan Pasha takes Tripoli for the Turks. 1552–7 Salah Reis, Beylerbey of Algiers.	
	1553 Wattasids temporarily restored by Turks at Fez.	1553 First Englishman, Capt. Windham, visits Benin with Francisco Pinteado. King of Benin able to speak Portuguese, which he had learned as a child. John Lok trading on Gold Coast. 1554 Songhai expedition against Katsina fails; battle of Karfata; Katsina regains independence.
	1554 13 Sept., Fez taken by Sharifs of Morocco; Marrakesh preferred as capital.	
	1556 Gafsa taken by Dragut.	
	1557–61 Hasan Pasha: second term at Algiers. 1557–74 Abu Abdallah Muhammad al-Ghalib, Sharif of Morocco.	1557 Exchange rate of 80 brass manillas to 1oz of gold.
	1558 Thirty-five galleys and twenty-five brigantines engaged in piracy from Algiers. Qayrawan taken by Dragut. 1559 Spanish fleet attacks Dragut in Jerba.	1558 Portuguese expel British traders from Shama, Gold Coast. post 1558 Portuguese fort built at Shama.
	1560 15 March, Dragut routs Spanish and retakes Jerba. Peñon de la Gomera ceded to Spain by Morocco.	c. 1560–1605 Farima, first Mani King of Loko.
		1561 Anglo-French fleet trading on W African coast.

EASTERN AFRICA	CENTRAL & SOUTHERN AFRICA	OTHER COUNTRIES
		1547 Turks occupy Aden.
		1547—53 Edward VI, King of England.
	1548—50 Jesuit mission in Kongo.	1548—9 New Testament in Geez printed in Rome.
		1549 Anglican first Book of Common Prayer.
c. 1550—*c.* 1900 Pangani (Muhembo) ruled by Zigua Jumbes.	*c.* 1550 António Caido, trader, adviser to Monomotapa; made Captain of the Gates by Vicecroy	1550 Mongols arrive in Peking.
	c. 1550—*c.* 1825 Inyanga, Rhodesia, occupied continuously.	
	c. 1550— 1612 Lunda empire founded by Kibinda Ilunga.	
		1551 Turks occupy Muscat. One-tenth of population of Lisbon African slaves.
		1552 *First Decade* of João de Barros, *Da Asia,* published in Lisbon. Council of Trent suspended. St Francis Xavier d.
1553 14 Jan., great consternation caused at Sire by an annular eclipse of the sun during the thirteenth year of the Emperor Galawdewos.		1553—8 Mary I, Queen of England.
1554 Abortive order for construction of a fort and mission in Mombasa.		
1554—5 Emperor Galawdewos defeats Galla, but fails to check their advance.		
	1556 Diogo I of Kongo badly defeated in war with Ngola.	1556 Charles V resigns in favour of Philip II (1556—89).
1557 André de Oviedo, S J, Bishop of Hierapolis, at Frēmonat; Turks seize Massawa and Arkiko, building fort at Dabarwa: monks massacred at Debra Damo; Tigre rises, driving Turks back to Suakin, Massawa and Arkiko: Zaila taken by the Turks from the Portuguese.	1557 Ngola Inene sends embassy to Portugal to request missionaries.	1557—78 Sebastião I, King of Portugal.
	1558 Mozambique becomes the capital of Portuguese East African possessions: building of fortress of S. Sebastião begun by architect Miguel de Arruola.	1558—1603 Elizabeth I, Queen of England.
		1558 The *Index* instituted. Francisco Alvarez, *Description of Ethiopia,* published in Antwerp.
1559 Harar attacks Ethiopia; Good Friday, Emperor Galawdewos killed in battle.		1559—65 Pius IV, Pope.
1559—63 Minas, Emperor of Ethiopia.		
	1560 Jesuit mission arrives in Angola with Paulo Dias as lay ambassador. Portuguese forbidden to visit Ngola. First Jesuit missions in Mozambique.	
	c. 1560 Markets set up at Louanze, Busuto and Massapa.	
	1561 Ngola refuse further co-operation with Portuguese; Jesuits in captivity to 1565. Afonso II, succ. as Mani Kongo, then killed at mass; Bernardo I succ. (—1566). Fr. Gonçalo da Silveira, S J,	

EGYPT & THE SUDAN	NORTHERN AFRICA	WESTERN AFRICA

	1562 Abortive attempt to expel the Portuguese from Mazagan. 1562–5 Hasan Pasha — second term. 1562–4 Rif tribesmen besiege Melilla. 1563 Systematic taxation by armed columns begun by Turks in Algiers.	*post* 1562 Annual English trading voyages to W Africa by 'interlopers'. 1562 Sir John Hawkins obtains 300 slaves from Sierra Leone.
	1564 Badis (Velez) ceded to the Spanish by Morocco; Peñon de la Gomera occupied by Spain. French consulate established at Algiers.	*c.* 1564–70 Abdallah b.Dunama, Mai of Bornu
1568 Sinan Pasha, governor of Egypt, sends expedition to Yemen.	1568–87 Eulj Ali, last Beylerbey of Algiers.	
1569–86 Dakin b.Nail, King of the Funj, great administrator.	1569 English Consulate-established at Algiers, but without privileges. 1569 Tunis taken by the Turks under Dragut and Eulj Ali.	
		c. 1570–1706 Katsina at war with Kano for control of Saharan trade terminus. *c.* 1570 Yoruba King Abipa leaves Igboho for Oyo. Susu occupy Port Loko. 1570 Jingereber mosque at Timbuktu rebuilt. 1571–1603 Idris Alooma, Mai of Bornu: introduces firearms from Ottoman Empire; many campaigns.
	1572 Epidemic in Algiers kills a third of the population.	1572 Portuguese Augustinians open a school at Elmina.
	1573–5 Abu Abdallah Muhammad II Sharif of Morocco. 1573 Don John of Austria attacks Tunis; fortifications at Algiers strengthened. 1574 Tunis finally taken for the Turks by Sinan Pasha.	

STERN AFRICA	CENTRAL & SOUTHERN AFRICA	OTHER COUNTRIES
	strangled at court of Monomotapa Nogomo at the instigation of Arab merchants.	1562–3 Final session of the Council of Trent.
3–97 Sarsa Dengel, Emperor of iopia. 3 One-third of Ethiopia under the la.	1563 Fr. Gouveia, SJ, writes from Ndongo recommending Portugal to seize the country to convert it to Christianity. King Ngola of Ndongo campaigns against King of Benguella.	1563 *The Thirty-nine Articles of Religion* promulgated in England. 1564–1616 William Shakespeare. 1564–1642 Galileo Galilei.
	1565 Ndongo embassy to Portugal; revolt of Kiluanji Kukakwango in Ndongo. 1566–7 Henrique I, Mani Kongo; war between Tyo and Kongo; Henrique I killed in battle.	1565 Malta resists Turkish invasion. Revolt of the Moriscos in Andalusia. 1566 The Low Countries revolt against Spain. *Catechism* of the Council of Trent promulgated. 1566–72 St Pius V, Pope. 1566–74 Selim II, Ottoman Sultan. 1567 Hawaii Is. discovered by Spaniards.
7 Galla devastate Harar and other ions. 568 Zanzibar invaded by 'Kafirs'. rkish raid on Cambo: queen, taken tive, throws herself into the sea.	1567–76 Alvare I, Mani Kongo. *ante* 1568 Bakuba migrating to present habitat, finally settling *c.* 1600. *c.*1568–1630 Early period of the Bakuba Kingdom. 1568 Jaga invasion of Kongo. 1569 Jaga capture Mbanza Kongo.	
59 Revolt in Harar: Talha elected tan. 59 A Portuguese fort begun at Mombasa. Monclaro, SJ, visits Kilwa, Mafia, mbasa, Malindi, Pate and Cambo; reto quells revolt at Pate; eastern st in economic decline; Cambo accepts rkish protection.	1569 Francisco Barreto's expedition against Monomotapa a failure.	1569–1639 Blessed Martin of Porres, OP, in America. 1569 All property of Englishmen in Portugal confiscated because of 'interlopers' in W Africa.
70 Segeju tribe first recorded near lindi. Galla still advancing, reaching hara and Begemder.	1570 Zimba first ravage country near R Zambezi.	1570 Inquisition established at Lima, Peru. Bull *Regnans in excelsis* excommunicates Elizabeth I of England.
71 Talha deposed in Harar; *jihad* claimed against Ethiopia.	1571 Portuguese force sent against Jaga in Kongo under Francisco de Gouveia; virtual Portuguese occupation (–1576). 1571–3 Francisco Barreto's expedition against Manica; Sena pillaged. *c.* 1572 Jaga routed and expelled; King of Kongo restored to full authority.	1571 Oct., Battle of Lepanto: Turkish fleet destroyed. 1572 Camoens, *Lusiads*. Massacre of St Bartholemew in France. Sir Francis Drake captures Spanish convoy from America. 1572–85 Gregory VIII, Pope. Gregorian Calendar instituted.
	1573 Francisco Barreto's second expedition: d. at Sena. 1574 Expedition from Sofala under Vasco Fernandes Homem reaches Manica, modern Umtali: little gold and silver found; garrison of Mozambique destroyed by African tribesmen. Embassy from	1574–95 Murad III, Ottoman Sultan. 1574–6 Akbar conquers Bengal.

EGYPT & THE SUDAN	NORTHERN AFRICA	WESTERN AFRICA
	1575–8 Abu Marwan Abd al-Malik I, Sharif of Morocco.	
	1576 Turkish expedition against Morocco to place pretender on the throne.	**1576** Portuguese fort at Accra destroyed by tribesmen.
		1577–8 Sidi Yahya mosque at Timbuktu restored.
	1578 4 Aug., Battle of the Three Kings or al-Makhazin; Portuguese army of 20,000 men annihilated at Kasr al-Kabir, near Fez; Sebastião of Portugal taken prisoner. **1578–1603** Abu al-Abbas Ahmad I, Sharif of Morocco: takes title of al-Mansur; supplied with arms by Elizabeth I of England; government of Morocco reorganized.	*c.* **1578**–*c.* **1606** Ehengbuda, Oba of Beni **1578** Sir Francis Drake attacks Portuguese shipping in Ribeira Grande.
	1580 Famine in Algiers.	**1580** Sir Francis Drake visits R Sierra Leone. *c.* **1580** Sankore mosque at Timbuktu rebuilt; fine salt introduced into Oyo.
	1581 Gourara and Touat oases taken by Morocco. Turkey and Spain agree to peace in N Africa; Spain retains Melilla, Mers al-Kebir and Oran.	
		1582 Aug., Edward Fenton explores R Sierra Leone. **1583** Mai of Bornu agrees to mention Sharif of Morocco as overlord in Friday Prayers. **1584** Abortive Carmelite mission south of C. Verde. **1585** Sir Francis Drake again attacks shipping at Ribeira Grande.
1586 Military revolt in Egypt.	**1586** Sharif of Morocco demands tribute from Askia Ishaq as an excuse for making war on Songhai.	

STERN AFRICA	CENTRAL & SOUTHERN AFRICA	OTHER COUNTRIES

CENTRAL & SOUTHERN AFRICA

Kongo to Portugal; Alvare I makes regulations to prevent cruelty to slaves.
1575 Portuguese trading centres already in existence at Massapa and Manica. Royal bodyguard in Kongo equipped with arquebuses. Paulo Dias arrives in Angola; received by friendly embassy. Treaty between Monomotapa Nogomo Sebastião and the Portuguese; Arabs expelled from his dominions.
1575–1610 Ralambo, Merina ruler, increases the extent of his kingdom.
1576–1614 Alvare II, Mani Kongo. Town of Luanda built.
c. 1576 Some Imbangala form kingdom under Kasanje on E coast of Angola.

STERN AFRICA

7 Harar army defeated by Ethiopians; of Sultanate of Harar; Galla raiding ar; new sultanate set up at Aussa.
7–1672 Sultanate of Aussa.
8 Turks and their allies defeated and ress of Dabarwa taken by the iopians.

1577 First Dominican mission in Mozambique.

1578 New colonists arrive in Angola; Benguela Velha built and then abandoned.
1578–86 Duarte Lopes travelling and trading in Kongo and Angola, with connections as far as the Great Lakes.

OTHER COUNTRIES

1576–1660 St Vincent de Paul, founder of the Lazarist Order and of the Sisters of Charity.
1576 40,000 African slaves in Spanish America.
1577–80 Sir Francis Drake rounds the Cape in the *Golden Hind,* circumnavigating the world.

1578 Confusion in Portugal after defeat in Battle of the Three Kings; Cardinal Henry, stop-gap King. Anglo-Portuguese treaty admits English traders to Madeira and Azores.

1580 *fl.* Fumo Liongo, Sultan of , hero of Swahili epics.

1579 War between Ngola and Portuguese; 2,000 soldiers sent out between 1575 and 1594.
c. 1580–90 Makua near Mozambique in revolt.
1580 Sept., Portuguese offensive against Ngola; army largely African.

1579 United Provinces established in Netherlands.

1580 Portugal subject to Spain (–1640).

1581 Portuguese expelled from Muscat. Embargo on Dutch trade at Lisbon forces Dutch to go east for spice trade. Dutch United Provinces become independent under William of Orange (1537–84). Fr Matteo Ricci (1552–1610) in China.

1583 Battle of Tala Ndongo; Portuguese build fort at Massangano.

1583 Pope declines concession of Kongo mines.

5 Amir Ali Bey rouses coast for kish Caliphate from Mogadishu to mbasa. Malindi alone loyal to tugal; João Rebello tortured to th for refusing to turn Muslim.
6 Sarsa Dengel leads expedition inst Sidama kingdom of Enarya; g converted to Christianity.
ir Ali Bey returns to Jidda from mbasa.

1584 Small Portuguese reinforcements arrive in Luanda.
1585 24 Dec., Portuguese badly defeated by Ngola.

1584 Virginia explored by Sir Walter Raleigh and Sir Richard Grenville.
1585 15,000 slaves in province of Pernambuco; alliance between England and Holland. Barbary Co. founded to trade with Morocco.

1586–97 Fr João dos Santos, OP, missionary in Mozambique.

1586 College of Cardinals reorganized.

EGYPT & THE SUDAN	NORTHERN AFRICA	WESTERN AFRICA
	1587 Turkish dominions in N Africa reorganized; three regencies, Tripoli, Tunis and Algiers; Algiers under Pashas with a 3-year term.	**1587–8** Portuguese fort built at Cacheu.
		c. **1588** Portuguese factories at Lagos, Warri, New and Old Calabar, and Cameroons R. **1588–90** John Bird, Newton, James Welsh and other Englishmen visit Benin.
1589 Troops mutiny in Egypt.	**1589** Arzila ceded by Spain to Morocco. **1590** Moroccan army under Judar Pasha sent to invade Songhai; troops include Spaniards, Italians, Greeks, French and English. Tunis ruled by Deys. New Qasba built at Algiers.	
		1591–1654 Moroccan Pashas of Timbuktu nominally subject to Marrakesh: 150 Pashas in 154 years: Judar Pasha, first Pasha. **1591** Slave trade across Sahara begins to increase. Feb., Judar Pasha's army arrives at Karabara on R Niger; Apr., Songhai army routed at Tenkondibo'o. Tuareg expand and control Niger bend, and eventually all southern Sahara from Timbuktu to L. Chad. **1591–4** Mahmud Pasha b.Ali b.Zarghun replaces Judar Pasha; Askia Ishaq defeated and murdered; puppet Askia installed in Timbuktu; Askia Nuh maintains resistance from Dandi.
		1593 1,200 slaves sent across Sahara to the Moroccan army.
		1594 Mahmud Pasha dies fighting Askia Nuh; succ. al-Mansur b.Abd al-Rahman (1594–7) kills Askia Nuh; end of Songhai empire. *c.* **1594** 700–800 confessions from Africans heard in Lent by the Portuguese chaplain in Cacheu. **1595** First Dutch voyage to the Gold Coast
	1595–6 al-Nasir, pretender, revolts against Sharif of Morocco.	**1595/6–1614/5** Mawura Saara, ruler of Gonja: vigorous Muslim activity. *c.* **1596–1655** Abd al-Rahman al-Sadi, historian, at Timbuktu.

EASTERN AFRICA	CENTRAL & SOUTHERN AFRICA	OTHER COUNTRIES

1587 Zimba horde from near R Zambezi reaches Kilwa: three-quarters of the population of 4,000 killed and eaten. Portuguese fleet from Goa puts down rebellion on the east coast.

1588 Zimba reach Mombasa: Tomé de Sousa repels Turks but fails to prevent sack by Zimba; Zimba attack Malindi; Segeju and Portuguese destroy Zimba horde; Bwana Bashir, King of Lamu, and others hanged for rebellion; Pate and Siu fined. Amir Ali Bey returns to Mombasa with four ships; Portuguese attacked in Pemba.

1589 Peace between Ethiopia and Turks.
1590 Wallo Galla at war with Aussa.
c. **1590** Settlement of Hatimii Arabs at Barawa, said to be from Andalusia. H. van Linschoten visits E Africa.

c. **1591** Nephew of ruler of Zanzibar converted to Christianity: sent to Goa for education by Dominicans; King of Pemba becomes Christian as Dom Felipe (d. 1607).
1591 Sir James Lancaster, first Englishman to water at Comoro Is. and at Zanzibar.

1590 28 Dec., Portuguese under Luis Serrão defeated by combined army of Ndongo, Kongo, Matamba and Jaga.
c. **1590–1610** Andrew Battel a prisoner of the Portuguese in Angola. First mention of the Jaga Kings in Angola as neighbours of Ndongo. Fort São Sebastião, Mozambique, completed.

1587 Mary, Queen of Scots, executed. Persecution of Christians in Japan. Sir Francis Drake pillages Cadiz.
1587–1629 Abbas I, Shah of Persia.

1588 Sir Francis Drake defeats Spanish Armada.

1589–1610 Henry IV, King of France.

1591 F.Pigafetta and D.Lopez, *Description of the Kingdom of the Congo.*
1591 Sir Richard Grenville killed fighting the Spanish fleet single-handed in the Azores.
1591–1605 Clement VIII, Pope.

ante **1592** Portuguese factory established in Zanzibar.

1592–3 Francisco d'Almeida, first royal governor of Angola, arrives with 600 men; forced by local Portuguese politics to withdraw to Brazil.
1592 Portuguese force from Sena and Tete routed by Zimba.
1593 Portuguese again routed by Zimba.
1593–4 Jerónimo d'Almeida, governor of Angola; brief campaign against Kisama.

1594–1602 João Furtado de Mendonça, Governor of Angola; 1 Aug., arrives with large army.

1592 Congregation for Affairs of the Faith established: beginning of modern missionary activity. Definitive edition of the *Vulgate.*

1593 Abjuration of Protestantism by Henry IV of France.

1593–6 Fort Jesus at Mombasa built by Giovanni Battista Cairatto.
c. **1593** Stambuli dynasty established at Faza.
1594 Portuguese customs house established at Mombasa, with export tariff of 6%.

1595 Bishopric created at São Salvador.

1596 Furtado de Mendonça's campaign up R Bungo, with 400 Portuguese and 15,000 Africans.

1595 First Dutch voyage round the Cape to Java.

c. **1596** Augustinians set up missions in Mombasa, Faza and Lamu; Brethren of the Misericordia established at Mombasa to care for Christian widows, orphans and converts.
1597–1603 Yaqub, Emperor of Ethiopia.

EGYPT & THE SUDAN	NORTHERN AFRICA	WESTERN AFRICA
1598 Troops again mutiny in Egypt.		**1598** Dutch trading stations established at Mori, Butre, Cormantin and Kommenda.
		late 16th c. Tobacco smoking in pipes introduced in W Africa.
c. **1600** Coptic ceases to be spoken, but still used as a liturgical language.		*c.* **1600** Temne, Bullon and Manes merged; Mani penetrating Sierra Leone region. Susu surrender Port Loko to the Temne. Twi-speaking Akwamu settle in Nsawam region, near Accra. Accra the capital of a Ga federation. Denkyera kingdom established. Kano conquered by the Jukun of Kworofa. Katsina invaded by Bornu. Hausa language begins to spread and develop. Efik moving towards present habitat. Edos (Binis) from Benin take possession of Lagos. Portuguese visits for slaves begin to be frequent. Yoruba vassal appointed by King of Benin as King of Lagos; tribute paid to Benin until 1830.
1601 Troops again mutiny in Egypt.		**1601** De Bry visits Benin.
		c. **1602** Dutch settlement at C. Mount, Sierra Leone.
1603 Keira dynasty founded at Darfur by Kuru (**1603**–*c.* **1640**).	**1603–7** Struggle for the succession in Morocco; Fez independent of Marrakesh. **1603–29** Zaidan, Sharif of Morocco.	**1603** Bornu empire in decline, following death of Mai Idris Alooma.
1604–5 Ibrahim Pasha, governor of Egypt: attempt at stern measures provokes troops to rebellion.		
1605 Sept., Ibrahim Pasha killed by troops.		**1605** 25 Sept., Balthazar Barreira, SJ, starts first mission in Sierra Leone.
1606–11 Adlan, King of the Funj: defeats Abdullab at Karkoj: court distinguished by numerous holy men: Islam spreads rapidly in the Gezira. **1607** Muhammad Pasha, governor of Egypt, known as Kul Kivan, 'Breaker of Mamluks'.		**c. 1606** Dutch, Flemish and Portuguese traders in Sierra Leone. **1607** William Keeling visits Sierra Leone with three ships.

ASTERN AFRICA	CENTRAL & SOUTHERN AFRICA	OTHER COUNTRIES

1598 Hasan b.Ahmad, Sultan of
Malindi, made Sultan of Mombasa
y the Portuguese.
1598—1612 Augustinian mission
stablished in Zanzibar.

1599 Muxima founded.

1598 Edict of Nantes. Spain occupies New Mexico.

ate 16th or early 17th c. Final
ettlement of the Bari.
7th c. Lwoo chieftainships begin in
rea now called Alur.
1600 Nandi settled in their present
abitat. Nyakyusa chieftainships instituted.
Buganda, with Sese Island allies, beats off
n attack from Bunyoro.
ost 1600 Galla moving southward,
aiding up to R Tana and Kilifi; end of
own life in Gedi.

17th c. Lozi kingdom founded by
Mboo son of Mbuyambwamba.
c. 1600 Imbangala warriors begin to
infiltrate Angola. About 400 Portuguese
in Mozambique. Gatsi Rusere ruling as
Monomotapa. Lunda empire founded
by Ilunga wa Lwefi (or Leu). Manioc
(cassava) introduced, possibly through
Kongo; widespread trade from Kongo to
Kasai. First Sakalava dynasty in
Madagascar: Andriandahifotsy, first ruler.
c. 1600—30 Foundation of Kasanje
kingdom on Upper Kwango.

1600 English East India Co. founded.
Akbar begins conquest of the Deccan.

1601—3 A.Battel living with the Jaga
near the Kuvo and Kwanza rivers.
1602—3 João Rodriguez Coutinho
governor of Angola; granted contract
for slaves for an annual fee.
1602 First French visit to Madagascar.
1603 Portuguese expedition on R Kwanza;
Coutinho d. of fever.
1603—7 Manuel Cerveira Pereira
temporary governor of Angola; cease-fire
with Ngola.
1604 Alvare II of Kongo asks to become
a feudatory of the Pope in return for
mining concessions. Cambambwe occupied
by Manuel Pereira; fort built. 17 June-25
Aug., Dutch blockade Mozambique.
1605 Town of Shilla Mbanza (Axilla
Ambanza) destroyed by Pereira.

1603—24 Fr Pais, SJ, in Ethiopia;
missionary activity in Tigre.
1603—4 Za Dengel, Emperor of
Ethiopia.

1601 First Poor Law in England. The
Dutch in Annam.
1602 The Pope again declines concession
of Kongo mines. Dutch East Indies Co.
founded.
1603—25 James I, King of England.
1603—4 Champlain's first voyage to
Canada.

1605—21 Paul V, Pope.
c. 1605/6—94 Palmares' 'Negro
Republic' in Pernambuco.
1605 Gunpowder plot.
1606 The Virginia Co. founded.
Anti-Catholic legislation in England.

1606 Fra Gaspar de S. Bernardino visits
eastern African coast.

1607 Philip, Christian King of Pemba, d.
Stephen, an infant, King of Pemba: sent
to Goa for education. W.Finck visits
Socotra. Yusuf b.al-Hasan, son of
Sultan of Malindi and Mombasa, b.

1607—11 Dom Manuel Pereira Forjaz,
Governor of Angola: policy of peace
with Mbundu.
1607 1 Aug., Portuguese treaty with
Monomotapa. March-May, Dutch besiege
Mozambique; 4 Aug., Dutch return; 20
Aug., siege again abandoned.
1607—8 Abortive attempt by Balthasar
de Aragão to cross Africa from Angola.
Portuguese expedition to seek gold and
silver near Chicoa; Monomotapa cedes
territory near Tete, granting mineral
rights throughout his kingdom.
1608 July-Aug., Dutch again besiege
Mozambique.

1607 Fr João dos Santos, OP, *Ethiopia
Oriental.* Virginia established as a British
Colony.

1608 Quebec founded by Champlain.
Treaty between England and the United
Provinces.

EGYPT & THE SUDAN	NORTHERN AFRICA	WESTERN AFRICA
1609 Uprising against Muhammad Pasha put down.	1609 80,000 Moriscos said to have arrived in Tunis.	1609 Ngazargarmu, capital of Bornu, taken by the Fulani.
	1610–37 Yusuf, Dey of Tunis: organizes piracy. 1610–13 Abu Mahalli, claims to be Mahdi and seizes Marrakesh. 1610 Larache ceded to Spain by Morocco. Morisco immigrants settle in numbers at Bou Regreg and commence piracy.	
1611–16 Badi Sid el Qom b.Abd al-Qadir, King of Sennar: repudiates alleged suzerainty of Ethiopia.		
		1612 Abortive French attempt to set up a station on the R Gambia. Dutch fort built at Mouri.
1616–45 Rubat b.Badi, Funj King of Sennar.		

EASTERN AFRICA	CENTRAL & SOUTHERN AFRICA	OTHER COUNTRIES
1609 4 May, Friday Mosque at Merca completed.	1609 Dom Nuno Alváres Pereira Captain-General of the Conquest of Mines of Silver; war between Simões Madeira and rebels Motoposso and Matuzianhe; Gatsi Rusere re-established as Monomotapa: further treaty with the Portuguese.	1609 Final expulsion of Muslims from Spain: about ½m. deported to N Africa. Bank of Amsterdam founded.
	1610 Sir H. Midleton's voyage. Monomotapa revolts; Estevão de Ataide sets up base for attack on Monomotapa at Tete; returns to Mozambique on rumour of new Dutch threat; desultory hostilities with Monomotapa (−1613). *c.* 1610 Tananarive becomes Merina capital. Kasanje swears fealty to Portugal. *c.* 1610−25 Bemba immigration from Lunda to N of L Bangweulu and then S.	1610 Jews again expelled from Spain. Henry IV of France assassinated. Galileo invents the telescope.
	1611−15 Bento Banha Cardoso, Governor of Angola: campaign against Mbundu and their Ngola.	1611−32 Gustavus Adolphus, King of Sweden. 1611 The Merchant Adventurers established at Hamburg.
1612 Portuguese lease Pemba to António Varella. *post* 1612 Pemba made subject to King of Malindi.	1612 *c.* 10,000 slaves shipped annually from Angola. Diocese of Mozambique separated from the Patriarchate of Goa. *c.* 1612 Portuguese territory in Angola invaded by Ndembu.	1612 Basilica of St Peter at Rome completed. Peace between Spain and France.
	1613 Diogo Simões Madeira in charge of operations against Monomotapa; Chombe decisively defeated. Mgr Vivès appointed permanent ambassador of Kongo to the Vatican. *c.* 1613 Emigration of Kasanje and his followers from Lukamba to Lui-Kwango plains. 1613−19 Fr Luis Mariano visits Madagascar.	1613 Thomas de Jesu, Carmelite friar, proposes a Congregation for the Propagation of the Faith. Beginning of Romanov dynasty in Russia (−1917).
1614 Portuguese bombard palace of Sultan of Mombasa; Sultan visits Goa to protest.	1614 Samuel Braun, trading on the R Congo, meets a French-speaking King with a Queen who spoke Flemish. May, fort of S. Miguel built at Chicoa. 1614−41 Struggle for succession in Kongo; seven Mani Kongo. 1614 Madeira's expedition from Tete to Chicoa; peace made with Monomotapa.	1614 Condé's rebellion in France.
1615 al-Hasan, Sultan of Mombasa, murdered by Nyika at instigation of the Portuguese; succ. Yusuf b.al-Hasan sent to Goa for education.	1615 Manuel Cerveira Pereira: 2nd term as Governor of Angola with commission to prepare conquest of Benguela. Sir Thomas Roe puts into Table Bay. Portuguese post at Chicoa obtains silver ore. 1615−16 Operations against Ango district and Libollo. *ante* 1616 Kapwhiti and Lundu Phin, Karonga leaders, settle on the R Wankurumadzi and R Mwanza. *c.* 1616 Kasanje dies. 1616 March, Gaspar Bocarro marches from Tete to Kilwa, visiting Maravi under Muzura, along an apparently organized trade route. 1616−20 Great drought in the Ambako region.	1615 William Harvey discovers the circulation of the blood.
	1617 Manuel Cerveira Pereira leaves for Benguela; Aug., Luis Mendes de Vasconcelos, Governor of Angola (−1621): operations against the Ngola (−1620). Dom Alvare III of Kongo complains to Pope Paul V of Portuguese conduct in Angola.	1617 Law of succession of Ottoman empire changed from primogeniture to the eldest male relative of the deceased ruler. 1617−18 Mustafa I, Ottoman Sultan.

EGYPT & THE SUDAN	NORTHERN AFRICA	WESTERN AFRICA

1618–19 Border forays between Sennar and Ethiopia.

1618 Morocco relinquishes control of Timbuktu; officers drawn from children of Moroccan officers by local women or *arma,* Pashas elected from *arma.*
c. **1618** Fort James built by British at Bathurst, Gambia.

1619 Pestilence in Egypt kills 330,000.

1620 Richard Jobson refuses to buy slaves on R Gambia.

1621 Dutch trading station set up at Gorée.

1622 English bombard Algiers.

c. **1622** 3,000 slaves sent annually from Guinea to Portugal.

1623 Troops in Egypt refuse super-cession of Mustafa Pasha as viceroy.

1625 Dutch fail to take Elmina from the Portuguese. Abomey conquered by Tacoodounu, chief of the Fons; Kingdom of Dahomey established.

EASTERN AFRICA	CENTRAL & SOUTHERN AFRICA	OTHER COUNTRIES
1618 Source of the Blue Nile discovered by Pedro Paez.	1618 Portuguese campaign against Ndongo. Ninety-four Ngola chiefs executed.	1618–48 Thirty Years War. 1618–22 Uthman II, Ottoman Sultan. 1618 Company of Adventurers of London trading into Africa chartered.
		1620 'Pilgrim Fathers' sail to America in the *Mayflower*. First African slaves landed in Virginia. *c.* 1620 *Historia do Reino de Congo*.
	1619–21 Nuno Alvares Pereira takes reinforcements to Mozambique from Goa; July, arrives at Tete; fails to find silver mines at Chicoa. *c.* 1620–50 Migration of Pende from E of R Lukala to Kasai. 1620 Portuguese leave Madagascar. Ngola driven on to an island in R Cuanza. June, Andrew Shilling and Humphrey Fitzherbert take possession of Saldanha Bay in the name of James I of England: colony refused by James I.	
1621 Jesuit church completed at Ghemb Mariam.	1621–3 João Correia de Souza, Governor of Angola: campaigns against Kasanje and Nambu a Ngongo. *c.* 1621–2 Ngola Mbandi sends his sister Nzinga (1582–1663) as ambassadress to Portuguese in Luanda: Portuguese recognize Mbandi as of equal status; Nzinga baptized as Dona Aña de Souza.	1621–3 Gregory XV, Pope. 1621–65 Philip IV of Spain and Portugal.
1622 Emperor Susenyos submits to Holy See; Wallo Galla raid Amhara.	1622 Anglo-Dutch task force abortively blockades Mozambique.	1622 6 Jan., Pope Gregory XV founds the *Sacra Congregatio de Propaganda Fide,* Sacred Congregation for the Propagation of the Faith; 22 June, Bull *Inscrutabili divinae* sets out the duties of the congregation in promoting missionary work. Persians expel Portuguese from Hormuz. Mustafa I, Ottoman Sultan, restored. 1623–40 Murad IV, Ottoman Sultan. 1623 Diet of Ratisbon.
	1623–4 Bp Simão de Mascarenhas Governor of Angola. 1623 Dutch attack on Luanda beaten off; Benguela temporarily occupied. Portuguese campaign against the Jaga. *c.* 1623 Xhosa and Tembu reach Umzimvubu R. 1623–69 Jesuit training college for the missions in São Salvador.	
1624 Seventy Christians at Faza. Fr Jerome de Lobo, SJ, missionary and explorer, at Malindi and R Juba. *c.* 1624 Ajuran and Madaule Somali migrate to El Wak region from R Shibeli.	1624–30 Fernão de Souza, Governor of Angola: attempts to revive Mbundi trade and Ndongo monarchy. 1624–63 Nzinga (Dona Aña de Souza) Queen of Mbundu: attempts to revive trade. 1624 Eight Jesuit missions on the Zambezi; typhoon destroys shipping in Mozambique harbour. Another Dutch attack on Luanda beaten off. Bungu (Bangu) destroyed by the Jaga.	1624 Fr Jerome de Lobo, SJ, leaves Goa for Ethiopia with Bp Alphonso Mendes, SJ, Latin patriarch of Ethiopia. Dutch found New Amsterdam and set up in Brazil.
1625–33 Fr Jerome de Lobo in Ethiopia.	*c.* 1625 Wambu Kalunga takes over Kingdom of Wambu (Huambo). 1625–1911 Kasanje empire one of the principal African states.	1625–49 Charles I, King of England. 1625 British take Barbados; French take St Christopher. St Vincent de Paul founds *Congrégation des Prêtres de la Mission*.

EGYPT & THE SUDAN	NORTHERN AFRICA	WESTERN AFRICA
		1626 Dieppe and Rouen Co. send Thomas Lambart to Senegal.
	1627—41 Bou Regreg independent as a republic.	1627 Ahmad Baba, writer, d. at Timbuktu.
	1628 French obtain coral monopoly in Algiers.	
		1629 Begho, Gyaman, famed for cloth weaving.
1630 Many Capuchins go to Cairo to evangelize Ethiopia.		1630 Cacheu separated from Cape Verde under a Captain-General.
1631 Musa Pasha, Viceroy of Egypt, suspended by grandees: Egypt ruled for twenty-five years by elected viceroy. 1631—56 Ridwan Bey al-Faqari, Amir al-Hajj (Commander of the Pilgrimage), effectively most influential grandee in Egypt, with his own faction known as al-Faqariyyah.	1631 Muhammad al-Sharif, chief of the Filali.	c. 1630—60 Oti Akenten, King of Ashanti. c. 1631 English trading post established at Cormantin.

1626–32 Bp Alphonso Mendez, SJ, in Ethiopia.

c. **1627** Yusuf b. al-Hasan returns to Mombasa as Sultan; enthroned by Portuguese with name Dom Hieronimo Chingulia; sends letter of obedience to the pope.
1627 Kilwa bordering on revolt through misconduct of Portuguese factor.
1628 Eleven Jesuit mission stations opened in Ethiopia; many imperial ordinances against the Ethiopian church.

1630 Somali pillage Zaila; town henceforward subject to Sharifs of Mukha.

1631 Aug., Pedro de Leitão, Captain of Mombasa, murdered by Sultan Yusuf b. al-Hasan in Fort Jesus with Portuguese chaplain; 20 Aug., Prior of Mombasa, two Portuguese Augustinians and many men martyred; 21 Aug., many women and children martyred; total of African and Portuguese martyrs about 250; Muslims in full control of Mombasa; Utondwe, Manda, Luziwa, Chwaka, Pate, Siu, Pemba refuse tribute to Portuguese; risings in Tanga and Mtangata.
1632 8 Jan., Portuguese fleet from Goa arrives at Mombasa to recover coast, withdrawing unsuccessfully on 19 March; 16 May, Yusuf b. al-Hasan abandons Mombasa; 5 Aug., Portuguese re-enter town peacefully. Emperor Susenyos of Ethiopia breaks with Rome: Susenyos d. 17 Sept.: Jesuits expelled: all Catholic missionaries banned under pain of death.
1632–67 Fasilidas, Emperor of Ethiopia. Axum Cathedral restored.

1626 Portuguese make war on Queen Nzinga: trade successfully re-established with Ari (Dom Felippe) as puppet ruler.

1627 Queen Nzinga attacks Portuguese and successfully makes her sister Queen of Ndongo. July, English blockade Mozambique but retire unsuccessfully to Comoro Is.

1628 French set up station at Ste Luce, Madagascar. Monomotapa attacks Portuguese; Fr Luis de Espirito Santo, OP, raises army of Portuguese and vassals defeating Monomotapa; Mavura Mhande made Monomotapa, (–1652).
c. **1629** First attempts to grow maize, manioc (cassava), sweet potatoes, pawpaw, coconuts, guavas and ground-nuts in small farms near Luanda.
1629 Monomotapa Mavura Philippe declares himself a vassal of Portugal and is baptized; treaty with Portuguese; flourishing Portuguese trading centres at Ruhanje, Bokoto, Tafuna, Chitom-borwizi, Hwangwa and Dambarare.
c. **1629–30** Queen Nzinga starts to recruit army.
c. **1630** Imbangala begin to conquer final settling place.
c. **1630–5** Queen Nzinga conquers Matamba.
1630–5 Dom Manuel Pereira Coutinho, Governor of Angola: war with Ndembu.
c. **1630–80** Flowering period of the Bakuba culture: marked development in administration and agriculture.
1630 Thirty Dominican missions in Mozambique.
1631 Kapararidze's revolt against Monomotapa defeated; June, Mono-Motapa organizes general rising against Portuguese.

1632 Diogo de Souza de Meneses attacks Karanga, winning decisive victory.

1626 Oct., Richelieu appointed Grand Master, Chief and Superintendent-General of the Navigation and Commerce of France. Peace of La Rochelle.
1627 Wallenstein expels the Danes from Germany. Siege of La Rochelle.

1628 La Rochelle capitulates. Buckingham assassinated.

1629 Beginning of conflict between Charles I and Parliament. Richelieu, principal minister in France. English take Quebec.

1630 Dutch take Pernambuco, Caracas and Surinam. Maine made a colony.

1631 Bohemia conquered by the Elector of Saxony.

1632 Colony of Maryland founded. Dutch take Curaçao.

EGYPT & THE SUDAN	NORTHERN AFRICA	WESTERN AFRICA
	1635 Treaty between France and Morocco: English expedition against Algiers. 1636 Maulai Muhammad succ. Muhammad al-Sharif as Filali sultan. 1636–43 Algiers at war with France.	1635 3 Nov., Fr Alexis de Saint-Lo founds the first mission at Rufisque.
		1637 Dutch fort at Mouri renamed Fort Nassau. 28 or 29 Aug., Portuguese surrender Elmina to the Dutch. Lambert sets up stations at Bieurt and Terrier Rouge, Senegal. Five French Capuchins found stations at Axim and Kommenda.
	1638 Maulai Muhammad seizes Tafilalet and much other territory.	1638 Dutch take Arguin from Spaniards. French build fort at St Louis, Senegal. c. 1638 English fort built at Cormantin.
c. 1640–70 Sulaiman Solong, Sultan of Darfur.	1640 Knights of Malta attack La Goulette. Tangier and Mazagan retained by Spain after Portuguese independence.	1640 Dutch trading lodge built at Anomabu.
	1641 Revolt of marabout al-Ayachi.	1641 Portuguese fort at Cacheu strongly fortified and garrisoned c. 1641 – c. 1700 Succession to the throne of Benin made rotatory. c. 1641 – c. 1661 Ahenzae, Oba of Benin.
		1642 Dutch take Axim fort from the Portuguese; Dutch attack English, taking all their forts except Cape Coast Castle.
1643 Pestilence in Egypt.		

EASTERN AFRICA	CENTRAL & SOUTHERN AFRICA	OTHER COUNTRIES

EASTERN AFRICA

1633–7 Petty revolts against Portuguese organized by Sultan Yusuf b.al-Hasan from Comoro Is. and from Jidda. Gondar built as the imperial capital of Ethiopia.
1633 Second Portuguese fleet dispatched to Mombasa; finds Sultan Yusuf b.al-Hasan fled to Jidda; coast recovered easily.

1635 Francisco de Seixas de Cabreira appointed Captain of Mombasa.

1636 Nov., Cabreira conducts punitive expedition against Pate, Siu, Manda and Luziwa; treaties imposed on their sultans, and on Faza and Lamu.

1640 Expulsion of all Portuguese missionaries from Ethiopia.

1642 Ethiopian embassy to Yemen.

1643 Sultan of Faza complains of Portuguese conduct on the island; Afonso Manoel, retiring Captain of Fort Jesus, sent for trial in Goa. Sultan of Pate warned against hostility towards Faza.

CENTRAL & SOUTHERN AFRICA

1633–5 War between Dembo and Portuguese.
1633 João da Costa reports on wealth of Karanga mines.
Dutch ship blockades Benguela.

1635–9 Francisco de Vasconcelos da Cunha, Governor of Angola.
1635 Peace with Ndembu.

1637 Scheme for colonization of Mozambique abandoned.

1638 Dutch occupy Mauritius. First French trading centre set up in Madagascar. Dutch settlement at the Cape.
1639 Dutch blockade mouth of R Congo.
1639–45 Pedro Cézar de Menezes Governor of Angola: fails to reach agreement with Queen Nzinga.

c. 1640 Dutch post established at Ambriz.
post 1640 Portuguese penetrating Changamire kingdom.

1641 First mention of Jaga state of Kakonda. 25 Aug., Dutch capture Luanda; 13,000 to 16,000 slaves exported annually; Portuguese retreat to Massangano. Boma kingdom already established. Dec., Dutch take Benguela.
1641–61 Garcia II, Mani Kongo; Capuchin mission revived in Kongo.

1643 17 May, Dutch attack Portuguese at Bango: governor captured but truce made. French station at Ste Luce receives seventy immigrants and ninety more in 1644: only seventy-two left by 1646. Pronis establishes French trading post at Fort Dauphin, Madagascar.

OTHER COUNTRIES

1634 Charles I levies Ship Money without the sanction of Parliament. Barreto de Rezende, *Livro de Estado da India* gives detailed account of E Africa.
1635 Franco-Spanish war. Colonies of Guadeloupe and Cayenne founded.

1636 Harvard University founded.

1637 Sultan Yusuf b.al-Hasan of Mombasa d. at Jeddah. Protestant synod in France holds that slavery is not condemned by the law of God.

1638 Trinitarian Order reformed. Solemn League and Covenant in Scotland.

1639 Alsace becomes French. Portuguese expelled from Japan. Pope Urban VIII forbids the deportation of natives of Paraguay and Uruguay as slaves and excommunicates all Catholics who engage in the slave trade. Peace of Berwick between England and Scotland.
1640–8 Ibrahim I, Ottoman Sultan.
1640 Portugal regains independence from Spain under Braganza dynasty (–1910). Dutch posts set up in Ceylon and Malacca. Long Parliament elected.
1640–56 João IV, King of Portugal.
1641 Strafford executed for treason. The Great Remonstrance.

1642 Treaty between England and Portugal of 1346 reaffirmed. French East India and Madagascar Co. founded. English civil war (–1648). Cardinal Richelieu d.; Cardinal Mazarin first minister (–1661); Galileo d. Tasmania and New Zealand discovered by Tasman. Montreal founded.
1643 Louis XIII of France d.; succ. Louis XIV (–1715). Bishops and the House of Lords abolished in England.

EGYPT & THE SUDAN	NORTHERN AFRICA	WESTERN AFRICA
1644 Mahsud Pasha deposed in uprising.		**1644** António de Mingo, half-caste King of Warri.
1645 Badi the Bearded (Dign), Funj King of Sennar: successful revolt by the Shaigia of Dongola.		
	1646 French Consulate building bought at Algiers.	**1646** Rising in Cacheu.
		1647 Feb., frigate *S. Teodosio* sent with troops to put down rising in Cacheu.
	1648–55 Ceuta beseiged by Ahmad Gailan, rebel Moroccan chieftain. **1648** French Consulate building bought at Tunis.	
		c. **1650** Jenne one of the great markets of the Muslim world. Obutong founded by Efik. Yoruba seize Dahomey. **1650–4** Abbasid rulers of Wadai. **1650–2** Swedish trading post at Butre. **1650** 15 Jan., Captain-General of Cacheu made subject to Governor and Captain-General of Cape Verde and the district of Guinea.
	1651 Dutch blockade Bou Regreg against pirates.	**1651** Germans from Courland build fort on St. Andrew's Is. in R Gambia. King of Warri asks Rome for missionaries;

EASTERN AFRICA	CENTRAL & SOUTHERN AFRICA	OTHER COUNTRIES
1644 Pemba at war with Faza.	1644 Dutch at war with Nzinga; Portuguese at war with Ngola. Monomotapa acknowledges suzerainty of Portugal in spite of Karanga disaffection. 1644–5, 1650 Unsuccessful English attempts to found colony at Nossi-Bé; Madagascar. 1645 First slaves exported from Mozambique to Brazil. 8 Feb, Portuguese reinforced with 260 white troops: all killed by Imbangala, 25 May, Twelve Spanish and Italian Capuchins arrive at Kongo. Oct., Francisco de Sotto Maior, governor of Angola (–1646) moves with 300 men; Massangano attacked by Queen Nzinga and the Dutch. 1645 or 1646 Portuguese ally with Kasanje. Ports of Libolo and Kasanje occupied. 1646 Francisco de Sotto Maior, Governor of Angola, d.; Triumvirate elected. Soyo recognized as independent by Kongo.	1644-1911 Ching dynasty in China. 1644 Sugar introduced into the Antilles Is. 1645 New Model Army raised by Cromwell. Laud executed. 1646 Charles I taken prisoner by Parliament. 1646–8 Confession of Westminster.
1647 Ali b.Daud makes Harar an independent sultanate. Ethiopian embassy to Yemen.	1647-74 Carmelite mission started in Madagascar; well received by Dian Ramaka, educated in Goa; Lazarists and Capuchins assist. 1647-8 The *Haarlem* wrecked in Table Bay; crew rescued after a year. 1648 Dutch, with Kongo and Matambo, defeat Portuguese; 12 Aug., Salvador Correia de Sà é Benavides, Governor (–1652): 24 Aug., recaptures Luanda; Mbundu and Kongo Ndembu recognize Portuguese suzerainty; Dutch withdraw. Flacourt becomes a Director of the French Co. of Madagascar: fortifies Fort Dauphin. 1649 Governor of the King of Kongo exiled from Luanda.	1647 Charles I escapes. London seized by Parliament. 1648 Treaty of Westphalia ends Thirty Years War. Parliament purged by Cromwell. 1648–87 Mehmed IV, Ottoman Sultan. 1649 30 Jan., Charles I of England beheaded; England declared a Commonwealth (–1660).
c. mid-17th c. Expansion of Lango, Jie, Teso and Karamojong peoples. Buganda, under Kabaka Kaberega, attacks Bunyoro: kingdom doubled in size: hereditary chieftainships created in Gombe and Butambala. Gedi finally abandoned.	*c.* 1650 Portuguese begin to export slaves from Mozambique; Imbangala open trade route between Kasanje and Musumba, Lunda capital, with Luanda. 1650 Oct., Portuguese recovery in Angola completed.	1650–80 Dutch conquest of Java. 1650 Cromwell invades Scotland. Omani Arabs recover Muscat from the Portuguese.
c. 1651 Delegation from Mombasa to Muscat asking Omani help to expel Portuguese.		1651 1 Jan., Charles II crowned King of Scots at Scone: abortive invasion of England. Navigation acts.

EGYPT & THE SUDAN	NORTHERN AFRICA	WESTERN AFRICA
		Capuchin mission established. (– 1682). The Guinea Company formed.
		c. 1651 Letter from the Pope to Oba of Benin brought by Fr Joseph.
		1651–8 Spanish Capuchin mission at Takoradi.
		1652 First Swedish trading voyage to Gold Coast; trading lodges built at Takoradi, Cape Coast, Osu and Accra, later Christiansborg Castle. Prince Rupert destroys the Commonwealth station on the R Gambia.
	c. 1653 Maulai al-Rashid emerges as a rival to Maulai Muhammad.	1653 Kwararafa at war with Katsina; city invested.
	1655 English bombard Algiers.	1655 *Tarikh al-Sudan* completed by Abd al-Rahman al-Sadi. Carolusborg Castle built at Cape Coast by the Swedes. c. 1655 *Kitab al-Fattash* completed by Ibn al-Mukhtar.
1656 Ridwan Bey d.: quarrel among beys concerning appointment of Amir al-Hajj.		1656 Dutch build Fort Batenstein at Butre.
		1657 Swedes driven out of all their Gold Coast trading lodges by Danes.
1658 Army of Upper Egypt descends in revolt on Cairo.	1658–70 Algiers ruled by Aghas with a council.	1658 Birni Ngazargarmu said to cover 6 square miles, with population 200,000.
		1658-61 Eleven Spanish Capuchins found station at Whydah.
1659 Expedition sent from Cairo to quieten Upper Egypt.		1659 Town of St Louis, Senegal, founded. Courlander fort on St Andrew's Is., R Gambia, bought by Dutch.
1660 'Conflict of the Beys': quarrel between the Faqariyyah and Viceroy of Egypt: 27 Oct., Faqariyyah beys beheaded.		1660 Accra chief Okai Koi defeated by Akramu. c. 1660–97 Obiri Yeboa, King of Ashanti.
	1661 French expedition against Algiers. Tangier (and Bombay) ceded by Portugal to England as part of Catherine of Braganza's dowry to Charles II.	1661 English seize Courlander fort in R Gambia: renamed Fort St James.

EASTERN AFRICA	CENTRAL & SOUTHERN AFRICA	OTHER COUNTRIES
1652 Omani raid Portuguese in Pate and Zanzibar; Augustinian Vicar of Zanzibar killed; King of Pemba raids Mafia and Kwale Is.; Queen of Zanzibar and Kings of Pemba and Utondwe pay tribute to Oman. 9 March, probable cipher date of the *Hamziya,* earliest known Swahili poem.	**1652** Monomotapa Manuza d.; succ. by a Dominican who declines throne; succ. Siti Kazurukumusapa, baptized as Dom Domingos (-1663). 6 April, Jan van Riebeeck founds Cape Colony as Commander, with Council of Policy.	**1652** Union of England and Scotland. War between England and Holland.
1653 Seixas de Cabreira again Captain of Mombasa; Zanzibar retaken; Pemba flotilla destroyed.	**1653** Armed expedition against raiding Hottentots.	**1653** Dutch expelled from Brazil. Rump Parliament dissolved by Cromwell.
	1654-7 Francisco de Lima, Captain of Mozambique.	**1654** Grand Vizier of the Porte becomes effective ruler of the Ottoman Empire. Treaty of Westminster: Anglo-Portuguese treaty again reaffirmed.
	1655 Dutch exploration beyond False Bay. Monomotapa d.; quarrel about succession; Dom Afonso succ. **1655** Plague in Angola: population said to have been halved.	**1655** Dutch seize Ceylon. English retake Jamaica.
		1656-83 Afonso VI, King of Portugal. **1656** Poland partitioned by Sweden and Brandenburg.
	1657 Dutch settlement at Liesbeeck valley. Dutch begin to import slaves from Madagascar and Java. Portuguese treaty with Queen Nzinga and with Garcia II. **1658-60** Dutch at war with Hottentots. **1658** Dutch abandon Mauritius.	**1657** New Parliament elected in England.
		1658 *Société des Missions Etrangères* established in France. Aurangzeb, Great Mogul. Cromwell d.
	1659-60 Army mutinies in Luanda.	**1659** *Instructiones* of the Sacred Congregation for the Propagation of the Faith urge the training of local clergy and the creation of seminaries in mission territories. Richard Cromwell abdicates.
1660 10 Dec., Omani raiders welcomed by Faza; support received by ships from Pate, Siu, Manda, Lamu, Simio, Mwera, Jasa and Oja. **1661** 12 Feb., Omani enter Mombasa with fleet from Swahili towns; 14 Feb., Portuguese town captured; 24 March, raiders disperse.	**1660-78** Bushmen raiding Dutch settlements. **1660-75** or **1675-90** Mwata Yamvo expands Lunda empire.	**1660-85** Charles II, King of England: monarchy restored in England.
		1661 Anglo-Portuguese treaty affirmed a third time. Board of Trade and Plantations created.

EGYPT & THE SUDAN	NORTHERN AFRICA	WESTERN AFRICA
1662 Ahmad Bey, Qasimi leader, assassinated.		*c.* 1662 or 1663 English build Cape Coast Castle. 1663 First English settlement built in Sierra Leone. English trading posts set up at Kommenda, Anashan, Egya and Winneba.
	1664 Maulai al-Rashid defeats his brother; begins to conquer Morocco. Abortive French attempt to take Djidjelli. 1664 - present day Sharifs of Morocco, Filali branch. 1664–72 Maulai al-Rashid b. Muhammad, Sharif. 1665 French expedition against Algiers.	1664 12 Sept., Dutch under Admiral de Ruyter attack English on Tasso Is., Sierra Leone. 1665 English at war with Dutch on west coast: Gorée, Shama, Cape Coast, Mori, Anomabu and Egya taken by English. English Fort at Cormantin taken by Dutch and re-named Fort Amsterdam.
	1666 6 June, Maulai al-Rashid seizes Fez and is proclaimed Sultan of Morocco.	1666 Dutch under Admiral de Ruyter retake all their trading posts except Cape Coast. Franciscan mission in Cacheu: local ruler baptized. *c.* 1666 Dutch fort completed at Conradsburg, Elmina. 1666-7 Villault de Bellefond visits western African çoast. 1667 Lemaire explores upper Senegal to see if it is connected with the Gambia.
	1668 English give Tangier a charter as a borough. Maulai al-Rashid destroys marabouts of Dila.	
		1669 Tizifan, King of Whydah, receives French mission under Elbée.
*c.*1670-82 Musa b. Sulaiman, Sultan of Darfur.	1670–1830 Algiers ruled by Deys and Pasha-Deys.	1670 Timbuktu overrun by Dambara from Segu. Villault de Bellefond visits Elbée and the Slave Coast. Ambassador of the King of Whydah sent to France. Kwararafa attack Kano and sack city; also attack Katsina. *c.* 1670 Gold from Begho being

EASTERN AFRICA	CENTRAL & SOUTHERN AFRICA	OTHER COUNTRIES
	1662 Jan van Riebeeck leaves the Cape for Malacca. **1663**-c. **1692** Monomotapa Mukombwe Afonso. **1663** First school at Cape Town: Dutch and Hottentots admitted. Dutch attack Mozambique, but fail to take it. Jan Blank's expedition to Madagascar. **1664-1710** Dutch re-occupy Mauritius.	**1663** Dutch seize Malabar. Louis XIV takes Lorraine. 'Company of Royal Adventurers of England trading with Africa' rechartered. **1664** Fifth French East India Co, with objects of colonization of Madagascar and empty lands in the East, and of trade with China. English take New Amsterdam (later New York) from the Dutch.
	1665 First Predikant (minister) appointed by the Cape government. Oct., Portuguese campaign to subdue Kongo; 29 Oct., battle of Mbwila; King of Kongo killed. Bourbon (Réunion) occupied by the French. **1665–1911** Sultanate of Wadai. **1666** Dutch settlements at Saldanha Bay and Vishoek. Fresh French attempt to increase colony in Madagascar fails. Alvare III, King of Kongo: murdered by the Count of Soyo: succ. Alvare IV. **1666** First Calvinist church at Cape Town built.	**1665** Five Mile Act. War between England and Holland. **1666** War between England and France. 2-6 Sept., Fire of London.
1667-82 Yohannes I, Emperor of Ethiopia. Many ecclesiastical reforms; first royal library and chancery built; separate walled quarter in Gondar for Muslims. **1667** W. Alley, first English visitor to Mombasa.	**1666-7** Cape Town Castle built. c. **1667** Maravi governed by King Karonga, with Makua subject to them. Lundu the second ruler of the Maravi empire from the R Zambezi to Quilimane. Betsimisaraka attack the Sihanaka but fail to conquer them; revolt of Sihanaka slaves put down by Labigorue.	**1667** Louis XIV conquers Holland. Dutch destroy the English fleet in the Thames. Treaty of Breda.
1668 Council at Gondar decrees that all Franks must leave Ethiopia unless they join the national church and that Muslims must live in villages separate from Christians.	**1667** Indians begin to arrive at the Cape. **1668** War in Zambezia between Monomotapa Domingos and Portugese.	**1688** Gambia Adventurers Co. established. Afonso VI of Portugal deposed; Pedro, regent. Revolt of the Moors in Spain. Diu sacked by Omani Arabs. **1669** Villault de Bellefond, *Relation des costes d'afrique appelées Guinée.*
1670 Omani raid eastern African coast as far as Mozambique; town sacked and burnt.	**1670** Portuguese destroy Soyo; Ndongo rebels. **1670-96** The Cape exports grain to Batavia.	

EGYPT & THE SUDAN	NORTHERN AFRICA	WESTERN AFRICA
		sent to the coast. Twi-speaking peoples expanding. c. 1670-5 Dutch build fortified trading post at Sekondi: later renamed Fort Orange. 1671 French fort built at Whydah.
	post 1672 Moroccan slave-raiding expeditions to the S. 1672 English bombard Algiers. 1672-1727 Maulai Ismail b. Muhammad, Sharif of Morocco.	1672 English fort built on Bunce Is., Sierra Leone.
	1673 Peñon de Alhucemas occupied for Spain by Principe de Monte Sacro.	
	1674 Sultan of Morocco attempts to take Ceuta from Spain.	
1676-80 Kutchuk Muhammad, Bashodabashi of Janissaries in Cairo: rivalry amongst troops in Cairo leads to unrest.		1676 Numerous Dutch traders on New Calabar R, and at Bonny. Companhia de Cacheu established.
	1677 June, Maulai Ismail takes Marrakesh: capital moved to Meknès; town greatly embellished.	
		1678 French take Arguin from the Dutch, and demilitarize fort. 1678-82 John Barbot in Benin.
	1679-84 Tangier besieged by Maulai Ismail with French aid.	1679-83 Christiansborg Castle held by Portuguese. 1679 Rulers of Mata and Mompataz rise against Portuguese after being forbidden to trade with foreigners. French Senegal Co. establishes rights on north bank of R Gambia. Gold and other trade with southern traders conducted at Begho by dumb barter.
1680 Kutchuk Muhammad banished. 1680-92 Unsa b. Nasir, Funj King of Sennar.		1680 Small English trading fort built at Anomabu. French rebuild Dutch fort at Gorée. c. 1680 Ga migration from Accra to Anecho (Little Popo) in Dahomey: Accra plain abandoned to the Akwamu: Ewe state of Anlo or Awuna already established.
	1681 al-Mamoura taken from the Spanish.	1681 French trading station at Albreda on R Gambia.

ASTERN AFRICA	CENTRAL & SOUTHERN AFRICA	OTHER COUNTRIES
	1671 Sept., Portuguese subjugate Ndongo. Madagascar declared a French royal property and named Ile Dauphine; immigration from France to Bourbon (Reunion). **1672 or 1673** Portuguese make Ngola Kanini II puppet King of Matamba. **1672-6** Isbrand Goske, first Dutch governor of the Cape. **1672** Cape peninsula formally bought from Hottentots.	**1671** George Fox, Quaker, urges Friends in Barbados to treat slaves well and set them free 'after certain years'. Dutch EIC dissolved. **1672-1750** Royal African Co. **1672** Turks attack Poland. England at war with Holland.
		1673 French Senegal Co. for slave trade founded. Richard Baxter, *Christian Directory,* denounces slave-hunting. French set up at Pondichéry.
674 Three Italian Franciscans illed in Gondar.	**1674** French evacuate Madagascar.	**1674** Dutch take Martinique.
c. post **1675** Masai begin to nter present-day Kenya.		**1675** Differential calculus invented by Leibniz. St Paul's Cathedral, London, rebuilt. **1676** O. Dapper, *Description of Africa,* published in Flemish at Amsterdam. Roemer first calculates the speed of light. **1677** William of Orange marries Mary of York.
	1677 All slave children under twelve ordered to attend school in Cape Colony. 2,000 colonists sent from Portugal to Mozambique. **1678** San Salvador completely destroyed in faction fights over the Kongo succession. Kingdom of Kongo fragments into principalities. **1679** Pedro d'Almeida's expedition to Mozambique; flagship overshoots town and takes a month to return; d'Almeida d.; fleet returns to India.	
678 Portuguese punitive expedition gainst Pate; rulers of Pate, Lamu, iu and Manda beheaded.		**1678** Anglo-Dutch treaty of alliance. Titus Oates's plot.
679 Fleet from Oman compels 'ortuguese to withdraw from 'ate to Mozambique: Pemba in evolt: queen expelled.		**1679** Second French Senegal Co. founded. Habeas Corpus Act. Treaty of Nimeguen: Gorée and Arguin ceded to France by Holland.
680 30 March, partial eclipse bserved at Bako, during the eign of Kabaka Juko.	**1680** 30 March, annular eclipse seen during the reign of Mbakam Mbomaneyeel of Bushoong. *Presidio* established at Caconda Velha. Portuguese population in Mozambique 50, with 200 mulattoes; colony greatly run down. *c.* **1680-1707** Majority of present Afrikaner stock arrive at the Cape. **1681** Portuguese defeated by Matamba.	**1680-1786** 2,130,000 slaves imported into British colonies in America and W Indies.
		1681 First plans in Brandenburg to trade in Africa.

EGYPT & THE SUDAN	NORTHERN AFRICA	WESTERN AFRICA
		1681-3 Capuchin Fr Celestin chaplain to R. Africa Co. at Whydah: starts schools for sons of chiefs and notables.
c. 1682–1722 Ahmad Bakr b. Musa Sultan of the Fur: spreads Islam, introducing mosques and schools: El Fasher founded; army reorganized.	1682 French embassy to Morocco under St Amand: 14 Dec., treaty exchanging prisoners taken at sea. French bombard Algiers.	1682 Dancourt travels by land from Cape Verde to St Louis. Mission at Benin inspected by Frs Francisco de Romano and Felipe da Figuar. Great Popo at war with Kwitta, Ardra and Whydah. Capuchins established at Warri.
	1683 French again bombard Algiers.	1683 French pirate Jean Hamlin takes seventeen English and Dutch ships off Sierra Leone disguised as an English man-o'-war. Christiansborg Castle recovered by Danes. 2 Jan., Brandenburgers lay out Gross-Friedrichsburg Castle as headquarters at Princestown. c. 1683-92 Brandenburger post set up at Dixcove.
1684 Serious famine in Sennar.	1684 5 Feb., English evacuate Tangier after destroying citadel and mole.	1684 English start trading post at Dixcove in a rented hut. Brandenburger Fort Dorothea begun at Akwida.
		1685-8 Dominican missions at Kommenda, Whydah and Benin. 1685 Arguin fort re-founded by Brandenburgers. Danish Fort Frederiksborg at Cape Coast sold to English. 1686 English rebuild post at Kommenda. Companhia de Cacheu dissolved.
1687 Kutchuk Muhammad returns to office but shortly replaced.	1687 Rif tribesmen attack Melilla.	1687 July, English factory established at Rio Nunez. Portuguese build fort at Bissau. Fort Dorothea captured by Dutch.
	1688 French expedition against Algiers; communication re-opened with Algiers and Tunis. 1688-9 Systematic breeding of negroes for Moroccan army instituted.	1688 June, English factory at Sherbro moved to York Is. Mission at Benin again suspended. O.Dapper visits Benin. Dutch Fort Vredenburg built at Kommenda.
	1689 French treaty with Algiers. Larache retaken by Morocco.	1689 Fort at York Is., Sierra Leone, begun. Lake Cayar explored. English seize French establishments on R Gambia.
		1690 Second Companhia de Cacheu established. Brandenburgers again in possession of Fort Dorothea. Franciscan chapel

ASTERN AFRICA	CENTRAL & SOUTHERN AFRICA	OTHER COUNTRIES
	c. 1681 Changamire, a subordinate chief, takes Butua; then attacks Portuguese in Mozambique: Monomotapa invades Butua and is routed; Portuguese withdraw on Sena and Tete.	
682-1706 Iyasu I the Great, mperor of Ethiopia: deeply eligious period of tranquillity; urkish influence in buildings nd decoration becomes marked.	1682-3 Expeditions from Cape to Namaqualand in search of copper.	1682 Law of Gravity discovered by Newton. Peter the Great proclaimed Emperor of Russia.
		1683 R. Africa Co. bankrupt. Turks defeated at Vienna; end of Turkish expansion in Europe. 1683-1706 Pedro II, King of Portugal.
	1684 Portuguese authority in Angola at its peak, but economic decline beginning. 1684-8 Luis Lobo da Silva, Governor of Angola. *c.* 1685 Successful wine-growing starts at the Cape.	1684-1750 R. Africa Co. re-formed. 1684 Massachusetts revolts. 1685 French Guinea Co. for slave trade formed. Revocation of the Edict of Nantes. 1685-8 James II, King of England.
686 Pate rebels against ortuguese; Sultan of Pate aken captive to Goa.	*c.* 1686 Gochu revolts against Monomotapa.	1686 St Cyr founded. Chandernagore founded. 1687-91 Sulaiman II, Ottoman Sultan. 1687 Cavazzi, *Relatio Historica Ethiopiae occidentalis.* Huguenots exiled from France.
688 Omani Arabs occupy Pate: Augustinian mission abandoned.	*ante* 1688 Changamire seizes Karanga territory. Many Canarins (Goanese) settle in Mozambique. 1688-9 200 French Huguenots settle at the Cape.	1688 War between Britain and France. James II goes into exile. Quakers of Pennsylvania condemn slavery. 25 Dec., Sultan and ten councillors from Pate executed in Goa. 1688-1702 William III and Mary II (-1694), King and Queen of England.
	1689 French East India Co. sends a Director to take charge of Bourbon Is. Port Natal bought from a Bantu chief for £1,700, but not occupied.	1689 John Locke, *Treatise on Civil Government,* condemns slavery. Ireland revolts against William III.
690 Solemn visit of Emperor yasu I to the Ark of Sion at Axum.	1690 Changamire attacks Monomotapa.	1690 British factory founded at Calcutta. Battle of the Boyne.

EGYPT & THE SUDAN	NORTHERN AFRICA	WESTERN AFRICA
		and hospice for missionaries built at Bissau.
	1691 Arzila retaken by Morocco.	
1692 Faqariyyah hegemony restored: Kutchuk Muhammad seizes Janissary headquarters in Cairo.		**1692** French take Fort St James, R Gambia, abandoning it after wrecking it. English take St Louis and Gorée. English begin fort at Dixcove.
	1693 French embassy to Morocco.	**1693** French expel English from St Louis and Goree. Akwamu temporarily seize Christiansborg Castle.
1694 Kutchuk Muhammad assassinated in Cairo. Nile flood exceptionally low, followed by famine and pestilence.	**1694** Morocco, assisted by France, again attempts to take Ceuta from Spain: blockade continued to 1720.	**1694** War between Dutch and Kommenda.
	1695 Twelve or thirteen corsair vessels of 30-40 tons operating from Salé.	**1695** Capuchins sent to visit Christians in Benin and find the churches lapsed into idolatry. French temporarily capture English fort on James Is., R Gambia.
	1696 Rif tribesmen attack Melilla.	**1696** First Capitão-mor of Bissau appointed: fort built. Companhia de Cacheu and Cabo Verde given a contract to export 10,000 slaves to S America in 6 years. English besieged by Ahanta at Dixcove.
1697 Ismail Pasha deposed by Janissaries; Achmet Agha, ruler (to 1703).	**1697** Rif tribesmen again attack Melilla.	**1697** Dutch Fort Patience built at Apam. French set up factory at St Louis, Senegal. **1697–1712 or 1717** Osei Tutu, Asantehene (King) of the Ashanti: beginning of the expansion of the Ashanti empire. **1697-1724** Andre Bruè explores Senegal, with erection of posts from Arguin to Sierra Leone. **1697** Hostilities at Bissau between the Portuguese and the Wolof, and at Cacheu with the Mandingo.
1698 Janissaries cause disturbances in Cairo. 10 June, Dr Poncet and Fr Brèvedent set out for Ethiopia to extend French and Catholic influence. **1699** 6 Jan., Poncet at Dongola; 10 June, at Sennar.	**1698** Treaty between France and Algiers: Algiers renounces Holy War.	**1698** Ogo Yoruba conquers Great Ardra. Wolof ruler Incinhate complains to the King of Portugal of the poor quality of imports and demands freedom of trade. Portuguese post established at Farim. **1699** David van Nyendael visits Benin. English reoccupy

EASTERN AFRICA	CENTRAL & SOUTHERN AFRICA	OTHER COUNTRIES
		1691-5 Ahmad II, Ottoman Sultan.
1692 Abuna Synnada replaced by Abuna Marcos as head of Ethiopian church; synod held to compose Christological differences. Massawa threatens Ethiopia with land blockade for attempt to raise customs duty; Turks apologize.		1692 French fleet defeated at La Hougue. Land tax in England.
	1693 Changamire, instigated by new Monomotapa Dembo Nyakambiro, attacks Portuguese marts; conquers territory as far as Tete, taking greater part of Monomotapa country. c. 1693 Rozwi entering Rhodesia.	1693 Dutch seize Pondichéry.
1694 Pemba still in rebellion and independent of Portuguese.	1694 Conde de Vila Verde ordered to organize Company in Mozambique; gold trade improves. Portuguese send relief expedition to Sena; quarrel between Changamire and Nhacunimbiri; Portuguese make Dom Pedro Monomotapa.	1694 Bank of England established.
	1695 Changamire again defeats Portuguese and then d.	1695-1703 Mustafa II, Ottoman Sultan.
1696 March, Saif b. al-Sultan, Sultan of Oman, besieges Fort Jesus, Mombasa, with a fleet and 3,000 men against 2,500 defenders.	1696 Portuguese gain access to silver mine in Chicoa; new Monomotapa, Dom Manoel.	1696 Third French Senegal and Cape Verde Co. founded. Board of Trade and Plantations established in London.
1697 Jan., plague reduces Portuguese in Fort Jesus to twenty men; Sept., small Portuguese force enters the fort.		1697 Fourth French Senegal Co. founded: André Bruë, director. French regain Pondichéry. Treaty of Ryswyck.
1698 Earliest dated carved door in Zanzibar. Dec., Fort Jesus, Mombasa, falls to Omani with only eleven survivors; Portuguese relieving fleet arrives later and sails away; Mogadishu temporarily occupied by Omani Arabs. 1699 Omani Arabs seize Zanzibar: Queen Fatuma b.Yusuf exiled to	1698 War between the Hanha (or Kakonda) and the Portuguese in Angola.	1698 Monopoly of trade of Royal Africa Co. in W Africa ended.

EGYPT & THE SUDAN	NORTHERN AFRICA	WESTERN AFRICA
		Fort St James, R Gambia. 20 Nov., slaves exported from Guinea required to be previously baptized. **1699-1700 or 1701** Ashanti at war with Denkyera.
		*c.***1700** Yoruba kingdom in decay. Franciscans in Bissau protest against the slave trade. Surame replaced by new capital of Birnin Kebbi. **1700** French build Fort St Joseph, R Senegal.
	1701 Maulai Ismail at war with Turks; 28 April, defeated.	**1701** 4 Feb., catechism made compulsory for all slaves in Guinea.
		1702 French set up factory at Arguin in Sierra Leone. Dispute between the French and the Portuguese at Bissau. David van Nyendael again visits Benin.
1703 Another Janissary Agha in power.	**1703** Fr Busnot visits Meknès to ransom Christian captives.	**1703** Contract of the Companhia de Cacheu and Cabo Verde comes to an end: fort at Bissau abandoned. **1703, 1704, 1708** French plunder English fort on St James Is., R Gambia.
1704 Du Roule, French Vice-Consul at Damietta, sent to Ethiopia but only reaches Sennar.		**1704** 17 July, English factory at Bunce Is., Sierra Leone, bombarded by French. French privateers take St James Is., R Gambia.
1705 Nov., De Roule murdered in Sennar as a magician.	**1705-1922** Tunis ruled by Beys of the Husainid dynasty from Crete. **1705-35** Husain b.Ali al-Turki,	**1705-6** Dutch build Fort Good Hope at Beraku.

EASTERN AFRICA	CENTRAL & SOUTHERN AFRICA	OTHER COUNTRIES

Muscat (to c. 1709).
Poncet and Brèvedent in
Ethiopia: 17 July, Brèvedent
d.; Aug., Poncet proceeds to
Gondar: treats Emperor Iyasu
successfully for skin disease.
  1699 Galla raids reaching
vicinity of Malindi.
  late 17th c. Present
structure of northern
Scholiland organized.
late 17th c. Tobacco smoking
in pipes introduced in E Africa.
18th c. Lango moving to their
present habitat.
  1700 Royal bodyguard
instituted in Buganda. Omani
governor installed in Zanzibar
marks beginning of gradually
extended Omani control of
the eastern coast from
Somalia to the R Ruvuma.
  post 1700 Elements of the
Luguru move from Ubena.

18th c. Rapid expansion of
copper trade between Lunda
Kingdom and W Coast. Tikar
migrating into the present
Cameroun. Khami, Rhodesia,
built.
c. 1700 Dhlo-Dhlo, Rhodesia,
built. The Vili organize slave
routes to San Salvador and all
central Kongo. Sakalava kingdoms
of Menabe and Beina established.
English pirates set up at
Libertalia.
Mboshi migrate from L Tumba to
R Nkeni and R Alima; Tyo lose
copper mines. Lunda general
establishes dominion near L
Mweru subject to Lunda empire:
title Kazembe (governor) applied
also to region. Antonian heresy
first reported in Kongo.
1700 Portuguese Mozambique
Company fails.

1700 Academy of Sciences created
in Berlin.

1701-14 War of the Spanish
Succession.
1701 Society for the Propagation
of the Gospel in Foreign Parts
(SPG) founded.
1702-14 Anne, Queen of England.
1702 First English daily newspaper:
The Daily Courant.

  1702 Franciscan Fr Joseph
visits Ethiopian court; given
letter from emperor to Pope
Innocent XI; seven young
Ethiopians go to Rome for
instruction.
  1703 Iyasu I leads expedition
against the six tribes of
Macha Galla.

1702 Xhosas cross Kei R and
hunt beyond the Fish R.

1703-30 Mahmud I, Ottoman Sultan.
1703-92 Muhammed b.Abd al-Wahhab,
religious reformer in Najd:
originator of Wahhabi sect.
1703 *Compagnie du St Esprit,*
first French missionary society,
founded. Lord Methuen's treaty
between England and Portugal.
1704 British occupy Gibraltar.
Battle of Blenheim.

  1704 Earthquake destroys many
buildings in Gondar.

1704 Benguela burnt by the
French.

  1705 Eldest son of Takla
Haimanot proclaimed emperor
in his father's absence from
Gondar; father asked to

EGYPT & THE SUDAN	NORTHERN AFRICA	WESTERN AFRICA
	first Husainid Bey of Tunis.	
1706 Janissaries again cause disturbances in Cairo.		**1706** English at Dixcove exchange presents with the King of Ashanti.
1707-11 Continuous tension caused by Janissaries in Cairo.		**1707** Fort at Bissau ordered to be demolished.
	1708 Spain loses Oran and Mers el-Kebir.	**1708** French privateers again hold St James Is. **1708-9** Dutch plant sugar plantation at Butre to make rum. **1709** English withdraw from St James Is. *c.* **1709** English fort at Sekondi rebuilt.
	1710 Tunis makes treaty with France. Succession to Beylik of Tunis confirmed in Husainid family.	
1711 Afranj Ahmad, Agha of the Janissaries, carried off; 22 April, battle outside Cairo; 18 June, further fighting; massacre of Janissaries; Ibrahim Bey, ruler (-1719).	**1711-1835** Karamanli dynasty of Tripoli, Pashas independent of Turkey.	**1711** Fort Dorothea taken by British and Dutch. Dixcove and Ahanta territory invaded by Chief John Conny. Two Italian Capuchins die on a journey to Katsina. **1712** *c.* Jan., Chief John Conny repulsed by English at Dixcove. *c.* **1712-55** Bambara Kingdom of Segu founded.
1714-24 Ismail Bey ibn Iwaz, effective master of Egypt. **1715-18** Unsa b. Badi, King of the Funj.	**1714** Tripoli becomes independent of Constantinople.	**1713** Fort St James recovered by R. Africa Co. **1714** Jesuit mission in Sierra Leone. French Senegal Co. sets up factories on the Guinea coast. *c.* **1715** Zamfara independent of Kebbi; penetration of Zamfara by Gobirawa begins.
	1716 Tunis makes treaty with England.	
1718 Unsa b.Badi deposed by Funj for immorality.		**1717** Dutch buy out Brandenburger forts on Gold Coast. **1718** Fort Dorothea becomes Dutch property.
1719 June, Cherkes Mahomet Bey attempts to seize power.		**1719** Pirates hold Bunce Is., Sierra Leone, for 7 weeks. Pirates seize James Is., R Gambia.

EASTERN AFRICA	CENTRAL & SOUTHERN AFRICA	OTHER COUNTRIES
abdicate because of his Catholic sympathies, but temporizes. **1706-8** Takla Haimanot I, Emperor of Ethiopia. **1706** Emperor Iyasu murdered; Emperor Takla Haimanot threatens to divert the Nile.		**1706-50** João V, King of Portugal.
		1707 Aurangzeb, Mogul Emperor, d.; Bahadur succ. (-1712). Act of Union between England and Scotland. **1708-78** William Pitt (later Earl of Chatham).
1708 Takla Haimanot murdered; Theophilus, brother of Iyasu I, succ. (-1711); beginning of an era of palace revolutions in Ethiopia.		
	1709 Kingdom of Kongo re-unified under Pedro IV.	**1709** Battle of Malplaquet.
c. **1710** Arab fort completed at Zanzibar on ruins of Portuguese church; garrison installed at Kilwa. **1711** Theophilus of Ethiopia d.; succ. Yostos I (—1716) only emperor not of Solomonic blood. **1711-28** Letters from Sultan and other notables of Kilwa sent to Goa to ask Portuguese to return.	**1710** Mauritius abandoned a second time by Dutch; a no-man's land until **1721**.	**1710** South Sea Co. founded. **1711** Abortive British attempt to take Canada. Marlborough disgraced.
		1712 Mogul war of succession between Bahadur's four sons. Treaty of Utrecht gives Britain 30-year monopoly of slave trade to Spanish colonies.
1715 Yostos I taken ill while superintending building of St Antonius's church at Gondar; witchcraft suspected; court revert to earlier practice of living in tents. **1716** David III proclaimed Emperor of Ethiopia (-1721); Yostos I, deposed, d. four days later and buried as a nobleman. **1716** Three Capuchins reach Gondar and are stoned to death.	**1713** Epidemic of smallpox at the Cape. **1714** Portuguese market set up at Zumbo at confluence of R Luangwa with R Zambezi. **1715** Islam first preached in Cameroun at Mandara. First commandos organized against Bushmen. First tax on wine at the Cape. **1716-22** War between the Hanha (or Kakonda) and Portuguese.	**1714-27** George I, King of England. Whig parliament elected. **1715-74** Louis XIV, King of France. **1715** Rebellion in Scotland. **1716** Turks beaten by Prince Eugène at Peterwardein.
		1717 Prussia sells her African colonies to the Dutch. **1718** Lady Mary Wortley Montagu introduces inoculation against smallpox. New Orleans founded. Quadruple Alliance formed.
1719 David III of Ethiopia poisoned; Asma Giorgis Bacaffa' proclaimed; great traveller, warrior and builder	**1719** Many Dominicans withdrawn from Mozambique.	**1719** Law concentrates all French overseas trading companies in 'La Grande Compagnie des Indes'. **1719-48** Muhammad Shah, Great Mogul.

EGYPT & THE SUDAN	NORTHERN AFRICA	WESTERN AFRICA
1720-6 Cherkes Mahomet Bey ruler of Egypt.	**1720** Tunis makes treaty with Spain.	**1720** Fort on Bunce Is., Sierra Leone, captured by a Welsh pirate. *c.* **1720** Ibo town of Onitsha receives Bini immigrants. **1721** English re-established on R Gambia. French capture Arguin.
		c. **1723** Agadja, King of Abomey, invades the kingdom of Allada.
1724-62 Badi Abu Shelukh, King of the Funj.		**1724** Andre Bruë leaves Senegal. Corps of Amazons founded as bodyguard in Dahomey; Great Ardra seized by Dahomey.
	1725 Tunis makes treaty with Austria. **1725-92** Algerian fleet and commerce decline.	*c.* **1725** *Jihad* begun in Futa Jalon by Karamoko Alfa and Ibrahima Suri. **1725-32** Famine in Bornu. **1725** Alfa Ba of Kuranko leads *jihad* in Futa Jalon against pagans: takes title of Almamy.
1726-9 Zulficar Bey, ruler of Egypt.		
	1727 Maulai Ismail d.: struggle for succession: Maulai Ahmad al-Dahabi, 1727-8; 1728-9 Maulai Abd al-Malik; 1729-30 Maulai Ahmad again. **1727** Ahmad Ali al-Rifi unsuccessfully assaults Ceuta.	**1727** Portuguese fort built at Whydah. 7 Feb., Dahomey army seizes European trading centres at Savi and Whydah. Dahomey conquers Sabi, capital of Whydah. Kingdom devastated by Agadja, King of Abomey.
	1728 Treaty between Morocco and Britain: all British slaves liberated in Morocco. Tunis makes treaty with Holland. French send squadron to La Goulette in protest against piracy. Tunis makes new treaty with France.	**1728** Africans wreck English fort on Bunce Is. King of Weme flees to Oyo; King of Whydah applies to Alafin of Oyo for an army; Dahomey defeated; strength of Oyo in cavalry.
1729 Cherkes Mahomet Bey attempts to regain power. **1729-39** Quatuorvirate under Uthman Kiaya rules Egypt.	**1729** Revolt of Ali Pasha in Tunis. **1729-57** Maulai Abdallah b. Ismail: quarrels *re* succession throughout reign.	**1729** Dahomey makes peace; begins to pay tribute to Oyo. **1729-31** Dahomey overrun by Yoruba. **1729-49** Pierre David directs French interests in Senegal. **1730** Growing of groundnuts first described in the Gambia.
1730 Abortive rising of Qasimiyyah in Egypt.		

CENTRAL & SOUTHERN
AFRICA

1730). Galla regiment formed:
any Galla promoted to high
ffice.

c. 1720 Sirhan b. Sirhan, *Annals
of Oman.* South Sea Co. fails.

1721 French annex Mauritius,
renaming it Ile de France.
1721-30 Dutch EIC hold Delagoa
Bay.

1721 Compagnie des Indes taken
over by French government.
Lenoir, director of French
establishments in India. Dutch
buy last Prussian factories in
West Africa.
1723 Compagnie des Indes
re-constituted. Parliament forbids
trade between American Colonies
and India.

1723-69 Ibrahim b.Yusuf,
ultan of Kilwa.
723 Sultan Ibrahim requests
ortuguese Governor of Mozambique
help expel Omani Arabs from
astern Africa.
724 Sultan of Kilwa repeats
equest to Portuguese.

1724 Thomas Benton d., leaving
his fortune to the Worshipful
Co. of Ironmongers, of which one
half was to redeem slaves in
Barbary and Turkey.
1725 8 June, Compagnie des Indes
re-chartered.

1725 Kilindi dynasty of Vuga
ounded by Mbega.

1726 Mahé, Seychelles Is.,
founded by La Bourdonnais.
1727 João Manuel de Noronha,
governor of Angola, deplores
the miserable state of the
missions.

1726 Montevideo founded.
Dean Swift, *Gulliver's Travels.*
1727-60 George II, King of
England.
1727 Slavery first publicly
denounced by the Quakers in
England.

727 First Mazrui deputy-
overnor of Mombasa; Sultan of
ate sends embassy to Goa asking
iceroy to expel Omani Arabs
rom eastern Africa.

728 *Utendi wa Tambuka,*
ated Swahili
oetical MS., but probably
omposed in the 17th c.
ortuguese reoccupy Pate and,
5 March, Mombasa; 28 Aug.,
ortuguese treaty with Pate.

729 25 April, Portuguese besieged
y Omani fleet in Fort Jesus,
Mombasa; 14 Aug., Portuguese
vacuate Pate; 26 Nov., Portuguese
inally evacuate Mombasa.

1729 First Turkish printing press.

730 Asma Giorgis (Bacaffa) d.
mpress Mentuab regent for
yasu II. Mombasa sends
elegation to Oman to ask for
governor: Muhammad b. Said
l-Ma'amri appointed; small
arrison sent to Zanzibar.
730-5 Iyasu II, Emperor of
thiopia: last eighteenth-century
mperor to exercise real authority.

1730-70 Andriambelomasina,
Merina ruler, fights off
Sakalava expansion.
? *c.* 1730 Yao make first contacts
with Arab traders on the coast.
c. 1730 Trekking into the
interior of the Cape begins.
c. 1730-54 Ratsimilaho, first
King of the Betsimisaraka.

1730-47 British forts in W Africa
given a subsidy by Parliament.
1730-44 Uthman III, Ottoman
Sultan.

EGYPT & THE SUDAN	NORTHERN AFRICA	WESTERN AFRICA
	1731 French send another squadron to La Goulette.	1731-42 Opoku Ware, Asantehene. *c.* 1731-43 War between Bornu and Kano.
	1732 Abortive Moroccan attempt to take Ceuta. Spain regains Oran (-1792) and Mers el-Kebir.	
	1734-*c.*1833 al-Zayyani, historian.	1734 Sultan of Bornu becomes overlord of Kano.
	1735 Ali Pasha besieges Qayrawan; effective ruler of Tunis.	*c.* 1735 Cowries the ordinary currency in Benin. *c.* 1735-50 Yorina Bussa, founder of the Amirate of Borgu.
1736 Quatuorvirate massacred; triumvirate under Uthman Bey (-1743).		
	1737/8-1815 Ahmad al-Tijani, founder of Tijaniyyah order.	1737-41 First Moravian mission on Gold Coast and at Anecho. 1737 War between Ashanti and Wassaw. *c.* 1738-47 Further Yoruba raids on Dahomey.
1738 Ethiopian embassy to Cairo to ask for new Abuna humiliated and imprisoned in Cairo. 1739 Qazdughiliyyah attempt to murder Uthman Bey: Uthman Bey defeated near Asyut. 1739-52 Abu al-Qasim, Sultan of Darfur: unsuccessful war against Wadai: expeditions against Rizeigat and Musabaat Arabs.		
	1740 Husain Bey murdered; Ali Pasha succ. as Bey of Tunis (—1756).	
		1742 Ashanti attack Danish fort at Ningo. 1742-7 Jakob Capitein, Dutch Reformed missionary, on the Gold Coast. 1742-70 Babari dan Ibn Ashe, King of Gobir; raids Katsina, Kano and Shirra. 1743 Ashanti overrun Accra and besiege Christiansborg Castle. *c.* 1744 or 1754 Uthman dan Fodio b. at Marata in Gobir.
1744-54 Ibrahim, commandant of the Janissaries, ruler of Egypt. 1744 Ethiopia attacks Sennar: defeated by Funj with Fur allies.		
		1745 English destroy French fort at Albreda, R Gambia. Dahomey cavalry defeated by Ashanti musketeers. French fort founded at Podor.

ASTERN AFRICA	CENTRAL & SOUTHERN AFRICA	OTHER COUNTRIES
		1731-42 Dupleix, Governor of Chandernagore.
		1732 John Barbot, *Description of the Coasts of North and South Guinea.* British colony of Georgia founded.
	1733 *Presidio* established at Soyo to prevent British and French trade. 1734-44 Bertrand Mahé de la Bourdonnais, Governor of Ile de France and Bourbon: sugar industry established.	
1735 or 1744 Ethiopia at war with Funj kingdom; Iyasu II defeated before Sennar.		1735 Russo-Turkish War.
1736 Total eclipse of the sun gives rise to prophecies of the fall of the Royal House of Ethiopia.	1736-42 George Schmidt, first protestant missionary at the Cape, evangelizes Hottentots.	1736-47 Nadir Shah of Persia.
		1738 Methodist revival begun by Wesley. First spinning-machine invented in England.
1739 Royal hunt to inaugurate manhood of Ethiopian Emperor Iyasu II. 1739-46 Muhammad b.Uthman al-Mazrui appointed governor of Mombasa; members of the Mazrui family governors and effective rulers of Mombasa until 1837.		1739 French East India Co. request for a base at Mombasa refused by Portugal. English courts reverse opinion of law officers of the Crown that slaves become free by being in England or by being baptized.
	c. 1740 Nganda Vilonda succ. Kanyembo as governor of L. Mweru region. Bemba settle in NE Rhodesia. Lunda kingdom of Kazembe founded. 1741 Alleged French East India Co. plan to seize Kerimba Is.	1741 Slavery in Brazil condemned by Pope Benedict XIV. 1742-54 Dupleix governor of French India.
1744 Muhammad b.Uthman al-Mazrui, Governor of Mombasa, declares Mombasa independent of Oman.	1744 Queen of Matamba attacks Portuguese in Ndongo.	1744 Further French East India Co. request for Mombasa refused by Portugal. 1744-8 War of the Austrian succession.
1745-75 Amba Iyasu, King of Shoa. 1745 Embassy from Oman recovers control of Mombasa.	1745 Governor of Mozambique reports that civil war in Oman had spread along eastern African coast. Majunga, Madagascar founded.	1745 J.B.N.D. d'Apres de Mannevillette, *Neptune Oriental*: first systematic collection of charts of eastern Africa and

EGYPT & THE SUDAN	NORTHERN AFRICA	WESTERN AFRICA

WESTERN AFRICA

*c.*1746 English Fort Vernon built at Prampram.

1747 Funj at war with Musabaat Arabs.
1748 Musabaat Arabs routed by Funj general Abu al-Kaylak: appointed governor of Kordofan.

1747 Dahomey finally conquered by Yoruba of Oyo.

1749-53 Senegal coast explored by Michel Adanson.
*c.*1749-54 Dan Juma, first Amir and founder of Gumel.
post **1750** Yoruba immigrants entering region of Porto Novo.
*c.*1750-67 War between the Ewe of Anlo and Krepi.
1750 Igbira establish kingdom at Panda in Nassarana.

1751-6 Thomas Thomson, Anglican chaplain to Cape Coast Castle, evangelizes among the Fante.
1752 First SPG missionaries arrive at Cape Coast Castle.

1752 Abu al-Qasim, Sultan of Darfur, killed in campaign against Kordofan.

1753 Portuguese post at Bissau re-established: fort rebuilt.
1753-70 Second English trading fort built at Anomabu.

1755-72 Ali Bey al-Ghazzawi, ruler; Houmam b.Yusuf al-Hawardi put down.

1757-90 Maulai Muhammad b. Abdallah, Sharif of Morocco: equilibrium restored.

1757 Abortive French attempt to take Cape Coast Castle.
1757-61 Jakob Protten chaplain at Christiansborg Castle.
1758 English treaty with Bai Samma, King of North Bullom.
British, having taken Senegal, rule it with Gambia as Senegambia.

1759-82 Ali b. Husain, Bey of Tunis.
Majunga, Madagascar, founded.

EASTERN AFRICA	CENTRAL & SOUTHERN AFRICA	OTHER COUNTRIES
		the Indian Ocean. Young Pretender's Rebellion in Scotland.
1746 Muhammad b. Uthman al-Mazrui murdered at Mombasa; his brother Ali made governor; Abdallah b.Said al-Busaidi, Governor of Zanzibar. 1747 Ali b.Uthman al-Mazrui seizes Pemba Is. 1748 Dutch begin to trade sporadically on the eastern coast.	1746 Plague of locusts at the Cape. 1746-59 Synod of Dutch Reformed Church at the Cape.	1746-73 Wahhabi state established in C Arabia by Muhammad b. Saud. 1746 French conquer Madras. 1747 Battle of Fontenoy. 1748 Peace of Aix-la-Chapelle. 1749 Ahmad b.Said al-Busaidi usurps throne of Oman and Muscat (-1783).
c.1750 Wallo Galla begin to be converted to Islam. Three Franciscans reach Gondar from Europe and return without encouragement. c. post 1750 Much of ruling class of Ugogo arrive from Uhehe. Sagara and Kaguru chieftainships organized.	c.1750 Bakweri (Bakwileh) arrive in Buea region. Marovcay, Boina capital, the largest town in Madagascar. Tembe disintegrate as a result of civil war and migrate southwards from near Delagoa Bay. Andriamanalina unites Betsileo in a kingdom. 1751-71 Ryk Tulbagh, Governor of the Cape. 1752 Administration of Mozambique separated from Goa: Francisco de Melo e Castro first Governor of Mozambique, Zambezia and Sofala. 1753 Laws relating to slavery codified at the Cape. 1753-8 Dom Antonio Alvares de Cunha, governor of Angola; describes colony as rotten, vicious and corrupt.	1750 Company of Merchants trading to Africa established by Parliament. 1750-77 Joseph, King of Portugal; Pombal, chief minister.
1753 Ali b.Uthman al-Mazrui murdered while on an expedition to seize Zanzibar: his cousin Masud b.Nasr governor of Mombasa (-1779).		
1755 Iyasu II d.; Ioas Emperor of Ethiopia (-1769), with Empress Mentuab as regent; court dominated by the Galla; monarchy in collapse.	1755 Smallpox epidemic at the Cape.	1754-7 Uthman II, Ottoman Sultan. 1755 Earthquake in Lisbon; many national and African records destroyed in the Tôrre do Tombo. Sermon by Bishop Hayter against the slave trade. 1756-63 Seven Years War. 1756 Basra seized by Ahmad b.Said al-Busaidi of Muscat and Oman. 1757-74 Mustafa III, Ottoman Sultan. 1758-9 Jesuits expelled from Portugal and its colonies.
1759 Kilwa sends embassy to Mozambique to ask help of Portuguese to expel Omani Arabs from E Africa.	1759 Presidio of St José d'Encoge established in the Leje valley. 1759-1803 642,000 slaves shipped from Luanda and Benguela to Brazil.	1759 J.B. Bourguignon d'Anville, Mémoires concernant les rivières de l'intérieur de l'Afrique, Paris. Samuel Johnson, History of Rasselas, Prince of Abissinia. 1759-1833 William Wilberforce,

EGYPT & THE SUDAN	NORTHERN AFRICA	WESTERN AFRICA
		*c.*1760-92 Perekule (or Pepple) King of Bonny. *c.*1760 Biu at war with Fulani; Oyo invades Borgu, but defeated; solemn celebration of Bebe (jubilee) festival for 3 years by Oyo. Sarkin Gobir Babari captures Birnin Zamfara; 15 year siege of Kiawa; Katsina subjected. 1760 15 April, Ahanta attack Dixcove at Dutch instigation; 18 April, town taken; 19 April, fort invested until 1761.
*c.*1761 Attempt to depose Badi, King of Funj. 1761—*c.* 1837 Makk Nasr al-Din, King of Berber.		
		1763-79 Senegambia a British Crown Colony. 1763 Catholic mission in Gorée.
		1764-9 Jakob Protten again at Christiansborg.
		1765 New constitution for Senegambia. 1765-83 Dutch maintain cotton plantations at Axim and Shama. 1765-1816 Philip Quaque, first Ghanaian Anglican deacon. 1766 English treaty with King Sumana in Sierra Leone. New fort of S. José built at Bissau.
	1767 Treaty of friendship and commerce between Morocco and Spain. 1768 French trading centre at Bizerta.	1768-76 Babba Zaki, King of Kano; establishes royal guard of musketeers. 1768 Yalunka, driven out of Futa Jalon, set up fortress town at Falaba. Moravian missionaries arrive on Guinea coast. 1768-83 English build Fort Apollonia at Beyin. 1769 J.F. Landolphe's first visit to Benin.
1769 Ali Bey, mentioned in Friday prayers as ruler of Egypt, subject to Turkey. Hamaj Muhammad Abu al-Kaylak, deposes Nasir, King of the Funj: Ismail made King (-1776) but Abu al-Kaylak real ruler (d.1772). Ali Bey makes alliance with Catherine II of Russia against Sultan Mustafa III.	1769 Venetian fleet attacks Tunis in reprisal for privateering. Maulai Muhammad forces Portuguese to abandon Mazagan; fails to evict Spaniards from Melilla, Ceuta, Peñon de Alhucemas and Peñon de la Gomera.	

EASTERN AFRICA	CENTRAL & SOUTHERN AFRICA	OTHER COUNTRIES
		advocate of the abolition of slavery.
1760 Kilwa allowed unrestricted trade with Mozambique. c.1760 Meru finally overcome Mweko.	1760 Jesuits expelled from Angola and Mozambique. Jacobus Cortsee crosses Orange R. Governor of Mozambique grants Sultan of Kilwa the right to buy grain from Mozambique. Abortive Portuguese attempt to re-establish market at Dambarare. c.1760 Kazembe III Ilunga succ.	1760-1820 George III, King of England. 1760 200,000 slaves in Virginia; blacks constitute 30% of the population in the thirteen English colonies. Sermon by Bishop Warburton against the slave trade.
	1762 Batavian sugar canes and mangoes introduced into Ile de France.	
c. 1763-80 Kyambugu, ruler of Buganda; first record of imports from east coast in Buganda. 1763-70 Mwana Khadija, Queen of Pate.		1763 Treaty of Paris ends Seven Years War; Senegal returned to France but Gorée retained by Britain. 1763-5 George Grenville, Prime Minister. 1764-1834 William Carey missionary. 1764 140,000 negroes in Jamaica.
1765 Further embassy from Kilwa to Mozambique; a 'Prince' Kombo goes to Mozambique to ask Portuguese to re-take Mombasa.	1765 Embassy from Kilwa to Mozambique asking Portuguese to expel Omani Arabs and return to their former possessions.	1765-7 Clive reforms Indian administration. 1765 23 March, Stamp Act passed. Hargreaves' 'Spinning Jenny' invented.
	1766 Blackwood (Albizzia lebbek) introduced into Ile de France.	1766-9 Bougainville's voyages in the South Seas.
	1767-70 De Mandave, administrator of French possessions in Madagascar. c. 1768 Yao on L. Malawi trading with Kilwa.	1768 First Secretary of State for the Colonies, Wills Hill, Earl of Hillsborough, (later Marquess of Downshire) appointed in Britain. 1768-1838 Zachary Macaulay. 1768-78 Captain Cook's voyages.
1769-1855 Period of masafent, or regional kings, in Ethiopia. 1769-72 James Bruce of Kinnaird in Ethiopia. 1769 March, Emperor Ioas murdered; succ. Yohannes II shortly dies; Takla Haimanot II, Emperor (-1777) Ras Michael Sehul expelled from court. Ibrahim b.Yusuf, Sultan of Kilwa, d.; succ. by his son	1769-72 Desroches, Governor of Ile de France.	1769 Muhammad Ali b. at Kavalla, Macedonia (-1849). Granville Sharp, The Injustice and dangerous tendency of tolerating slavery in England. French East India Co. dissolved. Napoleon Buonaparte b.

EGYPT & THE SUDAN	NORTHERN AFRICA	WESTERN AFRICA

1770 Ali Bey adds Syria and Arabia to Egypt: expedition to Mecca to settle Hashimite succession.

*c.***1770** Ashanti seize Gomba and enforce tribute until **1874**. Massacre of chiefs of Obutong by Akwa Akpa.

1771 Moroccans besiege Melilla.

1772 Ali Bey driven out of Egypt by Abu al-Dhahab, his son-in-law; Abu al-Dhahab is recognized as Ottoman Viceroy; James Bruce arrives in Cairo from Gondar.
*c.***1772** Hashim, Sultan of the Musabaat, takes Kordofan.
1773 Ali Bey d.

1772-93 French factory on Gambia Is., Sierra Leone.

1774 All Christian slaves liberated in Morocco. Spain declares war on Morocco: Spanish forts abortively attacked by Moroccans.

1775-98 Duumvirate of Ibrahim Bey and Murad Bey.

1775 Slaves in Algiers henceforward held only by the state and not by private individuals. Spanish expedition against Algiers.

1776 King of Funj deposed by Badi wad Regab: Funj kingdom in rapid decline.

*c.***1776** Islam introduced into Dahomey by Yoruba.
1776-84 Ewe war renewed.
1776 Abd al-Qadir, Terobe

EASTERN AFRICA	CENTRAL & SOUTHERN AFRICA	OTHER COUNTRIES
(1769-71); July, abortive Portuguese expedition to recover Mombasa leaves Mozambique, but passes Mombasa and goes to Malindi.		
1770-1803 Joseph, Abuna of Ethiopia.	**1770** Pierre Poivre, Intendant of Ile de France, introduces spice-bearing trees from Moluccas.	
1770-3 Umar, Sultan of Pate.		
1770 Jan., Portuguese expedition returns to Mozambique; March or April, internal troubles in Mombasa: independence proclaimed. Kilwa expels Omani governor.		
1771 Emperor of Ethiopia fights three battles against Ras Michael at Sarbakuse. Sultan of Kilwa deposed for drunkenness; his brother Yusuf b.Ibrahim, succ.	**1771-85** J. van Plettenburg, Governor of the Cape.	**1771** Egyptians take Damascus.
1772 Letter from Comoro Is. of a brother of the Sultan of Pate: first recorded Comorian Swahili prose MS.; Sultan of Kilwa deposed for incompetence: Hasan b.Ibrahim succ.	**1772-6** De Ternay, Governor of Ile de France.	**1772** Lord Mansfield's judgement disallows status of slavery in Britain.
1773 Sultan of Kilwa attempts to increase local taxation; forced to flee by a popular revolt; returns with an army but agrees not to fight and not to increase taxation. Governor of Ile de France recommends scheme to place a pretender in Mombasa with a view to setting up French base.	**1773-86** Benyowsky, a Hungarian, organizes colony at Antongil Bay, Madagascar, and declares himself independent.	**1773-1803** Abd al-Aziz b. Muhammad b.Saud greatly increases Wahhabi domains.
1773-6 Fumoluti b.Sheikh, Sultan of Pate.		**1773** Pope Clement XIV, by bull *Dominus ac Redemptor,* suppresses the Jesuits; 300 missions and *c.* 3,000 missionaries affected. The Boston Tea-Party.
	1774 Following numerous raids, Godlieb Opperman organizes commandos against Bushmen and Hottentots.	**1774** James Bruce returns to England and has his accounts of Ethiopia disbelieved. John Wesley, *Thoughts on Slavery.* Society of Friends decrees expulsion of a Friend for engaging in the slave trade.
	1774-6 War between the Portuguese and Mbailundu, Ndulu and Bihe.	**1774-89** Abd al-Hamid I, Ottoman Sultan.
1775-1808 Asfaha Wasan II, King of Shoa. *c. post* **1775** Masai expand, reaching Ngong Hills.	**1775-81** William Bolt holds Delagoa Bay in name of the Austrian Asiatic Co. *c.* **1775** Palo, chief of the Ama-Xhosa: tribe splits into Eastern Xhosa (Galeka) and Western Xhosa (Rarabe or Gaikas). Cape Town (Kaapstad) has 12,000 houses. Isihanaka organizes kingdom near Tamatave and Ivondro; Fohiloa also set up a kingdom in the same region.	**1775** Thomas Paine, *African Slavery in America.* Omani fleet burnt in Muscat harbour through neglect of crews. First efficient steam engine made by James Watt. *c.*1775 500,000 slaves in French West Indies.
1776 14 Sept., Treaty between Sultan of Kilwa and French slavetrader J.V.Morice to supply 1,000 slaves annually for 100	*c.*1776 First direct contacts between Dutch and Xhosa on Zeekse R. 1776 J.V. Morice brings first	**1776** Resolution in British Parliament that slavery is contrary to the law of God lost. American War of Independence:

EGYPT & THE SUDAN	NORTHERN AFRICA	WESTERN AFRICA
		Fulani (d. 1788), overthrows Denianke dynasty of Futa Toro; chosen Almamy; leads *jihads* against Walo, Jolof, Bondu and Galam.
1777 Rising of students in Al-Azhar against misappropriation of Waqf revenues by beys.		**1777-95** Bawa Jan Gwarzo, Sarkin of Gobir: encourages Uthman dan Fodio.
		1778-84 Holy Ghost Fathers in Senegal. **1778** Fernando Po ceded by Portugal to Spain; attempt at development a disaster. J.F. Landolphe's second visit to Benin with Beauvais, botanist. War between Dahomey and Yoruba; King of Appa flees to Weme; Allada beaten back by Oyo. **1779** Jan., French reoccupy St Louis, Senegal; Feb., and raze Fort James, R Gambia; May, British reoccupy R Gambia, and take Gorée.
	1780 Treaty of Aranjuez, of friendship and commerce, ends Hispano-Moroccan hostilities: boundaries of Spanish Moroccan possessions defined.	**1780-2** Desultory war between British and Dutch on the coast: Ahanta armed by Dutch against Dixcove.
	1781-2 Tijaniyyah order founded.	**1781-2** Dutch fort at Teme abandoned.
	1782-1814 Hammuda b.Ali, Bey of Tunis. **1783** and **1784** Spanish bombard Algiers. **1783** United States at war with Algiers; pays tribute to the pirates.	**1782** Spain abandons Fernando Po. **1782-5** British hold Dutch forts at Apam and Beraku. **1783** The Gambia ceases to be a colony and is placed under the Committee of the Company of Merchants. Third Companhia de Cabo Verde e Guine founded.
1784-5 War between Kordofan and Darfur.	**1784** Venice bombards Sousse.	**1784** Badagri invaded by Dahomey. Keta, last commercial fort set up in

...ASTERN AFRICA	CENTRAL & SOUTHERN AFRICA	OTHER COUNTRIES
ears. Dutch trader refused ...laves in Kilwa and Zanzibar. ...nnual caravan said to be ...rossing from Kilwa to Angola. ...776-1809 Bwana Fumomadi the ...reat, Sultan of Pate. ...777 French trading agency set ...p in Kilwa (-1781). ...777-9 Solomon II, usurper, ...mperor of Ethiopia.	slaves from Zanzibar to Ile de France. 1776-9 La Guirane, governor of Ile de France. 1777 Dominicans expelled from Mozambique. 1778 Boundary between Dutch and Xhosa demarcated on Fish R by Governor van Plettenberg.	4 July, Declaration of Independence. Adam Smith, *The Wealth of Nations*. Society of Friends makes manumission obligatory for any slaves owned by Friends. 1777-1816 Maria I, Queen of Portugal. 1778 States of Rhode Is., Connecticut, Philadelphia, Pennsylvania, Delaware and Virginia prohibit the import of slaves. 1778-1813 Sir Joseph Banks, President of the Royal Society, botanist.
...779-84 Takla Giorgis, Emperor ...f Ethiopia. ...779-80 Abdallah b.Muhammad ...l-Mazrui, Governor of Mombasa.	1779 Deputation of Cape Patriots to Netherlands to demand a written constitution and self-government. War between Dutch and Xhosa: Adriaan van Jaarsveld drives Xhosa back across Fish R, capturing 5,300 cattle. 1779-87 De Souillac Governor of Ile de France.	
....1780 Awallini dynasty of ...laggaro founded. ...780-1814 Ahmad b. Muhammad ...l-Mazrui, Governor of Mombasa.	1780-8 Franciscan and Benedictine missionaries working in Kongo. *c.*1780-1800 Some 10,000 slaves exported annually from Mozambique to S America.	1780 Britain abolishes office of Secretary of State for the Colonies; duties placed under War Office. Maria Theresa of Austria d.: her silver *thaler* (dollar) continues to be minted for export to Africa and Arabia with this date. Irish agitate for Home Rule.
....1781 J.V. Morice d., but French ...lave trade at Kilwa continues. ...781 Uthman dan Fodio becomes ...utor to the royal family of ...obir. F. Le Vaillant travelling ...long coasts of western Africa. ...)yo war with Dahomey, demanding ...ncreased tribute from Dahomey.	1781 Portugal gains Delagoa Bay from Austria.	
	1783 Famine in Luanda. Portuguese build fort at Cabinda. Portuguese operations against the Dembos. Cape patriots dissatisfied with minor reforms.	1783 Said b. Ahmad al-Busaidi, ruler of Oman and Muscat. Britain recognizes American independence. 3 Sept., Peace of Versailles. France recovers Gorée and Senegal with other possessions. Quakers petition Lord North to abolish slave trade and set up committee to press abolition. 1783-1801 William Pitt the Younger, Prime Minister.
...784 Takla Giorgis retires into ...xile; Ethiopia in the hands of	1784 F. Le Vaillant penetrates to Namaqualand from the Cape.	1784 'Meeting for Sufferings' publishes *The Case of our*

EGYPT & THE SUDAN	NORTHERN AFRICA	WESTERN AFRICA
1784 Civil war in Funj: Arbagi destroyed.		in W Africa, built by the Danes. 1784-9 Quarrels and dissension amongst Portuguese in Guinea.
	1785 Venetians destroy La Goulette.	
1786 Ottoman fleet under Hasan Pasha sent to assert Ottoman authority in Egypt: 10 Aug., Hasan Pasha arrives in Cairo, taking control of Lower Egypt; duumvirate in control of Upper Egypt.	1786 Moroccan treaty with USA and commercial convention with Kingdom of the Two Sicilies. Moroccan specie coined in Seville.	1786-1803 French fort at Amoku. 1786 Weme destroyed by Dahomey.
1787 Hasan Pasha withdraws from Egypt, leaving Ismail Pasha as viceroy: duumvirate resumes power (-1798). 1787-1802 Abd al-Rahman al-Rashid, Sultan of the Fur: settles capital on L. Tendelti, present El Fasher: governor of Kordofan shortly driven out by Musabaat.	1787 Plague kills 17,000 in Algiers. USA pays Morocco $10,000 for freedom from molestation by privateers.	1787 9 May, 400 freed slave colonists landed in St George's Bay; settlement made at Granville Town. Danish fort of Augustaborg built at Teshe. Dahomey raids Porto Novo (Ajashe).
1788 Funj Kings henceforward prisoners of Hamaj viziers. John Ledyard, preparing to cross Africa from Nile to Niger, d. in Cairo.		1788-92 French slaving depot at Benin (Gwatto). 1788 British settlement at Sierra Leone bought from a local chief. Danes establish plantation at Kpomko.
	1789 Ahmad al-Tijani moves to Fez. Lucas's expedition to explore the Niger driven back to Tripoli.	1789 Smallpox epidemic at Cape Coast Castle; slaves compulsorily vaccinated. J.F. Landolphe's third visit to Benin. Dahomey takes Ketu, and over 2,000 prisoners. St Louis, Senegal, sends *cahier* of grievances to French Estates-General. 1789-91 Daniel Houghton leaves Gambia for Bambouk. c.1789 Catholic faith firmly established in Warri.
	1790 Treaty between Tunis and Spain. 1790-2 Maulai Yazid b.Muhammad, Sharif of Morocco: ferocious persecution of Christians, Jews, and even Muslims: war declared on Spain. *c. post* 1790 Tijaniyyah order spreads rapidly in Mauritania.	c. 1790 Gidgid dynasty of Bedde begins to the established. Duke Ephraim (Effium) founds Duke's Town.

EASTERN AFRICA	CENTRAL & SOUTHERN AFRICA	OTHER COUNTRIES
great lords; economic decline: building in brick and stone only a memory; Iyasu III, Emperor -1788) again dwells in a tent. Saif b. Ahmad al-Busaidi, pretender to Oman and Muscat, attempts to stir up rebellion on eastern African coast. J. Crassons de Medeuil visits Kilwa: 4,193 slaves exported by French in preceding 3 years.	Fort at Cabinda destroyed by the French.	*fellow creatures, the oppressed Africans*. Pitt's India Bill.
1785 Saif b. Ahmad al-Busaidi d. at Lamu; 23 Jan., Ahmad b.Said the younger takes possession of Fort Jesus, Mombasa, for his father; 4 Nov., restoration of Portuguese fort at Kilwa completed by Omani governor.	1785 Jan., Cape Patriots again petition the States-General.	1785 US ships *Maria* and *Dauphin* captured by Algerian privateers near Gibraltar. 14 Apr., Louis XVI creates new French East India Company.
	1786 23 May., Benyowski killed in battle with French. Kingship disappears in Loango.	
	1787-1810 Andrianampoinimerina, King of the Merina, initiates policy of conquering the whole island; Betsilio, Benanozano, and Sihanaka occupied; Sakalava resist.	1787 Society for the Abolition of the Slave Trade founded in London.
1788 Ali, a chief of the Yajju, (Warra Sheikh) Galla, founds kingdom of Begemder in C and NW Ethiopia. Roussillon visits eastern African ports to settle slave prices for French traders.	1788 War between Portuguese and Marquis of Mosul.	1788 Wilberforce's anti-slavery motion in Parliament; his 'Ten Points' drawn up by William Wyndham Grenville; motion supported by William Pitt. 9 June, Association for Promoting the Discovery of the Interior Parts of Africa' founded in London.
1789-94 Hezekias, Emperor of Ethiopia. 1789 Mosque at Kipumbwi, capital of the Diwans of Mkwaja, built.	1789 Xhosa cross Fish R; allowed to remain 'without prejudice to the ownership of Europeans'.	1789-1807 Salim III, Ottoman Sultan. 1789 30 April., Washington elected President of USA. 5 May, French Estates-General meet: 14 July, Fall of the Bastille signalizes beginning of French Revolution. *The Interesting Life of Olandah Equiano or Gustavus Vassa, the African, written by himself,* London.
c.1790 Buganda greatly expands its frontiers and incorporates Buddu.	1790 Benguela Highlands mapped by Pinheiro de Lacerda. Marquis of Mosul tries to seize Luanda. 1790-1 David Charpentier de Cossigny governor of Ile de France. c.1790 Lunda empire at the height of its trading power. Kazembe Lukwesa Mpanga makes trade contacts with Tete.	1790 14 July, Feast of Reason in Paris. James Bruce, *Travels in the Highlands of Ethiopia.* F.Le Vaillant, *Voyage dans l'Intérieur de l'Afrique dans les années 1780-1785.*

EGYPT & THE SUDAN	NORTHERN AFRICA	WESTERN AFRICA
		1791 Crow visits Benin; Houghton killed at the R Kaarta: his report shows the Niger course. *c.***1791** King Pepple of Bonny seizes New Calabar. **1792** 1,190 negroes settled in Sierra Leone from Nova Scotia. British destroy French station at Benin (Gwatto). Oyo empire at its greatest extent. **1792-3** Abortive British attempt to found an agricultural colony on Bolama, Cape Verde Is.
	1792-1822 Maulai Sulaiman b. Muhammad, Sharif of Morocco: succession contested until 1796.	
1793-6 William George Brown visits Darfur from Asyut.	**1793** Further American ships taken by Algiers. Peace treaty between Algiers and Portugal. **1793-4** Sidi Muhammad b.Abd al-Rahman, founder of Rahmaniyyah order, d.	**1793** Kru men start seeking work in Freetown. **1793-4** James Watt and Matthew Winterbottom reach Timbo and Labé and return by the Rio Nunez. **1794-5 and 1796-9** Zachary Macaulay, Governor of Sierra Leone. **1794** Sept., French bombard Freetown.
		1795 Agwaragi of Katsina (1784-1801) defeats Bawa Jan Gwarzo of Gobir (1777-95) near Kiawa. **1795-7** Mungo Park reaches Segu and the Niger from Gambia.
	1796 US treaties with Tunis and Tripoli: Tripoli paid $83,000 a year for the safe conduct of US ships.	**1796** Wesleyan missionaries start work in Sierra Leone.
	1797 US treaty with Algiers: captives ransomed for $642,500 with annual payment of $21,600. **1797-8** Frederic Hornemann visits Siwa, Aujila, Mourzouk and Tripoli.	**1797** Capt. Hugh Crow wrecked off Bonny. French fort at Whydah evacuated.

EASTERN AFRICA | CENTRAL & SOUTHERN AFRICA | OTHER COUNTRIES

1791 6 May, Canada Constitution Act. 22 Aug., Negro rising in San Domingo. Revolt of slaves in Haiti. Sierra Leone Co. established to govern colony.

1792 Marquis of Mosul defeated by troops brought from Brazil and the Azores. Quarrel over succession leads to the division of the Douala into two sections. 13 March, 'Patriots' take control of Bourbon and the Ile de France. Moravians establish mission at Genadendal.

1792 499 petitions to Parliament against slavery. 2 Apr., Wilberforce wins anti-slavery motion by 230 to 85. 31 May, William Carey's sermon at Nottingham, 'An inquiry into the obligation of Christians to convert the heathen'.
French government abolishes all religious orders and societies.
Baptist Missionary Society founded in England.
1792-1816 Prince João, Regent of Portugal.
1793 Louis XVI of France executed.

1793 Bisa tribesmen trading with the Yao and with Goncalo Pereira, 5 days N of Tete. Apr., further hostility with Xhosa; Aug., peace made again.

1794-5 Takla Giorgis of Ethiopia: third restoration.

*c.*1794 Tembe occupying areas in Lubombo range.
1794 Ile de France ignores the abolition of slavery decreed by the French National Assembly.
1795 11 June, Britain occupies Cape on behalf of Prince of Orange. Sept., -1803, Feb., first British occupation: Lord Macartney Governor; many mild reforms. 16 Sept., following resistance, Dutch agree to capitulation of Rustenburg. Chokwe first mentioned between Bihe and the Lwena. Ovimbundu traders reaching Lwena in eastern Angola. June, burgers of Swellendamm elect own National Assembly. *c.*1795 Slaves outnumber Europeans at the Cape. **1795-6** Graaff-Reinet holds out but capitulates 17 Aug., 1796. *post* 1795 Trade between the Lozi and Angola.
1796 1 Oct., eclipse observed during the coronation of Mibambwe III Santabyo of Rwanda. Manuel Gaetano Pereira settles in Kazembe country. Portuguese build fort at Espirito Santo, Delagoa Bay; destroyed by the French.

1794 Britain takes Seychelles from the French. French National Assembly frees all slaves without compensation.

1795 Baeda Mariam II of Ethiopia.
1795-6 Takla Giorgis of Ethiopia: fourth restoration.

1795 Dutch surrender Ceylon and west coast of Sumatra to Britain. London Missionary Society founded.

1796-7 Solomon III of Ethiopia.

1796 Glasgow Missionary Society (Presbyterian) founded. Buonaparte in Italy.

1797-8 Ionas of Ethiopia.
1797 Sultan of Kilwa, Abu Bakr b.Hasan, protests against the seizure of a Kilwa vessel by the French.
1797-1814 Semakokiro, Kabaka of Buganda: Indian calico, cowries and copper bracelets imported

1797 South African Society for the Extension of the Kingdom of Christ founded at Rotterdam (Dutch Reformed Church).

1798 19 May, Napoleon Buonaparte sails with fleet from Toulon to conquer Egypt; 21 July, Battle of The Pyramids: Cairo taken; 1 Aug., Nelson destroys French fleet in Aboukir Bay; 21 Oct., rising in Cairo against French quelled. 25 July, Diwan of Cairo constituted by French; 5-20 Oct., general Diwan sits as advisory council with delegations from all parts of Egypt.

1799 Napoleon Buonaparte attacks Syria from Egypt; 24 May, checked by British at Acre; returns to Egypt, and defeats Turks at Aboukir, 24 July; 22 Aug., leaves secretly for France; Kléber left in command.

1799 Treaty of peace, trade, navigation and fishing between Morocco and Spain. USA fails to make treaty payments to Algiers, Tunis and Tripoli.

1798 10 June, Mungo Park returns to the Gambia, whence to the West Indies and England.

EASTERN AFRICA

from the coast; regular trade
conducted through Karagwe and
Nyamwezi country.
1798-9 Takla Giorgis of
Ethiopia: fifth restoration.

1799-1800 Demetrius of Ethiopia.

1798 27 Feb., ambassadors
from Kazembe at Tete seeking
trade relations. 3 July, Francisco
Lacerda's expedition leaves Tete
with fifty soldiers to cross Africa.
18 Oct., Lacerda d. at Kazembe
capital: Francisco Pinto takes over
expedition. 20 Nov., to 1799 9 Dec.,
Sir F. Dundas, Governor of Cape
Colony. Portuguese slave trading
centre at Delagoa Bay (— 1823).
1799 Dutch Reformed missionaries
working among Hottentots. First
London Missionary Society (LMS)
missionaries on Zak R. Famine in
Luanda. Jaga states of Ndulu,
Mbailundu, Bihe, Wambu, Ciyaka
and Ngalanga first mentioned.
late 18th c. Timbuka coalesce to
form a chiefdom.

1798 Malta taken by Napoleon
Buonaparte: 2,000 Muslim slaves
released.

1799 Mungo Park, *Travels in the
Interior of Africa.*
Napoleon Buonaparte, First Consul.
Church Missionary Society (CMS)
founded.
1799-1838 René Caillié, explorer.

EGYPT, THE SUDAN & NORTHERN AFRICA

1800 24 Jan., Kléber signs convention at al-Arish for evacuation of French troops. 20 March, Kléber defeats Turks and Mamluks at Heliopolis and, 14 June, is assassinated in Cairo.
1800/1-1840/1 Muhammad Fadhl, Sultan of the Fur: recovers Kordofan for 7 years.

1801 21 March, French defeated by British and Turks at Alexandria; 18 June, Cairo surrendered by French; 3 Sept., Alexandria surrendered; French evacuate; Khusrau Pasha, Viceroy of Egypt (-1803). Muhammad Ali arrives in Egypt with small force of local levies from Kavalla. Bey of Tripoli insists on increase of payment of safe-conduct money by USA.; Four Years War ensues.

1803 Albanian troops in Egypt mutiny over arrears of pay; commander shortly assassinated and succ. by Muhammad Ali.

1804 March, Muhammad Ali expels Mamluks from Cairo; Khurshid Pasha Viceroy of Egypt (-1805). Muhammad Kurra, real political power in Fur kingdom, murdered. Muhammad bu Dali, chief of the Darqawiyyah order, revolts against Uthman, Bey of Constantine.
1805 12 May, Muhammad Ali (1805-48) installed as Viceroy of Egypt: July, confirmed by the Porte.

1807 March, British occupy Alexandria briefly. Algiers

WESTERN AFRICA

1800 F. Hornemann visits Bilma, Kuka, Katsina and the Nupe: d. at Bokani. Maroon (Ashanti) rebels in Jamaica forcibly sent to Sierra Leone. Nova Scotian negro immigrants rebel in Sierra Leone.
1800-2 Britain holds Gorée.
*c.*1800 Muslim state fully established in Futa Jalon. Susu, Yalunka, Koranko and Mende reaching present habitats in Sierra Leone.
1801 18 Nov., Temne and Bulom attack Freetown: driven off by British, Loko and Maroons.

1802 11 Apr., renewed abortive Temne and Bulom attack on Freetown. Yunfa, pupil of Uthman dan Fodio, becomes Sarkin of Gobir.

1803 Uthman dan Fodio summoned from retirement to Gobir.

1804 21 Feb., Shehu Uthman dan Fodio's *Hijra* or flight to Degel; beginning of the *Jihad*: battle of Kwatto against Gobir: ruler of Sokoto (-1817).
c. **1804** Dutch abandon Akwida.
1804-14 British again hold Goree.
1805-6 Mungo Park, with thirty soldiers, attempting to reach R Niger, assassinated at the rapids.

1806 May, Ashanti defeat Fante at Abora, near Cape Coast: June, British at Fort William, Anomabu, offer mediation; 15 June, Ashanti take Anomabu and coast as far as Winneba.

1807 Ashanti-Fante war ended by smallpox and dysentery epidemic.

CENTRAL AFRICA

c. **1800** Mbailundu and Bilhe the principal purveyors of slaves, ivory and wax. Mangbetu move into the northern Congo from near L. Albert. Nyamwezi traders in Kazembe capital.

1801-10. The 'Pombeiros', P.J. Baptista and Amaro (or Anastacio) José, at the court of Kazembe IV.

EASTERN AFRICA	SOUTHERN AFRICA	OTHER COUNTRIES
*c.*1800-20 Galla kingdom of Enarea founded by Bofo (Abba Gomol).	*c.*1800 Betsilio become vassals of the Merina. *c.*1800-50 Export of slaves from Mozambique to S America rises to over 15,000 and up to 25,000 annually. 1800 Aug., First ocean mail post office opened at Cape Town.	1800 14 June, Battle of Marengo. 2 July, Act of Union between Great Britain and Ireland, effective 1 Jan., 1801. Missionary Institute founded in Berlin. *c.*1800 Estimated 776,000 negroes in Spanish America and 300,000 in Jamaica.
	1801 Réunion renamed Ile Buonaparte. Johannes van der Kemp, first LMS missionary, arrives at Cape Town.	1801 14 March, Pitt resigns: Addington Prime Minister (-1804). 9 Oct., Peace between France and Turkey: Egypt restored to Turkey. Elgin marbles brought to London.
*c.*1802-67 Kimweri the Great, Sultan of Vuga.	1802 John Trutor and William Somerville explore Bechuanaland. Lamboina, son of Andriantsirotso, chief of the Antankarana, frees them from Boina.	1802 27 March, Peace of Amiens between Britain and France. 2 Aug., Buonaparte appointed consul for life.
1803 Abuna Joseph of Ethiopia d.; no successor for 13 years.	1803 Xhosa claim all land from Fish R to Sunday R. 29 Feb., commando against Hottentots and Kaffirs. 1803 Feb. – 1806 Jan., Batavian Republic rules the Cape.	1803 25 Feb., Diet of Ratisbon. 18 May, Britain declares war on France. Denmark abolishes slave trade. 1803-4 Muhammad Bey al-Alfi, Mamluk, visits London.
1804 Bahadur, Omani governor of Zanzibar, with Yaqut as chief of customs.	1804 Decaen makes Tamatave the capital of French establishments in Madagascar.	1804 21 March, French *Code Civile* instituted. 10 May, Pitt again Prime Minister (-1806). 2 Dec., Napoleon crowns himself Emperor of the French. Mecca and Medina taken by Wahhabi. 1804-56 Sayyid Said b. Sultan, Sultan of Oman and Muscat.
	1805 July, British fleet returns to the Cape; capitulation of Papendorp.	1805 11 May, Treaty of St Petersburg between England and Russia. 19 Oct., Austria capitulates at Ulm. 21 Oct., Nelson destroys fleets of France and Spain off Trafalgar. 2 Dec., Battle of Austerlitz.
1806 Cyclone destroys coffee plantations on Bourbon Is.	1806 Jan., – 21 March 1877 Second British occupation of the Cape. Roman Catholic priests expelled from the Cape.	1806 23 Jan., Pitt d. William Wyndham (Lord) Grenville, Prime Minister (–1807). 15 Feb., Treaty of Paris between Austria and France against Britain. April, British blockade French coast. 21 Nov., Napoleon closes continental ports to Britain ('Continental System').
1807 Ahmad b. Said al-Mazrui, Governor of Mombasa, leads	1807 British stop slave trade at the Cape. Earl of Caledon,	1807 29 May, Selim III, Ottoman Sultan, deposed. 28 July, Mahmud

attacks Tunis. Special envoy
sent from Morocco to France.

Uthman dan Fodio takes Katsina.
The Gambia made a British Crown
Colony. Peace between the
Temne and the British.

1808 Fulani take Ngazargarmu;
retaken by Sheikh Hajj Muhammad
al-Amin. Uthman dan Fodio
conquers Bornu; Bornu remains
independent whilst Uthman dan
Fodio retires into private life:
brother Abdallahi establishes
amirate at Gwandu: son Bello
regent; Muhammad el-Kanemi
refuses throne of Bornu but
remains effective ruler with
title Shehu. Sierra Leone
becomes a Crown Colony:
population about 2,000.
Britain establishes a naval
patrol against slave traders in
W African waters.
1808-15 6,000 slaves captured
at sea released in Sierra Leone.

1809-14 Land reforms in Egypt.
1809-47 Abd al-Qadir ruler of
Taqdemt and Mascara.

1809-91 Samuel Ajayi Crowther,
first Yoruba to become an
Anglican Bishop.
Fante attack Accra and Elmina.

*c.*1810 Abiodun, Alafin of Oyo,
d.: Yoruba kingdom breaks up:
Afonja, governor of Ilorin,
attempts to seize power: Oyo
sacked: Ilorin made an independent
kingdom by Afonja: supplanted by
Mallam Alimi, who sets up an
amirate independent of Sokoto.
1810-14 Shaikh Ahmadu Lobo
(Hamadu Bari), Massina Fulani,
proclaims himself Amir
al-Muminin; conquers Massina.

1811 1 March, Mamluks in Cairo
massacred by Muhammad Ali; many
Mamluks flee to Sudan,
establishing camp at (New) Dongola.
1811-18 Berbers rebel in Middle
Atlas.

1811 Ashanti abortively attack
Fante to relieve Accra and
Elmina; Akim join in. Dutch
fort at Apam pillaged and
wrecked. Mutiny in Bissau:
governor alleged to be trading
on his own account. Methodist
mission at Freetown, Sierra
Leone, founded.
1811-12 Ngazargarmu taken by
Ibrahim Zaki.
*c.*1811 Fulani overrun Oyo as
far as Abeokuta.

1811 2 Feb., Baptista and José
regain Tete; May, they set out
to cross Africa, reaching Angola
1814.

1812 Muhammad Ali sends embassy
to urge Funj Sultan to expel
Mamluks from Dongola.

EASTERN AFRICA	SOUTHERN AFRICA	OTHER COUNTRIES
expedition against Pate and instals as sultan a vassal of Mombasa.	first British civil governor of Cape Colony.	II, Ottoman Sultan (-1839). 7-9 July, Peace of Tilsit. Oct., France and Russia declare war on Britain. Slave trade abolished by Britain (effective 1 March 1808). Congregation of Sisters of St Joseph founded. 1808 1 Jan., import of slaves into USA forbidden. 2 May, Spain rises against the French. 6 June, Joseph Buonaparte, King of Spain. 1 Aug., British expedition lands in Portugal.
1809-11 Henry Salt's expedition to Ethiopia. British take Rodrigues Is.	1809 Hottentots put under Colonial law.	1809 East India Co. agrees to Henry Salt's trade journey in Ethiopia. Metternich, Chief Minister in Austria (-1848). 22 Apr., Sir Arthur Wellesley (later Duke of Wellington) put in command in Portugal. 1 May, Pope Pius VIII taken prisoner by Napoleon.
	c.1810 Mthethwa, Ndandwe and Qwabe kingdoms dominate the Ngoni. 1810-28 Radama I: opens Madagascar to European influences. 1810 8 July, Britain takes Bourbon (Réunion); abortive British attempt to take Madagascar.	1810 American Board of Commissioners for Foreign Missions and Wesleyan Missionary Society founded. Anglo-Portuguese treaty against slavery. Spanish colonies revolt.
1811 Captain Smee's voyage along E African coast. British take Seychelles. Hydrographic survey of eastern African coast made by Capt. Philip Beaver in H.M.S. *Nisus*; visits Kilwa.	1811 Madagascar and Ile de France (Mauritius) taken by British.	1811 George III of England declared insane; Prince of Wales, later King George IV, Regent. Slave dealing declared a felony in England. 1811-18 Egyptian war against the Wahhabi.
1812-46 Sahela Selassie, King of Shoa.	1812 Xhosa driven back behind Fish R; block-houses garrisoned. Sultan of Anjouan asks aid from governor of Cape Colony against	1812 9 June, Lord Liverpool, Prime Minister (-1827). May, Napoleon invades Russia. 12 Aug., Wellington takes Madrid.

1813 Muhammad Ali initiates
policy of sending Egyptian
students abroad, to Austria,
England, France and Italy;
311 sent between 1811 and 1848.
Algiers again attacks Tunis; Tunis
becomes independent.
1813-14 J.L. Burckhardt explores
Upper Egypt and Nubia.
1814-24 Mahmud b.Muhammad,
Bey of Tunis.
1814-46 Colonel Warrington,
British Vice-Consul at Tripoli.

1814 Shehu Muhammad el-Kanemi
builds Kuka (or Kukawa).
American Baptists start work in
Liberia. Mutinous soldiers
attack the governor's residence
in Bissau. The Christian
Institution built by the CMS
in Freetown to train local
teachers and missionaries.
1814-16 Ashanti again attack
Fante and seize Accra. Fante
country becomes an Ashanti
province.

1814 Akwa declares himself
independent as a chief of the
Douala.

1815 US expeditions against
Algiers and Tripoli followed
by peace treaties.

1815 Temne start a secret
society to drive the Suen
chiefs from Port Loko. First
Prefect Apostolic of Senegal
appointed. Bissau in the hands
of a triumvirate of
mutineers.

c.1815-60 Namiembali, first King
of the Mangbetu dynasty, greatly
expands kingdom.

1816 Muhammad Ali founds School
of Engineering in Cairo. Anglo-
Dutch fleet under Lord Exmouth
destroys port and fleet of
Algiers.

1816 March, building of Bathurst,
Gambia, begun.

1816 Famine in Luanda.

1817 Sultan of Morocco forbids
privateering. Muhammad Uthman
al-Mirghani begins work as a
Muslim missionary amongst the
Bani Amir near Blue Nile.

1817 Uthman dan Fodio d.;
Muhammadu Bello, Sultan of
Sokoto (-1837), warrior, author
of works on history, geography,
and theology: sultanate includes
eleven emirates. French again
take possession of Senegal.
Cape Coast town accidentally
burned. 19 May, British mission
to Ashanti; 7 Sept., treaty between
Ashanti and British.

1818 Muhammad Ali, Viceroy of
Egypt, made Wali of Ethiopia:
son-in-law, Muhammad Bey Khusrau
the Daftardar, sent to tour Nubia.
1818-20 Sultan of Fezzan raises
taxes on 4,000 slaves passing
annually through his territory.

1819 Muhammad Ali tours Nubia.

1818 French military post set
up at Bakel, Senegal. Gray's
expedition to Senegal.
Committee of Merchants, with a
Mayor, constituted to govern
Bathurst, Gambia. Mollien
explores sources of rivers
Senegal and Gambia. Ashanti
war against Gyaman.
1819 French engagement with
Tratzas. Jan., Joseph Dupuis,

1819-21 Cotton cultivation
introduced into Angola.

EASTERN AFRICA	SOUTHERN AFRICA	OTHER COUNTRIES
	raiders from Madagascar. **1812-16** Radama I increases his territory.	Egyptians take Medina.
1813 Ahmad b.Said al-Mazrui attempts to seize Lamu: defeated at Shela: Omani governor installed at Lamu. **1813-7** Fumoluti Kipungu b. Fumoluti, Sultan of Pate.		**1813** EIC monopoly of trade in Indian Ocean, including eastern Africa, abolished. 7 Oct., Wellington enters France. 16-18 Oct., Napoleon defeated at Leipzig. Egyptians take Mecca. **1813-73** David Livingstone, missionary and traveller.
1814 Abdallah b.Ahmad al-Mazrui, governor of Mombasa (1814-21), declares Mombasa independent.	**1814-27** Lord Charles Somerset, Governor of Cape Colony. **1814** 13 Aug., Cape becomes a British Colony whilst other former Dutch colonies restored. 20 Nov., Britain retains Mauritius, Rodrigues and Seychelles by Treaty of Paris.	**1814** 30 March, Allies enter Paris; 11 Apr., Napoleon abdicates. Slave trade made illegal by Holland. 1 Nov., Congress of Vienna begins.
	1815 6 Apr., French reoccupy Bourbon.	**1815** 1 March, Napoleon lands in France. 18 June, Battle of Waterloo. 20 Nov., Treaty of Paris. Muslim slavery abolished in Sicily. Spain restricts her slave-traders to the seas S of the equator. Truce between Egypt and the Wahhabi. **1816-18** Egyptian war against Wahhabi resumed. **1816-26** João VI, King of Portugal. **1816** African Methodist Episcopal church of USA, Basel mission and Oblates of Mary Immaculate (OMI) founded. Compagnie du St-Esprit and Lazarist missionary seminaries reopened.
	1817 27 Oct., treaty between British and Radama at Tamatave, Madagascar, forbids slave trade.	**1817** British treaties with Portugal and Spain enable her to search their ships for slaves at sea. Portugal restricts slave trading to areas S of the equator. Sacred Congregation for the Propagation of the Faith (Propaganda) reformed.
*c.*1818 Cloves introduced into Zanzibar. **1818** Future Emperor Theodore II b., son of a minor chief of Kwara. **1818-21** Ioas II, Emperor of Ethiopia.	**1818** 15 Oct., French reoccupy Ste Marie, Madagascar. **1818** War amongst Xhosa; Nov., Gaika beaten at Amalinde by Dushane, son of Ndhlambi.	**1818** Slave trade made illegal by France. 30 Sept. - 21 Nov., Congress of Aix-la-Chapelle. Steamer *Savannah,* first to cross the Atlantic, takes 26 days.
1819 Joseph Senkovski, first Pole to visit Ethiopia.	**1819-51** Dr John Philip, LMS superintendent missionary:	**1819** Rhenish Mission founded. 12 hour day instituted for

first British consul appointed
to Kumasi. Court of Mixed
Commission set up in Freetown
to judge slave cases.

1820-1 The Sudan conquered by
Muhammad Ali as a private venture.
1820 July, Turkish, Albanian and
N African force of 4,000 leaves
Cairo under Ismail Kamil Pasha;
4 Nov., Shayqiyya defeated
near Kurti.

1820 23 March, new treaty between
Ashanti and British: not ratified by
British governor in Accra.

1821-81 The Sudan under Egyptian
administration.
1821 5 March, Berber submits to
Ismail Pasha; 20 Apr., second
column leaves Cairo under Ibrahim
Pasha; 12 June, Funj Sultan of
Sennar submits to Ismail Pasha;
Ibrahim Pasha dispatches slaves
for sale to help Muhammad Ali's
intervention in Greece; 20 Aug.,
column under Daftardar takes
Kordofan. *Jihadiyyah,* regular
troops recruited with slaves from
S Sudan, begin to be trained at
Aswan under French, Italian,
Spanish and Turkish officers.
Abidin Agha governor between
Second and Fourth Cataracts at
Dongola. Muhammad Ali introduces
cotton into Egypt from India and
the Sudan. Peace treaty between
Tunis and Algiers.
*c.*1822 Bulaq Press established.
1822-59 Maulai Abd al-Rahman b.
Hisham, Sharif of Morocco.
1822 Oct., or Nov., rising in
Shendi spreads rapidly through
central Sudan; Ismail Pasha and
retinue massacred; punitive
actions by Daftardar. Mahu
Bey Urfali governor of Berber.

1821 3 July, Sierra Leone, the
Gambia and Gold Coast joined as
British West Africa, with governor
at Freetown. Committee governing
Bathurst, Gambia, disbanded.
Richard Toll, Dagana and Bakel
founded at St Louis, Senegal;
peace treaties with the Trarzas
and Braknas.
1821-5 Walter Oudney, Dixon
Denham and Hugh Clapperton
in Nigeria: Chad, Kano and Sokoto
visited.

1822 Liberia founded as a colony
for freed slaves from USA.
Schools opened at Gorée and in
Senegal. Major Laing reaches
Timbuktu, but is assassinated in
the desert.

1822 Popular uprising and mutiny
of troops in Luanda: governor
replaced by a junta headed by
the bishop.

1823 Sept. - 1824 Aug., Egyptians
establish military patrols as far as
Ethiopian frontier; economic
chaos in the Sudan.

1823 Giovanni Belzoni d.
attempting to reach Timbuktu.
Society of Friends and Wesleyan
missions in Gambia; abortive
Catholic mission. Revolt of 300
degredados prevented in Santiago:
confrarias, local councils, set
up in Cacheu, Farim and Goba.
1823-31 Ashanti at war with
British.

ASTERN AFRICA	SOUTHERN AFRICA	OTHER COUNTRIES
	work started amongst the Bushmen.	labourers in Britain.
	1819 Cape troops out against Ndhlambi; Apr., Ndhlambi attacks Grahamstown; Oct., Ndhlambi beaten. 22 Nov., *Comité consultatif* set up in Réunion. French return to Fort Dauphin, Madagascar.	
1820 Habab tribe in Eritrea converted to Islam, with Marya and Bait Asgede in Tigre.	**1820-4** Unrest amongst south-east African Bantu.	**1820** 1 Jan. - 7 March, revolution in Spain. 24 Aug., revolution in Portugal. First iron steamship built in England.
	1820-1 About 5,000 British take up 100-acre farms in Cape Colony.	**1820-30** George IV, King of England.
	*c.*1820 War between Sakalava and Merina. Zulu *impis* organized by Dingiswayo, King of the Abatetwa.	
	1820 First LMS school opened in Madagascar and mission in Bechuanaland. Radama I ends export of slaves.	
	*c.*1821 Zwangendaba, sub-chief of Ndandwe Ngoni, leads horde beyond Delagoa Bay and raids Tsonga. Mthethwa Ngoni, under Shaka, lay waste region between Pondoland and Delagoa Bay.	**1821** March, Revolution in Naples. Apr., Greece revolts against Turks. 5 May Napoleon d. at St Helena. Africa Co. dissolved. Portuguese Ministry for Marine and Overseas abolished. Moresby treaty between Britain and Sultan of Muscat and Oman.
1822 Hamid b.Ahmad al-Busaidi, ent by Sayyid Said of Oman, ompels Barawa, Lamu, Pate and emba to acknowledge Omani uzerainty: Mazrui fleet destroyed ff Pemba. Abdallah b.Ahmad l-Mazrui asks for British protection r Mombasa against Oman. akalava raid Mafia Is.: Kua, uani Is., severely reduced.	**1822** English becomes official language of Cape Colony. *c.* 1822 Shaka reorganizes *impis*; drives Ngoni and Shangaa north.	**1822** 12 Aug., Castlereagh commits suicide. Canning, Foreign Secretary. Muhammad Ali of Egypt accepts Pashalik of Crete and quells Greek revolts. Oeuvre de la Propagation de la Foi founded; Société des Missions Evangéliques (SME) founded at Paris.
823 3-7 Dec., H.M.S. *Barracouta* t Mombasa: Mazrui demand for ritish protectorate refused. irst recorded caravan from anzibar, led by Indian Musa zuri, reaches L. Tanganyika.	*c.*1823 Makololo migrate across R Vaal into Bechuanaland thence to L. Ngami. Namaqua at war with Herero. **1823** Shaka attacks Natal: great chaos and movement amongst the tribes until *c.*1835. Robert Moffat visits Umzilikazi: people now known as Ndebele (Matabele). Capt. W.F.W.	**1823** 7 Apr., war between France and Spain. Portuguese Ministry for Marine and Overseas restored.

1824 Egyptian peasantry first
conscripted: many flee,
jeopardizing agriculture.
Aug.-Sept., Uthman Bey Jarkas
al-Birinji, commander-in-chief
in Sudan; fort built at Khartoum;
Sudanese exports made a
government monopoly (-1834).
1824-93 Ali Pasha Mubarak,
Egyptian Minister of Education.

1825 11 May, Uthman Bey d.;
Mahu Bey, commander-in-chief
Sudan (-1826); inaugurates
assembly of notables as gesture
of conciliation; mud-brick
citadel built in Khartoum: town
already developing; Egyptian
foreman cultivators and artisans
sent to develop Sudanese economy.
Kingdom of Sardinia sends fleet
to Tripoli to demonstrate against
privateering. British expedition
against Algiers.
1826 June, Ali Khurshid Agha,
commander-in-chief in Sudan, with
title as Governor of Sennar.
First Sudanese officers
commissioned. Systematic
cultivation of indigo begun in Sudan;
three shipyards established. Shilluk
raided for slaves. Sultan of
Darfur imprisons Muhammad Ali's
ambassador.
1827 Muhammad Ali founds School
of Medicine in Cairo primarily to
train army doctors. Ali Khurshid
Agha raids Dinka country for
slaves. Adolphe Linant de
Bellefonds journies to near Kawa.
Tunisian fleet, as allies of
Turkey, destroyed at Battle of
Navarino.

1828 First Egyptian newspaper
al-Waqai al-Misriyah founded as
a government organ. Funj and
Ingassana raided for tribute.

1824 21 Jan., Ashanti army
surrounds British force;
governor, Sir C. Macarthy,
commits suicide to avoid
capture: Osei Bonsu,
Asantehene, d.; fighting
becomes spasmodic. Denham
and Clapperton visit Muhammadu
Bello at Wurno: Muhammadu
alleged to have destroyed Hausa
records: Sokoto at war with
Bornu. Dynasty of Zaria becomes
rotatory between Mallawa, Bornawa
and Katsinawa Fulani.
1824-6 R. Caillié leaves Senegal
to travel amongst the Moors:
spends a year with the Braknas.
1825-6 Expedition under el-Kanemi
threatens Kano.
1825-7 Clapperton and R. Lander
reach Sokoto from Lagos.
1825 2-7 May, mutiny in Bissau.
Sept., Portuguese Guinea attacked
by Muslim elements from Sierra
Leone: Oct., and Dec., fort at
Cacheu attacked; 29 Dec., peace
arranged.

1826 7 Jan., Ashanti routed by
British at Dodawa. May, fresh
mutiny in Cacheu.

1827 13 Apr., Clapperton d. at
Jungarvie, near Sokoto. Britain
takes over Fernando Po from
Spain as a naval base and depot
for freed slaves. Basel Mission
starts work on Gold Coast.
Portuguese post established at
Bolama. The Christian Institution
refounded at Fourah Bay.
1827-9 R. Caillié explores R Niger,
reaches Timbuktu, and returns
via Morocco.
1828 20 Jan., Lander leaves for
England.
1828-43 British settlements on
Gold Coast ruled by Committee
of Merchants.

post 1825 The Bemba expanding
in the Bisa country.

1826 Bile, King of Bimbia,
takes the name of King
William.

1828-30 Douville exploring coast
and interior of Gabon.

EASTERN AFRICA	SOUTHERN AFRICA	OTHER COUNTRIES
	Owen makes treaties with chiefs near Delagoa Bay, seizing Inyaka and Elephant Is. for Britain. French settlement at Foulepointe destroyed by Radama I, but settlement on Ste Marie recognized.	
1824 Omani fleet sent to Mombasa to compel submission of Mazrui. Feb., Capt. Owen accedes to Mazrui demand for British protectorate: Lieut. Reitz governor—d. 29 May. Aug., Lieut. Emery, governor (-July, 1826). Swahili *History of Mombasa* translated into Arabic.	1824 Francis Farewell and James King buy land at Port Natal. Synod of Dutch Reformed Church at Cape Town revived. Rhenish mission working amongst Hottentots at Stellenbosch. Andriantsoly, Sakalava chief, does homage to Radama I. The Antankarana become vassals of the Merina. Sihanaka conquered by Radama I.	1824 Muhammad Ali of Egypt made Pasha of Morea: war in Morea until 1827. Crete taken by Egypt. Egyptians evacuate Najd, retaining Hijaz and Yemen. Louis XVIII of France d.; succ. Charles X (-1830). Trade unions permitted in England. Berlin Missionary Society founded. Britain declares slave-dealing to be piracy.
	1825 Advisory Council for government set up at Cape Town; a separate Advisory Council for the east set up at Grahamstown. French post at Fort Dauphin taken by Radama I.	1825 29 Aug., Portugal recognizes independence of Brazil. Samuel Crowther baptized.
1826 Oct., British withdraw from Mombasa. Sayyid Said of Oman orders the Mazrui to submit: the Mazrui agree to taxation but refuse to hand over Fort Jesus. Baeda Maryam III Emperor of Ethiopia for 4 days: Gigar restored (-1830).	1826 Three Griqua states established, Griquatown, Campbell and Philippolis. Thirty LMS schools open in Madagascar.	1826-57 Maria da Gloria, Queen of Portugal. 1826 Liberal constitution in Portugal. Janissaries massacred in Istanbul.
1827 Pangani founded. 1827 First visit of Sayyid Said of Muscat and Oman to E Africa; receives submission of Mazrui in Mombasa, and visits Zanzibar. British give treaty to Somali Habr Awal.	1827 Machinery of justice revised for Cape Colony. 1827-9 Portuguese garrison in present Lundazi District, Zambia.	1827 July, Russia, Great Britain and France blockade Morea. 20 Oct., Ottoman fleet defeated at Navarino. 8 Aug., Canning d. 5 Sept., Goderich Prime Minister.
1828-45 Hasan b.Ahmad al-Alawi, Mwenyi Mkuu of Zanzibar.	1828 30 Apr., Press ordinance guarantees freedom to the press at the Cape. Shaka murdered: Dingaan succ. Unsuccessful rising of Sakalava against Merina.	1828 25 Jan., Wellington, Prime Minister (-1830). 26 Feb., Dom Miguel becomes Regent of Portugal: 23 June, becomes King (-1834); constitution revoked. Aug., Egyptian forces withdraw from Morea.

EGYPT, THE SUDAN & NORTHERN AFRICA	WESTERN AFRICA	CENTRAL AFRICA

1829 Advisory Council *(Majlis al-Mashwara)* set up in Cairo.
1829 French Consulate established in Khartoum.

1829 15 Apr., further French treaty with the Trarzas.

1830 Agrarian law in Egypt specifies measures for repression of peasant revolts. Ali Khurshid Agha organizes expedition of 2,000 men against the Shilluk. 14 June, French attack Algiers; 4 July, Algiers taken; and later Bône, Bougie and Oran; 5 July, Dey signs Act of Capitulation: occupation restricted to near Algiers until 1840.

*c.*1830 Egba establish present town of Abeokuta. Ibadan occupied by Oyo refugees: Oyo rebuilt: Ibadan becomes Yoruba military headquarters. Dec., Sero-Kpera, King of Nikki, allies with the Yoruba against Ilorin. Lander brothers' expedition to Boussa and the Niger. Portuguese occupy Galinhas Is.
1830-43 Capt. George MacLean, Governor of the Cape Coast.

ante 1830 Luba army attack Kazembe: exterminated in the Luapula swamps.

1831-2 Ali Khurshid's Agha's expedition against the Hadendowa of the Taka with 6,000 men a costly failure.

1831-41 Temne-Loko war.
1831-49 Kebbi subdivided amongst various Fulani rulers.
1831 Apr., Ashanti make treaty with British and Fante.

1831 Kazembe IV Kaniemba refuses to trade with Tete.

---

*c.*1832-6 Frontier wars between Ali Khurshid Agha and Kanfu, ruler of Kwara, Ethiopia.
1832 Kordofan Province united with Khartoum Province. Abd al-Kadir assumes title of Amir: leads resistance to French until 1847.

1833 Egypt recognized as independent by Turkey. Ali Khurshid made a Bey and Mudir of the Sudan. Dongola brought under direct control of Khartoum. Sudan now wholly centralized. Abortive rising of peasants between Wadi Halfa and Dongola.
1833-4 General Voiral, French governor of Algeria, takes Mazagan.

1832 16 May, Portuguese colonies reorganized in provinces with a democratic administration. French make treaties to set up trading posts at Assinie, Grand Bassam and Dabou. Trarzas revolt against French.
1832-4 *Quorra* and *Alburkah,* small river steamers, start exploring R Niger under R. Lander.
1833 8 Sept.-17 Dec., *Junta* control of Cape Verde and Guinea; 17 Dec., Prefect appointed. Methodists start work on Gold Coast. American Episcopal Methodist, American Presbyterian, and American Board of Commissioners for Foreign Missions start work in Liberia.

1832 British commercial agency and Court of Equity established at Bimbia.

1834 22 July, Ordinance decrees military regime in Algeria under a governor-general: three divisions, Algiers, Oran and Constantine, each with a *Service des Bureaux Arabes.*

1834 Captaincies of Cacheu and Bissau merged. British naval establishment at Fernando Po returned to Spain.

1834 Angola ignores Portuguese abolition of the slave trade.

EASTERN AFRICA	SOUTHERN AFRICA	OTHER COUNTRIES
	1828-61 Ranavalona I, Queen of the Merina.	
	1829 Paris Evangelical Missionary Society (SME) starts work amongst the Bechuana and Hottentots. French expedition against Ranavalona of Madagascar; 11 Oct., Tamatave bombarded; 27 Oct., French checked at Foulepointe; 4 Nov., French withdraw.	1829 Apr., Roman Catholic Toleration Act in Britain. 14 Sept., Russo-Turkish war ends. British lease Aden as a coal depot.
1830-2 Iyasu IV, Emperor of Ethiopia: Protestant missionaries work near Adowa for a short while. c.1830 Galla kingdom of Jimar—Kakka emerges. Msiri (Ngelengwa) b. near Msene, Tabora. Quarrel over succession in Kilwa.	c.1830 Moshesh unites Baputi, Bamaru and Hlubi in a Basuto confederacy: beats off Zulus, Fingos, Griquas and Matabele. Umzilikazi lays waste country between Drakensburg and Witwatersrand. Conical tower and Great Outer Wall built at Zimbabwe. The Makua, led by Nairnwa, attack the Yao. Abdallah, Sultan of Anjouan. 1830 Full civil privileges granted to Roman Catholics in Cape Colony. French expedition withdrawn from Madagascar.	1830-7 William IV, King of England. 1830-1903 Robert Cecil, 3rd Marquess of Salisbury. 1830 4 Feb., Greece declared independent. 27-29 July, revolution in France: 7 Aug., Louis-Philippe elected King. 16 Nov., Grey, Prime Minister.
	1831 War between Matabele and Griquas and Koranas. Jean Laborde starts first iron and steel factories in Madagascar (d.1878). Gamitto, Portuguese explorer, visits Kazembe.	1831-46 Gregory XVI, Pope. 1831 Muhammad Ali dispatches Ibrahim Pasha to conquer Syria: occupied until 1840. 1 March, Reform Bill introduced. 4 June, Léopold of Saxe-Coburg elected King of Belgium (-1865) after separation of Belgium from Holland.
1832-3 Sayyid Said returns to Zanzibar: sends embassy to Madagascar to request marriage with Queen Ranavalona and 2,000 troops: marriage declined.	1832 Crown land in Cape Colony sold at auction instead of being free as before. *Prazero* system abolished in Mozambique.	1832 Edward Wilmot Blyden, negro patriot and writer, b. 4 June, Reform Bill passed in the House of Lords. 8 Aug., Greece elects Otto of Bavaria King. Nov., Holland forced to recognize Belgian independence. Turkey at war with Egypt, demanding cession of Syria.
1833 Gabra Krestos restored in Ethiopia: deposed in favour of Sahela Dengel (1833-40).	1833 Moshesh on friendly terms with Boer hunters and SME; other Bantu settle under him in Caledon valley. Seshongane with Ndandwe herds known as Abagaza, destroys fort at Delagoa Bay and raids eastern Rhodesia. New Constitution with Legislative Council, at Cape Town, with five to seven nominated non-officials. 1833-6 Portuguese posts in Delagoa Bay and raids eastern Shangaa.	1833 8 July, treaty between Russia and Turkey to close the Dardenelles to all but their own ships. 14 July, J. Keble, *National Apostasy*, starts the Oxford Movement. 29 Sept., civil war in Spain (-1840). Treaty of amity and commerce between USA and Muscat. Turkey recognizes virtual independence of Egypt, ceding Syria and Aden.
1834-5 Socotra first used by British as a coal depot.	1834 21 Dec., 12,000 Xhosa attack Cape Colony. Slaves emancipated at the Cape. Machinery of justice again revised in Cape Colony. Berlin	1834 26 May, Dom Miguel of Portugal d.; succ. Dom Pedro, d. 2 Sept., succ. Queen Maria da Gloria (-1853). Portuguese Ministry for Marine and Overseas

1835 Ali Khurshid Bey, made a Pasha
with a title of Hukamdar (commissioner),
reinforces Ahmad Kashif Ghassim,
who defeats Ethiopians at Kwara;
provincial administration systematically
organized. Two Sudanese regiments
raised for service against the
Wahhabi. Attempt to introduce
conscription into Sudan fails.
Tripoli retaken by the Turks under
Najib Pasha.
1835-6 Drouet-Erlon, first
governor-general of Algeria:
defeated at Macta.

1836 School of Languages established
in Cairo. Ahmad Kashif Ghassim
leads force against Kanfu of
Kwara. Arabic begins to replace
Turkish as offical language
in Sudan. Abortive rising of
Bishariyin. Mosque and school
built at Dongola. Clauzel
governor-general of Algeria:
attempt to take Constantine
fails. Successful operation
against Abd al-Kadir at Sikak.

1837 *Siyasetname* reforms Egyptian
administration, creating seven
government departments. Regular
steamship routes London-Alexandria
and Suez- Bombay established,
with 'Overland' route between.
First mosque in Khartoum
rebuilt because of growth of
town. April, Ahmad Kashif
Ghassim defeated by Ethiopians at
Wad Kaltabu: series of hostilities
between Sudan and Ethiopia to
1889. Clauzel replaced by
Damrémont; siege and capture
of Constantine; Damrémont d.;
replaced by Vallée. Treaty of
Ragna: Abd al-Kadir's authority
recognized in provinces of Oran,
Titéry and Algiers, but not in
towns.
1838-43 Ahmad Pasha Abu Widan,
governor-general of Sudan.
1838 Nov., Muhammad Ali visits
Khartoum; two parties of mineral
prospectors sent out; railway
link with Egypt projected as
far as Kordofan; Dec., Muhammad
Ali in S Sudan. Marshal Vallée

1835 Shehu Muhammad el-Kanemi
d.; succ. by son Omar; Sultan of
Bornu attempts to regain power:
defeated by Omar, who becomes
Shehu. 25 Feb., Miguelist
revolution in Portuguese Guinea.
American Episcopalian mission
starts work in Liberia.
Basel mission starts work in
Akropong; study of Ga and Twi
languages begun; coffee introduced
into Akwapim hills. J. Beecroft
ascends R Niger as far as
Lokoja in the *Quorra.*
*c.*1835 Quaker missionaries
working in the Gambia.
1836 The Bible translated into
Mandingo.

1837 First groundnuts exported
from Sierra Leone.

1838 22 Nov., agreement between
Ondonton, ruler of Intim, cedes
I.de Rei to Portuguese Guinea.
Capt. Bouët-Willaumez visits
W Coast of Africa to seek
suitable places for trading-posts
and a port; Gabon estuary,
Grand Bassam and Assinie

*c.*1835 Col. Nicholls makes treaties
with Cameroun chiefs.

1836 *Presidio* Duque de Braganza
established on land taken from
Matamba or Ginga.

1838 Governor of Angola removed
for trading in slaves.

EASTERN AFRICA	SOUTHERN AFRICA	OTHER COUNTRIES
	Mission starts work amongst the Korana. First exploration parties prepare for Great Trek; trek prevented by Kaffir war. **1834-5** Kaffir war.	again abolished. 1 Aug., slavery abolished throughout British Empire.
835-6 Combes and Tamisier exploring Ankober.	*ante* **1835** Rozwi state broken up by Zwangendaba. **1835** 1 March, Christians proscribed by Queen Ranavalona I. Sept., peace made between the Cape and the Xhosa. Oct., Great Trek begins. 20 Nov., Ngoni crossing of the R Zambezi near Zumbo dated by an eclipse of the sun.	**1835** 8 Apr., Peel resigns; Lord Melbourne Prime Minister. 7 Dec., first railway opened in Germany. Portuguese Ministry for Marine and Overseas restored.
1836-96 Sheikh Mzee b.Saif l-Stambuli, Sultan of Faza, ubject to Zanzibar.	**1836-7** War between Afrikaners and Ndebele. **1836** Great Trek: much of Transvaal and Free State reached: Dec., Potgeiter and Maritz set up rudimentary republic. March, Treaty of Friendship between Britain and Ndebele. Nov., only 60% of compensation for the emancipation of slaves in the Cape granted. Ngoni temporarily near L. Malawi. Portugal forbids slavery, but Mozambique suspends decree on grounds of 'absolute necessity'..	**1836-48** Chartist movement. **1836-47** Sir Thomas Stephen, British Colonial Under-Secretary. **1836** First US Consul appointed to Muscat. Bremen Mission and Leipzig Missionary Society founded.
837-48 Antoine, Arnauld and Charles Abbadie in Ethiopia. **837** Sayyid Said again in Mombasa and Zanzibar: eading Mazrui exiled to andar Abbas. US consulate stablished in Zanzibar. Amadi sets himself up as Mwenyi Mkuu of Tungi, aravan port for the Southern nterior.	**1837** Jan., Boards of Commissioners in Cape Colony towns levy local rates and manage municipal offices. Apr., Piet Retief with 400 followers joins Great Trek; elected Commandant-General and Governor. June, Xhosa cede half Natal to British; Nov., 9-days Boer battle with Ndebele along Marico R; Retief sets out for Natal; Dec., all of Natal offered to Retief by Dingaan; Retief murdered with all his followers at Dingaan's Kraal.	**1837** 20 June, William IV d.; succ. Queen Victoria (-1901). Aden Colony annexed by Britain. Morse invents the telegraph in New York.
838 Protestant missionaries xpelled from Tigre. Egyptian aid on Qalabat: panic in Gondar.	**1838** Sir George Napier tries to stop Great Trek; Port Natal occupied by Charters; May 2. Pretorius marches against Zulu; 16 Dec., Battle of Blood River; republican government moved to Pietermaritzburg.	**1838** 1 Aug., slavery abolished in India. 24 Sept., Anti-Corn Law League set up. Regular steamship services between Britain and America begin. Chartists issue the 'People's Charter'. Anglo-Turkish convention on free trade. First Afghan war.

takes further towns in Algeria.
Bishopric set up in Algiers.
Congress of united Algerians
under Abd al-Kadir at Bu
Khorshfa.
1839 13 Jan., Muhammad Ali
reaches Golden Mountains; 14
March, returns to Cairo. 1 July,
Turkish fleet surrenders in
Alexandria harbour.
1839-97 Jamal al-Din al-Afghani,
Egyptian religious teacher and
first Islamic modernist.
1839-40 Salim Qabudan explores
R Nile as far as Bor.
1840-1 Salim Qabudan's second
expedition as far as Gondokoro.
1840 Taka province taken by Abu
Widan; Kassala, capital.
Ahmad Pasha Abu Adham's expedition
against Hadendowa: ruler,
Muhammad Din, taken; Rufaa
Arabs pacified; slave raids as
far as Kurmuk. 12,000 Arabs
besiege Mazagan: defended for
4 days by 124 French.

occupied. Al-Hajj Omar returns
to Futa Jalon.
1838-90 Thomas Birch Freeman,
Methodist missionary, working
on Gold Coast.
1839-72 Methodist mission at
Kumasi.

*c.*1840 CMS and Wesleyans
spread rapidly amongst freed
slaves in Sierra Leone.
1840 Beecroft explores R Benin
and R Niger.

1839 9 Feb., King Denis, chief of
left bank of R Gabon, accepts
French treaty.

*c.*1840 Imbangala and Ovimbundu
caravans fighting each other on
the roads. Embassy from the
Bemba to the Kazembe: war magic
and kaolin provided.
post 1840 *Presidios* established
at Huila and Mossamedes: coffee
introduced in N Angola.

1841 Pashalik of Egypt made
hereditary in Muhammad Ali's
family; Muhammad Ali made
hereditary Viceroy of the Sudan.
Bureau of Translation attached
to School of Languages, Cairo.
General Bugeaud governor-general
of Algeria, with instructions
to pacify country; Mascara
taken.
1841-2 Salim Qabudan's third
expedition.
1842 Sebdna and Titéry province
taken by the French.
1842-6 Lazarist mission at
Khartoum.

1841 Palm-oil industry begun
in Dahomey. Baptist mission
starts work on Fernando Po.
R Niger expedition under naval
command with missionaries Schön
and Samuel Crowther. Wesleyan
missionaries visit Badagri and
Abeokuta.
1841-2 French commercial treaties
with Bonny and Old Calabar.

1842 Migration from Sierra Leone
to Abeokuta. J. Beecroft reaches
Cross R, exploring Old Calabar
R. CMS missionaries start work
at Badagri. Vicariate of the
Two Guineas established.
French treaty with the Black-
Will, Garroway, Ivory Coast,
ceding their country to France;
French confirm 1832 treaty with
King of Grand Bassam; French
treaties with Landownans and
Nalous in Guinea.

1842 18 March, King Louis, chief
of right bank of Gabon R, signs
treaty with French; 20 March,
similar treaty with King William
or Imale of Batanga; Apr.,
treaty signed by King Kaoko
recognizing French suzerainty.

EASTERN AFRICA	SOUTHERN AFRICA	OTHER COUNTRIES
*c.*1839 Frequent caravans from Zanzibar into the interior sent by Sayyid Said.	*ante* 1840 Ovimbundu trading with the Lozi. 1839 May, Dingaan acknowledges Boer claim to Natal.	1839-91 Abd al-Majid I, Ottoman Sultan. 1839 21 Apr., Turks invade Syria to expel Egyptians. 3 Dec., Pope Gregory XVI, Bull *In Supremo* condemns slavery and the slave trade. *Oeuvre des Noirs* founded by Fr F.M.P. Liberman in Haiti. Photography invented.
1840 Beke explores Gojjam. Sayyid Said moves definitively to Zanzibar. Embassy from Ethiopia to Egypt to obtain a new Abuna. Hasan b.Sulaiman, last Sultan of Kilwa, d. Government of India acquires Musha and al-Bab Is. from Sultan of Tadjoura: and Awbad Is. from Zaila.	*c.*1840 Ndebele trek to present Matabeleland, defeating Kalanga and Rozwi. Makololo migrate across R Zambezi to Tonga country. 1840 Feb., Dingaan d. in Swaziland. Sept., Pretorius sends delegates to Cape Town to treat for independence; Dec., leads war against the Pondo. Cape Town becomes a Municipality. Ngoni temporarily settle on Fipa plateau. Antankarana chief Tsimiaro takes refuge at Nossi-Mitsio; then cedes his territory to France. Capt. Passot's mission to Madagascar. French obtain Nossi-Bé and adjoining islands. 1840-1 Chiefs in Madagascar betrayed by the Hovas accept French treaties of protection: north-western Madagascar thus acquired.	1840 1d postage introduced in England. 10 Feb., Queen Victoria m. Albert of Saxe-Coburg-Gotha. 10 Feb., Upper and Lower Canada united. 15 July, Quadruple Alliance (Austria, Britain, Prussia, Russia) for protection of Turkey. 4 Nov., Acre bombarded by British; Egyptians forced to evacuate Syria. 1840-2 Opium war with China; 23 Aug., Hong Kong taken. 1840-52 Houses of Parliament rebuilt.
1841 British Consulate moved from Muscat to Zanzibar. Capt. Cornwallis Harris leads British Mission to the court of Shoa. Lieut. Jehenne visits Mayotte, Comoro Is.; 25 April, Amadi, Sultan of Mayotte, cedes rights to France for frs. 5,000 a year and free education for his children.	1841-3 James Rose-Innes, Superintendent-general of Education, reorganizes schools in Cape Colony.	1841 Feb., Peace between Turkey and Egypt. 13 July, Convention of the Straits between Turkey, England and France. 28 Aug., Melbourne resigns; Peel Prime Minister. Responsible government set up in Canada.
1842 J.L. Krapf, Protestant missionary, expelled from Ethiopia. *c.*1842 Mgr Justin de Jacobis and Lazarists arrive in Tigrai and modern Eritrea.	1842-3 War between British and Boers in Natal. 1842 June, Pretorius beats British column under Capt. T. Smith; July, republic begins to break down. Dr Philip recommends extension of Cape Colony to include Transorangia or treaties with Griqua and Basuto.	1842 1 Jan., British capitulate in Kabul. 9 Aug., treaty defining frontiers of Canada and USA. 29 Aug., Treaty of Nanking ends Opium war: Hong Kong ceded to England. Aug-Oct., Second Afghan War. Aug., Chartist riots in England. Anglo-American treaty USA to maintain a naval squadron in W Africa to suppress slave trade: treaty never observed.

EGYPT, THE SUDAN & NORTHERN AFRICA	WESTERN AFRICA	CENTRAL AFRICA
1843 End of Government monopoly of Sudanese exports attracts Greek and Italian traders to Khartoum. 6 Oct., Ahmad Pasha Abu Widan commits suicide; Ahmad Pasha Manikli, special commissioner, and then governor (-1845); provincial governors appointed answerable to Cairo. Sanusi sect founded by Sayyid Muhammad Ali al-Sanusi. Vicariate of Tunis established. Duc d'Aumale defeats Abd al-Kadir at Taguin. State and *habous* lands in Algeria confiscated by French: all other lands taken over and redistributed in plots.	**1843** 24 Aug., Mamadu Sanha, ruler of Badora, cedes territory of Ganjarra to Portuguese Guinea. British Crown resumes control of Gold Coast Settlements. Wesleyan mission established in Dahomey. French Protectorate over Assinie, Ivory Coast. Yoruba check attack on Ibadan by Fulani from Ilorin.	**1843** French take possession of right bank of R Gabon.
	1843-44 Bouët-Willaumez explores Falémé and Sénéboudou; treaty with Amady-Sadda, Almamy of Bondou; returns *via* Kéniéba gold mines. Raffenel and others explore Kéniéba gold mines.	
1844 Sudan re-centralized under Khartoum. Punitive expedition against Hadendowa. Aug., French at war with Morocco: 1 Aug., Tangier bombarded; 14 Aug., battle of Isly: Sultan of Morocco recognizes French occupation of Algeria. French occupy Laghouat oasis.	**1844** 6 March, 'The Bond of 1844', British treaty with Fante and other chiefs signed. 29 Dec., treaty between the Banhun of Goue and Cobone and Portuguese Guinea. Abortive attempt by Habe to regain Kano. West African Methodist Church started in Freetown. French receive territory between Atacla and Grand Bassam. Renewed Spanish occupation of Fernando Po.	**1844** Holy Ghost Fathers (CSSp) start work in Gabon. Protestant mission opened at Bimbia.
	1844-5 Many local risings in Portuguese Guinea.	
1845-9 Khalid Pasha Khusrau, governor of Sudan.	**1845** Jan., further treaties between Banhun tribes and Portuguese Guinea. William Fergusson, Governor of Sierra Leone, first British Governor of African ancestry. CMS Grammar School opened in Freetown. French expedition against slave trade; treaties with chiefs of Saint-André, Rio Fresco, Lahou, Jack-Jack, Ivory Town and others on Ivory Coast.	**1845** Baptist mission starts work at Douala under Alfred Saker. First mission schools in Douala. 4 Sept., new French treaty with King Kaoko, Gabon. Prize court established in Luanda.
1845 Sir J. Drummond Hay mediates in dispute between Morocco and Spain over boundaries of Ceuta.		
	1845-6 John Duncan travels beyond Abomey.	
1846 Suakin and Massawa leased to Muhammad Ali by the Turks. Apostolic vicariate of C Africa created with headquarters at Khartoum under Fr Ryllo, SJ,: church and school opened. First steamboat at Khartoum brought overland and assembled from sections. 2 Jan., French defeat Algerian rebels but with heavy losses. French begin to expropriate Algerian estates. Abd al-Kadir retires to Morocco.	**1846** 28 Dec., treaty between Cacheu and the rulers of Mata and Pecau. First CMS mission at Abeokuta; first Presbyterian mission in Calabar.	**1846-c.1860** Kapoko II, King of Wambu; walls of Samisasa completed. Aug., Pigéaud and Deschamps explore Rs Gabon and Como, reaching Gango; Mequet explores course of R Como.

EASTERN AFRICA	SOUTHERN AFRICA	OTHER COUNTRIES
1843 French treaty of alliance and commerce with King of Choa, Somalia. 13 June, French take possession of Mayotte. Walter Plowden and John Bell visit Ethiopia. **1843-62** French 'free emigration' labour scheme stimulates slave trade at Kilwa and Zanzibar.	**1843** Jan., British demonstration in force S of Orange R. 4 May, Natal proclaimed a British Colony. June, H. Cloete sent as Special Commissioner to Natal; Aug., Natal Volksraad submits. Nov.-Dec., treaties with Griqua and Basuto. 13 Dec., British Protectorate declared over Basutoland. French annex Mayotte and Mitsiou; French agent installed on Anjouan.	**1843** 18 May, schism in the Presbyterian Church of Scotland: Free Church of Scotland set up. *The Economist* first published. *Oeuvre de la Sainte-Enfance,* to support the evangelization of pagan children, established by Mgr Forbin-Jansen, Bishop of Nancy. Slavery abolished in India.
1844 Apostolic Prefecture of Madagascar established. Menelik b. J.L.Krapf starts LMS mission at Mombasa; shortly joined by J. Rebmann. First Arab arrives at Kampala. French consulate established at Zanzibar. *Alph,* first German vessel, visits Zanzibar. Turks temporarily occupy Arkiko. *c.*1844 Permanent Arab trading-centre established at Unyanyembe, near Tabora.	**1844** Apr., Boers from Natal set up new constitution of Thirty-Three Articles at Potchefstroom. Hendrik Potgieter settles at Delagoa Bay and acquires land for Transvaalers: loose constitution with Potgieter as Commandant. Faku recognized as ruler of Pondoland; boundaries defined. Natal and Cape Colony combined for administrative purposes. Missionaries permitted to return to Madagascar.	**1844-8** Maori risings in New Zealand. **1844** Baptist Missionary Society founded. Graham's Factory Act.
1845-50 Sahela Dengel (second restoration). **1845-65** Muhammad b. Ahmad al-Alawi, Mwinyi Mkuu of Zanzibar. **1845** Sayyid Said's expedition against Siu fails.	**1845** 13 May, Ranavalona declares all foreigners in Madagascar subject to local laws; 15 June, Anglo-French ultimatum: Tamatave bombarded; Christians massacred by Hovas. June, convention of Transorangian chiefs at Touwfontein. Aug., Natal annexed as a district of Cape Colony. *c.*1845 Zwangendaba, paramount chief of the Ngoni, d.; Ngoni break up; followers of Mpezemi and Mombera move from Fipa plateau to Malawi; remainder move to Songea, where other Ngoni had already settled; war, followed by further migration of part to Malawi.	**1845-8** USA at war with Mexico. **1845-6** Anglo-Sikh war.
1846 Vicariate of Central Africa and the Galla created under Mgr de Jacobis. Massawa leased by Turks to Muhammad Ali of Egypt.	**1846-8** Joaquim Rodrigues Graça explores headwaters of R Zambezi and Lunda territory. **1846-7** 100,000 Bantu in Cape Colony; eight reserves of 11½m. acres created. Klip River Republic W of Buffalo R. **1846-56** Livingstone's first journeys. **1846** March, war between Cape and Xhosa. Sir Harry Smith now governor of Cape Colony, and first High Commissioner.	**1846** 16 May, revolution in Portugal. 23 May, Corn Laws repealed. 16 June, Pius IX, Pope (-1878). 30 June, Lord John Russell, Prime Minister, with Lord Palmerston as Foreign Secretary.

1847 Marshal Bugeaud's expedition
against Kabylia; 23 Dec., Abd
al-Kadir surrenders to Lamoricière.
Chafarinas Is. occupied by Spain.

1848 Tunis sends embassy to
London without reference to the
Porte. Algerian divisions
become departments with prefects.
New port built in Algiers.

1849 2 Aug., Muhammad Ali d. at
Alexandria.
1849-54 Abbas I, Khedive of Egypt.
1849-1905 Muhammad Abduh, mufti
of Egypt, religious reformer.
1849-52 Massawa and Suakin revert
to government of the Hijaz. Abd
al-Latif Pasha Abdallah, governor
of Sudan, followed by short-term
puppet governors. French lay
waste Zaatcha oasis.

1850 School of Languages in
Cairo closed. Auguste Mariette
starts excavation of Memphis.
1850-2 Thirty-two doctors and
dispensers come from Egypt for
service in Sudan.
1850 French destroy oasis of
Nara. British expedition under
Barth leaves Tripoli for Fezzan
and Air. French officers start
to explore the Sahara.

1851 July, contract signed for
construction of Egyptian railway;
Oct., work begun under Robert
Stephenson.
1851-7 Catholic mission established
in Khartoum.
1851 C.Reitz, first Austrian consul,
appointed to Khartoum, with

1847 26 Aug., Liberia proclaimed
an independent republic.
First Spahis recruited. Blue
Sisters start work in Senegambia.
Bremen missionaries start
work at Christiansborg, then
moving inland (1853) and
working amongst the Ewe.
1848 First Senegalese Deputy
sent to French Assembly. Abbé
Boilat, first Senegalese
priest, returns home and
becomes inspector of schools;
opens first secondary school.
1848-50 Bouët-Willaumez
leads French expedition against
slave traders based in Liberia.
1848 L. Panet travels overland
from St Louis to Mogador.

1849-53 J. Beecroft, British
consul for Bights of Benin and
Biafra with jurisdiction from
Dahomey to the Cameroons:
mission to Kings of Dahomey to
offer 3-year subsidy to refrain
from slave trade rebuffed.
1849 Courts of Equity established
in areas under British influence in
Nigeria. Kebbi reunited under
Yakubu Nabame. CMS girls
secondary school opened in
Freetown.
*c.*1849 Outer wall of Ife built.
c. 1850 Mende moving into Sherbro
hinterland, with Temne, Fula,
Susu and Mandinka traders. 1850 Jan.,
Gold Coast separated from Sierra
Leone, with executive and
legislative councils. 8 Aug.,
administration of Cacheu
reorganized. British expedition
under Barth reaches Bornu, Kano
and Kuka. Panet crosses Sahara
from St Louis to Mogador. Hajj
Umar from Futa Jalon attacks
Bambara kingdoms of Segu and
Kaarta, and then Massina. Edward
Blyden emigrates to Liberia.
1851 Feb., J. Beecroft visits
Abeokuta. 5 June, garrison
mutinies at Bissau. 1 July,
commercial treaty between Guezo,
King of Dahomey, and France.
18 June - 9 July, Bissau fort
seized by French troops. 11 Aug.,
Portuguese relieving force reaches

1847 5 July, British treaty with
King William or Imale of Batanga.
Jaga Mbumba imposes duty on
spirits and tobacco at Cassange.

1848-52 Portuguese campaigns in
Bonde and at Cassange: Imbangala
retain monopoly of interior trade.

1848 Ladislas Magyar explores R Congo
as far as Yellela Falls and R
Kwanza as far as Kwango.
Victoria, in Ambas Bay, founded by
Alfred Salter, Baptist missionary
in Cameroun. 300 Portuguese of
radical tendencies migrate from
Brazil to Angola.

1849 Capt. Bouët-Willaumez founds
Libreville, Gabon, as a settlement for
freed slaves. First dispensary opened
in Douala.

*c.*1850 Ovimbundu traders reaching
the southern Lunda and Katanga.
post 1850 The Chokwe expand between
R Kasai, R Bushimai and R Cuanza.
1850 Du Mesnil explores R Como.
1850-2 Portuguese expedition
against the Imbangala.
1850-1930 Mgr Dupont, WF
missionary, apostle of the Bemba.
1850-65 Paul du Chaillu exploring
Gabon.

EASTERN AFRICA	SOUTHERN AFRICA	OTHER COUNTRIES
	Beginning of segregation in Natal; first location commission sets up reserves for immigrant Zulus. French territory in Madagascar increased.	
1847 Vicariate of Abyssinia created. *c.*1847 Future Emperor Theodore gathers a band of malcontents and overruns Gondar.	**1847-8** Antonio Francisco Ferreira da Silva Pôrto explores Barotseland. **1847** Dec., District of Victoria East annexed. British Kaffraria annexed. Xhosa gradually quietened.	**1847** 22 Feb., revolution in Portugal suppressed. 21 Oct.- 29 Nov., Sonderbund war in Switzerland. Straits Settlements made a Crown Colony.
1848 Muhammad b. Shaikh, Sultan of Pate, deposed for asserting independence from Oman. J.L. Krapf and J. Rebmann explore from Mombasa to Kilimanjaro. Walter Plowden returns to Ethiopia as British Consul.	**1848** Sir H. Smith annexes country between Orange and Vaal rivers. 29 Aug., Boers defeated at Bromplatz and retire across R Vaal. Vicariate Apostolic of Madagascar established. New draft constitution for Cape. Legislative Council for Orange River Sovereignty at Bloemfontein with nominated burghers. Robert Gray, first Anglican Bishop of Cape Town. British sovereignty proclaimed over whole area between Orange R, Vaal R and Drakensberg Mts.	**1848-9** Second Sikh war. **1848** Congregation of the Holy Ghost and the Congregation of the Sacred Heart of Mary amalgamated: Fr Libermann, Superior. Revolutions in Sicily, France, Austria and Hungary. 27 Apr., slavery forbidden in French colonies.
1849 Hamburg firm of O'Swald establishes agency in Zanzibar.	**1849** May, United Volksraad for all of Transvaal at Krugerspost; Potgeiter moves on to Zoutspansberg. 22 Nov., Cape Town forbids landing of convicts. *Jeruzalemgangers* of Marico talk of trekking down R Nyl to Sion. Warden zone for Basuto frontier: Moshesh agrees reluctantly. Livingstone explores L. Ngami and R Zambezi. **1849-50** Many British settle in Natal.	**1849** Risings in Canada. Navigation Acts repealed.
1850 Mbarak b. Rashid al-Mazrui, Wali of Gazi, attacks Rashid b. Hamis, Wali of Takaungu; Sayyid Said sends troops to restore *status quo ante*; Abdallah b. Hamis made Wali of Gazi (-1860). *c.*1850 Galla dominate region of R Tana. **1850-1** Yohannes III of Ethiopia restored.	**1850-65** Export of slaves from Mozambique to S America gradually dies out. **1850-3** Anglo-Kaffir war. **1850** Feb., new constitution at Cape with elective upper house. Governor of Cape deposes Gaika chief Sandile; Gaika refuse Chief Charles Brownlee; Sutu, widow of Gaika, set up. Francis Galton explores Damaraland. Jesuits take over Catholic missions in Madagascar.	**1850** Jan., Don Pacifico incident. 5 Aug., Australian Constitution Act. 17 Aug., Denmark sells Gold Coast possessions to Britain. Oct., Taiping rebellion. Society of Foreign Missions of Milan founded.
*c.*1851 Arab traders working west of Great Lakes. **1851-5** Sahela Dengel (third restoration).	**1851-2** Moshesh greatly increases Basuto territory. War with Kaffirs. **1852** Sand River Convention; Transvaal recognized by Britain. **1851-3** Basuto war. **1851** Another new draft constitution for the Cape prepared. Oblates of Mary Immaculate start work in Natal.	**1851** 1 May-15 Oct., Great Exhibition in London. May, gold discovered in New South Wales and Victoria. 4 July, Cuba declares itself independent: Sept., Spain suppresses Cuba. 2 Dec., Louis Napoleon seizes power in France.

duty of protecting Catholic
missionaries. General St
Arnaud's expedition to
Little Kabylia.

Bissau. 10 Sept., Portuguese
Guinea, Bissau and Cacheu
united under a single
governor. 25 Nov., Abortive
British attack on Lagos;
23-27 Dec., British attack
and fire Lagos. Barth
explores Kanem and Kuka.
Richardson d. at Bornu;
Barth and Overweg
explore L. Chad. Abeokuta
unsuccessfully attacked by
Dahomey. Soninki-
Marabout disturbances in
Gambia.

1852 French take Laghouat.
French occupy Ouargla oasis.

1852 1 Jan., Akitoye, King of
Lagos, signs treaty with Britain
for abolition of slave trade:
British vice-consul installed.
Apr., assembly of chiefs and
elders meets British governor
at Cape Coast: constitutes
itself first Legislative
Assembly: tax of 1/- *per capita*
raised under Poll Tax Ordinance.
African Steamship Co. begins
regular services to Nigeria.
Barth accompanies soldiers of
Sultan of Baghirmi to R Chari;
French make treaties of protection
with Ivory Coast chiefs.

1852 29 Apr., treaty between
Britain and seven Douala chiefs.
Naweej II, King of Lunda, d.:
Lunda empire at its zenith.
Swahili traders from Zanzibar
reach Benguela.
1852-61 Botanical survey of
Angola made by Friedrich
Welwitsch.

1853 Léopold I of Belgium
visits Egypt. Bayard Taylor,
first American tourist in
Sudan. Government school
in Khartoum with eighty-four
children. French take Géryville.

1853 Apr., revolt of traders
at Geba, Portuguese Guinea;
5 June, mutiny in the garrison
at Bissau. French fort built at
Dabou, Gold Coast. British
consulate for Lagos and Bight
of Benin established; Aug.,
hostilities in Lagos between King
and slave-traders: Sept., King
Akitoye d.; King Dosumu
installed. Regular courts set up
in Gold Coast.

1853-95 Kigeri IV Rwabugiri
Mwami of Rwanda: responsible
for present frontiers.

1854 13 July, Abbas I of Egypt
murdered; Muhammad Said Viceroy
(-1863). 15 Nov., Ferdinand
de Lesseps obtains concession for
construction of Suez Canal.
Great estates in Egypt subjected
to taxation. Dec., Muhammad
Said forbids slave trading in
Sudan. Cairo decree makes
hanging the penalty for murder
in the Sudan. Governor of
Kordofan brings Kababish and
Baqqara under control. French
take Ouargla and Touggart.

1854 *Jihad* (Holy War) preached
by Al-Hajj Omar; leaves Dinguiray
and invades Bambouk. *Pleiad*
exploring R Niger: quinine used
for the first time to prevent malaria
with total success. Mercantile
Courts of Equity set up by
black and white traders of Bonny;
King Pepple of Bonny deposed
by the British. Amatifou,
King of Ashanti, asks for French
protection. Baikie navigates
R Benue beyond Yola. Barth visits
Timbuktu. French campaign

ante **1854** Ovimbundu traders
crossing Africa to Mozambique.
1854 Feb., Livingstone exploring
Kasai region; reaches Luanda.
Court of Equity set up in
Victoria, Cameroun.

1852 Plowden makes treaty with
Ras of Begemder: Ras
overthrown by future Emperor
Theodore.
c.1852 Caravan from the coast
to Usambara cut off by the
Zigua: Kimweri, Sultan of Vuga,
appeals for help from Zanzibar:
military posts established at
Chogwe and Tongwe.

1852-4 da Silva Porto crosses
Africa from Benguela to Ibo.
1852 March, assembly of the
people at Rustenburg; Sand R.
Convention ratified, establishing
SA Republic. Dec., New
constitution with Legislative
Council elected for ten years.
Frontier armed and Mounted
Police raised.

1852-70 Napoleon III, Emperor
of the French.
1852 Right to elect deputies
withdrawn from all French
colonies except Martinique,
Guadeloupe and Réunion.
Responsible government granted
to New Zealand. 27 Feb.-18 Dec.,
Lord Derby, Prime Minister.
Harriet Beecher Stowe, *Uncle
Tom's Cabin.*

1853 Zanzibar customs post
established at Tungi, S of Cape
Delgado. Ras Kassa, son of the
chief of Kwara, reunites Ethiopia
by conquering Kings of Gojjam,
Begemder, Tigrai and Shoa:
future Emperor Menelik taken
as a hostage.

1853-1917 Leander Starr Jameson.
1853-6 Livingstone travels to
London and thence to Zambezi R
and Quelimane.
1853 1 July, Cape Colony granted
Constitution with elective
Legislative Council. Hendrik
Potgeiter and Andries Pretorius
d.; Volksraad appoints Marthinus
Potgeiter and Piet Pretorius
to succeed their fathers. Transvaal
treaty with Umzilikazi
forbidding traffic in firearms.
First Roman Catholic Vicar
Apostolic appointed in S Africa
(Rt. Rev. P.R. Griffith). Catholic
mission established at Baly,
Madagascar. Rev. W. Ellis, Methodist,
starts work in Madagascar.

1854 16 Apr., Sayyid Said leaves
Zanzibar for Oman: Khalid made
regent: on Khalid's death, Majid
regent. Future Emperor Theodore
recognized as ruler of Gondar and
Gojjam: successful war with Tigre.
1854-5 R.F. Burton and J.H. Speke
visit Harar.

c.1854 Land in Cape Colony:
8m. acres Crown Land; 13m.
native reserves; 11m. alienated.
1854-7 Railways built in SA.
1854 23 Feb., Convention of
Bloemfontein: British agree to
leave territory north of the
Orange R, leading to creation of
Orange Free State. 30 June,
First Cape Colony Parliament
meets. Sept., Josias Philip
Hoffman, first President of the
OFS, visits Moshesh. Maritzburg and

1854-6 Crimean war.
1854 De Koelle, *Polyglotta
Africana.* 14 June, Secretaryship
of State for the Colonies
separated from the War Office.
8 Dec., Doctrine of the
Immaculate Conception proclaimed
by Pope Pius IX.

against Wolof and Tekrur; fort
built at Podor.
1854-7 Exceptional appointment
of Amir Abdulsalami as Amir of
Zaria from Sulibawa Fulani.
1854-61 Colonel Faidherbe
governor of Senegal; Gorée
separated from Senegal.
1854-8 Posts set up in Senegal
from St Louis to Bakel and in
Oualo.

1855 Nov., Egyptian post set up
at Fashoda to check transport of
slaves: trade continues furtively.

1855-92 Soninki-Marabout wars in
Gambia.
1855 French build fort at Medina
against Al-Hajj Omar. Oualo
invaded by Trarza; rising of
Oualo and Braknas; French
annexe Oualo. French
pacification of Jack-Jack. Chiefs
on R Melakori attempt to engage
in slave trade: British repulsed
at Maligia with seventy-seven
dead. American Brethren in
Christ start work in Sierra
Leone. *New Era* newspaper
started in Freetown.

1855 23 Apr., chiefs of Elobey
Is. accept French suzerainty.
P. du Chaillu explores R.
Gabon estuary. War between
the Wovea (Berber) and King
William of Bimbia. Portuguese
occupy Ambriz and Bembe:
English company installed to
exploit copper mines.
Livingstone leaves Luanda.

1856 Cairo-Alexandria railway
completed. 5 Jan., second act
of concession for Suez Canal
project; 20 July, decree on
employment of Egyptian labour.
Khedive Muhammad Said visits
Sudan with Ferdinand de Lesseps
in his retinue: Berber handed
over to council of shaikhs:
provinces again decentralized
and made answerable to Cairo: Arakil
Bey al-Armani, a Christian, made
governor-general; camel-post
between Egypt and Sudan started,
railway projected; two government
steamboats reach (Old) Dongola
from Cairo. Bey of Tunis issues
a constitution (Destour).

1856-8 N'Diambour, Sine and
Saloun submit to the French.

1856-7 Arab traders reach Urua
(N Katanga).
*c.*1856-65 Tippu Tib trading
with the Luba.
1856 Msiri, a Nyamwezi, arrives
in the Kazembe capital.
c.post 1856 Muhammad b.Salih,
an Arab trader, established in
Kazembe country.

1857 Medjidieh Co. founded with
four steamships on Red Sea.
Cholera epidemic in Sudan.
Grand Kabylia conquered by
Marshal Randou. 17 June, 147
musabbalin (devotees) massacred
by French at Tishkert.

1857 Al-Hajj Omar lays siege to
Medina; 18 July, siege raised by
Faidherbe. Trarza rising put
down by Faidherbe. British
withdraw from Portendic, Senegal,
in return for French withdrawal
from Albreda. Pla or Grand Popo,
Dahomey, sold by the Minas to
France. MacGregor Laird
contracts with British Government
for annual visit of trading steamer
to Onitsha, Abo and Lokoja for
5 years: first steamer wrecked:
frequent attacks by locals on
this and subsequent steamers.

post 1857 Bakuba known as Leanda:
trade with Katanga, Stanley Pool
and Songye country.

1858 Arakil Bey al-Armani d.
J. Petherick appointed British
Vice-Consul in Khartoum.

1858 Kambia burnt by the British
in revenge for the Maligia
disaster. Apostolic Vicariate of
Sierra Leone established. French
treaties with Trarzas, Braknas

1858 14-15 Apr., Burton and Speke
at Wafanya, Burundi. Msiri sets up
trading station for ivory, copper and
slaves in Katanga.

EASTERN AFRICA	SOUTHERN AFRICA	OTHER COUNTRIES
	Durban become municipalities. DRC in Transvaal becomes independent of the Cape.	
1855 7 Feb., Ras Kassa crowns himself as Emperor Theodore II (-1868) at Mariam Deresse.	1855 Dec., Smithfield treaty: Basuto boundaries agreed. Nov., Victoria Falls discovered by Livingstone. Cape Colony abolishes British preference in favour of free trade. New constitution drafted for Transvaal. Divisional Councils elected for rural areas with 'colour blind' franchise.	1855 Enfield rifle adopted in British army. 6 Feb., Lord Palmerston Prime Minister. 19 May, Suez Canal Co. founded.
1856 19 Oct., Sayyid Said d. off Seychelles Is.; Sayyid Majid succ. as Sultan of Zanzibar (-1870), Sayyid Thuwaini Sultan of Oman and Muscat. R.F.Burton and J.H. Speke in Zanzibar and exploring Mombasa coast and Usambara Mts. 1856-7 Coptic Patriarch Querillos IV visits Emperor Theodore as ambassador of Muhammad Ali.	1856 2 May, Livingstone reaches Quelimane having crossed Africa from Luanda. Dec., new Transvaal constitution agreed; Pretoria named the capital. Dec., Zulu civil war. 16 Dec., South African Republic (Transvaal) set up; Marthinius Pretorius President. 8,000 Europeans in Natal, and 150,000 Bantu. Natal a Crown Colony by Royal Charter; elected majority on Legislation Council. Indentured Indian labour sent for from Natal. German legionaries, Crimean war veterans, settled in Kaffraria.	1856-1925 H. Rider Haggard, author. 1856 Britain and France renounce privateering at Conference of Paris. Livingstone appointed consul at Quelimane. Lyons Missionary Society (SMA) founded. Tasmania becomes self-governing. Anglo-Moroccan commercial treaty.
1857-9 R.F.Burton and J.H. Speke reach L. Tanganyika from Bagamoyo. Cholera epidemic at Kilwa Kivinje.	1857 Feb., Bantu in British Kaffraria reduced by death or dispersion from 105,000 to 37,000; Apr., Pretorius invades OFS; peace made by Paul Kruger. Pretorius renames Transvaal the South African Republic. First session of Natal Legislative Council. Conspiracy led by Prince Rakoto to overthrow Ranavalona in Madagascar.	1857 Sinn Fein Movement founded. 29 March, 'The Indian Mutiny'. 25 June, Prince Albert made Prince Consort. Dec., at Cambridge, Livingstone appeals to Oxford and Cambridge 'to join in making Africa free, civilized and Christian': Universities' Mission to C Africa founded. 1851-1941 Robert Baden-Powell (later Lord), founder of the Boy Scouts.
1858 J.H. Speke visits southern end of L. Victoria.	1858 Basuto, Bushmen, Koranas and Batalpin invade OFS and Transvaal; 29 Sept., treaty of Aliwal North: Basuto boundary redrawn. ORS and Natal DRC	1858 25 Feb., Lord Derby Prime Minister. 14 June, Ministry of Algeria set up in Paris, governing Algeria directly (-1860). 1 Nov., EIC abolished. Dec., Indian

and Douaichs, on left bank of
Senegal, setting up French
protectorate; Dinar, Senegal,
submits to France. French
construct fort at Dabou.

1859 25 Apr., construction of
Suez Canal begun. *Institut
Egyptien* founded. Telegraph
reaches Suakin. Duveyrier
fails to reach Touat. Anjera
tribesmen destroy Ceuta
boundary marks: war
declared on Morocco by Spain.

1859 Toro and Damga, Senegal
submit to French; French
treaties with rulers of Baol,
Sine and Saloun from Cape
Verde to Saloun estuary;
Rufisque, Portudal and Jaol
re-occupied.

1860 Duveyrier explores Tunisia
and Libya as far as Ghat. War
between Spain and Morocco:
Tetuan temporarily occupied by
Spain: 26 Apr., peace made:
Santa Cruz de Mar Pequeña ceded
by Morocco to Spain in
'perpetuity'. Ceuta and Melilla
made free ports.

1860 Aug.-Sept., rising against
the Portuguese in Cacheu of
Churo, Cacanda, Pecau and
Meta. Treaty between France
and Al-Hajj Omar: he agrees
to leave Senegal to the French
and retire to the Niger. Yolas
and Balantes submit to France.
Vincent visits Adrar. Pascäl
explores Futa Jalon and
Sénondébou. Apostolic
Vicariate of Dahomey and Benin
established. Yoni attack
Magbele and destroy CMS mission.
1860-1 Mage expedition from St
Louis to Tagant and back to
Senegal.

c.1860 Msiri teaches Kazembe the
Nyamwezi method of vaccination
against smallpox.
1860-1908 Mwesi IV Kissabo,
King of Burundi: continuous
struggle against refractory
chiefs.
1860-90 Principal development
of slave trade in the Congo
northwards and eastwards. Tuba,
King of Mangbetu, killed by
Dakpara, who usurps part of the
kingdom. Portuguese man fort
in San Salvador.

1861 American College for Girls
at Cairo begun as a primary
school. British Consulate
established in Khartoum.
1861-72 Jesuit and Franciscan
missions in the Sudan.
1861-5 Baker explores the
Sudan.
c.1861 Freebooter Muhammad Khair
al-Arqawi master of the Shilluk
country.

1861 Quarrel between De Sodji,
King of Porto Novo, and the
British: 23 Apr., town bombarded.
6 Aug., British Protectorate of
Lagos established. 27 Dec.,
Oranto and other Bissagos rulers
acknowledge Portuguese rule:
British established at Bolama.
Poll tax in Gold Coast produces
£1,500 only: thereafter abandoned.
Damel of Cayor cedes coast near
Cape Verde to France and gives
assurances of safe communication
between St Louis and Gorée.
Koya war with British. Bendu
annexed to Sierra Leone.
1861-4 R.F. Burton, British Consul
at Fernando Po.

1861 Lieut. Braouzec explores
R Como. 17 June, French treaty
with Chiefs Bechim and Longochila.
1861-2 Portuguese at war with
Jaga.

1862 Léopold I of Belgium
again visits Egypt.
c.1862 Chamber of Commerce
established in Khartoum.
1862 Jan.-Apr., twenty
Franciscans d. of disease on
Upper Nile. Musa Pasha

1862 Great Mosque of Zaria built
by Babban Gwani. Baikie visits
Bida, Zaria and Kano. Lagos
created a settlement. R.F.
Burton visits Benin. French
Evangelical mission starts work
in Senegal. Jauréguiberry

1862 1 June, French treaty with
Kings of C.Lopez. M. d'Aulnois,
French Commandant of Gabon.

EASTERN AFRICA	SOUTHERN AFRICA	OTHER COUNTRIES
	clergy form Transgariep Ring. 1858-64 Livingstone's Zambezi expedition.	Mutiny suppressed. First miracles at Lourdes. French colonial service separated from the Ministry of the Navy and made autonomous. Britain occupies Perim Is. Portugal decrees an end of slavery in 1878. 1858-1916 Fr Charles-Eugène, Vicomte de Foucauld, soldier, priest, explorer, linguist and apostle of the Sahara.
1859 Sayyid Said of Zanzibar signs treaty with Hanseatic towns. Sayyid Barghash deported to Bombay (-1861) after attempted *coup d'état*: Zanzibar bombarded by the British. Obock ceded to France. Consul Plowden murdered; John Bell shot protecting Emperor Theodore.	1859 26 Feb., 10 Aug., and 26 Sept., French treaties with chiefs in Madagascar. Companies and individuals allowed to mine gold in Cape on royalty basis. Some Chinese labour imported by Natal but returned. LMS mission founded at Inyati, first European settlement in S Rhodesia. CE bishop appointed to St Helena. Dopper Kerk leaves DRC. 1859-60 Durban railway built.	1859-1915 Booker T. Washington, American negro teacher and reformer. N.P 1859 18 June, Lord Palmerston, Prime Minister. Oil discovered in USA. Darwin, *Origin of Species.*
1860 Minaret of Malindi Mosque, Zanzibar, built. Apostolic prefecture of Zanzibar established. Catholic mission set up in Zanzibar. Mbarak b. Rashid al-Mazrui re-appointed Wali of Gazi: frequently in rebellion against Zanzibar. *c.*1860 H.A. Stern working amongst the Falasha. *c.*1860-70 Muhammad b. Abdallah, (the'Mad Mullah'), b. in Dulbahanta region of Ogaden. 1860-3 J.H. Speke and C. Grant discover the source of the Nile.	*c.*1860 Mariano, Portuguese half-caste, sets up slave-raiding base on Mt Morambula. 1860 3 Apr., Pretoria becomes capital of the Transvaal. British Kaffraria becomes a Crown Colony. Separation from Britain demanded in Cape Parliament. SA Republic and Republic of Lydenburg unite; 4 Apr., first united Volksraad at Pretoria. Mgr Maupoint, Bp of Réunion, decides to evangelize E Africa. 1860-3 Stephanus Schoemann and Willem Janse v.Rensburg, rival Acting Presidents in SA Republic.	1860 2 Nov., French Colonial Service again under Ministry of the Navy. Garibaldi's campaigns in Italy. France takes Savoy and Nice. Maori rising in New Zealand. Abraham Lincoln elected President of USA. Léon Godard, *Description et Histoire du Maroc,* suggests French conquest of Morocco.
1861 British naval force expels piratical 'Northern' Arabs from Zanzibar. Canning Award finalizes separation of Zanzibar from Oman. Siu rebels against Zanzibar: order restored by expedition under Sayyid Majid.	1861-4 UMCA sends abortive mission to Shire. 1861-3 Radama II, King of Merina; 12 Sept., signs treaty with France. 1861 Nov.–Dec., British take Inyaka Is. for Natal. Oblates of Mary Immaculate start work among the Sotho.	1861-76 Abdul Aziz, Ottoman Sultan. 1861-9 Luis I, King of Portugal. 1861-5 American Civil War: Britain neutral. 1861 18 Feb., Victor Emmanuel I proclaimed King of Italy. 14 Dec., Prince Albert d.
1862 11 March, France buys Obock for 10,000 Maria Theresa dollars. Abortive Egyptian expedition against Ethiopia: Egyptians forced to withdraw by smallpox epidemic. Emperor Theodore asks Queen Victoria for alliance	1862 J.S. Moffat founds first mission station in Matabeleland at Inyati. J.W. Colenso, Bp of Maritzburg, Natal, denies authenticity of the Pentateuch. Gazaland ceded to Portugal by Mzila b. Matshangana. Portuguese reoccupy Zumbo.	1862 29 March, Anglo-French commercial treaty. June, USA recognizes independent Liberia. 23 Sept., Bismarck Prime Minister of Prussia. Congregation of the Immaculate Heart of Mary (Scheut Fathers) founded.

Hamdi made governor-general
of Sudan with duty to restore
centralization. *Bibliothèque
Nationale* established in Algiers.
Rohlfs explores Morocco in
attempt to reach Timbuktu.

begins conquest of the Futa.

1863-79 Ismail Pasha, Khedive of
Egypt.
1863 Sultan Abdul Aziz of Turkey
visits Egypt. Egyptian Museum
founded for pre-Islamic Egyptian
studies. Sudan Co. (*Compagnie du
Soudan*) founded. Aziziya Misriya
Steamship Co. founded: regular
sailings Suez and Suakin and
Massawa begun. Jan., Sudanese
regiment embarked in Alexandria
to assist French army in Mexico.
Muhammad Khair al-Arqawi put
down. Baker expedition meets Speke
and Grant at Gondokoro. Tribal
holding land in Algeria abolished.

1864 Mutiny of Sudanese troops
at El Obeid. Sudan Government
takes over direct control of
customs. Line of Sudan railway
surveyed. British Consulate in
Sudan closed. Fr Daniele
Comboni publishes *Plan for the
Regeneration of Africa.* 5 Feb.,
Sharif Muhammad b. Abd al-Rahman
(1859-73) decrees absolute equality
for Jews in Morocco. Rohlfs
traverses the Sahara from west to
east.

1865 American College founded
at Asyut. Suakin leased to
Egypt by Turkey. Mutiny at
Kassala. Ahmad Mumtaz, governor
at Suakin (-1871): cotton
industry greatly expanded.
Massawa purchased from Turkey.
1865-71 Jafar Pasha Mazhar,
Governor-General of the Sudan.

1863 23 Feb., treaty of friendship
between Porto Novo and France.
Al-Hajj Omar captures Timbuktu;
capital at Hamdillahi near Segu:
empire from the Niger bend to
the upper Senegal. Dakar founded.
King of Porto Novo, Dahomey,
accepts French protection.
First Legislative Council election
in Sierra Leone.
1863-5 Faidherbe returns to
Senegal.
1863-74 Ashanti at war with
British on Gold Coast.
1863 Aug., British West Indian
troops landed and at once fall
sick.
1864-91 Samuel Ajayi Crowther,
a Yoruba (b. *c.* 1809), Anglican
Bishop of the Niger Territories.
1864 Al-Hajj Omar killed; succ.
his son Ahmadu Sefu (-1884).
Faidherbe drives Lat Dior from
Cayor, and annexes it to Senegal.
Holy Ghost Fathers mission
established in Sierra Leone. De-
Mikpon, King of Porto Novo,
invites a visit from HMS
Dialmath. Dahomey repulsed
in attack on Abeokuta. Little
Popo (Anecho) ceded to France.
Lagos Constabulary, later the
Nigerian Regiment, founded.
Dispute between the Ibadans
and the Egbas.
1865 Pinet-Laprade, governor
of Senegal; Saloun again
subdued; Prophet Maba defeated.
March, British send company of
West India Regiment to help
Egba siege of Ikorodu, near
Lagos. Mandingo near
Sancorla massacred by Fulas
under Mussa Molo. Geraldo de
Lema, Brazilian slaver, driven
out of Ada, raises army to take
town; 17 March, bombarded by
British; Ewe ally with
Asantehene. French temporarily
abandon Porto Novo; British
blockade Cotonou.
1865-7 Rohlfs's expedition from

1863 Kasanje independent of the
Portuguese. Lieut. Serval explores
R Ogooué.

1864 King Bell writes from
Douala asking the protection of
Queen Victoria. Lieut. Génoyer
explores R Como; Alligote and
Touchard explore R Ogooué.

*c.*1865 Tippu Tib trading with
Bemba and Lundaland. Ziber
Pasha established at Rabah as
master of the Azande trade in
some 25,000 slaves a year.

ASTERN AFRICA | SOUTHERN AFRICA | OTHER COUNTRIES

gainst Muslim powers: is
nored: therefore imprisons
ritish Consul and other
uropeans. Indigenous cotton
owing in Uganda first noted.
nited Methodist Free Churches
ission established near Mombasa.
hmad b.Fumoluti sets up
ultanate at Witu. Sayyid Majid's
rst visit to Mjimwema, to set
p new town, now Dar es Salaam.
H. Speke reaches Kampala.
863 Holy Ghost Fathers
stablished in Zanzibar. Menelik,
ing of Shoa. Emperor Theodore
sks Napoleon III for aid: response
egative: capital moved to
lagdala.

864 UMCA mission established
n Zanzibar. Baker discovers
.. Albert. Abuna Salama, head
f Ethiopian church, imprisoned.

865 Theodore II attempts
nsuccessfully to seize Shoa,
ndependent under Menelik.
ritish Consul Cameron
rrested.

SOUTHERN AFRICA

1862-1919 Louis Botha, statesman.
1862-3 Annexation of Transkei
rejected by Cape Parliament.

1863-8 Rasoherina, Queen of
the Merina.
1863 Dec., van Rensburg
sole President of SA Republic.
Mariano raiding up to Mlanji:
other Portuguese raiding near
Tete. CE Bishop appointed to
Bloemfontein. Bp Colenso
of Maritzburg, Natal, deprived
for heresy. Rt. Rev. A. Devereux
appointed Vicar Apostolic of
Eastern Province.

1864-5 Bantu extending throughout
SA.
1864 M.W. Pretorius, President of
SA Republic. Barotse (Lozi)
annihilate Makololo.

1865 27 March, Kaffraria
incorporated into Cape Colony.
June, OFS-Basuto war.
Cetewayo acknowledged leader
of the Zulu. British treaty with
Rasoherina.
1865-6 Economic depression
throughout SA.

OTHER COUNTRIES

Lassalle, *Working-Class Programme.*

1863-1945 David Lloyd George.
1863-6 Egyptian and Sudanese
force at Taif and Jidda.
1863 1-3 July, Battle of Gettysburg.
First underground railway in
London. J.S. Mill, *Utilitarianism.*

1864-1945 Frederick Lugard.
1864 22 Aug., Geneva Convention
starts the Red Cross Society.
Sept., British, French and Dutch
attack Japan. 8 Dec., Pius IX,
Quanta Cura and *Syllabus Errorum.*
Slave trade abolished by Napoleon
III. International Workers Association
founded. Privy Council decides Bp
Colenso's deprivation *ultra vires.*

1865-1909 Léopold II, King of
the Belgians.
1865 31 Jan., slavery abolished
in USA. 14 Apr., Abraham
Lincoln murdered. 18 Oct.,
Lord John Russell, Prime Minister.
Annexation of Algeria proclaimed
in Paris. Transportation of convicts
to Australia abolished.

EGYPT, THE SUDAN & NORTHERN AFRICA	WESTERN AFRICA	CENTRAL AFRICA

| | Tripoli reaches Bornu, Sokoto, Baguirmi, Benue and Lagos. | |
| **1866** Nov., Assembly of Delegates, quasi-parliament, set up for Egypt: seventy-five members, principally village headmen; powers limited by Organic Law. **1866-7** Egyptian military mission to Europe; Egyptian army re-equipped, including Krupp artillery and US Remington rifles. **1866** First Egyptian stamps issued. Baqqara raid Kordofan. | **1866** France acquires R Caramance, Rio-Cassinie, Rio Nunez, Rio Pongo and R Mellacorée on Guinea coast. Governor of Sierra Leone becomes Governor-in-chief of W African Settlements: separate Legislative Council for Sierra Leone. | **1866** War between Akwa and Bell tribes. Portuguese abandon Mpinda, San Salvador, Bembe and Encoje. |

| **1867-8** While officially neutral, Egypt assists British in Anglo-Ethiopian war. **1867** Apr., Sir Samuel Baker's expedition leaves Cairo for Gondokoro. First Sudanese made a Pasha; first two Sudanese made provincial governors. Elementary school started in Khartoum. Post Office opened in Suakin. Sudanese Regiment, reduced to a company in Mexican war, returns *via* Paris. | **1867** 5 March, Exchange of Gold Coast forts between British and Dutch: British take Mari, Kormantin, Apam and Accra; Dutch take Beyin, Dixcove, Sekondi and Kommenda. **1867-9** Egbas expel all European traders and missionaries from Abeokuta. | **1867** 10 May, French treaty with King of M'Goumbi and N'Doumbal Rakenga on R Ogooué. 8 Nov., Livingstone discovers L. Mweru. Bunza (or Munza), King of Mangbetu, builds new capital at Nangazizi. Tippu Tib trading with the Tabwa. James Holt Ltd founded at Douala. Livingstone visits Kazembe Mulonga. |
| **1868** *Jamiyyat al-Maarif* (publishing house) founded in Cairo, principally for publication of Arabic manuscripts. State system of education established in Egypt. **1868-71** Schweinfurth travels in the Sudan. **1868** White Fathers (Society of Missionaries of Our Lady of Africa) (WF) founded by Cardinal Lavigérie at Algiers. Sudan Co. liquidated. Elementary schools opened at Berber and Dongola. | **1868** Glé-Glé, King of Dahomey, cedes Cotonou to the French to prevent the British establishing themselves there; Minas sell Agoué to France; posts created at Boké and Benté, Guinea; French protectorate treaties on Ivory Coast. First educational grants-in-aid in Sierra Leone. Ashanti renew hostilities against British. *c.*1868 Creoles emerge as a distinctive people in Sierra Leone. | **1868** 14 Jan., new French treaty with Kings of Camma and Rembi; R Ogooué opened to European commerce. 18 July, Livingstone reaches L. Bangweulu. Trade treaty between Bunza and Abdal-Samad, Sudanese ivory merchant. **1868-70** Arabs and Swahili at war against Kazembe. |

| **1869** 17 Nov., Suez Canal opened by Empress Eugénie. 100 Sudanese boys admitted to primary school in Cairo. Tunis bankrupt. Britain, France and Italy take control. **1869-74** Gustave Nachtigal's journey to Bornu from Tripoli to Bornu and back *via* L.Chad, Darfur and the Nile. | **1869** March-Apr., W.H. Simpson, Acting Administrator of the Gold Coast, detained for 5 days by Akwamu; June, Ashanti attack Anum and Ho. 1 Dec., Bolama made the capital of Portuguese Guinea: government of Guinea reorganized. Lat Dior, instigated by Ahmadu Shehu of Toro, attacks French: defeated and flees abroad. Nachtigal visits Sheikh Omar of Bornu. | **1869** Msiri proclaims himself Mwami (King) of Garaganza (or Garenganze) with capital at Bunkeya. Bunza receives Schweinfurth. Arab trading post at Nyangwe established by Mwine Dugumbi: raids on Manyema, Lega and Songola country. *c.*1869-70 Tippu Tib trading with Bemba, Lungu and Kazembe with caravan of 4,000. **1869-70** Schweinfurth explores |

EASTERN AFRICA	SOUTHERN AFRICA	OTHER COUNTRIES
1866 Hormuzd Rassam, Asst. Political Officer in Aden, sent with Dr Blanc to obtain Cameron's release: both arrested and imprisoned: 17 Apr., Emperor Theodore upbraids British captives and demands British workmen to make munitions; Gondar rebels; prisoners taken to Magdala; 2 Dec., Gondar burnt; Theodore then fortifies Magdala. Building of Dar es Salaam begun by Sayyid Majid. Zanzibari expedition against Witu fails. Swedish Lutheran Missionaries established at Massawa. **1866-73** Dr Livingstone's last journey.	**1866** Jan., Amaxolo annexed by Natal. Apr., treaty of Thaba Bosigo: Moshesh accepts OFS annexations and promises compensation. Ciskei annexed to Cape Colony. Bishop Colenso secedes. Coolie supply to Natal stopped by Indian government. U.S. treaty with Rasonerina.	**1866** 6 July, Lord Derby, Prime Minister. Austro-Prussian War. Suakin and Massawa granted by Turkey to Khedive Ismail as hereditary possession. Mill Hill Fathers founded. Transatlantic cable laid. Klu-Klux-Klan founded.
1867 Jan., Livingstone travels up R Ruvuma; 1 Apr., reaches L. Tanganyika. Menelik proclaims himself independent as King of Shoa. Dec., British expedition of 68,000 men under Sir Robert Napier against Emperor Theodore arrives at Zulla.	**1867** Apr., diamonds found at Hopetown. Dec., Carl Mauch reports gold at Tati and in Mashonaland. Native Foreigners Act, directing the carrying of passes in Cape Colony, passed. Maseko Ngoni migrate from near Songea to S of L. Malawi. Dr José Lacerda, *Examen das viagens do Doutor Livingstone.*	**1867** 1 July, Canada becomes a Dominion. 22 Oct., Garibaldi's march on Rome. Nov., House of Commons votes £2m. to relieve British prisoners in Ethiopia. First Lambeth Conference. Verona Frs founded. K. Marx, *Das Kapital.*
1868 March, British prisoners in Ethiopia freed. 13 Apr., Napier captures Magdala: Emperor Theodore commits suicide. 500 manuscripts and other treasures seized for Britain. Napier supplies Ras Kassa with arms and returns home. Gondar sacked by Menelik, King of Shoa. Mission and orphanage for slave children opened at Bagamoyo. Magila, first UMCA mainland mission, founded. **1868-73** J. Kirk frequently Acting British Consul in Zanzibar. **1868-89** Yohannes IV, Emperor of Ethiopia. **1869** Italians purchase Assab. Djibouti replaces Obock as French coaling station. March, Livingstone reaches Ujiji. Sir Samuel Baker appointed Governor of the Equatorial Nile Basin (-1873).	**1868-70** War with Herero. 12 March, Britain annexes Basutoland. 8 Aug., France makes commercial treaty with Madagascar. Umzilikazi d.; Uncombata proclaimed regent.	**1868-1963** William E. Burghardt Du Bois, father of Pan-Africanism. **1868** 25 Feb., 8 Dec., Disraeli Prime Minister. 9 Dec., W.E.Gladstone Prime Minister (-1874).
	1869 London and Limpopo Mining Co. expedition to Tati. Dr William Macrorie consecrated Bishop of Maritzburg, as rival to Bishop Colenso. Diamond 'Star of S Africa' found; gold and diamond rush begins. Transvaal treaty with Portugal defines border and those of Gazaland: civil liberty given to Roman Catholics. Idols burnt in Madagascar. **1869-72** Baines explores Shire R.	**1869** 1 March, Irish Church disestablished. 4 March, Ulysses S. Grant, President of USA. 9 March, Hudson Bay Co. territory ceded to Canada. 8 Dec., First Vatican Council meets. Portugal makes all slaves *libertos,* with the right to wages before liberation.

Azande country.

1870 Khedivial Mail Line founded. American Staff Officers under Brigadier Charles P. Stone recruited to reorganize Egyptian army. Khedivial Library (now Egyptian National Library) founded. Telegraph line reaches Khartoum from Cairo. Sir Samuel Baker Pasha made Governor of Equatorial Province. 14 Oct., Décret Crémieux naturalizes all Algerian Jews as French citizens. On fall of Napoleon III, settlers attempt to govern Algeria through Commune d'Alger. French take El Goléa.

*c.*1870 National African Co. in practical, though unofficial, control of the R Niger.
1870 24 Nov., Portuguese recover Bolama from the British. French temporarily evacuate the Ivory Coast. Disastrous fire in Lagos.

*c.*1870 Bunza kills Dakpara and reunites Mangbetu kingdom.
1870 2,700 slave merchants estimated between Ubangi and Bahr al-Ghazal.

1871 March-1879 Sept., Jamal al-Din al-Afghani, pan-Islamic propagandist in Cairo, stirs up unrest, especially in al-Azhar University. *Muqabala* law grants ownership of land to Egyptian peasants paying *Muqabala* tax and redemption of half tax in perpetuity. Apr., Baker Pasha annexes Gondokoro for Egypt. Khartoum, Sennar and the White Nile provinces merged as 'Southern Sudan': Ahmad Mumtaz governor (-1872). 25 Oct., Tunis receives firman from Istanbul renouncing tribute: Bey still to be invested by the Porte and forbidden to cede territory or make war or peace. General rising against French in Algeria. Sultan of Morocco asks for a US protectorate: State Dept declines.
1872 Oct., Ahmad Mumtaz Pasha dismissed; replaced by Adham Pasha al-Arifi. Bunyoro annexed: negotiations with Mutesa, Kabaka of Buganda. Jafar Pasha Mazhar sends expedition to Bahr al-Ghazal: defeated by trader Zubair Rahma Mansur. Ismail Pasha Aiyub, governor-general of the Sudan: policy of economic retrenchment. Mgr Daniele Comboni appointed Vicar Apostolic of C Africa. Verona Fathers take charge of missionary work in the Sudan. Sanitary Council of resident foreign diplomats charged with public health in Tangier.

1871 Jan., governor of Portuguese Guinea assassinated by a grummet; Feb., rising suppressed. Senegal again sends a Deputy to Paris. French agreement with Lat Dior. Lagos again partly destroyed by fire. Attack on steamer *Nelson* on R Niger.

1871 March, Livingstone reaches R Lualaba. Sudanese merchants construct a zariba at Tangasi, near Nangazizi. Abd al-Samad replaced by Coptic Ghattas Co. Nyangwe the largest slave market in C Africa. American Presbyterian Mission starts work in Cameroun.

1872 6 Apr., British take over Dutch forts on Gold Coast. 26 Apr., riot at Elmina. 2 Sept., Asantehene threatens British with war. 9 Dec., Ashanti army leaves Kumasi. King Jaja sets himself up as chief at Opobo.

1872 Kibali basin explored by Giovanni Miani.

1873 Mixed Courts (*Tribunal Mixte*) established in Egypt. First girls' schools opened in Cairo. Peace made with

1873 9 Feb., Ashanti army defeats British at Assin Nyankumasi; 9 June, first British reinforcements arrive. 13 June, minor action at

1873 30 Apr., Livingstone d. near L. Bangweulu. Bunza killed by his own nephew. Nangazizi burnt: Mangbetu

EASTERN AFRICA

1870-88 Sayyid Barghash, Sultan of Zanzibar.
1870 Ajuran and Boran Galla drive Warday out of Wajir. Egyptians occupy Zaila and N Somalia as far as Cape Guardafui. Italians occupy Assab. Outbreak of cholera at Kilwa Kivinje.
*c.***1870** Kimweri, Sultan of Vuga.

1871-4 Nyungu ya Mawe, leader of a *ruga-ruga* warrior band in Unyamwezi.
1871 23 Oct., Livingstone back at Ujiji. 10 Nov., Stanley meets Livingstone at Ujiji. Mirambo destroys Tabora. Münzinger, a Swiss adventurer, governor of Massawa: bridge built across Keren hills.
1871-6 Menelik's campaigns against the Wallo Galla.

1872 15 Apr., hurricane devastates Zanzibar, Pemba and Mafia: two-thirds of clove and coconut plantations destroyed. Regular monthly mail service to Zanzibar begun by British India Steam Navigation Co. Mbarak of Gazi rebels and then swears allegiance to Zanzibar. Menelik corresponds with Victor Emmanuel II of Italy. Coronation of Yohannes IV of Ethiopia (-1889). Münzinger seizes Keren-Bilen region for Egypt. Egyptian force occupies Massawa.

1873-86 J. Kirk, British Consul at Zanzibar.
1873 15 March, V.L. Cameron leaves Bagamoyo to explore C

SOUTHERN AFRICA

1870 Anglican Synod in Cape Town: Privy Council decision *re* Bp Colenso rejected.
1870 June, Diggers' Republic proclaimed at Klipdrift: Stafford Parker, President. Aug., Orange Free State proclaims sovereignty over Campbell Lands. Dec., diamonds discovered in Orange Free State. Lobengula installed as succ. of Umzilikazi (-1893). London and Limpopo Mining Co. obtain rights at Tati. SA Gold Fields Exploration Co. obtains rights between R Gwelo and R Hunyani. Standard Bank of SA becomes government bank.
1870-1 Grandidier exploring Imerina country.
1871 5 Sept., Carl Mauch reaches Zimbabwe. Oct., Cecil John Rhodes treks from Natal to Kimberley. Basutoland annexed to Cape Colony and governed separately by proclamations. Britain annexes diamond fields of Kimberley and Griqualand West.

1872 1 July, T.F. Burgers elected President of Transvaal. Oct., Responsible government in Cape Colony: J.C. Molteno, first Premier. Griqualand West annexed to Cape Colony.

*c.***1873** 400 pupils, black and white, in schools in Mozambique.
1873 John Henry de Villiers, first local born Chief Justice

OTHER COUNTRIES

1870 13 July, French send ultimatum to Prussia. 18 July, Dogma of Papal Infallibility in faith and morals proclaimed. 19 July, France declares war on Prussia. 2 Sept., Napoleon III surrenders at Sédan. 4 Sept., revolution in Paris: Third Republic proclaimed. 20 Sept., Rome occupied by Victor Emmanuel II of Italy. End of First Vatican Council. H.M. Stanley sent by *New York Herald* to search for Livingstone. Elementary education made compulsory in England.

1871 18 Jan., William I, proclaimed German Emperor at Versailles. 28 Jan., Paris surrenders to the Prussians. 10 May, Franco-German Peace treaty. 29 June, Trade Unions legalized in England. 2 July, Rome becomes capital of Italy. 20 July, purchase of commissions abolished in England. 31 Aug., Thiers elected President of France. C. Darwin, *The Descent of Man.*

1872 8 Feb., Lord Mayo, Viceroy of India, murdered. Sept., Austrian, German and Russian Emperors meet in Berlin. France and Japan make conscription compulsory. Bureau of Released Slaves abolished in USA. Society of the Divine Word (SVD), and Pious Mothers of Nigritia founded.

1873 9 Sept., Prussian troops evacuate France. Germany and USA adopt the gold standard. Judicial system reformed in

Bahr al-Ghazal: Zubair Pasha
Rahma Mansur first governor.
Baker Pasha reaches Gondokoro
and then returns to England.
Zubair Pasha invades Darfur.
Post Offices opened at Korosko,
Wadi Halfa, Dongola, Berber
and Khartoum. Hospital in
Khartoum with 270 beds: other
hospitals in provincial capitals.
General George Gordon
appointed Governor of the
Equatorial Nile Basin.
1873-6 Egyptian General Staff
with Americans map the Sudan.
1873-6 Joubert's expedition.
1874-1908 Mustafa Kamil,
Egyptian nationalist.
1874 Jan., Zubair Pasha destroys
Darfur army at Shaka. Feb., Gordon
arrives in Egypt: March, reaches
Khartoum, and continues to Gondokoro:
series of military posts set up to
within sixty miles of L. Victoria.
Ruznameh tax imposed in Egypt.
Egyptian railway reaches Asyut;
Sudan Railway inaugurated. 2 Nov.,
El Fasher occupied. Paul
Soleillet's expedition.
Moroccan expedition against
Rif. D.Mackenzie establishes
factory at Tarfaya, Morocco.
Ceuta made the seat of the
Spanish Captania General
de Africa.
1875 Khedive Ismail accepts
Gordon's plan to extend
Egypt to include Eastern
Africa. Khedive (later
Royal Eygptian) Geographical
Society founded.
1875-1950 Ismail Sidky Pasha,
Egyptian statesman.
1875-6 Rohlfs travelling in the
Libyan desert.
1875-7 Largeau's expedition.

Elmina. 2 Oct., Major-General
Sir Garnet Wolseley sworn as
Civil Administrator. 20 Oct.,
ultimatum sent to Asantehene.
5 Nov., British attacked at
Abakrampa; 26 Nov., British
begin advance on Kumasi; Ashanti
retreat, having lost half of army
of 40,000, chiefly by disease.
Gbanya, chief of Kpa-Mende, sends
a contingent to assist the British
in the Ashanti war.

1874 31 Jan., British defeat
Ashanti at Amoafo. 4 Feb.,
Wolseley enters Kumasi and finds
town evacuated; town fired by
released Fante prisoners. 6 Feb.,
Wolseley returns to the
coast. 13 Feb., Asantehene
agrees to pay fine, free trade,
end of human sacrifices and open
road to Kumasi; 14 March, treaty
executed at Cape Coast. Lagos
put under the Governor of the
Gold Coast Colony; Sierra Leone
separated.

1875 King Jaja given a sword of
honour by Queen Victoria for
aid in Ashanti war. French
campaign against Ahmadu Shehu
of Toro; defeated at Boumdou;
Ahmadu d. Ashanti attack
Juaben. War on Bagru country.
Steamer *Sultan of Sockatoo*
attacked on R Niger.

again divided. Lieut. Grandy
explores R Congo. 456 boys
and 33 girls, black and white,
in schools in Angola. Marché
and de Compiègne explore
R Ogooué.

1874 Nyangwe comes under the
control of Tippu Tib.
1874-84 George Grenfell exploring
in Cameroun.
1874-7 H.M. Stanley exploring the
Congo.
1874-8 Savorgnan de Brazza's
first exploration of Rs Ogooué
and Alima, and then Congo basin.
1874-7 Pogge and Linx exploring
Angola and Congo as far as
Katanga.
1874-5 V.L. Cameron exploring
Katanga.

1875 6 Nov., Cameron reaches
Katombela, having crossed Africa.
Tippu Tib settles at Kasongo,
becoming virtual ruler of the
area. Slavery and forced
labour abolished in Angola.
post 1875 The Chokwe expand W
of R Kasai.

1876 May, Caisse de la Dette
Publique established in Cairo,
with Austrian, British, French
and Italian members; Oct.,
British and French controllers
appointed to supervise Egyptian
revenue and expediture: system
known as Dual Control. 1 Nov.,
G.J. Goschen and Joubert visit

1876 Brière de l'Isle governor
of Senegal. Cotonou ceded to
France. Fourah Bay College
affiliated to Durham University.
Sultan of Sockatoo again
attacked: trade at a stand-still
punitive expedition by the
Royal Navy on R Niger.
1876-84 *West African Reporter,*

1876 Papagiotis Potogos explores
sources of R Bili.

EASTERN AFRICA	SOUTHERN AFRICA	OTHER COUNTRIES
Africa. Mission under Sir Bartle Frere to Zanzibar: new treaty prohibits export of slaves and closes the slave market. Mbarak of Gazi again rebels. 5 June, Sayyid Barghash of Zanzibar abolishes slave market and the export of slaves: site of market used for Anglican cathedral.	of Cape Colony, appointed. Cetewayo crowned King of the Zulu. Anglican synod at Cape Town.	England. Flemish as well as French permitted in Belgian courts. Hanoi taken by François Garnier. Russia penetrates Chinese Turkestan. Guizot, *Histoire de la France*.
1874 18 Feb., V.L. Cameron reaches L.Tanganyika. 17 Nov., Stanley's second expedition leaves Bagamoyo. Yohannes IV appeals for Russian help against Muslims but receives no reply. **1874** Edward Steere, theologian, linguist, printer and architect, appointed Anglican Bp of Zanzibar (−**1882**).	**1874-81** Campaign for confederation of SA.	**1874-80** Benjamin Disraeli, Prime Minister. **1874** 13 Jan., Russia introduces conscription. 15 March, France proclaims protectorate over Annam. 18 Apr., Dr Livingstone buried in Westminster Abbey. 30 Aug., British Factory Act institutes 56½ hour week. 25 Oct., Britain annexes Fiji Is. Watch Tower or Jehovah's Witnesses founded in USA. Glasgow merchants subscribe £10,000 for a steamer on L. Nyasa.
1875 5 Apr., H.M. Stanley visits Kabaka Mutesa of Buganda. Nov., Barawa annexed by Egypt, followed by Kisimayu and Lamu. Zanzibari troops disarmed. Three Egyptian expeditions against Ethiopia: Münzinger's expedition annihilated by Sultan of Aussa; expedition from Massawa wiped out by Yohannes IV; expedition under Rauf Pasha against Harar successful; Egyptian puppet made Sultan. UMCA mission set up on R Ruvuma (now Diocese of Masasi). Nyungu ya Mawe occupies Kirurumo. **1875-93** LMS missions on L. Tanganyika. **1876** Sayyid Barghash issues proclamations forbidding conveyance of slaves by land and slave caravans from the interior coming to the coast: riots in Mombasa. General Gordon in Bunyoro. Jan., Egyptians withdraw from Barawa, Kisimayu and Lamu.	**1875** United Free Church of Scotland Missions set up at Blantyre and Livingstonia on L. Nyasa. Anglican Synod in Cape Town adopts new constitution. **1876** Blantyre founded. **1876-7** War with Secocoeni.	**1875-1965** Albert Schweitzer, theologian, missionary and musician. **1875** Aug., Carnarvon conversations on South African Federation. 19 Sept., Britain buys 176,602 Suez Canal shares from the Khedive for £4m. 15 Nov., H.M. Stanley writes letter in The *Daily Telegraph* appealing for missionaries to convert Uganda. Geographical Society of Lisbon founded. Parnell enters the House of Commons. German Socialist Labour Party founded. Turkey bankrupt. Sayyid Barghash, Sultan of Zanzibar, pays state visit to Queen Victoria at Windsor. **1876-1909.** Abd al-Hamid II, Ottoman Sultan. **1876** 26 Feb., China declares Korea independent. March, Cave report on Egyptian finances. May, Berlin conference. Sept., International Geographical Conference at Brussels founds International African Association.

Egypt to establish dual control.
Gordon resigns through ill
health. *Al-Ahram*, principal
Egyptian newspaper, founded.
Secret Society founded amongst
Egyptian army officers.
Moroccan expedition against Rif.

newspaper, founded.

1877-90 Gordon Pasha Governor-
General of the Sudan.
1877 Lyons missionaries (SMA)
start work in Egypt.

1877-86 War between Ibadan and
Egbas and Ijebus: Fulani from
Ilorin attack Ibadan.
1877 First visit of George
Goldie Taubman (later Sir
George Goldie) to the upper
Niger.

1877 1 Jan., Stanley arrives at
Stanley Falls; 12 March, at
Stanley Pool; 17 Oct., arrives
at Boma, having taken 999
days from Zanzibar.

1878 March, British and French govern-
ments demand international commission
of inquiry into Egyptian finances. 18
Aug., Nubar Pasha premier of Egypt; Sir
Rivers Wilson, Minister of Finance; 11
Dec., Dual Control in Egypt suspended on
introduction of ministerial government.
Cleopatra's Needle, given to England in
1819, dispatched from Alexandria to
London. Dem Ziber occupied by Gessi
Pasha: becomes capital of Bahr al-Ghazal.
Rohlfs visits Kufra oasis. Plan made for a
railway from Algeria to Senegal.
1879 17 Feb., Nubar Pasha and Sir R.
Wilson mobbed in Cairo; 18 Feb., fall
of Nubar Pasha's ministry. Apr., Sharif
Pasha forms ministry. 29 June, Khedive
Ismail deposed; Muhammad Tewfiq,
Khedive (-1892); International Committee
of Liquidation appointed. July, Assembly
of Delegates dismissed; Aug., Sharif
Pasha dismissed: Riyad Pasha, premier.
4 Sept., Dual Control reimposed:
Sir Evelyn Baring (later Lord Cromer)
British representative. Secret society
of Egyptian army officers emerges as the
Patriotic Party *(al-Hizb al-Watani)*,
hostile to the Khedive and foreigners.
Egyptian General staff disbanded: most
American officers discharged. Azande
recognize Egyptian suzerainty: ivory

1878 30 Dec., quarrel between
the people of Bolor and Jufunco
leads to the massacre of
Portuguese troops. Britain
besieged by Awuna in Fort
Prinsensten, Keta. Ibadan
army beats Fulani at Ikirun.

1879 Senegal granted financial
autonomy. United Africa Co.
founded by Sir George Goldie.
UAC station at Onitsha evacuated
because of local hostility. Cocoa
introduced into the Gold Coast
from Fernando Po and S. Tomé.
French establishments in the
Gulf of Benin attached to Gabon.
British occupy Ketonou.
1879-82 French war with
Moréah.

1878 LIM starts work in the
Congo.
1878-9 Serpa Pinto's journey
from Luanda *via* Bie to Durban.

1879 King Akwa asks the protection
of Queen Victoria. Rubber first
exported from Angola. 4 Aug.,
H.M. Stanley, with Zanzibar
porters, begins exploration of R
Congo. Fernando Po made a
penal settlement.
1879-86 Junker explores R Ouelle
and R Chari.

EASTERN AFRICA | SOUTHERN AFRICA | OTHER COUNTRIES

EASTERN AFRICA

-7 March, Ethiopian defeat
gyptians near Gura. May,
gyptians formally annex
erritory near L. Victoria and
.. Albert: no troops sent.
ept., Italian exploratory
aission under Count Orazio
ntinori arrives in Ethiopia
-1882). Fresh Egyptian
xpedition against Ethiopia
efeated at Gura: end of
gyptian pretensions in E
frica.
ohannes IV again asks
ussian help, sending gifts,
ut no reply. CMS start work
t Mpwapwa. First CMS
missionaries reach Uganda.
877 Slaves still being smuggled
om Kilwa: governor imprisoned.
loly Ghost Fathers mission
pened at Mhonda. Police,
vater-supply and street lighting
rganized in Zanzibar. Eastern
elegraph Co. links Zanzibar
o Aden. Menelik confirmed in
is title by Yohannes IV.
repel-Cambier expedition to
.. Tanganyika.
877-1901 General Matthews trains
anzibar regular army.

878 28 June, Lieut. Cambier's
xpedition leaves Bagamoyo.
Nyungu ya Mawe attacks White
Fathers' caravan. First White
Fathers' mission at Tabora.
talian trade expedition in
Ethiopia. Council of Ethiopian
Church at Borumieda: heretics
rdered to submit, and Muslims,
ews and pagans to be baptized.
878 or 1879 Hehe beat off the
Ngoni: war until 1881.
879 17 Feb., first White Fathers
each Entebbe. 27 May, Cambier
eaves Tabora; 12 Aug., arrives at
Jjiji: Fort Léopold built at Karema,
s post of International African
Association; Nov., joined by
urther expedition under Capt.
Poperlin. Mkwawa succ. Munyigamba
s chief of the Hehe. Gordon visits
Yohannes IV to make peace for
Egypt: Yohannes IV refuses,
lemanding recognition of
ncient frontiers. H.M. Stanley
eaves Zanzibar for the Congo.

SOUTHERN AFRICA

1877 31 March, Sir Bartle
Frere High Commissioner in S
Africa with instructions to work
for federation. 12 Apr., S
African Republic annexed by
Britain. Aug., first Kaffir war
(-1878). Oct., Britain makes
treaty of commerce with
Madagascar. François Coillard
explores Mashonaland. Zanzibar
Arabs set up a slave-raiding base
at Karonga, L. Malawi. Augusto
Cardoso's expedition to L. Nyasa.
1877-8 War with Galekas.
1878 18 March, Walvis Bay annexed.
May, Kruger and Joubert petition
Westminster against annexation of
Transvaal. 11 Dec., Britain sends
ultimatum to Zulus. Livingstonia
Central African Trading Co. (LCATC)
founded at Mandala near Blantyre.
Coffee first planted near Blantyre.
J. Stevenson founds company for
trade on L. Nyasa. Civil war in
Barotseland.

1879 12 Jan., to 1 Sept., Zulu
war; 22 Jan., British troops
massacred at Isandhlwana;
July, Prince Imperial killed.
4 July, principles of the
Afrikander Bond published.
28 Aug., Cetewayo captured;
1 Sept., peace signed; 16 Dec.,
Transvaal Republic proclaimed.
Fingoland and Griqualand East
annexed. Jesuit mission
established at Bulawayo.

OTHER COUNTRIES

Britain makes Socotra a
protectorate. Ottoman
constitution promulgated.

1877 1 Jan., Queen Victoria
proclaimed Empress of India.
17 March, first Turkish
Parliament meets. 14 Apr.-3
March 1878, Russo-Turkish
war. Livingstone Inland Mission
(LIM) founded in London. The
phonograph and the microphone
invented by Edison. The telephone
invented by Graham Bell.

1878-1903 Leo XIII, Pope.
1878 June, Boycott first practised
in Ireland. Sept., Anglo-African
war (-1880). 25 Nov., *Comité
d'Etudes du Haut-Congo* formed
in the Congo. H.M. Stanley agrees
to serve Léopold II for 5 years.
Flemish made an official language
in Belgium. Labour code instituted
for all Portuguese colonies: forced
labour abolished.

1879 Henry George, *Progress and
Poverty*. Fabri, pamphlet, *Germany's
need for Colonies*. Panama Canal Co.
founded. Edison and Swann make
the first electric light bulb.

made a state monopoly. Sayyid
Ali al-Mirghani b. Rising
against French in Algeria
finally quelled.
1880 Law of Liquidation in Egypt
allots 50% of revenue to
administration and 50% to Caisse
de la Dette. Rivalry between
France and Italy in Tunis.
1880-2 Muhammad Rauf,
Governor-General of the
Sudan.

*c.***1880** Freetown harbour fortified
as a naval coaling depot.
*c.***1880-4** Trade wars in the Sierra
Leone hinterland.
1880-4 Freer competition between
British and French companies on
Oil Rivers.
1880 St Louis, Rufisque and
Gorée made *communes de pleine
exercice*. French obtain railway
concession in Guinea. Lyons
mission (SMA) starts work
on the Gold Coast.
11 May, Dio attacked by Bambara,
but halted by order of Ahmadu,
Tekrur Sultan. Post at Bamako founded
by Galliéni.

*c.***1880** Msiri's kingdom at its
greatest extent, with caravans
to Angola and Zanzibar. Tyo
at war with Bobangi.
1880 19 Apr., post established
at Mswata. 30 Apr., Léopold
II proclaimed sovereign at Vivi:
Sir Francis de Winton appointed
Administrator-General. June,
Brazza sets up a post at
Franceville; Sept., makes treaties
with Congolese Kings; 1 Oct.,
Brazzaville founded. 9 Nov.,
Stanley and Brazza meet. First
missions of the Holy Ghost
Fathers in the Congo. Thirstland
Trekkers, under Jacobus Botha,
settle on Huila plateau, Angola;
Portuguese immigration to the
plateau increased.
1880-1 Serpa Pinto's second
journey.
1880-3 H. von Wissmann exploring
Congo.

1881 Feb., Colonels Ahmad Pasha
Urabi, Ali Fahmi and Abd al-Al
Hilmi, leaders of Patriotic Party,
court-martialled: mutiny of
Egyptian army secures their
release. 19 June, Muhammad Ahmad
b. Abdallah, a *faqih* from Dongola,
proclaims himself Mahdi in the
Sudan; period known as the
Mahdia (-1898). Aug., expedition
sent to seize the Mahdi fails.
9 Sept., nationalist rising in
Egypt under Ahmad Pasha
Urabi: new ministry under
Sharif Pasha. 30 Apr., French
navy seizes Bizerta; French army
invades Tunis from Algeria; 12
May, Treaty of Bardo: Bey of Tunis
accepts French protectorate.
July (-1883) rising against the
French in Algeria. *Code de
l'indigénat* established in Algeria.
1881-96 Administrative services
in Algiers under direct authority
of relevant ministries in Paris.
1882 Jan., Ahmad Pasha Urabi
made Secretary for War. 8 Jan.,
Anglo-French Note sent to Khedive;
5 Feb., new national ministry: 21
Feb., Ministry of the Sudan created.
in Egypt; 19-20 May, Anglo-French
fleet arrives at Alexandria; 11
July, British and French bombard
Alexandria; 22 July, Urabi
proclaimed a rebel; 13 Sept.,
British defeat Egyptian army

1881-2 UAC gives aid to Amir of
Nupe in struggle against rebels.
1881 Oct., Capt. Lonsdale visits
Asantehene on pacific mission
and to open northern trade routes.
French expedition to Kita;
Bosséyabès subdued in Guinea.
Annual slave raids from
Dahomey into Yorubaland.
Kwa Ibo territory raided by
King Jaja.
1881-8 French expeditions
against Almamy Samory.

*c.***1881** Simon Kimbangu, revivalist,
b. at Nkamba.
1881-5 Many other posts established
by the International African
Association in the Congo. Stanley
reaches Brazzaville; founds
Léopoldville on opposite bank of
R Congo; Dec., reaches Stanley Falls
in three boats. BMS starts work in
the Congo.

1882 Jan., Portuguese campaign
against Jubada. 28 June, Anglo-
French agreement on boundaries
of Sierra Leone and Guinea.
Friction between Ashanti and
Gyaman. First French Resident
at Cotonou. Hostilities between
Abomey and Porto-Novo. First
Gold Coast Education Ordinance.
UAC store destroyed at Asabu:
town bombarded by HMS *Flirt*.

1882 1 March, Britain refuses
the request of the Cameroun
kings and chiefs for a protectorate.
June, French post established on
R Alina, Congo. International
African Association posts
established at Mpala (by Storme)
and Stanley Falls (H.M. Stanley).
Kirundu founded. Tyo kingdom
accepts French protectorate.
Azanga, King of Mangbetu, submits to

EASTERN AFRICA	SOUTHERN AFRICA	OTHER COUNTRIES
1880 International African Association posts set up at Kondoa (French), Tabora and Kakoma (German). Freetown mission, Mombasa, attacked in Ramadhan by Arabs and Swahili for harbouring escaped slaves. Menelik defeats Galla and prepared to take Harar; sends expedition against Kaffa. *c.***1880** 50,000 Muslims, 20,000 pagans and ½m. Galla said to have been baptized in forced conversion by Ethiopian Church. **1880-1950** Siti binti Saad, Swahili poetess. **1880-1** Rohlfs visits Ethiopia.	**1880** 13 Oct., Transvaal Republic declares its independence; 16 Oct., Britain and Transvaal at war; 16 Dec., Transvaal rises in War of of Independence; Republic again proclaimed. 30 Dec., Republic proclaimed with Paul Kruger as President. Cape-Basuto War (-**1881**). De Beers mining corporation formed by Cecil Rhodes.	**1880-3** Gladstone, Prime Minister. **1880** March, Roman Catholic orders expelled from France. 19 June, Tahiti annexed by France. St Gothard tunnel completed. The bicycle invented. Typhoid bacillus discovered. *Compagnie française de l'Afrique équatoriale)CFAE)* founded.
1881 Menelik's expedition against Arusi. Yohannes IV pays Coptic Patriarch 12,000 Maria Theresa thalers for consecration of four abunas (bishops). France requires Egypt to remove the Egyptian flag from Ras Bir, near Obock. French occupy Obock.	**1881** 28 Jan., Boers repulse British at Laing's Neck; and 27 Feb., at Majuba Hill; 27 Feb., armistice between Boers and British; 21 March, Transvaal self-governing under a Triumvirate; Apr., Treaty of Pretoria, Britain recognizes Boer republic; Aug., Pretoria Convention defines boundaries. *c.***1881** Caravans of up to 5,000 slaves passing through Mwembe to Kilwa. **1881** Work in Nyasaland resumed by UMCA. **1881-2** Fighting on western Transvaal border.	**1881** 13 March, Alexander II of Russia murdered. 19 Apr., Lord Beaconsfield (B. Disraeli) d. 3 July, Turkey cedes Epirus and Thessaly to Greece. Revised Version of the New Testament published. Vatican Archives opened to students.
1882 Dec., Italy establishes colony of Eritrea. Menelik's expedition against Gojjam; Galla kingdom of Gudru seized; Sultan of Jimma becomes vassal of Menelik. Mkwawa, chief of the Hehe, campaigns against Nyamwezi and Ngoni.	**1882** Marianhill Abbey founded by the Trappists. Friction between French and government in Madagascar.	**1882** 6 May, Phoenix Park murders. 6 June, Hague Convention of 3-mile limit for territorial waters. House of Commons resolution recommends the transfer of all administrative responsibility in W Africa to the 'natives' except 'probably' in Sierra Leone. Von der Goltz mission to Istanbul. Leopold II establishes International Association for the Congo. First US legislation on emigration.

EGYPT, THE SUDAN & NORTHERN AFRICA	WESTERN AFRICA	CENTRAL AFRICA
under Urabi at Tel el-Kebir; British occupation of Egypt and Sudan begun; 15 Sept., British take Cairo: Urabi banished to Ceylon; 9 Nov., Lord Dufferin arrives to re-establish Dual Control. Jules Ferry proposes a school in every hamlet in Algeria. **1883** Jan., The Mahdi captures Bara. 1 May, 'Organic Law' in Egypt sets up Legislative Council and General Assembly under authority of British Agent. 5 June, Convention of Marsa: France gains effective control of Tunisia. 11 Sept., Sir Evelyn Baring, (later Lord Cromer, 1841-1917) arrives as British Agent (-1907). 5 Nov., Mahdi defeats Anglo-Egyptian force at El Obeid: Britain decides to evacuate Sudan. 23 Dec., Rudolf von Slatin Pasha, Governor of Darfur, having become Muslim, submits to Mahdi. **1883-90** Nubar Pasha, premier of Egypt. **1884** 18 Feb., Gordon reaches Khartoum with orders to evacuate Egyptians; Mahdi refuses to negotiate; Mahdi takes Qedaref and, 13 Oct., Omdurman.	UAC reorganized as the National African Co. Ltd. **1883** Feb., Asantehene Mensah Bonsu deposed by chiefs for friendliness towards British: year of anarchy ensues in Ashanti. March, Fula rising against Portuguese at S. Belchier. Dec., French begin conquest of upper Niger. French reoccupy Grand Bassam, Assinie and Dabou, Ivory Coast. Consul Hewett recommends deportation of King Jaja of Opobo for cruelty to Africans. **1884** Apr., Germany occupies Togo. Apr., Portuguese expedition against Jebelor, Jeboucer and Beri. Merchants of the Benin River complain that they have had no consular visit since 1879. 1 July, treaty between Britain and Opobo. 5 July, German treaty with Chief Nlapa in Togo. 1 Nov., treaty between Britain and Asabu. 19 Dec., further treaty between Britain and Opobo stipulating freedom of trade. Treaties between National African Co. and Sokoto and Gwandu. Rio de Oro, (later Villa Cisneros), occupied by Emilio Bonelli: Spanish Protectorate between Cape Bojador and Cape Blanco proclaimed.	Sudanese mercenaries in Egyptian pay. **1882-3** Harry Johnston in Angola and the Congo. **1883** 30 Jan., commercial agreement between King Akwa and German merchant E. Schmidt. 23 Aug., German treaty with Pass-All, Cameroun chief. Brazza, Commissioner-General in West Africa. Joseph Thomson explores region between Lakes Nyasa and Tanganyika. **1883-4** H. von Wissmann exploring northern Cameroun. **1883-5** Brazza with others explores and occupies French Congo. **1884** 8 June, H.M. Stanley leaves the Congo for Europe, having set up 40 posts and made 400 treaties. 12 July, Douala chiefs sign protectorate treaty with firm of E. Woermann, 14 July, German Protectorate over Kamerun inaugurated by Dr. G. Nachtigal; 19 July, abortive British attempt to proclaim a protectorate. Grenfell explores Oubangui in order to set up missions. **1884-5** Mangbetu again independent as a result of the Mahdia. H. von Wissmann explores Lakes Tanganyika and Nyasa, reaching coast at Quelimane. **1884-6** Tippu Tib at Stanley Falls: requested by Sultan of Zanzibar to seize eastern half on Congo in his name. Dias de Carvalho's expedition to Katanga.
1885 26 Jan., Mahdi takes Khartoum; Gordon d. 28 Jan., British relief force arrives; Sudan evacuated. 22 June, Mahdi d., succ. by Khalifa Abdallahi b. Muhammad; 30 July, Dervishes take Kassala and control all Sudan except ports. **1885-1959** Sayyid Abd al-Rahman al-Mahdi, posthumous son of the Mahdi.	**1885** 1 June, treaty between Britain and Sokoto. 5 June, British establish Protectorate over 'Niger Districts'. July, German flag raised at Agbanekin; Sept., Portuguese flag raised at Whydah, Godomey and Cotonou: claims later withdrawn in favour of France. 11 Nov., boundary between Sierra Leone and Liberia defined; French garrison established at Cotonou.	**1885-1902** German penetration of N Kamerun. **1885-1911** German penetration of southern and central Kamerun. **1885** 9 Jan., Spain proclaims protectorate over Spanish Guinea. 24 Dec., Franco-German convention on boundaries of Kamerun and Gabon. Chokwe invasion of Lunda territory.

EASTERN AFRICA   SOUTHERN AFRICA   OTHER COUNTRIES

1883 French vessel *l'Inferne* sent to reconnoitre Obock with a view to setting up a post. Mahdist raid on Gondar. Bukumbi, first White Fathers' mission on L. Victoria, founded. Vicariate Apostolic of Uganda established.

1883 16 Apr., Paul Kruger President of the SA Republic; 24 Apr., Germany begins settlements in SW Africa and Angra Pequena: Britain states it an infringement of her rights. 1 June (-Dec. 1885) French war with Madagascar; 14 Dec., Portugal grants railway concession from Delagoa Bay to Transvaal to US promoter. Sept., Boer republic of Stellaland founded in Bechuanaland. British consul appointed to Malawi region, accredited to the 'Kings and Chiefs of Central Africa'. Oblates of St Francis de Sales start work on the Orange R. 1883-4 civil war in Zululand.

1883-1950 Earl Wavell. 1883-1945 Benito Mussolini. 1883-1968 Earl Attlee. 1883 3 Jan., Lord Granville circulates powers stating Britain's intention to withdraw from Egypt as soon as the state of the country permits. Annam becomes a French Protectorate. Tongking expedition. First skyscraper built in Chicago.

1884 9 Apr., Sultan of Gobad recognizes French authority at Obock. 3 June, Menelik signs treaty with Britain for alliance against the Mahdi and suppression of the slave trade. 24 June, Lagarde opens French post at Obock as 'Commandant'; 21 Sept., Sultan of Tadjoura recognizes France. Nov., Gobad and Tadjoura ceded to France. Nov., Dr Karl Peters lands in Zanzibar and makes treaties with eleven mainland chiefs. Dec., Britain establishes British Somaliland Protectorate based on Zaila. Mutesa, Kabaka of Buganda, d. Abdallah b. Muhammad b. Ali Abd al-Shakur made ruler of Harar. Keren-Bilen territory restored by Egypt to Ethiopia.

1884 Feb., Cetewayo driven out of Zululand. March, British Protectorate proclaimed in Basutoland. May, Dinizulu, son of Cetewayo, crowned King of the Zulu in return for land ceded to settlers. Aug., German Protectorate proclaimed over SW Africa. Sept., Goshen annexed by the Transvaal. Sept., rebellion against Lewanika in Barotseland. Nov., Britain annexes St Lucia Bay to Natal, to prevent Boer access to E coast. Maseko raid across the Kirk Mts; Yao slave raiding temporarily interrupted. Galekaland and Tembuland annexed by the Cape. *Imvo zaba Ntsundu*, first Xhosa newspaper, published. Tembu National Church formed in Transkei. A. Schultz and A. Hammar explore R Chobe. H. Capello and R. Ivens cross Africa from Angola to Quelimane *via* Barotseland.

1884 1 Feb., *Oxford English Dictionary* begins publication. 26 Feb., Anglo-Portuguese Treaty recognizing Portuguese right to the mouth of the R Congo: Léopold II and Germany protest. 27 Feb., Convention of London regulates status of the Transvaal. Society for German Colonization founded. 26 Apr., Britain denounces Anglo-Portuguese Congo Treaty. 18 June, International Conference on Egyptian finances. London. 15 Nov. (-24 Feb.. 1885), Berlin Conference: recognizes free trade on R Congo with abolition of slavery and the slave trade.

1885 5 Jan., Five CMS converts martyred in Buganda. 6 Feb., Italy occupies Massawa; 25 Feb., Germany annexes German East Africa. 26 March, Lagarde signs treaty with Somali chiefs of Gubbet-Kharab and Ambado. Tadjoura and Djibouti occupied. Aug., German naval demonstration off Zanzibar; German claims on mainland recognized. 29 Oct., Bp Hannington murdered on

1885 22 Jan., Treaty of friendship between SA Republic and Germany. 31 March, British Protectorate over North Bechuanaland ends Stellaland republic. Sept., Bechuanaland proclaimed a Crown Colony. 17 Dec., French treaty with Madagascar: Resident installed. Gold discovered in the Transvaal. Cape railway reaches Kimberley. Transvaal formally denies all Indians civil and political rights. Cape Parliament Houses

1885 12 Feb., Karl Peters' German East Africa Co. chartered. 23 Feb., International Congo Association formally recognized. 25 Feb., Berlin Act. 30 Apr., Léopold II proclaimed sovereign of the Congo Free State. 1 Aug., Constitution of CFS proclaimed. 30 Oct., Separate cabinet and *Force Publique* instituted for CFS. Trans-Canadian railway completed. Lord Salisbury, Prime Minister (-1886).

24 Dec., Franco-German
convention; Germans receive
Porto Seguro and Little
Popo; French Guinea
possessions recognized by
Germany; boundaries of Togo
agreed. British abandon
Kétonou. Trade treaties
between Sokoto and Gwandu
on behalf of R Niger Co.
Further complaints from
Benin at the lack of consular
visits. Court of Equity on
Brass R compelled by local
chiefs to reverse decisions.
King Jaja of Opobo objects
to freedom of trade agreed
at the Berlin Conference.

1886 Prefecture Apostolic of the
Nile Delta established. Emin
Pasha withdraws to southern
Equatoria.

1886 13 Jan., Colony of Lagos
separated from Niger Rivers;
governor independent of Gold
Coast. 12 May, Franco-
Portuguese convention on
Dahomey and Guinea. 14 July, British
and Germans agree 2½ miles of
Gold Coast-Togo boundary.
Anglo-German agreement on
the boundary of Nigeria with
Kamerun. Portuguese campaign
against Fulas led by Mussa Molo
near Sancorla. King Agoué
accepts French protection.
Adansi massacre 150 Ashanti
traders; June, Ashanti army drives
Adansi people across R Pra.
British arbitration ends Yoruba
war. Naval force attacks Niger
delta villages after attacks on
Royal Niger Co.'s vessels. Royal
Niger Co. Constabulary founded.
1886-7 Togo-Dahomey frontier
delineated by France and Germany.
1886-8 Galliéni's expeditions
against Samory and Bambara.
1886-1951 *Sierra Leone Weekly
News,* newspaper.
1887-96 Civil war in Ashanti.
1887-9 Binger travels from
Bamako to Grand Bassam, Ivory
Coast, *via* Kong and the Mossi.
1887 Dakar separated from Gorée and
made a *commune de pleine exercice.*
Executive Council in Gambia
expanded, including two Africans.
Basel (Calvinist) Mission
replaces the English Baptists in
the Gold Coast. Gléglé, King of
Dahomey, demands French
withdrawal from Cotonou. Dispute
between Britain and King Jaja;
Aug., King Jaja deported to West
Indies. Governing Councils
replace Courts of Inquiry on
Oil Rivers.

1886 12 May, Franco-Portuguese
convention on the boundary of
the French Congo; 29 June,
colonies of Gabon and French
Congo under single rule: Brazza,
Commissioner-General. 24 Aug.,
post at Stanley Falls attacked
by Arab traders under Rashid,
nephew of Tippu Tib. Dec.,
Sanford Exploring Expedition
granted a concession in the
upper Congo. 23 Dec., Bremen
mission starts work in Douala.
Force Publique established in
the Congo for military and police
duties. Plymouth Brethren
mission established in Katanga.
American Presbyterians replaced.
by *Société des Missions
Evangéliques* in Gabon.

1887 22 May, Britain signs
convention with Egypt to
withdraw in 3 years. Fighting
on Sudan frontier with
Ethiopia.

1887 Feb., Tippu Tib made
Governor of Stanley Falls District
in the Congo Free State. 29 Apr.,
Convention between France and
the Congo Free State on Congolese
boundaries. Chokwe expelled by
brothers Mushiri and Kawele.
Baptist Mission in Ambas Bay
bought out by Germany; British
claim to Ambas Bay withdrawn.

EASTERN AFRICA	SOUTHERN AFRICA	OTHER COUNTRIES

Buganda boundary. 20 Dec., Germany acquires customs privileges at Dar es Salaam and Pangani. Yohannes IV gives permission for a Russian colony and monastery in Ethiopia. Italians occupy Massawa. British occupy Berbera and Zaila. H.H. Johnston in the Kilimanjaro region. Benedictine nuns start work in Dar es Salaam.

completed. Lewanika regains control of Barotseland. Independent Congregational Church of Bechuanaland started.

1886 3 June, Catholic and Anglican converts martyred in Buganda. 2 Dec., Mirambo d. Bethel Lutheran Mission starts work in German East Africa. Yohannes IV declares war on the Mahdi. Sultan of Harar defeats Italian expedition.

1886 6 Jan., French Protectorate established over Grand Comoro; 21 Apr., French Resident refused by Anjouan: French troops disembark; 26 Apr., French Protectorate established in Mohéli. 30 Dec., German-Portuguese agreement on boundaries of Angola and German SW Africa. Part of Zululand annexed.

1886 1 Feb.-26 June, Gladstone, Prime Minister, succ. Salisbury. 10 July, Royal Niger Co. chartered. 1 Nov., Anglo-German agreement on spheres of interest in E. Africa. H. de la Martinière, *Essai de Bibliographie Marocaine,* again suggests French conquest of Morocco. Slavery abolished in Cuba. Burma annexed by Britain.

1887 Jan., Ras Alula defeats Italians at Sagati; Ethiopian army withdraws because of Galla rising; June, attacked by Mahdists; Gondar burnt and pillaged; another Mahdist expedition defeated; Harar taken by Menelik: Sultan deposed. 13 Dec., Stanley discovers L. Albert Edward Nyanza. France occupies Dougaretta; British, in exchange for French evacuation, recognize French possession of Mouscha Is. Relief expeditions of Stanley and Karl Peters seeking for Emin Pasha. British declare protectorate over N Somalia. Benedictines of

1887 26 March, Anjouan accepts French Protectorate and Resident. 21 June, Britain annexes all Zululand. 30 July, Treaty between Lobengula and the Transvaal. Dinizulu banished to St Helena. Rhodes acquires control of De Beers. Gold Fields of SA Ltd, later Consolidated Gold Fields of SA Ltd, founded by Rhodes.
1887-9 Fighting between LCATC and Arabs under Mlozi at N end of L. Nyasa.

1887 4 Apr., first Colonial Conference in London. 29 Apr., Agreement on French and Belgian Congo boundaries. 26 May, Imperial British EA Co. chartered. 18 June, Reinsurance Treaty between Germany and Russia. 21 June, Queen Victoria's Golden Jubilee. 12 Dec., Triple Alliance between Austria, Britain, and Italy. *Compagnie du Congo pour le Commerce et l'Industrie* founded in Brussels. Independent Labour Party founded in Britain.

1888-91 Archinard's expedition
against Samory.
1888 11 Dec., French protectorate treaty
with Almamy of Futa, Guinea. New
Anglo-German agreement on Gold
Coast-Togo boundary. Treaty
with the Alafin of Oyo places
all Yorubaland under British
protection.

1888 29 Apr., Stanley finds
Emin Pasha. 11 Dec., Gabon
and French Congo declared a
single colony: Brazza,
Commissioner-General. All
British missionaries replaced
by Germans in Kamerun.
Tippu Tib claims Rwanda as
being its supplier of arms.
*c.*1888-1933 Njoya, King of
Foumbau: inventor of Bamoun
script of seventy-three letters
and ten figures. Scheut Frs
replace the Holy Ghost Frs
in the Congo. Yaoundé
founded.

1889 *al-Muayyad*, political journal
founded in Cairo by Shaikh Ali
Yusuf. Emin Pasha leaves
Equatoria with H.M. Stanley's
relief mission. Budget surplus
restored in Egypt.

1889 10 Jan., France declares
Protectorate over the Ivory
Coast. 10 Aug., Anglo-French
convention on frontiers of
Guinea, Sierra Leone, Gold
Coast and Lagos. Corraim,
ruler of Ganadu, revolts against
the Portuguese. Aug., punitive
expedition. Gléglé invades
Porto Novo and then d.
Major MacDonald, Special
Commissioner, investigating
allegations against R Niger Co.
Lieut. Mizon enters R Niger
mouth with French warship:
hostilities with local Africans.
Final pacification of R Niger
at Opobo. Anglo-French
agreement on the boundary of
Dahomey with Nigeria.

1889 22 Dec., eclipse observed
during the coronation of Mibambwe
IV Rutarindwa of Rwanda.
Simon Kimbangu comes under
influence of BMS. Léopold II
declares all 'vacant' land in the
Congo state property. First
hospital built at Boma.

1890-1 Riyad Pasha, premier of
Egypt.
1890 Apr., Uthman Digna, Governor
of Dongola. 12 March, King Idris
I of Libya b. 12 Nov., Cardinal
Lavigérie's 'Algiers Toast'
calls on all Frenchmen to rally to
the Constitution, in an attempt
to improve relations between
Church and State.

1890 March, Béhanzin, son of
Gléglé, attacks Cotonou;
settlement made by French
includes payment of rent
for Cotonou and Porto Novo.
5 Aug., Franco-British
declaration in London on
French West Africa; France
gives up rights in Sokoto in
exchange for recognition of
protectorate in Madagascar.
Dec., Asantehene refuses
British protectorate.
Rising in Carantamba,
Chenhaba, Julabu, Denadu and

1890 Apr., Tippu Tib returns to
Zanzibar to answer a law suit
filed by Stanley. 25 Oct.,
Pallotine Fathers start work in
Kamerun. Ponel mission explores
R Oubangui. Cholet explores
R Sangha as far as N'Goko.
Prince d'Arenbourg and H. Alis
found committee for French
Africa, for penetration to
L. Chad and to join up Algeria,
Sudan and the Congo.
Nord-West Kamerun Gesellschaft
established.
1890-1 Lemarinel mission to

Ottilien arrives in Dar es
Jaam.
₹87-94 Menelik subdues additional
alla and Sidama territory.
₹88 French move post from
bock to Djibouti; 8 Feb., move
cognized by Britain. Abu
aihiri's rebellion in German
ast Africa. Ethiopians sent to
ussia to join in 900th anniversary
lebration of the introductior.
Christianity. IBEA sets up
ase in Mombasa; 'coastal strip'
ased from Sultan of Zanzibar.

₹89 18 Jan.-17 Feb., Russian
pedition settles in fort at
agallo; 17 Feb., fired on and
urrendered to French: March,
pedition returned to Russia.
) March, Yohannes IV killed in
ittle of Metemna; Menelik
oclaims himself Emperor.
May, Italy signs Treaty of
cciali with Menelik, and
aims this implies a protectorate.
alians make treaty of protection
ith Sultan of Obbia, Somalia.
Aug., Italians occupy Asmara.
alian treaty of friendship and
ade with Shoa. 6 Sept., Kabaka
lwanga of Buganda deposed: succ.
iwewa. 18 Oct., Muslims expel
Christian missionaries from
uganda: Kiwewa deposed:
acc. by Muslim Kabaka Kalema:
ountry antagonized by
ompulsory circumcision.
eligious freedom restored to
luslims in Ethiopia.
1890 Rinderpest destroys many
ittle in E Africa, followed by
neumonia: serious outbreaks of
mallpox: Masai, Kikuyu and
amba especially affected. Islam
eginning to spread near Tanga
ıd Dar es Salaam. Allidina
'isram (b.1863) leading figure
Zanzibar mercantile community
890 4 Jan., revolt led by Bwana
leri defeated. May, von Wissmann
ccupies Kilwa Kivinje and Lindi.
aly reorganizes Red Sea
rritories as Colony of Eritrea.
Aug., Sultan of Zanzibar signs

1888 11 Feb., Lobengula of the
Matabele accepts British
Protectorate; 30 Oct., grants
mining rights to Cecil Rhodes:
Rhodes amalgamates Kimberley
diamond companies. 30 Oct.,
Lobengula signs 'Rudd Concession'
for all mines and metals in his
kingdom to Rhodes group.
Rhodes gains control of Kimberley
industry. LCATC absorbed by
British SA Co. under the name
of the African Lakes Corporation.
Portuguese refuse passage of
artillery for use against Mlozi
to African Lakes Co. and send
expedition under Serpa Pinto
to occupy Shire Highlands.
Bechuanaland Exploration Co.
formed. Barotse campaign
against the Ila.
1889 March, De Beers Consolidated
formed. May, H.H. Johnston
takes up duties as Consul for
Mozambique. 29 Oct., British
SA Co. under Cecil Rhodes
given a charter extending its
territory at the expense of
Transvaal. Dec., British Protectorate
of Nyasaland proclaimed. H.H.
Johnston makes treaties in Nyasaland.
L.S. Jameson makes treaties in
Mashonaland. Salisbury, Rhodesia,
founded. Truce made with the
Arabs at Karonga. Britain
declares Makololo country and
the Shire hills under her
protection. Witwatersrand
Chamber of Mines formed.
1889-1918 Seventy-six Ethiopian
churches founded in S Africa.

1890 27 June, BSA Co. signs treaty
of protection with Barotseland.
17 July, Cecil Rhodes premier of
Cape Colony. Aug., first Swaziland
convention. BSA Co. Pioneer
Column sets up posts at Fort Tuli,
Fort Victoria and Fort Charter
and, 10 Sept., Fort Salisbury:
12 Sept., British flag ceremoniously
raised. 14 Nov., Anglo-Portuguese
agreement on the Zambezi and the
Congo. Bechuanaland placed
under a British Governor.

1888 6 Aug., Corinth Canal
opened. 20 Oct., Suez Canal
Convention at Constantinople
declares canal open to all
nations in war as in peace.
Missionary Sisters of the Precious
Blood and African Society of
German Catholics founded.
Slavery abolished in Brazil.
Cardinal Lavigérie ordered by
Leo XIII to undertake a crusade
against slavery.
1888-1918 William II, German
Emperor.

1889 July-Aug., International
Colonial Congress in Paris. 18
Nov., Colonial Conference in
Brussels. 20 Oct., British SA
Co. incorporated with powers
in all southern Africa north of
Bechuanaland. Brazil proclaimed
a Republic. Eiffel Tower built.
Panama Canal Co. bankrupt.
1889-1908 Carlos, King of
Portugal.

1890 20 March, Bismarck dismissed.
24 May, Mackinnon Treaty between
Léopold of Belgium and BEAC
recognizes Léopold's rights west of
the Upper Nile in return for
territory near L. Tanganyika.
1 July, Anglo-German convention:
Britain cedes Heligoland in return
for Zanzibar and Pemba. 2 July,
Anti-Slavery Conference in
Brussels to eradicate slave trade
and liquor traffic amongst
underdeveloped peoples. 9 July,
part of Léopold II's will made
public, leaving the CFS to Belgium,

EGYPT, THE SUDAN & NORTHERN AFRICA	WESTERN AFRICA	CENTRAL AFRICA
	Xime led by Moli Boia: Portuguese punitive expedition sent. Sierra Leone Protectorate proclaimed. Fr Dorgère, ambassador to the court of Abomey. Dr Crozat explores Mossi. Archinard's second expedition against Ahmadu. Treaty between Royal Niger Co. and Sultan of Sokoto. Anglo-German agreement on boundaries of Nigeria and Kamerun. Anglo-French agreement on boundaries of Nigeria. 1890-3 Col. Monteil explores Say, Kano, Bornu, Chad and returns to Tripoli, after making treaties with Kong and others. 1890-4 Explorations made in Guinea by Parvisse, Brasselard and Faidherbe, and Madrolle. *post* 1890 Syrian traders arriving in Freetown.	Katanga; Msiri refuses to recognize Congo Free State. 1890-1902 Ovimbundu kingdoms in Angola subjected by Portugal. *post* 1890 Balanced budgets in Congo Free State.
1891-3 Mustafa Pasha Fahmi, Premier of Egypt. 1891 Plot in Omdurman to supersede the Khalifa. Feb., Anglo-Egyptian expedition from Suakin routs Uthman Digna and captures his headquarters near Tokar.	1891 Dood's campaign in Senegal. 20 Oct., French treaty with Adrar. Numerous French explorations in Ivory Coast. 12 Dec., Dr Ballay, Governor of Guinea. 3 Dec., Ballot, Governor of Benin (Dahomey). Department of Native Affairs set up in Sierra Leone. Government of Oil Rivers reorganized. African Banking Corporation, first bank in Nigeria, opened. 1891-2 Col. Humbert's expedition against Samory.	1891 May, first expedition of Katanga Co.: Oct., refused recognition by Msiri. 21 Sept., ivory and rubber made state monopolies in the Congo. Basanga revolt against Msiri. Dec., Msiri refuses to recognize Stairs mission. 20 Dec., Msiri killed by Capt. Bodson: end of kingdom of Garaganza. Crampel mission on Rs Oubangui and Chari. French posts established at Ouesso and on R Kemo. Albertville established as a post by Capt. Joubert. 1891-4 War between Arabs and Congo Free State. 1891-2 Bia-Francqui expedition to Katanga: copper deposits described by J. Cornet.
1892 Health Commission of members of foreign colonies in Tangier. 1892-1914 Abbas II Khedive of Egypt, hostile to Britain.	1892 French treaty with Tiéba, King of Sikasso. Ménard's expedition: 4 Feb., killed at Seguela. Binger's expedition delimits Ivory Coast frontier with Gold Coast. May, Egbados subdued by British. 9 Aug.-17 Sept., Béhanzin, King of Dahomey, attacks French. 17 Nov., French take Cana and Abomey; Béhanzin flees; 3 Dec.,	1892 5 Apr., Joubert defeated by Rumaliza at Kalonda; Albertville besieged; Dec., relieved by Lieut. Long. May, Ngongu Lutebo defeated at Batugenge; Sefu b. Tippu Tip, with 10,000 Arabs, defeats Belgian force under Hodister. Sept., O. Baumann exploring Burundi: believed by the Hutu to be a liberator from Tutsi

EASTERN AFRICA	SOUTHERN AFRICA	OTHER COUNTRIES

Anti-Slavery Decree. 1 Aug.,
Emin Pasha, Langheld and
Stuhlmann at Tabora: local
Arabs accept German suzerainty.
Sept., Langheld establishes
stations at Mwanza and Bukoba.
28 Oct., Germany takes over
German East Africa from
German EA Co. 4 Nov.,
British Protectorate over
Zanzibar proclaimed: Foreign
Office responsible to 1913.
18 Dec., F. Lugard occupies
Uganda for BEAC. Mbatian,
Laibon of the Masai, d.:
Sendeu and Lenana quarrel
for the succession.

thus obtaining loan from
Belgian Parliament. 5 Aug.,
Anglo-French convention
defines spheres of interest
in Nigeria, Zanzibar and
Pemba, and Madagascar. 20
Aug., Anglo-Portuguese
agreement on Nyasaland and
Mashonaland.
1890 Charles de Gaulle b.

1891-2 Julius von Soden, first
Governor of German East Africa.
1891-3 H. von Wissmann's
expedition to L. Nyasa *via*
R Zambezi and R Shire: post
set up at Langenburg.
1891 9 Feb., Menelik of Ethiopia
denounces Italian claims to a
protectorate. Aug., IBEA set up
administration in Kisimayu.
16 Aug., Emil von Zelewski
severely defeated by Hehe
people under Mkwawa. Oct.,
control of Sultan of Zanzibar's
finances taken over by British:
Sir Lloyd Matthews, First Minister:
administration reorganized on
British colonial lines.
1891 Sisal first introduced into
German East Africa. First
British officer posted in Busoga.
Berlin Society Missionaries start
work amongst the Makonde.

1891 Jan., Harry Johnston
appointed first Commissioner
of the British Central Africa
Protectorate. 2 Feb., Sultan
Abdallah of Anjouan d.; civil
war over succession; Said Ali
raises revolt in Grand Comoro
and is deported. 10 June,
L.S. Jameson, administrator
of BSA Co.'s territories. 11
June, Anglo-Portuguese
convention on boundaries
of N and S Rhodesia;
Nyasaland proclaimed a British
Protectorate. First hospital in
Salisbury opened by Dominican
Nuns. First Anglican Bishop
of Mashonaland appointed.
Hut tax introduced in Nyasaland.
Joseph Booth starts Baptist
Zambezi Industrial Mission at
Blantyre. BSA Co. extends
operations into future N
Rhodesia.
1891 Mozambique Co. established
to exploit Manica and Sofala
districts; Niassa Co. established
N of R Lurio.
1891-2 Special mission on
administrative reform in
Mozambique.

1891 Feb., agreement between
British government and BSA Co.,
extending the company's
operations beyond the R Zambezi.
15 Apr., Anglo-Italian agreement
on Ethiopia, defines their
colonial boundaries. Katanga
Co. founded. 9 May, powers
to appoint magistrates and to
raise revenue granted to BSA Co.
15 May, Leo XIII, *Rerum Novarum*.
21 May, Portugal agrees to new
boundaries of Angola and Congo
Free State. 1 June, Anglo-
Portuguese convention on
Mozambique boundaries. 26
June, Franco-British agreement
on boundaries of Guinea. 31
July, British sphere beyond the
Zambezi formally constituted.

1892 June, German force defeated
by Chagga people near Moshi:
new expedition quells Chagga. 23
July, Tafari Makonnen (later
Emperor Haile Selassie) b. Hehe
raid on Kilosa kills all of German
garrison. Quarrel between
Catholics and Protestants in
Uganda.

1892 1 Aug., Ndebele begin to
raid Mashona in Fort Victoria
area. 23 Aug., French occupy Iles
Glorieuses. Sept., first train
reaches Johannesburg; and, Dec.,
Pretoria. 19 Oct., French occupy
St Paul Is.; and, 27 Oct.,
Amsterdam Is. Primitive Methodist
mission set up in Barotseland. Berlin
Missionary Society starts work in.
S. Rhodesia.

1892 2 Feb., Leo XIII, *Inter
Sollicitudines*. 14 June, Portugal
bankrupt. 18 Aug., Gladstone's
fourth ministry (-1894). 15
Oct., Anglo-German Convention
on Kamerun.

French Protectorate of Dahomey proclaimed. 21 May, administration of Portuguese Guinea reorganized. 8 Dec., Franco-Liberian convention on Ivory Coast frontier. Civil war in Kano following disputed succession. Fresh rising led by Moli Boia. Divine Word Fathers (SVD) start work in Togo. Oil Rivers Irregulars, later Niger Coast Constabulary, founded.
1892-3 Combes' expedition cuts Samory's communications with Futa Jalon and Sierra Leone.

domination. Oct., Emin Pasha murdered in Congo. 22 Nov., Belgians suppress rising of Arab slave-holders in the Congo.
1892-4 General war in Kasai.
1892-3 Delanghe's campaign in NE Congo.

1893-4 Riyad Pasha, Premier of Egypt.
1893 17 Jan., Khedive Abbas dismisses pro-British minister. Moroccans obstruct extension to fortifications of Melilla: war of Melilla between Spain and Morocco.

1893 10 March, French colonies of Guinea and Ivory Coast formally established. 15 Nov., Anglo-German agreement on boundary of Nigeria and Kamerun. 21 Nov., French governor installed in Soudan. 12 Dec., French reach Timbuktu. Oil Rivers Protectorate renamed Niger Coast Protectorate. British obtain treaties of trade and friendship at Abeokuta, Oyo and Ilorin. Rabeh, former slave of Zubayr Pasha, leads an army from the eastern Sudan into Bornu: Shehu of Bornu defeated: Rabeh proclaimed Sultan (-1900).

1893 26 Feb., confused fighting on R Lualaba between Arabs and *Force Publique*; 4 March, Nyangwe occupied. 18 May, Arabs expelled from Stanley Falls. 6 Aug., Arab camp destroyed at Utia Mutongo. Revolt of Dahomey troops in Kamerun. Jesuits start work in the Congo.
1893-4 Decazes mission on R Oubangui. *Force Publique* operations against Rumaliza.

1894 Jan., Khedive Abbas Hilmi II inspects Egyptian army after reform by Kitchener. 17 July, Italians take Kassala from the Dervishes; clashes between Belgians and Dervishes.
1894-5 Nubar Pasha, Premier of Egypt.
1894-1908 Abd al-Aziz b. Hasan, Sultan of Morocco, aged 14; Bu Ahmad, negro slave, vizier (-1900), effective regent.
1894 Agreement of Marrakesh between Spain and Morocco ends war of Melilla.

1894 Nov., rising in Bissau. 10 Jan., Col. Bonnier killed by Tuareg. Béhanzin captured in Dahomey; 22 June, Ballot governor of Dahomey: Dahomey proclaimed a French Colony. 10 Nov., Capt. Lugard signs treaty with French expedition under Capt. Decoeur. Aug., expedition against Itsekiri. Fabert and Donnet missions to Adrar.

1894 15 March, Franco-German agreement on the boundaries of French Congo and Kamerun. 18 March, Mahdist troops attack Congo Free State post at Mundu and are repelled with losses. 12 May, Anglo-Congolese treaty on boundary of Congo with Uganda; Germany and France protest; 14 Aug., Franco-Congolese convention gives French access to Nile; French occupy former Belgian posts on Upper Oubangui. G.A. von Götzen explores Rwanda: June, received by Mwami Rwabugiri of Rwanda; 16 June, discovers L. Kivu. *Force Publique* campaign against Kibonge. Arabs in Kasai finally defeated.
1894-1900 French exploration

893 10 March, IBEA hands over
Uganda to British Government.
Dec., Italians defeat Mahdist attack
on Eritrea near Agordat. Dec.,
British build four forts in Bunyoro.
Sayyid Ali of Zanzibar d.; Sayyid
Khalid b. Barghash takes palace;
jected by British and Zanzibar
roops. Sayyid Hamid b.
Thuwaini installed by British:
ultan's powers henceforward
eremonial. Lieut. Prince routs
Nyamwezi under Siki. Meli,
Chagga chief, defeated by
Germans. First German
Government school opened
t Tanga. Leipzig Mission starts
vork in German East Africa.
893-5 J. von Schele, Governor
f German EA.
893-9 Finance, Agricultural,
urvey, Justice, Medical and
ublic Works Departments
rganized in Dar es Salaam.
893-1905 Tanga-Mombo railway
uilt.

894 3 March, treaty establishes
oro Confederacy, bringing Toro
to British sphere of influence.
1 Apr., Uganda declared a British
rotectorate; 5 May, Anglo-Italian
greement on E Africa assigning
arar to Italy. Oct., new German
xpedition against Hehe:
Ikwawa defeated. Rising under
Hasan b. Omari near Kilwa suppressed.
heikh Mbarak al-Mazrui allowed
o settle near Dar es Salaam with
,000 followers. 30 Oct., Capt.
rince takes Hehe fortress of
Kalenga. Lugard partitions
uganda between Protestants,
Catholics and Muslims, giving
rotestants premier position:
wo prime ministers (Katikiro),
ne Protestant, one Catholic.
Rising on coast of German EA

1893 Jan., France occupies
Kerguelen Is. 10 May, Natal
granted self-government. July,
Matabele rising against BSA Co.
13 Nov., Britain agrees to the
annexation of Swaziland by
Transvaal. Nov., Jameson
crushes Matabele revolt and
occupies Bulawayo. Nov.,
abortive meeting of second
Swaziland convention. Nov.,
Lobengula flees and then d.
Zombe (Abercorn) and Ikawa
(later Fife) made British posts.
Treasury grant of £10,000 p.a.
agreed for the Nyasaland
Protectorate.

1894 Jan., Rhodes wins elections
in the Cape and also becomes
Minister for Native Affairs. Jan.,
Jameson completes occupation
of Matabeleland. Aug., Glen
Grey Act inaugurates new native
policy. Britain annexes Pondoland,
connecting Natal and Cape
Colony. 10 Nov. – Jan., 1896,
French conquest of Madagascar.
24 Nov., BSA Co. cease to control
British Central African Protectorate
(Nyasaland). Gold discovered in
Transvaal. Dec., French occupy
Tamatave. Bulawayo begins to
develop rapidly: 400 gold
prospecting licences issued,
11,000 claims registered; Native
Hut Tax of 10% p.a. instituted in

1893 Jan., Armenian massacres
begun by the Turks. Feb., USA
makes Hawaii a Protectorate.
15 Nov., Anglo-German agreement
on Shari District. Rome removes
ban on the translation of the
Bible into African vernaculars.
António Enes, *Moçambique*, sets
out bases of Portuguese colonial
policy. Women granted votes in
New Zealand.

1894 10 Feb., Harold MacMillan b.
3 March, Gladstone resigns; succ.
Lord Rosebery. 12 Apr., Anglo-
Congolese agreement on the
boundaries of Uganda and the
Congo. 5 May, Anglo-Italian
agreement on EA. 22 June-
10 July, Colonial Conference
at Ottawa. 1 Aug., Japan at war
with China (-1895). 14 Aug.,
Belgo-French agreement on
Congo boundaries.

and occupation of Chad.

1895-1908 Mustafa Pasha Fahmi
again premier of Egypt.
1895 D. Mackenzie's factory at
Tarfaya bought out by Sultan
of Morocco for £50,000.

1895-1964 Sir Milton Margai.
1895-1914 Sierra Leone railway
built.
1895 1 Jan., British Niger Co.
proclaims protectorate over
Busa and Nikki. Oyo bombarded
and temporarily garrisoned.
29 Jan., Brass towns attack
Royal Niger Co.'s factory at
Akassa; 43 African captives
killed and eaten; Sir John
Kirk sent to investigate as
Special Commissioner; 22 Feb.,
British take Nimbe and other
Brass Towns. March, Ashanti
embassy sent to London.
Apr.-May, rising in Bissau
put down by troops from
Angola; revolt in Forrea led
by Mamadu Pate Bulola: Aug.,
punitive expedition dispatched.
15 June, *Afrique Occidentale
Française (AOF),* French West
African Federation, established.
comprising Senegal, Soudan,
Guinea, Ivory Coast and
Dahomey. SMA start work in
the Ivory Coast. Anglo-French
agreement on the boundary of
Sierra Leone.

1895 5 Feb., Franco-Belgian
agreement on Congolese
possessions; French post
established at Tamboura.
4 July, Batetela in the *Force
Publique* revolt; 9 Oct.,
mutineers defeated at
R Lomami; 18 Oct.,
mutineers decisively defeated.
Chokwe defeated by Ngongo
Letata, an ally of Tippu Tib.
Slave trade forbidden in
Kamerun.
1895-7 Chaltin's campaigns in
NE Congo.

1896 16 March, Lord Cromer
dispatches Anglo-Egyptian force
to the Sudan. 23 Sept., Kitchener
retakes Dongola with Anglo-Egyptian
force.
1896-1903 Aswan Dam built.

1896 British expeditionary force
sent to Ashanti; 20 Jan.,
Asantehene deposed and
imprisoned with other notables;
March, Apr., disturbances in
Ilorin. 16 Aug., British
Protectorate over Ashanti
proclaimed; similar treaties
with neighbouring chieftains.
Anglo-French Convention on
boundary of Dahomey and
Nigeria.

1896 15 June, Crown Lands
Ordinance in Kamerun. 24 July,
Marchand mission to occupy
Fashoda disembarks at Loango.
Mibambwe IV Rutarindwa of
Rwanda murdered for 'unpopularity
and greed': succ. Yuhi V
Musinga. German post established
at Usumbura. First White
Fathers' Mission in Burundi
established at Muyaga. Trappists
start work in the Congo.
Pallotine Fathers start work in
Kamerun. Congo station
established at Uvira.

ASTERN AFRICA   SOUTHERN AFRICA   OTHER COUNTRIES

der Bwana Heri. Menelik
mpaigns against Walamo
person. Boundary between
alian Somalia and Ethiopia
fined. Mill Hill Fathers
art work in Uganda.
94-1925 Sir Apolo Kagwa,
atakiro of Buganda.

95 1 Feb., British instal Shaikh
ashid b. Salim al-Mazrui as
aikh of Takaungu. 25 March,
alian troops enter Ethiopia.
ne, quarrel with Shaikh Mbarak
Rashid al-Mazrui leads to civil
ar. 18 June, British Protectorate
er IBEA territory in Kenya
oclaimed in Mombasa as the
ast African Protectorate. British
ce-consul appointed in Pemba.
ne, British quarrel with Sayyid
amid of Zanzibar: private
dyguard formed: 17 Dec.,
ghting between bodyguard and
ritish. 1 July, British East
frican Protectorate, including
esent Kenya, Uganda and
anzibar: Sir Arthur Hardinge,
rst Commissioner. 7 Dec.,
thiopians defeat Italy at Amba
lagi. 12 Dec., Uganda-Usoga
greement: Busoga incorporated
to Uganda. Jubaland declared
British Protectorate. 'Mad
ullah' settles at Berbera and
en begins to propagate
ervish' doctrines. IBEA
rrenders its charter. George
ilson, Resident in Buganda:
rst baraza (National Council)
tablished as the Lukiko. Only
British officials in Uganda.
rst bush schools started by
MS in Uganda.
95-1912 British gradually
ccupy Northern Frontier
istrict of Kenya.
95-6 Hermann von Wissmann,
overnor of German EA.

96 March, Indian regiment
rought to quell Mazrui war.
March, Ethiopians defeat
alians at Adowa: Italy forced
sue for peace. 9 Apr., Kingdom
f Koki and parts of Bunyoro
corporated into Kingdom of
uganda. 20 May, decree sets up
Côte Française des Somalis et
épendences', subject to Minister
f France to Ethiopia. 25 Aug.,
ayyid Hamid d.; Sayyid Khalid
gain seizes palace; 26 Aug.,
ritish bombard Zanzibar and
stal Sayyid Hamud b. Muhammad

BSA Co. area. Coal first located
in S Rhodesia, later Wankie
Colliery Ltd. Europeans begin
to occupy 'gold belt areas', richer
lands in Matabeleland. Shangani
and Gwaai Reserves designated
in S Rhodesia. Lourenço Marques
attacked by Africans. Gungunhana,
chief of Gaza, deported to Lisbon.
1895 Feb., third Swaziland
Convention makes Swaziland a
Protectorate of the Transvaal.
15 Feb., French occupy Majunga.
2 May, battle of Ampasilova.
2 May, BSA Co. territory south of
Zambezi organized as Rhodesia.
16 May, battle of Ambodimonty.
20 June, battle of Tsarasoatra.
30 June, BSA Co. assumes control N
of the R Zambezi. 8 July, Delagoa
railway provides outlet for
Transvaal. 29 Sept., Tananarive
bombarded and occupied. 1 Oct.,
treaty establishes French
Protectorate in Madagascar. Nov.,
Arab half-caste Mlozi defeated by
Johnston at Karonga: over 1,000
slaves freed: Mlozi hanged after a
trial by Makonde chiefs. 11 Nov.,
'British' Bechuanaland annexed to
Cape Colony. 29 Dec., Jameson's
raid into Transvaal from Bechuanaland.
Transkeian General Council formed.
Telegraph reaches Blantyre and
Zomba. Swaziland becomes a
protectorate of the SA Republic.
Northern Copper Co. obtains 500
mile concession in the Kafue region.
'Kaffir Boom' in mining shares
spreads to London, Berlin and Paris.
Civil circumscriptions introduced in
Mozambique.
1895-9 Native risings in Mozambique.

1896 2 Jan., Jameson surrenders
at Doornkop. 3 Jan., William II
of Germany sends 'Kruger telegram'.
6 Jan., Rhodes resigns premiership
of Cape Colony; committee of Cape
Assembly reports Rhodes engineered
Jameson raid; Pretoria and
Johannesburg fortified. 13 Jan., Sir
Gordon Sprigg becomes Prime
Minister of the Cape. 21 Feb.,
Rainilaiarivony, Prime Minister of
Madagascar, deported to Algeria:
rebellion throughout island. 17
March, offensive and defensive
alliance between Transvaal and

1895 13 March, Anglo-Moroccan
agreement. 28 March, Sir E. Grey,
Foreign Secretary, states Britain
would regard French occupation
of Upper Nile an unfriendly act.
5 Apr., French protest. 22 June,
Lord Salisbury, Prime Minister.
1895-1903 Joseph Chamberlain,
Colonial Secretary. 1-8 Aug., William
II of Germany visits England:
Salisbury suggests partition of
Turkey. Marconi invents wireless
telegraphy.

1896 3 Jan., 'Kruger telegram'
provokes Anglo-German crisis;
March, Britain decides to retake
Sudan, to prevent French advance.
30 Sept., Franco-Italian convention
on Tunis, Italy abandoning many
claims. First electric submarine
built in France. First modern
Olympic Games held in Athens.

1897 Apr., Marchand mission
reaches Bangui; Dem Ziber
occupied; May, Kitchener's
force advances; 3 Aug.,
Marchand mission reaches
Semio; Nov., Marchand on
R Such at Wan; 25 Dec., Italy
cedes Kassala to Egypt.

1897 4 Jan., British Consul-
General Phillips, with large party,
massacred attempting to reach
Benin. Jan., further trouble
in Ilorin; 27 Jan., British occupy
Bida; 16 Feb., Ilorin occupied.
18 Feb., British force takes Benin.
Fresh revolt led by Mamadu Pate
Bulola. West African Frontier
Force (WAFF) enrolled to protect
British Protectorates. Ashanti
Goldfields Corporation starts
operations in the Gold Coast.

1897 Jan., Rwanda explored by
Hauptmann Ramsay. 14 Feb.,
mutiny at Dirfi: **1897-9**
Operations against mutineers.
1897 Mutiny of Congolese troops
at Uvira. Sept., Batelas rise in
Upper Congo.

1898 8 Apr., Kitchener defeats Amir
Mahmud at R Atbara; 10 July,
Marchand occupies Fashoda; 12
July, French flag ceremonially
hoisted; 7 Aug., Anglo-Egyptian
force takes Abu Hamed; and,
2 Sept., Omdurman; 3 Sept.,
Marchand makes treaty with
Shilluk; 19 Sept., Kitchener
reaches Fashoda; 4 Nov.,
Marchand ordered to evacuate
Fashoda; 11 Dec., French
evacuate Fashoda.

1898 1 Jan., Hut Tax instituted
in Sierra Leone Protectorate:
27 Apr., general rising: settled
by W African regiment; Sarkin
Damagaram from Zinder
abortively invades Kano.
Railway construction begun in
the Gold Coast. Lagos lit by
electricity. Anglo-French
agreement on Nigerian
boundaries.
1898-1900 Foureau and Lamy
explore Bornu and Wadai.

1898 Tyo revolt unsuccessfully.
The Chokwe defeated by the Lunda.
Sud-Kamerun Gesellschaft established.
Oct., territory near L. Kivu and the
Ruzizi and Mfumbiri Mts occupied
by Germany.
1898-1900 Richard Kandt explores
Rwanda and Burundi.

EASTERN AFRICA	SOUTHERN AFRICA	OTHER COUNTRIES

EASTERN AFRICA

as Sultan. 28 Aug., Administrator appointed for French Somaliland. 26 Oct., Treaty of Addis Ababa: Italian Protectorate withdrawn. Aussa annexed by Menelik. Military post established at Iringa. **1896-1901** Uganda railway built from Mombasa to Kampala.

1897 20 March, Ethiopian-French treaty defining Somali border. 5 Apr., Legal status of slavery abolished in Zanzibar: slaves to be freed on their demand with compensation to owners; courts reorganized and High Court set up. 14th May, Ethiopian-British treaty: Britain abandons certain claims in Somaliland but Ethiopia declines to abandon claims on Upper Nile. 6 July, Kabaka Mwanga of Buganda rebels against British and flees to Buddu: infant son Daudi Chwa made Kabaka. Sept., mutiny amongst British Sudanese mercenaries in Eldama Ravine, Kenya, and in Uganda. Dec., Mwanga defeated by British; Indian troops arrive in Mombasa and disarm some Sudanese. German punitive expedition against Ngoni. Native Courts Regulation in Kenya recognizes 'chiefs and headmen' in certain tribes. Translation of Bible into Luganda completed. Menelik's expedition under Walda Giorgis takes Kaffa. **1897-1900** Ethiopia annexes much Somali territory in various expeditions. **1897-8** Operations against Hehe under Mkwawa: Mkwawa commits suicide. **1897-9** Famine amongst Kikuyu, Kamba and neighbouring peoples. **1898** Aug., Sudanese mutineers defeated by Indians at Mouli. Famine in Busoga and Bunyoro. Lijj Iyasu b. **1898-1900** Civil war between Masai.

SOUTHERN AFRICA

Orange Free State. March to Sept. **1897** Matabele rising in Rhodesia. 18 Aug., France annexes Madagascar. 9 Sept., General Galliéni takes charge as Resident-General of Madagascar. 27 Sept., slavery abolished in Madagascar. Serious rinderpest in Ndebele territory. **1896** Expeditions against the Yao and the Chewa. **1896-1900** Resistance to French in Madagascar. **1897** 28 Feb., Queen of Hovas deposed; 30 July, Galliéni Governor-General of Madagascar. Aug., Sir Alfred Milner arrives as High Commissioner for S Africa. 4 Nov., Cape railway reaches Bulawayo. 1 Dec., Zululand annexed to Natal. Natal makes it a criminal offence for a white man to marry an Indian. First demand for a white Legislative Council in S Rhodesia made by Bulawayo Literary and Debating Society.

1898 Jan., British operations against the Ngoni in N Rhodesia. 9 Feb., Kruger re-elected as President of Transvaal with large majority. 25 June, Lawlev treaty between the Barotse and the BSA Co. Legislative Council with elected and official members in S Rhodesia. Ngoni in Fort Jameson area subjugated. Anglo-Portuguese expedition against Yao chief Mataka. Railway from Beira to Umtali completed. Jacobus Johannes Fouché b.

OTHER COUNTRIES

1897 18 March, Crete unites with Greece. 18 Apr., Greece at war with Turkey. 15 June, Second Colonial Conference, London: Joseph Chamberlain presides. 22 June, Queen Victoria's Diamond Jubilee. July, report of Parliamentary Committee into Jameson Raid censures Cecil Rhodes, but clears Chamberlain and Colonial Office. 18 Sept., Anglo-French agreement on Tunisia. 16 Dec., Peace of Constantinople.

1898 Feb., Chamberlain suggests Anglo-German alliance. 28 March, German Navy Bill. 4 Apr., war between USA and Spain. 19 May, Gladstone d. 14 June, Anglo-French convention on boundaries of Nigeria and Gold Coast. 30 Aug., secret Anglo-German agreement on Portuguese African territories: Britain to lease Delagoa Bay, Germany to have parts of Angola and Mozambique. 10 Dec., USA acquires Guam,

1898-1916 Ali Dinar, last Sultan
of Darfur.

1899-1956 Anglo-Egyptian Condominium over the Sudan.
1899 19 Jan., Anglo-Egyptian
Convention on the Sudan. 21
March, Anglo-French Convention
on Libyan hinterland ends Fashoda
crisis: Italy protests at large
concessions to France in the
Sahara. Nov., The Khalifa
killed on the White Nile.

1899 9 Aug., Britain buys
possessions of the Royal Niger
Co. 14 Nov., Britain and
Germany agree on the frontiers
of Togo and the Gold Coast.
French bring Ullemmeden
Tuareg and other Moorish
peoples on the Niger bend
under control. First
Government school in Nigeria
opened. Gold Coast-Togo
boundary finally agreed.
ante **1900** Tuareg undisputed
masters of southern Sahara.

1899 3 and 4 June, Mahdists
temporarily occupy Rejaf.
Dispute between Congolese and
German troops near L.Kivu:
23 Nov., Bethe-Hecq agreement.
New labour law in Angola
reintroduces forced labour.

1900 *al-Liwa,* Egyptian Nationalist
newspaper, founded. Ibrahim
Abboud b. French occupy Touat,
Gourar and Colomb-Béchar.
Communication with L. Chad
area becomes effective. 14 Dec.,

1900-2 French occupation of
Zinder territory.
1900 1 Jan., British Government
assumes control of all Royal
Niger Co.'s territories.
Protectorate of Northern Nigeria

1900 23 Jan., Franco-Portuguese
convention on boundary of French
Congo. 27 June, Franco-Spanish
agreement on boundary of Rio
Muni. 5 Sept., Chad proclaimed
a French military protectorate.

EASTERN AFRICA   **SOUTHERN AFRICA**   **OTHER COUNTRIES**

1898-9 Bishop Dupont, WF, becomes a chief of the Bemba.

Philippines and Puerto Rico. 10 Dec., Cuba independent. Zeppelin invents the airship. Portugal appoints committee to study the problems of Portuguese Africa. Southern Rhodesia Order in Council establishes constitution for BSA Co. government until 1923.

1899 9 Jan., Administrator of French Somaliland raised to Governor; Marchand at Djibouti. Apr., Kabaka Mwanga and Mwami Kabarega of Bunyoro deported to Kisimayu and thence to Seychelles Is. Sept., 'Mad Mullah' proclaims himself Mahdi; raids on British and Italian Somaliland. Building of Nairobi begun. Lord Delamere travels for the first time through the Kenya Highlands. Ankole brought under British control. Boran Galla subjected to Ethiopia.
1899-1900 General unrest in German EA; 2,000 Africans said to have been killed resisting hut tax.
1899-1902 Sir Harry Johnston, Commissioner in Uganda.

1899 24 March, Johannesburg Uitlanders petition Queen Victoria on their grievances against the Boers; 31 March-5 June, Milner and Kruger fail to agree on Transvaal franchise. 11 July, Transvaal enfranchises immigrants after 7 years' residence. 27 July, Transvaal rejects British proposal of joint inquiry into franchise bills. Rising at Moroni, Grand Comoro: 9 Sept., Governor of Comoro installed at Dzaoudzi. 9 Oct., Kruger sends ultimatum to Britain. 11 Oct., Orange Free State follows suit; 12 Oct.-31 May 1902, Boer War. 15 Oct., secret Treaty of Windsor: Portugal undertakes to prevent transit of munitions from Delagoa Bay to Transvaal. 17 Oct., Boers defeated at Glencoe. 30 Oct., Boers victorious at Nicholson's Nek. Oct., British operations against Kazembe. Nov., Boers take Ladysmith. 11 Dec., Boers repulse British at Magersfontein. and, 15 Dec., at Colenso. Dec., Canadian and Australian volunteers land in S Africa. Railway reaches Salisbury, Rhodesia. Education Ordinance in S Rhodesia provides grants for mission schools. Silver King and Sable Antelope mines discovered near R Kafue. Anti-malarial campaign in S Rhodesia undertaken by Dr A.M. Fleming. Matabeleland Native Labour Bureau set up. Rhodesia Regiment established. Last engagement in Nyasaland against Arab slave traders. Tanganyika Concessions Ltd. formed.
1899-1968 Theophilus Ebenhaezer Donges.
1900 10 Jan., Lord Roberts becomes Commander-in-Chief with Lord Kitchener as Chief of Staff. 18 Feb., Piet Cronje surrenders at Paardeberg. 28 Feb., Redvers Buller relieves Ladysmith. 13 March,

1899 4 Feb., Philippines revolt against USA. 21 March, Anglo-French Agreement on the Sudan. Apr., Anglo-Russian agreement on the partition of China. 9 Aug., Britain buys out Royal Niger Co. 23 Dec., Germany obtains Baghdad railway concession. North-Eastern Rhodesia Order-in-Council. Barotseland-NW Rhodesia Order-in-Council.

1900-4 Four British expeditions against the 'Mad Mullah'. 24 June, Franco-Italian agreement on boundaries of French Somaliland guaranteeing Italian access to Aussa caravan route. 26 June,

1900 27 Feb., (British) Labour Party founded. 28 Feb., Russia suggests France and Germany put pressure on Britain to end Boer War. 3 March, Germany rejects proposal. 19 June, *Compagnie de Katanga* becomes *Comité Spéciale*

secret Franco-Italian agreement on respective interests in Morocco and Tripoli. Sultan of Morocco shows weakening resistance to French expansion. Egyptian population *c.* 10 m.

replaces Royal Niger Co.: Sir F. Lugard High Commissioner (-1907): indirect rule instituted, 'the most significant development in British colonial policy', subsequently extended in numerous Ordinances throughout British colonial possessions. Nov., Ashanti rising suppressed by British. Northern Nigerian Regiment founded. Carter and Denton Bridges in Lagos completed; Lagos to Ibadan railway opened; MacGregor Canal cut. French defeat Rabeh in L.Chad region. Canhabaque rising against the Portuguese.

Dec., mixed Belgian-German survey of L.Kivu region.

1901 20 July, Morocco grants France control of frontier police. 27 July, Delcassé states policy of French predominance in Morocco. 7 Dec., Anglo-Italian agreement on the Sudan frontier. *Tertib,* tax on income from land and livestock, introduced into Morocco.

1901 British campaigns to put down slave raiding in Kantagora and Nupe. 1 Apr., Slavery Proclamation abolishes status of slavery in Nigeria. Apr., Kolumbo taken by French; July, Baoulé chiefs submit. Jufunco rising against Portuguese. 25 Sept., Kingdom of Ashanti annexed to Gold Coast Colony; Protectorate proclaimed. Sept., Yola taken by British. Incident at Argungu between French and British: Capt. C.V. Keyes shot. Administrator of the Gambia made Governor.

1901-9 Buéa the capital of Kamerun.

1902 15 Aug., Britain and Ethiopia agree Sudan frontier. Dec., Aswan dam opened. Algerian law provides special 'Organization of the Southern Territories of the Sahara'. 1902-9 Bu Hamara, or al-Rogui, pretender to the Moroccan throne, starts revolt at Taza.

1902 Feb., Bauchi taken by British; Bornu submits. March, French expedition to Sout-el-Ma, Mauritania. 18 Apr., Lieut. Moncorge and Sgt Richard killed by Coniaguis at Boussara, Guinea. Further French operations against Baoulé:

1902 18-21 June, Seven Protestant missions in the Congo meet to discuss common problems, 9 Feb., Léon Mba b. at Libreville. 19 Aug., Samisasa taken by Portuguese. Germans arrive in Foumbau. Portuguese campaign on the Bié plateau. 1902-3 Anarchy and terrorism

EASTERN AFRICA

oro agreement. Uganda
greement: Buganda made
province of Uganda: Ganda
» pay hut tax for British
dministration: Lukiko constituted
legislature and court of appeal,
1900 Kakunguru develops
fluence in Bukari; recognized
s Kabaka by Sir H.H. Johnston.

901 Uganda railway reaches
. Victoria from Mombasa.
nglo-German agreement on
oundaries of Nyasaland and
erman East Africa. Aug.,
nkole agreement: small
cal kingdoms included in
nkole. Italians make
ultanate of Mijurtein, Somalia,
protectorate. Uganda railway
fluences settlement policies in
enya. Labour bureau set up
 Zanzibar. Sleeping-sickness
rypanosomiasis) first
iagnosed in Uganda by Drs.
H. and A. Cook. Last
udanese mutineers in
ganda rounded up. British
dministrative officer
ppointed to oversee Kakunguru
 Budaka; Kakunguru moves
 Mbale. Cecil Rhodes's
ranscontinental Telegraph
o. line reaches Ujiji from
bercorn.
902 Jan., first political
eeting of white settlers in
enya forms Colonists'
ssociation. 6 Feb., Franco-
thiopian agreement on finance
f Djibouti-Addis Ababa
ilway provokes protests from
ritain and Italy. 1 Apr., Eastern
rovince of Uganda transferred

SOUTHERN AFRICA

Roberts captures Bloemfontein;
attempts to negotiate peace with
Boers fail. 17 May, relief of
Mafeking. 24 May, Britain annexes
Orange Free State. 5 June.,
Pretoria captured. 4 July, armies
of Roberts and Buller unite at
Vlakfontein. Aug., (-1902) Boers
steadily gathered into concentration
camps, eventually totalling 200,000
men. Kruger flees to Marseilles.
27 Aug., Botha defeated at
Bergendal. 31 Aug., Johannesburg
occupied. 15 Sept., R.T. Coryndon
appointed first Administrator of
Barotseland and NW Rhodesia.
17 Oct., treaty between Barotse and
BSA Co. 25 Oct., Britain annexes
Transvaal. Indemnity Act passed
by Cape Parliament.
Nov., many Boer guerilla actions.
Dec., mobile commandos become
active. Martial law proclaimed
throughout SA outside ports and
native areas. African taxation
introduced in NE Rhodesia.
Basutoland 'Ethiopian' Church
established by Willie Mokalapa.
Labour board of S Rhodesia set up.
Labour tax introduced in Nyasaland.
1901 Jan., Kitchener uses scorched
earth policy to counter Boer
guerillas; Feb., Botha's raid on
Natal, and De Wet and Hertzog's
invasion of Cape Colony fail;
26 Feb., Kitchener and Botha
meet at Middleburg but fail to
agree. Graded Civil Service set up
in NE Rhodesia.

1902 2 March, Municipal councils
established in Madagascar. 31
May, Peace of Vereeniging ends
Boer war: Boers accept British
sovereignty; British promises
representative government and
£3m. for restocking farms.
Cecil Rhodes d. Labour Party
organized in SA. African People's

OTHER COUNTRIES

de Katanga. 29 July, King
Umberto of Italy murdered:
succ. Victor Emmanuel III.
6 Oct., Kruger flees to Europe :
refused audience by Kaiser.
16 Oct., 'Khaki' election in
Britain: Conservatives obtain
sweeping victory. 16 Dec.,
Franco-Italian agreement on
Tunisia. Boxer rebellion in
China.

1901-10 Edward VII, King of England.
1901 22 Jan., Queen Victoria d. 6
Sept., President McKinley murdered:
succ. Theodore Roosevelt (-1909).
8 Sept., Hendrik Verwoerd b. at Ouderkerk,
near Rotterdam. 27 Dec., Britain
breaks off negotiations for a German
alliance.

1902 30 June-11 Aug., Colonial
Conference in London. 10 May,
Portugal again bankrupt. 12
July, H.J. Balfour, Prime
Minister. 1 Nov., Franco-Italian
agreement on N Africa. 8 Nov.,
Spain refrains from agreement on
Morocco with France for fear of
antagonizing Britain. 18 Dec.,

| | June, post established at Sakassou. Senegal separated from new Protectorate area of Sénégambie-Niger. Oio rising against the Portuguese. British campaigns in Yola, Bornu and Zaria. Zungeru made headquarters in N Nigeria. CMS mission opened in Zaria. 1902-5 Coppolani mission amongst tribes in Mauritania. | in Burundi. |

1903 *Al-Sudan,* first Arabic newspaper in the Sudan. Sultan of Morocco borrows £800,000 from British, French and Spanish syndicates.

1903 Jan., Kano offers ineffective resistance to British occupation. 1 Feb., Anglo-French agreement on boundary of Gold Coast with Ivory Coast. British campaigns against Sokoto and Kano: 3 Feb., Kano submits. 15 March, British conquest of N Nigeria completed. J.Biker, Governor of Portuguese Guinea, exposes contract labour scandal in Angola.

1903-10 Railway system built in Congo Free State.
1903-11 Kamerun railway built.
1903 Construction of Benguela-Katanga railway begun. June, German expedition against Kissabo, King of Burundi.
1903-5 Congo Free State expedition to Bahral-Ghazal.

1904 Apr., special regime created for Tangier. 18 May, Maulai Ahmad b. Muhammad al-Raisuli kidnaps Ion Perdicaris, Greek resident in Tangier: British and US fleets sent to Tangier. USA pays ransom of $/70,000: al-Raisuli made governor of Tangier.

1904 Nnamdi Azikiwe b. Portuguese expedition against Xura (or Churo). 8 Apr., Anglo-French convention on boundaries of the Gambia, Senegal, French Guinea, Sierra Leone and Zinder. 25 Apr., Anglo-French agreement on boundaries of the Gold Coast. 18 Oct., French territory of Haut-Senegal-Niger constituted under Governor Ponty. 5 Nov., Franco-Portuguese agreement on Guinea boundaries. Dec., France recognizes W African Colonies as French West Africa; capital at Dakar. Village chief at Satiru declares himself the Mahdi: arrested and replaced by his son. Serious famine in N Nigeria. French punitive expedition against the Conaguis.
1904-5 French post at Agadès.

1904-11 French campaigns to pacify the Fang, Bakota and Mitshogo.
1904-5 Royal Commission of Inquiry sent to the Congo. Five White Fathers' missions already established in Rwanda.

1905 31 March, Kaiser William II visits Tangier: sets off Moroccan crisis. 17 May, Britain proposes discussions on Morocco. 8 July, France agrees to discussions. 28 Sept., France and Germany agree to conference. Sultan of Morocco obtains further loan from France.

1905 Risings in French Guinea; French operations against Baoulé, Agbas and Ebries; 7 June, Algerian-*AOF* boundary of defined; French Mauritania reorganized.

1905 Feb., insurrection in Welle district, Belgian Congo; Nov., report of Commission of Inquiry into Belgian atrocities in Congo excuses Léopold II. May, Chief Machoncho attempts to kill German administrator von Grawert, and is shot by him. Oct., Mwami Kissabo formally

EASTERN AFRICA	SOUTHERN AFRICA	OTHER COUNTRIES

to the EA Protectorate. 27 Sept., Kenya Crown Land Ordinance inaugurates white settlement of Highlands. Village Headmen Ordinance in Kenya appoints headmen. Joseph Chamberlain, Colonial Secretary, visits Kenya: recommends area between Mau escarpment and Nairobi for Jewish settlement. Sultan of Zanzibar recognizes Italian suzerainty over Banadir.
1903 June, Lord Delamere settles permanently in Kenya: forms Kenya Planters and Farmers Association. Sir C. Eliot begins discriminatory policy against Indian land ownership in EA Protectorate. Berlin II Mission starts work in German East Africa. First cotton seed imported into Uganda.

Organization founded in Capetown by Dr Abdallah Abdurahman. Broken Hill Co. formed. Portuguese campaign in the Barue region.

1903 Feb., Joseph Chamberlain visits SA: policy henceforward aimed at conciliation of Boers. March, Customs Conference at Bloemfontein anticipates later federation of S Africa. Nov., Commission in Transvaal favours using immigrant Chinese labour in Rand mines. Afrikaner Bond becomes the S African Party. Swaziland under the government of the Transvaal. Tobacco introduced in S Rhodesia. State education for Europeans in S Rhodesia begun. Rhodesia Native Labour Bureau established.
1903-5 Lagden Native Affairs Commission.

first meeting of Committee of Imperial Defence in London. J.A. Hobson, *Imperialism*. Portugal forbids sale of rum to Africans. Uganda Order-in-Council. Abuna Mateos, Ethiopian Bishop, visits Russia.

1903-14 St Pius X, Pope.
1903 18 March, religious orders dissolved in France. Apr., Edward VII visits Lisbon and Rome. May, Sir Roger Casement's report on Belgian atrocities in the Congo published; 20 May, question raised in Parliament by Herbert Samuel. May, Edward VII visits Paris. Aug., Sixth Zionist Congress in Vienna. 3 Nov., Panama independent. First Ford motor factories established.

1904 Telegraph lines open from Dar es Salaam to Tabora and Mwanza, and from Tanga to Korogwe. Dar es Salaam to Morogoro railway built. Agricultural exhibition in Dar es Salaam. First power-gin built in Kampala.

1904 Feb., Chinese coolie labour recruited for the Transvaal. 22 Feb.-2 Feb. 1908, Dr L. Starr Jameson, Prime Minister of Cape Colony. 3 Oct.- 1908 rising of Herero and Hottentots in German SW Africa. Rhodes University College, Grahamstown, founded. First Zionist church in Johannesburg founded by Daniel Bryant. Rhodesia Agricultural Union formed. African taxation introduced in NW Rhodesia.

1904 8 Feb., Japan at war with Russia. 8 Apr., *Entente Cordiale* between Britain and France: differences on Morocco, Egypt and Newfoundland settled; Britain recognizes Suez Canal Convention and surrenders claim to Madagascar. 4 July, construction of Panama Canal begun. 10 Aug., Russian fleet destroyed at Vladivostock. 6 Oct., Franco-Spanish agreement delimits respective zones of influence in Morocco. First Algerians arrive in France to work in Marseilles sugar refineries.

1905 19 May, Acting Provincial Commissioner in Ankole speared to death: Ankole agreement suspended. Planters and Farmers Association (Kenya) becomes the Colonists' Association, Delamere losing control. Nandi Field Force raised to control Nandi tribe: expedition against Sotik and Kisu.

1905 Jan., Botha forms *Het Volk* organization to agitate for responsible government in the Transvaal. 25 Apr., Transvaal granted constitution: regarded by Botha as inadequate. Railway bridge over Victoria Falls completed.

1905-61 Dag Hammarskjöld, later Secretary-General of the United Nations.
1905 3 March, Reforms announced in Russia. Oct., mutiny on the *Potemkin*. 7 June, Norway decides to separate from Sweden. 5 Sept., Treaty of Portsmouth between Russia and Japan. 28 Sept.,

recognized by Germany as ruler
of Burundi. Franco-German
treaty on Kamerun frontiers.

1906-10 Saad Zaghlul, Egyptian
Minister of Education.
1906 Dispute between Britain
and the Porte on Egyptian
boundary in the Gulf of Aqaba
(Taba incident). Dinshaway
incident: affray between
British shooting party and
Egyptian villagers. Sultan
of Morocco obtains another
loan from France.

1906 Battle between Hausa and
Jukon traders at Abinsi: Tiv join
Jukon, overwhelm Hausa and
destroy Royal Niger Co. store.
Rising at Satiru: many British
killed: 10 March, punitive
expedition. 9 Apr., Anglo-
French convention on boundary
of N Nigeria. 1 May, Colony of
Lagos amalgamated with
Protectorate of S Nigeria as
Colony and Protectorate of
Southern Nigeria. 7 July,
French reoccupy Agadès.
Bêtès in Haut-Sassandra revolt;
agitation in French Niger.
Expedition against the Tiv in
N Nigeria. Lyons missionaries
(SMA) start work in Liberia.

1906 Apr., Kissabo's power as King
of Burundi consolidated.
Agreement between Congo Free
State and the Vatican that each
Catholic mission would include
a school. Mill Hill Frs start
work in the Congo.

1907 al-Raisuli outlawed by
Sultan of Morocco. 22 March,
French physician Mauchamp
murdered at Marrakesh. 29
March, Ujda taken by French
as reprisal. 4 Aug., French fleet
bombards Casablanca after
anti-foreign demonstrations:
Casablanca and Rabat occupied.
7 Dec., first Nationalist
Congress in Egypt under
Mustafa Kamil. Dec., Mts
of Beni Suassen taken by
French in further reprisal
for murder of Mauchamp.
al-Hizb al-Watani, Patriotic
Party, founded by extreme
Egyptian nationalists. *Hizb
al-Umma* (Party of the Nation)
founded in Cairo as moderate
nationalist party. *Al-Jarida,*
moderate Egyptian nationalist
newspaper, founded. Bank of
Rome opens branch in Tripoli.
1907-11 Sir Eldon Gorst,
British Agent and Consul-
General in Egypt.
1908 National University
founded in Cairo. 7 June,
Maulai Hafid usurps his
brother: proclaimed Sultan
of Morocco at Fez. Aug.,
Abdul Aziz defeated by
Sultan at Marrakesh; 25

1907 March, French mission in
southern Sahara. June, further
rising against French in Haut-
Sassandra. 18 Sept., Franco-
Liberian agreement on
frontiers of Liberia, Ivory
Coast and Guinea. 8 Dec.,
Félix Dubois arrives at
Timbuktu, having crossed Sahara
without any other European.
Rising in Cuór region, Portuguese
Guinea. Northern Territories
Constabulary established in the
Gold Coast.
1907 William Ponty, Governor-
General of *AOF.*
1907-14 Lagos harbour improved
for ocean vessels.

1907-10 Portuguese campaigns
against the Dembo. Education
conference at Douala. Population
of Rwanda about 1½m. Bielefeld
Mission established in Rwanda.

1908 Dec., Adrar pacified by Col.
Gouraud. Rising in Bissau
region.
1908-11 Railway built from
Bara to Kano, and joined to
Lagos railway; general
manager of Nigerian railways

1908-12 Many small wars by chiefs
in Burundi.
1908 26 June, *Afrique Equatoriale
Française (AEF)* established by
decree. 20 Aug., Léopold II
hands over Congo to Belgian
Government; 18 Oct., confirmed

EASTERN AFRICA

Responsibility for Uganda transferred from Foreign Office to Colonial Office. **1905-7** Local organizations form Pastoralists' Association in Kenya. **1905-7** Maji-Maji rebellion in German EA: southern area chiefly affected. **1905** Sept., Bp Cassian Spiess murdered. **1906-12** Baron F. von Rechenburg, Governor of German EA: first governor to speak Swahili: develops a 'plantation' colony. **1906** 4 July, Britain, France, and Italy guarantee independence of Ethiopia. 13 July, Toro agreement revised: Toro Confederacy becomes Kingdom of Toro. Winston Churchill visits EA Protectorate. Large areas in Uganda near L. Victoria evacuated because of sleeping-sickness epidemic. Zanzibar administration reorganized.

1907-8 Uganda-Congo Boundary Commission: Kivu mission successfully avoids contact with Belgian force. **1907** Aug., first Kenya Legislative Council meets: Land Board appointed. 6 Dec., frontier of British East Africa defined by Britain and Ethiopia. Emperor Menelik paralysed: Lijj Iyasu nominated as successor; Ras Tasamma appointed regent. Education Dept.,established in Zanzibar: Roman script officially used for writing Swahili instead of Arabic script. Commissioner for Uganda made Governor. Unrest in Bunyoro: fifty chiefs deported.

1908 March, Lord Delamere leads settler demonstration outside Government House, Nairobi, on Labour Policy. Central Committee of Associations formed in Kenya. Convention between Italy and Ethiopia on boundaries of Italian Somalia.

SOUTHERN AFRICA

1906 Feb., African rising in Natal against the poll tax. 6 Dec., self-government granted to Transvaal and Orange River Colonies. **1906 or 1907** Watch Tower movement starts in Nyasaland. **1906-10** Portuguese campaigns on the Mozambique coast.

1907 23 May, Legislative Council instituted in Mozambique. 1 July, revised constitution for Orange River Colony. July, Selborne memorandum proposes a federation of S Africa. 21 Sept., rising in German SW Africa suppressed. Swaziland transferred to the jurisdiction of the High Commissioner for SA. Mahatma Gandhi first organizes passive resistance amongst Transvaal Indians. S African Labour Party formed. Strike of miners in the Rand. Dutch Reformed Church takes over missions of Berlin Missionary Society in Rhodesia. Unofficial majority in S Rhodesian Legislative Council. Livingstone made the capital of NW Rhodesia. Roy Welensky b.

1908 3 Feb.-30 May, 1910 J.X. Merriman, Prime Minister of Cape Colony. 9 Apr., Comoro Is. attached to Madagascar. May, Railway and Customs conference in Pretoria: J.C. Smuts moves for union of S Africa and also

OTHER COUNTRIES

Franco-German agreement on Morocco. 28 Nov., Sinn Fein Party founded in Dublin. 5 Dec., Sir H. Campbell-Bannerman Prime Minister. 6 Dec., Church and state separated in France.

1906 16 Jan.-8 Apr., Algeciras Conference on Morocco. 8 Apr., Algeciras Act signed. 6 May, Russian Constitution proclaimed. May, Anglo-Belgian agreement on boundaries of the Congo and the Sudan. 18 June, Anglo-German agreement on the boundaries of Uganda and German East Africa. 13 Dec., Anglo-Italian agreement on Ethiopia. *Union Minière du Haut Katanga* established. School of Tropical Medicine opened in Brussels. H.W. Nevinson, *A Modern Slavery*, on contract labour in Angola.

1907 Feb.-Apr., Edward VII visits Paris, Madrid and Rome. 14 May, Anglo-Spanish agreement on the Mediterranean. Colonial Reform Act in Portugal. Encyclical *Pascendi Gregis* against modernism. Boy Scouts founded. Shell Co. founded.

1908 1 Feb., King Carlos of Portugal and the Crown Prince murdered. 8 Apr., H.H. Asquith, Prime Minister. 1 May, Hijaz railway reaches Medina from Damascus. 24 July, Young Turk rising. 20 Aug.-9 Sept., Belgian Parliament votes annexation of the

Sept., Casablanca incident:
German deserters from French
Foreign Legion taken by force
from German consular official.

complains that African-owned
motor transport is undermining
railway profits on Iddo to
Ibadan line.

by Belgian Act of Parliament.
Local councils established in
Kamerun.

1909 25 March, press censorship
in Egypt to control nationalists.
Bu Hamara attacks Melilla:
Spaniards reply with force of
90,000: Bu Hamara captured
and exhibited in an iron cage,
and then thrown to lions.
Limits of Melilla enlarged.
German instructors sent to
Moroccan army.

1909 18 Sept., Kwame Nkrumah
b. Gen. Christopher Soglo b.
French occupy Wadai, Chad.
Teachers Training College and
Technical School set up in
Accra.

1909 Apr., Prince Albert of
Belgium visits the Congo.
New Franco-German treaty
on Kamerun frontier.
Agricultural Department
organized in the Belgian
Congo. Jules Renkin,
Minister for the Belgian
Congo, tours country for
4 months. Government
school established in
Usumbura. Yaoundé
becomes the capital of
Kamerun after an earthquake
in Buéa. 12 June, Anglo-
Belgian clash near L.Kivu.

1910 20 Feb., Butros Ghali,
premier of Egypt, assassinated
by a Muslim fanatic. Proposal
to extend concession to Suez
Canal Co. to 1968 by 40 years
rejected by Egyptian General
Assembly. Saad Zaghlul,
Egyptian Minister of
Justice. French loan to
Morocco.

1910 Jan., French post at
Agboville occupied temporarily
in revolt of Abbeys. March,
Kano railway completed. Oct.,
- 1911 March, French force
suppresses Baoulé, Ivory
Coast. Beit-el-mal (Native
Treasury) established in Zaria.
Hanns Visscher, first Director
of Education in N Nigeria,
appointed.

1910 15 Jan., Gabon, Middle Congo
and Ubangi-Chari-Chad federated
as French Equatorial Africa (*AEF*).
March-May, extensive reforms in
Belgian Congo. 14 May, Anglo-
Belgian agreement assigns west
shore of L.Albert to Belgian
Congo. Grants-in-aid given to
mission schools in Kamerun:
agricultural school opened.
1910-11 Portuguese operations
against Kasanje and Mahungo:
Lunda province occupied.
1911 'Police' and 'Government
chiefs' instituted in Rwanda.
Neukirchner Missiongesellschaft
established in Angola.
post **1911** Civil circumscriptions
introduced in Angola.

1911 Apr., Fez taken by France.
June, Spain occupies Larache and
Alcazarquivir (al-Ksar al-Kabir),
1 July, German gunboat *Panther*
arrives at Agadir, thus creating
international tension. 5 Nov.,
Italy annexes Tripolitania and
Cyrenaica. 26 Nov., Italy takes
Tripoli. Sheikh Ali Yusuf d.:
Party of Constitutional Reform
in Egypt collapses.
1911-4 Lord Kitchener, British
Agent and Consul-General in
Egypt.

1911 French detach Térritoire
Militaire du Niger from province
of Haut-Sénégal-Niger.

EASTERN AFRICA | SOUTHERN AFRICA | OTHER COUNTRIES

aly gains basin of R Juba. Elgin ledge that, as a matter of dministrative convenience, Indians vould not be given land in the .enya Highlands. Famine in usoga.

909 Jan., Native Courts roclamation in Buganda: rotectorate Native Courts rdinance for remainder of Jganda. Boran Galla driven rom Wajir. Complete abolition f slavery in Zanzibar. A.M. eevanjee, first Indian appointed o Kenya Legislative Council. 909-19 Nyabingi spirit ossession cult gives trouble to Jganda authorities: leader Muhumsa, widow of former uler of Rwanda. .1909 Sixty-seven Catholic nission stations in Germany EA vith 30,000 converts; seventy-hree Protestant stations with 1,000 converts. Somalis first each R. Tana. .1910-11 Toro becomes a lourishing centre for Congo vory trade. .910 Convention of Associations et up by Kenya settlers.

1911-60 Sayyid Khalifa b. Harub, Sultan of Zanzibar, following abdication of Sayyid Ali because of increasing British control. 1911 Zanzibar henceforward controlled by British Resident answerable to Governor of EA Protectorate. British Indian silver rupees made the standard coinage of Zanzibar. Native Tribunal Rules recognize traditional councils of elders in Kenya. Feb., first meeting of Convention of Associations of Kenya settlers. Ras Tasamma d.: Lijj Iyasu rules Ethiopia with Council. Permanent patrol of Kings African Rifles against Ethiopian gun-runners instituted in Acholi. Rinderpest in Karamoja destroys 70% to 90% of the cattle.

S Rhodesia. 12 Oct.-5 Nov., and 23 Nov.-3 Feb. 1909, National Convention in Durban and then Cape Town drafts constitution for a Union of S Africa. First tobacco factory in Nyasaland built at Limbe. 1908-12 Portuguese campaigns against the Yao in Niassa district. 1909 Rhodesian railways link with the Congo railway.

1910 27 Apr., Botha and Hertzog found South African Party. 24 May, Jameson founds Unionist Party: 31 May, Union of South Africa proclaimed. Lord Gladstone, first Governor-General. 1 July, Union of South Africa becomes a Dominion. 15 Sept., South African Party win first elections: Botha premier. Israelite church incident at Bulhoek. Mohéli Is. attached to Madagascar. 1911 West Pondoland District Council formed.

Congo Free State. 28 Oct., *Daily Telegraph* publishes interview with William II. Slavery abolished in S Tomé Principé and Angola. National Association for Advancement of Coloured Peoples (NAACP) founded by W.E.B. du Bois.

1909 9 Feb., Germany recognizes France's special interests in Morocco in return for economic concessions. 4 March, Taft, President of USA. 27 Apr., Young Turks depose Sultan Abdul Hamid: succ. Muhammad V (-1918). 19 May, Anglo-German agreement on the boundaries of Uganda and German E Africa near L. Kivu. 30 Nov., Lords reject Lloyd George's Finance Bill. 17 Dec., Léopold II of Belgium d.; succ. Albert (-1934). W. Cadbury, *Labour in Portuguese West Africa*: boycott of S Tomé cocoa instituted. Lado enclave ceded by Belgium from Congo to the Sudan.

1910 Feb.-May, British and German Conference on L.Kivu-Mfumbiro region. 6 May, Edward VII d.; succ. George V (-1936). 4 Oct., Revolution in Portugal: henceforward a Republic. 4-5 Nov., Nicholas II of Russia and William II of Germany meet a Potsdam. Dec., Liberals win general election in Britain on reform of the House of Lords: H.H. Asquith, Prime Minister. World Protestant missionary conference at Edinburgh. Swiss railways nationalized. 1911 23 May, Imperial Conference at London. 6 July, Parliament Act limits powers of House of Lords. 18 Aug., Republican Constitution in Portugal agreed. 29 Sept., Italy declares war on Turkey in order to take Tripoli. 4 Nov., Franco-German convention: France to have a free hand in Morocco in return for territory in the Congo for Kamerun. 30 Dec., Chinese Republic proclaimed. Caseley Hayford, *Ethiopia Unbound*. Negro Society for Historical Research founded in USA.

EGYPT, THE SUDAN & NORTHERN AFRICA

1912 30 March, Sultan of Morocco signs treaty making Morocco a French Protectorate: Marshal Lyautey, first Resident-General; 12 Aug., Sultan abdicates. 27 Nov., Franco-Spanish convention on their respective zones in Morocco: Spanish zone to be governed by a Khalifa of the Sultan.
1912-25 Gradual French penetration and occupation of Morocco.

1913 Apr., Maulai al-Mahdi, Khalifa in Spanish Protectorate, arrives in Tetuan. al-Raisuni leads opposition to Spanish Protectorate. Legislative Assembly, superseding previous bodies, created in Egypt with wider powers.

1914 Sir Henry McMahon, British High Commissioner in Egypt (–1919). 18 Oct., Egyptian Legislative Assembly prorogued, never to meet again. 2 Nov., martial law proclaimed in Egypt; 17 Dec., British Protectorate proclaimed; 18 Dec., Abbas II deposed: Husain Kemal installed as Khedive. *Code de l'Indigénat* in Algeria modified. Motor vehicles first used in the Sahara.

1915 4 Feb., Turks driven back from Suez Canal. 24 March, Sanusi revolt in southern Tunisia; Oct., and Nov., revolt spreads to Hoggar. Spanish

WESTERN AFRICA

1912 West Africa Currency Board constituted. Rising in Abeokuta.

1913-25 Dissension and local civil war concerning the building of a Friday Mosque at Porto Novo.
1913 Further rising in Abeokuta. Indirect rule established in the Gambia.

1914 1 Jan., Northern and Southern Nigeria amalgamated; Executive and Legislative Councils for Nigeria established.
Jan., rising N of Porto Novo.
July-Aug. 1916, rising in Niger, *AOF*.
8 Aug. Britain and France occupy Togo; 26 Aug., Germans capitulate.
2 Sept., Convention of Lomé divides Togoland into British and French sectors. 16 Sept., Egbaland incorporated into the Protectorate of Nigeria. Blaise Diagne, first Senegalese elected to the Chamber of Deputies. All Nigerian forces combined in the Nigerian Regiment of the West African Frontier Force. French occupy Tibesti. Railway from Port Harcourt to Udi completed. Gold Coast Regiment serves in conquest of Togo and Kamerun.
1914-19 Sir F.D. Lugard, Governor-General of Nigeria.

1915 March, risings in Bélédougou, near Bamako, and in Goumbou and Nara regions against recruitment. 15 Aug., administration re-organized and

CENTRAL AFRICA

1912 15 Aug., German Residency moved from Usumbura to Kitega. African Inland Mission (AIM) starts work in the Belgian Congo.

1913 11 March, Anglo-German agreement on the frontier of Nigeria and Kamerun. Bakongo rise against Portuguese; campaign near Vila Luso. Hospital at Lambaréne founded by Albert Schweitzer. Methodist Mission of South Congo (MMSC) starts work in the Belgian Congo.
1913-18 Portuguese at war with the Congo.

1914 Aug., German troops from E Africa penetrate Congo in spite of Belgian declaration of neutrality. 8 Aug., Chief Rudolf Manga Bell hanged in Douala. Kamerun campaign against Germans: 29 Aug., Nigerian troops occupy Tebe; 30 Aug., Nsanakang occupied; 27 Sept., Douala surrenders; 2 Oct., French take Victoria, Kamerun. 4 Oct., Germans defeat Belgian attempt to take Kisenyi, Rwanda. 2 Dec., Germans defeat Belgian attack on Rwanda. First general tax collected in Rwanda. Methodist Mission of the Central Congo (MMCC) starts work. Campaign against sleeping-sickness inaugurated in Kamerun.

1915-66 Mwambutsa, Mwami (King) of Burundi.
1915 Feb., British liaise with Belgians to co-ordinate war against the Germans in East Africa. May-Jan. 1916, Germans

EASTERN AFRICA	SOUTHERN AFRICA	OTHER COUNTRIES
1912 Tanga railway reaches Moshi. *Uganda Herald* first printed. Uganda Witchcraft Ordinance. Southern half of Lado enclave ceded from the Sudan to Uganda as W Nile Province: Bari-Lotuka area ceded to the Sudan.	**1912** 1 Feb., SA Cabinet reconstituted; June, J.C.Smuts as Finance Minister. 25 July, formal annexation of the Comoro Is. to Madagascar. 2 Dec., Botha resigns; 20 Dec., forms new cabinet without Hertzog. 20 Dec., Botha cabinet again reconstituted, with J.C. Smuts as Defence and Finance Minister. SA Defence Act provides for force of 27,500. African National Council organized in SA. Northern Rhodesia Police formed.	**1912** 10 Feb., French Senate ratifies Moroccan agreement. 8-11 Feb., Haldane visits Berlin. 16 July, Franco-Russian naval convention. 12 Aug., Decree defining French citizenship in W Africa. Sept., Anglo-French naval convention. 17 Oct.-3 Dec., First Balkan War. 28 Oct., Turkey cedes Tripoli to Italy by Treaty of Ouchy. 6 Nov., Woodrow Wilson elected President of USA (-1921). 27 Nov., Franco-Spanish convention delimiting boundaries of Moroccan Protectorates. 5 Dec., Triple Alliance renewed.
1913 1 July, Zanzibar incorporated in British East African Protectorate, with control transferred from Foreign to Colonial Office. 12 Dec., Emperor Menelik d.: Ras Mikael effective ruler of Ethiopia. Cotton becomes Uganda's principal industry, providing over 50% of exports; fifty-seven markets officially gazetted. Buganda agreement (Allotment and Survey). 5,536 Europeans in German EA, of whom 4,107 Germans.	**1913** July, Troops fire on striking miners at Kleinfontein. Cape Federation of Trades founded. Natives Land Act (SA). Gandhi arrested after a demonstration. Salvation Trust Ltd. formed. Famine in Mozambique. Nguru migrate into Shire Highlands.	**1913** 17 Jan., Poincaré President of France (- 1920). 3 Feb.-23 Apr., second Balkan War. 19 May-10 Aug., third Balkan War. 24 July. Lords reject Home Rule Bill for Ireland a second time. 7 Aug., France increases conscription to 3 years. 20 Nov., Anglo-German agreement on Portuguese colonies. Arab Congress in Paris. Einstein describes theory of relativity.
1914 March, Central Railway reaches Kigoma, L.Tanganyika, from Dar es Salaam. March, East African Indian National Congress formed. Aug., Kabaka Daudi Chwa comes of age. 8 Aug., British bombard Dar es Salaam wireless station: town surrendered. 20 Sept., H.M.S. *Pegasus* disabled by German cruiser *Königsberg* in Zanzibar harbour. Nov., Anglo-Indian expedition of 8,000 ambushed by General Lettow-Vorbeck in attack on Tanga. Abamalaki, separatist movement from C. of E. in Uganda, begins. Ras Mikael crowned Negus of Wallo and Tigrai.	**1914** Jan., SA Federation of Trades declares a general strike: martial law proclaimed. June, Indian Relief Act; Smuts - Gandhi agreement on Indian problems. Aug., Northern Rhodesian Police occupy German post at Schuckmannsberg, Caprivi strip. 10 Aug., SA troops destroy German coastal wireless stations at Luderitzbucht and Swakopmund, German SW Africa. 21 Aug., patrol from German SW Africa violates Union territory. 8 Sept., Germans attack Karonga. Sept.-Oct., abortive pro-German rebellion in the Transvaal: martial law proclaimed; 27 Oct., Beyer's commando destroyed by Botha; 12 Nov., De Wet routed; 20 Dec., rebellion declared ended. Grand Comoro becomes a French colony. **1914-15** 7,500 S Africans go independently to Europe to fight Germany.	**1914** 10 March, suffragette riots in London. 15 June, Anglo-German agreement on Baghdad railway. 23-25 June, enlarged Kiel canal opened. 28 June, Archduke Ferdinand of Austria murdered at Sarajevo. 26 July, Irish Nationalist rising in Dublin. 28 July, Austria declares war on Serbia. 1 Aug., Germany declares war on Russia. 1 Aug., Universal Negro Improvement Association and African Committees League founded by Marcus Garvey in Jamaica. 2 Aug., Germany declares war on France. 3 Aug., Germany invades Belgium. 4 Aug., Britain declares war on Germany. 7 Nov., *Jihad* (Holy War) proclaimed against allies in Istanbul. Extensive autonomy granted to Portuguese Colonies. *Journal of Egyptian Archaeology* first issued.
1915 Railway built from Voi to Taveta, Kenya, to facilitate British attack on German EA. Begemder and Gojjam put under Ras Mikael. S Africans, based on	**1915** 13 Jan., SA troops occupy Swakopmund in German SW Africa. 23 Jan.-3 Feb., uprising in Nyasaland led by John Chilembwe. 12 May, Windhoek	**1915** 2 Feb., Germans initiate submarine warfare. 1 March, total blockade of Germany declared by the Allies. 22 Apr., Germans first use poison gas.

recognize al-Raisuni as governor
of many Moroccan tribes.

decentralized in Portuguese
Guinea. 22 Aug.-15 Feb.
1916, rebellion and guerilla
warfare in Dahomey. Nov.,
revolt near Dédougou. 13
Dec., Sanusi rebels reach
Agadès; and 28 Dec., Bilma.
Religious revival in Opobo
leads to formation of Christ's
Army and the Delta Church.
Gambia constitution revised.

defeat Belgian attacks on Kisenyi.
14 May, Chad placed under a
French civil governor. 11 June,
Garna, Kamerun, surrenders to
Nigerians and French; 29
June, Ngaundere captured; 30
Sept., Douala taken; 5 Nov.,
fortress of Banyo taken.
Unrest in Belgian Congo results
in twenty-one armed operations.
Congo Evangelistic Mission
(CEM) starts work in Katanga.
Southern part of the Huila
plateau brought under
Portuguese control.

1916 24 Jan., Spanish royal decree
organizes administration in
Spanish Morocco. Many tribes
submit to Protectorate: communications
between Tetuan, Tangier and
Larache secured. 1 Dec., Fr
Charles de Foucauld murdered
at Tamanrasset. Sayyid Idris
al-Sanusi becomes Amir of
Cyrenaica.
1916-17 Sanusi rising continues.

1916 Feb., rising in Koutiala
district. March, risings in San
and Bandiagara districts.
Feb.-May 1919, French
operations against the Sanusi.
Oct., King of Nikki rebels
against French in Borgou.
Spanish occupy Juby. Riots
in Iseyin and Lagos. Gold
Coast constitution revised.

1916 1 Jan., British and Nigerians
enter Yaoundé unopposed by
Germans. 18 Feb., last Germans
surrender in Kamerun. 6 March,
part of Kamerun detached and
administered with Nigeria,
(renamed Cameroon). 3 Apr.,
and 5 Sept., French decrees
placing reminder of Kamerun.,
as renamed Cameroun, under
AEF. 12 Apr., Chad
incorporated into *AEF*. 20
Apr., Belgians invade Rwanda
and Burundi: 21 May, in
complete control of Rwanda;
27 June, Usumbura capitulates;
all Burundi taken. Oct.,
German Pallotine Fathers replaced
by French Holy Ghost Fathers
(CSSp) in Cameroun. Seventh
Day Adventists (SDA) start
work in the Belgian Congo.
Population of Burundi about
1½m.

1917 Ahmad Fuad, Khedive of
Egypt. Egyptian population
over 17m.

1917 May, rising in the Bijagos
Is. May, Joost van Vollenhoven
Governor-General of *AOF*. 21
Aug., French Commissioner for
Togo put under Governor-
General of *AOF*. Dec.-Aug.,
1918, rising in Dida district,
Ivory Coast.

1917 18 Aug., female slavery
forbidden in Cameroun by
French. First African Catholic
priest ordained in the Belgian
Congo. Heart of Africa Mission
(HAM) starts work in the
Belgian Congo.
1917-19 All German Protestant
missionaries expelled from
Cameroun and replaced by
Paris Missionary Society.

EASTERN AFRICA	SOUTHERN AFRICA	OTHER COUNTRIES

Karonga, advance on Neu Langenburg (Tukuyu). Two 4½ ton British launches, *Mimi* and *Toutou* capture German gun-boat on L. Tanganyika.

occupied by Botha. 21 June, Christian de Wet surrenders at Bloemfontein. 9 July, Germans in SW Africa surrender to Botha. Oct., anti-German riots in S Africa follow the sinking of the *Lusitania*. 20 Oct., Hertzog's Nationalist Party gains majority in SA Parliament. 13 Dec., Balthazar Johannes Vorster b. War on War Group breaks away from Labour Party in Johannesburg; International Workers of Africa (IWA) organized, with newspaper, the *International*. Port traffic in Beira reaches 200,000 tons.

May, Convention of Damascus. 3 June, Allies take Kut al-Amara. 11 Oct., Nurse Cavell shot. July-March 1916 correspondence between Sir Henry McMahon and Sharif Husain of Mecca on Arab nationalist movement.

c.1916 Lijj Iyasu, Emperor of Ethiopia, adopts Islam.
1916 General Smuts in command of British forces in E Africa: 2 March, attack on Moshi-Tanga railway begun: 13 March, Moshi taken; Apr., Kondoa Irangi taken; Belgian offensive against German E Africa: 6 May, Kigali, Rwanda, taken; 6 June, Usumbura taken; 13 June, Smuts captures Wilhelmstal (Lushoto). 29 July, Kigoma and Ujiji taken. Aug., Central railway reached by Smuts at Morogoro. 4 Sept., British take Dar es Salaam. 19 Sept., Tabora taken by the Belgians. 24 Sept., Lijj Iyasu escapes to Diredawa. 27 Sept., Lijj Iyasu formally deposed. Menelik's daughter Zawditu (Judith), Empress of Ethiopia: Ras Tafari (later Emperor Haile Selassie) regent and heir to the throne. 2 Nov., Ethiopian army returns to Addis Ababa having defeated supporters of Lijj Iyasu. Allidina Visram d.: end of his trading empire; Narandas Rajaram and Co. Ltd. begins operations in Uganda, establishing ginneries. Palace and finances of Kabaka reformed; Buganda central administration and judicial system reformed. Sir Horace Byatt made Civil Administrator of northern part of German EA.
1917 11 Feb., Zawditu crowned Empress of Ethiopia in Addis Ababa. March, East African Women's League formed to promote women's suffrage. Many small actions in southern German EA; 15 Oct., battle of Mahina: British 2,700 casualties out of 4,900 infantry; Nov., Lettow-Vorbeck crosses R Ruvuma into Mozambique.

1916 Rhodesia Railway Workers Union formed: promotes general strike. May, S African and N Rhodesian troops advance into German E Africa. Cape Town and Stellenbosch Universities chartered. Lewanika d.

1916 3 Feb., conscription introduced in Britain. Feb., battle of Verdun. 16 May, so-called Sykes-Picot agreement. 31 May, Battle of Jutland. June, Arab revolt proclaimed in Hijaz. 1 July-23 Oct., S African brigade heroically defends Delville Wood, R Somme. School of African and Oriental Studies, London, founded.

1917 May, a republic openly canvassed in S Africa. SA Native Administration Act. Industrial and Commercial Workers Union formed at Cape Town for Africans. Anglo-American Diamond Corporation formed. Responsible Government Association formed in Rhodesia. Rising in Barue region.

1917 15 March, Nicholas II of Russia abdicates. 2 Apr., USA declares war on Germany. 2 Nov., Balfour Declaration promises Jewish people a national home in Palestine. 3 Nov., Baghdad taken by the British. 7 Nov., Bolsheviks seize power in Russia. 20-30 Nov., battle of Cambrai: Hindenburg line broken. 22 Nov., Peace conference between Germany and Russia at Brest-Litovsk. 9 Dec.,

1918 3 Nov., Saad Zaghlul demands independence for Egypt from British High Commissioner. 27 Nov., British refuse delegation (Wafd) of Egyptian Nationalists. Husain Rushdi Pasha resigns as Prime Minister.

1918 Blaise Diagne appointed Commissioner-General for Recruitment of Troops in Black Africa. July-Feb. 1919, rising amongst the Adja of Mono.

1919 8 March, Saad Zaghlul Pasha and three other nationalists ordered to be deported to Malta: riots ensue. 21 March, Allenby becomes High Commissioner in Egypt. 7 Apr., Zaghlul released in Malta; proceeds to Conference of Paris. Dec., Lord Milner heads commission on reform of Egyptian constitution (-Dec., 1920). General Berenguer, Spanish High Commissioner: more Moroccan tribes submit.

1919 10 July, Anglo-French agreement on the partition of Togo. 30 July, force of 23,000 men raised in *AOF,* followed by annual contingents of 12,500. Sir Frederick Lugard leaves Nigeria after 25 years service. Risings amongst the Egbas. Mauritania constituted a separate governorate in *AOF,* with St Louis as capital.

1919 Fraternal Lutheran Mission starts work in N Cameroun.

c. **1920** *Parti Communiste Algérien (PCA)* founded.
1920 Feb., first aircraft flight across the Sahara. Destour (Constitution) Party (DP) formed in Tunisia to secure independence of Tunisia as a nation. *Aliwiyya* order founded at Mazagan (Algeria) by Mustafa b. Aliwa. Abdelkrim (Abd el-Karim), Qadi (Cadi) of the Beni Uriaghel, revolts in the Rif Mts.

1920 6 Nov., Lycée Faidherbe opened at St Louis. 4 Dec., *AOF* reorganized into different provinces. National Congress of British West Africa founded in Accra. Control of Niger. Co. acquired by Lever Bros Ltd. La Guera occupied by Spanish. King of Lagos deposed for acting as a focus for political adventurers.

1920 30 May, *Union Générale des Ouvriers du Congo* established in Elizabethville. Extensive reforms of local government in the Belgian Congo with partial indirect rule. Diamang *(Companhia de Diamantes de Angola)* starts operations. Bwiti cult started in Gabon and spread to Spanish Guinea. Kiyoka cult started in Angola.

1921 Feb., Britain proposes abolition of protection in Egypt and negotiation of a treaty: March, Adli Pasha Yegen, Egyptian Premier: leads delegation to London; 28 May, Egyptian nationalist riots in Alexandria. 21-22 July, Abdelkrim defeats Spanish General Silvestre near

1921 1 Jan., boundary between Mauritania and French Soudan shifted: latter gains 185,000 in population. 23 March, administration of French Togo reorganized. 13 Dec., Niger becomes a French Colony, capital Zinder. Katsina training college founded.

1921 15 March, Rwanda and Burundi ceded to Belgium; 22 March, Kigoma ceded by Belgian Congo to Tanganyika. 23 March, Cameroun organized as a French colony separate from *AEF.* Simon Kimbangu organizes Messianic sect. 14 Sept, Simon Kimbangu arrested. African Education

EASTERN AFRICA	SOUTHERN AFRICA	OTHER COUNTRIES
Buganda Treasury opens bank account. **1918** British occupation of Teso and Lango completed. **1918-19** Major famine in Busoga and neighbouring regions; rinderpest in Buganda and W Province of Uganda.	**1918** Feb., Lettow-Vorbeck's column in Mozambique. May, white municipal workers strike in Johannesburg; June, Bantu workers follow. Sept., Lettow-Vorbeck attacks Fife; 14 Nov., surrenders in N Rhodesia. South African Native College started at Fort Hare. N Rhodesian Legislative Council elected by 589 white voters. Income Tax introduced in S Rhodesia.	Jerusalem taken by the British. **1918** Jan., suffrage for women of thirty and over agreed in Britain. 8 Jan., President Wilson issues the 'Fourteen Points'. 3 March, treaty of Brest-Litovsk. 4 Sept., Germans retreat on the western front. 14 Sept., Austria asks for peace. 18 Oct., Turkey asks for an armistice. 10 Nov., William II of Germany flees to Holland 11 Nov., allies concede an armistice to Germany. **1918-19** World-wide epidemic of Spanish influenza.
1919-22 Major-General Sir Edward Northey, Governor of Kenya. **1919** 31 Jan., Sir Horace Byatt becomes Civil Administrator of all German EA occupied by British troops: Dec., some schools reopened. Famine in Kondoa-Irangi. Moyale and Wajir garrisoned by regulars for the first time.	**1919** March-Apr., African National Union organizes meetings, with burning of passes. 8 Apr., Ian Douglas Smith b. 30 May, part of SW Africa transferred to Belgium. 28 Aug., Botha d.; 3 Sept., Smuts, Prime Minister (-1924). Responsible Government campaign led by Sir Charles Coghlan in S Rhodesia.	**1919** 18 Jan., Peace Conference opens in Paris. 25 March, League of Nations Covenant adopted. 6 May, Conference of Paris makes German E and SW Africa, Togo and Kamerun 'B' class mandates. 14-15 June, the Atlantic first crossed by aeroplane. 28 June, Treaty of Versailles. 22 Aug., Rwanda-Burundi made a 'B' class mandate. 12 Sept., Franco-Italian agreement on boundary of Tripolitania and Niger. **1919-48** Sir Ralph Furse in charge of recruitment at the Colonial Office.
1920 July, East African Protectorate becomes Kenya Colony, except for coastal strip, which becomes Kenya Protectorate. East African Currency Board constituted with florin as basic unit. 22 July, Sir H. Byatt becomes Governor of Tanganyika Territory. Sept., first Director of Education appointed in Tanganyika. Educational Commission in Zanzibar. Kikuyu Association formed: Harry Thuku, secretary. Final British expedition against 'Mad Mullah' in Somaliland: he dies of influenza. Uganda Legislative Council instituted , with five officials, two Europeans and one Indian: Indians boycott Council in protest. British Convention with Italy cedes 33,000 sq. miles of Jubaland to Somalia. **1921** 8 Feb., Indian rupee notes demonetized in EA. 22 March, Belgian mandate proclaimed over Rwanda-Urundi, formerly in German EA. 1 Sept., European non-officials in Dar es Salaam protest against closer union with Kenya. Dec., Taxpayers Protection League formed in Kenya. Young Kikuyu Association formed.	**1920** Feb., first flight from London to the Cape. 71,000 Bantu strike in the Rand. March, SA general election: coalition government under Smuts; Sept., SA Party and Unionist Party merge. SA Native Affairs Commission set up to advise the Prime Minister, and to provide for the extension of the Transkei system and to summon conferences of notables. Gold payments suspended from SA. Witwatersrand University chartered. College buildings at Fort Hare burnt in protest against poor food. **1921** Council of Advice set up for SW Africa with equal numbers of Afrikaners and Germans. Feb., SA general elections: enlarged SA Party victorious: 8 Feb., Smuts gains majority of twenty. May, Israelite Ethiopian sect under prophet Enoch fired on by the police at Bulhoek.	**1920** 10 Jan., Treaty of Versailles and League of Nations comes into force. 16 Jan., US Senate rejects joining League of Nations. Prohibition of alcohol instituted in USA. 20-23 March, first Malines Conference between Anglicans and Roman Catholics. 18-26 Apr., San Remo Conference: Anglo-French agreement on Mesopotamia. 16 May, St Joan of Arc canonized. 20 June, Imperial Conference in London. 22 July, Order-in-Council formally establishes Tanganyika Territory. 15 Nov.-18 Dec., first General Assembly of the League of Nations. 15-22 Dec., Brussels Conference: Germany required to pay £13,450 m. in forty-two years. Royal Institute of International Affairs, London, founded. Further autonomy granted to Portuguese Colonies. **1921** 3 Jan., first Indian Parliament meets. 24-9 Jan., Conference on German reparations in Paris: Germans to pay £11,300 m. in 42 years. 21-26 Feb., Near East Conference in London. 4 March, Harding President of USA. 12 Nov., Disarmament Conference in Washington (-8 Feb. 1922). 6 Dec., Treaty between Britain and

Anual: General Silvestre commits suicide; Aug., Abdelkrim takes Zeluan, Nador and Monte Arruit: Melilla threatened; Republic of the Rif proclaimed. Spanish counteraction against Abdelkrim; Dec., R Kert reached. Spanish operation against al-Raisuni's stronghold at Beni Aros. 23 Dec., Zaghlul and associates again deported. Public Health Decree organizes health service in Spanish Morocco.

Commission in Angola. Swedish Free Mission established in Kivu.

1922 21 Feb., British Protectorate in Egypt declared ended: Egypt independent for the first time since 323 BC. 16 March, Britain formally recognizes Kingdom of Egypt, with joint Anglo-Egyptian sovereignty over the Sudan. General Berguete, Spanish High Commissioner in Morocco: Oct., agreement made with al-Raisuni: western zone of Morocco pacified. Nov., Lord Carnarvon and Howard Carter discover tomb of Tutankhamun at Luxor. Dec., Señor Silvela, Spanish High Commissioner in Morocco. Liberal-Constitutional Party (al-Ahrar al-Desturiyyun) constituted in Egypt. Tripolitanian representatives recognize leadership of the Amir of Cyrenaica. Bey of Tunis threatens to abdicate in support of claims of DP.

1922 3 March, Haut-Sénégal and Niger reconstituted by separation of Haute-Volta, capital at Ougadougou. First elections in Nigeria. Achimota College founded near Accra. Enlarged Legislative Council with some elected members instituted in Lagos. Committee for Trade and Taxation in British West Africa set up.

1922 15 July, 244 followers of Simon Kimbangu transferred to Huri district. Kisaka region ceded by Belgian Congo to Tanganyika. Evangelization S Africa Mission (ESAM), Pentecostal Union of Missionaries of Great Britain and Ireland, Unevangelized Africa Mission, Berean Missionary Society and Mission Baptiste de Kivou start work in the Belgian Congo.

1923 15 March, Fuad I declared King of Egypt (-1936); 19 Apr., new constitution proclaimed. 20 Apr., Egyptian Constitution adopted. General elections to Chamber of Deputies in Egypt: Wafd Party victorious; Saad Zaghlul, Premier. Amir of Cyrenaica retires to Egypt. Abd al-Salam Bennouna, 'father of Moroccan nationalism', founds free school in Tetuan. *Etoile Nord Africaine (ENA)*, Algerian nationalist party, founded. **1923-4** Continuous guerilla warfare in Spanish Morocco.

1923 School established for sons of chiefs at Georgetown, Gambia. **1923-7** Minor risings on the borders of southern Sahara.

1923 25 Dec., many Kimbangist churches opened. Slavery forbidden in Cameroun. Njoya, King of Fumbau, deposed.

1924 May, Abdelkrim repulsed by

1924 1 Jan., *Institut de Biologie*

1924 Catholic missions in the

EASTERN AFRICA	SOUTHERN AFRICA	OTHER COUNTRIES
Three-day meeting in Nairobi on the question of Indian rights in Kenya. African population of Nairobi 12,000. Government trade school opened at Makerere. Lijj Iyasu caught and imprisoned.	Oct., conference in Cape Town on union of S Rhodesia with the Union of SA. Dec., Smuts-Churchill Agreement guarantees British naval base at Simonstown under protection of SA. Seretse Khama b.	Ireland. Pan-African Congress in Paris. Native Assistance code for Portuguese Colonies. Lloyd George suggests that German EA be administered by USA.
1922 Jan., Florin replaced by shilling as basis of EA currency. March, Harry Thuku deported to Kismayu. 1 June, Customs Dept. started in Tanganyika. 6 Sept., Wood-Winterton report received in Kenya: rejects restrictions on Indian immigration representation and segregation, except in the 'White' Highlands: common roll for electorate proposed: 'Interests of the African natives must be paramount' sets future precedent. Gold discovered S and E of L.Victoria. Status of slavery abolished in Tanganyika. Medical and teacher-training courses opened at Makerere. Julius Kambarage Nyerere b. 1922-5 Sir Robert Coryndon, Governor of Kenya.	**1922** Jan.-Feb., strikes in the Rand. 26 Jan., S Rhodesia Legislative Council agrees to responsible government. 6 March, Communist Council of Action gains control of the Rand. 10 March, martial law in Johannesburg. 15 March, Defence Force suppresses strike. 1 Apr., SA denounces Mozambique convention of 1909. 6 Nov., referendum on responsible government in S Rhodesia: 8,774 votes for; 5,089 favour union with S Africa.	**1922** Jan., Pope Benedict XV d.; Pius XI elected. 4-13 Jan., Cannes Conference postpones payment of German reparations. 22 Jan., first meeting of the Hague International Court. 6 Feb., Washington Naval treaty. 20 July, League of Nations Council approves mandates for Togo, Cameroun, Tanganyika and SW Africa. 10 Sept., Convention of St Germain-en-Laye on missions in Africa. 15 Oct,, Conservatives win general election in Britain: Bonar Law Prime Minister. 28 Oct., Mussolini's march on Rome: Fascist Party in control of Italy. 1 Nov., Mustafa Kemal proclaims Turkey a republic: end of the Ottoman sultanate. 26 Dec., 'deliberate default' of Germany declared by Reparation Commission. Sir F.D. Lugard, *The Dual Mandate in Tropical Africa.*
1923 1 Apr., British introduce poll tax in Tanganyika. 28 Sept., Ethiopia admitted to the League of Nations. Credit to Natives (Restriction) Ordinance in Tanganyika limits amount of credit that traders may sue for. Kavirondo Taxpayers' Welfare Association formed. Railway reaches Jinja from Mombasa. Encouragement of coffee-growing by Africans in Uganda begun. 1923-8 Discussions on 'Closer Union' in EA.	**1923** Apr., alliance between Nationalist and Labour Parties in SA, the 'Pact'. 1 Sept., S Rhodesia formally annexed as a Crown Colony: government to be by an elected Legislative Assembly. 1 Oct., S Rhodesia obtains responsible government: Sir Charles Coghlan sworn as first Prime Minister (-1927). Responsible Government Party renamed the Rhodesian Party. Rhodesian Congo Border Concession Ltd. formed. Native conferences at Bloemfontein and Pretoria under 1920 Act. SA Urban Areas Act closes towns to influx of Bantu. 1923-5 Voluntary repatriation of Indians from SA encouraged: 5,250 return home.	**1923** 1 Jan., USSR established. 10 Jan., French occupy Ruhr. 22 May, S. Baldwin Prime Minister. July, White Paper on Indians in Kenya: common roll denied: five Indian representatives in Kenya Legislative Council. 26 July, Treaty of Lausanne. 2 Aug., Harding d.: Coolidge President of USA (-1928). 13 Sept., General Primo de Rivera dictator of Spain. 26 Oct.-8 Nov., British Empire Conference: right of Dominions to make foreign treaties recognized. 8-9 Nov., attempted coup by Hitler fails. 6 Dec., general election in Britain: Labour Government with Liberal support. 18 Dec., Britain, France and Germany sign convention on special international status of Tangier. Advisory Committee on Native Education in Tropical Africa set up in London.
1924 Extension of railway from	**1924** 1 Apr., N Rhodesia taken	**1924** 21 Jan., Lenin d.; Stalin in

Spanish at Wadi Lau, near
Tetuan. 25 June, Britain
refuses to leave the Sudan in
face of Egyptian demand for
evacuation. Oct., General
Primo de Rivera takes over
High Commissionership of
Spanish Morocco: methodical
withdrawal of Spanish army
begun. 19 Nov., Sir Lee Stack
murdered in Cairo. 30 Nov.,
Egyptian Premier accepts British
terms of compensation demanded
for Stack's murder. Egyptian
Parliament dissolved; anti-Wafd
coalition established. Legislative
Assembly set up in Tangier:
French administrator (-1940).
1925 Jan., al-Raisuni attacked
and defeated by Spanish: Apr.,
d. Abdelkrim attacks French
Morocco along R Warqa: repulsed
from Fez. 26 Aug., Pétain takes
command of French army in
Morocco. 8 Sept., Spanish
force disembarks and starts
operations against Rif: Abdelkrim
attacks Kudia Tahar; Sept.,
Ajdir taken by Spanish: new
Khalifa, Hasan b. al-Mahdi, succ.
his father in Tetuan: General
Sanjurjo succ. as High Commisioner:
Abdelkrim negotiates for peace.
6 Dec., Italian agreement with
Egypt on Cyrenaica. Sudan
Defence Force formed. Union
Party (al-Hizb al-Ittihad) formed
in Egypt.

at Dakar affiliated to the
Institut Pasteur, Paris.
1 May, general reorganization
of education in AOF. New
Constitution in Sierra Leone.
Polo introduced into Katsina.
British Mandated Territory of
the Cameroons administered as
an integral part of Nigeria.

Congo receive government
grants for schools.

1925 30 March, African elected
members introduced into
Conseils d'Administration in
Soudan, Guinea, Ivory Coast
and Dahomey. New Education
Ordinance in the Gold Coast.
Prince of Wales visits Nigeria.
New constitution in Gold
Coast.

1925 6 Feb., Kimbangist sect
banned in Kasai. Romo
Nyirenda, Mnyasa, introduces
Kitawala or Kitower cult into
Katanga, proclaiming himself
Muana Lesa (Son of God).
University of Louvain
establishes medical and
agricultural institutes in
the Congo.

1926 27 May, Rif war in Morocco
ends: Abdelkrim surrenders to
France. 1 Aug., Muhammad
Bennouna, Ahmad Balafrej and
six others determine to work
for Moroccan independence.
25 Aug., Shauen reoccupied.

1926 28 Dec., capital of Niger
transferred from Zinder to
Niamey. Geological survey
made in Sierra Leone.

1926 Friendly Balali Society
founded by André Matswa.
Treaty of St Paul de Loanda
on frontier of Angola and
Congo.

EASTERN AFRICA

SOUTHERN AFRICA

OTHER COUNTRIES

Tabora to Mwanza approved. Kilimanjaro Native Planters' Association, of Chagga Coffee-planters, formed. N. Leys, *Kenya,* causes a stir amongst Kenya settlers. Indians in Kenya refuse taxes in protest against lack of equal status with Europeans. Local Native Councils instituted in Kenya. Ras Tafari tours Middle East and Europe. Ormsby-Gore Commission in Kenya. Rev. Dr. Arthur, Presbyterian missionary, appointed to Kenya Executive and Legislative Councils to represent Native interests.

1925 29 June, Jubaland transferred to Italian administration. Oct., Education Conference in Dar es Salaam: beginning of standardization of Swahili. Lord Delamere holds conference at Tukuyu, Tanganyika, of white settlers from EA, Nyasaland and N Rhodesia. 19 Oct., Italy completes occupation of Italian Somaliland under terms of **1889** Protectorate. 145 ginneries in Uganda, 100 Indian owned. Kikuyu Central Association replaces Young Kikuyu Association; Kavirondo Taxpayers' Welfare Association divides into Bantu and Luo branches. Governor of Kenya ceases to be responsible for Zanzibar: British Resident now answerable direct to Colonial Office.
1925-30 Sir Edward Grigg (later Lord Altrincham), Governor of Kenya.
1925-31 Sir Donald Cameron, Governor of Tanganyika Territory.
1926 Oct., Milton Obote b. 7 Dec., first meeting of Tanganyika Legislative Council with thirteen official and seven non-official members. Ras Tafari takes personal command of Ethiopian army. Native Authority Ordinance formalizes indirect rule in Tanganyika. Conference of East African governors in Nairobi. Labour Dept. set up in Tanganyika. Sir Apolo Kagwa, Katakiro of Buganda, resigns: British administration in Buganda more influential. First non-official members appointed to Zanzibar Legislative Council.

over from the BSA Co. by the Crown. 30 June, general election in S Africa: J.B.M. Hertzog, Prime Minister (-1933) with Pact ministry. Indians in SA deprived of municipal franchise. Bondelswarts Hottentots rebel against a dog tax: more than 100 persons killed. Germans in SW Africa become British by nationality unless they refuse. African Education Commission in Mozambique. General elections in S Rhodesia: Rhodesian Party gains twenty-four out of thirty-six seats.

1925 Apr., scuffle between police and native demonstrators at Waaihoek location. 7 July, S African Senate rejects colour-bar bill. Afrikaans recognized in SA as an official language on an equality with English and Dutch. Indian residence segregated in SA by Areas Reservation Act. Suffrage granted to women in S Rhodesia. Morris Carter Land Commission in S Rhodesia. First demands for union of the two Rhodesias and Nyasaland. N Rhodesian unofficial members attend Tukuyu Conference. European Education Dept. opened in N Rhodesia with sub-department for Native Education in the Dept. for Native Affairs.

1926 June, Non-European Conference at Kimberley attended by ANC and SA Indian National Congress. SA Immorality Act forbids carnal connection between persons of differing colour. Statutory colour bar imposed in SA by Mines and Works Amendment and Colour Bar Acts. Rising of rival groups of Bastards at Rehoboth, SW Africa, put down by force. Progressive Party organized in S Rhodesia by Lieut.-Col. F.W. Johnson. S Rhodesia Native Welfare Association headed by D.F. Gwebu *alias* Fish. Conference of unofficials from E Africa and N Rhodesia at Victoria Falls reject federation.

control of USSR. 23 Jan., J. Ramsay MacDonald Prime Minister. 2 Feb., Caliphate abolished by Turkey. 19 Feb., Reza Khan seizes power in Persia. 16 July - 16 Aug., London Reparations Conference accepts Dawes plan. 29 Oct., Conservatives win sweeping victory at general election. 5 Nov., civil war begins in China. 6 Nov., S. Baldwin, Prime Minister. *Etoile Nord Africaine (ENA)* founded near Paris.

1925 3 Jan., Fascist Party made the sole political party in Italy. June-July, Franco-Spanish conference on Morocco in Madrid. 1 July, evacuation of the Ruhr begun. 20 July, Druse rising in Lebanon and Syria. 31 Oct., Reza Khan proclaimed Shah of Persia. 1 Dec., Locarno treaties signed. 6 Dec., Egyptian agreement with Italy on Cyrenaica. Anglo-Italian agreement recognizes Ethiopia as a sphere of Italian influence: Ras Tafari's protest published with it by League of Nations. Dominions Office separated from Colonial Office. St Thérèse of Lisieux canonized.

1926 28 Feb., Encyclical *Rerum Ecclesiae gestarum* on indigenous clergy and the evolution of African missions into dioceses published in Rome: looks forward to decolonization. 3-12 May, general strike in Britain. 24 May, minerals and oil nationalized in Mexico. 28 May, *coup d'état* in Portugal. 1 July, Anglo-Portuguese agreement on boundary of SW Africa and Angola. 8 Sept., Germany admitted to the League of Nations. 25 Sept., International convention on slavery. 19 Oct.-18 Nov., Imperial Conference in London: Britain and the Dominions declared autonomous communities equal in status. Copper Exporters Inc. formed in USA. Protestant

EGYPT, THE SUDAN & NORTHERN AFRICA	WESTERN AFRICA	CENTRAL AFRICA
1927 9 March, revocation of self-government in Libya. Sidi Muhammad b. Yusuf, Sultan of Morocco. Mopping up operations continue in Rif to 10 July. 23 Aug., Nahas Pasha becomes leader of the Wafd Party. Oct., King Alfonso XIII and Queen Victoria Eugenia of Spain visit Spanish Morocco. Egyptian population over 14m. *ENA* accepts Communist Hadj Ben Ahmed Messali (or Messali Hadj) as leader.	**1927** 2 Sept., domestic slavery abolished in Sierra Leone. Dr Aggrey, African educationist, Vice-Principal of Achimota College, d. NA Council founded in Katsina.	**1927** Railway system in Cameroun completed.
1928 16 March-25 June, Nahas Pasha, Premier of Egypt. 29 Apr., British ultimatum compels Egypt to allow freedom of public meetings. 19 July, *coup d'état* in Egypt; Parliament dissolved for 3 years, freedom of press suspended. 25 July, Italy signs Tangier Statute, giving Spain a freer hand. Italian and Portuguese representatives join Committee of Control of Tangier.	**1928** Bathurst Trade Union formed. First Catholic priest ordained in Dahomey. First N Nigerian girls' school opened in Ilorin.	
1929 31 Oct., Egyptian constitution restored. Muslim Brotherhood founded by Hasan al-Banna at Ismailia. Taha Husain, *al-Ayyam* (The Book of Days). *ENA* dissolved.	**1929** Women's riots in E Nigeria. NA Police formed in Katsina.	**1929** Electric light installed in Douala. **1929-30** Angola population about 3 m., with about 35,000 whites.
1930 1 Jan., Nahas Pasha again premier of Egypt. 21 June, Ismail Sidky Pasha premier of Egypt. Court of Cassation established in Egypt. Motor rally from the Mediterranean to the R Niger. **1930-5** Constitution suspended in Egypt.	**1930** Elementary Training College for Teachers established in Katsina. *c.* 1930 Church of the Lord (Aladura) founded at Ogere, W Nigeria.	**1930** 14 Oct., Joseph Mobutu b. French grant of 3 m. francs to combat sleeping-sickness in Cameroun. Pointe-Noire to Brazzaville railway complete. *c.* 1930 Pro-German newspaper *Mbale* (Truth) in Cameroun.

EASTERN AFRICA | SOUTHERN AFRICA | OTHER COUNTRIES

1927 Nov., Conference of Indian Associations of East Africa in Nairobi: Isher Dass becomes leader in Indian non-cooperation. Sukuma Federation of Chiefs gazetted. Archbishop Hinsley appointed Apostolic Visitor to British Africa (–1934). Clove Growers Association established in Zanzibar as a co-operative: 9,000 members join. In spite of Indian ban, A.H. Malik returned as member to Kenya Legislative Council.

1928 2 Aug., Italy signs 20 year treaty of friendship with Ethiopia. *Coup d'état* in Ethiopia : Ras Tafari takes control; 17 Oct., Ras Tafari crowned Negus by Empress Zawditu. Much railway development in East Africa. Foundation stone of Tabora school laid by Sir Donald Cameron. Nyamwezi Federation of Chiefs gazetted.

1929 Jan., Hilton Young Commission report on Kenya land and racial questions: 'paramountcy' of African interests reiterated. Negus Tafari initiates many reforms in Ethiopia. Tanganyika African Association (TAA) formed. Board of Agriculture formed in Kenya. Church of Scotland presses attack on female circumcision amongst the Kikuyu: Kikuyu Central Association agitate against this and on land rights. Clerical course instituted at Makerere. Commission on cotton industry in Uganda reports. Government departments in Uganda instructed if possible to appoint Africans; and Indians only on a temporary basis.

1930 March, Ras Gugsa Wolfie, brother of Empress Zawditu, revolts against Negus Tafari; 31 March, Ras Gugsa defeated and killed. 2 Apr., Empress Zawditu d.: 3 Apr., Ras Tafari proclaimed Emperor as Haile Selassie: Nov., crowned in Addis Ababa. Ministry of Education set up in Ethiopia. Harry Thuku released from deportation order. Serious fall in prices in Tanganyika.
1930-5 Belgian military mission trains Ethiopian Imperial Guard.

1927 Jan., SA Conference with Indian government representatives in Cape Town. 28 Aug., Sir C. Coghlan d.; H.U. Moffat, Prime Minister of S Rhodesia. Nov., Indian Government Agency set up at Cape Town. SA Native Adminstration Act. Pondoland General Council, embracing E and W Pondoland, formed. First strike of African workers in S Rhodesia. Interterritorial Railway Commission created for N and S Rhodesia and Bechuanaland.
1928 May, strike of SA Native Clothing Workers' Union and Witwatersrand Tailors' Association. 31 May, new flag first flown in SA. 11 Sept., Portuguese- S African treaty regulating transport and labour recruitment. Nov., Botha cabinet reconstituted. SA Communist Party reorganized, with an increasingly Bantu membership. 400 Boer families transferred from Angola to SW Africa. General election in S Rhodesia. Rhodesian Anglo-American Corporation formed.
Mozambique population 4 m., of which 17,800 whites, 8,500 Indians, 8,350 half-castes and 900 Chinese.
1929 Jan., 'Black Peril' general election: Hertzog returned to power with an increased majority. Nov., white mobs attack Bantu and Coloured meetings in Durban. The word *'apartheid'* first used. Land Settlement Board set up in N Rhodesia to encourage white settlement. Portfolio of External Affairs created in SA.
1929-30 Malaria eliminated from N Rhodesian Copper Belt. Indirect rule instituted in N Rhodesia.

1930 19 May, white women given votes in S Africa. SA Riotous Assemblies Act. Quota Act reduces Jewish immigration into SA. Pretoria University chartered. Progressive and Country Parties in S Rhodesia merged as the Reform Party. Education for European children between seven and fifteen made compulsory in S Rhodesia. Land Apportionment Act in S Rhodesia divides land between Africans and Europeans. Union between N and S Rhodesia shelved. Unofficials gain parity with officials in N Rhodesian Legislative Council: general elections include Roy Welensky.
c. **1930** Welfare Societies organized amongst Africans in N Rhodesia, airing local grievances. Makape 'cleansing' cult starts in Nyasaland.

Missionary Conference at Le Zoute.
1927-31 Jan., military control of Germany ended. 2-25 May, World Economic Conference at Geneva. 20 May, Britain recognizes Saudi Arabia. 20-21 May, C. Lindbergh makes first solo air crossing of the Atlantic. 27 May, Britain breaks off diplomatic relations with Russia. 20 June, –4 Aug., Naval Disarmament Conference at Washington. 27 July, Belgium and Portugal agree on boundary adjustments in the Congo. 14 Dec., Treaty between Britain and Iraq. Canada admitted to the Council of the League of Nations.
1928 20 Feb., Transjordan independent. Apr., Dr. Salazar, Minister of Finance in Portugal. 7 May, suffrage extended to all women over twenty-one in Britain. 25 July, Italy adheres to Tangier Statute. 2 Aug, treaty of friendship between Ethiopia and Italy. 27 Aug., Kellogg Pact signed in Paris . 6 Oct., Chiang Kai-Shek elected President of China. 7 Nov., H. Hoover elected President of the USA. Advisory Committee on Native Education in Tropical Africa re-established as Advisory Committee on Education in the Colonies.

1929 11 Feb., Lateran Treaty between Pope Pius XI and Italy recognizes territorial sovereignty of Vatican City. 30 May, Labour Party wins general election in Britain. 5 June, MacDonald's second ministry. 3 Oct., Diplomatic relations between Britain and Russia restored. 28 Oct., New York Stock Exchange collapses: world economic crisis begins. 13 Nov., Bank for International Payments founded at Basle. Portuguese Colonial Act.
1929-30 Warren Fisher Committee on training of the Colonial Service.

1930 21 Jan.-22 Apr., Naval Disarmament Conference in London. 12 March, Gandhi begins civil disobedience campaign in India. 22 Apr., Five Power Treaty for Naval Disarmament. 8 May, London talks on Egypt and the Sudan break down. June, Labour Government issues White Papers *Conclusions on Closer Union* (in EA) and *Memorandum on Native Policy in East Africa.* 30 June, Iraq independent; Rhineland wholly evacuated.
1 Oct. - 14 Nov., Imperial Conference in London. 12 Nov – 19 Jan. 1931, Round Table Conference on India. Statute of Westminster defines independent status of Dominions. Geneva Act forbids forced labour in Colonies. Portuguese Colonial Act.

1931 22 Apr., Treaty of Friendship between Egypt and Iraq. Berber *Dahir* (decree) recognizes Berber customary law in Morocco: provokes Islamic nationalist reaction. Apr., Spanish electtions result in Spanish demonstrations in Morocco: General Jordana, High Commissioner, flees from Tetuan; General Sanjurjo High Commissioner; 5 May, Moroccan workers demonstrate for 8 hour day and equality of wages; June. Señor Lopez Ferrer. High Commissioner: Dec., Derkawah confraternity rising at Bab Taza.

1931-4 Further small risings in southern Sahara.
1931 Diamonds discovered in Sierra Leone. First Nok culture portrait heads found at Nok, S of Zaria.

1931 1 July, Benguela-Katanga railway opened: first trans-African railway completed.

1932 15 Jan., France completes pacification of French Morocco. Muslim Brotherhood headquarters moved to Cairo.

1932 5 Nov., Haute-Volta split between Soudan and Niger.

1932 Baptist Mid Mission established in Belgian Congo.

1933 *ENA* revived. Development plan drawn up for Spanish Morocco.

1933 Odumegwu Ojukwu, an Ibo, b. in Nigeria. District Economic Boards set up in Katsina.

1933 More than 1 m. Catholics in Belgian Congo.
1933-46 Léon Mba exiled from Cameroun for sedition.

1931 1 June, Anglo-Italian agreement on boundary of British and Italian Somaliland. 13 Nov., Lord Delamere d. Joint Select Committee on Closer Union in EA. African population in Nairobi 27,000. Kikuyu Association changes name to Kikuyu Loyal Patriots. Railway from Jinja reaches Kampala. New constitution in Ethiopia: unitary state with a Senate and House of Representatives with limited duties. Ethiopian troops occupy Ogaden. First girls' school opened in Ethiopia. Bank of Ethiopia founded: currency issued to replace Maria Theresa thalers.
1931-7 Sir Joseph Byrne, Governor of Kenya.
1932 Feb., Standing Economic Committee in Kenya with parity between official and non-officials. Official salaries in Tanganyika reduced by amounts varying from 5% to 10%: economy of Tanganyika severely criticized by Sir Sydney Armitage-Smith for over-expenditure on social services. Germans in Tanganyika pressing for right to be elected to Legislative Council. Lord Moyne's report on financial and other questions in Kenya. Gold discovered at Kakamega, Kenya. Sir Alan Pim, *Report on the Financial Position and Policy of the Zanzibar Government*. Emperor Haile Selassie announces total abolition of slavery to be completed by 1952.
1933 March, Lord Francis Scott, settler leader, takes anti-Income Tax petition from Kenya to London. Kenya Land Commission. Uganda Indians restricted to special trading centres. Bunyoro Agreement. Uganda Cotton Zone Ordinance.

1930-2 United Transkeian Territories General Council formed from the Transkeian and Pondoland Councils.
1931 Jan., Earl of Clarendon appointed Governor-General of SA on the advice of SA ministers: High Commissionerships for S Rhodesia, Basutoland, Bechuanaland and Swaziland separated. Quota Act in SA for immigrants from central Europe. European suffrage in SA freed from financial and educational restrictions. SA Natives' Urban Areas Amendment Act further restricts African residence rights. Dr Godfrey Huggins resigns from Rhodesian Party over Public Services Economy Act; becomes leader of Reform Party. Many N Rhodesian mines close, followed by acute unemployment.

1932 Jan-Feb., conference between SA and India fails to settle SA – Indian problem. Apr., SW Africa Legislative Council obtains extended powers, with recognition of German as an official language. Aug., S Rhodesia makes tobacco agreement with Britain. 27 Dec., Judge Tielman Roos demands a non-racial government in SA with abandonment of the gold standard. SA Native Service Contract Act. Civil and military police separated in N Rhodesia.

1933 7 Jan., SA abandons the gold standard. 30 March., Hertzog and Smuts form National Coalition Party of 144; opposition 6. Sept., Tshekedi Khama, Regent of the Bamangwato, deposed by the British Government for exceeding his powers: subsequently reinstated. 6 Sept., following S Rhodesian general elections, Dr. G, Huggins, Prime Minister. Jewish immigration into SA increases rapidly: local agitation follows. SA Communist Party collapses. Afrikaans Bible published. Roy Welensky elected Chairman of Railway Workers Union in Broken Hill. Pressure for union of N and S Rhodesia revived. Africanization begun in N Rhodesia. N Rhodesia Regiment established. Native Authorities set up in Nyasaland.

1931 4 March., civil disobedience ended in India. 14 Apr., revolution in Spain: King Alfonso XIII flees. 15 May., Encyclical *Quadragesimo anno*. 2 July., British Government declares that amalgamation of N and S Rhodesia will not be considered for the time being. 28 Aug., Coalition Government in Britain: MacDonald Prime Minister. 18 Sept., Japan attacks Manchuria. 21 Sept., Britain gives up gold standard. 27 Oct., general election in Britain: coalition 558 seats with 56 opposition. 1 Dec., second India Conference in London. BBC Empire service opened.

1932 4 Jan., Gandhi arrested: Indian Government assumes special powers. 2 Feb., Disarmament Conference in Geneva opens. 5 May, President Doumer of France murdered. 26 May., draining of Zuider Zee completed. July, Dr Salazar Prime Minister of Portugal (−1968). 21 July-20 Aug. Imperial Economic Conference at Ottawa. 5-20 Sept., Stresa Conference. 8 Nov., F.D. Roosevelt elected President of USA. 19 Nov., −24 Dec., third India Conference in London. Dec., Copper Conference in New York. International agreement on copper prices. Imperial Airways route from London to Cape Town opened.

1933 30 Jan., Hitler Chancellor of Germany. 14 Feb., Bank crisis in USA. 27 Feb., Reichstag burnt down. 26 March., new Portuguese constitution. 30 Apr., USA abandons gold standard. 14 July, Nazis forbid other parties in Germany. 15 July, Four Power Pact signed in Rome. 14 Oct., Germany leaves Disarmament Conference and League of Nations. 12 Nov., Nazis win elections with 95% of votes. 16 Nov., Liberals join opposition in England. Imperial Organic Charter and Overseas Administrative Reform Act in Portugal. Charles te Water, SA High Commissioner in London, elected President of the League Assembly. Germany presses Permanent Mandates Commission for rights equal with British subjects in Tanganyika.

1934 19 Oct., Major-General
Yakubu Gowon b. at Zaria. Senegalese
branch of *SFIO (Section Française de
l'Internationale Ouvrière)* founded. *Air-
Afrique* (later absorbed in *Air France*)
formed. Law school opened in Kano with
Shaikhs from Gordon College, Khartoum,
Smara, in interior of Sanguiat al-Hamra,
occupied by Spanish. Ifni reoccupied.
1934 or 1935 *Parti Socialiste Senegalais
(PSS)* founded by Lamine Gueye.

1935 Jan., Abd al-Salam Bennouna d.
12 Dec., Egyptian Nationalists demand
restoration of 1923 constitution.
Association of Ulama founded in
Algeria by Shaikh Abd al-Hamid b. Badis.

1935 Ousmane Socé Diop., *Karim.*

1935 Port of Douala greatly developed.
Salvation Army starts work in Belgian
Congo.

1936 28 Apr., (-21 July, 1952) Farouk,
King of Egypt. 10 May, Nahas Pasha,
Premier of Egypt. 10 May-1937, 31 July,
Wafd government in Egypt. 17 July,
Melilla the first Spanish city to rise
against the Popular Front. 26 Aug., British
end military occupation of Egypt except
for Canal Zone; Anglo-Egyptian treaty
for 20 years allows Britain to station
10,000 men in Egypt. Blum-Violette
reforms of administration in Algeria:
attempt to give French citizenship to
21,000 Muslims abortive.
Parti-Populaire Algérien (PPA) founded by
Messali Hajj. Islah (Reform) Party founded
in Spanish Morocco by Abd al-Khalek
Torres.

1936 First air mail service from
England reaches Kano.

EASTERN AFRICA | SOUTHERN AFRICA | OTHER COUNTRIES

1934 May, Kenya Land Commission report. Anglo-Ethiopian Boundary Commission on Ethiopian-Somali frontier: 22 Nov., Italian fort found at Wal-Wal halts commission: British claim provocation by Italians and withdraw: 5 Dec., hostilities between Italians and Ethiopians. Military college opened at Holeta, Ethiopia, under Swedish officers.

1935 1 Feb., Italy sends troops to Eritrea and Italian Somaliland. March, Ethiopia appeals for protection to League of Nations. July, Lijj Iyasu d. 10 Sept., white settlers in Kenya denounce government, advocating closer union with Uganda and Tanganyika. 3 Oct., Italy invades Ethiopia, using aircraft and poison gas. 6 Oct., Adowa occupied. 8 Nov., Makalle and Tigre occupied.

1936 31 March-2 Apr., Ethiopia defeated at Battle of Maichew; 2 May, following decision of Council of Ministers, Emperor leaves Ethiopia to keep international negotiations open. 5 May, Italians occupy Addis Ababa; 9 May, Ethiopia formally annexed by Italy; Victor Emmanuel III of Italy proclaimed Emperor; Marshal Graziani Viceroy; Ethiopian guerilla resistance continues under Ras Imru and the Black Lions; Dec., Ras Imru surrenders. Tribute to chiefs in Uganda abolished: salaries instituted.

1934 Feb., Prince George (later Duke of Kent) visits SA. 5 June, Smuts's South African Party and Hertzog's followers in Nationalist Party form United S African Nationalist Party; rump of Nationalist Party re-formed under D.F. Malan. 12 June, South African Status Bill: Cape Parliament retains right to secede from Commonwealth. July-Oct., Nazi and Hitler Youth organizations banned in S Africa. Reform Party and Rhodesian Party merge to form United Party; Nov., general elections give Huggins a crushing victory.

1935 14 Jan., Lower Zambezi railway bridge opened. May, Lusaka formally inaugurated as capital of N Rhodesia. 20-31 May, African strikes and riots on the Copper Belt. Grey Shirt movement in SA in imitation of Nazi Brown Shirts. Demand of ruling United Party in SW Africa to unite with SA referred to a Commission of Inquiry. Government Archives of S Rhodesia instituted.

1936 7 Apr., S African Native Representation Bill: Africans allowed to elect three Europeans to represent them in Parliament: native representative council set up with advisory powers. June-July, Hertzog expresses hopes of the transfer to SA of Swaziland, Bechuanaland and Basutoland: chiefs and others oppose the proposal. Sept., Empire Exhibition at Johannesburg. Dec., SA Government states categorically that it will not transfer SW Africa to any other power. *Federasie van Afrikaanse Kultur Verenigings (FAK)* founded to promote and defend Afrikaner culture. SA Lands Act: Bantu to have as reserves 37.5 m. acres out of Union's total of 30.2 m. acres. Transvaal Asiatic Land Tenure Amendment Act enables Indians to own property. Native Authorities and Courts established in N Rhodesia. N Rhodesia Mine Workers Union organized with all-white membership.

1934 Jan., Stavisky scandal in France. 17 Feb., Albert of Belgium d.; succ. Léopold III. 24 March, Philippines independent. 30 May, Nazi 'Purge'. 14-15 June, Hitler meets Mussolini in Venice. 20 June, British — Italian agreement on frontier of Sudan with Libya. 25 July, Dollfuss, Chancellor of Austria, murdered by Nazis. 18 Sept., Russia joins League of Nations. 29 Dec., Japan denounces Washington Naval Treaty of 1922. *L'Etudiant Noir* founded by Léopold Sédar Senghor and Aimé Césaire. Religious orders suppressed in Portugal.

1935 Jan., Ethiopian protests against Wal-Wal incident to League of Nations. 7 Jan., Franco-Italian agreement on Somali boundaries. 13 Jan., Saar plebiscite votes return to Germany. 16 Jan., Germany repudiates military articles in the Treaty of Versailles. 7 June, S.Baldwin, Prime Minister. Sept., League of Nations exonerates both parties to Wal-Wal incident. 15 Sept., Swastika made the official German flag: Jews outlawed in Germany. 7 Oct., League of Nations imposes partial sanctions on Italy. 14 Nov., General election in Britain won by National Party. 9 Dec., Hoare-Laval proposals for Ethiopia announced in London. 19 Dec., Sir S. Hoare resigns: A.Eden, Foreign Secretary. 18 Dec., Baldwin states in House of Commons that no colonial territories will be handed over without regard to the interests of the people concerned. Conscription restored in Germany.

1936 Jan, 20, King George V d. 20 Jan. — 10 Dec., Edward VIII King of England. 16 Feb., Popular Front elected in Spain. 7 March, German army occupies the Rhineland: Hitler demands the return of former German colonies. 28 June, Emperor Haile Selassie addresses General Assembly of League of Nations. 15 July, League of Nations ends sanctions against Italy. 18 July, Rising in Spain against Popular Front. Aug., General Franco returns to Spain. 2 Aug., Non-intervention in Spain proposed by France. 14 Aug., Spanish Nationalists take Badajos. 9 Sept., Non-Intervention Committee meets in London. 1 Oct., Franco becomes Chief of the Spanish State. 1 Nov., Rome-Berlin Axis proclaimed by Mussolini.

1937 March, *ENA* revived as *PPA*
(Parti du Peuple Algérien). 16 March,
Mussolini visits Libya. 26 May, Egypt joins
League of Nations. Aug., General
Beigbeder, High Commissioner of
Spanish Morocco. 30 Dec., Liberal
Constitution Party forms government in
Egypt. Capitulations abolished in Egypt.
Economic crisis in Morocco: *Kutlat al-
Amal al-Watani* (National Action bloc)
splits into *al-Hizb al-Watani* (National
Party) under Allal al-Fasi and *al-Harakat
al-Qaumiya* (Popular Movement).
Allal al-Fasi exiled for 9 years to Gabon.
Moroccan Unity Party *(al-Wahdat al-
Maghribiya)* founded in Spanish Morocco
by Mekki Nasiri.
Abuna Abraham of Ethiopia, with twelve
bishops consecrated by him,
excommunicated by Coptic Synod of
Alexandria.
c. **1938** *UPA (Union Populaire
Algérienne)* formed by Ferhat Abbas.
1938 1-6 June. Daladier, French Prime
Minister, visits Algiers, Corsica and
Tunisia to counter Mussolini's demand
for colonies in N Africa. 9 Apr.; civil disobedience campaign in Tunisia, organized by Habib Bourguiba, results in
riot in Tunis: Bourguiba and others court-
martialled: NDP dissolved, but continues
underground. 25 Oct., Libya declared to
be part of Italy, *RFMA (Rassemblement
Franco-Musulman Algérien)* formed by
Ben Djelloul.

1939 *PPA* dissolved but continues
clandestinely.
General Asensio, High Commissioner
of Spanish Morocco.
Education re-organized in Spanish
Morocco. Liberal Party in Spanish
Morocco founded by Khalid al-Raisini.

1940 3 July, British sink French fleets in
Oran and N Africa. 14 July, Spanish
force occupies Tangier in the name of
the Khalifa: international regime
suppressed. 3 Sept., Italian army reaches
Sidi Barrani in attack on Egypt defended
by Britain. 9 Dec., British under Wavell
attack Sidi Barrani; 15 Dec., Italians
driven across Libyan border.

1937 Quota-system for cocoa
introduced by foreign firms trading
in the Gold Coast.

1938 Apr., Gold Coast cocoa freed from
quota system. *PSS* and *SFIO* branch in
Senegal fused. 20,000 troops recruited
in *AOF*, of whom 7,000 were sent to
France in addition to 18,000 *tirailleurs*
in *AOF* and 29,000 already in France
and N Africa. *Institut Français d'Afrique
Noire (IFAN)* established at Dakar.

1939 Airport built at Hastings, Sierra
Leone. Nigerian regiment raises fifteen
battalions. German estates in Cameroun
seized by the Nigerian Government.

1940 June, 130,000 troops recruited in
AOF under arms: treated by Germans
with especial cruelty. 22 June, part of
Niger frontier with Libya demilitarized
by Franco-Italian armistice. 8 July,
British attack *Richelieu* in Dakar harbour.
26 Aug., Niger and Chad declare in
favour of De Gaulle. 23-25 Sept., Anglo-
French expedition to take Dakar fails;
opposed by Governor Boisson.

1937 2 Dec., Ntari V of Burundi
(Charles Ndizeye) b.

1938 President Carmona of Portugal
visits Angola.

1939 *Mission des Noirs,* later known
as the Khaki movement, founded by Simon
Pierre Mpadi. 100,000 attending schools
in Cameroun. 6,000 km. of roads in
Cameroun as against 600 km. in 1914.

1940 27 Aug., Cameroun taken over by
Free French under De Gaulle. 28 Aug.,
Brazzaville taken over by Free French.
8 Nov., Gabon taken over by Free French.
Capt. Michel Micombero b. Mvungi cult
emerges on R Cuango; Tonsi movement
starts in W Angola as the Tawa cult.

EASTERN AFRICA | SOUTHERN AFRICA | OTHER COUNTRIES

1937 Feb.. grenades thrown at Viceroy in Addis. Ababa: 3-day Black Shirt reign of terror; Nov., Duke of Aosta made Viceroy of Ethiopia; sporadic resistance continues; Dec., Abuna Abraham, blinded by poison gas, made head of Ethiopian church by Italians.

1937 2 Apr., S Africa prohibits political activity by foreigners in SW Africa. Aug., report of Commission on Cape Coloured Folk. Dec., first meeting of the Native Representation Council. Sir Patrick Duncan, first South African born Governor-General, appointed. SA Native Laws Amendment Act gives government greater powers to enforce segregation. SA Aliens Act, intended primarily to control influx of Jews.
Rhodes-Livingstone Institute established at Livingstone.
N Rhodesian African Congress established.

1937 March, Encyclical *Mit brennender Sorge* against Nazism smuggled secretly to all German Catholic churches. 1 Apr., new constitution in India. 8 May., Montreux Convention ends capitulations in Egypt. 14 May–15 June, Imperial Conference in London, following coronation of George VI. 28 May, Baldwin resigns: succ. Neville Chamberlain.
23 June, Germany and Italy withdraw from Non-Intervention Committee. 1 Oct., Higher Arab Committee banned in Palestine. 17-21 Nov., Lord Halifax visits Hitler. *ENA* dissolved. Dec., Italy leaves League of Nations. Constitutional conference on N Rhodesia in London. Jomo Kenyatta, *Facing Mount Kenya.*

1938 Tanganyika League, with headquarters in Nairobi, formed to resist return of the territory to Germany. African population of Nairobi 40,000. Uganda Cotton Commission.
1938-40 Sandford Committee on resources of Tanganyika.

1938 May-June, census of SA urban natives to enforce segregation. 18 May, United Party under Hertzog confirmed in power by general election. Sept., Cape Town and Durban harbours re-fortified; SA Air Force enlarged; preparations for munitions factories at Pretoria begun. 9 Sept., Cabinet reshuffle in SA. African Native Healing Church founded. Centenary of the Great Trek celebrated. The Copper Belt Urban Advisory Councils and Native Advisory Committees set up. N Rhodesia Regiment European Reserve formed. Bledisloe Commission on closer co-operation between Rhodesia and Nyasaland.

1938 25 Feb., Lord Halifax, Foreign Secretary. March, Germany seizes Austria. 16 Apr., Britain recognizes Italian sovereignity in Ethiopia. Sept., first Czechoslovak crisis. 15 Sept., Chamberlain meets Hitler at Berchtesgarten; and 22-23 Sept., at Gödesburg. 29 Sept., Munich Conference of Chamberlain, Daladier, Hitler and Mussolini. 25 Oct., Libya declared part of Italy. 8 Nov., violent attacks begun on Jews in Germany. 10 Nov., Mustafa Kemal Atuturk d. 10 and 14 Nov., Stanley Baldwin reiterates that government does not intend handing over any colonial territories.

1939 20 July, convention of British non-officials at Iringa backs closer union; Oct., Dar es Salaam Chamber of Commerce asks for amalgamation of EA. Continued Ethiopian resistance holds down fifty-six Italian battalions.
1939-45 87,000 Tanganyika Africans give service in the war. Rapid economic development in Uganda doubles revenue.

1939 4 Sept., Hertzog attempting to declare SA neutral, defeated by 80 votes to 67. 5 Sept., Smuts forms coalition government and declares war on Germany.
Major harbour improvements in Table Bay. Registration of manpower in SA made. Common Court of Appeal established in N and S Rhodesia. N Rhodesian Regiment African Reserve formed. President Carmona of Portugal visits Mozambique.
1939-45 N and S Rhodesians serve in Africa, Middle East, Madagascar, and Burma.

1939 Feb., Pius XI d. ; succ. Pius XII. 15 March, Hitler seizes Czechoslovakia. 28 March, Madrid surrenders to Franco. 31 March, Britain guarantees Polish independence. 7 Apr., Mussolini seizes Albania. 13 Apr., Britain guarantees Greek independence. May, conscription instituted in Britain. 22 May, German-Italian military alliance. 1 Sept., Germany invades Poland. 3 Sept., Britain and France declare war on Germany. Nov., British Government announces it will buy all W African cocoa. First two African Catholic bishops of modern times consecrated by Pope Pius XII.

1940 Italians attack British Somaliland from Ethiopia: July, Moyale, Kenya, taken by Italians; Aug., Italians advance on Berbera; Sept., British withdraw from British Somaliland; Sept., small British force working with Ethiopian guerillas. 16 Dec., Italians driven from El Wak in Somaliland. Income tax introduced in Tanganyika and Zanzibar. First African doctor in government service in Tanganyika.

1940 1 Jan, Price control established in SA. Feb., Colonial Development Fund approved by Parliament. Apr., strikes at N Rhodesian mines. 21 July, Smuts broadcasts to Britain and USA on an 'international society of free nations'. Europeans conscripted in N Rhodesia.

1940 Feb., Colonial Development Fund approved by Parliament. 9 Apr., Germany invades Norway. 7 May, Portuguese concordat with the Vatican and agreement on missions. 10 May, Germany invades Belgium, France and Luxembourg. Churchill replaces Chamberlain as Prime Minister. 15 May, Holland capitulates. 28 May, Belgium capitulates. 10 June, Italy declares war on allies and attacks France. 14 June, Germans take Paris. 22 June, armistice between France and Germany. 23 June, armistice between France and Italy. 8 Aug. - 6 Sept., Battle of Britain.

1941 3 Jan., Italians surrender Bardia.
19 Jan., British take Kassala. 30 Jan.,
British take Derna and advance on
Benghazi; 6 Feb., British take Benghazi.
31 March, Germans open counter-
offensive in N Africa. 7 Apr., British
evacuate Benghazi in planned withdrawal.
13 Apr., Germans take Bardia. 20 Apr.,
Germans attack Tobruk.
1 July, Auchinleck replaces Wavell in
Middle East. 18 Nov., British renew
offensive against Germans and Italians
in Libya. 19 Dec., Rommel begins withdrawal in Libya; British reoccupy
Benghazi and regain Cyrenaica.
1941-5 General Orgaz, High Commissioner
of Spanish Morocco.

1941 Combined Free French and
British force unsuccessfully raids
Dakar.

1941 Sixty killed in an uprising at
Luluabourg.

1942 9 June, British recapture Bardia.
3 Feb., British evacuate Derna. 23-30
Apr., reinforcements sent to Rommel
in N Africa whilst he bombards Malta.
2 June, British fall back from line
Gazala-Bir Hakim. 10 June, Free French
surrender Bir Hakim to Germans. 13 June,
British lose 230 tanks. 19 June, British
withdraw to line Sollum-Sidi Omar on
Egyptian frontier. 21 June, Germans
take Tobruk. 25 June, British
withdraw to Mersa Matruh; and, 28 June,
to El Alamein. Racialist laws made by
Vichy regime in Algeria: Muslims
forbidden markets, cinemas and bathing
beaches at the same time as Europeans,
or even to sit beside them. 1 Aug., French
Mayor of Zeralda murders twenty-seven
Muslims by asphyxiation. 19 Aug., Alexander replaces Auchinleck in command of
Middle East; Montgomery given command
of Eighth Army. 31 Aug., German offensive
renewed at Alam Halfa but held by British.
23 Oct., Eighth Army under Montgomery
begins battle of El Alamein. 4 Nov.,
Allied First Army under Eisenhower lands
in Algeria. Nov., Moncef Bey forms
nationalist government in Tunisia. 10 Nov.,
all Germans expelled from Egypt. 11 Nov.,
Eisenhower recognizes Admiral Darlan as
French Chief-of-State in North Africa:
Britain indignant. 13 Nov., British Eighth
Army retakes Tobruk; and, 21 Dec.,
Algiers. Sultan of Morocco declines to
join in General Noguès's resistance to
Americans. Wafd government in Egypt
declares martial law and censorship.
24 Dec., Darlan assassinated by a
Frenchman at Algiers.

1942-6 W African troops serving in
Burma. 7 Dec., *AOF* joins the allies.
Viscount Swinton, as Resident
Minister for W Africa, establishes
headquarters at Accra.

1942 State insurance for African and
European workers in the Belgian Congo
with old age pensions.

EASTERN AFRICA   SOUTHERN AFRICA   OTHER COUNTRIES

16 Sept., compulsory military service in USA. 27 Sept., Tripartite Pact between Germany, Italy and Japan. 28 Sept., Italy attacks Greece. 8 Oct., Germany occupies Rumania. Fabian Colonial Bureau founded.

1941 20 Jan., Emperor Haile Selassie crosses from Sudan into Ethiopia on foot. 26 Jan., British take Biscia, Eritrea. 30 Jan., S Africans drive Italians from Kenya. Pro-British rising in Ethiopia. 19 Feb., British attack Italian Somaliland. 7 March, British invade Ethiopia with agreement of Emperor. 19 March, Berbera retaken. Jijiga occupied by Nigerian troops. 27 March, British take Keren and Harar. 5 Apr., British take Addis Ababa; and, 6 Apr., Massawa. 20 May, end of British campaign in Ethiopia. British Military Administration set up with Sir Philip Mitchell as Chief Political Officer. 1 Aug., Governor's Conference at Nairobi sets up *EA Economic Council.* Economic Control Board set up in Zanzibar to control prices and distribution.

1941 Feb., riot after pro-Nazi *Ossewabrandung* meeting in Johannesburg. N Rhodesian Labour Party formed by R. Welensky: gains majority at election. War Supplies Committee set up in Salisbury for N and S Rhodesia and Nyasaland. Rhodesian mines agree to 'closed shop' for white labour.

1941 9 Feb., British bomb Genoa and raid Livorno: fail to stop Germans under Rommel crossing to N Africa in support of Italians. 11 Feb., Lend-Lease Bill signed by Roosevelt. 28 March, British defeat Italian navy off Cape Matapan. 6 Apr., Germany invades Yugoslavia and Greece. 10-11 May, House of Commons destroyed in air raid on London. 4 June, William II of Germany d. 8 June, British invade Syria. 22 June, Germany invades Russia. 12 July, alliance between Britain and Russia. Aug., General Smuts gazetted Field-Marshal. 11 Aug., Churchill and Roosevelt sign Atlantic Charter. 5 Oct.–6 Dec., Germans fail to take Moscow. 7 Dec., US fleet destroyed by Japanese in Pearl Harbour. 8 Dec., Japan declares war on Britain and USA. 11 Dec., Japan, Germany and Italy declare war on USA. 19 Dec., Japanese take Hong Kong. Portuguese Missionary Statute.

1942 31 Jan, Anglo-Ethiopian military convention: Britain retains Ogaden and Reserved Area as military occupied territory: Emperor of Ethiopia resumes administration with British advisers at his own request. Serious tribal clashes on Ethiopian-Kenya border. Zanzibar copra given guaranteed prices by British Ministry of Food. Kitawala revolt in Uganda.

1942 5 May, British invade Madagascar: General de Gaulle recognized. King's African Rifles from Tanganyika take part in Madagascar operations. Oct., Commodity Supply Directorate established in SA. Oct., Hertzog d. Africans at Broken Hill boycott Indian traders.

1942 1 Jan., United Nations Declaration by twenty-six countries. 15 Feb., Japan takes Singapore. May and June, German offensive in Russia. 1 May. Japan cuts Burma Road. 11 June, Lease-Lend extended to Russia. 13 July, campaign of civil disobedience begins in India. 11-12 Aug., violent riots in India. 11 Nov., Germany occupies 'unoccupied' France. 20 Nov., Beveridge plan for social insurance published. Colonial Labour Advisory Committee, Advisory Committee on the Welfare of Coloured People in the United Kingdom, and Interdepartmental Committee on Locust Control formed. Germans release Habib Bourguiba from prison in France.

1943 23 Jan, Eighth Army enters Tripoli; and, 10 Feb, reaches frontier of Tunisia. 10 Feb., Ferhat Abbas, *Manifesto of the Algerian People.* 21 Feb., Allied Armies in N Africa all placed under Eisenhower. 24 Feb., Germans withdraw at Kasserine Pass. March, Habib Bourguiba returns to Tunisia. 7-11 March, heavy German counter-attacks repulsed by Eighth Army in Tunisia. 29 March, Mareth Line broken. 6 Apr., German retreat through Gabès Gap. Eighth Army links with allies under Eisenhower. 8 Apr., Arnim succ. Rommel as commander of German Afrika Korps. 10 Apr., Eighth Army occupies Sfax. 7 May, allies take Tunis and Bizerta. Germans retire to Cape Bon. 12 May, Germans surrender in Tunisia. 10 May, Moncef Bey, premier of Tunisia, deported by French: Lamine Bey badly received by Tunisian populace: new ministry under Salaheddin Boccouche. June, General de Gaulle comes to power in Algiers. 3 June, General de Gaulle and General Giraud become co-Chairmen of French Committee of National Liberation. 12 Dec., de Gaulle speaks at Constantine promising extension of franchise to Algerian Muslims. Private schools begin to increase in Morocco. Moroccans begin to join Trade Unions.

1944 11 Jan., Independence of Morocco first demanded by Nationalist Party: Ahmad Balafrej arrested: riots in Rabat and Fez. March, *AML (Amis du Manifeste et de la Liberté)* founded by Ferhat Abbas rapidly gains ½m. members. Oct., Wafd government dismissed in Egypt. 27 Nov., schools plan for Algeria published. *Code de l'Indigénat* abolished in Algeria.

1945 1 Jan., Wafd boycott Egyptian general election; Ahmed Pasha premier of Egypt. 24 Feb., Ahmed Pasha assassinated after announcing Egypt's declaration of war on Germany. 8 May., Algerian nationalist procession in Sétif clashes with police: riots follow and also in Kabylie: some 10,000 killed in following repression by French army and police.

1943 First Africans appointed to Gold Coast Executive Council.

1944 30 Jan. – 8 Feb., Brazzaville Conference on French policy in Africa promises decolonization. Annual conference of Protectorate Chiefs established in the Gambia.
1944–5 H. Balfour (later Lord Balfour of Inchrye), Resident Minister for West Africa.

1945 4 Nov., Lamine Gueye, Léopold Senghor (Senegal), Félix Houphouët-Boigny (Ivory Coast), Apithy Sounou Migan (Dahomey), Fily Dabo Cissoko (Soudan) and Yacine Diallo (Guinea) elected to represent *AOF* in French Constituent Assembly. 25 Dec., *CFA (Côte Française d'Afrique) francs* created.

1943 Mennonite Mission established in Belgian Congo.

1944 20 Feb., *Force Publique* mutinies at Luluabourg. 18 Dec., *Syndicats du Confédérés du Cameroun (USCC)* founded. Edéa barrage begun in Cameroun.

1945 24-25 Sept., strike in Douala. Dec., Dr. L.P. Anjoulet and Prince Aléxandre Douala-Manga Bell elected as first deputies for Cameroun. More than 2 m. Catholics in the Belgian Congo. 3,000 Europeans in Cameroun.

EASTERN AFRICA	SOUTHERN AFRICA	OTHER COUNTRIES
1943 French Somaliland occupied by allies: Somali for the first time under single British control. SYL (Somali Youth League) formed. 11th (East African) Division sent to Ceylon in preparation for Burma campaign. Dec., New Anglo-Ethiopian agreement on Ogaden and Reserved Area.	1943 July, general election in SA won by Smuts. Partly elected councils set up in Bechuanaland. Regional Councils established throughout N Rhodesia: Barotseland continues with *Khotla*.	1943 Feb., Japanese evacuate Guadalcanal. 15 May, *Conseil National de la Résistance* created in France. 18 May-1 June, UNRRA founded. 10 July, allies disembark in Sicily. 25 July, fall of Mussolini. 11-24 Aug., Quebec Conference. 17 Aug., allies take Messina. 4 Sept., allies disembark in Italy. 8 Sept., allies grant Italy an armistice. 10 Sept., Germans occupy Italy N of Rome. 14 Oct., Japan proclaims the Philippines independent. 19-30 Oct., Moscow Conference. 13 Nov., Italy, recognized as an allied co-belligerent, declares war on Germany. 22-26 Nov., Cairo Conference. 1-24 Dec., Teheran Conference. 4 Dec., Marshal Tito forms government in Yugoslavia. French mandate in Lebanon terminated. Colonial Projects Research Council, Colonial Social Welfare Advisory Committee, and Colonial Fisheries Advisory Committee formed.
1944 Dec., Tanganyika Government publishes *An Outline of Post-War Development Proposals*. Town Councils stablished for Zanzibar and Ngambo. Protectorate Government of Buganda reorganized. *c.* 55,000 Uganda Africans serving in the army.	1944 16 March, Nationalist mob attacks meeting of 5,000 garment workers in Johannesburg. Non-official majority in N Rhodesian Legislative Council. Nyasaland African Congress (NAC) formed.	1944 Feb. — March, R Don basin liberated by Russia. 7 March, French Ordinance gives Algerian Muslims fifteen deputies in the National Assembly and seven senators in the Council of the Republic. 12 Apr., Victor Emmanuel III of Italy abdicates. 1-16 May, Conference of Dominion Prime Ministers in London. 4 June, allies enter Rome. 6 June, D Day, allies land in Normandy. 12 June, flying bombs first used by the Germans. 1-22 July, Bretton Woods Conference. 7 Aug., French decree recognizing trades unions in overseas territories. 17 Aug., battle of Falaise. 21 Aug.—7 Nov., Dumbarton Oaks Conference. 25 Aug., Free French, under General de Gaulle, enter Paris. 3 Sept., allies enter Brussels. 6 Sept., provisional constitution in France. 19-28 Sept., battle of Arnhem. 9—21 Nov., Moscow Conference. 17 Dec., German counter-offensive. 28 Dec., German counter-offensive crushed. Colonial Social Science Research Council and Tsetse Fly and Trypanosomiasis Committee formed.
1945 First African appointed to Zanzibar Legislative Council. Zanzibar receives £750,000 from CD and W Funds. Chiefs David Makwaia and Abdiel Shangali first African members appointed to Tanganyika Legislative Council. Riots in Buganda partly motivated by low producer prices.	1945 April, Central African Council set up in Salisbury for the Rhodesias and Nyasaland. 22 Aug., Madagascar to send five elected representatives to Parliament in Paris. 15 Oct., Labour and Dominion parties withdraw from SA coalition government; Smuts remains as premier in United Party Government. Pius XII College founded at Roma: subsequently	1945 1 Jan., German offensive in Lorraine. 13 June, Russian offensive begins. 4 March, allies reach the Rhine. 8 April, Germans encircled in Holland. 12 Apr., F.D. Roosevelt d.; H.S. Truman, President of USA. 25 Apr., Russians reach Berlin suburbs. 25 Apr.—26 June, San Francisco Conference draws up UN Charter. 18 Apr., Mussolini hanged. 30 Apr.,

23 Sept., Egypt demands revision of
Anglo-Egyptian Treaty, with end of
military occupation and return of the
Sudan. 11 Oct., Spanish forces evacuate
Tangier: international regime restored.
20 Oct., Egypt, with Syria, Lebanon,
and Iraq, warn US that the creation of a
Jewish state in Palestine will lead to war.
Arab League founded in Cairo. Egypt
declares war on Germany and Japan
in order to gain entry to UNO. Habib
Bourguiba flees from Tunis to Cairo.
Rising against French in Algeria; 100
French and 100,000 Algerians killed.
1945-6 *PPA* reorganised as *UDMA*
*(Union Démocratique du Manifeste
Algérien).*
1945-51 Lieut.-Gen. Varela, High
Commissioner of Spanish Morocco.
1945-6 Severe drought leads to
famine in Spanish Morocco.

1946 Feb., general strike in Cairo.
8 May, nationalist riots in Algeria. June,
*MTLD (Mouvement pour le Triomphe
des Libertés Démocratiques)* founded
by Messali Hajj. Nov., Lord Stansgate
leads unsuccessful British mission in
Cairo to revise Anglo-Egyptian treaty.
Nov., *PPA* re-emerges as *MTLD:* obtains
five out of fifteen seats in French National
Assembly. *UDMA* obtains eleven out of
thirteen seats in Constituent Assembly
and ten out of fifteen seats in National
Assembly in general elections.

1946 29 March, new constitution in
Gold Coast: first British colony in Africa
to have an African majority in the
legislature. Gold Coast Chiefs complain
of high prices and black market. 11 Apr.,
forced labour abolished in *AOF*. 30 Apr.,
native customary law abolished throughout *AOF*. 7 May, French citizenship
extended to all colonial subjects with
limited franchise: general councils set up
for all territories, and Grand Council for
AOF. 30 June, *AOF* representatives
re-elected to new French Constituent
Assembly. 3 July, administration of
justice reorganized in *AOF*. 17 July,
railway system of *AOF* centralized. ·
18 Oct., Congress of African deputies and
other nationalists at Bamako: *RDA
(Rassemblement démocratique africaine)*
party elected. *RDA* founded by Félix
Houphouët-Boigny in Ivory Coast, with
branches in other French W African
territories. *PPS* wins Senegal elections.
Gambia Executive and Legislative
Councils reorganized. District Councils
instituted in Sierra Leone. Cameroons
Development Corporation set up: former
German estates leased. 150 'leopard'
murders in Calabar Province. *AOF* sends
seventeen representatives to the three
Assemblies in Paris.

1946 6 Apr., creation of *Syndicats
professionels indigènes* authorized in the
Belgian Congo. 23 Dec., *Conseil d'Etat*
instituted for Belgian Congo. *UNISCO
(Union des intérêts sociaux congolais)*
founded: Joseph Kasavubu, President.
Bloc Démocratique Africain founded in
Gabon by Léon Mba.

University of Basutoland, Bechuanaland and Swaziland. African railway strike in N and S Rhodesia. African Mineworkers Union strike involves 70,000 workers in SA.

Hitler commits suicide. 2 May, Russians take Berlin. Germans capitulate in Italy. 8 May, all German armies surrender unconditionally. 21 May, Labour Party leaves Coalition in Britain. 28 June, UN Charter promulgated. 5 July, Labour Party wins general election in Britain: C.R. Attlee Prime Minister. 17 July– 1 Aug., Potsdam Conference. 6 Aug., atomic bomb dropped on Hiroshima, and 9 Aug., Nagasaki, 11-31 Aug., Paris Conference on Tangier. 2 Sept., Japan surrenders unconditionally.. 18 Oct., Nuremburg trial of Nazi leaders begun. Dec., East African High Commission and Legislative Assembly proposed. Placide Tempels, *La Philosophie Bantoue.* Second British C.D and W Act. Colonial Medical Research Committee and Committee for Colonial Agriculture, Animal Health and Forestry Research formed. World Federation of Trade Unionists demands equal pay for equal work at Paris conference of colonial representatives.

1945-54 France at war in Indo-China.

1946 Apr., Britain proposes a Greater Somalia under British trusteeship. Somali Youth League (SYL) growing in membership. Aug., A.Creech-Jones, Labour Colonial Secretary, visits Tanganyika. 28 Aug., clash in Asmara between Eritreans and British Sudanese troops. Sept., Jomo Kenyatta returns to Kenya after 15 years abroad. Williamson Diamond Mine at Mwadui, Tanganyika, found to be the largest in the world. Development plan for Uganda issued. First village council established at Chwaka, Pemba.

1946 Central African Airways set up. Rhodesian Court of Appeal extended to Nyasaland. Various joint services agreed for N and S Rhodesia. African Christian Council formed in N Rhodesia.

1946 6 Jan., Ministère de la France d'Outre-Mer sets up Ten Year Plan organization. 20 Jan., General de Gaulle resigns and retires into private life. 1 Feb., Trygve Lie elected Secretary-General of UN. 5 March, Churchill's Fulton speech. 28 March, Frank Samuel submits Ground Nut Scheme for Kenya, Tanganyika and Rhodesia to Labour Government. 11 Apr., forced labour abolished in French overseas territories. 30 Apr., *FIDES (Fonds d'investissement et de développement économique et social)* set up for French colonial development. May, Mrs Pandit and Vyshinsky attack Smuts's Indian and SW African policies in UNO. 1 May, Bank of England nationalized. 1 June, Lamine Gueye law gives French citizenship to all inhabitants of French overseas territories. 2 June, plebiscite in Italy votes for a republic. 3 June, mixed *Communes* established in all French territories. 2 Aug., Ferhat Abbas, leader of *Union Démocratique du Manifeste Algérien,* lays before National Consituent Assembly in Paris draft law for an Algerian Republic federated with France. 27 Oct., constitution of French sub-Saharan territories become *l'Union Française.* Dec., United Africa Co. made agent for Ground Nut Scheme. 14 Dec., United Nations rejects S African proposal for incorporation of SW Africa in the Union. Colonial Economic Research Committee Advisory Committee on Co-operation in the Colonies, Colonial

1947 26 Jan., Egypt breaks off diplomatic relations with Britain, claiming that Britain has revised 1926 treaty unilaterally and because of British statement that the Sudan will be prepared for self-government. Egyptian population over 19 m. Algerian coal industry nationalized. General Juin, Resident General of Morocco. Sultan of Morocco demands satisfaction of legitimate Arab national aspirations in a speech at Tangier. Abdel-krim. Moroccan nationalist, given asylum in Egypt by King Farouk: Maghreb Office opened in Cairo to co-ordinate nationalist movements.

1947 1 Jan., Nigeria becomes self-governing with new constitution subject to certain restrictions: unofficial majorities in Legislative Council and in regional Houses of Assembly. 1 July, Markala barrage on R Niger comes into use. 29 Aug., *AOF* Grand Council meets at Dakar. 4 Sept., Territory of Haut-Volta reconstituted; Hodh region transfered from Soudan to Mauritania. 10 Oct(-19 March 1948). strike on Dakar-Niger railway. New constitution in Sierra Leone with an African majority in the Executive and Legislative Councils. *Présence Africaine* founded by Alioune Diop. President Vincent Auriol visits *AOF*. Cocoa marketing boards established in Lagos and Accra. University College of the Gold Coast established.

1947 *Société de colonisation Belge du Katanga* established to promote immigration of Belgian agriculturalists. 29 Aug., *AEF* Grand Council meets at Brazzaville.

1948 2-4 Apr., police strike in Alexandria. Apr., elections for Algerian Assembly: results believed rigged. 28 Dec., Nokrashi Pasha, Egyptian Premier, assassinated.
1948-9 Egypt at war with Israel.
1948 or 1949 Clandestine *OS (Organisation Spéciale)* formed within *MLTD* to secure Algerian independence by force.

1948 18 Jan., Ibadan University opens to first pupils as a University College. 26 Jan.—11 Feb., boycott of European imports organized in the Gold Coast. 28 Feb., serious riots in Accra with looting and sack of the prison; subsequent riots in Koforidua, Kumasi and other Gold Coast towns. 22 Sept., Apostolic Delegation established at Dakar. Nov., *Bloc Démocratique Sénégalais (BDS)* founded by Léopold Senghor, with newspaper *Condition Humaine*. Yundum Egg Scheme inaugurated in the Gambia.

1948 10 Apr., *Union des Populations du Cameroun (UPC)* founded. Family allowances instituted in the Belgian Congo, and theoretical minimum salaries. Native *colonato* (farm colony) started at Canonda, Angola.

1949 Dec., Socialist Party founded in Egypt. First Four-Year Plan for development of Algerian agriculture.

1949 Jan.—Aug., Coussey Committee on constitutional reforms on Gold Coast. June, Convention People's Party (CPP) founded by Kwame Nkrumah. Oct., Oil-Palm Produce Marketing Board, Cotton Marketing Board and Ground Nut Marketing Board set up in Nigeria. 18 Nov., serious disturbance at Enugu Colliery, with twenty-one killed; riots at Aba, Galabar, Onitsha and Port Harcourt.

1949 21 Feb., University of Lovanium established by decree. *Evolution Sociale Camerounaise (ESOCAM).* founded. Ten Year Plan instituted in the Belgian Congo to encourage internal markets. Red Star movement started in Angola.

Development Corporation, Colonial Economic and Development Council, Inter-University Council for Higher Education in the Colonies, and Colonial University Grants Committee formed. India bans trade with S Africa.

1947 30 Jan., Ground Nut Scheme begun at Kongwa, Tanganyika. May, Abdelkrim, Moroccan nationalist, released from banishment in Réunion. Zanzibar Legislative Council reformed with two African, three Arab, one European and two Indian non-official members. Local government councils set up throughout Zanzibar and Pemba. Zanzibar clove crop fails. East African High Commission established. African population of Nairobi over 70,000. Ethiopian Air Force reorganized.

1947 21 Jan., Smuts declines to put SW Africa under UN trusteeship. King George VI and Queen Elizabeth visit SA. 21 Feb., King George VI opens SA Parliament in person. 29 March – July, nationalist revolt against French in Madagascar. SA Bureau of Race Relations set up at Stellenbosch to promote *apartheid*. African trade unions first formed in N Rhodesia.

1947 1 Jan., coal nationalized in Britain. 2 Feb., allied peace treaties with Bulgaria, Finland, Hungary, Italy and Rumania. 1 March, martial law proclaimed in Palestine. 4 March, Treaty of Dunkirk. 25 March, Indonesia independent. 14 Apr., new party created by De Gaulle. 5 June, Marshall plan for European recovery announced. 1 July, general mobilization in China against the Communists. 6 Aug., Sir Stafford Cripps announces austerity programme in Britain. 15 Aug., India and Pakistan become independent. 27 Aug., Statute of Algeria creates Algerian Assembly with financial and some administrative powers. 12 Dec., Burma independent.

1948 Jan., Four Power Commission (Britain, France, USA, USSR, visits Mogadishu: SYL clashes with pro-Italian Somalis: fifty-one Italians and seventeen Somalis killed. 6 Apr., first session of East African Central Legislature in Nairobi. 1 May, East African Railways and Harbours amalgamated. 24 July, Four Power Commission signs Protocol with Ethiopia. 23 Sept., Ethiopia resumes administration of Jijiga and Dagabur; takes control for first time of Gabridare, Qalafu, Warder and eastern Ogaden; SYL and Somali National League appeal to UNO for a united Somalia. SYL proscribed in Kenya. General strike in Zanzibar. Dejazmatch Balcha Hospital, staffed largely by Russians, opened in Addis Ababa. Agitation for independence in Harar Province. Ethiopia.

Jan., Smuts visits SWA: legislature offered wider powers and representation of territory in SA Parliament. 26 May, Smuts leading United and Labour parties, defeated in general election; Nationalist Afrikaner Party wins on *apartheid* platform; 3 June, D.F. Malan premier. Natal University chartered. Sept., Seretse Khama marries Ruth Williams in London. Ngwato refuse to accept Seretse Khama as chief because of his marriage to an English woman. General election in S Rhodesia, Huggins gaining twenty-four out of thirty seats. Constitutional reform in N Rhodesia extends Legislative Council to 5 years.

1948 1 Jan., railways nationalized in Britain. 30 Jan., Gandhi murdered. 10 March, Jan Masaryk commits suicide. 17 March, Treaty of Brussels. 1 Apr., electricity nationalized in Britain. 1 Apr., Overseas Food Corporation take over Ground Nut Scheme from UAC: Sir L. Plummer, Chairman. 14 May, mandate in Palestine terminated by Britain. State of Israel proclaimed. 15 May, Egyptian and other Arab League troops enter Palestine to support Arabs. 18 June, Russia blockades W Berlin. 5 July, National Health Service inaugurated in Britain. 22 Aug., World Council of Churches inaugurated in Amsterdam. 17 Sept., Count Bernadotte murdered by Jewish terrorists. 24 Sept., conference of representatives from British African Colonies in London. 2 Nov., H.S. Truman elected President of USA. 27 Dec., Cardinal Mindzsenty arrested. Rapid increase in Algerian migration to France.

1949 2 Dec., Mathew Commission, under Sir Charles Mathew, appointed to recommend new constitution for Tanganyika. Disappointing harvest in Ground Nut Scheme. Makerere made a university college. Arabs and Indians in Zanzibar Legislative Council demand elections as a step towards self-government within the Commonwealth.

1949 Jan., Zulu-Indian riots in Durban. 29 June, SA Citizenship Act suspends automatic grant of citizenship to Commonwealth immigrants after 5 years' residence: bans marriages of mixed race. SA pound devalued. Rhodes University, including Fort Hare, chartered. SW African Affairs Amendment. Act. Unofficial conference at Victoria Falls determines in favour of a federation of the Rhodesias and Nyasaland.

1949 24 Feb., armistice between Israel and the Arab States. 8 March, Vietnam independent within the French Union. 23 March, *FERDES (Fonds d'équipment rural et de développement économique et sociale)* set up for French colonial development. 5 May, Council of Europe established. 4 Apr., North Atlantic Treaty signed at Washington. 18 Apr., Eire leaves the Commonwealth. 11 May, Israel admitted to UN. 12 May, Russian blockade of Berlin ended. 21 Sept., UN makes Italian Somalia a trusteeship for 10 years under Italy. 21 Sept., Chinese Peoples' Republic

1950 Jan or Feb., Mohammed Ben Bella, leader of clandestine *OS.* 3 Jan. Egyptian general election: Wafd return to power with two-thirds of seats. 12 Jan., Egyptian government includes all ministers dismissed in 1944. Egypt proclaims 'neutralist' foreign policy over Korea. French promise Tunisia self-government by negotiated stages.

1950 Jan., *Institut des hautes études* set up at Dakar. 5 Jan.,–1 Feb., political demonstrations in the Ivory Coast. Oct., *RDA* disclaims connection with the Communist Party. 19 Oct., *CFTC (Confédération Française de Travail Catholique)* conference at Lomé. Sierra Leone Peoples' Party (SLPP) founded by Milton Margai. Port at Abidjan reconstructed. Territorial Sports Committee set up in Dahomey. *IOM (Groupe Parlementaire Indépendent Outre-Mer)* formed. Lagos Town Council becomes elective.

1950 Labour inspectors instituted in Belgian Congo. Textile factories set up in the Belgian Congo. *ABAKO (Association des Bakongo)* founded. 60% of government doctors in Cameroun now of local origin. *Colonato* started at Damba. 30,000 *assimilados* in Angola out of a population of 4 m.

1951 9 Apr., provisional government formed in Libya: Mahmud Bey Muntasser, Prime Minister. 12 May, Bey of Tunis demands a Tunisian Parliament. 27 Oct., Egypt denounces 1936 treaty with Britain and 1899 agreement on the Sudan: Farouk takes title of King of Egypt and the Sudan. 16 Nov., Egypt offers to allow future of Sudan to be decided by plebiscite subject to UN supervision. 1 Dec., Kingdom of Libya independent under King Idris I al-Sanusi. French put pressure on Sultan of Morocco to disavow Nationalist Party. Republican Socialist Party formed in the Sudan. Alliance formed between *MTLD,* Ulema and *PCA* as Algerian Front for the Defence and Respect of Liberty. Lieut.-General Garcia Valino, High Commissioner of Spanish Morocco: political detainees released. **1951** Dec.–1952 Guerilla war against British Forces in Canal Zone. **1951-2** Joint front of Algerian political parties.

1951 Feb., Yundum Egg Scheme in the Gambia collapses, having cost more than £900,000. Feb., Democratic Party formed in Gambia. *AOF* representation increased to twenty-one. *BSS* wins majority of Senegalese votes in French general election. General election in Sierra Leone: SLPP gains overwhelming victory over the National Council in Sierra Leone. Election in Gold Coast: CPP triumphant; Kwame Nkrumah Leader of Government Business in new Assembly. Disorders in Benin prevent elections. Abdullahi Bayero Mosque opened in Kano. New constitution in Nigeria with Council of Ministers and House of Representatives. Gambia constitution again revised, with elections from a common roll. United Party formed in Gambia.

1951 Dec., Municipal elections in the Belgian Congo : triumph for *ABAKO* led by Joseph Kasavubu. Simon Kimbangu d. *Conscience Africaine,* journal founded by Abbé Joseph Maloula. *Union des Syndicats Autonomes du Cameroun* founded. *Mouvement d'Action Nationale Camerounaise (MANC)* founded.

1952 14 Jan., Tunisia fails in appeal to Security Council to state case for independence. Riots in Casablanca. 18 Jan., Habib Bourguiba arrested, followed by other nationalist leaders in Tunisia. 26 Jan. large scale incendiarism in Cairo: 277 fires: army intervenes to restore order. 27 Jan., - 1 March, Ali Maher Pasha Premier of Egypt. 1 March, Naquib al-Hilali, Premier of Egypt. 18-27 March, anti-British riots in Egypt. 30 March, anti-French riots in Tangier. 10 Nov., International Committee

1952 Jan., Muslim Congress Party formed in Gambia. 21 March, Kwame Nkrumah first Prime Minister of the Gold Coast. *BDS* gains forty-one out of fifty seats in Senegal *Conseil-général.* Territorial Assembiy set up in Dahomey.

1952 Mwata Yamvo Ditende Yawa Naweji III succ.: father-in-law of M.Tshombé. International trade union congress in Douala.

proclaimed. 15 Dec., Trusteeship agreement for Italian Somalia approved. S Africa informs UN that 'in the interests of efficiency' it will no longer report on SW Africa: question referred to the International Court at The Hague.
1950 Jan., Conference of Commonwealth Finance Ministers in Colombo. 26 Jan., India becomes a republic. 31 Jan., President Truman gives order for manufacture of 'H' bomb. 14 Feb., Thirty year alliance between China and Russia. 24 Feb., general election in Britain: Labour Party wins with majority of six: C.R. Attlee Prime Minister. 1 March, K. Fuchs imprisoned for espionage. 25 June, Korean war begins. July, International Court rules that SW Africa is still under mandate. 31 July, Léopold III of Belgium abdicates: succ. Baudouin I. Aug., Labour Government gives instructions to wind up Ground Nut Scheme: £30 m. lost. 28 Sept., Indonesia admitted to UN. 7 Oct., Tibet invaded by China.

1950 1 Apr., Britain returns Somalia to Italy as UN Trusteeship: conditional on independence in 1960. Abnormally large clove crop in Zanzibar. Ethiopia appoints *Abuna* (Patriarch) independently of Cairo for the first time. University College founded in Addis Ababa. Somali clan elders in British Somailand made 'local authorities'.

1950 29 Jan., racial riots in Johannesburg. 1 May, anti-*apartheid* demonstration in the Rand by ANC and SA Indian National Congress: police kill eighteen persons and wound thirty. 26 June, ANC and Indian protest against *apartheid*. 11 Sept., Smuts d. 13 Dec., SA declines to place SW Africa under UN trusteeship, Dutch Reformed Church demands repatriation of all Indians. SA Immorality Act forbids Europeans carnal intercourse with non-Europeans. Population Registration Act makes carrying a 'pass' incumbent on all. Suppression of Communism Act gives Minister of Justice semi-dictatorial powers. Potchefstroom University chartered. 4,353 *assimilados* in Mozambique in population of 5.7m.

1951 19 Jan., Abuna Basilios, first Ethiopian to become Metropolitan of Ethiopia, enthroned. Apr., Ethiopian expeditionary force sent to serve in Korean war. 17 Nov. – 12 Dec., Meru evicted from farm in Sanya corridor, N Tanganyika: unrest follows. Dec., Institutes of higher education in Ethiopia formed into Haile Selassie I University. Mathew Commission reports on Tanganyika constitution: Legislative Council to have seven Africans, seven Europeans and seven Asians.

1951 19 Jan., six members from the SWA House of Assembly take their seats for the first time in the SA Parliament. Feb., SA Prime Minister and leader of the opposition protest against appointment of Kwame Nkrumah as Chief Minister in the Gold Coast. 11 March, demonstrations in Cape Town against Separate Representation of Voters Bill: 28 May, demonstrations by Torch Commando lead to riot and bloodshed: 100,000 members claimed. 2 Apr., British naval base at Simonstown handed over to SA. Second Victoria Falls Conference on federation; Nov., British Government agree. Hastings Kamazu Banda and Harry Nkumbula, *Federation in Central Africa*. African Local Government School opened at Chalimbana, N Rhodesia. Government Geological Survey started in N Rhodesia. 20 March, SA Supreme Court pronounces Separate Representation of Voters Act invalid.

1951 4 Jan., Commonwealth Prime Ministers' Conference in London. 9 Jan., White Paper on Ground Nut Scheme. 9 Feb., World Muslim Congress in Karachi. March, Colonial Secretary permits Tshekedi Khama to return to Ngwato reserve. 15 March, Anglo-Egyptian agreement on sterling balances. 23 Apr., H. Wilson reigns from being President of the Board of Trade. 28 Apr., Dr Musaddiq, Prime Minister of Persia. 2 May, oil nationalized in Persia: Abadan crisis. 2 June, Pius XII. encyclical *Evangelii Praecones,* on missions. 23 June, USSR propose ceasefire in Korea. 28 June, British cruiser sent to Abadan. 1 July, Egypt detains British ship *Empire Roach*. 22 July, Gen. Craveiro Lopes elected President of Portugal. 23 Aug., treaty of friendship between Israel and USA. 1 Sept., UN Security Council calls on Egypt to end restrictions in the Suez Canal. 25 Sept., British staff ordered to leave Abadan. 16 Oct., Liaqat Ali Khan, Prime Minister of Pakistan, murdered. 25 Oct., Conservatives return to office: Churchill Prime Minister. Portuguese colonies made provinces of Portugal.

1952 11 Sept., Eritrea federated with Ethiopia. 20 Oct., State of Emergency proclaimed in Kenya as a result of 'Mau Mau' rising; leaders of Kenya African Union arrested. General elections in Eritrea; July, Eritrean Assembly approves constitution and receives ratification from Haile Selassie. Tanganyika Election Committee under Professor W.J.M. Mackenzie recommends one-man official majority in Legislative Council.

1952 28 March–15 Apr., tercentenary of the arrival of van Riebeeck celebrated by whites in SA: thousands of Bantu protest themselves 'an oppressed people' and pledge a relentless struggle. 22 Apr., Bill introduced to make SA Parliament a High Court, to circumvent Supreme Court's invalidation of racial legislation: 3 June, SA High Court of Parliament Bill receives Assent. 29 Aug., SA Supreme Court rules High Court of Parliament Bill invalid. Oct., uranium first extracted at the W Rand Consolidated Mine. 18 Oct., riot in Port

1952 5 Jan., Churchill visits USA: 17 Jan., addresses Congress. 31 Jan., Princess Elizabeth and the Duke of Edinburgh leave Britain for Kenya. 6 Feb., King George VI d.: succ. Elizabeth II. 20-25 Feb., NATO Council agree at Lisbon on entry of Morocco and Tunisia. 1 March, Heligoland restored to German Federal Republib. 10 March, revolution in Cuba. 28 April., peace treaty between the allies and Japan effective. 2 May, jet air service from London to Johannesburg opened. 6 May, Dr Rajendra Prasad elected

of Control in Tangier enlarged. May, Messali
Hadj deported from Algeria. 29 June-23
July, ministerial crisis in Egypt, with several
cabinets. 23 July, Committee of Free
Officers under Gamal Abd al-Nasr (Nasser)
and Abd al-Hakim Amer seizes control in
Egypt: General Muhammad Naquib (Neguib)
made commander-in-chief. 26 July, King
Farouk forced to abdicate and go into exile:
infant Fuad II proclaimed King. Sept.,
National Front Party formed in the Sudan.
7 Sept., new Egyptian government formed
by Neguib. 9 Sept., Agrarian law limits
land-holding in Egypt; 14 Sept., personal
waqfs abolished. 13 Oct., Egyptian agreement with Britain on the Nile waters in
the Sudan. 29 Oct., Egypt recognizes right
of the Sudan to self-determination. 7 Dec.,
riots in French Morocco. 10 Dec., Egypt
abolishes 1923 Constitution. Umma party
formed in the Sudan. Free Morocco *(al-
Maghrib al-Hurr)* Party in Spanish Morocco
founded by Muhammad Zeriouh.

1953 12 Jan., Constitutional Commission
formed in Egypt; 16 Jan., all political
parties dissolved in Egypt; 23 Jan., Rally
of the Liberation proclaimed sole party;
10 Feb., Neguib voted dictatorial powers
for three years with provisional
constitution, 12 Feb., Anglo-Egyptian
agreement on the Sudan: British and
Egyptian forces to evacuate. May,
charitable *waqfs* nationalized in Egypt.
18 June, Republic proclaimed in Egypt;
Neguib first President; Lieut.-Col. Nasser,
Vice-President. 30 July, British-Libyan
treaty of alliance. 20 Aug., France deposes
Sultan of Morocco; Sidi Muhammad b.
Arifa installed but ignored by majority
of Moroccans in French zone: Spanish
Moroccans protest. 25 Nov., general elections in the Sudan: majority for union
with Egypt. Egyptian defence treaties with
Saudi Arabia and Yemen. Oil prospecting
begins in Sahara.

1953 12 Feb., *IOM* conference at Bobo-
Dioulasso envisages federation of
France and African territories. May, inter-
tribal riots in Kano: northerners attack
Yoruba and Ibo. Dec., Alhaji Muhammadu
Sanusi succ. as Emir of Kano; programme
of land and other reforms. Dr Albert Margai
becomes Chief Minister in Sierra Leone.
*ORANA (Organisation pour la recherche
sur l'alimentation et la nutrition en Afrique)*
set up at Dakar. Institute of Tropical
Ophthalmology set up at Bamako.
Campaign against malaria organized in
Dahomey.

1953 Jan., *Union Sociale Camerounaise
(USC)* founded: opposed by *Bloc Démocratique Camerounais*. Kintwadi movement
starts on the lower Congo. Angolan group
protests to UN of Portuguese brutality.
Geological Survey of Angola carried out.
Riot in S. Tomé: 100 killed.

1954 Jan., mass meeting in Tetuan protests
against deposition of Sultan of Morocco.
9 Jan., Ismail al-Azhari, Prime Minister of
the Sudan. 25 Feb., Col. Gamal Abd al-
Nasr (Nasser) seizes power in Egypt; 27
Feb., Neguib again in power. 1 March,
Sudanese Parliament opened: violent anti-
Egyptian demonstrations in Khartoum.
25 March, political parties again permitted
in Egypt: general elections announced:
29 March, freedom again withdrawn. 18 Apr.,
Nasser premier and military governor of
Egypt. May *UGTA* headquarters moved to
Tunis. 31 July, Mendès-France promises
internal autonomy to Tunisia in Carthage.

1954 15 June, CPP again wins Gold
Coast general election; 21 June, Kwame
Nkrumah forms new government;
National Liberation Movement (NLM)
opposes CPP with Northern Peoples' Party
(NPP). Gambia minerals scheme set up.
Apr., Gold Coast constitution revised. New
constitution in Nigeria: British Northern
and Southern Cameroons separated:
Nigeria organized as a Federation. Major
revision of the Gambia constitution.
Harbour constructed at Ifni. General elec-
tions in the Gambia.

1954 15 Jan., first thirty Africans
admitted to pre-university course at
Lovanium, of whom only eleven pass.
21 March, Joseph Kasavubu, President
of *ABAKO*. University established at
Elizabethville. President Craveiro Lopes
of Portugal visits Angola. Union of
Angolan Peoples (UAP), African
Nationalist Party, organized.
1954-5 Many strikes in Cameroun.

Elizabeth leads to chain of anti-European riots as far as the Rand. Nov., riots in Kimberley. 10 Nov., riots in E London. 28 Nov., meetings of more than ten 'natives' forbidden in SA.

President of India. 27 May, European Defence Treaty signed in Paris. 18 June, British publish plan for Central African Federation (FCA). 20 June. President Truman signs Foreign Aid Bill. July, Meru case heard by UN Trusteeship Council. 19 July, Olympic games open in Helsinki. 23 July, Pius XII addresses encyclical to 'all the peoples of Russia'. 11 Aug., King Talal of Jordan deposed: succ. Husain. 10 Oct., new Five Year Plan in USSR. 22 Oct., Persia breaks off diplomatic relations with Britain. Britain approves self-government for the Sudan. 10 Nov., Trygve Lie, Secretary-General of UN, resigns. 29 Nov., Commonwealth Economic Conference in London.

1953 8 Apr., Jomo Kenyatta and five others convicted of 'managing' 'Mau Mau'. June, KAU proscribed; 15 July, Kenya Supreme Court quashes Kenyatta's conviction; 24 Aug., Kenya Government calls on 'Mau Mau' to surrender. 22 Sept., African Court of Appeal upholds conviction. 24 Dec., Emergency declared against 'Mau Mau' in Tanganyika: 640 Kikuyu arrested: 15,000 subsequently taken into custody. Julius Nyerere elected President of Tanganyika African Association. Pastoral letter, *Africans and the Christian Way of Life,* issued by Bishops of Tanganyika.

1953 16 Jan., SA Government takes emergency powers. 15 Apr., general election in SA: Nationalists maintain majority in record 87.8% poll. Union Federal Party in Natal and Liberal Party formed. 20 Aug., demonstration in Nyasaland by Nyasaland African Congress. 1 Sept., appointment of a Commission to institute *apartheid* in SA Universities announced. 16 Sept., third reading of Separate Representation of Voters Amendment Bill again fails. Oct., Malan demands that Britain hand over High Commission territories to SA. Oct., Federation of Central Africa (N and S Rhodesia and Nyasaland) comes into being. Dec., young Europeans join SA Resistance movement: unlawful meeting held in Germiston Native Location. 15 Dec., Sir Godfrey Huggins forms Federal Party Ministry. Nyasaland chiefs visit London to prevent federation. The Rev. Michael Scott tours preaching non-violence as the proper method of resistance to federation of the Rhodesia and Nyasaland.

1953 1 Jan., London Conference on FCA. 20 Jan., General Eisenhower sworn President of USA. 5 Feb., British Government publishes scheme for FCA. 5 March, Stalin d.: 6 March, Malenkov succ. 7 Apr., Dag Hammarskjöld elected Secretary-General of UN. 2 June, Queen Elizabeth II crowned. 3 June, Commonwealth Prime Minister's Conference in London. 30 July, treaty of alliance between Britain and Libya. Aug., £20m. collected in India for Resistance Movement against *apartheid*. 10 Sept., London Conference on N Rhodesia constitution. Nov-Dec. sixty nation Special Political Committee of UN debates *apartheid*. 2 Nov., Pakistan declared a Republic. 8 Nov., *União Nacional* wins Portuguese general election. 22 Dec., Queen Elizabeth visits New Zealand. Spain refused to endorse French deposition of Sultan of Morocco. Portuguese Organic Overseas Law: status of *assimilado* abolished in Portuguese colonies: all natives obtain Portuguese citizenship.

1954 March, party of 'Mau Mau' Kikuyu raid Mt Meru area: many speared by Meru tribesmen. 14 Apr., Societies Ordinance requires registration of all associations in Tanganyika. 31 May, state of emergency proclaimed in Buganda. 7 July, Tanganyika African National Union (TANU) formed, replacing TAA: Julius Nyerere President: constitution based on CPP. 4 Nov., High Court supports legality of Uganda government in withdrawing recognition of Kabaka. Ethiopia requests Britain to withdraw from Haud; 29 Nov., agreement signed: strong Somali protests. Third UNO visiting mission, led by Mason Sears, in Tanganyika.

1954 1 Jan., SA Bantu Education Act comes into force. 3 Feb., first opening of Parliament of FCA. 22 Apr., S Rhodesian Parliament resolves that the title of the country be the State of S Rhodesia. June, drainage scheme for 10,000 acres of swamp near L Shirwa launched. Sept., inaugural Conference of African Chambers of Commerce. 25 Sept. –9 Oct., Prince Bernhard of the Netherland visits SA. 30 Nov., J.G.Strijdom elected leader of the Nationalist Party: Malan retires. Rhodesian University College founded: Dr. W. Adams, first Principal. 1,286 native churches in SA, with 761,000 members.

1954 25 Jan.-18 Feb., Berlin Conference of Foreign Ministers of Britain, France, USA and USSR. 3 Feb.–May, Queen Elizabeth visits Australia, Ceylon, Libya, Malta and Gibraltar. March, *CRUA (Comité Révolutionnaire pour l'Unité et l'Action)* founded as military organization for Algerian independence in Berne, Switzerland, by Mohammed Boudiaf, Ben Bella and seven others. 1 March, USA explodes hydrogen bomb in Marshall Is. 28 Apr., Conference of Asian Prime Ministers at Colombo. 7 May, fall of French post of Dien Bien Phu, Indo-China. 26 May, Emperor of Ethiopia visits USA. 29 June, Potomac

13 Aug., *MTLD* counter-Congress in Algiers.
19 Oct., Anglo-Egyptian agreement on the
evacuation of the Canal Zone. Nov., nationalist rising in Algeria (-1962); principal centres
Constantine and Batna: ten Europeans
killed: 2,000 members of political parties
arrested: *MTLD* dissolved. 1 Nov., *CRUA*
renamed *FLN (Front de Libération
Nationale)* ; army known as *ALN (Armée de
Libération Nationale)*. 14 Nov., President
Neguib put under house arrest; 17 Nov.,
Nasser Head of State in Egypt. 23 Dec.,
France sends 20,000 troops to Algeria.

1955 Feb., Jacques Soustelle, Governor-
General of Algeria (-Jan 1956) with special
mission to solve crisis: Communist Party
declared illegal: Nationalist press
suppressed. 10 Feb., Robert Lacoste,
Resident Minister of Algeria. 2 March,
mutual defensive alliance between Egypt
and Syria. 31 March, State of Emergency
declared in Algeria in limited areas. 17 Apr.
Nasser attends Bandoeng Conference. 27
Apr., commercial agreement between
Egypt and USSR. June, Soustelle outlines
plan for integration of Algeria with France.
20 Aug., riots in Morocco: riots in Algeria
kill many French non-combatants: many
Muslims killed as reprisal. 30 Aug., State of
Emergency extended to all Algeria. Sept.,
PCA dissolved. 26 Sept., Nasser announces
large purchase of arms from Czecho-
Slovakia. 17 Oct., Sultan of Morocco with-
draws to Tangier; Council of the Throne
abolished. 30 Oct., puppet Sultan of
Morocco abdicates. 1 Nov., Moroccan
'Army of Liberation' attacks French posts
in the Rif and Middle Atlas. 18 Nov., Sultan
Muhammad V restored in Morocco:
coalition government formed under Col. Si
Bekkai. *MLTD* replaced by *MNA
(Mouvement National Algérien)*. *ALN* head-
quarters set up in Algiers by Belkacem Krim.
Union Moroccaine de Travail, first all-
Moroccan trade union.

1955 10 Jan, first session of Nigerian
Federal Council. 16 Apr., constitutional
changes in Togo. 4 July, independence
promised for Togo.
1955-8 Nicholas Grunitzky, premier of
Togo.

1955 13 July, UPC dissolved by decree.
Dieudonné movement in Madimba,
Kasangula and Thysville. Oil struck near
Luanda. King Baudouin visits the
Belgian Congo.

1956 Jan., General Catroux appointed
Governor-General of Algeria: appointment
cancelled becaused of opposition of
Europeans in Algeria. 1 Jan., The Sudan
proclaimed an independent republic. 1 Jan,
sixty-one Muslim members of Algerian
National Assembly resign: Assembly
dissolved. Resident Minister of Algeria
nominated. 1 Jan., new economic and financial charter for Spanish Morocco. 5 Jan.,
President Tito visits President Nasser in
Cairo. 7 Jan., general election in Libya.
16 Jan., new constitution announced in

1956 Jan.-Feb., Queen Elizabeth II visits
Nigeria. Jan., Oil first struck at Oloibiri,
Niger delta. Jan., breakaway *CGT* con-
ference at St Louis. 2 Jan., in French
general election *RDA* obtain seven seats,
IOM six seats, *SFIO* one; Houphouët-
Boigny, Minister. 9 March, British
Togoland votes in favour of absorption
into Gold Coast. 8 July, *CATC
(Confédération Africaine de Travailleurs
Croyantes)* formed at Ouagadougou. 17
July., general election in Gold Coast:
increased CPP majority. 3 Aug., Gold Coast

1956 3 Feb., Lovanium officially made
university. 30 June, *Conscience Africair*
publishes a manifesto criticizing Prof. B
Comité national d'organisation (CNO)
formed in Cameroun. Campaign of civil
violence and murder by *CNO,* with man
attacks on missions. Dec., *CNO* boycott
elections. Dec., Abbé Fulbert Youlou
elected *Maire* of Brazzaville. 23 Dec.,
general election in Cameroun. Léon Mba
elected *Maire* of Libreville. Districts and
circumscriptions reorganized in Angola.
Craveiro Lopes Dam at Biopio complete

Charter issued. 15 July, *MTLD* Congress in Belgium called by Messali Hadj. 5 Aug., agreement between Persia and western countries on Persian oil. 24 Aug., Labour Party delegation under Attlee visits Peking. 9 Sept., treaty granting USA use of-air bases in Libya. 10 Oct., CRUA resolves on military insurrection in Algeria on 1 Nov. 1954. 19 Oct., Anglo Egyptian agreement on Suez Canal base. 23 Oct., four-power agreement to end occupation of Germany. 4 Dec., riots in Athens on Cyprus. 16 Dec., special prayers for SA in St Paul's Cathedral, London.

1955 18 Jan., Kenya Government sets out terms for surrender of 'Mau Mau'. 20 March, new constitution in Tanganyika. 15 Aug., Britain signs transitional agreement with Buganda. 17 Oct., the Kabaka returns to Buganda. 10 Dec., United Tanganyika Party (UTP) inaugurated at Dodoma. Ethiopian constitution revised. 1944 Anglo-Ethiopian agreement revised: Ethiopia takes over Ogaden and 'Reserved Area'. Ethiopian Navy established with international technical assistance.

1955 21 Jan., prolonged constitutional crisis over Entrenched Clauses of SA Act. 25 March, SA Appeal Court increased from six to eleven members. 20 June, SA Senate enlarged from forty-eight to eighty-nine members, giving Nationalist majority of seventy-seven. 4 July, Britain offers to return Simonstown base to SA while retaining right to use it. Lourenço Marques-Transvaal railway connected to N Rhodesia. Nyasaland constitution revised: African representatives only admitted to the Legislative Council.

1955 23 Feb., Bangkok Conference. 24 Feb., Baghdad pact for mutual defence between Britain, Turkey, Iraq, Iran and Pakistan. 28 Feb., Israelis defeat Egyptians near Gaza. 2 March, defensive alliance between Egypt and Syria. 7 March, Julius Nyerere addresses UN Trusteeship Council. 5 Apr., Sir W. Churchill resigns: 6 Apr., A. Eden, Prime Minister. 17-24 Apr., Bandoeng Conference attended by twenty-four African and Asian states. 5 May, end of allied occupation of W Germany. 26 May, Conservatives win general election in Britain. 3 June, Franco-Tunisian agreements signed. 4 July, defence agreements between Britain and SA. 10 Aug., treaty of friendship between France and Libya. 30 Sept., UN General Assembly debates Algeria. 2 Oct., France withdraws from UN General Assembly in protest against hostile attitude on Algeria. French policy statement on Morocco. 5 Oct., British White Paper on High Commission Territories. 6 Nov., Declaration of La Celle St Cloud: France to terminate Moroccan protectorate. 9 Nov., S Africa withdraws from UN General Assembly in protest against Cruz report on *apartheid*. Dec., Professor Bilsen produces plan for the independence of the Congo after 30 years. 7 Dec., C.R. Attlee resigns leadership of Parliamentary Labour Party: succ. H. Gaitskell. Portuguese Native Statute for Angola and Mozambique.

1956 Jan., Bibi Titi binti Mohamed, woman nationalist leader, enters Tanganyika politics. 29 May, Lord Lloyd, Under-Secretary for the Colonies, states British policy in Hargeisa, British Somaliland: early internal self-government indicated. General elections in Eritrea.

1956 1 Feb., SA requests USSR to withdraw consulates. 27 Feb., SA Act Amendment Act abrogates Entrenched Clauses protecting Cape Coloured voters. 27 March, Tomlinson Commission Report on socio-economic development of Bantu areas in SA. 18 May, Cape Supreme Court declares Senate Act and SA Act Amendment Act valid. Sept.–1 Jan., 1957, State of Emergency in N Rhodesian copper belt after strikes by African miners. 31 Oct., Lord Malvern resigns after 23 continuous years in office: Sir Roy Welensky,

1956 2 Jan., general elections in France. 11 Jan., Arab states offer to replace British grant-in-aid to Jordan. 19 Jan., Republican Front government elected in France on platform of 'peace in Algeria': Guy Mollet, premier. 23 Jan., treaty between Italy and Libya. 2 Feb., Eisenhower and Eden issue Washington Declaration. 25 Feb., Communist Party Conference in Moscow denounces Stalinism and the cult of the individual. 2 March, General Glubb dismissed from command of Arab Legion. 5 March,

Egypt. 19 Jan., Sudan joins Arab League.
Feb., *USTA (Union Syndicale des
Travailleurs Algériens)* founded by
Messali Hadj; March, rival *UGTA (Union
Général des Travailleurs Algériens)* founded
by Ben Khedda. 6 Feb., Guy Mollet visits
Algiers: pelted by Europeans. March, much
of Aurés and Nementcha Mts., Kabylia and
Constantine in *ALN* hands. March, govern-
ment of Tahar b. Ammar organizes
elections for Constituent Assembly in
Tunisia. 2 March, France recognizes
Moroccan independence. 20 March, France
recognizes Tunisian independence: Habib
Bourguiba first President. 7 Apr., Hispano-
Moroccan agreement for independence of
Spanish Zone and the reunity of Morocco
completed. 21 Apr., Egypt. Saudi Arabia and
the Yemen sign military alliance. 4 June,
Egypt declares she will not extend Suez
Canal Co.'s concession after its expiry in
1968. 13 June, last British troops evacuate
Canal Zone. 23 June, Nasser elected
President of Egypt: referendum in Egypt
confirms new constitution: 94.84% of votes
stated to be in favour. 30 June, bomb
explosion in *UGTA* headquarters in Algiers
marks beginning of European counter-
terrorist activity. 2 July, Libyan government announces creation of an Air Force
and a Navy, with British and US aid. 5 July.
Protocol of the Powers recognizes authority
of the Sultan of Morocco over Tangier:
29 Oct., international regime abolished.
19-20 July, Britain and USA inform Egypt
they cannot finance Aswan High Dam.
26 July, Nasser nationalizes Suez Canal. 2
Aug, British and French nationals leave
Egypt. 12 Aug., Nasser refuses to attend
proposed London conference. 20 Aug.,
ALN conference at Soummam attended
by 200 delegates: *CNRA (Conseil National
de la Révolution Algérienne)* set up. 10
Sept., Nasser rejects Dulles' Plan. 22 Oct,
Ben Bella and other *FLN* leaders
kidnapped on a Moroccan aircraft and
deported to Paris. Forty French settlers
massacred at Meknès, Morocco, in reprisal.
25 Oct., Egyptian High Command unified
with Jordan and Syria under Egyptian
control. 29 Oct., Israel invades Egypt in
Sinai Desert. 30 Oct., Anglo-French
ultimatum to Egypt and Israel demanding
cease-fire and withdrawal of Israel to within 10 miles from Suez: accepted only by
Israel. 31 Oct., Anglo-French force bombs
Egyptian airfields. Nov., cabinet reorganized in
Morocco. 3 Nov., Britain and French accept
Middle East cease-fire if UN will keep peace.
5 Nov., British land paratroops at Port Said.
7 Nov., Anglo-French cease-fire in Egypt:
Britain declares troops will be evacuated
only on arrival of UN force. 15 Nov., UN
emergency force arrives in Egypt. 5 Dec.,
British and French begin withdrawal
(completed 22 Dec.) 27 Dec., UN begins

asks Britain for independence. 18 Sept.,
Britain agrees to independence of Gold
Coast on 1 March 1957. 10 Dec., *CGT* and
*CGTA (Confédération Générale des Trav-
ailleurs Africains)* conference at Cotonou.
BDS again wins Senegalese seats in French
general election. Port of Dakar modernized.
Sierra Leone Legislative Council
renamed the House of Representatives.
Volta R bridge built.

Prime Minister of FCA. 21 Nov., Sir de Villiers Graaf elected leader of the United Party. 5 Dec., 140 Africans, Asians and Europeans arrested for treason in SA. 19 Dec., preliminary hearing of 150 accused begun in Johannesburg. Districts and circumscriptions reorganized in Mozambique President Craveiro Lopes of Portugal visits Mozambique.

Italy agrees to pay £5.8m. reparations to Ethiopia. 9 March, Abp Makarios deported to Seychelles Is. 18 Apr., Khruschev and Bulganin visit Britain. 30 May, Bandoeng Conference of African and Asian students. 23 June, *loi-cadre* on French overseas territories. 28 June Commonwealth. Prime Ministers' Conference in London. 13 July, Lord Radcliffe appointed constitutional commissioner for Cyprus. 15 July, Italy awarded £15 m. contract for Kariba dam. 26-31 July, Britain, France and US make financial retaliations against Egypt. 2 Aug., Britain rejects request of FCA for Dominion Status in the Commonwealth. 2 Aug., Tripartite Declaration by Britain, France and US protests against nationalization of Suez Canal. 16-23 Aug., Suez Canal Conference in London: boycotted by Nasser. 21 Aug., Dulles' plan for Suez. 29 Aug., French contingent stationed in Cyprus. 1 Sept., 285 boarding schools opened in USSR. 4 Sept., UN convention on Slavery approved. 19 Sept., second London Conference on Suez: 21 Sept., establishes Canal Users' Association. 23 Sept., Britain and France refer Suez dispute to UN Security Council. 13 Oct., UN Security Council adopts British and French resolution on Suez: vetoed by USSR. 23 Oct., insurrection in Hungary. 24 Oct., Soviet troops intervene in Hungary. 29 Oct., Israel invades Sinai. 31 Oct., USA sends aid to Israel against Egypt. 1 Nov., Jordan forbids use of RAF bases against Egypt. 2 Nov., Gaza taken by British. 4 Nov., UN General Assembly agrees to send international force to Middle East. UN resolution on Hungary vetoed by USSR. USSR forces attack Budapest. 5 Nov., USSR threatens rocket attacks if Britain and France do not cease fire in Suez. 6 Nov., Eisenhower re-elected President of US. 12 Nov., UN observers refused permission to visit Hungary. 19 Nov., Emperor of Ethiopia visits Japan. 20 Dec., Nyerere again addresses UN Trusteeship Council.

clearance of Suez Canal. 29 Dec., anti-
Muslim riots in Algiers. Dec., Sultan of
Morocco visits USA. Dec., *CRFC Comité
pour le Renaissance de France) and
ORAF (Organisation de la Résistance de
l'Algerie Française)* dissolved by
R. Lacoste: activities continue clandestinely.
FLN (Front de Liberation Nationale)
founded in Cairo for liberation of Algeria.
FLN gains majority support in Algeria.
*Union Générale des Travailleurs Algériens
(UGTA)* founded. 450,000 French con-
scripts serving in Algeria. *ALN* lays siege to
Tlemcen. Several oil deposits found in
Algeria. General strike of students in Algeria
ordered by *FLN.*

1957 Jan., Algerian law creates
*Organisation Commune de Régions
Sahariennes* for administration of Sahara,
including parts of French Sudan, Niger and
Chad. Jan., plural marriage abolished in
Tunisia. Jan., General Faure's conspiracy
exposed. 6 Jan., Treaty of 'brotherhood and
good neighbourliness' between Libya and
Tunisia. 15 Jan., foreign banks, insurance
companies and agencies 'Egyptianized'.
16 Jan., attempt on life of General Salan.
March, Vice-President Nixon visits Morocco
and Tunisia. 9 March., Franco-Tunisian
agreement for supply of 3,500 French
officials and teachers to Tunisia: some
French judges seconded to Tunisian
courts. 20 March, French delegation
withdraws from Tunisian Independence
Day celebration in protest against *FLN*
representatives. 28 May, National Union
proclaimed the sole political party in
Egypt. 25 July, Bey of Tunis deposed:
Tunisian Republic proclaimed: Habib
Bourguiba, first President. 3 Aug.,
Decree grants Moroccan nationality
to shipping registered in Tangier.
26 Aug., Royal Charter enables
Tangier to continue as a free port. 6 Nov.,
first *ALN* attack on oil prospectors. 26 Dec.,
Conference in Cairo attended by forty-four
neutralist nations. Titles of King and
Kingdom of Morocco replace Sultan and
Sharifian Empire: Prince Maulai Hasan
proclaimed successor to the throne. 500
Muslims only amongst 5,000 students at
University of Algeria. Afro-Asian Solidarity
Conference in Cairo.

1957 11-13 Jan., *MSA (Mouvement
socialiste Africain)* congress at Dakar.
16 Jan., *CGT* conference at Cotonou.
28 Feb., *Institut des Hautes Etudes* at
Dakar becomes a University. March,
British Togoland united to Gold Coast.
6 March, Gold Coast becomes independent with new name of Ghana. 31 March,
elections in all *AOF* territories.
March, *RDA* gains overwhelming
electoral majorities in Soudan, Guinea
and Ivory Coast: dominant party in
Upper Volta coalition: opposition in
Niger and Dahomey. 4 Apr., *AOF*
territories obtain financial autonomy
and extended powers. 15 May, Grand
Council of *AOF* elected: F. Houphouet-
Boigny, President. 18 May, village
committees instituted in *AOF*. 26 July,
Nouakchott becomes capital of
Mauritania. 8 Aug., Eastern and Western
Regions of Nigeria become self-
governing; Alhaji Abubakar Tafawa
Balewa, first Federal Prime Minister.
25 Sept., International Conference of
RDA at Bamako. General election in Sierra
Leone won by SLPP. Irregulars make attacks
in Rio de Oro and French Mauritania; rising
of Ba Amran in Ifni demanding unity with
Morocco. College of Technology set up at
Kumasi.

1957 Feb., Health insurance instituted
for workers in the Belgian Congo. 10 March
Federation of Baptist and Evangelical
Churches in Cameroun. 26 March,
municipal government in the Belgian
Congo reorganized with local elections.
4 Apr., *AEF* territories obtain financial
autonomy and extended powers. 16 June,
riots in Léopoldville following a football match. Dec., 9,284 colonists in
the Belgian Congo, of whom 60%
Belgians. 14 Dec., Deputy Samuel
Wanko murdered in Cameroun, followed
by many other murders of Africans and
Europeans. 115,000 Muslims in the
Belgian Congo. General election in
Gabon.

1958 Feb., French garrisons concentrated
on Bizerta. 8 Feb., French bomb Sakiet,
Sidi Yusuf, Tunisia, in reprisal for aid to
ALN. 4 March, first locally produced oil
leaves Algeria. 5 March, United Arab
Republic (UAR) proclaimed, with Egypt
and Syria, as provinces; two vice-presidents
for each and separate councils: 8 March,
joined by Yemen. Apr., Abdelkrim refuses

1958 Jan., Ifni and Spanish Sahara
declared Spanish metropolitan
provinces. Feb.. first shipment of
crude oil from Nigeria. March,
Parti du Régroupement Africain (PRA)
formed, with object of setting up federation of French W African territories.
26 March conference at Dakar of all
political parties, except *RDA* and *Parti*

1958 Aug., General de Gaulle announces
independence for all French Africa at
Brazzaville. Parmehutu Party founded in
Rwanda. Uprona Party founded in Burundi
by Prince Rwagasore. Oil refinery complete
at Luanda. More than 4 m. Catholics in
the Belgian Congo.

1957 Nov., Convention of Tanganyika
Chiefs held at Iringa. Ethiopian Coffee
Board set up.

1957 9 Jan.-15 Sept., Johannesburg treason trial continues. 4 March,
Rhodes University College, Salisbury,
opened. 4 Apr., SA Native Laws Amendment Bill forbids Africans to worship
in European churches. 8 Oct., Earl of
Dalhousie sworn as new Governor-
General of FCA. 19 Oct., Constitution
Party founded at Lusaka. 17 Dec.,
charges against sixty-one accused in
the Johannesburg treason trial withdrawn.

1957 8 Jan., UN agreement with Egypt
on clearance of Suez Canal. 9 Jan., Sir
A.Eden resigns: 10 Jan., H.MacMillan,
Prime Minister. 21 Jan., 5,881 Egyptian
prisoners of war released by Israel in
exchange for four Israelis. 30 Jan., UN
General Assembly votes against apartheid
and SA refusal to negotiate with India
and Pakistan on 'Asians': SA delegate
walks out. 3 Feb., thirteen French decrees
on overseas territories. 6 Feb.,
Franco-Moroccan agreement on
administrative and technical co-operation.
27 March, Compagnie Française du
Sahara formed. 2 Apr., trade
agreement between Morocco and USA.
25 March, Belgium, France, W. Germany,
Holland, Italy and Luxembourg sign
Common Market Treaty in Rome.
6 Apr., Abp Makarios released. 27 Apr.,
Pius XII, encyclical Fidei Domum,
on nationalism. May-June Nigerian
Constitutional Conference. 2 June,
Ministry of the Sahara created by
France. 26 June-5 July, Commonwealth
Prime Ministers' Conference. 7 July,
four agreements between Morocco and
Spain. 11 July, Agha Khan d.; succ.
Prince Karim. 26 July, Channel Tunnel
Study Group set up. 31 Aug., Malayan
Federation becomes independent.
10 Sept., Ghana and Israel agree to set
up Black Star Shipping Line. 11 Oct.,
Radio telescope at Jodrell Bank first
operated. Nov., Loi-cadre for Algeria
creates local regional councils. 26 Nov.,
International Court of Justice rules
itself competent to judge dispute on
Portuguese territories in India. Dec.,
UN appoints tribunal to settle Ethiopian
boundary with Italian Somaliland.
5 Dec., Indonesia expels Dutch nationals.

1958 Jan., TANU Conference at Tabora.
July, Attorney-General of Tanganyika
prosecutes Nyerere for criminal libel: 9
July, trial opened: 15 July, Attorney-
General apologizes for contempt of court.
15 July, Sir R.Turnbull sworn as Governor
of Tanganyika (-1961). 11 Aug., Nyerere
pays £150 fine. Sept., first half of elections
in Tanganyika. 1958-9 District Councils

1958 11 Jan., cabinet crisis in S
Rhodesia. 30 Jan., treason trial of ninety-
one accused begun at Pretoria. 16 Apr.,
general election in SA won by Nationalists. June, UN Good Offices Committee
visits SWA. 5 June, United Federal Party
wins S Rhodesian election: Sir E.
Whitehead, Prime Minister. 6 July, Dr.
H.K.Banda returns to Nyasaland and,

1958 1 Jan., Common Market Treaty
comes into force. 14 Jan., Spanish decree
separates Ifni from Spanish Sahara:
both made Lieut-Governorships under
Governor-General of Canary Is.: headquarters in Sidi Ifni and al-Aiun. 20 Jan.,
Dr. Vivian Fuchs's expedition reaches
S Pole. 1 Feb., financial agreement

pension from King of Morocco. 27-30
Apr., Conference for Maghreb Unity held in
Tangier. May, new government in
Morocco: Ahmad Balafrej Prime Minister:
government reorganized as constitutional
monarchy: National Deliberative Assembly
created. 13 May, European demonstrations
against the Government in Algiers:
General Massu acclaimed President of the
Committee of Public Safety. 16 June,
General Salan becomes Delegate-General of
the French Government in Algeria. 16 Sept.
Provisional Algerian Government set up in
Cairo: Ferhat Abbas, Prime Minister. Nov.,
Franco-Moroccan conversations on
Algerian-Moroccan frontier. 17 Nov.,
Military *coup* in Sudan led by General
Ibrahim Abboud. 30 Nov., local elections in
Algeria. 8-11 Dec., Cairo Economic
Conference. 15 Dec., Paul Delouvrier,
Delegate-General of French Government in
Algeria; General Maurice Challe in com-
mand of army; change in operations against
ALN. Oil pipe-line from Hajji Messaoud to
Touggourt begun in Algeria: much other
petroleum found. Group of Mauritanian
notables formed at Rabat to make propa-
ganda to incorporate Mauritania as a province
of Morocco.

Africain Indépendent (Senegal). 15-22 Apr.,
Accra Conference attended by Libya,
Liberia, Morocco, Sudan, Tunisia,
UAR and Ghana. 27 Apr., Togo
independent: Sylvanus Olympio,
President of Togo. 3-4 May, serious
riots in Conakry. 1 June, F.Houphouët-
Boigny again becomes Minister of State
in de Gaulle Government. 7 June,
Guinea demands immediate internal
autonomy within an African-French
Community. 8 June, senatorial elections in
Niger, Senegal and Upper Volta.
Spanish West African administration
reorganized in three districts: Apr.,
northern district ceded to Morocco.
25-27 July, *PRA* conference at
Cotonou demands African Independence
without French participation. 24 Aug.,
General de Gaulle visits Abidjan, meeting
Ivory Coast and Upper Volta
representatives; 25 Aug., Conakry, where
Sekou Touré demands total independence; 26 Aug., Dakar. 25 Sept.,
referendum by universal suffrage in *AOF*:
all territories except Guinea ask
for a French community. 29 Sept.,
simultaneous declaration in Conakry,
Dakar and Paris of the independence of
Guinea: Sekou Touré, President.
23 Nov., paper Ghana-Guinea Union
announced by Nkrumah and Sekou
Touré. 20 Nov., Soudan, 25 Nov.,
Senegal, and 28 Nov., Mauritania
elect for independence within the French
Community. 28 Nov., R Niger bridged
at Gaya. 5-13 Dec., Pan-African
political parties, trade unions and student
movements meet. 4 Dec., Ivory Coast votes
unanimously for independence outside the
French Community: Dahomey votes for
independence within it, followed on 11
Dec., by Upper Volta, and on 18 Dec., by
Niger. Nigerian Federal Government
takes control of armed forces. Nigerian
Currency Board instituted. Nigerian
Navy created.

1959 Jan., Provisional Algerian Government
moved to Morocco. 13 Jan., General de
Gaulle announces amnesty for Algerian
insurgents. 18 March, oil struck at Bir
Tlaksin, near Tripoli. Apr., extension of
railway to Darfur opened. 16 Apr., oil
struck at Zelten, Libya. 18 Apr., bombs
exploded in Algiers and many other cities
during municipal elections. May, British
financial agreement with Libya: Britain to
pay £3.25 m. for 5 years. 11 Nov., *CEMN*
(Comité d'Entente des Mouvements
Nationaux) formed by European extremists
in Algeria.

1959 17 Jan., Federation of Senegal,
Soudan, Upper Volta and Dahomey
promulgated: two latter soon withdraw:
rump known as Mali. 23 Jan., Mali
constitution approved. 24 Jan., Senegal
constitution approved. 13 Feb., Dahomey
leaves Mali federation. 15 Feb., Dahomey
constitution approved. 28 Feb., Upper
Volta constitution approved: Upper
Volta leaves Mali federation. 8 March,
elections in Mali. 12 March, Niger
constitution approved. 15 March,
Northern Region of Nigeria becomes
self-governing. 22 March, Mauritania
constitution approved. 22 March,
elections in Senegal. 24 March, *Parti de la*
Fédération Africaine (PFA) founded
in Dakar. 26 March, Ivory Coast

1959 1 Jan., Cameroun gains internal self-government. 4 June, *ABAKO*
meeting in Léopoldville banned: three
days of rioting follow. 11 Jan., *ABAKO*
dissolved. Kasavubu and other Congolese
leaders imprisoned. 14 March, *ABAKO*
leaders released. 17 March-13 May,
Kasavubu and other leaders visit Belgium.
7-12 Apr., conference of Congolese
political parties at Luluabourg; Patrice
Lumumba demands independence in
Jan. 1961. Friction between the
Baluba and the Bena Lulua. 6 May,
chief of the Lulua demands recognition
of Belgium as an independent sovereign.
June, many violent outbreaks in
Cameroun. 3 Aug., Albert and Evariste
Kalondji, and Albert Nyembwe imprisoned

set up in Tanganyika. Severe famines in Tigre and Eritrea following drought and locusts.

1 Aug., becomes President of NAC. 24 Aug., J.G. Strijdom, Prime Minister of SA, d. 2 Sept., H.F. Verwoerd, Prime Minister of SA. 29 Sept., train derailed at Lusaka, allegedly by nationalists. 12 Oct., indictments in SA treason trial withdrawn. 14 Oct., Madagascar becomes independent. Oct., Zambia African Congress formed. 22 Nov., new indictments served in SA treason trial.

between France and Morocco. 9 Feb., agreement between Turkey and Libya. 6 March, first UAR cabinet announced in Damascus. 8 March, Yemen joins UAR. 27 March, Kruschev elected chairman of USSR Council of Ministers. 1 Apr., Fidel Castro announces revolution in Cuba. 30 Apr., State of Emergency in Malta. 2 May, State of Emergency in Aden. 29 May, General de Gaulle invited to form 'government of national safety'. 1 June, de Gaulle again becomes Prime Minister of France. 2 June, French National Assembly Admiral Amérigo Tomàs elected President of Portugal. 13 July, de Gaulle declares for a federation with internal autonomy for French overseas territory as the French Community. 1 Aug., State of Singapore created. 13 Aug., France agrees to pay Egypt £20 m. compensation for Suez crisis. 18 Aug., Belgian Ministry of the Colonies becomes Ministry of the Belgian Congo and of Rwanda-Urundi. 23 and 31 Aug., racial disturbances in Britain. 25 Sept., ten-year cultural agreement between India and UAR. 29 Sept.–27 Oct., Nigerian Constitutional Conference in London. 9 Oct., Pope Pius XII d. 28 Oct., Cardinal Roncalli elected Pope as John XXIII. 5 Nov., General de Gaulle announces five-year plan for Algeria. 18 Nov., Belgian Prime Minister announces that relations with the Belgian Congo will be reconsidered. 19 Dec., constitution of French Community enacted; 21 Dec., General de Gaulle elected President of France and the Community. 22 Dec., Franco-Egyptian commercial agreement.

1959 Apr., Jomo Kenyatta released from prison, and put under house surveillance. Feb., second half of elections in Tanganyika. 17 July, *Zinjanthropus* skull found at Olduvai by Mrs L.S.B. Leakey. Emperor of Ethiopia makes state visit to USSR: Ethiopia obtains $100 m. loan. Tax amnesty granted in Eritrea.

1959 23 Jan., H.F. Verwoerd explains Bantustan policy in Parliament. 15-17 Feb., serious riot in Karonga: Fort Hill seized by insurgents; 28 Feb., Fort Hill recovered by Tanganyika police; 2 March, state of emergency declared in Nyasaland. 24 March, Bantu Self-Government Bill introduced in SA Parliament. May, Umtata established as capital of Transkei. 7 July, meeting of the French Community at Tananarive. Aug., Malawi Congress Party (MCP) formed as successor to NAC. Eight 'Bantustans' voted by SA Parliament. Dr Banda imprisoned in S Rhodesia. SA universities reorganized: Cape Town and Witwatersrand closed to non-Europeans.

1959 8 Jan., Agreement signed between Italy and UAR. 24 Jan., French *Ministère de la France d'Outre-Mer* abolished. 3-4 Feb., first meeting of French Community in Paris. 9 Feb., cultural agreement between UAR and Yugoslavia. 11 Feb., Federation of Arab Amirates of the South inaugurated at al-Ittihad, Aden. 16 Feb., Fidel Castro sworn as Prime Minister of Cuba. 17 March, rising in Tibet: Dalai Lama flees to India. 18 March, Hawaii becomes 50th state of USA. 15 Apr., J.Foster Dulles, US Secretary of State, resigns. 25 Apr., technical and economic agreement between Ethiopia and W Germany. 18 May, Cuba expropriates US sugar interests. 22 May, USA agrees to give

constitution approved. Apr., Gambia minerals scheme collapses. 2 Apr., elections in Dahomey. 4 and 7 Apr., agreements between Ivory Coast and Upper Volta and Niger on common services: *Conseil de l'Entente Sahel-Benin* formed. 6 Apr., *AOF* formally dissolved. 12 Apr., elections in Ivory Coast. 19 Apr., elections in Upper Volta. 17 May, elections in Mauritania. 29-30 May, *Conseil de l'Entente Sahel-Benin* meets at Abidjan, with addition of Dahomey. 9 June, Customs Union between Dahomey, Ivory Coast, Mauritania, Niger and Upper Volta. 16-19 July, Presidents Nkrumah, Sekou Touré and Tubman meet at Sanjquelli, Liberia, to plan a union of free African states. 19 Oct., government falls in Niger. Dec., Federal elections in Nigeria, followed by coalition government. 11-12 Dec., meeting of French Community at St Louis, Senegal: Senegal and Soudan demand independence and bring about the collapse of the Community. 14 Dec., general elections in Nigeria. 18 Dec., coalition government under Hamani Diori.

widespread rioting with many thousands killed in the Congo. 23-9 Oct., riots in Stanleyville set off riots and attacks on Europeans throughout the Congo. Dec., body of Simon Kimbangu moved to Nkamba, the 'New Jerusalem'. 20 Dec., elections in the Belgian Congo boycotted by *ABAKO*. 24-7 Dec., conference of federalist parties at Kisantu. Eighty-four political parties registered in Cameroun. Léon Mba, Prime Minister of Gabon. White population of Angola about 175,000. Forty-five Africans and *assimilados* and seven Europeans arrested for subversion in Angola. Bishop of Luanda's secretary expelled from Angola for alleged nationalist involvement.

1960 2 Jan., European riots in Algiers: state of siege and curfew proclaimed. 19 Jan., reshuffle in Algerian Provisional Government: General Staff formed under Houari Boumédienne. 30 Jan., African Peoples' Congress in Tunis calls for volunteers to help *ALN*. Feb., National Bank of Egypt and Banque Misr nationalized; Ten Year Plan for development inaugurated. 13 Feb., First French nuclear device exploded at Reggan in the Sahara. 27-9 May., local elections in Algerian Government rejects French proposal for an *FLN* delegation to France. 8-12 Dec., General de Gaulle visits Algeria; 10 Dec., European and Muslim riots. Egyptian population over 26 m.

1960 1 March, Guinea creates a separate currency. May, Conference of African Heads of State at Monrovia, Liberia. 20 June, Mali independent: Modibo Keita, President. Aug., Senegalese Assembly declares Senegal independent of Mali; Dahomey and Niger independent. 20 Aug., Modibo Keita and other Soudanese arrested and deported to Bamako; end of federation. Oct., University of Nigeria at Nsukka opened. 1 Oct., Federation of Nigeria becomes independent; Sir J.Robertson, first Governor-General; 3 Oct., first Federal Parliament opens. Afro-Asian Solidarity Conference in Conakry. New constitution in the Gambia, followed by general election. Progressive People's Party (PPP), led by David Jawara, formed in Gambia. Democratic Party and Muslim Congress in Gambia merge as the Democratic Congress Alliance. Fourah Bay College becomes the University of Sierra Leone. David Diop, Senegalese poet, d.

1960 Jan., The Bakongo proclaim a separate Republic of Lower Congo. 1 Jan., Cameroun independent. Apr., Kamdem Ninyim, first Prime Minister of Cameroun. Apr., Kongo quarter of Cameroun burnt. 1 Apr., Spanish Guinea divided into two metropolitan provinces of Spain, as Rio Muni and Fernando Po: Africans given full rights as Spanish citizens. 19 May, *loi fondamentale* on constitution in the Congo (L). June, Kasai divides itself into two independent areas. 13 June, following general elections in Congo (L), Lumumba fails to form a government. 17 June, Kasavubu likewise fails. 21 June, Lumumba at last succeeds and becomes Prime Minister. 22 June, Kasavubu elected President. 30 June, Congo(L) declared independent. 5 July, *Force Publique* mutinies in Thysville; and 7 and 8 July, at Léopoldville. 1 July, Katanga secedes from Congo (L) as an independent republic under Moïse Tshombé. 12 and 13 July, Kasavubu and Lumumba ask for UN assistance against Tshombé. 8 Aug., South Kasai declared independent by Albert Kalondji; 9 Aug., Belgian Embassy in Léopoldville closed. 11 Aug., Republic of Chad becomes independent. 17 Aug., Gabon becomes independent. 25 Aug., Katanga and S Kasai confederated. 26-31 Aug., Pan-African conference in Léopoldville. 2 Sept., University of Lovanium given internal recognition. 5 Sept., Lumumba

the Sudan $10 m. to construct textile factories. 9 June, first US Polaris submarine launced. 29 June, agreements signed between Yugoslavia and the Sudan. 3 July, French worker-priest movement ordered to be discontinued. 28 July-21 Oct., incidents on Chinese-Indian border. 11 Aug., Dr Nkrumah sworn as a Privy Councillor. 26 Aug-3 Sept., President Eisenhower visits Bonn, London and Paris. 12 Sept., Soviet rocket reaches the moon. 16 Sept., General de Gaulle offers Algeria secession, integration or self-government in association with France. 8 Oct., general election in UK increases Conservative majority. 28 Oct., UK trade agreement with Guinea. 10 Nov., UN General Assembly condemns *apartheid* and any other form of racial discrimination. 19-27 Nov., President of Guinea visits Moscow. 1 Dec., UK — USSR cultural agreement. 22 Dec., International Bank grants $56½m. to improve the Suez Canal.

1960 Jan., Dag Hammarskjöld visits Dar es Salaam. Kilombero Valley rice scheme inaugurated. Apr., UN visiting mission in Tanganyika. 26 June, British Somaliland becomes independent. 1 July, Somalia, including former British and Italian territory, becomes independent: 500 miles of frontier with Ethiopia still undefined. 8 Aug., general election in Tanganyika follows changed composition of Legislative Council. 1 Sept., Nyerere forms government as Chief Minister: Tanganyika achieves responsible government. Dec., Emperor of Ethiopia makes state visit to Liberia and Brazil. 13 Dec., group of army officers and others seize power in Ethiopia; 14 Dec., Addis Ababa under their control; Crown Prince proclaimed Emperor; Abuna Basilios, Patriarch, leads protest against conspirators; 15 Dec., fighting between conspirators and loyalists; 17 Dec., Emperor Haile Selassie returns to Addis Ababa and resumes control. Ban on SYL removed in Kenya; replaced by Northern Province People's Progressive Party (NPPPP). Mozambique African opposition groups form in Dar es Salaam.

1960 1 Jan, Fort Hare university restricted to Xhosa students. 24 Jan., four white and five African police murdered by a mob at Cato Manor, Durban. 3 Feb., H.MacMillan's 'wind of change' speech at Cape Town condemns *apartheid*. March, new constitution in Bechuanaland. 21 March, demonstrations by Pan-African Congress lead to riot at Sharpeville: sixty-seven Africans killed, 180 wounded. 28 March, day of mourning for Sharpeville observed in African locations near Johannesburg. 30 March - 31 Aug., State of Emergency in SA. March, Chief Albert Luthuli arrested for condemning the Sharpeville massacre as genocide. 2 Apr., Rt. Rev. A. Reeves, Bp of Johannesburg, flees secretly to Swaziland. 9 Apr., attempt to murder Dr. Verwoerd at Johannesburg. 10 Sept., Bp Reeves returns to SA and is then deported. 5 Oct., referendum in favour of a republic in SA. Legislative Council set up in Basutoland. Nyasaland Legislative Councils gains an African majority. Seven farming co-operatives in Zavala circumscription, Mozambique. White population of Mozambique about 85,000. Liceu Salazar at Lourenço Marques has 1,000 pupils, of whom thirty are Africans. Portuguese Bishop of Beira speaks out repeatedly against repressive practices in Mozambique.

1960 16-18 June, abortive Cyprus Conference in London. 20 Jan.-20 Feb., Brussels Round Table Conference on Congo political problems. 6 Feb., Spain grants concessions to six US oil companies to exploit Spanish Sahara. 13 Feb., trade agreement between Cuba and USSR. 14 March, Portugal announces dispatch of a fleet and troops to Angola as precautionary measures. 26 March, economic agreement between UAR and USA. 20 Apr.-4 May, Sierra Leone Constitutional Conference in London. 20 Apr.-9 May, UAR boycotts US shipping in reprisal for picketing of a UAR ship in New York. 26 Apr.-26 May, Brussels conference on Congo economic problems. 2-12 May, British Somaliland Constitutional Conference in London. 7-10 June, Nasser visits Greece. 13-20 June, Nasser visits Yugoslavia. 1 July agreement between Britain and Cyprus announced. 20-21 July. UN agrees to send troops to Congo (L), immediately. 25 July-4 Aug., Nyasaland Constitutional Conference in London. 19 Aug., USA refuses to permit countries enjoying US aid to buy sugar from Cuba. 25 Aug., cultural agreement between Ghana and USSR. 1 Sept., Franco-Moroccan agreement on French evacuation. 30 Sept., Bechuanaland Protectorate Constitution published. 10 and 31 Oct., devastating cyclones in E Pakistan. 1 Nov., MacMillan announces UK agreement to US Polaris submarine base at Holy Loch, Scotland. 8 Nov., John FitzGerald Kennedy elected President of USA. 2 Dec., Archbishop

government dismissed by President
Kasavubu: Lumumba 'dismisses' Kasavubu
13 Sept., Joseph Iléo, Prime Minister. 14
Sept., Col. Joseph Mobutu seizes power
with *Collège des Commissaires* (19 Sept.-9
Feb., 1961). Nov., A.Gizenga takes contro
of Eastern Province, Congo(L). 3 Dec.,
Lumumba interned. *UPA* issues manifesto
*The Struggle for the Independence of
Angola*: leadership challenged by the
Popular Movement for the Liberation of
Angola *(MPLA)*. Fifty-two Africans,
including the Chancellor of the Archdioce
of Luanda, arrested for subversion.
7,000 white unemployed in Angola. 350,0
attending schools in Cameroun. 13,000 km
of roads in Cameroun. 15,000 Europeans
in Cameroun.

1960-3 Jan., Katanga *de facto* independen

1961 17 Jan., Lumumba transferred
to Katanga. 25 Jan-16 Feb., abortive
round table conference in Léopoldville.
4 Feb., Civil war in Angola starts
with a rising in Luanda. 9 Feb.,
provisional government in Congo (L)
with Joseph Iléo as Prime Minister.
11 Feb., S Cameroons votes to join
Cameroun. 11 Feb., N Cameroons
votes to join with Nigeria. 12 Feb., Léon
Mba elected President of Gabon. 13 Feb.,
Lumumba's death announced. 15 March,
terrorism begins in Northern Angola.
17 Feb., agreement between UN and
President Kasavubu on UN intervention
in the Congo (L). 24 Apr.-28 May,
Coquilhatville Conference on
federation in Congo (L). 22 July-2Aug.,
Congolese (L) Parliament meets at
Lovanium; Katanga and Eastern
Province members absent. 2 Aug.,
Cyrille Adoula, Prime Minister of the
Congo (L). 24 - 28 Aug., expulsion of
foreign and mercenary soldiers from
the Congo ordered. 13-20 Sept., UN
operations in Katanga result in cease-fire
(20 Sept.). 21 Sept., Dag Hammarskjöld
killed in aircraft accident. 1 Oct.,
Cameroons joins Republic of Cameroun.
13 Oct., Prince Louis Rwagasore of
Burundi assassinated. 20 Dec., Kitona
agreement between Congo (L) government and Katanga on end of secession.
MPLA publishes programme.

1961 3-7 Jan, Casablanca conference on
the Congo (L). 6-8 Jan., referendum for the
self-determination of Algeria. 22 Apr.,
Generals Salan, Challe, Jouhaud and Zeller
proclaim that the armed forces have taken
over Algeria; *OAS (Organisation Armée
Secrète)* becomes public; 26 Apr., Generals'
Revolt fizzles out, May, *OAS* terrorism
begins. 20 May, French cease firing in
Algeria; 20 May-16 June, 6,200 Algerian
internees released. 31 May, Algerian
Chief of Police murdered by *OAS*. July, all
banks and insurance companies in UAR
nationalized together with all major enter-
prises except petroleum. July, Agrarian Law
reduces land holding in Egypt to 100 feddans:
land distributed between co-operatives and
small-holders. 6 Aug., Ben Khedda replaces
Ferhat Abbas as Prime Minister. 5 Oct.,
Nasser recognizes Syria as independent
but preserves name UAR. 26 Dec., union
with Yemen dissolved.

1961 8 Apr., Kwame Nkrumah makes
Dawn Speech in Accra. 27 Apr., Sierra
Leone independent. 1 June, Northern
Cameroons joins Federation of Nigeria
after referendum. 19 Aug., treaty of
friendship between Ghana and Communist
China. Oct., Ahmadu Bello University
opened at Zaria. 16 Oct., Dr. Nnamdi
Azikiwe becomes Governor-General of
Nigeria. P.S. N'Jie, Chief Minister of the
Gambia. Republic of Dahomey takes
over fort at Whydah (Ajuda) from
Portugal.

1962 Jan., *OAS* terrorism increased. 19
March, French cease-fire in Algeria.
Christian Fouchet, as High Commissioner,
replaces Delegate-General in Algeria.
21 May, National Congress summoned in
Cairo to approve a National Charter. 31 May
OAS terrorism ceases. 15-16 June,
Conference of Heads of State of Casablanca
Pact. 3 July, formal declaration of Algerian
independence. 9-18 July, Economic
Conference in Cairo of underdeveloped
countries. 27 Sept., new provisional con-
stitution promulgated in Egypt. 21 Oct.,

1962 5-10 Jan., A.Mikoyan, first Vice-
President of USSR, visits Ghana and
Guinea; 9-14 Jan., Conference of the
Confederation of African Syndicalists
at Dakar. 12-15 Jan., Mikoyan visits Liberia
14 Jan., *Juvento*, opposition party
in Togo, dissolved. 15-18 Jan., H.
Lubke, President of German Federal
Republic, visits Guinea. 19 Jan.,
National Assembly dissolved in Chad. 22-
24 Jan., Conference of African Heads
of State at Lagos. 3 Feb., economic
agreement between USA and Guinea

1962 11 Jan., M. Foucha, Prime Minister of
Cameroun. 24 Jan., A.Gizenga placed unde
house arrest in Léopoldville. 9 March, new
constitution in Congo (L). 15 March,
Tshombe returns to Léopoldville. 5 Apr.,
Provisional Government of Angola constitu
ed in Léopoldville. 24 Apr., first meeting
of National Federal Assembly of Cameroun
25-6 Apr., Conference of Heads of State
of Equatorial Africa at Libreville. 8 May,
Congolese (L) Parliament rescinds parliamentary immunity of A.Gizenga. 18 May,
conversations between Tshombé and

of Canterbury visits the Pope at the Vatican. 11 Dec., cultural agreement between W Germany and USSR. *Journal of African History* first issued.

1961 10 Feb.-28 March, conspirators in abortive Ethiopian *coup* tried; 30 March conspirators executed. 27 March, Constitutional Conference in Dar es Salaam. 1 May, Tanyanyika achieves internal self-government. 2 June, Somalia – USSR agreements signed. Oct., Kivukoni College, Dar es Salaam, set up. 9 Dec., Tanganyika becomes independent as a member of the Commonwealth: Sir R. Turnbull, Governor-General. NPPPP candidate for NFD returned unopposed, demanding secession of NFD from Kenya to Somalia. Law Faculty inaugurated in Dar es Salaam.

1961 14 Feb., decimal currency adopted in SA. March, rebellion against the Portuguese in Angola begins. 8-12 March, Tananarive conference on the Congo (L). May, All-in African National Action Council led by Nelson Mandela demands three-day strike to coincide with inauguration of SA Republic: 31 May, SA becomes a Republic: C.R.Swart, first President. 30 June, treason trial ended in Johannesburg with acquittal of remaining accused. Oct., universities announced for Lourenço Marques and Luanda. 18 Oct., Nationalists again win SA general election. Nov.-Dec., riots in Nyasaland. Nov., Suskei created. Dec., Chief Albert Luthuli awarded the Nobel Peace Prize. 6 Dec., new Constitution in S Rhodesia. 12 Dec., Mafeking made the capital of a Tswana Bantustan. Mauritius obtains internal self-government. Rhodesian Front Party formed. MCP wins all seats at Nyasaland general election.

1961 3 Jan., USA, with eleven other states, breaks off diplomatic relations with Cuba. 22 Jan., Capt. H.Galvão seizes Portuguese liner *Santa Maria* off Curaçao, but fails to start rising in Angola. 31 Jan.-17 Feb., abortive constitutional talks on N Rhodesia in London. 14 Feb., USSR demands resignation of Dag Hammarskjöld and end of UN operations in the Congo (L). 20-21 Feb., UN Security Council demands cease-fire in the Congo (L) with UN force to keep peace. 8 March, Commonwealth Prime Ministers' Conference in London. 10 March, UN Security Council debates Angola. 15 March, UN calls on Portugal to end colonialism. 7 Apr., UN General Assembly condemns SA policy in SWA. 20 May, peace talks on Algeria begin at Evian. 9 June, UN resolution calls on Portugal to end repression in Angola. 19 June-20 Sept., USA–USSR talks on disarmament. 25 June-22 Dec., Kuwait crisis. 25 July-3 Aug., Nyasaland Constitutional Conference in London. 1-6 Sept., Belgrade Summit Conference of non-aligned states. 10 Sept., Pope John XXIII appeals for world peace on radio and television. 28 Sept., Syria unilaterally leaves UAR following military *coup.* 10 Oct., Britain applies for membership of Common Market. 1 Nov., UK Commonwealth Immigrants Bill published. 18 Dec., India takes Goa from Portugal.

1962 Jan., Nyerere resigns: Rashidi Kawawa, Prime Minister of Tanganyika. 15 Feb., commission to institute single party government set up in Tanganyika. 22 Feb., first general election with universal franchise in Uganda announced. 1 March, Uganda obtains internal self-government. 25 Apr., new government formed by Milton Obote with Uganda People's Congress (UPC). 15 June., Waruhui Itote, known as 'General China', released from prison in Kenya. July, Ethiopian University at Abbis Ababa closed after student

1962 8 March, FCA Parliament dissolved. 27 Apr., general election in FCA. 4 May, new government formed by Sir R.Welensky. 5 May, proposed Transkei Constitution signed by 129 chiefs. 22 May, Constitution of Madagascar modified: President of the Republic to be elected by universal adult suffrage; 26 May, President Tsiranana voted special powers. Pretoria statement signed by representatives of UN Special Committee on SWA acquits SA of

1962 30 Jan., UN resolution demands independence for Angola. 23 Feb., UN recommends independence of Rwanda - Burundi as a single federated state. 14 Feb. -6 Apr., Kenya Constitutional Conference in London. 28 Feb., new Rhodesian Constitution presented to Parliament. 7 March., final negotiations on Algeria at Evian. 19 March-6 Apr., abortive Zanzibar Constitutional Conference in London. 3-8 Apr., President Tsiranana of Madagascar visits Taiwan: treaty of friendship with Nationalist China. 8 Apr., French referendum on Algeria: 90% in favour. 9-10 Apr., Brussels conference of African

Egyptian treaty with Yemen, promising support for 5 years: 40,000 Egyptian troops support Republicans in Yemen. 1-5 Nov., Regional Conference of FAO at Tunis: eighteen nations demand expulsion of S Africa. Nov., estimated that only 150,000 Europeans remained in Algeria, out of approximately 1m. a year previously. 7 Dec., Socialist Arab Union proclaimed the sole political party in UAR.

signed. 4 March, general election in Chad; 14 Apr., new constitution voted in Chad; 22 Apr., François Tombalbaye elected President. May, PPP wins seventeen out of twenty-five seats in Gambia general election. 4 May, new government formed in Chad. 25 May, general election in Sierra Leone. 26-7 May, conference at Labé of Presidents of Guinea and Senegal. 6 June, Dr Jawara, Prime Minister of the Gambia. 1 July, National Bank and *franc* established in Mali; 20 July, riots in protest. 29 July, CPP Congress. 2 Aug., attempt on President Nkrumah's life fails. 4 Aug., Rt. Revd. Richard Roseveare, Anglican Bishop of Accra, expelled from Ghana. 1 Sept., Ghanaian ministers Ako Adjei and Tawia Adamafio arrested. 9 Sept., bomb exploded near State House, Accra. 23-27 Sept., President Nehru makes state visit to Nigeria. 26 Sept., Chief Obafemi Awolowo put under surveillance. 2 Oct., Nkrumah refuses life presidency, but agrees to one-party state. 26 Oct., television inaugurated in Ivory Coast. 27 Oct., trade fair in Lagos. 5-10 Nov., bauxite mines in Guinea assigned to US concessionaire. 28 Dec., International Congress of Africanists at University of Ghana. 17 Dec., abortive *coup d'état* in Dakar. 18 Dec., President Mamadou Dia arrested. New government formed in Senegal. 24 Dec., Ghana announces discovery of a plot organized by Ghanian refugees in Togo. 31 Dec., end of state of emergency in Nigeria: Chief Akintola heads a coalition government. Amir Abdurrahman of Daura celebrates golden jubilee on the throne. Gambia National Union Party formed.

Adoula in Léopoldville: 24 June, conversations break down. 1 July, Rwanda and Burundi become independent. 17 July women's riots in Elizabethville. 15 Aug., provinces of Congo (L) reconstituted. 24 Aug., R.Gardiner, special representative of UNO, arrives in Elizabethville with U Thant's plan for Katanga. 25 Aug., Congo (B) announces intention of setting up single party government. 15 Sept., Government of Katanga accepts broad lines of U Thant's plan. 16 Sept., incidents between Congolese and Gabonese after a sporting event in Brazzaville. 20 Sept., Congolese (B) expelled from Gabon. 10 Oct., Christophe Gbenye, leader of the opposition in Congo, arrested. 16 Oct., project for a Congolese federal constitution published. 26 Oct., CAR becomes a one-party state. 30 Nov., censure motion on Adoula government rejected. 21 Dec., American military mission to end Katanga secession arrives in Léopoldville. 24 Dec., first incidents between UN force and Katangese troops. 28 Dec., UN troops take Elizabethville and end Katanga secession. 29 Dec., PAFMECSA Conference in Léopoldville. 30 Dec., Elizabethville brought under control by UN troops.

1963 May – 1964 1 Feb., elections in Egypt. Oct.-Nov., frontier incidents between Algeria and Morocco. 14 Oct., French evacuate Bizerta.

1963 1 Jan., new government in Guinea. 13 Jan., President Sylvanus Olympio of Togo found murdered outside US Embassy, Lomé. 14 Jan., Communist Party banned in Ivory Coast. 15 Jan., parliamentary immunity withdrawn from seven members in Ivory Coast. 16-18 Jan., *Conseil de l'Entente* meets at Abidjan and Yamoussoukro. 17 Jan., Nicholas Grunitzky President of Togo. 24-6 Jan., Monrovia Group Conference in Lagos. 29 Jan., new government in Ivory Coast. 7 Feb., foundation stone of Abidjan University laid. 3 March, new constitution in Senegal. 2 Apr., Ghana Seven Year Plan published. 5-9 Apr., eighty-five notables tried for subversion at Yamoussoukro, Ivory Coast. 7 Apr., five persons condemned to death for treason in Accra. 9 Apr., Senegal protests against bombing of Boumack by Portuguese

1963 3 Jan., Jadotville taken by UN troops; 15 Jan., end of secession of Katanga. 14 March, Ignace Ndimaya, Minister of Public Works in Burundi, arrested for treason. 23 March, Thaddée Siyuyurumunsi, President of Burundi Legislative Assembly, arrested. 13 Aug., general strike in Congo (B). 15 Aug., Abbé Fulbert Youlou resigns Presidency of Congo (B); Alphonse Massemba-Debat President. 9 Nov., Congolese (L) *franc* devalued. 20 Nov., Soviet Embassy expelled from Congo (L).

monstrations. July, Jomo Kenyatta
sits Mogadishu on behalf of KANU: Aug.,
onald Ngala visits Mogadishu for KADU.
July, Chiefs cease to be salaried in Tang-
nyika. 6-10 July, Secretary of State for
ie Colonies visits Nairobi. 21 Nov., Jomo
enyatta and Tom Mboya declare
pposition of KANU to secession of
FD; Oct-Dec., NFS commission
nds overwhelming support for
:cession from Kenya to Somalia. 10 Sept.,
hristopher Kasanga Tumbo heads People's
emocratic Party in Tanganyika. 27 Sept.,
:eventive Detention Act in Tanganyika.
Oct., Uganda becomes independent. 11
ct., President Kenyatta calls on former
1au Mau' forest fighters to cease activity.
1 Oct., KANU accepts Indian members.
·5 Nov., Julius Nyerere obtains 97% of
otes in presidential election. 18 Nov.,
1alcolm MacDonald, Governor of Kenya.
0 Nov., new government in Somalia under
r Abdi-Rashid Ali Shirmarke. 9 Dec.,
anganyika proclaimed a republic:
yerere installed as first elected President
f Tanganyika.
RELIMO headquarters set up in Dar
 Salaam by Eduardo Mondlane with the
»ject of liberating Mozambique from
ortugal.

1963 14 Jan., one-party government
roposed in Tanganyika. 4-10 Feb., Afro-
sian Solidarity Conference at Moshi,
anganyika. March, NFD (Kenya) renamed
1orth-Eastern Region. 8 March, Duncan
andys, Colonial Secretary, announces in
1airobi the NFD is to be a seventh region:
lots in Mogadishu: 14 March, Somalia breaks
ff relations with Britain. 8 Apr., new
onstitution in Kenya; 18-25 May, general
lections; KANU successful: 1 June, Jomo
Lenyatta, Prime Minister. 22-6 May,
onference of thirty African Heads of
tate in Addis Ababa: Charter of Organiza-
ion of African Unity (OAU) approved.
· June, Nyerere, Obote, and Kenyatta meet
1 Nairobi to discuss projected East African
'ederation. 24 June, Makerere University
:ollege, with the Royal College in Nairobi
nd University College, Dar es Salaam
malgamated as the University of East Africa.
: July, Sayyid Abdallah b. Khalifa, Sultan
-f Zanzibar, d.; succ. Jamshid b. Abdallah;

genocide and excessive military occupation. 11 Aug., Northern Sotho Bantustan
created. 1 Sept., capital of Comoro Is.
transferred from Dzaoudzi to Moroni.
1 Sept., new constitution in N Rhodesia.
20 Sept., ZAPU banned in S Rhodesia; 2
Oct., Joshua Nkomo arrested; 30 Oct.,
general election in N Rhodesia. 21 Nov.,
riots at Paarl, near Cape Town. 14 Dec.,
first African government in N Rhodesia;
coalition between Kaunda and Nkumbula.
General election in S Rhodesia: Winston
Field: thirty-five seats; Sir Edgar Whitehead: twenty-eight. 22 Dec., Comoro Is.
granted internal self-government.

1963 14 Jan., R.A.Butler visits FCA.
30 Jan. Butler announces working party to
arrange dissolution of FCA. 7 Feb., Dr
Hastings Kamuzu Banda sworn as first
Prime Minister of Nyasaland. 3 Apr.,
S Rhodesia demands independence: 9
Apr., refused by Britain. 3 May, SA
Government takes discretionary powers
against subversion under General Law
Amendment Act: May-Nov, 543 persons
detained under ninety-day clause. 28 June
3 July, Victoria Falls Conference of
FCA to discuss dissolution of federa-
tion. 12 July, split in ZAPU; 8 Aug.,
ZANU (Zimbabwe African National
Union) founded by Rev. Ndabaningi
Sithole. Aug., ZANU and PCC (People's
Caretaker Council) outlawed in S Rhodesia
22 Nov., general elections in Transkei. 7
Dec., Chief Kaiser Mantanzima elected head
of the government in Transkei. 11 Dec.,
Transkei Legislative Assembly inaugurated.
31 Dec., FCA dissolved.

states associated with the
Common Market. 13 Apr.-12 May Mennen
Williams, Assistant in US Secretariat of
State, visits Guinea, Sierra Leone, Dahomey,
Cameroun, CAR, Togo, Congo (L), Rwanda-
Urundi, Kenya and Upper Volta. 13 Apr.,
London agreement with rulers of Bunyoro,
Toro and Ankole. 21 Apr., commercial
agreement between Ghana and USSR. 9
May., banking agreement between Ghana
and USA. 6-16 May, President Mba of
Gabon visits Israel: co-operative agreement
signed. 17 May, UN technical assistance
treaty with Madagascar. 5-23 June,
President Mamadou Dia visits eastern
Europe. 12 June, Uganda Constitutional
Conference in London. 28 June, UN
General Assembly demands independence
with universal franchise for S Rhodesia. 23
July., Treaty of friendship and technical
and cultural co-operation between Israel
and Ivory Coast. 31 July, U Thant appeals
to UN for peaceful settlement in the Congo
(L). 3 Aug., UN Special Committee on
SWA disowns Pretoria statement of 26 May.
10 Aug., U Thant plan for federal con-
stitution in Congo (L). 10-19 Sept.,
Commonwealth Prime Ministers'
Conference in London 27 Sept., Yemen
military *coup* gains highland area only:
Egypt intervenes in immediate support.
11 Oct.-8 Dec., Second Vatican Council
begun: includes seventy-three bishops and
archbishops of African origin. 22 Oct-20 Nov.,
Cuba crisis between US and USSR. 6 Nov.,
UN General Assembly recommends diplomatic and economic sanctions against
apartheid in SA. 12-23 Nov., Nyasaland
Constitutional Conference in London. 30
Nov., U Thant elected Secretary-General
of UN. 14 Dec., General Assembly of UN
demands an end to Portuguese Colonies
and an effective UN presence in SWA.

1963 28 Jan.-14 Feb., Swaziland Constitutional Conference in London. 29 Jan.,
Britain's attempt to join Common Market
breaks down. 14 Feb., Harold Wilson elected leader of the Labour Party. 25 Feb.,
C.Adoula visits Belgium. 25 Feb., Melville
Herskovits d. 20-9 March, London talks on
dissolution of FCA. 22 March, J.Profumo,
British Secretary of State for War, makes
statement on his personal affairs. 11 Apr.,
Pope John XXIII, encyclical *Pacem in
terris*. 17-24 Apr., UN examines Senegal's
complaint against Portugal. 10 May, UN
Special Committee on *apartheid* asks
Security Council to re-examine racial
discrimination in SA. 15 May, Chief
Enahoro extradited from Britain. 3 June,
Pope John XXIII d. 4 June, J. Profumo
admits that he misled the House of
Commons. 17 June, African delegates at
ILO Conference at Geneva walk out in
protest at the presence of a SA delegate.
18 June, dissolution of FCA announced in

aircraft. 19 Apr., President
Nkrumah publishes scheme for African
unity. 1 May, President Modibo
Keita of Mali awarded Lenin Peace
Prize. 5 May, general elections in
Togo. 7 May, William Tubman elected
President of Liberia for the fifth time.
17 May, trial of Chief Enahoro in Lagos.
2-12 Aug., Conference of Foreign Ministers
of OAU in Dakar. 10 Aug., Nigerian
Parliament approves new constitution
making Nigeria a Federal Republic. 25 Aug.,
SA aircraft impounded after a forced
landing in Niger. 7 Sept., Chief Antony
Enahoro imprisoned for 15 years.
10 Sept., cabinet crisis in Ivory Coast.
12 Sept., Chief Obafemi Awolowo
imprisoned for 10 years. 2 Oct.,
Dr Nnamdi Azikiwe elected President of
Nigeria. 4 Oct., The Gambia achieves
internal self-government. 27-8 Oct.,
military *coup* in Dahomey. 1 Dec.,
general elections in Senegal. 2 Dec.,
Hubert Maga, President of Dahomey,
dismissed. 2-5 Dec., OAU Commission
on Algeria and Morocco meets at Bamako.
11 Dec., Sir Arku Korsah, Chief Justice of
Ghana, dismissed by President Nkrumah.
12-18 Dec., International Congress of
Africanists at Accra. 15 Dec., constitutional congress in Dahomey. 15 Dec.,
referendum of self-government in
Fernando Po and Rio Muni. 22 Dec.,
general election in Chad.

1964 23 March, provisional constitution
abrogated in Egypt: replaced by National
Assembly of 350 members elected by
universal secret suffrage. 26 March, new
National Assembly meets. 13-21 July, conference of Foreign Ministers, and, 17-21
July, Heads of State of OAU in Cairo. July,
Arab League meets in Cairo; Sept., another
meeting. 5-10 Oct., Conference of non-
aligned countries in Cairo: Tshombé refused
admission. 21 Oct., student riots in Khartoum; 25 Oct., Field-Marshal Abboud assumes
sole power; 30 Oct., civilian caretaker
government takes power; 16 Nov., Abboud
resigns. 7 Dec., riots in Khartoum.

1964 2 Jan., attempt on President
Nkrumah's life. 5 Jan., Presidential
election in CAR: David Dacko, the
sole candidate. 8 Jan., Dr J.B.Danquah,
Leader of Opposition in Ghana, arrested.
26 Jan., referendum in Ghana institutes
one-party state. 15 March, general election in CAR. 19-20 March, Sir A.
Douglas-Home, British Prime Minister,
visits Lagos. 12 Apr., general elections
in Mali, 28 Apr., Sir Milton Margai,
Prime Minister of Sierra Leone, d.; succ.,
his brother, Albert Margai. 13 Oct.,
opposition in Senegal banned. Four
members of the opposition in Niger
shot. Oct., strike of teachers in
Nigeria. 17 Nov., ex-President Hubert
Maga of Dahomey set free. 19 Nov.,
Abidjan University inaugurated. 27 Nov.,
Soirou-Migan Apithy deposed from being
President of Dahomey. 22 Dec., General
Christophe Soglo formally takes power in
Dahomey, and dissolves Assembly, all
councils and political parties. 30 Dec.,
general election in Nigeria.

1964 3 Jan., eight terrorists executed in
Cameroun. 10 Jan.-13 Apr., Constitutional
Commission in Congo (L). 11-19 Jan.,
many thousand Tutsi massacred in Rwanda.
18 Feb., elements of Gabon army seize
public buildings. 19 Feb., French troops
intervene at Gabonese request. 23 Feb.,
Gabonese government dissolved. 15 March,
provincial government collapses in Katanga.
16-20 March, P.H. Spaak, Prime Minister of
Belgium, visits Congo (L). 31 March, government collapses in Burundi: 7 April, new
cabinet under Abin Nyamoya. 12 Apr.,
general election in Cameroun. 18 May,
Kouilou Province, Congo (L), revolts. 27
May, rebels seize Albertville. 26 June,
Tshombé returns to Congo (L). 30 June,
Adoula government collapses. 2 July,
single party state in Congo (L) under
Mouvement National de la Révolution.
9 July, new government in Congo (L),
under Tshombé. 11 July, all political
prisoners in Congo (L) released. 23 July,
Gaston Soumialot announces provisional
government of eastern Congo, with
another for western Congo under Pierre
Mulele. 4 Aug., troops of Soumaliot
government take Stanleyville. 1 Sept.,
Stanleyville retaken by Tshombé government; 2-4 Sept., Tshombé visits Albertville.

July, general election in Zanzibar. 4 Oct., Kabaka Mutesa II of Buganda elected President of Uganda. Nov., Foreign Ministers Conference of OAU in Addis Ababa. 13-18 Nov., OAU commission appointed to adjudicate Algerian-Moroccan frontier dispute. 17 Nov., elections for Territorial Assembly in French Somaliland. 20 Nov., Tutsi refugees flee from Burundi into Rwanda. 10 Dec., Zanzibar becomes independent: 25 Dec., State of Emergency proclaimed.

Parliament. 21 June, Pope Paul VI (Montini) elected. 18 July, UN Special Committee on *apartheid* recommends an embargo on arms and oil until SA abandons *apartheid*. 31 July, UN Security Council demands independence for Portuguese colonies. 5 Aug., USA and USSR sign nuclear test ban treaty in Moscow. 12 Aug., President Salazar speaks on Portuguese overseas policy. 25 Aug., Rome Conference between Britain and Somalia with Kenya represented: Somalia claims deliberate British misrepresentation: Kenya refuses secession of NFD. 28 Aug., negro demonstrations in Washington for civil rights. 20-4 Sept., Zanzibar Constitutional Conference. 25 Sept.-19 Oct., Kenya constitutional Conference. 18 Oct., H. MacMillan, Prime Minister, resigns. 18 Oct., Sir A. Douglas-Home, Prime Minister, having resigned his earldom. 22 Nov., President Kennedy murdered. 4 Dec., final session of Vatican Council. 5 Dec., SA expelled from FAO regional meetings. 14 Dec.-1964, 5 Feb., Chou-en-Lai, Prime Minister of China, visits UAR, Algeria, Morocco, Tunisia, Ghana, Mali, Guinea, Sudan, Ethiopia and Somalia. 18 Dec., African students in Moscow demonstrate after death of Ghanaian student.

1964 12 Jan., revolution in Zanzibar: 'Field-Marshal' John Okello seizes power: Shaikh Abedi Karume acclaimed President. 12-15 Jan., incidents between Somalis and Ethiopian police. 20 Jan., troops mutiny in Dar es Salaam. 21 Jan., President Nyerere asks for British troops to restore order. 23 Jan., troops mutiny in Uganda and seize Minister of Interior: British troops requested. 24 Jan., troops mutiny in Kenya: British troops asked for: 25 Jan., British disembark in Dar es Salaam. 7 Feb., fighting between Ethiopian and Somali troops. 12 Feb., President Nyerere addresses special meeting of OAU. 11 March, 'Field-Marshal' Okello forbidden to remain in Zanzibar. 10 Apr., meeting of heads of state of Kenya, Tanganyika, Uganda, and Zanzibar in Nairobi. 22 Apr., treaty of Union between Tanganyika and Zanzibar. 28 Apr., Union of Tanganyika and Zanzibar publicly ratified. 18 May, Conference at Addis Ababa on African Administration. June, Emperor of Ethiopia pays state visits to Kenya, Uganda and Tanganyika. 5-10 Sept., OAU Conference in Addis Ababa. Oct., Shaikh Amri Abedi, Tanganyikan Minister of Justice, poet, author and Swahili translator of the Koran, d. 16-18 Oct., Conference in Dar es Salaam of heads of state of Kenya, Tanganyika

1964 7 Jan., N Rhodesia achieves internal self-government 20-21 Jan., general election in N Rhodesia: 23 Jan., Dr Kenneth Kaunda forms first government. 14 Apr., Winston Field's government collapses in S Rhodesia; replaced by cabinet under Ian Smith. 30 Apr., *Odendaal* Plan on the development of SWA published. 6 May, SA Bantu Laws Amendment Act strengthens *apartheid*. 12 June, Rivonia trial concluded, with life imprisonment of eight SA African nationalist leaders, including Nelson Mandela. 6 July, Nyasaland becomes independent as Malawi. Disturbances in Chinsali District, N Rhodesia, caused by Lumpa prophetess Alice Lenshina: 2-3 Aug., fifty persons killed at Lundazi: 11 Aug., Alice Lenshina gives herself up. 8-9 Sept., three ministers resign and three dismissed in Malawi cabinet crisis: 25 Sept., armed subversion begun by *FRELIMO* in Mozambique. 1 Oct., Sir Roy Welensky beaten in by-election. 3 Oct., State of Emergency proclaimed in Malawi. 9 Oct., presence of guerillas alleged on Tanganyika-Mozambique frontier. Liberation Front of Mozambique *(FRELIMO)* announces general armed insurrection. 24 Oct., N Rhodesia becomes independent with new name of Zambia. 4 Nov., referendum on S Rhodesian independence.

1964 4-7 Jan., Pope Paul VI makes 3 day pilgrimage to the Holy Land. 30 Jan., *coup d'etat* in S Vietnam. 10 Feb., Pope Paul VI appeals for peace in Rwanda. 4 March, UN mediator appointed for Cyprus dispute. 11 March, SA withdraws from ILO. 14 Apr., London international conference on economic sanctions against SA. 20 Apr.-15 May, Basutoland Constitutional Conference in London. 5-19 May, N Rhodesia Constitutional Conference in London. 26 May - 4 June, General Abboud, President of the Sudan, makes state visit to London. 18 June, UN Security Council resolution on *apartheid* in SA. 19 June, US Civil Rights Bill passed by Congress. 8 July, Conference of Commonwealth Prime Ministers in London. 19-26 July, negro riots in Harlem, Brooklyn and Rochester, USA. 22-30 July, Gambia Constitutional Conference in London. 2 Aug., N Vietnam attacks US warships. 5 Aug., first US air raids on N Vietnam. 4-11 Sept., Ian Smith visits London for talks on Rhodesia. 27 Sept., Warren Report on President Kennedy's murder published. 10-24 Oct., Olympic Games in Tokyo. 14 Oct., Dr Martin Luther King awarded Nobel Peace Prize. 15 Oct., Labour Party wins British general election. 19 Oct., twenty-two Uganda martyrs canonized

1965 8-12 Feb., Official visit of Queen Elizabeth II to the Sudan. 9 Feb., Sudan African National Union (SANU) appeals for an end to fighting in S Sudan. 16 Feb., Juba attacked by insurgents. 18-28 Feb., new government in the Sudan: Serr al-Katim Khalifa, Prime Minister. 15 March, Nasser re-elected President of Egypt by 99.9% of votes cast. 16-29 March, round table conference on S Sudan in Khartoum. 21 Apr., general elections in northern Sudan. 10 June. Muhammad Ahmed Mahgoub, Prime Minister of the Sudan: 8 July, Ismail al-Azhari elected President. 29 July, Algerian oil agreement with French. Sept., Wafdist and Muslim brotherhood demonstrations in Egypt following death of Muhammad al-Nahas.

1965 14-18 Jan., *Entente* Council meets at Abidjan and Yamoussoukro. 6 Feb., death of Dr. J.B. Danquah made public in Ghana. 8 Feb., former Ministers Ako Adjei and Tawia Adamafio sentenced to death in Accra. 10-12 Feb., conference of French-speaking African heads of state at Nouakchott: *Organisation Commune Africaine et Malgache (OCAM)* created. 18 Feb., The Gambia proclaimed independent. 31 March, coalition government in Nigeria. 9 May, general elections in Mauritania. 8 June, general elections in Ghana. 11 June, Kwame Nkrumah re-elected President of Ghana. 9 July, new coinage instituted in Ghana. 27 July, Ghana-Togo frontier re-opened. 30 Sept., Hamani Diori re-elected President of Niger. 3 Oct., Maurice Yaméogo re-elected President of Upper Volta. 7 Nov., general elections in Upper Volta. 21-6 Oct., OAU conference at Accra. 21 Oct., general elections in Niger. 26-9 Oct., Nasser visits Ghana. 7 Nov., general elections in Ivory Coast; F.Houphouët-Boigny re-elected President.

8 Sept., Popular Republic of the Congo proclaimed by Radio Stanleyville with Gbenye as President. 16 Oct.-9 Nov., Tshombé government offensive against rebels in Stanleyville. 24 Nov., Belgian parachutists relieve Stanleyville. 26 Nov., parachute operation at Paulis. 9 Dec., Customs and Economic Union formed by Congo (B), Central African Republic, Chad, Cameroun and Gabon.
1965 9 Jan., new government formed by Pierre Ngendadumwe in Burundi: 15 Jan., assassinated: 25 Jan., Joseph Bamina, Prime Minister. 30 Jan., diplomatic relations between Burundi and China broken off. 5 March, Burundi National Assembly dismissed. 18 March, general election in Congo (L). 25 March, Abbé Fulbert Youlou, President of Congo (B) flees to Congo (L). 31 March, Burundi ministers suspended. 6 Apr., new government in Congo (B). 18 July, African Games at Brazzaville. 4 Sept., Dr Albert Schweitzer d. at Lambaréne. 3 Oct., general election in Rwanda; Grégoire Mayibanda elected President. 18 Oct., new government in Congo (L) under Evariste Kimba. 14 Nov., Evariste Kimba receives a vote of no confidence. 25 Nov., General Mobutu deposes J.Kasavubu and becomes President of Congo (L). 28 Nov., new government in Congo (L) under Col. Mulamba.

1966 25 July, Mahgoub loses vote of confidence in Sudanese Parliament; 27 July, Sadek el-Mahdi, leader of Umma Party, forms new government. 15-16 Sept., Treaty of Friendship and Solidarity between Morocco and Senegal.

1966 1 Jan., Col. Jean Bedel Bokassa seizes power in CAR; 3 Jan., Dahomey breaks off diplomatic relations with China. 4 Jan., Col. Sangoulé Lamizana seizes power in Upper Volta. 6 Jan., CAR breaks off diplomatic relations with China. 11-12 Jan., Commonwealth Conference at Lagos. 15 Jan., military *coup d'état* by Ibo officers in Nigeria. 17 Jan., General Aguiyi Ironsi becomes head of Nigerian government. 20 Jan., murder of Sir Abubakar Tafawa Balewa, and other leading Nigerian personalities, confirmed. 9 Feb., racial riots in Mauritania: curfew imposed. 24 Feb, Kwame Nkrumah overthrown in Ghana by army and police; Lieut.-Gen. J.A.Ankrah heads military council; general rejoicing in Accra.

1966 10 Jan., US Ambassador expelled from Burundi. 22 March. General Mobutu signs a decree giving the President of Congo (L) legislative power. 23 March, Congo (L) provinces reduced from twenty-one to fourteen. 6 May, new government in Congo (B) under Ambroise Noumazalay. 30 May, Evariste Kimba, Jérome Ananay, Emmanuel Bamba and Aléxandre Mahamba arrested for plotting against General Mobutu: 31 May, condemned to death: 2 June, executed. 30 June, Léopoldville renamed Kinshasa; Elizabethville renamed Lumumbashi; Stanleyville renamed Kisangani; Coquilhatville renamed Mbandaka; Banningville renamed Bandundu; and Paulis, Isoro. 8 July, Prince Charles Ndizewe announces that he has seized power in Burundi: 12 July, new government under Capt. Micombero. 1 Sept.,Prince Charles

and Uganda with Prime Minister of N Rhodesia: railway from Lusaka to Dar es Salaam agreed. 29 Oct., Tanganyika and Zanzibar become the United Republic of Tanzania. 17 Nov., J.S.Mayanja-Nkangi elected Prime Minister of Buganda.

in Rome. 18 Nov., British Government puts embargo on the export of arms to SA. 2-5 Dec., Pope Paul VI visits Bombay. 4 Dec., Alex Quaison-Sackey, Ghanaian delegate, elected President of UN General Assembly. 9-30 Dec., UN Security Council debates Congo (L).

1965 1-8 Feb., Queen Elizabeth visits Ethiopia. 10 Feb., Uganda closes frontier with Congo (L). 13 Feb., Congo (L) aircraft bomb two Uganda villages. 25 Feb.-9 March, OAU *ad hoc* Commission on the Congo in Nairobi. 4-7 June, Chou en-Lai, Prime Minister of China, visits Tanzania. 5 July, one-party government formally adopted in Tanzania. 30 Sept., Julius Nyerere re-elected President of Tanzania.

1965 11 Jan., SA takes powers to imprison potential state witnesses for 180 days. 29 Jan., Bechuanaland constitution revised with a Senate and an Assembly elected by universal suffrage. Feb., armed raid on Fort Johnston *boma*, led by Henry Chipembere, Malawi exminister. 21 Feb., Arthur Bottomley and Lord Gardiner visit Rhodesia. 1 March, general election in Bechuanaland: Seretse Khama, Prime Minister, victorious. 30 March, Rhodesian Parliament dissolved. 1,5 and 11 May, racial riots in Mauritius. 8 May, general elections in Rhodesia: Ian Smith's Rhodesian Front Party victorious. 8 Aug., general election in Madagascar. 4 Sept., Dr Verwoerd states that a New Zealand Football team would be unacceptable in SA if it included Maoris. 25-30 Oct., Harold Wilson, British Labour Prime Minister, in Rhodesia. 11 Nov., Ian Smith proclaims Rhodesia independent.

1965 11 Jan., Adoula's 'African Plan' for Congo (L) published. 24 Jan., Sir Winston Churchill d. 28 Jan-6 Feb., Financial agreement between Belgium and Congo (L) signed in Brussels. 17-24 Feb., President Nyerere visits Peking. 4 March, Afro-Asian student demonstrations in Moscow: 6 March, in Peking. 24 March, US spacecraft lands on the moon. 30 Apr.-6 May, UN Security Council debates Rhodesia. 17-25 June, Commonwealth Prime Ministers' Conference in London: Vietnam peace mission proposed. 22 June, 700th anniversary of British Parliament celebrated. 2 July, General de Gaulle receives Presidents of Gabon, Ivory Coast, Niger, Togo, Upper Volta, CAR and Congo (B) in Paris. 7-24 Sept., Mauritius Constitutional Conference in London. 8 Sept., Rhodesian diplomat appointed to Lisbon in spite of British protests. 2 Oct., campaign of violence in Aden begins. 4 Oct., Pope Paul VI addresses UN. 4-11 Oct., Smith meets British ministers in London. 9 Nov., death penalty for murder suspended in Britain. 13 Nov., UN Security Council condemns Rhodesian declaration of independence. 15 Nov., Guinea and Tanzania break off diplomatic relations with Britain, followed by Ghana (16 Dec.), UAR (17 Dec.), Sudan and four other African states. 17 Nov., UN Security Council orders Britain to put down the Rhodesian rebellion. 20 Nov., UN Security Council orders oil embargo on Rhodesia. 8 Dec., Vatican Council ends.

1966 22 Feb., Milton Obote arrests five ministers in Uganda and announces that he has taken full powers. 31 March, Summit Conference of eleven eastern and central African states at Nairobi. 14 Apr., Oginga Odinga ceases to be Vice-President of Kenya. 15 Apr., new constitution in Uganda: unitary state with presidential government. 3 May, cabinet reconstructed in Kenya; Joseph Murumbi, Vice-President. 4 May, Economic agreement between Burundi, Ethiopia, Kenya, Malawi, Mauritius, Tanzania and Zambia. 10-23 May, constitutional crisis in Uganda; 24 May, Obote seizes royal palace: Kabaka escapes. 25-6 Aug., General de Gaulle visits Djibouti: referendum on independence promised: 27-29 Aug., visits Addis Ababa. 31 Oct-9 Nov., meeting

1966 23 March, trial at Pretoria of Abram Fischer, QC, for communism: sentenced to life imprisonment. 30 March, general elections in S Africa: United Party victorious. 5 Apr., *Ioanna IV*, having been stopped by the British Navy, reaches Beira. 11 Apr., oil tanker *Manuela* turns back from Beira. 20 May, Dr Hastings Kamazu Banda elected President of Malawi. 25-7 June, *OCAM* conference in Tananarive. 6 July, Malawi becomes a republic. 6 Sept., Rhodesian Parliament votes for preventive detention. 6 Sept., H. Verwoerd, Prime Minister of SA, assassinated in House of Assembly. 13 Sept., B.J.Vorster, Prime Minister. 30 Sept., Bechuanaland becomes independent as Botswana. 4 Oct., Basutoland becomes independent as Lesotho. 5 Dec., 'working document' rejected by Rhodesian Cabinet. 27 Dec., riot at Thaba Bosigo, Lesotho,

1966 1 Jan., Pope Paul VI appeals again for peace in Vietnam. 18-24 Jan., Sir Hugh Beadle, Chief Justice of Rhodesia, visits London for talks. 31 Jan., Britain imposes complete trade ban on Rhodesia. 7 March, G.Mennen Williams, US Assistant Secretary of State for African Affairs, dismissed. 22-3 March, Archbishop of Canterbury visits Rome for talks on church unity. 7 Apr., Britain demands meeting of UN Security Council on the oil embargo against Rhodesia: 9-10 Apr., Security Council meets. 21 Apr., UN Committee on Decolonization resolution on Rhodesia. 9 May, talks on Rhodesia in London. 19 May, UN Security Council meets on Rhodesia. 8 June, Basutoland Constitutional Conference in London. 12-21 July, race riots in USA. 18 July, International Court of the Hague rejects Ethiopia and Liberia's

2 March, Kwame Nkrumah proclaimed co-President of Guinea. 4 March, Britain recognizes the new Ghanaian government. 10 March, Sékou Touré announces his readiness to send troops to Ghana. 20 Apr., new government in Chad. May and Sept., many Ibos massacred in N Nigeria. 24 May, General Ironsi announces that Nigeria is no longer a federation, and will be a republic. 28 May, riots in Kano. 29 July, military counter-*coup* in Nigeria: Lieut.-Col. Yakubu Gowon takes over: Lieut.-Col. Ojukwu challenges Federation. General Ironsi killed. 1 Aug., General Yakubu Gowon takes power. 2 Aug., Chief Awolowo freed. 7 Aug., Moktar Ould Daddah re-elected President of Mauritania. 12 Aug., constitutional conference in Lagos. 29 Sept., riots in Nigeria between Ibos and others. 3 Oct., constitutional conference in Lagos adjourns for 3 weeks. 29 Oct., Guinea delegation to OAU arrested in Accra. 16 Nov., Nigerian constitutional conference adjourns *sine die*. 21 Nov., attempted *coup d'état* in Togo; 26 Nov., new government formed. 12 Dec., Col. Lamizana, President of Upper Volta, proclaims that the army will assume power for 4 years. 26 Dec., ex-President Yaméogo attempts suicide.

enthroned as King Ntare V of Burundi. 5 Oct., Congo (K) breaks off diplomatic relations with Portugal and closes foreign consulates. 26 Oct., General Mobutu assumes functions of Prime Minister. 28 Nov., Ntare V of Burundi deposed: Republic proclaimed. with new government under Capt. Michel Micombero. 9 Dec., negotiations between Congo (K) and the *Union minière du Haut-Katanga* break down. 17 Dec., cabinet reconstructed in Congo (K). 31 Dec., *Union Minière du Haut-Katanga* compulsorily liquidated: replaced by *Générale Congolaise de Minerai*

1967 4-6 Apr., conference in Cairo of 'revolutionary heads of state' of Algeria, Mauritania, Tanzania and UAR. 15 May, Sadek El Mahdi resigns; 18 May, Muhammad Mahgoub, Prime Minister of the Sudan. 22 May. agreement between Ethiopia and the Sudan on rebels in Eritrea. 30 June 1 July, Moïse Tshombé kidnapped in an aircraft and taken to Algiers. 21 July, Algerian Supreme Court agrees to the extradition of Tshombé.

1967 4-5 Jan., conference on Nigeria with Ghanaian participants at Aburi, Ghana. 12 Jan.,Lieut-Col. Etienne Eyadéma seizes power in Togo. 13 Jan., President Grunitzky of Togo deposed. 1 March Guinea cabinet reconstructed. 10 March, Nigerian Supreme Council accepts Aburi recommendations. 16 March, federal constitution restored in Nigeria. 16 March, general elections in Sierra Leone: 21 March, the army takes power: Siaka Stevens appointed Prime Minister of Sierra Leone. 22 March, abortive attempt to assassinate President Senghor of Senegal. 24 March, second military *coup* in Sierra Leone: Lieut.-Col. Juxon-Smith, President of the National Reform Council. 14 Apr., Lieut. Col. Eyadéma becomes Head of State in Togo: new government constituted. 17 Apr., abortive *coup d'état* in Ghana: General Kotoka killed. 1 May, Africanization of the clergy announced in Guinea. 2 May, President Tubman of Liberia re-elected for the sixth time. 6 May, Mali *franc* devalued by 50%. 9 May, two Ghanaian officers executed and one imprisoned for 30 years for the attempted *coup d'état*. 12 May, Papal Pro-Nuncio protests against Guinea Africanization of their

1967 12 Feb., conference on the security of eastern and central Africa at Kinshasa. 16-17 Feb., agreement between Belgium and the Congo on copper. 15 Feb., Gabon constitution revised. 13 March, Moïse Tshombé condemned to death *in absentia*. 19 March, general and presidential election in Gabon. 4 June, referendum on new constitution in Congo (K): 90% vote yes. 24 June, new currency created in Congo (K) with the *zaïre* as the unit. 5 July, military uprising in eastern and northern provinces of Congo (K). 13 July, foreign mercenaries flee from Kisangani. 9 Aug., column of mercenaries enters Bukavu. 11-14 Sept., OAU summit conference at Kinshasa: 20 Sept., all mercenaries to be evacuated. 5 Oct., nine ministers dismissed in Congo (K); cabinet reconstructed. 6 Oct., *Fondation Léon Mba* for tropical diseases set up in Gabon. 13 Oct., universities closed in the Congo: students required to teach. 3 Oct., fighting in Bukavu..Armed column from Angola enters Dilolo region of Congo(K) under Bob Dénard. 4 Nov., Congolese army takes Bukavu: mercenaries and gendarmes flee to Rwanda. 5 Nov., Dénard column retires to Angola. 11 Nov., special committee of OAU meets in Kinshasa to discuss mercenaries. 28 Nov., Bernard Albert Bongo, Vice-President, becomes

of foreign ministers and then heads of state of OAU at Addis Ababa.

following a quarrel between the King and the Prime Minister; 28 Dec., King Moshoeshoe II placed under house arrest.

complaint concerning SWA by majority of one. 31 July, British Colonial Office abolished: responsibilities taken over by Commonwealth Office. 6-15 Sept., Commonwealth Prime Ministers' Conference in London. 27 Sept., racial riots in USA. 14 Oct., UN Security Council unanimously supports Congo (K) complaint against Portugal. 21 Oct., slag tip disaster at Aberfan, Wales. 22 Oct., UN General Assembly votes for universal suffrage in Rhodesia. 27 Oct., UN General Assembly votes for an end to the S African Mandate over SWA. 17 Nov., UN General Assembly resolution on Rhodesia. 2-4 Dec., Ian Smith and Harold Wilson meet on *HMS Tiger:* 4 Dec., 'working document' approved by British Cabinet. 12 Dec., UN General Assembly recommends sanctions against Portugal. 16 Dec., UN Security Council votes for sanctions against Rhodesia. 20 Dec., UN General Assembly votes on Djibouti.

1967 5 Jan, Daniel Arap Moi, Vice-President of Kenya. 17 Jan., seven Italian missionaries expelled from Uganda, for having aided the liberation movement in southern Sudan. 5 Feb., President Nyerere makes the 'Arusha declaration', stating the aims of Tanzania. 8 Feb., demonstrations in Zanzibar. 11 Feb., banks, principal industries and insurance companies in Tanzania nationalized: Kenya, Uganda and Zambia reassure foreign companies that they do not intend to follow suit. 23 March, referendum in French Somalia; 22,555 vote to remain with France, 14,666 against. 6 June, East African Community established by Kenya, Uganda, and Tanzania. 11 June, fresh constitutional reforms announced in Uganda. 16 July, new government in Somalia under Mohammed Ibrahim Egal. 28 Oct., treaty of friendship between Ethiopia and Somalia signed at Arusha. 1 Dec., President Nyerere proclaims the birth of East African Community at Arusha. 15-16 Dec., conference of eastern and central African heads of state in Kampala.

1967 3 Jan., police attacked at Leribe, Lesotho. 5 Jan., King of Lesotho agrees to work as a constitutional monarch. Chief Leabua Jonathan, Prime Minister of Lesotho, visits Cape Town for talks on aid. Feb., Dr T.E.Donges elected President of S Africa. 19 Apr., general elections in Swaziland: King Sobhuza II's party overwhelmingly victorious. 8 July, United People's Party formed in Botswana. 19 July, Albert Sylla, Madagascar Minister for Foreign Affairs, killed in an aircraft accident. 22 July, Chief Albert Luthuli d., aged seventy-nine. 7 Aug., general elections in Mauritius: 15 Aug., Sir Seewoosagur Ramgoolam forms new government. 12 Oct., Yatuta Chisiza shot dead at Mpatamanga, near Blantyre, while leading a gang to assassinate Dr Banda. 8 Nov., G. Thomson, British Commonwealth Secretary, visits Zambia, S Africa, Botswana and Rhodesia. 2 Dec., first human heart transplanted at Groote Schuur Hospital, Cape Town.

1967 15-24 Jan., H.Wilson and G.Brown tour Common Market capitals. 27 Jan., treaty between UK, USA and USSR banning use of nuclear weapons in outer space. 15 Feb., financial agreement between France and Mali. 13-21 March, student 'sit-in' in London School of Economics. 20 March, Encyclical *Populorum progressio* published. 2 Apr., abortive UN mission to Aden. 16 Apr., De Gaulle blocks British entry into European Common Market. 24 Apr., UN debate on SWA. 19 May, UN General Assembly resolves to set up a council to administer SWA. 13 June, Constantine Stavropoulos appointed Commissioner *ad int.* 5-10 June, war between Israel and Arab States: Israel seizes W bank of Jordan and Sinai. 17 June, China explodes hydrogen bomb. 7 July, agreement between France and Niger on uranium. 11 July, UN Security Council condemns recruitment and training of mercenaries. 14-24 July, race riots in USA. 24 July, President de Gaulle visits Quebec. 10 Aug., UN debate on SWA. 25 Sept., cease-fire in Aden. 26 Oct., Belgium resolves to give technical aid again to the Congo (K). 31 Oct., the Pope sends a message to Africa. 15 Nov., UN Security Council censures Portugal for allowing Angola to be used as a base for mercenaries. 17 Nov., UN General Assembly recommends sanctions against Portugal

clergy. 12 May, political parties
abolished in Togo. 16 May, Dahomey
cabinet reconstituted. 22 May, Papal
Pro-Nuncio, Cardinal Zougrana, and
Archbishop of Conakry protest against
Guinea Africanization of the clergy.
24 May, Togo Development Bank
set up. 27 May-1 June, seventy-
three priests and fifty-five nuns
expelled from Guinea. 27 May, Nigeria
Federation reorganized into twelve states
with Federal Executive Council. 30
May, Lieut.-Col. Odumegwu Ojukwu
proclaims former Eastern Region
of Nigeria independent as the Republic
of Biafra: civil war ensues. 8 June,
meeting in Lagos of the governors of the
new regions. 13 June, cabinet recon-
struction in Nigeria admitting civilian
ministers. 15-16 June, Catholic
Bishops of W Africa meet at Dakar to
protest against Guinea Africanization of
the clergy. 19 June, constitutional
reform in Senegal. 29 June, Mustafa Lo
executed for attempted murder of
President Senghor. 7 July, Nigerian
federal forces attack Biafra; 31 July,
Nsukka captured; 26 July, Bonny
captured; 10 Aug., West Central Province
liberated: new government formed.
22 Aug., National Committee for the
Defence of the Revolution assumes full
powers in Mali. 11-18 Sept., France
and Ivory Coast hold joint manoeuvres.
21 Sept., Guinea announces the freeing
of Ivory Coast prisoners. 25 Sept., Ivory
Coast frees political prisoners from
Guinea. 2 Oct., Sékou Touré re-elected
as Supreme Leader of the Revolution.
22-23 Nov., OAU consultative mission
recommends the preservation of
federation in Nigeria. 11-20 Dec., 2nd
International Congress of Africanists at
Dakar 17 Dec., military *coup d'état*
in Dahomey: provisional government
under Commandant Maurice Kouandéte.
20 Dec., President Soglo of Dahomey
dismissed. 22 Dec., Lieut.-Col. .
Alphonse Alley elected President of
Dahomey.

Head of State *ad int.* in Gabon.

1968 1 Jan., President Boumédienne
begins the 'Year of the Party', con-
solidating his political organization by
conferences at all levels. 7 Feb.,
Constituent Assembly dissolved in the
Sudan; troops called out to prevent
riots; 8 Feb., deputies protest and
demand a change of Prime Minister.
Feb., Sayed Ali al-Mirghani, head of the
Khatmia sect since 1899, d. in Sudan,
aged about 88. 31 March, President

1968 1 Jan., Sékou Touré re-elected
President of Guinea. 3 Jan., Nigerian
currency notes exchanged for a new
issue. 10 Jan., Captain Hachémé,
President of the Military Revolutionary
Committee of Dahomey, deposed.
16 Jan., National Assembly of Mali
dissolved. 19 Jan., Captain Kérékou
becomes President of the Military
Revolutionary Committee in Dahomey.
19 Jan., Guinea cabinet re-shuffled.
22 Jan., National Assembly of Mali

1968 12 Jan., cabinet reshuffle in Brazza-·
ville: Massemba-Debat heads government.
1 Feb., General Mobutu proposes the
creation of a Union of States of C Atrica,
consisting of Congo (Kinshasa), Chad and
CAR. 26 Feb., at Brazzaville, the African
Superior Council for Sport decides to
withdraw all African countries from the
Olympic Games in Mexico in protest
against the participation of SA. 2 Apr.,
Charter of the Union of States of C Africa
signed at Bangui: creates a common

to compel her to give independence to her overseas territories. 18 Nov., Labour Government in Britain devalues sterling. 26 Nov., People's republic of S Yemen proclaimed in Aden. 28 Nov., President Léon Mba of Gabon d. in Paris. 29 Nov., British evacuate Aden. 12 Dec., Britain and UAR resume diplomatic relations. 28 Dec., Hubert Humphrey, Vice-President of USA, leaves to visit Ivory Coast, Liberia, Ghana, Congo (K), Zambia, Ethiopia, Somalia and Tunisia.

1968 20-24 Feb., Conference of Ministers of OAU at Addis Ababa: Britain condemned for not taking Rhodesia by force; France condemned for refusing to decolonize Djibouti; *apartheid* denounced vigorously. 13 Apr., Tanzania recognizes Biafra as an independent state. Alleged tax-defaulters die in Mwanza, Tanzania, through overcrowding in cells. 21 May, Uganda complains of 'aggression' from the Sudan. 23-31 May, abortive conference at Kampala on a cease-fire in Biafra.

1968 1 Jan., Malawi sends official diplomatic mission to SA. President Kaunda reproaches British government for not taking more active steps in Rhodesia: claims that Britain 'deliberately violated' the Declaration of Human Rights. 10 Jan., Dr T.E.Donges, President-elect of SA, d. 29 Jan., Court of Appeal in Salisbury denies the right of Rhodesians to appeal to the Privy Council. 4-6 Feb., President Kaunda, shocked by 'tribal wranglings' at UNIP

1968 16 Jan., extensive economy decisions announced in UK, involving withdrawal of forces from Persian Gulf and Far East. 22-4 Jan., British Prime Minister visits Moscow. 1 Feb., UN conference on Commerce and Development in New Delhi. 2 Feb., Pope Paul VI sends message to General Gowon on Biafra. 15 Feb., International Olympic Games Committee decides by a majority postal vote (not two-thirds) to admit S Africa to the Olympic Games in Mexico. 19-23 Feb., Swaziland

Nasser makes 'Declaration' on constitutional and political reforms. 5 Apr., Libyan Petroleum Corporation signs agreement with two French oil companies for development and exploitation. 18 Apr., elections in the Sudan: Democratic Unity Party gain almost an overall majority. 2 May, unanimous referendum in UAR endorses President Nasser's 'Declaration'. 27 May, new Constituent Assembly meets in Khartoum: Ismail el-Azhari, President of the Supreme Council; Muhammad Mahgoub, Prime Minister. 1 June, new government in the Sudan. 4 June, refugees from Eritrea entering the Sudan. 16-22 July, meeting of the Committee of Eleven on African Liberation Movements at Algiers. 22-6 July, meeting of the Committee of Five on Rhodesia at Algiers. 23 July, Israeli aircraft hijacked by Palestinian commando and taken to Algiers. 13-16 Sept., OAU Summit Conference at Algiers: majority condemn secession of Biafra. 21 Nov., student riots at El Mansoura, UAR. 25 Nov., student riots in Alexandria, UAR. 28 Nov., Muhammad Mahgoub, Prime Minister of the Sudan, has heart attack: is taken to London.

replaced by delegated legislation under President Modibo Keita. 29 Jan., Biafra issues own currency. 2-8 Feb., Admiral Amérigo Tomàs, President of Portugal, visits Portuguese Guinea. 25 Feb., Léopold Sédar Senghor re-elected President of Senegal. 24 March, Organization of the Riverain States of the Senegal, consisting of Guinea, Mali, Mauritania and Senegal, created. 24 Feb.-9 March, Commonwealth Education Conference in Lagos. 21 March, Nigerians capture Onitsha. 31 March, General Gowon offers Biafra peace talks: refused. 31 March, new Dahomey constitution approved by referendum. 18 Apr., Colonel Juxon-Smith, President, arrested by military elements in Sierra Leone. 22 April, Sir Banja Tejan-Sie, Chief Justice of Sierra Leone, appointed Governor-General *ad int.* 22-4, Apr., conference of WA Heads of State at Monrovia. 26 Apr., civilian rule restored in Sierra Leone. 27 Apr., Siaka Stevens appointed Prime Minister of Sierra Leone. 5 May, elections in Dahomey: less than 26% vote. 14 May, Ivory Coast recognizes Biafra. 15 May, Nigeria breaks off diplomatic relations with Ivory Coast. 18 May, Port Harcourt taken by Nigeria from Biafra. 18 May, student strike in Dakar; 29 May, Dakar University closed. 30-1 May, state of emergency proclaimed in Dakar. 10 June, Lamine Gueye, President of Senegalese National Assembly, d. 20-6 July, abortive conference on ceasefire in Biafra; General Gowon and Colonel Ojukwu present, under chairmanship of Emperor Haile Selassie, at Niamey. 26 June, Dr Emile Derlin Zinsou appointed President of Dahomey. 2 July, Britain announces emergency relief for Nigeria and Biafra: relief team sent under Lord Hunt. 4 July, Ojukwu refuses British aid for Biafra so long as Britain sends arms to Nigeria. 28 July, Dr Zinsou confirmed as President of Dahomey by referendum. 31 July, Military Revolutionary Committee dissolved in Dahomey: constitutional rule restored. 4 Sept., Nigerians capture Aba. 10 Oct.-28 Feb., 1969, two Soviet trawlers, charged with operating without licence in Ghanaian territorial waters, detained at Takoradi. 7 Nov., Constituent Assembly constituted in Ghana. 19 Nov., Military Liberation Committee seizes power in Mali: President Modibo Keita detained. 20 Nov., following disturbances in Bo and Kemena, Sierra Leone, Government declares state of emergency: confirmed by Parliament, 23 Nov. 21 Nov., Nigeria and USSR sign agreement for economic and technical co-operation. 22 Nov., new government formed in

market. 17 Apr. - 22 June, second constitutional conference on Spanish Equatorial Guinea. 24 Apr., 112 mercenaries, refugees in Rwanda, repatriated to Europe. 8 May, Gabon recognizes Biafra. 1 Aug., National Assembly dissolved in Brazzaville. 2 Aug., Massemba-Debat, having lost military support for his government, leaves Brazzaville; Lieut. Augustin Poignet made acting head of state. 15 Aug., referendum in Spanish Equatorial Guinea on independence: 63.1% votes in favour, 35% against. 23 Aug., Congo (K) signs agreement with Belgium for scientific and technical co-operation; Belgian property in Congo, frozen in 1960, released; interest on Belgian capital in Congo made transferable. 28 Aug., government of Chad requests French military intervention to restore order in Tibesti. 4 Sept., Massemba-Debat, President of Congo (Brazzaville), deposed by the military. 5 Sept., Capt. Alfred Raôul, Prime Minister, becomes acting President. 6 Sept., Massemba-Debat disappears. 22 Sept., general election in Spanish Equatorial Guinea. 7-8 Oct., Pierre Mulele, former Education Minister, and principal instigator of the Kouilu rebellion, Congo (Kinshasa), condemned to death: 9 Oct., executed. Congo (B) breaks off diplomatic relations with Congo (K) following execution of Pierre Mulele. 12 Oct., (Spanish) Equatorial Guinea becomes independent: Francisco Macias Nguema, first President. 21 Dec., Equatorial Guinea orders cessation of mercy flights from Fernando Po to Biafra.

4 July, Sudan apologizes to Uganda for 'acts of aggression' and offers compensation. 26 July, at Arusha, economic agreement between Kenya, Tanzania, and Uganda. 4 July, Tanzania resumes diplomatic relations with Britain, broken since 1965. 5-9 Aug., further abortive conference at Addis Ababa on cease-fire in Biafra. 21 Aug., Tanzania-Zambia Railway Authority formed to control proposed rail link. 2 Sept., oil pipeline from Dar es Salaam to Ndola opened, 1,058 miles long. 18 Oct., editor of Uganda review *Transition* arrested for sedition. 20 Nov., curfew in Zanzibar for military exercises. 31 Dec., Kenya Minister of Commerce and Industry announces that 700 non-citizens had been refused trading licences and estimated that 3.000 would be refused in the following 6 months.

National Council, resigns as President of UNIP and of Zambia: persuaded to withdraw both resignations. 9 Feb., nineteen men, found guilty of terrorism in SWA, sentenced to life imprisonment; nine others to 20 years imprisonment. 19 Feb., Jacobus Johannes Fouché elected President of SA unopposed. 24-7 Feb., Sir Alec Douglas-Home and Lord Goodman visit Salisbury for secret talks. March - April, guerilla offensives from Zambia into Rhodesia. mounted by Zimbabwe African People's Union and ANC of SA. 6 March, three African nationalists, reprieved by the Queen, executed in Salisbury. 12 March, Mauritius becomes independent within the Commonwealth. 19 March, Rhodesian National Party (RNP) formed by Len Idensohn. 9 Apr., Whaley commission, on the Rhodesian constitution, reports. 19 Apr., Mulungushi Reforms announced in Zambia: 51% state participation in twenty-five major companies. 20 May, Zambia recognizes Biafra. 4 June, Zambia announces amnesty for followers of Alice Lenshina. 9 June, Luangwa Bridge, Zambia, destroyed by unknown terrorists: diesel fuel supply from Malawi to Zambia temporarily cut off. 17 July, Rhodesia announces intention of forming a republic. July, further guerila offensive from Zambia into Rhodesia. 2 Aug., Rhodesian government announces that it will disregard Privy Council judgements. 7 Aug., student demonstration in Cape Town protests against government refusal to allow the appointment of an African to a university post in anthropology. 9 Aug., Rhodesian judge sentences thirty-two Africans to death for possession of arms, declaring that Rhodesian Government possessed 'internal *de jure* status'. 13 Aug., political riot at Chililabombwe, Zambia: six killed. 14-24 Aug., 400 students occupy Cape Town University: student demonstrations in Johannesburg, Pretoria, Pietermaritzburg, and Durban. 14 Aug., United Party proscribed in Zambia. 16 Aug., Balthazar Vorster, Prime Minister of SA, speaks at Heilbron, OFS, stating that the government cannot tolerate student breaches of law and order. 25 Aug., Pan-African Congress (PAC), SA African nationalist movement in exile, proscribed in Zambia. 29 Aug., Centre Party formed in Rhodesia. Aug., SA Minister for Foreign Affairs visits Malawi. 6 Sept., Swaziland, last British colonial territory in Africa, becomes independent within the Commonwealth: constitutional monarchy under King Sobhuza II: currency linked with the SA *rand*: new name of country, Ngwane. 11 Sept., Lord James Graham (Duke of Montrose) resigns from Rhodesian

Constitutional Conference in London prepares for independence. 27 Feb., emergency legislation in Britain to stem Asian immigration from Kenya. 1 March, new British Immigration Act comes into effect, particularly to control entry of East African Asians into Britain: more than 1m. recent coloured immigrants already in Britain. 31 March, President Johnson announces he will not stand for re-election; partial halt to bombing in Vietnam. 3 Apr., Vietnam agrees to negotiate peace with USA. 4 Apr., Revd. Martin Luther King assassinated. 9 Apr., UK Race Relations Bill published. 10 Apr., US Civil Rights Bill passed. 24 Apr.-27 May, Emperor Haile Selassie visits Thailand, Cambodia, Indonesia, Australia, S Korea, Malaysia and Singapore. 24 Apr., SA not to participate in the Olympic Games in Mexico. 3 May-17 June, students riot in Paris, followed by workers' strikes and general unrest in France. 13 May, Vietnam peace talks open in Paris: procedural shilly-shally until the end of the year. 29 May, UN Security Council imposes mandatory sanctions on Rhodesia. 5 June, Senator Robert Kennedy assassinated. 12 June, UN General Assembly again condemns SA for its refusal to hand over SWA to UN. 18 June, House of Lords rejects mandatory sanctions on Rhodesia. 30 June, General de Gaulle wins landslide general election. 18 July, sanctions order on Rhodesia passed by House of Lords. 29 July, Papal Encyclical, *Humanae Vitae*, on contraception, published. 20 Aug., Soviet and allied troops occupy Czechoslovakia. 30 Sept.. World Bank loans Guinea $64.5 million for a bauxite extraction project at Boko. 9-13 Oct., Ian Smith, Prime Minister of Rhodesia, and Harold Wilson, British Prime Minister, meet on HMS *Fearless* off Gibraltar: discussions abortive. 22 Oct., *'Fearless'* proposals for Rhodesia receive all party support in House of Commons. 5 Nov., Richard Nixon elected President of USA. 7 Nov., UN General Assembly votes economic sanctions against Rhodesia. 29 Nov., UN General Assembly demands independence for Portuguese terrorities in Africa. 3 Dec., UN General Assembly condemns *apartheid* in SA.

Mali: Lieut. Moussa Traoré, President. 27 Nov., 200 persons under arrest for political reasons in Sierra Leone. 11-16 Dec., Lord Shepherd visits Nigeria for talks with General Gowon. 17 Dec., Ghanaian Government announces discovery of a plot to return Nkrumah to power: Air Marshal Otu arrested.

1969 8 Jan., Elections in Egypt; Ali Sabry dismissed, allegedly for personal contacts with Russia. 12 Jan., President Nasser annuls Supreme Court decision to try forty-six students, arrested for rioting in Alexandria. 25 May, military *coup* in Khartoum, led by Col. Ja'afar al-Nimeiri, successful without a shot fired: all political leaders arrested in bed: Muhammed Ahmed Mahgoub overthrown. 29 June, Moïse Tshombé, former Prime Minister of Katanga, d. at Algiers, aged 49. 30 June, Ifni handed over by Spain to Morocco. 8 July, UAR gives full diplomatic recognition to E Germany. 21 July - 1 Aug., Pan-African Festival of Culture in Algiers. 25 Aug., meeting of Arab Foreign Ministers in Cairo to discuss reconquest of the Holy Places. 26 Aug., Ismail el-Azhari. former President of Sudan, d. 31 Aug., Supreme Court of Justice set up in Egypt to deal with constitutional matters and to arbitrate between government departments. 1 Sept., King Idris I of Libya deposed in a military *coup*. 4 Sept., Palestine National Congress held in Cairo. 22-4 Sept., World Islamic Conference at Rabat. 24 Oct., following torrential rains in Tunisia, 700 estimated dead. 30 Oct., Libya asks UK to withdraw military bases. 8 Nov., Arab League Defence Council meet in Cairo. UAR destroyers bombard Israeli-occupied Sinai. 11 Nov., air battle over Suez Canal. 8-13 Dec., talks in Tripoli, Libya, on UK withdrawal from military bases: UK to withdraw by March 1970. 27 Dec., Libya, Sudan and UAR agree to form military, economic and political alliance.

1969 14 Jan., General Eyadéma announces return to liberty of political activity in Togo. 17 Jan., all political activity forbidden in Togo following demonstrations. 3 Feb., trial of Air Marshal Otu begun in Ghana. 25 March, strike of secondary school children in Senegal. 26 March, Nigerian offensive against Biafra: bombardment lasts 3 days. 27-31 March. H.Wilson, British Prime Minister, visits Nigeria to obtain first hand knowledge of civil war. 2 Apr., General Ankrah, President of National Council of Liberation, Ghana, deposed for alleged corruption: succ. by General Akwasi Afrifa. 14-15 Apr., Marcelo Caetano, Prime Minister of Portugal, visits Portuguese Guinea. 18-19 Apr., Consultative committee of OAU on Nigeria meets in Monrovia. 23 Apr., Nigerian troops take Umuahia, capital of secessionist Biafra. 24 Apr., Biafra regains Owerri. 1 May, ban on political activity lifted in Ghana (imposed Feb. 1966). 5 May, plot against government discovered in Cotonou, Dahomey. 8 May, Ex-President Yaméogo of Upper Volta condemned to 5 years hard labour. 9 May, twenty-nine European oil technicians, of whom twenty-four Italian, captured by Biafra near Kwale: eighteen held as prisoners. 11 May. National Council of the Revolution in Guinea proclaims itself a revolutionary tribunal. 13 May, three new political parties authorized in Ghana: Progress Party (PP) led by Dr Kofi Busia; People's Popular Party (PPP) led by Dr Lutterodt; All People's Party (APP), led by Dr E.V.C. de Graft Johnson: electoral campaign opened. 13-15 May, strike of post office workers in Senegal. 14 May, fourteen persons condemned

1969 8 Jan, relief air lift from Fernando Po to Biafra interrupted. 24 Jan., CAR suspends diplomatic relations with Congo (K). 24 Jan., diplomatic relations established between Equatorial Guinea and Nigeria. 16 Feb., elections in Gabon. 24 Feb., riots against Spanish Consulate and barracks at Bata, capital of Equatorial Guinea; Spanish flag burnt by mob. 1 March, Prince Albert of Belgium visits Congo (K), heading economic mission. 1 March, President of Equatorial Guinea asks for UN observers: state of emergency and curfew proclaimed. 5 March, abortive *coup* in Equatorial Guinea, led by Foreign Minister Atanasio Nelongo, who dies later in hospital. 8 March, UN representative sent to Bata. 14 March. commission of Spanish economists arrives in Bata, with an economic aid plan for Equatorial Guinea. 10 Apr., abortive *coup d'état,* led by Lieut.-Col. Aléxandre Banza, frustrated in CAR. 12 Apr., of 7,000 Spanish citizens in Equatorial Guinea before the troubles only 1,352 remain: country paralysed by lack of technicians and specialists. 12 Apr., Col. Banza executed. 16-17 Apr., Portuguese Prime Minister visits Luanda, Angola. 16-18 Apr., Summit Conference of E and CA states in Lusaka. 31 May, Jacques Debert condemned to forced labour for life in Congo. 4 June, serious student riots in the University of Lovanium: probably 30 dead; 400 arrested. 1 Aug., cabinet reshuffle in Congo(K): Adoula becomes Prime Minister. 5-8 Nov., President of Gabon pays official visit to Cameroun. 8 Nov., abortive *coup d' état* in Brazzaville. 14 Nov., revolutionary court in Brazzaville tries authors of the *coup d' état:* Kolela condemned to death; 21 Nov., Massemba-Debat and Noumazalaye acquitted.

Cabinet, following disagreement with Ian Smith on constitution. 22 Sept., Chichewa (formerly Chinyanja) and English made the offical languages of Malawi. 1 Oct., SA government published constitution for Ovamboland, SWA, giving a legislative council and an executive council. 17 Oct., new Ovamboland Legislative Council meets at Okashiti: forty-two members, all African. 18 Oct., Rhodesia rejects *'Fearless'* proposals. 22 Oct., Smith sends documents to London to keep negotiations open. 23 Oct., elections in Transkei. 2-16 Nov., George Thomson, Commonwealth Secretary, visits Salisbury for fresh talks; 10 Nov., Rhodesia adopts new national flag; 18 Nov., reports deadlock. 25 Nov., fourteen villages in Mwinilunga district, Zambia, burnt, allegedly by ANC terrorists trained in Angola. 19 Dec., Dr. Kaunda re-elected President of Zambia with overwhelming parliamentary majority.

1969 3 Feb., Dr Eduardo Mondlane, leader of *FRELIMO,* assassinated in Dar es Salaam; succ. Dr Uria Simango. 17-22 Feb., Foreign Ministers of OAU meet in Addis Ababa. 3 March, university and schools closed in Addis Ababa. 23 March, anti-Arab demonstration in Addis Ababa. 26 March, general elections in Somalia. 31 March, H.Wilson visits Addis Ababa. 22 May, new government formed in Somalia by President Egal. 5 July, Tom Mboya, Kenyan political leader, assassinated in Nairobi, aged 43. 28 July, first symposium of Episcopal Conferences of Africa and Madagascar in Kampala. 30 July-1 Aug., Pope Paul VI visits Uganda: venerates Uganda martyrs: consecrates twelve African bishops; holds talks to promote peace in Biafra. 27 Aug., Council of Ministers of OAU meet in Addis Ababa. 1 Sept., Abdallah Kassim Hanga, Othman Shariff, and Ali Mwange Tambwe, former ministers, arrested in Dar es Salaam for alleged 'plotting' against the Zanzibar Revolutionary Government. 6-10 Sept., conference of OAU heads of state at Addis Ababa. 8 Sept., Benedict Kiwanuka, former Uganda Prime Minister and leader of the opposition, arrested. 25 Sept., Agreement signed at Arusha, Tanzania, between the East African Economic Community and EEC. 4 Oct., Michael Kamaliza, former minister, Bibi Titi Binti Mohamed, and four army officers detained on charges of subversive activities in Dar es Salaam. 15 Oct., President Shirmarke of Somalia assassinated in northern Somalia. 21 Oct., military *coup* in Somalia; constitution abolished: General Muhammad Syad takes power. 25 Oct., President Kenyatta visits Kisumu: seven killed in riot. 27 Oct., Oginga Odinga, former Vice-President of Kenya, and eight other KAPU leaders

1969 13-15 Jan., representatives of EEC hold Conference of Parliamentary Association with (Francophone) African states in Madagascar. 3-12 Feb., trial of Rev. Ndabaningi Sithole, Rhodesian African nationalist: sentenced to 6 years imprisonment for incitement to murder. 17-20 Apr., Portuguese Prime Minister visits Mozambique. 20 May, Ian Smith says he despairs of negotiations with Britain. 21 May, new Rhodesian constitution published: House of Assembly to have 66 members: 50 Europeans, representing 220,000 persons; 16 Africans, representing more than 4 million persons: franchise based on earnings or property. 17 June, referendum to amend the constitution in Zambia, to give Parliament power over property rights. 20 June, referendum in Rhodesia on the proclamation of a republic and a new constitution. 24 June, Sir Humphrey Gibbs, last British Governor of Rhodesia, resigns. 11 July, L.Gandar and B.Pogrund, SA journalists, sentenced in Johannesburg to 6 months imprisonment for publishing in the *Rand Daily Mail* allegedly false information about SA prisons. 14 July, President Kaunda of Zambia disputes High Court judgement freeing two Portuguese soldiers found infringing Zambian border with Angola. 15 July, Chief Justice of Zambia, Mr James Skinner, defends High Court judgement: mob wrecks High Court. 11 Aug., President Kaunda announces nationalization of copper in Zambia: government to have 51% share in copper companies. 17 July, Chief Justice Skinner leaves Zambia; two other judges resign. 25 Aug., Vice-President Simon Kapwepwe of Zambia resigns, but agrees to stay in office until August 1970. 5 Sept., Botswana Parliament dissolved.

1969 4 Jan., Spain renounces claim to Ifni. 7-15 Jan., Commonwealth Conference in London: Prime Minister of Uganda announces his intention to expel 40,000 Asians. 19 Jan., Prime Ministers of Denmark, Norway, and Sweden offer their good offices to end the Nigerian civil war. 24 Jan.-19 Feb., following student riot London School of Economics closed. 18 Feb., three Palestinian Arab terrorists attack Israeli civil airliner at Zurich. 10 March, James Earl Ray sentenced to 99 years imprisonment for the murder of the Rev. Martin Luther King. 28 March, Vatican names two new African cardinals, Mgr Malula, Abp of Kinshasa, and Mgr Véron Rakatomalala, Abp of Tananarive. 4 Apr., Middle East peace talks held in New York between France, UK USA and USSR. 1 June, Lord Hailey d. 13 June, UN Security Council debate on Rhodesia. 15 June, Georges Pompidou elected President of France. 20 June, Jacques Chaban-Delmas appointed Prime Minister of France. 24 June, British government announces severance of surviving official links with Rhodesia. 21 July, Neil Armstrong, US astronaut, is first man to set foot on the Moon. 22 July, UN Security Council debates Zambia's complaint of frontier violation by Portugal. 8 Aug., France devalues *franc* by 11.11% 10 Aug., Francophone African states agree to follow the devaluation of the *franc*. 12 Aug., bitter fighting breaks out in N Ireland between Protestants and Catholics. 14 Aug., British troops sent to N Ireland. 27 Sept., Nicolas Grunitzky, former President of Togo, d. in Paris, following a car crash in Abidjan. 15-18 Oct., Conference of the African Studies Association of USA and Canadian Council for Africa in Montreal: disturbances caused by American

to death by revolutionary tribunal in
Guinea. 15 May, thirteen participants in
alleged imperialist plot in Senegal condemned to death, nine hard labour for
life and others from 11 to 20 years hard
labour. 16 May, Senegalese cabinet
reshuffled. 16 May, cabinet reshuffled
in Guinea. 17 May, strike of petrol-pump
attendants in Senegal. 20 May, strike of
civil servants in Dahomey. 23 May,
Ivory Coast recalls its embassy from
Moscow. 24 May, following a student
strike, Abidjan University closed. 31 May,
Ivory Coast breaks off diplomatic relations with USSR; Abidjan University
reopened. 1 June, Biafran tribunal
condemns eighteen Italian technicians
to death. 2 June, strike of bank employees
in Senegal. 5 June, Biafra releases the
eighteen Italian technicians. 10 June,
International Red Cross suspends
relief flights to Biafra from Cotonou,
Dahomey. 11 June, general strike in
Senegal: state of emergency proclaimed.
30 June, Nigerian National Commission
of Rehabilitation (NCR) takes over all
relief operations in Biafra. 5 July, NCR
announces that neutral teams may join
in inspection of relief supplies to Biafra.
21 July, agreement between Nigeria and
the International Red Cross on mercy
flights to Biafra. 23 Aug., Ghanaian
Constituent Assembly promulgates new
constitution in its final sitting. 28 Aug.,
Dr Azikiwe, former President of Nigeria,
declares himself in favour of a united
Nigeria. 29 Aug., elections in Ghana:
PP 105 seats; National Liberal Alliance,
29 seats; others, 6. 2 Sept., Second
General Assembly of African Churches
at Abidjan. 3 Sept., Dr. Kofi Busia
becomes Prime Minister of Ghana.
7 Sept., Dr. Busia forms new government
in Ghana. 26 Sept., ex-Colonel Alphonse
Alley, former President, tried in Dahomey.
30 Sept., charges against Air-Marshal Otu
withdrawn in Ghana: reinstated and given
special employment in Prime Minister's
office. Military government in Ghana
terminated. 2 Oct., agreement signed by
Nigerian government ending International Red Cross in Nigeria: work to be
taken over by Nigerian Red Cross. 4 Oct.,
Alphonse Alley sentenced to 10 years
imprisonment. 19 Nov., aliens without
residence permits required to leave
Ghana within 2 weeks. 25 Nov., Gbedem-
ah, Leader of the Opposition in the
Ghana Parliament, found guilty of abuse
of power, declared to be ineligible for
parliament. 2 Dec., many thousands of
aliens, especially Nigerians, begin to
leave Ghana. 7 Dec., Nigeria offers to
meet representatives of Biafra in Addis
Ababa. 9 Dec., Senegalese constitution

19-20 Nov., forty French technicians
expelled from CAR. 15 Dec., conference
of Foreign Ministers of Congo (K),
Burundi and Rwanda at Gisenyi.

arrested in connection with Kisumu riot. 30 Oct., KAPU banned. 1 Nov., new government formed in Mogadishu under General Mohamed Said Barre. 7 Nov., National Assembly dissolved in Kenya. 6 Dec., general elections in Kenya. 16 Dec., Nigerian and Biafran delegations in Addis Ababa. 18 Dec., Biafran delegation leaves Addis Ababa, refusing to negotiate under OAU auspices. 19 Dec., attempt on life of President Milton Obote: state of emergency declared in Uganda. 20 Dec., new cabinet formed in Kenya.

24 Sept., election of the forty members of Representative Council of the Coloured Population. 4 Oct., Dr Albert Herzog, ultra-conservative leader, expelled from the government party in SA. 8 Oct., a new Bantustan, Vendaland, in N Transvaal, inaugurated. 18 Oct., general elections in Botswana. 1 Nov., new African party, Progressive National United Party, formed in Rhodesia. 18 Nov., new constitution adopted by Rhodesian Parliament. Bill passed in Malawi giving local courts increased powers in criminal and civil cases: permitted to impose death penalty. 21 Nov., all four expatriate judges in Malawi resign. 2 Dec., President Tsiranana forms new government in Madagascar. 30 Dec., agreement between SA and USA on gold. 31 Dec., midnight, Zambia formally takes over copper companies.

'Black Caucus'. 15 Oct., peaceful demonstrations in USA against Vietnam war. 3-6 Nov., General Mobutu visits Belgium. 5 Nov., anti-*apartheid* demonstrations at Rugby Football match at Twickenham, London, between Oxford University and the Springboks, 21 Nov. former Kabaka of Buganda, Sir Edward Frederick Mutesa, d. in London. 1 Dec., UN General Assembly demands sanctions against S Africa on account of SWA. 8 Dec., UN Security Council, following a complaint from Senegal, condemns Portugal. 19 Dec., Spanish Foreign Minister announces that Spanish Sahara has choice of independence, or autonomy in association with Spain, or incorporation into one or other neighbouring state. 22 Dec., UN Security Council orders Portugal to cease immediately from violating the sovereignty and territorial integrity of Guinea.

revised. 10 Dec., military *coup* in
Dahomey; President Zinsou overthrown.
12 Dec., Provisional Military Directory
formed in Dahomey. 14 Dec., general
election in Chad.

1970 6 Jan., treaty of 'brotherhood, good
neighbourliness and co-operation' signed
between Algeria and Tunisia. 10 Jan.,
names of Revolutionary Command Coun
cil, which overthrew King Idris I of Libya,
made public: headed by Col. Moamer
al-Qadafi. 26-8 Jan., Summit Conference of East and Central Africa held
in Khartoum. 1 Feb.–mid-April,
frequent clashes in Suez Canal area
between UAR and Israel. 7 Feb., Iraq,
Jordan, Syria, Sudan. and UAR hold
confrontation' meeting on Israel in
Cairo. 20-22 Feb., Marshal Tito,
President of Yugoslavia, visits the Sudan.
29-31 March, Mahdist plot discovered
in the Sudan: army seizes Aba Is.: Imam
El Mahdi killed. 22 Apr., UAR becomes
official member of GATT (General
Agreement on Tariffs and Trade). 29
Apr., USSR announces that Soviet
pilots are flying operationally in
UAR. 19-20 May, Algeria recognizes
E Germany. 25 May, banks and many
foreign businesses nationalized in the
Sudan. 27-28 May, Presidents of UAR
and of Libya visit Khartoum. 28 May,
King Hasan II of Morocco meets
President Boumédienne of Algeria at
Tlemcen, settling long-standing frontier
dispute: agree to co-operate in
exploiting iron ore deposits. 1 June,
President Bourguiba returns to Tunis,
after 5 months in hospital in Paris.
8 June, King Hasan II receives President
of Mauritania at Casablanca. Formation
of new government begun in Tunisia.
6 July, UAR signs new industrial protocol with USSR. 21 July, Aswan High Dam
begins operation. 24 July, referendum
in Morocco approves new constitution.
28 July, Algerian cabinet reorganized.
7 Aug., US plan for 90-day cease-fire
accepted by UAR, Israel, and Jordan.
4-8 Sept., General Gowon visits Cairo.
28 Sept., President Gamal Abd el-
Nasser d. in Cairo. 29 Sept., Vice-President Anwar Sadat of UAR sworn as
Acting President. 15 Oct., Anwar Sadat
elected President of UAR. 4-9 Nov.,
Libya, Sudan, and UAR hold summit
meeting in Cairo. 8 Nov., Libya, Sudan
and UAR agree to form Federation:
joined by Syria on 27 Nov.

1970 2-19 Jan., U Thant, Secretary-
General of UN, visits Mauritania,
Senegal, Guinea, Liberia, Ghana,
Cameroun, Togo, Niger, Upper Volta,
Ivory Coast, and Nigeria. 5 Jan., Ivory
Coast cabinet reorganized. 10 Jan.,
Ojukwu leaves Biafra. 12 Jan., General
Effiong asks for an armistice in Biafra.
12 Jan., Lord Hunt sent to Lagos to
report on relief work in Nigeria. 13 Jan.,
Government of Nigeria, refuting Vatican
fears on genocide, states that Vatican
unnecessarily prolonged Biafran conflict by sustaining the rebels with supplies.
15 Jan., General Gowon announces
end of civil war in Biafra. 3 Feb., thirty-
two RC missionaries, chiefly Irish,
expelled from Nigeria for illegal entry.
11-24 Feb., Portugal alleges frontier
violations of Portuguese Guinea by
Senegal. 22 Feb., referendum amends
Senegalese constitution to create office
of prime minister and to give president
wider powers. 28 March-3 Apr., elections
suspended, and then annulled, in
Dahomey. 9 Apr., government reorganized in Mauritania. 23 Apr., The
Gambia becomes a republic, remaining
within the British Commonwealth. 1
May, Presidential Council of three
members set up in Dahomey.
Hubert Maga elected President of the
Council. 23 May, Conference at Bamako
of WA heads of states which form the
Customs Union of the Economic Community of WA. 27 May, Otumfuor Sir Osei
Agyeman Prempeh II, Asantehene of Ashanti,
Ghana, 1935-70, d. aged 78. 5 June, Nana
Matthew Polu elected Asantehene as
Opoku II. 14 June, new constitution
in Upper Volta confirmed by referendum.
30 July, General Andrew Juxon-Smith,
former head of the military government in
Sierra Leone, condemned to death for treason,
9 Aug., attempted *coup d'etat* discovered in
Togo: seventeen persons arrested. 19 Aug.,
at Abidjan, Second Symposium of the
Episcopal Conferences of Africa and
Madagascar. 31 Aug., former Chief
Justice Sir Edward Akufo-Addo elected
President of Ghana. 11 Sept.,
diamond industry nationalized in Sierra
Leone. 15 Sept., state of emergency
proclaimed in Sierra Leone, following
political violence. 1 Oct., Hamani Diori
re-elected President of Niger. 11 Oct.,
incident near Largeau, Chad: eleven French
soldiers killed, ten wounded. 4 Nov.,
President Houphouët-Boigny of Ivory

1970 3 Jan., new constitution promulgated
in Brazzaville. 10 Jan., friendly relations
re-established between Presidents of CAR,
Chad, and Congo (B) at meeting at
Yaounde, also attended by U Thant, and
Presidents of Gabon, Ivory Coast,
Mauritania, Niger, Senegal, and Upper
Volta. 28-30 Jan., Mauritius joins Joint
African Malagasy Organisation *(OCAM)*
at conference at Yaoundé: name
changed to *Organisation africaine,
malagache et mauritienne
(OCAMM)*. 23 March, attempted *coup*
in Brazzaville. 28 March, President Ahidjo
of Cameroun re-elected. 29 March, eleven
persons condemned to death on account
of the attempted coup in Brazzaville. 16
May, new government formed in
Cameroun. 7 June, elections in Cameroun.
16 June, normal relations restored between
Congo (B) and Congo (K). 17 June, King
of the Belgians and Queen Fabiola visit
Congo (K). 27 Aug., Bp Albert Ndongmo,
RC Bishop of Nkongsamta, Cameroun,
arrested for complicity in a rebellion,
after returning from Rome, where he
had been reproached for his performance
in the temporal affairs of his diocese.
1 Nov., General Mobutu re-elected President
of Congo (Kinshasa). 7 Dec., government
re-organised in Congo (K): eleven ministers
lose their positions. 26 Dec., treason and
rebellion trial opened at Yaoundé,
Cameroun.

1970 1 Jan., Trade Licensing Act becomes effective in Uganda, restricting foreign traders to specified commodities. 13 Jan., following deputation to President Kenyatta by Luo M.Ps. many political detainees released. 24 Jan., two hand-grenades thrown in Djibouti restaurant: sixteen Europeans injured; special security measures imposed. 26 Jan.-2 Feb., Marshal Tito, President of Yugoslavia, visits Tanzania. 12 Feb., Marshal Tito visits Kenya. 27 Feb.-6 March, meeting of Foreign Ministers of OAU in Addis Ababa: message sent supporting UAR in struggle with Israel. Feb., *Tanzania Standard* taken over by Tanzanian Government. 13-17 Apr., preparatory meeting of representatives of non-aligned countries in Dar es Salaam: fifty-nine out of seventy-four nations invited attend. 27 Apr., failure of 'counter-revolutionary plot' announced in Somalia. 1 May, President Obote announces that, in pursuance of 'Common Man's Charter' in Uganda, export and import trade, except oil, will be nationalized, and that government will acquire 60% share in major companies. 3 May, Brian Lea, British diplomatist in Uganda, reported kidnapped: hoax subsequently uncovered: dismissed from Foreign Service. 6 May, six persons sentenced to life imprisonment in Kampala for attempt on President Obote's life. 14 May, Uganda and Zambia threaten to withdraw from the Commonwealth Games if SA cricket team visits Britain. 25 June, treason trial opens in Dar es Salaam: accused include Oscar Kambona, former Foreign Minister, *in absentia,* Bibi Titi binti Mohamed, women's leader, Michael Kamaliza, former Minister of Labour, and four others. 20 Aug., World Alliance of Reformed Churches and International Congregational Council ally formally at ceremony in Nairobi to form World Alliance of Reformed Churches (Presbyterian and Congregational), representing 55m. people. 1 Sept., meeting of heads of state of OAU in Addis Ababa: condemns sale of arms to SA. 22 Sept., Presidents Kaunda, Nyerere and Obote meet in Dar es Salaam to concert strategy against UK sale of arms to SA: warnings to London that Tanzania, Uganda and Zambia may leave Commonwealth if sales are concluded. Sept., four girls of reputed 'Shirazi' origin alleged to have been forced into marriages in Zanzibar. 26 Oct., at Dar es Salaam, and 28 Oct., at Kapiri Mposhi,

1970 8 Jan., cabinet reorganized in Zambia. 27 Jan., general election in Lesotho: opposition Congress Party wins with thirty-two seats; 30 Jan., Prime Minister Leabua Jonathan suspends constitution, declaring elections invalid because of opposition intimidation; leaders of the opposition arrested. 2-8 Feb., Marshal Tito visits Zambia. 16 Feb., twenty-two Africans in SA tried under Suppression of Communism Act: prosecution withdrawn, all acquitted. All then detained but subsequently released. Feb., estimated in Mozambique that 12,000 rebels had deserted *FRELIMO.* 2 March, Rhodesia proclaimed a Republic: eleven out of thirteen countries withdraw consuls thereafter, leaving only Portugal and SA.Lesotho cabinet reformed. 9-10 March, USA, France, Italy, West Germany, and Holland close their consulates in Salisbury. 11 March, Botswana establishes diplomatic relations with USSR. 22 March-8 Apr., controversy between Smith government and Anglican, RC, and other Christian bodies over the Land Tenure Act. 3 Apr., King Moshoeshoe of Lesotho leaves for exile in Holland. 10 Apr., general election in Rhodesia. 14 Apr., Clifford Dupont nominated President of Rhodesia. 13 Apr., Botswana has boundary dispute with SA. 15 May, SA excluded from the International Olympic Committee. 16 May, general election in SA: Nationalist Party returned with reduced majority. 19 May, student riot in Johannesburg in protest at detention of Africans without trial: thirty-seven arrested, but only twenty-nine ultimately charged and fined. 19-21 May, B.Vorster, Prime Minister of SA, visits Malawi and new capital of Lilongwe being built with SA aid: 21-22 May, visits Rhodesia. 22 May, Samora Moises Machel appointed President of *FRELIMO.* 23 May, Portuguese offensive against African guerillas in Angola. 25 May, President Tsiranana returns to Madagascar after 4 months in hospital in Paris. 28 May, African guerilla centre destroyed in Angola by Portuguese. 11 June, Zulu Territorial Authority set up in SA under Chief Gatsha Buthelezi. 4 July, Nacala rail link, joining Malawi with Mozambique, opened. 14 July, agreement signed between USSR and Mauritius on the use of Mauritian ports by Soviet fishing vessels. 20 July, SA Prime Minister introduces Uranium Enrichment Bill to establish Uranium Enrichment

1970 2 Jan., British foreign currency restrictions relaxed. MCC forced to cancel cricket tour of SA after pressure by Kenya, Uganda, and Zambia against cricket tour in England. 11 Jan., Pope Paul VI states that genocide is feared in Biafra following cessation of hostilities. 19 Jan., H. Wilson pays tribute in Parliament to the 'magnanimity in victory' of General Gowon. 19 Jan., twelve cricket grounds in England damaged by anti-*apartheid* demonstrators against visit of SA cricket team. 28-30 Jan., UN Security Council makes renewed attempt to compel SA to withdraw from SWA. 7-23 Feb., W.P. Rogers, US Secretary of State, visits Morocco, Tunisia, Ethiopia, Kenya, Zambia, Congo(K), Cameroun, Nigeria, Ghana, and Libya. 12 Feb., SA cricket team tour of England reduced to twelve matches from twenty-eight. 3 March, at request of Britain UN Security Council condemns Rhodesia's 'purported assumption of republican status'. 8 March, attempt to assassinate President Makarios in Cyprus. 11 March, Misuse of Drugs Bill published in London. 16 March, *New English Bible* published in London. 16-22 March, Arab Petroleum Congress in Kuwait, 18-19 March, UN Security Council condemns the proclamation of the Rhodesian Republic. 23-6 March, Permanent Secretariat of Foreign Ministers of Islamic countries set up, following conference in Mecca. Davis Cup Committee expels SA from tennis competition in protest against *apartheid*. 28 March, Rogers's Report on US policy in Africa published in Washington. 1-3 Apr., troops sent to quell disturbances in Northern Ireland. 4 May, serious student riot at Kent State University, Ohio, followed by riots on many other US campuses. 4-9 May, modest Labour gains in UK local elections. 20 May, US announces measures against SA on account of her continued occupation of SWA. 22 May, SA cricket tour of UK cancelled. 3 June-17 July, Vorster visits Portugal, Spain, and Switzerland. 18 June, Conservatives win election in UK from Labour with majority of thirty-one: Edward Heath, Prime Minister. 24 June, Sir A.Douglas-Home, Foreign Secretary, announces readiness to discuss resumption of arms talks with SA. 30 June, negotiations for British entry into Common Market re-opened. 2 July, Pope Paul VI receives three revolutionary leaders from Angola and Mozambique at the Vatican. 10 July, Vatican Radio broadcasts the text of a note sent by the Pope to Portugal.

Coast agrees to a dialogue with SA. 7
Nov., general election in Ivory Coast;
President Houphouët-Boigny re-elected.
22 Nov., armed attack on Conakry,
Guinea; President Sékou Touré claims
it a Portuguese aggression: denied by
Portugal. 24 Nov., students from Chad,
Dahomey, Togo, and Upper Volta
join riot in support of Guinea; 27 Nov.,
expelled by presidential decree. 25 Nov.,
UN mission arrives at Conakry,
Guinea, and finds alleged evidence of
Portuguese aggression. 29 Nov.,
Political prisoners in Guinea escape
to Bissau, Portuguese Guinea. 9-12
Dec., special meeting of Foreign
Ministers of OAU at Lagos to discuss
situation in Guinea. 20 Dec., elections
in Upper Volta. 24 Dec., Archbishop
Tchidimbo of Conakry arrested.
29 Dec., some one hundred W Germans
expelled from Guinea: recall of the
W German ambassador requested.

1971 2 Jan., eight students arrested in
Algiers for alleged subversion. 13 Jan.,
USSR President Podgorny visits Egypt. 15
Jan., National Union of Algerian Students
dissolved by government. Aswan High
Dam inaugurated. 18 Jan., Egyptian
peace plan announced. 20-2 Jan., Summit
Conference of Libya, Sudan, Syria and
UAR in Cairo. 27 Jan., UAR sends
ambassador to Tunisia, after 6 years of
diplomatic coldness. 4 Feb., UAR extends
cease-fire with Israel to 7 March and offers
to open Suez Canal in exchange for Israeli
withdrawal from Sinai: Israel refuses to
withdraw before a peace treaty. 12 Feb.,
government reshuffled in Sudan in order
to include all parties except Communists.
14-20 Feb., President Tito visits UAR. 7
March, cease-fire between Israel and UAR
expires, but decision made to 'withhold
fire' on Suez Canal; 18 March, President
Sadat of Egypt rejects Israeli border
proposals. Khartoum University closed.
1 Apr., President Sadat offers concessions
for settlement of dispute with Israel:
refused (4 Apr.). 2 Apr., Libyan
government agreement with international
oil companies on oil prices, royalties and
taxes. 10 Apr., cabinet reshuffle in UAR.
10 Apr., military conscription and a single
party organization announced in the
Sudan. 17 Apr., in Benghazi, President
Sadat announces new Federation

1971 5 Jan., Portuguese military
communiqué in Bissau announces
895 guerillas known killed. 740
wounded, and 86 taken prisoner
in Portuguese Guinea during 1970.
19 Jan., seminar on African boundary
disputes held in Accra. 25 Jan., 58
Portuguese mercenaries executed in
Conakry. Sentence of life imprisonment
with hard labour on Archbishop of
Conakry confirmed. 27 Jan., major
cabinet changes made in Ghana. 29
Jan., Guinea breaks off diplomatic
relations with W Germany for alleged
subversion. 29-30 Jan., *OCAM*
conference at Fort Lamy, Chad.
1 Feb., 1 student killed, 6 wounded
and 5 policemen in riot at Ibadan
University. 3-13 Feb., President
Pompidou visits Mauritania, Senegal,
Ivory Coast, Cameroun and Gabon.
12 Feb., National Consultative Assembly
instituted in Dahomey. 13 Feb., coalition
government formed in Upper Volta. 17 Feb.
President Mobutu of Congo (K), visiting
Senegal, states that he will not agree to
'dialogue' with SA. 22 Feb., cabinet
reshuffled in Guinea. 23 Feb.,
Nigeria, followed by other governments,
protests against British supply of
certain arms to SA. 26 Feb.,
University of Dakar closed following
student strikes and unrest. 28 Feb.,

1971 15 Jan., Vice-President and two
deputies executed in Cameroun for
rebellion; Archbishop Ndongmo's
death sentence commuted to life
imprisonment. 25 Jan., cabinet
reshuffled in Cameroun. 5 Feb.,
cabinet reshuffled in CAR. 9 Feb.,
cabinet reshuffled in Congo (B). 4
March, cabinet reshuffled in
Burundi. 9 March, cabinet changed
in Cameroun. 28 March, President of
CAR announces readiness for
contact with SA. 30 March, Fr
Andrade, Catholic priest, sentenced
for 'trying to separate Angola from the
mother country'. 2 Apr., Cameroun
establishes diplomatic relations with
China. 3-7 Apr., Gen. Gowon pays
official visit to Cameroun. 20 Apr.,
Emperor Haile Selassie pays official
visit to Burundi. 26 Apr., cabinet
reshuffled in CAR. 10 May, 150
political prisoners released in Chad.
14 May, 5 persons sentenced in Congo
(B) for harming national security and
spreading false news. 23 May, cabinet
reshuffled in Chad. 4 June, Lovanium
University closed, following student
unrest and demonstrations. 6 June,
CAR formally recognizes Republic of
SA. 9 June, 83 guerillas announced
killed, and 44 wounded in Angola.
14 June, cabinet reorganized in Congo

official ceremonies held to inaugurate the beginning of the construction of the Tanzanian-Zambian Railway with funds loaned by China. 30 Oct., general and local elections in Tanzania: no voting permitted in Zanzibar. 16 Dec., state of emergency proclaimed in Eritrea: insurgents alleged to be from 2,000 to 10,000.

Corporation of SA Ltd. 28 July, *FRELIMO* forces in Mozambique stated to be retreating into Tanzania. 6 Sept., general elections in Madagascar. 8-10 Sept.,Third Non-Aligned Summit Conference, attended by more than fifty nations, held in Lusaka. 14 Sept., nineteen Africans, previously acquitted under Suppression of Communism Act, tried and acquitted under Terrorism Act. 15 Sept., SA Prime Minister states that Bantustans may request independence at any time. 22 Oct., SA now announced as capable of producing napalm bombs. 9 Nov., preliminary talks between UK and Rhodesia begun in Pretoria, to see if a basis can be found for a negotiated settlement. 10 Nov., completion of Mulungushi reforms announced in Zambia: all banks, insurance agencies, building societies, and large companies taken over: all expatriates to lose wholesale and retail trading licences from 1 Jan. 1972. 19-21 Nov., co-operative agreement signed between Republics of Madagascar and SA. Nov., US loans 6m. dollars to Botswana to construct a road from Francistown to Livingstone, Zambia. 4 Dec., King Moshoeshoe returns to Lesotho after 9 months of exile. 31 Dec., Guy Clutton-Brock, of Cold Comfort Farm, Rhodesia, deprived of Rhodesian citizenship.

12 July, China grants Tanzania loan of £169m. repayable over 30 years from 1973, for Tanzania-Zambia railway. 20 July, Iain Macleod, Chancellor of the Exchequer, d. 23 July, CS gas bombs thrown in House of Commons. UN Security Council passes a resolution ordering the reinforcement of the embargo on the supply of arms to SA. 27 July, Dr Antonio de Oliveira Salazar. Prime Minister of Portugal, 1932-68, d. 3 Sept., Executive Committee of World Council of Churches announces gift of $200,000 (£83,250), from a Special Fund to Combat Racism, to oppressed racial groups, including nineteen African revolutionary groups 'for relief and legal aid.' 6 Sept., four aircraft hijacked by Palestinian guerillas. 11 Oct., President Nyerere revisits British Prime Minister to protest that Tanzania will leave Commonwealth if arms are sold to SA by UK. 16 Oct., President Kaunda visits London and protests against sale of arms by UK to SA. 6-9 Nov., Emperor Haile Selassie visits Italy. 9 Nov., General de Gaulle d., aged 80: homage paid to him by every African head of state. 24 Nov., UN Security Council special mission to inquire into aggression in Portuguese Guinea. 3 Dec., special mission reports, blaming Portugal: denied by Portugal, who blames refugees from Guinea. 2 Dec., Dr Caetano, Prime Minister of Portugal announces wide increases of autonomy for Angola and Mozambique. 8 Dec., UN General Assembly adopts six resolutions condemning *apartheid.*

1971 8 Jan., Tanzanian Government announces new syllabus to 'revolutionize' education. 10 Jan., Central Committee of World Council of Churches meets in Addis Ababa. 12 Jan., 7th anniversary of the Zanzibar Revolution: *Tanzanian Standard* calls for permanent constitution in place of an *interim* one. 25 Jan., military *coup* led by Major-General Idi Amin overthrows President Obote's government in Uganda. 26 Jan., President Nyerere condemns Uganda military *coup.* 2 Feb., General Amin announces composition of cabinet in Uganda, chiefly of former senior civil servants, declaring himself Head of State: all courts suspended. 5 Feb., Radio Dar es Salaam continues to attack General Amin. 12 Feb., Tanzanian troop movements reported on Uganda frontier. 15-16 Feb., OAU African Liberation Committee meets at Moshi, Tanzania. 19 Feb., four persons, including Bibi Titi binti Mohamed, sentenced to life imprisonment in Tanzania for allegedly plotting the overthrow of the government. 20 Feb., Emperor of Ethiopia offers amnesty to bandits in Eritrea. 23 Feb.-5 March. Archbishop of Canterbury and delegates from many countries attend Anglican Consultative Committee at Limuru, Kenya.

1971 1 Jan., six ministers, suspended for alleged misappropriation in Zambia, reinstated. 6 Jan., Guy Clutton-Brock ordered to leave Rhodesia by 4 Feb., 15 Jan., Cold Comfort Farm Society declared an unlawful organisation in Rhodesia. 19 Jan., Portuguese communiqué in Mozambique announces 651 guerillas killed and 1,804 taken prisoner during 1970; 132 Portuguese troops killed. 21 Jan., cabinet announced by Chief Minister in Comoro Is. 22 Jan., Very Rev. Gonville ffrench-Beytag, Anglican Dean of Johannesburg, arrested for alleged subversive activities. 23 Jan., Radio Johannesburg gives details of USSR naval forces in virtual control of the Red Sea and Indian Ocean. 26 Jan., Commission of Inquiry into alleged corruption set up in Zambia. 27 Jan., SA Government offers plebiscite to enable SWA to decide its future. 8 Feb., anti-racial descrimination law in Mozambique published. SA releases letter to Hague Court proposing plebiscite in SWA: court refuses without reasons given. 18 Feb., new government, principally former ministers, in Madagascar. 14 Feb., 20 Africans, Asians and Coloureds reported arrested in SA under Terrorism Act. 3 March, Mrs Nelson (Winnie) Mandela given 1 year's im-

1971 5 Jan., peace talks between Israel, Jordan and UAR resumed in New York. 8 Jan., Israel announces plan for peace with Jordan, Lebanon and UAR. 14-21 Jan., Conference of Commonwealth Heads of Government in Singapore. 20 Jan.-8 March, Post Office strike in UK. 4 Feb., Law Officers issue White Paper stating British obligation to supply maritime helicopters and other naval spares to SA. Receiver appointed to manage Rolls Royce Co. 15 Feb., UK recognizes change of government in Uganda. 11 Feb., 40 nations, including UK, USA and USSR, sign treaty banning atomic weapons from the sea bed. 15 Feb., decimal currency introduced in UK. 22 Feb., Foreign Secretary states that British Government will honour legal obligations to SA. 24 Feb., new UK Immigration Bill published. Feb., measures announced in Lisbon to give elected legislatures to Angola, Mozambique and Portuguese Guinea. 1-2 March, President Sadat visits Moscow. 13 March, Prime Minister of Israel gives interview to the London *Times,* outlining boundaries desired by Israel. 26 March, East Pakistan declared independent as Republic of Bangla Desh: several million persons flee from Pakistani forces in India, 30 March-8 Apr., 8 vol. *General History of Africa* announced as a UNESCO project following a conference in Paris.

of Arab Republics, incorporating UAR, Libya and Syria, and that draft constitution would be prepared. 23 Apr., cabinet reshuffle in Morocco. 2 May, Ali Sabry dismissed from being Vice-President of UAR. 13 May, Egyptian Ministers of the Interior and of War dismissed: seven others resign. 14 May, new cabinet formed in Egypt: plot against President Sadat disclosed. 25 May, fighting reported in Khartoum on National Day celebrations between communists and government supporters. 3 June, Tunisia expresses hope to re-establish diplomatic relations with China. 11 June, Libya recognizes China. 2-8 July, Archaeological Conference in Rabat to co-ordinate research in Algeria, Morocco and Tunisia; 10 July, abortive military *coup* in Morocco: fighting at party to celebrate birthday of King Hasan II: 100 killed, including Belgian ambassador. 13 July, ringleaders of *coup* executed in Rabat. 19 July, Free Officers' Organization seizes power in Sudan: Chairman: Lieut.-Col. Babikr Nur Osman; 22 July, Libya forces BOAC passenger aircraft carrying Lieut.-Col. Babikr Nur Osman and other Sudanese leaders down at Benghazi. Counter-*coup* launched in afternoon by General Nimeiri, successfully regaining power in the Sudan. Four officers implicated in the *coup* executed. 25 July, Maltese Prime Minister holds talks with Libya in Tripoli 26 July, further executions in the Sudan, including Lieut.-Col. Babikr Nur Osman. 28 July, Abdel Khalek Mahgoub, leader of Sudanese Communist Party, hanged, 29 July, Algeria suspends diplomatic relations with Jordan. 31 July, Summit Conference in Algiers, attended by certain Arab powers only, condemns Jordan *in absentia* for treatment of Palestinian guerillas. 3 Aug., major cabinet reorganization in Sudan. 6 Aug., new cabinet announced in Morocco: Karim Lamrami, Prime Minister. 13 Aug., provisional constitution announced in the Sudan. Libyan cabinet reorganized, bringing in more civilians. 25 Aug., trial for treason of Ali Sabry, former Vice-President of Egypt, and seventy others, begun in Cairo: suspended after uproar. Sept., Libya announces British cancellation of agreement to supply Chieftain tanks, 12 Sept., extensive cabinet changes in UAR. 12-15 Sept., UK Foreign Secretary, Sir Alec Douglas Home, visits President in Cairo: states he is certain that UAR desires 'peace based on justice' with Israel. 15-18 Sept., UK Foreign Secretary visits Morocco. 7 Oct., Col. Qadafi, Chairman of the Revolution Command Council, Libya, resigns, but withdraws resignation. 15-20 Oct.,

Union of Senegalese Students and Dakar Students' Union dissolved by decree. 8-11 March, 3rd Anglo-American Dialogue held in Lagos. 11 March, Whiteney Young, American Civil Rights leader, d. in Lagos. 14 March, riot following strike at Samrebori, Ghana: 3 killed. 16 March, Family Planning Council inaugurated in Accra. 19 March, Mauritanian Education Minister dismissed following student unrest. 22 March, Ghanaian Foreign Minister indicates readiness to visit SA. 23 March, two abortive attempts to assassinate Prime Minister of Sierra Leone by soldiery. 23-9 March, Ivory Coast, Madagascar, CAR and Ghana accept SA policy of dialogue: Nigerian and Zambian newspapers demur. 24 March, defence and security agreement made between Gambia and Senegal. 26 March, mutual defence treaty between Guinea and Sierra Leone, 28 March, Guinean troops called in to protect Prime Minister of Sierra Leone. 29 March, University of Dakar re-opened. 30 March, Abidjan University closed. 31 March, Mr Justic C.O. Stevens sworn in as Acting Governor-General of Sierra Leone *vice* Sir Banja Tejan-Sie. 6 Apr., Local Administration Act decentralizes local governments in Ghana. 8 Apr., a torture plot discovered in Mali. 12-17 Apr., conference on Negritude in Dakar. 19 Apr., President Senghor of Senegal favours SA policy of dialogue. Sierra Leone becomes a republic. 28 Apr., at Abidjan President Houphouët-Boigny makes important declaration on dialogue with SA. 4 May, President William Tubman re-elected President of Liberia. 28 May, Ghana-Ivory Coast Co-operation treaty signed, covering many fields of common interest. 7 June, Nigeria and Tanzania resume diplomatic relations. 8 June, cabinet reorganized in Ivory Coast. 20 June, cabinet reshuffled in Guinea. 1 July, President Houphouët-Boigny of Ivory Coast re-affirms policy of dialogue with SA. 19 July, new Ghana People's Party formed in Accra. 23 July, Vice-President William Tolbert sworn in as successor to President Tubman for 6 months. 30 July, Nigeria announces expulsion of 30 East European diplomats. 15 Aug., President Ould Daddah of Mauritania re-elected for the third time. 24 Aug., Ghana Parliament passes Act banning restoration of

(B). 15 June, Lovanium University renamed Kinshasa University. 23 June, delimitation of Cameroun-Nigeria border agreed. Cholera epidemic reported in Chad. 25 June, rebel activities officially reported in Chad. 29 June, government reorganized in Gabon. 2 July, four ministers dismissed in Congo (K); government reorganized. 6 July, President Bongo of Gabon supports dialogue with SA. 10 July, CAR Air Force disbanded. 4 Aug., Rwanda-Uganda border re-opened. 23-5 Aug., OAU Middle East Peace Committee meets in Kinshasa: peace delegation sent to Egypt and Israel. 5 Oct., two former ministers and a general arrested in Kinshasa for subversive associations. 19 Oct., cabinet reshuffled in CAR. 27 Oct., Congo Democratic Republic (K) changes official name to Republic of Zaïre. 15 Nov., student strike in Brazzaville. 15 Dec., cabinet reshuffled in CAR. 16 Dec., party purge and government reorganization in Congo (B).

26 Feb., OAU Ministerial Council meets in Addis Ababa: Uganda delegation excluded. 14 March, partial elections in Territory of the Afars and Issas. 15 March, Eritrean Liberation Front (ELF) claims successes against Ethiopia, with 70 Ethiopian soldiers killed. 23 March, all political activities suspended in Uganda. 27 March, Oginga Odinga released from detention in Kenya. 31 March, Dar es Salaam Radio strongly opposes SA policy of dialogue. 1 Apr., two Rhodesian Africans sentenced in Nairobi for possession of prohibited (Chinese) literature. 4 Apr., former Kabaka, Sir Edward Frederick Mutesa, entombed near Kampala. 6 Apr., campaign against tribalism announced in Somalia. 7 Apr., new Abuna, Tewoflos, elected Patriarch of Ethiopia. 21 Apr., alleged hostile acts complained of by Uganda on the part of Tanzania and the Sudan. 4-8 May, General Gowon visits Ethiopia. 5 May, abortive plot in Somalia: two generals accused. 8-12 May, General Gowon visits Kenya. 9 May, Vice-President of Zanzibar announces death sentence for 19 men arrested for an attempted *coup* in Zanzibar in August 1970. 12 May, strike of University students in Ethiopia. 13 May, Uganda government offers 1m. shillings to anyone who brings former President Obote back to the country. 19 May, 'Ten Commandments', outlining policy in religious matters, announced by General Amin in Kampala. 25 May, eleven schools closed in Ethiopia following strikes. 4 June, *FRELIMO* headquarters in Dar es Salaam claims guerilla successes in Mozambique and to be threatening Cabora Bassa dam. 11-19 June, OAU Council of Ministers meets in Addis Ababa. 21-3 June, OAU Summit Conference at Addis Ababa: majority reject dialogue with SA. 7 July, compulsory education in Zanzibar extended from 7 to 10 years. 8 July, Uganda closes border with Tanzania, claiming 70 officers and 600 other ranks killed by Tanzanians. 10 July, US Vice-President Spiro Agnew begins tour of Ethiopia, Kenya, Congo (K) and Morocco. 11 July, army purge in Uganda. 14 July, President Amin claims Tanzanian forces attacking Uganda including Chinese Communist instructors. 19 July, President Nyerere

prisonment for violating banning order. 5 March, self-rule for Tswanaland announced by SA. Bantu languages made official in Bantu Homelands. 7 March, riot of Coloureds at Port Elizabeth: 6 wounded, 10 police injured, 22 persons arrested. 19 March, SA Prime Minister gives interview explaining SA policy of dialogue without preconditions with other African countries, reserving internal affairs. 25 March, University of Tananarive closed following student strike. 26 March, Prime Minister of Swaziland visits SA Prime Minister in Cape Town. 31 March–1-2 Apr., abortive rising in Madagascar quashed. 13 Apr., Transkei Chief Minister demands transfer from SA of all departments still under SA control, additional land (including 'white districts'), more money, and re-orientation of labour policy. 14 Apr., Rhodesian Prime Minister rejects Five Principles as a basis for negotiation with U.K. 16 Apr., SA Minister of Bantu Administration and Development rebuts Transkei demands. 19 Apr., result of General Election in Malawi announced: all candidates selected by President and returned unopposed. 21 Apr., SA Prime Minister announces details of further land to be handed over to Bantustans. 21 Apr., SA Prime Minister describes President Kaunda of Zambia as a 'double talker', disclosing attempts to have a friendly dialogue since 1968. 3 May, Chief Minister of Transkei makes further demands from SA.: *apartheid* to be applied 'in reverse' until it ends in SA. 14 May, Mauritius Foreign Minister visits SA. 15 May, Malawi government seizes all property of members of the Lumpa sect. 28 May, Mozambique government expels WF missionaries, some 40 priests and over 100 lay brothers. 1 June, Venda and Cisker legislative assemblies instituted. 21 June, fighting near Cabora Bassa dam. 2 July, President Banda of Malawi announces he will visit SA and that the Malawi Legation in Pretoria will be an Embassy. 6 July, President Banda of Malawi sworn President for life. 7 July, Lusaka University students demonstrate outside French Embassy against French supply of certain arms to SA. UK-Rhodesian talks concluded. 12 July, Lusaka University students send letter criticizing President of Zambia. 13 July, guerilla force from Zambia repelled near Cabora Bassa dam. 15 July, Lusaka University closed for 'indiscipline and lawlessness'. 27 July, SA Prime Minister completes two-month tour of N Sotho, Tswana and Venda homelands. Malawi and SA

Apr., UK reduces 7% bank rate to 6%. 10 Apr., US table tennis team visits China. 25 Apr., 200,000 persons demonstrate in Washington against Vietnam war. 14 May, Hague-Court rejects application for a plebiscite in SWA. 18 May, Father-General of the White Fathers announces withdrawal of White Father missionaries from Mozambique. 7 June, EEC and UK make satisfactory agreement on sugar. 21 June, Hague Court states SA under an obligation to withdraw from SWA: judgement not accepted by SA. 28 June, Lord Goodman holds talks with Rhodesian Government in Salisbury. 30 June, anti-*apartheid* demonstration at Adelaide, Australia, during Rugby match against Springboks. 7 July, White Paper published on British entry into EEC. 11-18 July, President Amin of Uganda pays private visit to Israel and UK. 22 July, UK protests 'most energetically' at Libyan interference with BOAC aircraft, demanding release of all passengers. 23 July, official French statement that France will fulfil only current arms ontracts with Portugal, Rhodesia or SA. President Tubman of Liberia d. in London: body transported by RAF to Monrovia for burial. 28 July, China denies Ugandan charges. 15 Aug., President Nixon announces measures to counter US currency crisis. 18 Aug., Summit Meeting of Federation of Arab Republics (Libya, Syria, UAR) in Damascus: Sudan to join Federation later. 2 Sept., UK reduces 6% bank rate to 5%. 6 Sept., UK Trade Union Congress rejects terms for UK entry into EEC. 10 Sept., World Council of Churches announces donation of $200,000 to African liberation movements. 30 Sept., Synod of Bishops in Rome: rule of celibacy for clergy of the Latin rite re-affirmed. 6-12 Oct., Emperor Haile Selassie visits China. 11 Oct., President Sadat visits Moscow. 14 Oct., 25th centenary celebrations of founding of Persian Empire. 25 Oct., UN General Assembly votes to admit China, and expel Taiwan. 28 Oct., House of Commons votes overwhelmingly for Britain to enter EEC. 2-5 Nov., OAU Middle East Peace Mission visits Israel, and then Cairo. 11 Nov., US Senate votes lifting of sactions on import of Rhodesian chrome ore into USA. 2 Dec., House of Commons approves Anglo-Rhodesian settlement proposals by 297 votes to 267. 6 Dec., Republic of Bangla Desh recognized by India. 20-1 Dec., Prime Minister Heath and President Nixon meet in Bermuda to discuss China and international monetary crisis. 22 Dec., Dr Kurt Waldheim elected Secretary-General of UN, *vice* U Thant (retired with effect from 31 Dec.).

General Nimeiri elected President of
the Sudan: cabinet of 26 ministers
announced, 29 Oct., new government
announced in Tunisia. 5-9 Nov., OAU
Middle East Peace Mission visits Cairo. 16
Nov., King Idris I of Libya sentenced to
death *in absentia*. 28 Nov., Jordanian
Prime Minister assassinated in Cairo. 7
Dec., Libya nationalizes BP assets in Libya.
9 Dec., former Vice-President Ali Sabry
and three other former ministers sentenced
in Cairo, three to life imprisonment and
one to 15 years. 15 Dec., fighting on
border of Sudan and Uganda. 23 Dec.
UK protests against Libyan nationalization
of BP assets.

Kwame Nkrumah or his party. 27
Aug., abortive *coup d'état* in Chad;
6 Sept., Chad claims Libyan complicity
in recent *coup d'état*. 28 Sept., Radio
Lomé announces that military rule
will continue in Togo. 14 Oct., 15 army
officers arrested in Nigeria for fraud
and embezzlement. Nigerian
Executive Council reshuffled.
10 Nov., 16 former 'Biafran'
officers dismissed from Nigerian
Army and 15 discharged. 19 Nov.,
Professor Justin Obi hanged
in Monrovia for murder of
Liberian Bp Brown. 27 Dec., cabinet
reshuffle in Chad.

of Tanzania states Ugandan charges to be 'lies'. 1 Aug., Frene Ginwala, Editor of *Tanzania Standard and Tanzania Sunday News,* dismissed: replaced by President Nyerere as Editor-in-Chief. 5 Aug., Baganda people at mass meetings in Kampala, demand restoration of monarchy: refused by President Amin. 24 Aug., fighting between Tanzania and Uganda confirmed. 1 Sept., mediation agreed to between Tanzania and Uganda. 16 Sept., Secretary-General of OAU announces diplomatic offensive against SA control of SWA. 28 Sept., President Amin of Uganda announces intention of sending delegation to SA to open dialogue. 10 Oct., President Amin states that monarchy will not be restored in Buganda. 18-19 Oct., Summit Conference of E and CA States in Mogadishu: 'Declaration of Mogadishu' issued, uring armed struggle to liberate Southern Africa. 20 Oct., further border clashes between Tanzania and Uganda. 21 Nov., Tanzania-Uganda border reopened.

exchange ambassadors. 1 Aug., United United Progressive Party (UPP), led by former ministers Justin Chimba and Simon Kapwepwe, formed in Zambia, protesting against corruption and victimization by ruling party. 4 Aug., SA grants limited independence to Damara in SWA. 16-20 Aug., President of Malawi visits SA. 29 Aug., 7 *FRELIMO* guerillas killed and 1 captured in Rhodesia. 14 Sept., SA announces measures to consolidate 29 Zulu areas, including cession of white-occupied land. 15-21 Sept., Lord Goodman visits Salisbury for further talks with Rhodesian Government. 20 Sept., President of Zambia arrests 75 political opponents, including many UPP members. 24-5 Sept., President of Malawi pays official visit to Mozambique. 1 Oct., formation of Front for the Liberation of Zimbabwe (FROLIZI) announced: Shelton Siwela as Chairman. 6 Oct., SA Prime Minister announces 1 police officer killed and 4 constables wounded pursuing terrorists in Caprivi Strip. Delegation from Ivory Coast visits Pretoria. 7 Oct., Zambia alleges SA violation of frontier. 8 Oct., SWAPO admits liability. 21-7 Oct., further talks in Salisbury between Rhodesia and UK. 1 Nov., Dean of Johannesburg sentenced to 5 year's imprisonment under Terrorism Act: released on bail pending appeal. 3 Nov., Transkei Territorial Government authority extended over 1½m. Xhosa living outside the territory: National Boards to be set up in all SA urban areas with more than 100 Xhosa inhabitants. 15-24 Nov., British Foreign Secretary visits Salisbury for talks with Rhodesian Prime Minister: 24 Nov., communiqué reports agreement on proposals for constitutional settlement 4 Dec., Prince Goodwill Swalithini installed as Paramount Chief of the Zulu. 8 Dec., Malawi purchases 8 armoured scout cars from SA. 13 Dec., 6,000 Ovambo strike at Winhoek, 16 Dec., African National Council (ANC) formed in Rhodesia, coalition of all African parties. 16 Dec., state of emergency proclaimed in Mauritius following strike in essential services. 20 Dec., 7 by-elections in Zambia: UNIP wins 6 seats; Simon Kapwepwe, UUP leader, wins 1 seat.

Index

1907, 1931, 1960, 1961, 1962, 1967
Banningville, 1966
Bannockburn, battle, 1314
Banque Misr, 1960
Bantu, 186±150, *c. ante* 1500, 1864-5
Bantu Education Act, 1954
Bantu languages, 1971
Bantu Laws Amendment Act, 1964
Bantu Self-Government Bill, 1959
Bantustans, 1959, 1970
Banu Abd al-Wad, 1235-1554; *see also* Abdulwadids
Banu Amir, 1817
Banu Ghaniya, 1199-1222
Banu Hammad, 1007-9
Banu Hilal, 1052-3, 1057, 1152
Banu Marin, *c.*1150, *c.*1215, 1244-58, 1248, 1253; *see also* Marinids
Banu, Saad, 1505, 1510-1653, 1525, 1541
Banu Sulaim, *c.*1052, 1184, 1209
Banyo, 1915
Banza, Lieut.-Col. Aléxandre, 1969
Baol, 1859
Baoulé, 1901, 1902, 1905, 1910
Baptista,P.J., 1801-11, 1811-14
Baptist missions, 1792, 1814, 1841, 1844, 1845, 1891, 1922, 1932
Baputi, *c.*1830
Baqdoura, battle, 742
Baqqara, 1854, 1866
Bara, 1883, 1908-11
Barawa, 1105, 1417-19, 1506, 1541, *c.*1590, 1822, 1875, 1876
Barbarossa, *see* Abu Yusuf Aruj *and* Khair al-Din
Barbary Company. 1585
Barbosa, Duarte, *c.*1517-18
Barbot, John, 1678-82, 1732
Barca, *c.*500 BC, 642
Barcelona, 1114
Bar-Cochba, 132-5
Bardia, 1941-2
Bardo, Treaty, 1881
Barghash, Sayyid, Sultan of Zanzibar, 1859, 1870-88
Bari, 840
Bari, settlement of the, late 16th or early 17th c.
Bari-Lotuka, 1912
Baring, Sir Evelyn, *see* Cromer, Lord
Barmecides, 803
Barotse *and* Barotseland, 1847-8, 1864, 1878, 1884,

1885, 1888, 1890, 1898, 1900, 1943
Barqa, 869
Barquq, Mamluk Sultan, 1382-99
Barracouta, HMS, 1823
Barre, Gen. Mohamed Said, 1969
Barreira, Balthazar, SJ, 1605
Barreto, Francisco, 1569, 1573
Barros, João de, 1552
Barsbay, Mamluk Sultan, 1422-37
Barth, H., explorer, 1850-4
Bartolomeo of Tivoli, Bp, 1330-50
Barué, 1902, 1917
Bas, Tunka, 1062
Basanga, 1891
Basel Mission, 1816, 1827, 1835, 1887
Basil of Caesarea, St, 330-79
Basilides, gnostic, *c.*130
Basilios, Abuna, 1951, 1960
Basiliscus, 468
Basle, Council of, 1433, 1438-43
Basra, 634
Bassam, Grand, 1832, 1838, 1842, 1844, 1883
Bastards, rising, 1926
Basuto *and* Basutoland, *c.*1830; relations with Britain, 1842-3, 1851-3, 1868, 1871, 1880; boundaries, 1849, 1855, 1858, 1865-6; British Protectorate, 1884-1966; independence as Lesotho (q.v.), 1966
Bata, 1969
Batalpin, 1858
Batanga, 1842, 1847
Batelas, 1897
Batetela, 1895
Bathurst (Gambia), 1618, 1816, 1818
Battel, Andrew, *c.*1590-1610, 1601-3
Batugenge, battle, 1892
Bauchi, *c.*900, 1902
Baudouin I, King of the Belgians, 1950, 1955
Baumann, O., 1892
bauxite in Guinea, 1962, 1968
Bawa Jan Gwarzo, ruler of Gobir, 1777-95
Baxter, Richard, 1673
Bayazid II, Ottoman Sultan, 1481
Baybars, Sultan, 1260-77
Baybars, Mosque of, 1303
Beadle, Sir Hugh, 1966
Beauvais, botanist, 1778
Beaver, Capt. Phlip, R.N., 1811

Bechim, 1861
Bechuanaland, 1802, 1820, 1823, 1829, 1883, 1885, 1890, 1895, 1936, 1943, 1960, 1965; independence as Botswana, 1966
Bechuanaland Exploration Co., 1888
Bedde, *c.*1300, *c.*1790
Bede, the Venerable, 731
Bedr al-Jamali, 1073-6, 1077
Beecroft, J., 1835, 1840, 1842, 1849-53, 1851
Begemder, 1570, 1788, 1852, 1915
Begho, early 15th c., 1629 *c.*1670, 1679
Behanzin, King of Dahomey, 1890, 1892, 1894
Beigbeder, General, 1937
Beina, Kingdom of, *c.*1700
Beira, 1898, 1915
Beirut, 1109, 1182
Beit, Sir Alfred, 1853
Beja, 404-369 BC., *ante* 300 BC, *c.*250-350, *c.*320-55, *c.* 690, 831, 834, 854
Beke, explorer, 1840
Bekkai, Col. Si, 1955
Belbeis, 640
Bélédougou, 1915
Belem, 1502, 1515-20
Belezina, 905
Belgian Congo, *see* Congo
Belgium *and* Belgians: activity in Congo, 1878f; on Upper Nile, 1890; war with Germans, 1914-15; acquire Rwanda-Burundi, 1921; in Ethiopia, 1930-5
Belgrade Conference, 1961
Belisarius, 533-47
Belkacem, Krim, 1955
Bell, King of Douala, 1864, 1914
Bell, Prince Aléxandre Douala-Manga, 1945
Bell, Chief Rudolf Manga, 1914
Bell, John, 1843, 1859
Bell tribe, 1866
Bellefond, Villault de, 1666-70
Bellefonds, Adolf Linant de, 1827
Bello, Regent of Sokoto, 1808
Belzoni, Giovanni, 1823
Bemba, *c.*1610-25, 1740, *post* 1825, *c.*1840,*c.*1865, '1898
Bembe, 1855, 1866
Bemoim, João, 1486
Benanozano, 1787-1810
Ben Bella, Mohammed, 1950,

1954, 1956
Ben Djelloul, 1938
Bendu, 1861
Benedict, St, *c.*480-577
Benedict XIV, Pope, 1741
Benedict XV, Pope, 1922
Benedictine missions, 1780-8, 1885, 1887
Benghazi. 1941
Benguela, *c.*1483, 1578, 1615, 1617, 1623, 1633, 1641, 1704, 1759-1803, 1790, 1852
Bengui, 1968
Beni Aros, 1921
Beni Suassen Mts, 1907
Beni Uriaghel, 1920
Benin *and* Bini: art, 1140-1360, *c.*1299, *c.*1360-1500; constitutions, *c.*900, *c.*1176, *c.*1200, *c.*1481-4, *c.*1641-*c.*1700; missions in, 1485-6, *c.*1504-50, 1682, 1685-8, 1695; relations with England, 1553, 1588-90, 1585, 1897; with Portugal, *c.*1485-6, *c.*1504-50; wars, *c.*1280, *c.*1450, *c.*1484-1504, *c.*1504, 1515-16; other references, *c.*1283, *c.*1500, *c.*1600-1830, *c.*1651, 1699, 1702, *c.*1720, 1769, 1788-92, 1951, 1967
Benjamin of Tudela, 1171
Ben Khedda, 1956, 1961
Benté, 1868
Benton, Thomas, 1724
Benyowski, 1773-86
Ber, 1840-1
Beraku, 1705-6, 1782-5
Berber (town), 1821, 1856, 1868
Berbera, 1518, 1885, 1895, 1940, 1941
Berberistan, *c.*1550
Berbers, 144-52, 253, 289-95, 496-530, 534, 546-8, 565-78, 7th c.; conquests, 4th c.-*c.*750, 608, 711-12, *c.*800, 944; relations with Arabs, 642, 647-710, 702, 705, 734-42, 771; Muslim conversion, *c.*1000, 14-15th c; other references, 1811-18, 1856, 1931, 1934
Berean Missionary Society, 1922
Berenguer, General, 1919
Berenice, 221-220 BC; *see also* Adulis
Bergendal, battle, 1900
Berghwata, *c.*744
Berguete, General, 1922
Beri, 1884
Beri-Beri tribe, *c.*800
Berlin Academy of Sciences, 1700
Berlin Conference on Congo,

Lyons Mission (SMA), 1856, 1859, 1877, 1880, 1906

Maaqil Arabs, 14th - 15th c.
Maba, prophet, 1865
Mabveni, 180 ± 100
Macarthy, Sir C., 1824
Macartney, Lord, 1795
,Macaulay, Zachary, 1768-1838, 1794
Maccabees, 167 – 143 BC
MacDonald, Major, 1889
MacDonald, Malcolm, 1962
MacDonald, J. Ramsay, 1924
Macedon, c.338 BC; treaty with Syria, 202 BC
Macedonian heresy, 381
MacGregor Canal, 1900
Macha Galla, 1703
Machel, Samora Moises, 1970
Machili Forest, 90 ± 220
Machoncho, Chief, 1905
Mackenzie, D., 1874, 1895
Mackenzie, Prof. W.J.M., 1952
Mackinnon Treaty, 1890
MacLean, Capt. George, 1830-43
MacLeod, Iain, 1970
McMahon, Sir Henry, 1914-5
MacMillan, Harold, 1894, 1957, 1960, 1963.
Macrinus, Roman Emperor, 217
Macrorie, Dr. William, 1869
Macta, battle, 1835-36
Madagascar, ?c.700-1500, c.915, post 1100, 1110 ± 80, c.1540-75, c.1600;
Portuguese activities in, 1500, 1505, 1506, 1508, 1620;
British activities, 1644-5, 1810, 1811, 1817, 1845, 1865, 1877, 1904, 1942;
French activities, 1602, 1628, 1638, 1648, 1666, 1671-4, 1804, 1818, 1819, 1829-30, 1840, 1846, 1883-5;
French treaties with, 1859, 1861, 1868, 1885, 1895;
under French rule, 1890, 1894-6, 1895, 1896-1900, 1945, 1947;
independent, 1958, 1962, 1965, 1969, 1970, 1971;
other references, 1529, 1647-74, 1663, 1831,

1832-3, 1844, 1866
Maderia, Diogo Simões, 1609, 1613, 1614.
Madeira Is., ante 1147, 1351, 1418-20, 1578
Madimba, 1955
'Mad Mullah', see Muhammad b. Abdallah, 'Mad Mullah',
Madrolle, explorer, 1890-4
Madule Somali, c. 1624
Mafeking, 1900, 1961
Mafia Is., 1569, 1652, 1822, 1872
Maga, Hubert, 1963, 1964, 1970
Maga dynasty, 4th c. c. 750
Magbele, 1860
Magdala, 1843, 1863, 1866, 1868
Magellan, 1519-22
Magersfontein, battle, 1899
Magha, ruler of Mali,, c.1332-6
al-Maghili, Shaikh, 1463-99
Maghrawa, 976
Maghreb Office in Cairo, 1947
Maghreb Unity Conference, 1958
Maghumi dynasty of Bornu, c. 570
Magila, 1868
Magna Carta, 1215
Magonids, c.479 BC
Magyar, Ladislas, 1848
Mahamba, Alexandre, 1966
al-Mahalla al-Mansura, 1299-1306
Mahamusa, 1909
Mahdi, Imam el- 1970
al-Mahdi, Maulai, 1913
al-Mahdi, Muhammad Ahmad b. Abdullah, 1881-5
al-Mahdi, Sadek, 1966-7
al-Mahdia, c.912, 944, 1057, 1087, 1104, 1148-60, 1151, 1199-1222, 1550
Mahdis, c.1079-c.1130, 1125, 1610-13, 1881, 1899, 1904
Mahdists, Sudani, 1886-7, 1893, 1894
Mahe, 1726
Mahgoub, Muhammad Ahmad, 1965-9
Mahina, 1917
Mahmud I, Ottoman Sultan, 1898
Mahmud al-Kati, historian, c.1468, 1519
Mahmud Bey Muntasser, 1951
Mahmud b. Muhammed, Bey of Tunis, 1814-24
Mahmud of Ghazna, 997-1030

Mahmud Pasha b. Ali b. Zarghun, 1591-4
Mahsud Pasha, 1644
Mahu Bey Urfali, Governor of Berber, 1822, 1825-6
Mahungo, 1910-11
Mai Ali of Bornu, 1503
Maichew, battle, 1936
Maisara, 739-40
maize, post 1500, c.1629
Majid, regent of Zanzibar, 1854-6; Sultan, 1856-70
Maji-Maji, 1905-7
Makada, c.1500
Makake cult, c.1930
Makalanga, 1506, 1514
Makalle, 1935
Makape, cult. 1930
Makarios, Archbishop, 1956-7
Makerere, 1921, 1922, 1929, 1949, 1963
al-Makhazin, battle, 1578
Makhzumi dynasty, c.898-1285, 1277-85
Makk Nasr al-Din, King of Berber, 1761-c.1837
Makololo, c.1823, c.1840, 1864, 1889
Makonde, 1891, 1895
Makua, c.1580-90, c.1677, c.1830
Makwaia, David, 1945
Malacca, 1511, c.1512-15
Malabar, 1663
Malan, D.F., 1934-54
malaria, 1899, 1929-30, 1953
Malawi, 1845, 1883, 1964, 1966, 1968, 1969, 1970, 1971
Malawi Congress Party (MCP), 1959, 1961
Malchus, c. 550 BC
Maldives, 1505
Malfante, traveller, 1447
Mali (ancient), 1240, c. 1255-70, c.1270, ante 1312, 1325, c.1331, 1336-1433, 1360, 1374, 1400, 1450, 1473
Mali, 1959, 1960, 1962, 1964, 1967, 1968
Maligia, battle, 1855
Malik, A.H., 1927
al-Malik, jurist, c.712 or 719-91
al-Malik al-Adil, Mamluk, 1215
al-Malik al-Adil Muhammad b. Sulaiman, Sultan of Kilwa, c.1412-21
al-Malik al-Adil Muhammad b. al-Husain, Sultan of Kilwa, c.1520
al-Malik al-Ashraf Khalil, Mamluk, 1290-3
Malindi, 1412-22, 1415, 1498, 1500, 1506-8, c.1512-15, 1541-2, 1585, c.1699, 1769

Malines Conference, 1920
Mallam Alimi, Amir of Ilorin, c.1810
Malocello, Lanzarote, ante 1336
Maloula, Abbé Joseph, 1951
Malplaquet, battle, 1709
Malta, 1530-51, 1565, 1640, 1798, 1942, 1971
Malula, Cardinal, 1969
Malvern, Lord, 1956
Mamadu Pate Bulola, 1895, 1897
Mamadu Sanha, 1843
Mamluks see Bahri Mamluks and Burji Mamluks
al-Mamoura, 1681
Mamun, Caliph, 813
Manda, 1631-6, 1636, 1660, 1678
Mandala, 1878
Mandates, 1919, 1922
Mandave, De, 1767-70
Mandela, Nelson, 1961, 1964
Mandela, Mrs Nelson (Winnie), 1971
Mandingo, 2nd c., 4th c. c.750, c.1043, c.1230, 1697, 1836, 1865
Manes, c.1550, c.1600
Manetho, historian, c.275 BC
Mangbetu, c.1800, c.1815-60, 1867, 1870, 1873, 1882, 1884
Mani, gnostic, c. 216-76
Mani kings of Kongo, 14th c., 1483
Mani kings of Loko, c.1560-1605
Mani people, c.1600
Manica, 1571-3, 1574, 1575, 1891
Manichaeans, c.216-76, 477-84
manioc (cassava), c.1600, c.1629
Mannu dynasty of Futa Toro, c.1250-1300
Mannu dynasty of Tekrur, c.1040
Manoel, Afonso, 1643
Mansa Musa, see Kankan Mansa Musa
Mansa Ule, King of Mali, c.1255-70
Mansfield, Lord, 1772
Mansoura, El, 1968; see under al-Mansura
al-Mansur, Caliph, 754-75
al-Mansur, Abu Abbas Ismail, 946-52, 976-1008
al-Mansur, Abu Yusuf b. Abu Yusuf al-Mohad, 1184, 1196
al-Mansur, Hammadid Amir, 1090

1630
Perpetua, St, 203
Persepolis, c.500 BC
Persia and Persians: treaties with
Carthage, c.550 BC, c.484-483
BC; invasions of Egypt, 525-
404 BC, 486 BC, 460 BC, 404-
399 BC, 380 BC, 378 BC, 373
BC, 343 BC, 616-29; relations
with Greeks, c.525 BC,
c.522 BC, 499-493 BC, 449-
448 BC, 396-386 BC; wars with
Romans, 231-2, 241-4, 281,
338-50, 363-4, 421-2, 502-6;
relations with Byzantines, 532,
539-62, 572-91, 603-9, 611-14,
629; Arab conquest of, 632,
641-3; Mongol conquests of,
1235-9, 1253-8, 1386, defeated
by Turks, 1514; rule in Arabia,
572-628; in E Africa, 1107
Pétain, Marshal, 1925
Peter, St, 67
Peter, of Alexandria, c.300-11
Peter, Patriarch of Alexandria,
477
Peter I, of Cyprus, 1365
Peter Nolasco, St, 1218
Peters, Dr Karl, 1884, 1885,
1887
Peter the Great, Czar, 1682
Peterwardin, battle, 1716
Petherick, vice-consul, 1858
Petronius, 23 BC
Pharisees, 90 BC
Pharos (Alexandria), 280 BC
Pharsalus, battle, 48 BC
Philae, 380-343 BC, 553-4
Philip, Dr John, 1819-51,
1842-3
Philip, King of Macedon,
359-336 BC
Philip V, King of Macedon,
215 BC
Philip, King of Pemba,
1607
Philip, Roman Emperor,
244-8
Philip II, Holy Roman
Emperor, 1556-89
Philip IV, King of Spain,
1621-65
Philippa of Lancaster,
Queen of Portugal, 1385-
1483
Philippe Augustus, King of
France, 1191
Philippolis, 1826
Phillips, Consul-General,
1897
Philo of Alexandria, 40
Phoceans, 525 BC
Phoenicians, c.1100 BC –
814 BC, c.900 BC, c.610
BC, c.450 BC, 360 BC,
345 BC
Phraortes, Medean ruler,
c.660 BC

Piankhy, King of Meroe,
c.751-730 BC
Pietermaritzburg, 1838
Pigafetta, F., 1591
Pigeaud, 1846
Pilgrim Fathers, 1620
Pillar tombs in E Africa,
1364
Pim, Sir Alan, 1932
Pinet-Laprade, Governor of
Senegal, 1865
Pinteado, Francisco, 1798
Pinto, Serpa, 1878-9,
1880-1, 1888
Pious Mothers of Nigritia,
1872
pirates and piracy: British,
1700, 1720:
Mediterranean, 1057,
1369-93, 1390, 1435-87,
1529, 1534, 1558, 1610-
37, 1695, 1728, 1783; Red
Sea, 630-40, 699, 702; in
W Africa, 1719
Pirès, Tomé, writer, c.1512-15
Pisa, 1034, 1087, 1104, 1271,
1409, 1462-1517; treaties:
with Tunis, 1228; with
Hafsids, 1264
Pisistratus, Tyrant of Athens,
561-528 BC
Pitt, William (Earl of
Chatham), 1708-78
Pitt, William, the Younger,
1783-1806
Pius II, Pope, 1462
Pius III, 1503-13
Pius IV, 1559-65
Pius V, St, 1566-72
Pius VIII, 1809
Pius IX, 1846-78
Pius X, St, 1903-14
Pius XI, 1922-39, 1929
Pius XII, 1939-58
Pius XII College, 1945
Pla (Grand Popo), 1857
plagues, 1346, 1348-55, 1619,
1643, 1655-7, 1787
Plataea, battle, 479 BC
Platea Is., c.ante 800 BC
Plato, 428-347 BC
Plettenburg, J. van, 1771-85
Pliny the Elder, 77
Plotinus, 205-70, c.255
Plowden, Walter, 1843, 1848,
1852, 1859
Plummer, Sir L., 1948
Plymouth Brethren, 1886
Podgorny, President of USSR,
1971
Podor, 1745, 1854
Pogge, explorer, 1874-7
Pogrund, B., 1969
Poignet, Lieut. Augustin,
1968
Poincaré, President of France,
1913-20

Poitiers, battles, 732, 1356
Poivre, Pierre, 1770
Polu, Nana Matthew,
Asantehene, Prempeh II, 1970
Polycarp, St, 156
Polybius, navigator, 149-146
BC
Pombal, Marquis of, 1750-77
'Pombeiros', 1801-10
Pompey the Great, 65 BCf
48 BC
Pompidou, George, President
of France, 1969
Poncet, Dr, 1698-99
Pondo and Pondoland, 1840,
1844, 1894, 1911, 1927,
1930-2
Ponel, explorer, 1890
Pontius Pilate, c.25-30
Ponty, William, 1904, 1907
Poperlin, Captain, 1879
Popo, Grand, 1682, 1857
Popo, Little, 1864, 1885
Popular Front (Spain), 1936
Popular Movement for
Liberation of Angola (MPLA),
1960
Population Registration Act
(S Africa), 1950
porcelain, c. 1475
Porphyry, philosopher,
c.232-304, c.270-80
porphyry quarries, 41-54
Port Elizabeth, 1952, 1971
Portendic, 1857
Port Harcourt, 1914, 1949,
1969
Port Loko, c.1600, 1815
Porto de Cavaleiro, 1441
Portolan, Laurentian,
geographer, 1351
Port Novo, post 1750, 1787,
1861, 1863, 1865, 1882,
1889, 1890, 1913-25, 1914
Porto Seguro, 1885
Port Said, 1956
Portudal, 1859
Portugal and Portuguese, 1128,
1143, ante 1147, 1180, 1385,
1551, 1578, 1580-1640, 1640,
1910; in N and W Africa,
1431f, 1437, 1443, 1466,
1481, 1684; in E Africa,
1497f, 1502-12, c.1580-90,
1631-7, 1679, 1729; relations
with Ethiopia, 1520-7, 1534,
1541f; trade monopolies,
1454, 1456, 1504, 1519,
1532, 1558; colonial policies,
1832, 1914, 1920, 1929,
1930, 1933, 1951, 1953,
1956; UN activities against,
1962, 1963, 1966, 1967;
Anglo-German agreements on
colonies, 1898, 1913; treaties
with Britain, 1372, 1578,
1642, 1654, 1661, 1703; see

also under Missions
postal Services, 1866, 1867,
1873
potatoes, sweet, c. 1629
Potchefstroom, 1844;
University, 1950
Potgeiter, Hendrik, 1836,
1844, 1849, 1853
Potgeiter, Marthinus, 1853
Potogos, Papagiotis, explorer,
1876
Potsdam Conference, 1945
pottery: Bigo, c.1500;
Channelled ware, 90 ± 220,
186 ± 150, 1080 ± 180,
Dimple-based ware, 825 ± 150
c. 900; Gokomere, 330 ± 150,
Greek 360 BC 15,
Stamped ware, c.1-600
Prampram, c.1746
Preachers, Order of: see under
Dominic, St and Dominican
missions
Premis, c.203
Prempeh II, Asantahene, 1970
Presbyterian missions, 1796
Présence Africaine, 1947
Prester John, 1165, 1487
Pretoria, 1856, 1860, 1881,
1892, 1896, 1900, 1923;
treason trial, 1958-61
Pretoria University, 1930
Pretorius, Andries, 1838, 1840,
1853
Pretorius, Marthinius, 1856,
1864
Pretorius, Piet, 1853
Primo de Rivera, Gen. 1923,
1924
Prince Imperial, the, 1879
Prince, Captain T. von, 1893,
1894
Princestown, 1683
Príncipe, Is. 1476, 1908
Printing c.1300, 1729, c.1822
Privy Council appeals, 1968
Probus, Roman Emperor, 274,
276-82
Procopius, historian, post 500-
562
Progress Party (PP) (Ghana),
1969
Progressive National United
Party (Rhodesia), 1969
Progressive Party (S Rhodesia),
1926, 1930
Progressive People's Party (PPP)
(Gambia), 1960, 1962
Pronis, 1643
Proterios, 451, 454
Protten, Jakob, 1757-61, 1764-9
Provence, Arab raids on, 849-50
Prussia, 1717, 1721, 1870
Psammetichus I, Pharaoh, 664-
610 BC
Psammetichus II, 595589 BC
Psammetieus III, 526-525 BC

Ptolemais Epitheras, c. 629-264 BC

Ptolemy I Soter, King of Egypt, 323-285 BC

Ptolemy II Philadelphus, 285-247 BC

Ptolemy III Euergetes I, 247-221 BC

Ptolemy IV Philopator, 221-200 BC

Ptolemy V Epiphanes, 200-1819 BC

Ptolemy VI Philometor, 181-145 BC

Ptolemy VII Euergetes II, 145-116 BC

Ptolemy VIII Soter II, 116-108/7 BC, 88-80 BC

Ptolemy IX Alexander I, 108/7-88 BC

Ptolemy X Alexander II, 80 BC

Ptolemy XI Auletes, 80-51 BC

Ptolemy Apion, King of Greece, 96 BC

Ptolemy, Claudius, geographer, c.90-168, c.150, c.400, c.ante 800

Ptolemy, King of Mauritania, 40

Punic Wars, 264-241 BC, 218-201 BC

Punt, post c.510 BC

Pygmies, c.450 BC

Pyramids, battle, 1798

Qadafi, Col. Moamer, 1970, 1971

Qadi al-Fadil, 1134-92

al-Qadir, Caliph, 1011

Qadiriyyah order, 1198, c.1500

Qait Bey, 1467-96, 1472, 1881

Qala, 1007-9, 1017

Qalabat, 1838

Qalafu, 1948

Qalaun, Mamluk Sultan, 1279-90

Qanbalu, c.747-54

Qansuh al-Ghauri, Mamluk Sultan, 1516

Qarmatian republic, 899

Qasimiyyah rising, 1730

Qayrawan, 670, 683, 732-55, 758, 761, 771, 800-909, 1057, 1348, 1540, 1558, 1735; buildings at, 772-4, c.817, 836, 874-902, 1276

Qazdughliyyah, 1739

Qedaref, 1884

Quadi, 169

Quaison-Sackey, Alex, 1964

Quakers: condemnation of slavery, 1671, 1688, 1727, 1774, 1776, 1783; missions, 1823, c.1835

Quaque, Rev. Philip, 1765-1816

Quelimane, 1498, 1544, 1853-6

Querillos IV, Coptic Patriarch, 1856-7

quinine, 1854

Qumr, c.915

Qwabe, c.1810

Rabah, 1865

Rabat (Ribat al-Fath), 1150, 1163, 1907, 1971

Rabeh, 1893-1900

Race Relations Bill (British), 1968

Racial disturbances in Britain, 1958

Radama I, King of Merina, 1810-28

Radama II, 1861-63

Raffenel, explorer, 1843

Rahmaniyyah order, 1793-94

Railway Workers Union, 1933

railways: in Egypt and Sudan, 1838, 1851. 1856, 1863, 1874, 1959; C. African, 1903-11; E African, 1893-1905, 1896, 1898, 1899, 1901, 1902, 1904, 1912, 1914, 1915, 1923, 1924, 1928, 1931, 1955, 1964, 1968, 1970; Southern African, 1854-7, 1859-60, 1883, 1885, 1892, 1895, 1897, 1899, 1927, 1955, 1970; W Africa, 1878, 1880, 1895-1914, 1898, 1900, 1908, 1909, 1910, 1914, 1930, 1931, 1947

Rainilaiarivony, Premier of Madagascar, 1896

al-Raisuli, Maulai Ahmad b. Muhammad, 1904, 1907

al-Raisuni, 1913, 1915, 1921-2, 1925

Rakoto, Prince, 1857

Rakotomalala, Cardinal Véron, 1969

Ralambo, Merina ruler, 1575-1610

Rally of the Liberation (Egypt), 1953

Ramgoolam, Sir Seewoosagur, 1967

Ramire II, 939

Ramleh, battle, 1102

Ramsay, Hauptmann, 1897

Ramsay, Michael R., Abp of Canterbury, 1966, 1971

Ranavalona, Queen of Merina, 1828-61

Rand Daily Mail, 1969

Randou, Marshal, 1857

Raoul, Capt, Alfred, 1968

Raphael, King of Nubia, 1006

Raphia, battle, 720 BC

Raqqada, 874-902, 909, 910

Rarabe (Gaikas), c.1775

Ras Bir, 1881

Rashid, Arab trader, 1886

al-Rashid b. Muhammad, Sharif of Morocco, c.1653, 1664-72

Rashid b. Hamis, Wali of Takaungu, 1850

Rashid b. Salim al-Mazrui, 1895

Rasoherina, Queen of Merina, 1863-8

Rassam, Hormuzd, 1866

Rasselas, History of, 1759

Rassemblement Franco-Musulman Algérien. 1938

Rassemblement Démocratique Africaine (RDA), 1946, 1950, 1956, 1957, 1958

Ratisbon, Diet of, 1623

Ratsimilaho, King of Betsimisaraka, c.1730-54

Rauf Pasha, see Muhammad Rauf Pasha

Ravasco, Ruy Lourenço, 1502-3, 1505

Ravenna, Treaty of, 442

Rawa, King of Zandoma, c.1283

Ray, James Earl, 1969

Raydan, c.300

Rebello, João, 1585

Rebmann, J., 1844, 1848

Rechenburg, Baron F. von, 1906-12

Red Cross Society, 1864, 1969

Red Sea, see Nile-Red Sea canal and under Piracy

Red Star Movement (Angola), 1949

Reeves, Bp A., 1960

Reform Party (S Rhodesia), 1930, 1931, 1934

Reggan, 1960

Regulus, General, 256 BC

Reheboth (S Africa), 1926

Rehreh, 404-369 BC

Reitz, C., 1851

Reitz, Lieut., 1824

Rejaf, 1899

Rembi, 1867

Renkin, Jules, 1909

Rensburg, Willem Janse v., 1860-3

Republican Socialist Party (Sudan), 1951

Rerum Ecclesiae Gestarum, encyclical, 1926

reserves in Cape Colony, Bantu, 1846-7

Responsible Government Association (S Rhodesia), 1917, 1923

Retief, Piet, 1837

Réunion (Bourbon), c.1513, 1801; see also Bourbon

Rex Regum, Papal Bull, 1443

Reyes de Taifas, 1031

Reza Khan, Shah, 1924, 1925

Rezende, Barreto de, 1635

Rhapta, c.41-54

Rhenish mission, 1819, 1824

Rhode Is., 672, 807

Rhodes, Cecil J., 1871-1902

Rhodesia: prehistoric, c. post 500 BC, c.ante 400, c.11th c., 1058 ± 65, 1388 ± 60, 15th c., 1428 ± 60, c.ante 1500, c.1450-80, c.1550 – c.1825; see also Zimbabwe

Northern: constitutional changes, 1918, 1924, 1937, 1943, 1944, 1945, 1948, 1953, 1962, 1964; independence, 1964; NR Regiment, 1916, 1933, 1938, 1939; African Congress, 1937; other references, 1929, 1932, 1956; see also Federation of Central Africa and Zambia

Southern: 1895; constitutional changes: 1897-9, 1907, 1922, 1923, 1945, 1953, 1954, 1961, 1963; elections and referenda, 1922, 1928, 1958, 1962, 1964; proposed union with S Africa, 1921-2; Land Apportionment Act, 1930; Land Tenure Act, 1970; detention powers, 1963; tobacco 1903, 1932 UDI status, 1965f; republic proclaimed, 1970; new constitution 1969; UN activity on, 1965f; sanctions, 1965, 1966, 1968; elections and referendum, 1965, 1969, 1970; relations with Portugal, 1965; relations with USA, 1971; preventive detention, 1966; guerilla activity in, 1968, 1971

Anglo-Portuguese boundary convention, 1891

Rhodesia Railway Workers Union, 1917

Rhodesian Anglo-American Corporation, 1928

Rhodesian Congo Border Concession Ltd., 1923

Rhodesian Front Party, 1961, 1965

Rhodesian National Party, 1968

Rhodesia Native Welfare Association, 1926

Rhodesian Party, 1924, 1934
Rhodes-Livingstone
Institute, 1937
Rhodes University College,
1904, 1949, 1954, 1957
Ribat-al-Fath, 1163, *see also*
Rabat
Ribeira Grande, 1578, 1585
Ricci, Fr Matteo, 1552-1610,
1581
Richard I, King of England,
1189-99
Richard, Sgt, 1902
Richard Toll, 1821
Richelieu, Cardinal, 1626-42
Ridwan Bey, 1631-56
Riebeeck, Jan van, 1652,
1662, 1952
Rif rebellions, 1562-4, 1687,
1696, 1876, 1920, 1921,
1924-7, 1955
Rimini, Council of, 359
rinderpest, *c.*1890, 1896,
1911, 1918-19
Rio de Oro, 1346, 1436, 1884,
1957
Rio Muni, 1900, 1960, 1963
Rio Nunez, 1687, 1793-4
Rivonia trial, 1964
Riya Arabs, 1284
Riyad Pasha, Premier of
Egypt, 1879, 1890-1, 1893-4
Rizeigat Arabs, 1739-52
Roberts, Lord, 1900
Robertson, Sir J., 1960
Robert the Bruce, 1306
Rock paintings, Saharan, *c.*
300 BC
Roderick, King of Visigoths,
711
Rodriguez Is., 1809-11
Roe, Thomas, 1615
Roger II, King of Sicily,
1130-54
Rogers Report on US Policy,
1970
al-Rogui, 1902-9
Roha, 1137
Rohlfs, explorer, 1862,
1864-7, 1875-6, 1878,
1880-1
Romano, Fr Francisco de,
1682
Rome *and* Romans, *c.*753 BC,
*c.*616 BC, 509 BC, 471 BC,
451-449 BC, 381 BC, 343 BC,
326 BC, 264-241 BC,
218-201 BC, 120 BC; treaty
with Jews, 161 BC; in
60 BC; in Egypt, 80 BC,
59 BC, 65 BC, 30 BC;
Parthian wars, 114-16, 195;
Persian wars, 231-2, 241-4,
281, 338-50, 363-4, 421-2,
502-6; partition of Empire,
293, 314, 395; fall of, 410,
452, 455, 536, 546, 547;

Arab raid on, 846; trade
treaties with Carthage, 348 BC,
327 BC, *c.*306 BC; Church of,
relations with Constantinople,
418-519, 1054, 1439, 1452;
see also under missions, orders
and councils
Rommel, Field-Marshal, 1941,
1943
Romo Nyirenda, Mnyasa, 1925
Roncevaux, battle, 778
Roos, Judge Tielman, 1932
Roosevelt, F.D., President of
USA, 1932-45
Roosevelt, Theodore, President
of USA 1901-9
Rose-Innes, James, 1841-3
Roseveare, Bp Richard, 1962
Rosetta, 919-20, 1310-41
Rosetta Stone, post 200 BC
Roule, du, 1704-5
Roussillon, 1788
Royal Adventurers of England
Co., 1663
Royal Africa Co., 1672-1750,
1683,
Royal Institute for
International Affairs, 1920
Royal Niger Co., 1886, 1889,
1890, 1899, 1900
Rozwi, *c.*1693, *ante* 1835,
*c.*1840
Rubat b. Badi, King of Sennar,
1616-45
rubber, 1879
Rufaa Arabs, 1840
Rufisque, 1635, 1859, 1880
Ruhanje, 1629
rum, distillation of, 1708-9
Rumaliza, 1892-4
Rupert of the Rhine, Prince,
1652
Russadir, *c.* 450 BC
Rusere, Gatsi, Monomotapa,
*c.*1600
Rusguniae, *c.*450 BC
Rusicade, *c.*450 BC
Russell, Lord John, 1846
Russia, 1613-1917, 1769,
1885, 1888, 1889, 1904-5,
1918; *see also* USSR
Rustamid Imams, 716-908
Rustenburg, 1795, 1852
Rusucurru, *c.*450 BC
Ruvuma, R, 1867
Ruyter, Admiral de, 1664-
1666
Ruzibis, *c.*450 BC
Rwabugiri, Mwami of Rwanda,
1894
Rwagasoré, Prince Louis, of
Burundi, 1958, 1961
Rwanda, *c.*900, *c.ante* 1400,
1888, 1894, 1897, 1898-1900;
Belgian, 1907, 1914, 1916,
1919, 1921, 1962;
independent, 1962, 1963,
1964, 1967, 1968

Ryllo, Fr, SJ, 1846
Ryswyck, Treaty of, 1967

Saad al-Din II, Sultan of Ifat,
1415
Saad Zaghlul Pasha, 1906-23
Saba, *c.*300, *c.*320; *see also*
Sheba
Sabakon, *see* Shabako
Sabbatarianism, 320
Sabi, 1727
Sabr al-Din, Governor of Ifat,
1328
Sabratha, *c.*450 BC
Sabry, Ali, 1969, 1971
Sacred Congregation for the
Propagation of the Faith
(Propaganda), 1622, 1659, 1817
Sadat, Anwar, President of
Egypt, 1970, 71
Sa'e Benavides, Salvador Correia
de, 1648-52
Safi, 1508, 1541
Sagallo, 1889
Sagara, *c.post* 1750
Sagati, battle, 1887
Sagres, 1419
Saguiat al-Hamra, 1934
Saguntum, 219 BC
Sahara, *c.*1300 BC – *c.*600 BC,
*c.*1000 BC, *c.*300 BC, *c.*250 BC,
*c.*300; trade, 1000 BC, *c.*300,
742, *c.*1000, 1325, 1445,
*c.*1570-1706, 1591, 1593;
oil, 1914, 1953, 1960
Sahara, French, 1957
Sahara, Spanish, 1958, 1960,
1969
Sahela Dengel, Emperor of
Ethiopia, 1833-40, 1845-50,
1851-5
Sahela Selassie, King of Shoa,
1812-46
Sahh, Berber translator, *c.*744
Said b. Sultan al-Busaidi,
Sayyid, Sultan of Oman and
Muscat, 1804-56, 1822, 1826,
1827, 1832-3, *c.*1839
Said Ali, Comoro rebel,
1891
Said b. Ahmad al-Busaidi,
ruler of Oman, 1783
Said b. al-Husain
(Ubaidullah al-Mahdi),
900-3, 909-34
Said Ibrahim, Prince, Prime
Minister of Comoro Is.,
1971
Saifa Harud, Emperor of
Ethiopia, 1344-72
Saifawa dynasty of Kanem,
*c.*734-1846
Saif al-Dawla, 944-5
Saif b. Ahmad al-Busaidi,
1784-5
Saif b. al-Sultan of Oman,
1696

St Amand, 1682
St Andrew's Is., 1651, 1659
St Arnaud, General, 1851
Ste Catherine, 1475
Ste Luce, 1628, 1643
Ste Marie, 1818, 1823
St Esprit, Compagnie du,
1703, 1816
St Germain-en-Laye, 1922
St Helena Is., 1502, 1505,
1859
St James Is., 1695, 1703-8,
1709
St Joseph, Sisters of, 1807
Saint-Lô, Fr Alexis de,
1635
St Louis (Mauritania), 1919
St Louis (Senegal), 1638,
1659, 1692-3, 1697, 1779,
1789, 1880, 1959
St Lucia Bay, 1884
St Paul de Loanda, Treaty
of, 1926
St Paul Is., 1892
Sais, *c.*517 BC, 404-399 BC
Sakalava, *c.*1600, *c.*1700,
1730-70, 1787-1810, *c.*
1820, 1822, 1824, 1828
Sakassou, 1902
Saker, Alfred, 1845
Salazar, Dr Antonio de Oliveira,
1928, 1932-70
Saldae, *c.*450 BC
Saldanha, 1518
Saldanha Bay, 1620, 1666
Saldoun, 1865
Salé, 1260, 1695
al-Salih Najim al-Din, Ayyubid
ruler, 1240-9
Salim III, Ottoman Sultan,
1789-1807
Salim Qabudan, 1839-40,
1841-2
Salisbury, 3rd Marquess of,
1830-1903, 1885-6, 1895
Salisbury (Rhodesia), 1889,
1891, 1899, 1957
Sallust, historian, 86-35 BC,
47 BC
Saloum, *post* 1200
Saloun, 1856-8, 1859
salt,? *c.* 300-400
Salt, Henry, 1809-11
Salter, Alfred, 1848-52
Salvation Army, 1935
Salvation Trust Ltd., 1913
Samaria, *c.*854 BC, 1183
Samarra, 836-92
Samian War, 441-439 BC
Samisasa, 1846 – *c.* 1860,
1902
Samory, Almamy, 1881-8,
1888-91, 1891-3
Samrebori, 1971
Samuel, Frank, 1946
Samuel, Herbert, (later
Viscount) 1903
Sanchez, João, 1506-8

427-413 BC, 415 BC, c.409 BC, 400 BC, 345-340 BC, 310-307 BC, c.275 BC, 264-241 BC; Vandals in, 439, 476; Muslims in, 668 or 669, 827-909, 902; Norman rule, 1071, 1091, 1122, 1130-65; treaty with Tunis, 1228; slavery abolished, 1815; Allied landings, 1943

Sidama, *ante* 1428, 1533, 1586 1887-94

Sidi Barrani, 1940

Sidi Bu Madian, c.1197

Sidi Daudi, mystic, 1011

Sidon, c.1000-500 BC, 1110, 1204

Sierra Leone, c.1400, 1448 1482, 1517, 1580, 1582, 1602, 1663, 1672, 1702, 1788, c. 1800, 1801, 1802; British rule in, 1808, 1821, 1837, 1850, 1863, 1864, 1866, 1868, 1874, 1800-4, 1890, 1891, 1924, 1946, 1947, 1956, 1960; independent 1961, 1962, 1967-8. 1970, 1971; settlement of slaves in, 1787, 1792, 1800, 1808-15; University of, 1960; frontier agreements, 1885, 1889, 1895, 1904; republic, 1971; Gambian troops in, 1971

Sierra Leone Co., 1791

Sierra Leone Peoples' Party (SLPP), 1950, 1951, 1957

Sierra Leone Weekly News, 1886-1951

Sigisvult, Count of Africa, 428

Sihanaka, c.1667, 1787-1810, 1824

Sijilmasa. c..705. 742. 771-976, 790-823, c.900-3, 909, 921, 933-5, 976, c.1045, 1055, 1524-5, 1274

Sikak, 1836

Sikasso, 1892

Siki, 1893

Silko, King of the Nobatae, 543

Silva, Luis Lobo da, 1684-8

Silva, Simão de, 1512

Silva Porto, António Francisco Ferreira da, 1847-8, 1852-4

Silveira, Fr Gonçalo da, SJ, 1561

Silvela, Senor, 1922

Silvestre, General, 1921

Simancas, battle, 939

Simango, Dr Uria, 1969

Simeon, King of Aloa, c.985

Simonstown, 1921, 1951, 1955

Simpson, W.H., 1869

Sinan Pasha, 1551, 1574

Sine, *post* 1200, 1856-8, 1859

Sirhan b. Sirhan, historian, c.1720

Sisal, 1891

Sithole, Rev. Ndabaningi, 1963, 1969

Siti binti Saad, poetess, 1880-1950

Siti Kazurukumusapa, Monomotapa, 1652-63

Sittius, bandit, 46 BC

Siu, 1588, 1631-6, 1660, 1678, 1845, 1861

Siuna. 1152

Siwa, 525-404 BC, 331 BC, 1797-8

Siwela. Shelton, 1971

Sixtus II, Pope, 258

Siyuyurumunsi, Thaddée, 1963

Skinner, Chief Justice James, 1969

Slatin Pasha, Rudolf von, 1883

slavery *and* slave trade, 256 BC, 747-54, 1198, 1424, 1501, 1510, 1521, 1576, 1585, 1591, 1620, *post* 1672; Arab, 666, 868-92, 899, 1877, 1880, c.1881, 1899; in Egypt and Sudan, 651, 1073-6, 1818, 1821, 1840, 1854, 1855, c.1865, 1870; in China, 1179; British, 1562, 1620, 1680-1786, 1712, 1739, 1760, 1769, 1772; in Cape Colony, 1677, 1753, c.1795; Christians in N Africa, 1535, 1724, 1728, 1774; French, 1637, 1673, 1685, c. 1775, 1776, 1776-9, 1784, 1788-92; Muslims in Malta, 1798; Portuguese, 1441, 1485, 1506, 1513-15, 1526, c.1530, c.1550-1, 1602-3, 1612, c.1622, 1645, c.1650, 1696, 1759-1803, 1800-50, 1850-65; Christian protests against, 1435, 1462, 1537, 1639, 1671, 1673, 1688, c.1700, 1727, 1741, 1755, 1760, 1783, 1787-8, 1792, 1839, 1888; restrictions on, 1808, 1810, 1815, 1817, 1842, 1848; abolition of, 1794, 1803, 1807, 1808, 1814, 1818, 1834-6, 1838, 1848, 1858, 1864, 1865, 1869, 1873, 1876, 1890, 1895, 1897, 1908, 1917, 1927, 1932; baptism of slaves, 1699, 1701; international conventions on, 1926, 1956

sleeping sickness, 1901, 1906, 1914, 1930, 1944

smallpox, 1713, 1718, 1755, 1789, c.1860, 1862. c.1890

Smara, 1934

Smee, Captain, 1811

Smith, Adam, 1776

Smith, Sir Harry, 1846, 1848

Smith, Ian Douglas, 1919, 1964f

Smith, Captain, T., 1842

Smithfield Treaty, 1855

Smuts, J.C., Field-Marshal, 1908, 1912, 1916, 1939, 1950

Smyrna, 1097-8

So, 7th c., c.800

Soares, Fernão, 1506, 1512-Sobhusa II, King of Swaziland, 1967, 1968

Socialist Arab Union (Egypt) 1962

Socialist Party (Egypt), 1949

Social Science Research Council, 1944

Social Welfare, Advisory Committee on Colonial, 1943

Société de Colonisation Belge du Katanga, 1947

Société des Missions Evangéliques, 1822, 1886

Society of Jesus, *see* Jesuits

Society for the Propagation of the Gospel (SPG), 1701, 1751-6

Society of the Divine Word, 1872, 1892

Socotra, 1503, 1507, 1511, 1542, 1607, 1834-5, 1876

Socrates, c.468-399 BC

Soden, Julius von, 1891-3

Sodji, De, King of Porto Novo, 1861

Sodre, Vicente de, 1503

Sofala, c.915, c.945, 950, c.1120, c.1300, 1488-90, 1500, 1502, 1505-7, 1512-15, c.1526, 1891

Soglo, Gen. Christophe, 1909, 1964, 1967

Sohag, 333-451

Sokoto, 1804-17, 1821, 1824, 1884, 1885, 1890, 1903

Soleillet, 1874

Solik, 1905

Solomon, King of Israel, c. 970-930 BC

Solomon II, Emperor of Ethiopia, 1777-9

Solomon III, Emperor of Ethiopia, 1796-7

Solomon, Prefect of Africa, 534, 539

Solon, law-giver, c.612-599 BC

Somali and Somalia, 9th-11th c., c.950, 12th c., 1105, 1414-29, c.1500, 1527, c.1624, 1630, 1827, 1870; British Somaliland, 1884, 1887, 1895-1900, 1920, 1940, 1941, 1950, 1956, 1960; French

Somaliland, 1885, 1896, 1943, 1963, 1967, 1971; Italian Somalia, 1889, 1901, 1925, 1948, 1949, 1950, 1960; independent Somalia, 1960, 1961, 1963, 1967, 1969; frontiers. 1894, 1897, 1900, 1908, 1920, 1931, 1934, 1935, 1946, 1954, 1957, 1960, 1964, 1967

Somali National League, 1948

Somali Youth League (SYL), 1943, 1946, 1948, 1960

Somerset, Lord Charles, 1814-27

Somerville, William, 1802

Somme, battle, 1916

Songea, 1845

Songhai, 7th c., c.890, c.1000, 1100, 1332-6, 1464f, 1473, 1493-1535, 1512, c.1515-61, 1554, 1586-91, 1594

Songo Mnara Is., 1390 1055, 1077

Soninke, c.770-1240, c.800, 1055, 1077

Soninki, 1851, 1855-92

Sonni Ali (Ber) the Great, King of Songhai, 1464-92

Sonni Baru, King of Songhai, 1493

Sonni Ma Gogo, c.1400

Sonyo, c.1483

Sorko Farau, c.690

Sosso kingdom, c.8th c., c.1078-80, c.1230

Sotho Bantustan, 1962

Sotik, 1905

Sotto Maior, Francisco de, 1645-9

Soudan, 1893, 1895, 1921, 1925, 1958, 1959

Souillac, de, 1779-87

Soumangouroun, 1200-1235

Soumialot, Gaston, 1964

Soummam, 1956

Sousa, Tomé de, 1588

Sousse, 1511, 1540, 1784

Soustelle, Jacques, 1955-6

Sout-el-Ma, 1902

South Africa, Republic of, 1961, 1964, 1966, 1968, 1970

South Africa, Union of, 1908, 1910, 1912, 1914, 1917, 1930-1, 1934. 1939, 1952-3, 1955, 1956, 1960; Citizenship Act, 1949; High Commission Territories, 1955; elections, 1929, 1933, 1958; Entrenched Clauses, 1955, 1956; Federation of Trades, 1917; High Court of Parliament Bill, 1952; Lands Act, 1936; Native Administration Act, 1917, 1927; Native Affairs Commission, 1920; Native Laws Amendment Act, 1957;